A Problem Solving Approach to
Mathematics for Elementary School Teachers

About the Cover: **Start at the upper left-hand corner and connect the dots until you can move across the spine at the bottom left-hand corner. You may only move horizontally or vertically, and you may only connect dots whose numerical values differ exactly by one (1). What is the least number of dots you can connect to find a path through the maze? What is the minimum sum of the numbers on the dots that create a path through the maze? Can the solution to each of the questions be obtained using the same path? How do the answers to these questions change if diagonal movements are allowed? We invite you to send your solutions to the authors in care of The Benjamin/Cummings Publishing Company.**

A Problem Solving Approach to
Mathematics for Elementary School Teachers

Rick Billstein
Shlomo Libeskind
Johnny W. Lott
**University of Montana
in Missoula**

The Benjamin/Cummings Publishing Company, Inc.
Menlo Park, California • Reading, Massachusetts
London • Amsterdam • Don Mills, Ontario • Sydney

To Jane and Carolyn.
To Molly, Ran, Nureet, and John.

Sponsoring Editor: Susan A. Newman
Production Editors: Margaret Moore, Ruth Cottrell, Steven Sorensen
Book and Cover Designer: John Edeen
Technical Illustrator: Pat Rogondino
Chapter Opener Illustrator: John Edeen

Library of Congress Cataloging in Publication Data

Billstein, Rick.
   A problem solving approach to mathematics for
elementary school teachers.

   Bibliography: p.
   Includes index.
   1. Mathematics--Study and teaching (Elementary)
2. Mathematics--1961-   . 3. Problem-solving.
I. Libeskind, Shlomo, joint author. II. Lott,
Johnny W., 1944-   joint author. III. Title.
QA135.5.B49   372.7   80-28421
ISBN 0-8053-0851-2

abcdefghij-DO-8987654321

The Benjamin/Cummings Publishing Company, Inc.
2727 Sand Hill Road
Menlo Park, California 94025

Preface

OUR GOALS

In search of a suitable textbook for our mathematics content course for prospective elementary school teachers, we found that no one text fully met our needs. We wrote this book to satisfy our needs and to meet these general goals:

- to survey the appropriate mathematics in a way that is both intelligible and entertaining;
- to present and use the heuristics of problem solving as an integral part of mathematics;
- to encourage our students to extend their learning beyond the classroom by providing a diversity of problems (both elementary and challenging), discussion topics, and bibliographies for further reading.

This book is the result of our many years of combined experience working with pre-service and in-service teachers. Preliminary versions of the book were class-tested for over two years with more than 700 students. We listened carefully to students' reactions to our material and observed their successes and failures. We tried to present the material in the most interesting and comprehensible way. Also, as we wrote we tried to anticipate students' questions, common misconceptions, and difficulties.

Since the mathematics preparations of students who take this course vary widely, we have written the book so that the material can be used by students with diverse backgrounds.

We have included enough topics to allow instructors to adapt this text to a variety of course lengths and organizations. Sections preceded by an asterisk * are optional and can be omitted without loss of continuity.

CONTENT FEATURES

Problem Solving

The National Council of Teachers of Mathematics (NCTM) in *An Agenda for Action: Recommendations for School Mathematics of the 1980's* lists as its first recommendation that "problem solving be the focus of school mathematics in the 1980's." In our text we have stressed and integrated problem solving whenever possible. For instance, in many worked examples, we show students why we have chosen to work a problem a certain way by discussing the problem solving processes involved. The following are other ways in which we have taken a problem solving approach:

Problem solving chapters (Chapters 1 and 13) are devoted to the problem solving techniques used throughout the text. Chapter 1 develops a four-step problem solving method, based upon Polya's work, that is used throughout the rest of the text:

- understanding the problem
- devising a plan
- carrying out the plan
- looking back at the problem

This chapter presupposes only minimal mathematics skills from students. Chapter 13 reviews problem solving strategies and presents challenging problems based upon topics covered in the preceding chapters.

A **preliminary problem** begins Chapters 1 through 12. Each problem poses a question that students can answer after mastering the material in that chapter. We encourage our students to attempt to solve the preliminary problem before starting the chapter so that they might develop a sense of what is needed to solve the problem. The final section of each of these chapters gives a solution to the preliminary problem using the four-step method presented in Chapter 1.

Brain teasers supplement many of the problem sets. They are challenging and entertaining problems related to the subject matter of the sections in which they appear. Solutions to the brain teasers are in the Instructor's Resource Manual that accompanies this textbook.

Sets and Relations

We present these topics (Chapter 2) in a way that allows instructors to cover less than the complete chapter if they wish.

Number Theory

Number theory concepts (Chapter 5) afford an excellent opportunity to develop the concept of proof. We have proved many of the properties in this chapter in a way that we believe is most meaningful to students at this level.

Probability and Statistics

We cover probability and statistics from an experimental point of view. We present many topics in probability (Chapter 7) through the use of tree diagrams, rather than the traditional formula-oriented approach. Formulas for combinations and permutations are developed later in this chapter. Statistics (Chapter 8) is presented with an emphasis on organizing, presenting, and interpreting data.

Geometry

Chapters 9, 10, 11, and 12 cover informal geometry. Chapter 9 introduces basic concepts of geometry. Motion geometry and geometric constructions are taught in Chapter 10 by using compass and straightedge, paper folding, and Miras. Work with Miras can be omitted if they are not available. Chapter 11 deals with the Pythagorean Theorem and notions of measurement. Chapter 12 presents the fundamentals of coordinate geometry.

Metric Measurement

We integrate metric measures with other geometric concepts in Chapters 10 and 11. We believe that this is a more natural, intuitive approach than many other textbooks take. We use metric units throughout the text and emphasize estimations and metric to metric conversions, rather than metric to English conversions and vice versa.

Logic

Appendix I: Informal Logic is a brief, self-contained overview of logic that emphasizes the precise use of language. We have included this appendix for those instructors who believe that an introduction to logic is necessary in this course. Appendix I can be taught at any time during the course or omitted entirely without any loss of continuity.

Calculator Usage

Recommendation 3 in *An Agenda for Action* from NCTM states that "Mathematics programs must take full advantage of the power of calculators and computers at all grade levels." With this in mind, we wrote Appendix II: Calculator Usage and designed it so that the material can be taught as a separate unit or incorporated into the text. Appendix II contains sections on how to choose a calculator, flowcharting, and over one-hundred calculator problems that are cross-referenced to the text's problem sets. A calculator symbol   🖩   appears at the end of most problem sets in the text and refers students to the appropriate problems in the appendix. Appendix II can be skipped entirely without any loss of continuity.

PEDAGOGICAL FEATURES

We usually present each new topic in a way that could be used in an actual school situation.

We have set off other pedagogical features in the design of the book, in the end-of-section features, and in the end-of-chapter features.

In Design

- Key terms, definitions, theorems, and other important concepts are highlighted in **boldface** type. Key terms are repeated in the margins to help students review the material.
- Graphs, charts, geometric drawings, cartoons, and other kinds of illustrations reinforce the content presented.
- A functional use of color in the text material and illustrations helps to emphasize various concepts.
- **Sample textbook pages** from several elementary mathematics series are reproduced throughout the book. These pages show how various topics are introduced to students in grades kindergarten through 8.

In End-of-Section Features

Laboratory activities are suggested at the end of many sections. These may be used to aid in the learning or in the eventual teaching of mathematics content. **Problem sets** at the end of each section include large numbers of problems generally arranged in order of increasing difficulty. Stars ★ indicate the most challenging problems. Answers to odd-numbered problems are included at the back of the book.

In End-of-Chapter Features

Questions From the Classroom appear at the end of each of Chapters 2-12. This feature is a collection of the kinds of questions students might ask their teachers about the material presented in that chapter. These questions can be discussed in class or assigned as research questions. Our students have found that this feature provides valuable experience in preparing for their future teaching. This feature is based upon *Mathematical Questions From the Classroom* by Richard Crouse and Clifford Sloyer (Prindle, Weber, Schmidt, 1977). Suggested answers to these questions are available in the Instructor's Resource Manual.

  Chapter outlines are included to help students review the chapter in outline form. **Key terms** are presented in boldface type in these outlines. **Chapter tests** provide an opportunity for students to test themselves on important concepts developed in each chapter. **A selected bibliography** concludes each chapter. These bibliographies can be assigned for outside reading or extra credit; they can be used as reference for answering many of the Questions From the Classroom; or they can complement the text for those students who wish to read further on a particular topic.

THE INSTRUCTOR'S RESOURCE MANUAL

This supplement contains:
- answers to *both* odd- and even-numbered problems
- solutions to the problems in Chapter 13
- sample chapter tests that may be used as test questions or as make-up tests
- suggested answers to Questions From the Classroom
- solutions to the brain teasers

ACKNOWLEDGMENTS

We would like to thank the students we have taught over the past several years for their patience and suggestions as we have class-tested and refined this text. Our sincere thanks also go to the Mathematics Department of the

University of Montana in Missoula, especially Vera and Valerie. The reviewers of our work (an alphabetical list is provided below) offered us excellent guidance, and we are grateful to them for the care they took with their reviews. Finally, we would like to thank our editor, Susan Newman, to whom this book also holds special significance. She and her colleagues at Benjamin/ Cummings, particularly Margaret Moore, have worked extremely hard on this text and have looked forward to its publication with the same excitement we have.

R.B.
S.L.
J.L.

List of Reviewers

Leon J. Ablon, College of Staten Island (CUNY)
James R. Boone, Texas A and M University
Donald J. Dessart, University of Tennessee, Knoxville
Glenadine Gibb, University of Texas, Austin
Boyd Henry, College of Idaho
Allan Hoffer, University of Oregon
Robert Kalin, Florida State University
Steven D. Kerr, Weber State College
Helen R. Santiz, University of Michigan, Dearborn
C. Ralph Verno, West Chester State College
John Wagner, Michigan State University
Grayson Wheatley, Purdue University

Special consultant on problem solving: G.L. Alexanderson, University of Santa Clara

Acknowledgments

We gratefully acknowledge the following sources for allowing us to reprint selected textbook pages from their elementary mathematics series:

p. 8:   From Robert E. Eicholz, Phares G. O'Daffer, and Charles R. Fleenor, *Mathematics In Our World,* Grade 3, p. 281. Copyright © 1978 by Addison-Wesley Publishing Company, Inc.

p. 42:   From Eugene D. Nichols, Paul A. Anderson, Leslie A. Dwight, Frances Flournoy, Robert Kalin, John Schluep, and Leonard Simon, *Holt School Mathematics,* Grade 8, p. 10. Copyright © 1974 by Holt, Rinehart and Winston, Publishers.

pp. 61, 228, and 262:   From Robert E. Eicholz, Phares G. O'Daffer, and Charles R. Fleenor, *Mathematics In Our World,* Grade 6, pp. 101, 226, and 284. Copyright © 1978 by Addison-Wesley Publishing Company, Inc.

pp. 98 and 114:   From Walter E. Rucker and Clyde A. Dilley, *Heath Mathematics,* Grade 4, pp. 46 and 60. Copyright © 1979 by D.C. Heath and Company.

p. 110:   From Eugene D. Nichols, Paul A. Anderson, Leslie A. Dwight, Frances Flournoy, Robert Kalin, John Schluep, and Leonard Simon, *Holt School Mathematics,* Grade 6, p. 69. Copyright © 1974 by Holt, Rinehart and Winston, Publishers.

p. 118:   From *Scott, Foresman Mathematics,* Grade 5, p. 84, by L. Carey Bolster, et al. Copyright © 1980 by Scott, Foresman and Company. Reprinted by permission.

p. 149:   From *Growth in Mathematics* (Silver), by David W. Wells, et al., p. 310. Copyright © 1978 by Harcourt Brace Jovanovich, Inc. Reprinted and reproduced by permission of the publisher.

pp. 170 and 300:   From Series m: *Mathematics,* Level 7, p. 356 and Level 6, p. 333. Tina Thoburn and Jack E. Forbes, Senior Authors. Copyright © 1978 Macmillan Publishing Co., Inc.

p. 189:   From Walter E. Rucker and Clyde A. Dilley, *Heath Mathematics,* Grade 6, p. 93. Copyright © 1979 by D.C. Heath and Company.

p. 290:   From *Scott, Foresman Mathematics,* Grade 5, p. 246, by L. Carey Bolster, et al. Copyright © 1980 by Scott, Foresman and Company. Reprinted by permission.

p. 326:   From *Scott, Foresman Mathematics,* Grade 4, p. 119, by L. Carey Bolster, et al. Copyright © 1980 by Scott, Foresman and Company. Reprinted by permission.

p. 330:   From *Growth in Mathematics* (Brown), by David W. Wells et al., p. 256. Copyright © 1978 by Harcourt Brace Jovanovich, Inc. Reprinted and reproduced by permission of the publisher.

p. 419 and 544:   From Robert E. Eicholz, Phares G. O'Daffer, and Charles R. Fleenor, *Mathematics In Our World,* Grade 8, pp. 50 and 294. Copyright © 1979 by Addison-Wesley Publishing Company, Inc.

p. 497.   From Walter E. Rucker and Clyde A. Dilley, *Heath Mathematics,* Grade 8, p. 134. Copyright © 1979 by D.C. Heath and Company.

p. 615:   From *The Random House Mathematics Program,* Grade 8 © 1974 by Random House, Inc.

We also wish to acknowledge the following sources for allowing us to reprint their material:

p. 284:   B. C. by permission of Johnny Hart and Field Enterprises, Inc.

p. 480:   From *Experiencing Geometry* by James V. Bruni. © 1977 by Wadsworth Publishing Company, Inc., Belmont, California 94002. Reprinted by permission of the publisher.

p. 140:   From Morris Kline, *Mathematics for Liberal Arts,* © 1967 by Addison-Wesley Publishing Company, Inc., pp. 74–75. Reprinted with permission.

Brief Contents

Detailed Contents

Note: Each numbered section ends with a problem set. Chapters 2–12 end with Questions From the Classroom, chapter outline, chapter test, and selected bibliography. The remaining chapters and the appendices have selected bibliographies.

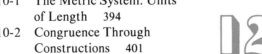

Introduction to Problem Solving

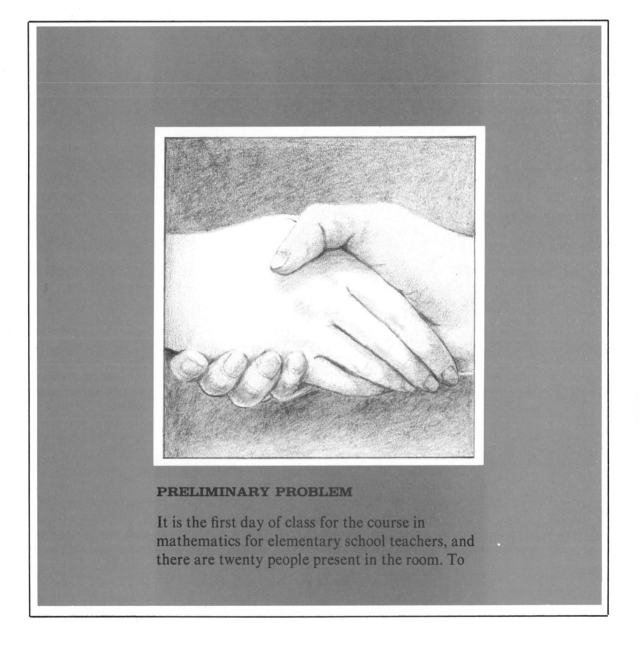

PRELIMINARY PROBLEM

It is the first day of class for the course in mathematics for elementary school teachers, and there are twenty people present in the room. To become acquainted with one another, each person shakes hands just once with everyone else. How many handshakes take place?

INTRODUCTION

The preliminary problem may seem beyond your capabilities. However, we urge you to spend some time trying to discover a strategy for solving it. If you try to solve the problem but are unable to do so, the solution at the end of the chapter will be valuable in expanding your problem-solving abilities.

Many students *and* teachers dislike doing problems, mainly because they have not had success in solving problems. Not seeing an immediate solution to a problem, they often give up, convinced that the problem is beyond their capabilities. Problem solving, in many cases, does take time.

How do you become a good problem solver? In this chapter, we present various strategies to help you develop problem-solving skills. Most of the examples in this text are mathematical, but many of the problem-solving techniques can be applied to situations outside mathematics.

1-1 EXPLORATION WITH PATTERNS

Discovering patterns is a very important strategy in problem solving. In mathematics, we refer to examining a variety of cases, discovering patterns, and forming conclusions based on these patterns as **inductive reasoning.** Scientists use inductive reasoning when they perform a number of experiments to discover various laws of nature. Statisticians use inductive reasoning when they form conclusions based on collected data. Inductive reasoning usually leads to what mathematicians call a **conjecture,** a statement thought to be true but not yet proven as either true or false. Inductive reasoning is an extremely helpful technique, but it should be used cautiously. There are examples where a certain pattern works for a number of cases but eventually breaks down.

Study the following examples and problems and look for some special property that all terms share. Different people may observe different patterns.

inductive reasoning

conjecture

Example 1-1

Find the next three terms to complete a pattern.

A26, B25, C24, _____, _____, _____

Analysis

Solution

Consecutive letters of the alphabet are listed, starting with A. The numbers are listed in decreasing order, starting with 26. Thus, using this pattern, the next three terms are D23, E22, and F21.

Example 1-2

Find the next three terms to complete a pattern.

1, 2, 4, ____ , ____ , ____

Solution

The difference between the first two terms is 1; the difference between the second two terms is 2; consequently, the difference between the next two terms might be 3, then 4, and so on. Thus, the completed sequence might appear as follows.

1, 2, 4, 7, 11, 16

Another property that 1, 2, 4 share is based on powers of 2. Notice that $1 = 2^0$, $2 = 2^1$, and $4 = 2^2$. The next terms could be 2^3 or 8, 2^4 or 16, and 2^5 or 32. Thus, the completed sequence might appear as follows.

1, 2, 4, 8, 16, 32

It becomes evident that more than one pattern is possible. Consequently, either solution is correct.

Example 1-3

Find the next three terms in the sequence.

1, 4, 7, 10, 13, ____ , ____ , ____

Solution

Each term is 3 units greater than the previous term.

Sequence   1   4   7   10   13

Difference   3   3   3   3

If this pattern continues, the next three terms will be 16, 19, and 22.

sequence

arithmetic sequence

In each example, the terms were given in an ordered arrangement. The word **sequence** will be used to describe terms given in a definite order. If each successive term in a sequence is obtained from the previous term by the addition of a fixed number, then the sequence is called an **arithmetic sequence.** The sequence in Example 1-3 is an arithmetic sequence. The fixed number is 3. Neither pattern in Example 1-2 illustrates an arithmetic sequence since no fixed number has been added.

Sometimes it is helpful to identify a general term for a sequence to solve a problem. Tables are useful aids for predicting the value of any term in a sequence. Consider the following table for the sequence of Example 1-3. The column headed "number of term" refers to the order of term in the sequence. The column headed "term" lists the accompanying terms of the sequence. We *ellipsis* use an **ellipsis,** denoted by three dots, to indicate that some terms are missing.

Number of Term	Term
1	1
2	$4 = 1 + 3$
3	$7 = 1 + 3 + 3 = 1 + 2 \cdot 3$
4	$10 = 1 + 3 + 3 + 3 = 1 + 3 \cdot 3$
5	$13 = 1 + 3 + 3 + 3 + 3 = 1 + 4 \cdot 3$
.	.
.	.
.	.

Notice that the number of 3's in each term is one less than the number of the term. Thus, the tenth term could be $1 + 9 \cdot 3$ or 28, and the one-hundredth term could be $1 + 99 \cdot 3$ or 298. The nth term, or general term, could be $1 + (n - 1) \cdot 3$, which, we shall see in Chapter 3, is the same as $3n - 2$.

Example 1-4   Find the next three terms and the nth term in the sequence.

2, 4, 8, 16, 32, . . .

Solution   Each term is double the preceding one. If this pattern continues, the next three consecutive terms will be 64, 128, and 256. This type of sequence is *geometric sequence* called a **geometric sequence.** Each successive term of a geometric sequence is obtained from its predecessor by multiplication by a fixed number. In this example, the fixed number is 2. To find the nth term, examine a table for the sequence.

Number of Term	Term
1	$2 = 2^1$
2	$4 = 2 \cdot 2 = 2^2$
3	$8 = 2 \cdot (2 \cdot 2) = 2^3$
4	$16 = 2 \cdot (2 \cdot 2 \cdot 2) = 2^4$
5	$32 = 2 \cdot (2 \cdot 2 \cdot 2 \cdot 2) = 2^5$
.	.
.	.
.	.

The table reveals a pattern. Following this pattern, the tenth term is 2^{10}, the one-hundredth term is 2^{100}, and the nth term is 2^n.

Example 1-5

The Greeks were fascinated by the way numbers appear geometrically. The following arrays represent the first four terms of what sequence of numbers? What is the nth term in the sequence?

Solution
square numbers

Notice that each array forms a square. The sequence of numbers suggested is that of the **square numbers,** namely, $1^2, 2^2, 3^2, 4^2, \ldots$ The following table shows the pattern.

Number of Term	Term
1	$1 = 1^2$
2	$4 = 2^2$
3	$9 = 3^2$
4	$16 = 4^2$
5	$25 = 5^2$
6	$36 = 6^2$
7	$49 = 7^2$
.	.
.	.
.	.

If the pattern continues, the tenth term will be 10^2, the one-hundredth term will be 100^2, and the nth term will be n^2.

Example 1-6
triangular numbers

Because of their shape, the following triangular arrays of dots represent the first four terms of a sequence of numbers called **triangular numbers.** What is the pattern for the set of triangular numbers?

Solution

The sequence 1, 3, 6, 10, . . . is suggested by these arrays. Each successive triangular array is obtained by adding another row of dots. The fifth array is obtained by adding 5 dots, the sixth by adding 6, the seventh by adding 7, and so on. The following table suggests a pattern.

Number of Term	Term
1	1
2	$3 = 1 + 2$
3	$6 = 1 + 2 + 3$
4	$10 = 1 + 2 + 3 + 4$
5	$15 = 1 + 2 + 3 + 4 + 5$
6	$21 = 1 + 2 + 3 + 4 + 5 + 6$
7	$28 = 1 + 2 + 3 + 4 + 5 + 6 + 7$
.	.
.	.
.	.

Following this pattern, the tenth term is $1 + 2 + 3 + \cdots + 10$, the one-hundredth term is $1 + 2 + 3 + \cdots + 100$, and the nth term is $1 + 2 + 3 + \cdots + n$. Later in this chapter we will show that, as a small boy, Karl Gauss, the famous German mathematician, discovered a simpler expression for the sum of $1 + 2 + 3 + \cdots + n$.

Example 1-7

Find the seventh term in the following sequence.

$5, 6, 14, 29, 51, 80, \ldots$

Solution

The pattern for the differences between successive terms is not easily recognizable. To discover the pattern, we look at the second difference.

Sequence   5   6   14   29   51   80

First difference   1   8   15   22   29

Second difference   7   7   · 7   7

Since the second difference is a fixed number, 7, the first difference row is an arithmetic sequence. Thus, the sixth term in the first difference row is $29 + 7$ or 36, and hence the seventh term in the original sequence is $80 + 36$ or 116. What number follows 116?

The general term for this sequence can algebraically be found to be $(7/2)n^2 - (19/2)n + 11$. However, justifying the general term for this particular sequence is beyond the scope of this text.

Example 1-8

Find the seventh term in the sequence.

$2, 3, 9, 23, 48, 87, \ldots$

Solution First, compute the differences.

Sequence 2 3 9 23 48 87

First difference 1 6 14 25 39

Second difference 5 8 11 14

Third difference 3 3 3

Since the third difference is a fixed number, the second difference is an arithmetic sequence. The fifth term in the second difference sequence is 14 + 3 or 17, the sixth term in the first difference sequence is 39 + 17 or 56, and the seventh term in the original sequence is 87 + 56 or 143.

Page 8 is a sample from the Addison-Wesley series *Mathematics In Our World,* 1978, Grade 3, showing that patterns appear early in elementary school mathematics.

PROBLEM SET 1-1

1. List the terms that complete a possible pattern. Then describe the pattern.
    (a) 2, 6, 10, 14, 18, _____, _____, _____
    (b) 0, 5, 10, 15, 20, _____, _____, _____
    (c) 1 × 2, 2 × 3, 3 × 4, 4 × 5, _____, _____, _____
    (d) □, 00, □ □ □, 0000, □ □ □ □ □, _____, _____, _____
    (e) 61, 57, 53, 49, _____, _____, _____
    (f) 5, 6, 8, 11, _____, _____, _____
    (g) 2, 5, 10, 17, _____, _____, _____
    (h) 1, ½, ¼, ⅛, _____, _____, _____
    (i) X, Y, X, X, Y, X, X, _____, _____, _____
    (j) 1, 3, 1, 8, 1, 13, _____, _____, _____
    (k) 1, 1, 2, 3, 5, _____, _____, _____
2. The following geometric arrays suggest a sequence of numbers.

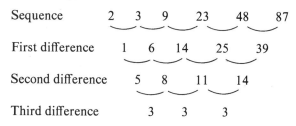

    (a) Find the next three terms.   (b) Find the one-hundredth term.
    ★(c) Find the *n*th term.

Finding the Pattern

The last card in each row is turned down.
Can you tell what number is hidden?

Example:

1. 2   4   6   8   10   12   14   ?

2. 3   8   13   18   23   28   33   ?

3. 1   2   4   8   16   32   64   ?

4. 1   6   7   12   13   18   19   ?

5. 1   2   4   7   11   16   22   ?

3. List the next three terms to complete a pattern in each of the following. (Finding differences may be helpful.)
    (a)   5, 6, 14, 32, 64, 115, 191, _____, _____, _____
    (b)   0, 2, 6, 12, 20, 30, 42, _____, _____, _____
    ★(c)   10, 8, 3, 0, 4, 20, 53, _____, _____, _____
4. Consider the following geometric arrays of pentagonal numbers. The numbers are formed by counting the dots. Find the first six numbers suggested by this sequence.

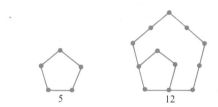

5. Find the nth terms for each of the following.
    (a)   1, 3, 5, 7, 9, 11, . . .   (b)   2, 4, 6, 8, 10, 12, . . .
    (c)   9, 13, 17, 21, 25, 29, . . .   (d)   1, 8, 27, 64, . . .
    ★(e)   2, 6, 18, 54, . . .
6. Classify each sequence in Problem 5 as *arithmetic, geometric,* or *neither.*
★7. Find the first five terms of the sequence with the nth term given as follows.
    (a) $n^2 + 2$ (b) $5n - 1$
8. In Appendix II, do Problems 6, 16, 17, 18, 22, 27, and 32.

1-2 HOW TO SOLVE PROBLEMS

BRAIN TEASER

Find the next three terms of the following sequences.

O, T, T, F, F, S, S, E
1, 2, 4, 3, 7, 5, 11, 6

exercises   What is a problem for one person may be an exercise for another. Solving **exercises** involves performing a routine procedure for finding solutions. On the other hand, according to the National Council of Supervisors of Mathematics (1977), solving problems involves "applying previously acquired knowledge to new and unfamiliar situations." For example, solving $12 \times 4 = \square$ is an exercise for most eighth graders, but it is a problem for most second graders. In the cartoon on page 10, Peppermint Patty tries to substitute another kind of exercise for a problem.

People rarely encounter computational exercises outside the classroom, but they do encounter problems. Thus, problem-solving skills are important for their success. One well-known mathematician and educator, George Polya, describes the experience of problem solving in his book, *How To Solve It.*

© 1978 United Feature Syndicate, Inc.

A great discovery solves a great problem but there is a grain of discovery in the solution of any problem. Your problem may be modest; but if it challenges your curiosity and brings into play your inventive facilities, and if you solve it by your own means, you may experience the tension and enjoy the triumph of discovery. Such experiences at a susceptible age may create a taste for mental work and leave their imprint on mind and character for a lifetime.

One way to become a good problem solver is by attempting a variety of problems. Techniques developed in solving these problems can be used to help solve new problems. As part of his work in problem solving, Polya developed a four-step process similar to the following.

1. Understanding the Problem
    (a) Can you state the problem in your own words?
    (b) What are the unknowns?
    (c) What information do you obtain from the problem?
    (d) What information, if any, is missing or not needed?
2. Devising a Plan
    The following list of strategies, although not exhaustive, is very useful.
    (a) Try a simpler problem.
    (b) Draw a table, diagram, or model.
    (c) Look for a pattern.
    (d) Break down the problem into special cases.
    (e) Write an equation.
    (f) Use trial and error.
3. Carrying Out the Plan
    Perform the necessary computations.
4. Looking Back
    (a) Check the results in the original problem. (In some cases, this will require a proof.)

(b)   Interpret the solution in terms of the original problem.

(c)   Determine whether there is another solution, perhaps a more direct one.

(d)   Determine whether there is another method of finding the solution.

(e)   Determine whether there are other related or more general problems for which the techniques will work. *How can you re-word the problem to create a new one.*

Step 4, looking back, is an important step for developing students' problem-solving skills. At this stage, students examine and describe their own thinking. Not only do they benefit, but other students who hear the description will benefit.

It is not necessary to memorize these four problem-solving steps. They will come naturally with practice. You will be asked to use the strategies discussed in this chapter but not always in the detail seen here. This four-step process does not assure a solution to a problem, but it gives valuable guidelines when there is no obvious way to proceed. Most of the problems presented in this chapter are solved without algebra since many elementary students do not have the tools of algebra.

Problem solving is not a spectator sport. The more problems you attempt, the better you become. The following discussion illustrates how the four-step process is helpful in solving problems.

One interesting problem whose solution is usually attributed to a famous German mathematician, Karl Gauss (1777–1855) (see Figure 1-1), involves finding the sum of the first one hundred counting numbers. According to legend, when Gauss was a child, his teacher became infuriated with the class and, as punishment, required the students to find the sum of the first 100 counting numbers. The teacher expected this problem to keep the class occupied for a considerable amount of time. Gauss gave the answer almost immediately. Can you? This problem will now be analyzed using the four-step process just described.

FIGURE 1-1
Karl Gauss

Understanding the Problem

The problem is to find the sum $1 + 2 + 3 + 4 + \cdots + 100$.

Devising a Plan

One story reports that Gauss noticed the relationship given in Figure 1-2. By considering $1 + 100, 2 + 99, 3 + 98, \ldots, 50 + 51$, he observed that there are 50 pairs of numbers, each having a sum of 101.

FIGURE 1-2

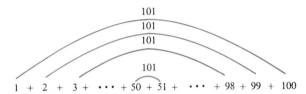

Carrying Out the Plan

Since there are 50 pairs, each with the sum 101, the total sum is 50(101) or 5050.

Looking Back

It is easy to check the computation involved. It is also easy to see that the method is mathematically correct since addition can be performed in any order, and multiplication is repeated addition. A more general problem is to find the sum of the first n numbers, $1 + 2 + 3 + 4 + 5 + \cdots + n$, where n is any natural number. Use the same plan as before and notice the relationship in Figure 1-3.

Since there are n numbers in the sum, there are $n/2$ pairs of numbers. The sum of each pair is $n + 1$. Therefore, the sum $1 + 2 + 3 + \cdots + n$ is given by $(n/2)(n + 1)$. This approach works nicely if the number of terms is even. Does the same formula work if n is odd?

FIGURE 1-3

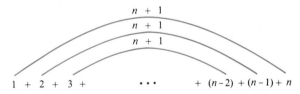

FIGURE 1-4

If you follow only certain patterns in attacking problems, there is a danger that you may form a *mind set*. A mind set occurs when you draw a faulty conclusion by assuming that you know the answer to a problem without really examining the problem. For example, spell the word "spot" three times aloud. "S-P-O-T! S-P-O-T! S-P-O-T!" Now answer the question: "What do you do when you come to a green light?" Write your answer. If you answered "Stop," you may be guilty of forming a mind set. You do not stop at a *green* light.

Examine Figure 1-4. Do you see anything unusual? Many people do not notice that the "the" appears twice in the sign. They have formed a mind set.

Consider the following problem.

A man had 36 sheep. All but 10 died. How many lived?

Did you answer "10"? If you did, you are catching on and are ready to try some problems. If you did not answer "10," then you should reread the problem and make sure you really *understand the question*.

The next series of problems illustrates how the four-step process can be used with a variety of other problems. These are the types of problems that appear in elementary school textbooks.

Problem 1   A shopkeeper is packaging soda pop in cartons that hold 8 bottles each. She has 420 bottles. How many cartons does she need?

Understanding the Problem

This problem may be an exercise for you, but it is a real problem for many elementary students. The problem is easy to understand; one carton holds 8 bottles, two cartons hold 16 bottles, and so on. How many cartons does it take to hold 420 bottles? Assume that there must be a full set of 8 bottles before a carton is needed.

Devising a Plan

A plan for solving this problem usually depends on the level of the students. One student might reason that if one carton holds 8 bottles, then ten cartons hold 80 bottles, twenty cartons hold 160 bottles, and so on, developing a table such as the one that follows.

Cartons	1	10	20	30	40	50
Bottles	8	80	160	240	320	400

A more advanced student may recognize that the problem is a division problem that asks how many groups of 8 are in 420.

Carrying Out the Plan

The preceding table shows that 50 cartons hold 400 bottles with 20 bottles left over. Since only full cartons will be packed, the 20 bottles fill an additional two cartons. Four bottles are left over.

Division yields the same result: 52 cartons with 4 bottles remaining.

$$
\begin{array}{r}
52 \\
8\overline{)420} \\
\underline{40} \\
20 \\
\underline{16} \\
4
\end{array}
$$

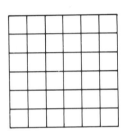

FIGURE 1-5

Looking Back

The answer is correct since $(8 \cdot 52) + 4 = 420$.

The problem can be varied by changing the number of bottles, by changing the size of the carton, or by asking how many full cases it would take to package the cartons if a case holds six cartons.

Problem 2   Using the existing lines in Figure 1-5, how many different squares are there?

Understanding the Problem

Before proceeding, it is important to know what is meant by square and, also, what is meant by "different squares." A square is a four-sided figure whose sides are line segments of equal length and whose adjacent sides meet at right angles. Two squares are different if they have either different dimensions or different locations. For example, the colored lines in Figure 1-6 show four different squares.

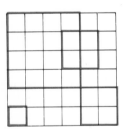

FIGURE 1-6

Devising a Plan

The strategy of looking at simpler problems is one of the most important strategies in problem solving and will be used repeatedly in this text. This strategy appears to be appropriate here. The simplest problem to consider is: How many different squares are there in a 1×1 grid? This is very easy; only one. How about a 2×2 grid? There are four 1×1 squares and one 2×2 square for a total of five squares.

How many squares are in a 3×3 grid?

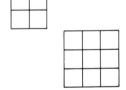

There are nine 1×1 squares, four 2×2 squares, and one 3×3 square for a total of fourteen squares. How many squares are in a 4×4 grid?

The problem now becomes more involved. Making a table to record the information is helpful.

Grid Size	1 × 1	2 × 2	3 × 3	4 × 4	Total Squares
1 × 1	1 or 1^2				1
2 × 2	4 or 2^2	1 or 1^2			5
3 × 3	9 or 3^2	4 or 2^2	1 or 1^2		14
4 × 4	16 or 4^2	9 or 3^2	4 or 2^2	1 or 1^2	30

Notice that each total is a sum of perfect squares and that the total of 30 is obtained by finding $1^2 + 2^2 + 3^2 + 4^2$. The table reveals a pattern that is very helpful for counting squares with larger grids. Thus, in a 5 × 5 grid, the total is given by $1^2 + 2^2 + 3^2 + 4^2 + 5^2$ and, in a 6 × 6 grid, the total is $1^2 + 2^2 + 3^2 + 4^2 + 5^2 + 6^2$.

Carrying Out the Plan

The only computation involved is finding $1^2 + 2^2 + 3^2 + 4^2 + 5^2 + 6^2$, namely 91.

Looking Back

The more general problem is to find the number of squares in an $n \times n$ grid. Following the preceding pattern, it seems that the number of squares in such a grid is $1^2 + 2^2 + 3^2 + \cdots + n^2$. However, we cannot be absolutely certain of this answer since the observation of a pattern from a few cases does not assure that the pattern always holds. As problem solvers learn more mathematics, they will be able to complete proofs. *Observing a pattern from a few cases does not constitute a proof.*

Problem 3   Given any 30 points on a circle, join them in pairs by segments in all possible ways. What is the greatest number of nonoverlapping regions into which the interior of the circle can be separated? Find a pattern that helps to answer the question for n points, where n is any number.

Understanding the Problem

To better understand what is meant by nonoverlapping regions, consider Figure 1-7. All possible segments joining 2 distinct points separate the circle into 2 regions. With 3 distinct points, 4 regions are formed. With 4 distinct points, 8 regions are formed. The problem is to find the number of regions formed when there are 30 distinct points on a circle connected in pairs by segments in all possible ways. We are then to generalize the problem to n points.

FIGURE 1-7

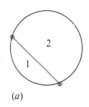

(a)

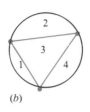

(b)

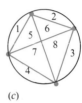

(c)

Devising a Plan

One possible strategy for 30 points is to draw a circle, mark the points, draw the segments, and count the regions. This strategy is not very helpful because the picture is complicated by many segments and regions.

Another strategy, suggested by Figure 1-7, is to examine simpler problems and look for a pattern. A table for the first three cases follows.

Number of Points	Number of Regions
2	2
3	4
4	8

It appears that as the number of points increases by 1, the number of regions doubles. Based on this observation, it appears that 5 points would yield 16 regions. Figure 1-8 verifies this idea.

Based on the pattern established, the number of regions for 6 points is 32. To solve the original problem, you could extend the following table to 30 points and generalize to n points.

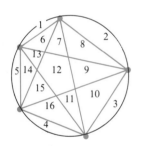

FIGURE 1-8

Number of Points	Number of Regions
2	2 or 2^1
3	4 or 2^2
4	8 or 2^3
5	16 or 2^4
6	32 or 2^5

Carrying Out the Plan

According to the pattern suggested by the preceding table, the number of regions for 30 points is 2^{29}, and the number of regions for n points is 2^{n-1}.

Looking Back

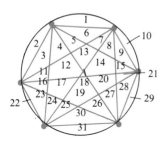

FIGURE 1-9

Part of looking back includes checking the answer to make sure that it is correct. Although you cannot realistically check the problem for 30 points or n points, you can check it for 6 points. The maximum number of regions for 6 points is shown in Figure 1-9. In reality, the answer is *not* 32 as we expected, but rather 31. Hence, the conclusions for 30 points and n points are not valid. This may be shocking since most of us put our complete faith in the continuation of a simple pattern once we have been fortunate enough to discover it. Patterns are very helpful, but there is always a possibility that they may break down unless it can be proved that they work for all cases. A pattern in mathematics leads only to an educated guess, not to a sure solution.

Although the sequence 1, 2, 4, 8, 16, 32, . . . does not work in the given problem, there is a pattern to the sequence 1, 2, 4, 8, 16, 31, ... It is possible, but somewhat difficult, to find the next terms using the difference technique discussed earlier.

Problem 4   How many ways are there to make change for a quarter using only dimes, nickels, and pennies?

Understanding the Problem

There are no limits on the number of coins to be used. Nickels, dimes, and pennies need not all be used; that is, 25 pennies is an acceptable answer, as would be 2 dimes and 1 nickel.

Devising a Plan

Organize a chart to keep a record of all possibilities as they are examined. First, consider the possibilities when the number of nickels and dimes is zero and the number of pennies is 25. Continue the chart by trading nickels for pennies. Are there other combinations? What about dimes? To finish the problem, consider all possibilities using dimes.

D	N	P
0	0	25
0	1	20
0	2	15
0	3	10
0	4	5
0	5	0

Carrying Out the Plan

Start with combinations using one dime. With one dime, the greatest number of pennies possible is 15. Next, trade nickels for pennies.

D	N	P
1	0	15
1	1	10
1	2	5
1	3	0

The last case to consider is possibilities with 2 dimes. Proceeding as before, we obtain the following.

D	N	P
2	0	5
2	1	0

By putting all three cases together, we obtain the following table.

D	N	P
0	0	25
0	1	20
0	2	15
0	3	10
0	4	5
0	5	0
1	0	15
1	1	10
1	2	5
1	3	0
2	0	5
2	1	0

Thus, there are 12 ways to make change for a quarter using only dimes, nickels, and pennies.

Looking Back

Check each row to see that it shows change for one quarter. The systematic listing used in the chart shows that all cases have been considered.

The problem can be extended easily by starting with an initial amount other than one quarter.

An interesting related problem is as follows. Given the number of coins it takes to make change for a quarter, is it possible to determine exactly which coins they are? (*Hint:* Look at the large table listing the 12 different combinations. Is the number of coins in each combination different?) If you think you know the answer, try it with a friend to see if it works.

The discussions in this section demonstrate only a few of the problem-solving strategies that can be taught in the elementary grades. The general ideas can be used at almost any grade level. Variations or combinations of these strategies are adaptable to problems encountered in everday life.

PROBLEM SET 1-2

The first thirteen problems are warm-up problems or puzzles that have been around in one form or another for many years. They will help you begin to think and to understand what is really being asked in a problem. Beware of mind sets. (The strategies discussed in Chapter 1 will be useful in Problems 14–30.)

1. How much dirt is in a hole 2 ft long, 3 ft wide, and 2 ft deep?

2. Two U.S. coins have a total value of 55¢. One coin is not a nickel. What two coins are they?

3. A farmer went to sleep at 8:00 P.M. He set his alarm for 9:00 A.M. How long did he sleep before he was awakened?

4. Divide 30 by ½. Add 12. What is the answer?

5. Sal owns 20 blue and 20 brown socks which he keeps in a drawer in complete disorder. What is the minimum number of socks that he must pull out of the drawer on a dark morning to be sure he has a matching pair?

6. A heavy smoker wakes up in the middle of the night and finds herself out of cigarettes. The stores are closed, so she looks through all the ashtrays for butts. She figures that with five butts she can make one new cigarette. She finds 25 butts and decides they will last her till morning if she smokes only one cigarette every hour. How long does her supply last?

7. You have 8 sticks. Four of them are exactly half the length of the other 4. Enclose 3 equal squares with them.

8. Suppose you have only one 5-liter container and one 3-liter container. How can you measure exactly 4 liters of water if neither container is marked for measuring?

9. It takes 1 hour and 20 minutes to drive to the airport, yet the return trip takes only 80 minutes using the same route and driving at what seems to be the same speed. How can this be?

10. What is the minumum number of pitches possible for a pitcher to make in a major league baseball game, assuming he plays the entire game, and it is not called prior to completion?

11. Consider the following banking transaction. Deposit $50 and withdraw it as follows:

withdraw $20	leaving $30
withdraw 15	leaving 15
withdraw 9	leaving 6
withdraw 6	leaving 0
$50	$51

Where did the extra dollar come from? To whom does it belong?

12. A businessman bought four pieces of solid-gold chain, each consisting of three links.

He wanted to keep them as an investment, but his wife felt that, joined together, the pieces would make a lovely necklace. A jeweler charges $10.50 to break a link and $10.50 to melt it together again. What is the minimum charge possible to form a necklace using all the pieces?

13. An alternate version of the story of Gauss computing $1 + 2 + 3 + \cdots + 100$ reports that he simply listed the numbers in the following way to discover the sum.

$$
\begin{array}{l}
1 + \quad 2 + \quad 3 + \quad 4 + \quad 5 + \cdots + \quad 98 + \quad 99 + 100 \\
\underline{100 + \quad 99 + \quad 98 + \quad 97 + \quad 96 + \cdots + \quad 3 + \quad 2 + \quad 1} \\
101 + 101 + 101 + 101 + 101 + \cdots + 101 + 101 + 101
\end{array}
$$

Does this method give the same answer? Discuss the advantages of this method over the one described in the text.

14. How many different squares are in the following figure?

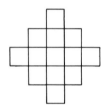

15. What is the largest sum of money—all in coins and no silver dollars—that I could have in my pocket without being able to give change for a dollar, a half-dollar, a quarter, a dime, or a nickel?

16. Arrange the numbers 1 through 9 in squares arranged like the ones at the left so that the sums of every row, column, and diagonal are 15. (The result is called a *magic square*).

17. Molly is building a staircase out of blocks in the pattern at the left. How many blocks will it take to build a staircase that is 25 blocks high?

18. How can you cook an egg for exactly 15 minutes if all you have are a 7-minute and an 11-minute timer?

19. How many different ways can you make change for a $50 bill using $5, $10, and $20 bills?

20. How many different four-digit numbers have the same digits as 1984?

21. There are four volumes of Shakespeare's collected works on a shelf. The volumes are in order from left to right. The pages of each volume are exactly 2 inches thick. The covers are each ⅙ inch thick. A bookworm started eating at page 1 of Volume I and ate through to the last page of Volume IV. What is the distance the bookworm traveled?

22. A woman goes into a store and says to the owner: "Give me as much money as I have with me, and I will spend $10." It is done. Then the woman repeats the operation in a second and a third store, after which she has no money left. How much did she have at the start?

23. Looking out in the backyard one day, I saw an assortment of boys and dogs. Counting heads, I got 22. Counting feet, I got 68. How many boys and how many dogs were in the yard?

24. A bottle and a cork together cost $1.00. The bottle costs 96¢ more than the cork. How much does the cork cost?

25. A cat is at the bottom of an 18-foot well. Each day it climbs up 3 feet, and each night it slides back 2 feet. How long will it take the cat to get out of the well?

26. A pioneer moving west had a goose, a bag of corn, and a fox. He came to a river. The ferry was large enough to carry him and one of his possessions. If he were to leave the fox and the goose alone, the fox would eat the goose. If he were to leave the goose and corn alone, the goose would eat the corn. How did he get himself and his possessions across the river?

27. In a horse race:
    (a) Fast Jack finished a length ahead of Lookout.
    (b) Lookout did not finish in last place.
    (c) Null Set finished 7 lengths ahead of Bent Leg.
    (d) Fast Jack finished 7 lengths behind Applejack.
    (e) Bent Leg finished 3 lengths behind Fast Jack.
    What was the finishing position of each horse?

28. Eight marbles all look alike, but one is slightly heavier than the others. By using a balance scale, how can you determine the heavier one in exactly:
    (a) 3 weighings?   (b) 2 weighings?

29. Marc went to the store with $1.00 in change. He had at least one of each coin less than a half dollar, but he did not have a half-dollar coin.
    (a) What is the least number of coins he could have?
    (b) What is the greatest number of coins he could have?

30. Ten women are fishing all in a row in a boat. One seat in the center of the boat is empty. The five women in the front of the boat want to change seats with the five women in the back of the boat. A person can move from her seat to the next empty seat, or she can step over one person without capsizing the boat. What is the minimum number of moves needed to exchange the five women in front with the five in back?

31. You are given a checkerboard with the two squares on opposite corners removed and a set of dominoes such that each domino can cover two squares on the board. Can the dominoes be arranged in such a way that all of the 62 remaining squares on the board can be covered? If not, why not?

32. Would you rather work for a month (31 days) and get one million dollars or be paid 1¢ the first day, 2¢ the second day, 4¢ the third day, 8¢ the fourth day, and so on?

33. In Appendix II, do Problems 23, 24, 25, 26, 28, 36, 37, 38, 55, 56, 57, 61, and 65.

LABORATORY ACTIVITY   Place a half dollar, a quarter, and a nickel in position *A* as shown in the figure. Try to move these coins, one at a time, to position *C*. At no time may a larger coin be placed on a smaller coin. Coins may be placed in position *B*. How many moves does it take? Now, add a penny to the pile and see how many moves it takes. This is a simple case of the famous Tower of Hanoi problem in which ancient Brahman priests were required to move a pile of 64 disks of decreasing size, after which the world would end. How long would this take at a rate of one move per second?

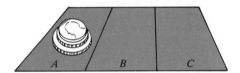

SOLUTION TO THE PRELIMINARY PROBLEM

Understanding the Problem

There are 20 people in the room, and each person shakes hands with each other person only once. It takes two people for one handshake; that is, if Maria shakes hands with John and John shakes hands with Maria, this counts as one handshake, not two. The problem is to find the number of handshakes that take place.

Devising a Plan

One plan that would certainly work is to take 20 people and actually count the handshakes. Although this plan provides a solution, it would be nice to find a less elaborate one. First, look at some simpler problems. With one person in the room there are no handshakes. If a second person enters the room, there is 1 handshake (remember, 2 persons shaking hands counts as 1 handshake). If a third person enters the room, he or she shakes hands with each of the other persons present, so there are 2 additional handshakes for a total of 1 + 2. If a fourth person enters the room, he or she shakes hands with each of the other three members present, so there is an addition of 3 shakes for a total of 1 + 2 + 3. If a fifth person enters the room, an additional 4 shakes take place. Make a table to keep track of the shakes. The following table has been carried out for five people.

Number of People	Number of Handshakes
1	0
2	1
3	$1 + 2 = 3$
4	$1 + 2 + 3 = 6$
5	$1 + 2 + 3 + 4 = 10$

Notice that the last number in the sum, $1 + 2 + 3 + 4$, is one less than the number of people shaking hands. To complete the problem, we could complete the chart to 20 people and compute the sum.

Carrying Out the Plan

Following this pattern for 20 people, the answer is given by $1 + 2 + 3 + 4 + \cdots + 19$. The technique used by Gauss (Section 1-3) to find sums is very useful in performing this computation.

$$1 + 2 + 3 + 4 + \cdots + 19 = \frac{19(20)}{2} = 190$$

Looking Back

Another way of working this problem is to look at diagrams rather than tables. A diagram showing a handshake between persons A and B can be indicated by a line segment connecting A and B as shown.

```
●————————●
A        B
```

The diagram showing handshakes for three, four, and five people is given in Figure 1-10.

FIGURE 1-10

3 people
3 handshakes
(a)

4 people
6 handshakes
(b)

5 people
10 handshakes
(c)

From the diagrams, we see that the problem becomes one of counting the different line segments needed to connect various numbers of points. In looking at the problem for five people (Figure 1-10(c)), we see that person A shakes hands with persons B, C, D, and E (4 handshakes). Person B shakes hands with persons A, C, D, and E (4 handshakes). In fact, each person shakes hands with 4 other people. Therefore, it appears that there are 5 · 4 or 20 handshakes. However, notice that the handshake between A and B is counted twice. This dual counting occurs for all five persons. Consequently, each handshake was counted twice; thus, to obtain the answer, we must divide by 2. The answer is (5 · 4)/2 or 10. This approach leads to the answer of 190 handshakes for 20 people and can be generalized for any number of people.

CHAPTER OUTLINE

I. Mathematical patterns
   A. Patterns are an important part of problem solving.
   B. Patterns are used in **inductive reasoning** to form conjectures. A **conjecture** is a statement that is thought to be true but not yet been proven.
   C. A **sequence** is a group of terms in a definite order.
      1. **Arithmetic sequence:** Each successive term is obtained from the previous one by the addition of a fixed number.
      2. **Geometric sequence:** Each successive term is obtained from its predecessor by multiplying it by a fixed number.
      3. Finding differences for a sequence is one technique for finding the next terms.

II. Problem solving
   A. Problem solving should be guided by the following four-step process:
      1. Understanding the problem
      2. Devising a plan
      3. Carrying out the plan
      4. Looking back
   B. Important problem-solving strategies include:
      1. Try a simpler problem.
      2. Draw a table, diagram, or model.
      3. Look for a pattern.
      4. Break down the problem into special cases.
      5. Write an equation.
      6. Use trial and error.
   C. Beware of mind sets!

SELECTED BIBLIOGRAPHY

Billstein, R. "Checkerboard Mathematics." *The Mathematics Teacher,* **86**(December 1975):640–646.

Butts, T. *Problem Solving in Mathematics.* Glenview, Ill.: Scott, Foresman, 1973.

Fisher, B. "Calculator Games: Combining Skills and Problem Solving." *The Arithmetic Teacher,* **27**(December 1979):40–41.

Gathany, T. "Involving Students in Problem Solving." *The Mathematics Teacher,* **72**(November 1979):617–621.

Green, D. "Ant, Aardvark and Fudge Brownies." *The Arithmetic Teacher,* **27**(March 1979):38–39.

Greenes, C., R. Spungin, and J. Dombrowski. *Problem-mathics.* Palo Alto, Calif.: Creative Publications, 1977.

Greenes, C., J. Gregory, and D. Seymour. *Successful Problem-Solving Techniques.* Palo Alto, Calif.: Creative Publications, 1977.

Hecht, A. "Environmental Problem Solving," *The Arithmetic Teacher,* **27**(December 1979):42–43.

Hughes, B. *Thinking Through Problems.* Palo Alto, Calif.: Creative Publications, 1976.

Krulik, S. "Problem Solving: Some Considerations." *The Arithmetic Teacher,* **25**(December 1977): 51–52.

LeBlanc, J. "You Can Teach Problem Solving." *The Arithmetic Teacher,* **25**(November 1977):16–19.

Leder, G. "Sex Differences in Mathematics Problem Appeal as a Function of Problem Context." *Journal of Educational Research,* **67**(April 1974): 351–353.

Lester, F. "Ideas about Problem Solving: A Look at Some Psychological Research." *The Arithmetic Teacher,* **25**(November 1977):12–14.

Liedtke, W. "The Young Child as a Problem Solver." *Arithmetic Teacher,* **25**(April 1977):333–338.

Lindquist, M., and M. Dana. "Almanac Facts." *The Arithmetic Teacher,* **27**(January 1979):4–7.

Linquist, M. "Problem Solving with Five Easy Pieces." *The Arithmetic Teacher,* **25**(November 1977):7–10.

Lott, J. "Behold! A Magic Square." *The Arithmetic Teacher,* **24**(March 1977):228–229.

Masse, M. "More Problems Please." *The Arithmetic Teacher,* **26**(December 1978):11–14.

Morris, J. "Problem Solving with Calculators." *The Arithmetic Teacher,* **25**(April 1978):24–26.

Nelson, D., and J. Kirkpatrick. "Problem Solving." In *Mathematics Learning in Early Childhood,* ed. J. N. Payne. 37th Yearbook of National Council of Teachers of Mathematics. Reston, Va.: NCTM, 1975.

Position Paper on Basic Mathematical Skills, National Council of Supervisors of Mathematics, January 1977.

Payne, J. N. (ed.). *Mathematics Learning in Early Childhood.* 37th yearbook of National Council of Teachers of Mathematics. Reston, Va.: NCTM, 1975, (Chapters 9 and 10.).

Polya, G. *How to Solve It.* Princeton, N.J.: Princeton University Press, 1957.

Polya, G. *Mathematical Discovery.* Vol. I. New York: John Wiley & Sons, 1962.

Polya, G. *Mathematical Discovery.* Vol. II, New York: John Wiley & Sons, 1965.

Richardson, L. L. "Role of Strategies for Teaching Pupils to Solve Verbal Problems." *The Arithmetic Teacher,* **22**(May 1975):414–421.

Robinson, E. "On the Uniqueness of Problems in Mathematics." *The Arithmetic Teacher,* **25**(November 1977):22–26.

Suydam, M., and F. Weaver. "Research on Problem Solving: Implications for Elementary School Classrooms, *The Arithmetic Teacher,* **25**(November 1977):40–42.

Szetela, W. "Analogy and Problem Solving: A Tool for Helping Children to Develop a Better Concept of Capacity." *The Arithmetic Teacher,* **27**(March 1980):18–22.

Thomas, D. "Geometry in the Middle School: Problem Solving with Trapezoids." *The Arithmetic Teacher,* **26**(February 1979):20–21.

Thompson, M. *The Experiences in Problem Solving.* Reading, Mass.: Addison-Wesley Publishing Company, 1976.

Troutman, A., and B. Lichtenberg. "Problem Solving in the General Mathematics Classroom." *The Mathematics Teacher,* **67**(November 1974):590–597.

Underhill, R. "Teaching Word Problems to First Graders," *The Arithmetic Teacher,* **25**(November 1977):54–56.

Walter, M., and S. Brown. "Problem Posing and Problem Solving: An Illustration of Their Interdependence." *The Mathematics Teacher,* **70**(January 1977):4–13.

Wheatley, G. "The Right Hemisphere's Role in Problem Solving." *The Arithmetic Teacher,* **25**(November 1977):36–39.

Whitin, D. "Patterns with Square Numbers." *The Arithmetic Teacher,* **27**(December 1979):38–39.

Wickelgren, W. *How to Solve Problems.* San Francisco: W. H. Freeman, 1974.

Zalewski, D. "Magic Triangles—More Discoveries!" *The Arithmetic Teacher,* **27**(September 1979): 46–47.

Zweng, M. "The Problem of Solving Story Problems." *The Arithmetic Teacher,* **27**(September 1979):2–3.

Sets and Relations

2

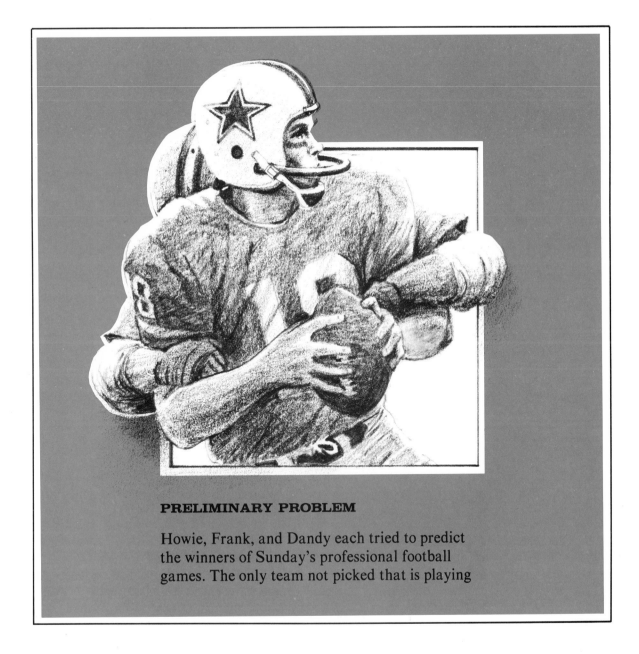

PRELIMINARY PROBLEM

Howie, Frank, and Dandy each tried to predict the winners of Sunday's professional football games. The only team not picked that is playing

Sunday was the Giants. The choices for each person were as follows.

Howie: Cowboys, Steelers, Vikings, Bills
Frank: Steelers, Packers, Cowboys, Redskins
Dandy: Redskins, Vikings, Jets, Cowboys

If the only teams playing Sunday are those just mentioned, which teams will play which other teams?

INTRODUCTION

set theory

It was George Cantor, in the years 1871–1884, who created a new and special area of mathematics called **set theory.** Cantor was born in Russia and educated in Germany. Much of his professional life was spent at the University of Halle, now in East Germany. Cantor's later years were spent in controversy over his work on set theory, causing him to spend some time in a mental institution. He finally won recognition for his work before he died. His theories have had a profound effect on mathematical research and on the teaching of mathematics.

The language of set theory was implemented into elementary schools in the 1960s in the post-Sputnik era. It contained words such as **set, subset, union,** and **intersection.** In the 1970s, numerous people felt that the new language caused confusion for children as well as for teachers and other adults. The following cartoon illustrates the feelings of many of these people.

Many mathematics educators are convinced that the basic set concepts are simple enough to be taught in the early grades. The concepts clarify many mathematical ideas that are much harder to understand without the use of sets.

2-1   DESCRIBING SETS

set
elements
In mathematics, undefined terms are usually terms that are very basic, and we usually have a clear picture of them. The word set is such a term. In mathematics, the word **set** refers to any collection or group of objects. The individual objects in a set are called **elements** or **members** of the set. If we are speaking of the set of students in your mathematics class, each student is an element or a member of that set. If we consider the set of letters in the English alphabet, each letter is an element of that set. We let capital letters stand for sets and use braces to enclose the elements of the set. The set of letters of the English alphabet can be written as

$$A = \{a, b, c, d, e, f, g, h, i, j, k, l, m, n, o, p, q, r, s, t, u, v, w, x, y, z\}$$

The set consisting of the first four counting numbers can be written as

$$B = \{1, 2, 3, 4\}$$

The order in which the elements are written makes no difference, and each element should be listed only once.

well defined
    For a given set to be useful in mathematics, it must be **well defined.** This means that if we are given a set and some particular object, we must be able to tell whether the object does or does not belong to the set. For example, the set of all citizens of Hong Kong who ate rice on January 1, 1981, is well defined. We do not know if a particular resident of Hong Kong ate rice or not, but we do know that person either did or did not.

    Consider the set A consisting of the letters of the English alphabet. This set is well defined. We know that m is an element of set A. This can be written in symbols as $m \in A$. The number 12 is not an element of A. We write this as $12 \notin A$.

    Consider the set of all the tall students in your mathematics class. This set is not well defined since the decision as to whether a student belongs to this set can be left to personal opinion. Different people have different views on what it means to be tall. Similarly, the set of good mathematics teachers is not well defined since not everyone agrees on the definition of a good mathematics teacher.

    We use sets to define mathematical terms. For example, the set of
natural numbers **natural** or **counting numbers** is defined by the following.

$$N = \{1, 2, 3, 4, \ldots\}$$

infinite set
finite set
The three ellipsis dots indicate that the list continues indefinitely. The set of natural numbers N is an example of an infinite set. An **infinite set,** informally described, is a set that contains an unlimited number of elements. In contrast, a set is called a **finite set** if the number of elements in the set is zero or a

natural number. For example, the set of letters in the English alphabet is a finite set since it contains exactly 26 elements.

equal sets   Two sets are **equal** if they contain exactly the same elements. The order in which the elements are listed does not matter. If A and B are equal, written $A = B$, then every element of A is an element of B, *and* every element of B is an element of A. If A does not equal B, we write $A \neq B$.

Example 2-1   Tell which of the following pairs of sets are equal.

    (a) $A = \{a, b, c\}$ and $B = \{b, c, a\}$
    (b) $C = \{a, 1, 2\}$ and $D = \{a, 1, 3\}$
    (c) $E = \{2, 4, 6\}$ and $G = \{2, 4, 6, 8, 10\}$

Solution   (a) $A = B$ (b) $C \neq D$ (c) $E \neq G$

roster method   When all the elements of a set are listed, we say that the set has been named by the **roster method.** Each element in the set is listed only once. Using the roster method, the set of letters in the word "book" can be written as follows.

$\{b, o, k\}$

set-builder notation   Sometimes a set has so many elements that the roster method is not a practical way of describing it. In other cases, the individual elements of a set are not known. Sets of this kind can often be indicated by describing a property common to all the elements. The sets are named using **set-builder notation.** The set of animals in the San Diego Zoo can be described as follows.

$Z = \{x \mid x$ is an animal in the San Diego Zoo$\}$

This is read: "*Z is the set of all elements x* such that *x* is an animal in the San Diego Zoo." The vertical line is read: "such that."

Example 2-2   Write the set of natural numbers greater than 50 and less than 500 using (a)   the roster method and (b)   set-builder notation.

Solution   (a) $\{51, 52, 53, 54, \ldots, 498, 499\}$
    (b) $\{x \mid x$ is a natural number greater than 50 and less than 500$\}$

Example 2-3   Write the set of even natural numbers greater than 4 and less than 6 using set-builder notation.

Solution | $\{x \mid x$ is an even natural number greater than 4 and less than 6$\}$

It is impossible to list the elements in Example 2-3 using the roster method. There are no even natural numbers greater than 4 and less than 6. empty set   The set has no elements. A set that contains no elements is called an **empty set** or **null set.** The empty set is designated by the symbols $\varnothing$ or $\{\ \}$. (The empty set is often incorrectly recorded as $\{\varnothing\}$. This set is not empty. It contains one element, namely $\varnothing$. Likewise, $\{0\}$ does not represent the empty set.) Two examples of empty sets are:

$F = \{x \mid x$ was a female president of the United States before 1900$\} = \varnothing$

$G = \{x \mid x$ is a natural number smaller than 1$\} = \varnothing$

universal set   The **universal set,** or the **universe,** is the set that contains all elements that are being considered in a given discussion. The universal set is denoted by U. While the empty set never changes, the universal set may vary from one discussion to another. For this reason, you should be aware of what the universal set is in any given problem.

If the universal set is given by $U = \{a, b, c, d, \ldots, x, y, z\}$, every set discussed must contain only letters of the English alphabet. $\{1, 2, 3\}$ cannot be considered. It does not belong to the universe being discussed since it contains elements other than letters of the English alphabet.

Suppose $U = \{x \mid x$ is a person living in California$\}$ and $A = \{x \mid x$ is a female living in California$\}$. The universal set and set A can be represented by a diagram. The universal set is usually indicated by a large rectangle, and particular sets are indicated by geometric figures inside the rectangle as Venn diagram   shown in Figure 2-1. This figure is an example of a **Venn diagram,** named after the Englishman John Venn. He published a book called *Symbolic Logic* in which he used diagrams like Figure 2-1 to illustrate ideas in logic.

Consider the sets $A = \{1, 2, 3, 4, 5, 6\}$ and $B = \{2, 4, 6\}$. Notice that all the subset   elements of B are contained in A. We say that B is a **subset** of A and write $B \subseteq A$. In general, we have the following definition.

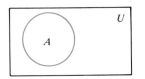

FIGURE 2-1

DEFINITION

> B is a **subset** of A, written $B \subseteq A$, if and only if every element of B is also an element of A.

Notice that this definition is written with the words "if and only if." This means: if B is a subset of A, then every element of B is also an element of A *and* if every element of B is also an element of A, then B is a subset of A.

proper subset

All definitions can be written in "if and only if" form.

We say that B is a **proper subset** of A if B is a subset of A and there is at least one element of A that is not an element of B. We write $B \subset A$.

Example 2-4

If $U = \{1, 2, 3, 4, 5\}$, $D = \{1, 3, 5\}$, and $E = \{1, 3\}$, (a) Which sets are subsets of each other? (b) Which sets are proper subsets of each other?

Solution

(a) $D \subseteq U$, $E \subseteq U$ and $E \subseteq D$. Notice also that $D \subseteq D$, $E \subseteq E$, and $U \subseteq U$.

(b) $D \subset U$, $E \subset U$ and $E \subset D$.

When a set A is not a subset of another set B, we write $A \not\subseteq B$. To show that $A \not\subseteq B$, you must find at least one element of A that is not in B. If $A = \{1, 3, 5\}$ and $B = \{1, 2, 3\}$, then A is not a subset of B since there is an element, namely 5, belonging to A but not to B. Likewise, $B \not\subseteq A$ because there exists an element, namely 2, belonging to B but not to A. (Note that $\{2\} \subseteq \{1, 2\}$ and $2 \in \{1, 2\}$, but $\{2\} \notin \{1, 2\}$ and $2 \not\subseteq \{1, 2\}$.)

Is the empty set a subset of every set? For example, is it true that $\varnothing \subseteq \{1, 2\}$? Suppose $\varnothing \not\subseteq \{1, 2\}$. Then there must be some element in $\varnothing$ that is not in $\{1, 2\}$. Since the empty set has no elements, there cannot be an element in the empty set that is not in $\{1, 2\}$. Consequently, $\varnothing \not\subseteq \{1, 2\}$ is false, and therefore $\varnothing \subseteq \{1, 2\}$ is true. The same reasoning can be applied in the case of the empty set and any other set. *Thus, for any set A, $\varnothing \subseteq A$.* In particular, $\varnothing \subseteq \varnothing$.

How many subsets does a given set have? That is, is there a formula for finding the number of subsets of a set with n elements? To emphasize the process used in solving this problem, we use the four steps outlined in Chapter 1.

Understanding the Problem

There are n elements in a set. We are to determine a formula for finding the number of subsets for this given set no matter what n is.

Devising a Plan

To obtain a general formula, try some simple cases first.
1. If $A = \varnothing$, then A has 1 subset, itself.
2. If $B = \{a\}$, then B has 2 subsets, $\varnothing$ and $\{a\}$.
3. If $C = \{a, b\}$, then C has 4 subsets; namely, $\varnothing$, $\{a\}$, $\{b\}$, and $\{a, b\}$.

4. If $D = \{a, b, c\}$, then D has 8 subsets; namely, $\varnothing$, $\{a\}$, $\{b\}$, $\{c\}$, $\{a, b\}$, $\{a, c\}$, $\{b, c\}$, and $\{a, b, c\}$.

Using the information from these cases, make a table and search for a pattern.

Number of Elements	Number of Subsets
0	1
1	2 or 2^1
2	4 or 2^2
3	8 or 2^3
.	.
.	.
.	.

This table suggests that for 4 elements, there are 2^4 or 16 subsets. Is this guess correct? If $E = \{a, b, c, d\}$, then all of the subsets of $D = \{a, b, c\}$ are also subsets of E. Eight new subsets are also formed by adjoining the element d to each of the 8 subsets of D. These 8 new subsets are $\{d\}$, $\{a, d\}$, $\{b, d\}$, $\{c, d\}$, $\{a, b, d\}$, $\{a, c, d\}$, $\{b, c, d\}$, and $\{a, b, c, d\}$. Thus, there are twice as many subsets of set E (with 4 elements) as there are of set D (with 3 elements). Thus, there are indeed 16, or 2^4, subsets of a set with 4 elements. Extending the pattern, there are 2^5, or 32, subsets of a set with 5 elements, and 2^6, or 64, subsets of a set with 6 elements.

Carrying Out the Plan

Notice that in each case the number of elements and the power of 2, which is used to obtain the number of subsets, match exactly. Thus, if there are n elements in a set, there are 2^n subsets that can be formed.

Looking Back

In this problem, the answer was based on more than simply observing patterns in a table. It was observed that adding one more element to a set doubled the number of possible subsets. The formula 2^n subsets for a set with n elements is based on this doubling factor. Notice also that this formula implies that $2^0 = 1$, which is a true statement. The fact that $a^0 = 1$, $a \in N$ is investigated in Chapter 3. Another question this problem suggests is: Given a set with n elements, what is the number of subsets each having exactly one element, exactly two elements, exactly three elements, and in general exactly k elements?

PROBLEM SET 2-1

1. Which of the following sets are well defined?
   (a) The set of wealthy school teachers
   (b) The set of great books
   (c) The set of students taking this class
   (d) The set of natural numbers greater than 100
2. Write the following sets using either the roster method or set-builder notation.
   (a) The set of letters in the word "mathematics"
   (b) The set of pink elephants taking this class
   (c) The set of months whose names begin with J
   (d) The set of natural numbers greater than 20
3. Rewrite the following statements using mathematical symbols.
   (a) B is equal to the set whose elements are x, y, z, and w.
   (b) 3 is not an element of set B
   (c) The set consisting of the elements 1 and 2 is a proper subset of the set consisting of the elements 1, 2, 3, and 4
   (d) The set D is not a subset of set E
4. Indicate which symbol, $\in$ or $\notin$, makes each of the following statements true.
   (a) 3 _____ $\{1, 2, 3\}$ (b) 2 _____ $\{2\}$
   (c) 0 _____ $\varnothing$ (d) a _____ $\varnothing$
   (e) $\{1\}$ _____ $\{1, 2\}$ (f) $\varnothing$ _____ 1
   (g) $\varnothing$ _____ $\varnothing$ (h) $\{1, 2\}$ _____ $\{1, 2\}$
   (i) $\{1\}$ _____ $\{\{1\}, \varnothing\}$ (j) $\{1, 2\}$ _____ $\{1\}$
5. For each of the statements in Problem 4, indicate which symbol, $\subseteq$ or $\not\subseteq$, makes the statement true.
6. The set of all subsets of $\{x, y\}$ is $\{\{x\}, \{y\}, \{x, y\}, \varnothing\}$. Find the set of all subsets of $\{x, y, z\}$.
7. Write each of the following using set-builder notation.
   (a) The set of states in the United States
   (b) The set of elementary school teachers
8. If $A = \{a, b, c, d, e, f\}$, how many subsets does A have? How many proper subsets does A have?
9. If a set B has n elements where n is some natural number, how many proper subsets does B have?
10. Which of the following represent equal sets?

    $A = \{a, b, c, d\}$ $E = \varnothing$
    $B = \{x, y, z, w\}$ $F = \{\varnothing\}$
    $C = \{c, d, a, b\}$ $G = \{0\}$
    $D = \{x \mid x$ is one of the first four letters of the alphabet$\}$ $H = \{\ \}$

11. If $B \subset C$, what is the least possible number of elements in C? Why?
12. What relationship exists between C and D if $C \subseteq D$ and $D \subseteq C$?
13. Is $\varnothing$ a proper subset of every set? Why?
14. Is it always true that $A \not\subseteq B$ implies $B \subset A$? Why?
15. Classify each of the following as true or false. If your answer is "false," tell why.

(a) $\{\ \} = \varnothing$ (b) $\{\varnothing\} = \{\ \}$
(c) If $A = B$, then $A \subseteq B$ (d) If $A \subseteq B$, then $A \subset B$
(e) If $A \subset B$, then $A \subseteq B$ (f) If $A \subseteq B$, then $A = B$

The brain teaser is a version of Russell's paradox named after Bertrand Russell, and it was one of the causes of controversy over Cantor's set theory.

BRAIN TEASER

A soldier, Joe, was ordered to shave those soldiers, and only those soldiers, of his platoon who did not shave themselves. Let $A = \{x \mid x$ is a soldier who shaves himself$\}$ and $B = \{x \mid x$ is a soldier who does not shave himself$\}$. Notice that every soldier must belong to one set or the other. To which set does Joe belong?

2-2 OPERATIONS ON SETS

Suppose that a person inherits two different stamp collections and decides to sell or exchange all duplicates. The person must identify the set of all stamps that are common to the two collections. If we name the two stamp collections A and B, the set of stamps duplicated in the collections is called the **intersection** of the two collections.

intersection

DEFINITION

> The **intersection** of two sets A and B, written $A \cap B$, is the set of all elements common to both A and B.

Using set-builder notation, we write this as $A \cap B = \{x \mid x \in A \text{ and } x \in B\}$.

Example 2-5   Find the intersections for each of the following pairs of sets.

(a) $A = \{\text{Charlie, Snoopy, Lucy}\}$ and $B = \{\text{Snoopy, Lucy, Linus}\}$
(b) $F = \{1, 2, 3\}$ and $G = \{1, 2, 3, 4, 5\}$
(c) $H = \{1, 2, 3, 4\}$ and $J = \varnothing$
(d) $M = \{1, 2, 3, 4, 5\}$ and $N = \{6, 7, 8\}$

Solution | (a) $A \cap B = \{\text{Snoopy, Lucy}\}$ (b) $F \cap G = \{1, 2, 3\}$
         | (c) $H \cap J = \emptyset$ (d) $M \cap N = \emptyset$

disjoint sets   When sets such as M and N in the preceding example have no elements in common, we call them **disjoint sets.** In other words, two sets A and B are disjoint if and only if $A \cap B = \emptyset$.

Venn diagrams can be used to picture the intersection of sets. For example, Figure 2-2 shows pictures for four different conditions for $A \cap B$. Set A contains lines in one direction. Set B contains lines in another direction. The intersection of the two sets is indicated by the shading.

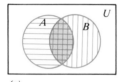

(a)

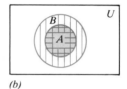

(b)

FIGURE 2-2

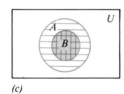

(c)

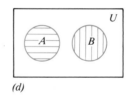

(d)

Depending on the elements of A and B, one of the four pictures must describe $A \cap B$. In Figure 2-2(a), the sets have some elements in common. In Figure 2-2(b), $A \subseteq B$ and $A \cap B = A$; in Figure 2-2(c), $B \subseteq A$ and $A \cap B = B$; in Figure 2-2(d) $A \cap B = \emptyset$. Notice the lack of shading in Figure 2-2(d) since A and B are disjoint.

Remember the stamp collection at the beginning of this section? If the stamp collector combines the two stamp collections, A and B, into one collection in such a way that there is only one of each stamp, we say that the new stamp collection is the **union** of A and B.

union

DEFINITION

> The **union** of two sets A and B, written $A \cup B$, is the set of all elements in A, in B, or in both A and B.

Using set-builder notation, $A \cup B = \{x \mid x \in A \text{ or } x \in B\}$.

The key word in the definition of union is "*or*." In everyday language, the word "or" usually means one thing or another but not both. For example, "I am going to the ballgame or to the play." In mathematics, usually, "or" means *one or the other or both*.

Example 2-6   Find the union of the sets in each of the following pairs.

    (a) $A = \{$Charlie, Snoopy, Lucy$\}$ and $B = \{$Snoopy, Lucy, Linus, Schroeder$\}$

    (b) $X = \{1, 2, 3, 4\}$ and $Y = \{5, 6, 7, 8\}$

    (c) $C = \{1, 2\}$ and $D = \varnothing$

    (d) $E = \{1, 2, 3\}$ and $F = \{2, 3, 4, 5\}$

Solution   (a) $A \cup B = \{$Charlie, Snoopy, Lucy, Linus, Schroeder$\}$

    (b) $X \cup Y = \{1, 2, 3, 4, 5, 6, 7, 8\}$

    (c) $C \cup D = \{1, 2\} = C$

    (d) $E \cup F = \{1, 2, 3, 4, 5\}$

Remark   It is important to notice that although elements may be listed in each set, they are listed only once in the union of the sets.

Venn diagrams showing the union of sets A and B for four different conditions are given in Figure 2-3. In each case, the union is indicated by the shaded region.

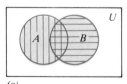
(a)

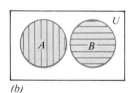
(b)

FIGURE 2-3

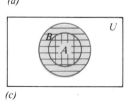
(c)

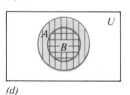
(d)

In Figure 2-3(*c*), $A \subseteq B$ and $A \cup B = B$, and in Figure 2-3(*d*), $B \subseteq A$ and $A \cup B = A$.

Suppose $U = \{1, 2, 3, 4, 5, 6\}$ and $A = \{1, 3, 5\}$. The set of all the elements of the universe that are *not* in A is $\{2, 4, 6\}$ and is called the complement **complement** of A.

DEFINITION

> The **complement** of a set A, written $\overline{A}$, is the set of all elements in the universal set U that are not in A.

Using set-builder notation, $\overline{A} = \{x \mid x \in U \text{ and } x \notin A\}$.

Example 2-7   If $U = \{a, b, c, d\}$ and $B = \{c, d\}$, find (a) $\overline{B}$ and (b) $\overline{U}$.

Solution   (a) $\overline{B} = \{a, b\}$ and (b) $\overline{U} = \varnothing$.

Example 2-8   If $U = \{x \mid x \text{ is a student in a mathematics class}\}$ and $F = \{x \mid x \text{ is a female student in a mathematics class}\}$, find $\overline{F}$.

Solution   Since the individual students in a particular mathematics class are not known, $\overline{F}$ must be described using set-builder notation.

$\overline{F} = \{x \mid x \text{ is a male student in a mathematics class}\}$

Venn diagrams can also be used to represent complements. The shaded region in Figure 2-4 represents $\overline{A}$.

FIGURE 2-4

Example 2-9   Draw a Venn diagram for $\overline{A \cup B}$.

Solution   Since the complement bar is over the expression $A \cup B$, first find $A \cup B$ and then find its complement. $A \cup B$ is the shaded portion of Figure 2-5.

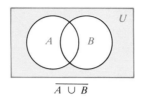

FIGURE 2-5

$\overline{A \cup B}$

If A is the set of students taking a mathematics class and B is the set of students taking physics, then the set of all the students taking physics but not
complement of A relative to B mathematics is called the **complement of A relative to B.**

DEFINITION

> The **complement of A relative to B,** written $B - A$, is the set of all elements in B that are not in A.

$B - A$ is also read "the set difference of B and A." Using set-builder notation, $B - A = \{x \mid x \in B \text{ and } x \notin A\}$. A Venn diagram representing $B - A$ is given in Figure 2-6.

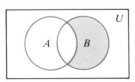

FIGURE 2-6

Example 2-10

If $A = \{d, e, f\}$ and $B = \{a, b, c, d, e\}$, find: (a) $B - A$, (b) $A - B$, (c) $A - A$.

Solution

(a) $B - A = \{a, b, c, d, e\} - \{d, e, f\} = \{a, b, c\}$
(b) $A - B = \{d, e, f\} - \{a, b, c, d, e\} = \{f\}$
(c) $A - A = \{d, e, f\} - \{d, e, f\} = \varnothing$

The set difference of two sets can be written as the intersection of two sets in the following way.

$B - A = B \cap \overline{A}$

This result can be illustrated using Venn diagrams as shown in Figure 2-7.

FIGURE 2-7

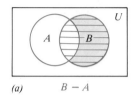 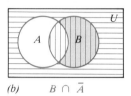

(a) $B - A$ (b) $B \cap \bar{A}$

Not only can Venn diagrams be used to represent various sets and set operations but portions of Venn diagrams can be described in set notation.

Example 2-11   Use set notation to describe the shaded portions of the following Venn diagrams. (There are many solutions.)

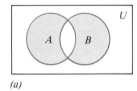   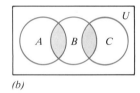

(a)   (b)

Solution   (a) $(A \cup B) \cap \overline{(A \cap B)}$ or $(A \cup B) - (A \cap B)$
(b) $(A \cap B) \cup (B \cap C)$ or $B \cap (A \cup C)$

Example 2-12   Suppose M is the set of all students taking mathematics and E is the set of all students taking English. Identify the students described by each region in Figure 2-8.

FIGURE 2-8

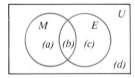

Solution   Region (a) contains all students taking mathematics but not English. Region (b) contains all students taking both mathematics and English. Region (c) contains all students taking English but not mathematics. Region (d) contains all students taking neither mathematics nor English.

Some descriptions of sets involve combinations of union, intersection, and set difference. Parentheses indicate which operations are performed first.

Example 2-13   Let $U = \{1, 2, 3, 4, 5, 6, 7, 8, 9, 10\}$,

$A = \{2, 3, 6, 8, 10\}$,
$B = \{1, 3, 5, 7, 9\}$,
$C = \{1, 2, 3, 4, 5\}$,

Find $(A \cap C) \cup B$.

Solution $(A \cap C) \cup B = (\{2, 3, 6, 8, 10\} \cap \{1, 2, 3, 4, 5\}) \cup \{1, 3, 5, 7, 9\}$
$= \{2, 3\} \cup \{1, 3, 5, 7, 9\}$
$= \{2, 3, 1, 5, 7, 9\}$

The ideas of sets and Venn diagrams are helpful for solving certain types of problems.

Example 2-14   Suppose a survey was taken of college freshmen to determine something about their high school backgrounds. The following information was gathered from interviews with 110 students.

25 took physics
45 took biology
48 took mathematics
10 took physics and mathematics
  8 took biology and mathematics
  6 took physics and biology
  5 took all three subjects

How many students took biology but neither physics nor mathematics? How many did not take any of the three subjects?

Solution   To solve this problem, build a model using sets. Since there are three distinct subjects, draw a Venn diagram with the 3 sets and 8 regions. In Figure 2-9, P is the set of students taking physics, B is the set taking biology, and M is the set taking mathematics. The shaded region represents the 5 students who took all three subjects. The lined region represents the students who took physics and mathematics but who did not take biology.

Since a total of 10 students took physics and mathematics, and since 5 of those also took biology, $10 - 5$ or 5 students took physics and math but not biology. The other numbers in the diagram were derived using similar reasoning. After completing the diagram, interpret the results. Of all the students, 36 took biology but neither physics nor mathematics, and 11 did not take any of the three subjects.

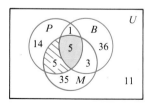

FIGURE 2-9

The following sample is taken from *Holt School Mathematics*, 1974, Grade 8. It shows a problem similar to the one in Example 2-14. (The notation $n(P)$ means the number of elements in set P.)

SOLVING PROBLEMS USING SETS

Consider this problem.

28 girls.
20 of them have long hair.
16 of them have curly hair.
12 of them have both long and curly hair.

How many girls have long hair, but not curly hair?
How many girls have curly hair, but not long hair?
How many girls have neither long hair nor curly hair?

To answer these questions, we shall use a Venn diagram. Let $P = \{girls\}$, so $n(P) = 28$. $G = \{girls$ having long hair$\}$, so $n(G) = 20$. $B = \{girls$ having curly hair$\}$, so $n(B) = 16$ and $n(G \cap B) = 12$.

Each dot represents a girl.

1. We know that $n(G) = 20$ and that $n(G \cap B) = 12$.

   a. How many are in G, but not in $G \cap B$?

   b. How many have long hair, but not curly hair?

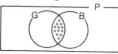

2. We know that $n(B) = 16$ and that $n(G \cap B) = 12$.

   a. How many are in B, but not in $G \cap B$?

   b. How many have curly hair, but not long hair?

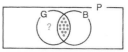

3. We know that $n(P) = 28$.

   a. What is $n(G \cup B)$?

   b. How many have neither long hair nor curly hair?

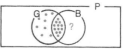

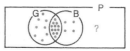

10

PROBLEM SET 2-2

1. Given $U = \{f, i, n, a, l, s, o, v, e, r\}$ and $A = \{f, i, n, a, l, s\}$, $B = \{a, r, e\}$ and $C = \{o, v, e, r\}$, find each of the following.
    (a) $A \cup B$ (b) $A \cap B$ (c) $\overline{A} \cup C$ (d) $A \cap \overline{C}$
    (e) $(A \cup B) \cup C$ (f) $B \cap \overline{C}$ (g) $\overline{C} \cup A$ (h) $\overline{C \cup A}$
    (i) $C \cap \overline{B}$ (j) $B - C$

2. Tell whether each of the following are true or false. If false, tell why.
    (a) For all sets A, $A \cup \varnothing = A$.
    (b) For all sets A and B, $A - B = B - A$.
    (c) For all sets A, $A \cup A = A$.
    (d) For all sets A and B, $\overline{A \cap B} = \overline{A} \cap \overline{B}$.
    (e) For all sets A and B, $A \cap B = B \cap A$.
    (f) For all sets A, B, and C, $(A \cup B) \cup C = A \cup (B \cup C)$.
    (g) For all sets A, $A - \varnothing = A$.

3. If $B \subseteq A$, find a simpler expression for:
    (a) $A \cap B$ (b) $A \cup B$.

4. For each of the following, indicate the portion of the Venn diagram that illustrates the set.
    (a) $A \cup B$ (b) $\overline{A} \cap B$ (c) $A \cap \overline{B}$ (d) $(A \cup B) \cap \overline{C}$
    (e) $\overline{A \cap B}$ (f) $(A \cap B) \cup C$ (g) $(A \cap B) \cup (A \cap C)$ (h) $(\overline{A} \cap B) \cup C$

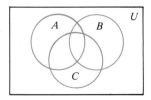

5. Use set notation to identify each of the following shaded regions.

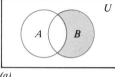

(a)

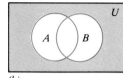

(b)

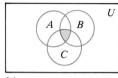

(c)

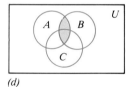

(d)   *(e)*   *(f)*

6. Given that the universe is the set of all humans, $B = \{x \mid x$ is a college basketball player$\}$, and $S = \{x \mid x$ is a college student more than 200 cm tall$\}$, describe each of the following in words.

   (a) $\overline{B \cap S}$ (b) $\overline{S}$ (c) $B \cup S$

   (d) $\overline{B \cup S}$ (e) $\overline{B} \cap S$ (f) $B \cap \overline{S}$

7. If S is a subset of the universe U, find each of the following.

   (a) $S \cup \overline{S}$ (b) $S \cup U$ (c) $\emptyset \cup S$ (d) $\overline{U}$ (e) $S \cap U$

   (f) $\overline{\emptyset}$ (g) $S \cap \overline{S}$ (h) $S - \overline{S}$ (i) $U \cap \overline{S}$ (j) $\overline{\overline{S}}$

8. Answer each of the following and justify your answer.

   (a) If $a \in A \cap B$, is it true that $a \in A \cup B$?

   (b) If $a \in A \cup B$, is it true that $a \in A \cap B$?

9. For each of the following, find $A - B$.

   (a) $A \cap B = \emptyset$ (b) $B = U$ (c) $A = B$ (d) $A \subset B$

10. For each of the following, draw a Venn diagram so that sets A, B, and C satisfy the given conditions.

   (a) $A \cap B \neq \emptyset, C \subset (A \cap B)$

   (b) $A \cap C \neq \emptyset, B \cap C \neq \emptyset, A \cap B = \emptyset$

   (c) $A \subset B, C \cap B \neq \emptyset, A \cap C = \emptyset$

11. Shade the portion of the diagram that represents the given sets.

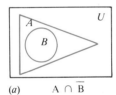 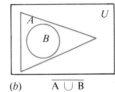 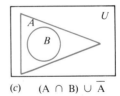

   (a) $A \cap \overline{B}$ (b) $A \cup B$ (c) $(A \cap B) \cup \overline{A}$

★12. Using set notation, describe the shaded region shown below.

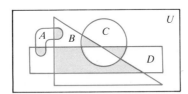

13. Suppose P is the set of all eighth-grade students at the Paxson school, with B the set of all students in the band and C the set of all students in the choir. Identify in words the students described by each region of the following diagram.

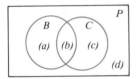

14. Of the eighth-graders at the Paxson school, there were:
     7 who played basketball,
     9 who played volleyball,
    10 who played soccer,
     1 who played basketball and volleyball only,
     1 who played basketball and soccer only,
     2 who played volleyball and soccer only, and
     2 who played volleyball, basketball and soccer.
    How many played one or more of the three sports?

15. In a fraternity with 30 members, 18 take mathematics, 5 take both mathematics and biology, and 8 take neither mathematics nor biology. How many take biology but not mathematics?

16. Three types of antigens are looked for in blood tests; they are A, B, and Rh. Whenever the antigen A or B is present, it is listed, but if both these antigens are absent, the blood is said to be type O. If the Rh antigen is present, the blood is said to be positive; otherwise it is negative. Thus, the main blood types are:

    $\{A^+, A^-, B^+, B^-, AB^+, AB^-, O^+, O^-\}$.

    A Venn diagram for blood types is shown at the right.

    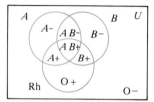

    (a) Indicate the area representing the people who react positively to the A antigen but not the B antigen nor the Rh antigen.
    (b) Suppose a laboratory technician reports the following results after testing the blood samples of 100 people. How many of the 100 people were classified as O negative?

Number of Samples	Antigens in Blood
40	A
18	B
82	Rh
5	A and B
31	A and Rh
11	B and Rh
4	A, B, and Rh

17. Two families each having three children are assembled for a birthday party. Each of the six children has either blue or brown eyes, and brown or blond hair. Children in one family may differ by at most one characteristic. The following are descriptions of the six children.
    Tom: blue eyes, brown hair   Harry: blue eyes, blond hair
    Dick: brown eyes, blond hair   Jane: blue eyes, brown hair
    Mary: brown eyes, brown hair   Abby: blue eyes, blond hair

    Separate the children into two families.

BRAIN TEASER

Every doodad is a doohickey. Half of all thingamajigs are doohickeys. Half of all doohickeys are doodads. There are 30 thingamajigs and 20 doodads. No thingamajig is a doodad. How many doohickeys are neither doodads nor thingamajigs?

2-3 PROPERTIES OF SET OPERATIONS

Consider the sets A and B where $A = \{1, 2, 3\}$ and $B = \{2, 3, 4, 5\}$. Since $A \cap B = \{2, 3\}$ and $B \cap A = \{2, 3\}$, in this case $A \cap B = B \cap A$. In fact, it is always true that for any two sets A and B, $A \cap B = B \cap A$.

Using the same sets, we see that $A \cup B = \{1, 2, 3, 4, 5\}$ and $B \cup A = \{1, 2, 3, 4, 5\}$. In general, it is true that for any sets A and B, $A \cup B = B \cup A$.

commutative properties

These properties are called **commutative properties.**

Property | For all sets A and B,
(1)   Commutative Property of Set Intersection. $A \cap B = B \cap A$
(2)   Commutative Property of Set Union. $A \cup B = B \cup A$

Another property of sets involves the grouping of three sets under the operation of intersection. Consider $A \cap B \cap C$. Since operations are performed on pairs of sets, $A \cap B \cap C$ can be interpreted as $(A \cap B) \cap C$ or as $A \cap (B \cap C)$. Are these two interpretations the same? Let $A = \{a, b, c\}$, $B = \{b, c, d\}$, and $C = \{b, c, d, e, f\}$, and examine the two cases.

$$(A \cap B) \cap C = (\{a, b, c\} \cap \{b, c, d\}) \cap \{b, c, d, e, f\}$$
$$= \{b, c\} \cap \{b, c, d, e, f\}$$
$$= \{b, c\}$$

$$A \cap (B \cap C) = \{a, b, c\} \cap (\{b, c, d\} \cap \{b, c, d, e, f\})$$
$$= \{a, b, c\} \cap \{b, c, d\}$$
$$= \{b, c\}.$$

In this example, $(A \cap B) \cap C = A \cap (B \cap C)$. Venn diagrams are useful for examining the general cases. (Remember, always perform the operation in parentheses first.) The shaded regions for $(A \cap B) \cap C$ and $A \cap (B \cap C)$ in Figure 2-10 are the same, and thus, in general $(A \cap B) \cap C = A \cap (B \cap C)$. A similar situation holds for union of sets; that is,

$(A \cup B) \cup C = A \cup (B \cup C)$. (The justification of this property using Venn diagrams is left as an exercise.) These grouping properties are referred

associative properties   to as **associative properties.**

FIGURE 2-10

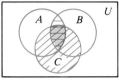 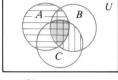

(*a*) $(A \cap B) \cap C$ (*b*) $A \cap (B \cap C)$

Property | For all sets A, B, and C,
(1) Associative Property of Set Intersection.
$(A \cap B) \cap C = A \cap (B \cap C)$
(2) Associative Property of Set Union.
$(A \cup B) \cup C = A \cup (B \cup C)$

As a result of the associative properties for union and intersection of sets, we simply write $A \cap B \cap C$ or $A \cup B \cup C$. It is not necessary to specify how the operations should be performed.

Is grouping important when two different operations are involved? For example, is it true that $A \cap (B \cup C) = (A \cap B) \cup C$? To investigate this, let $A = \{a, b, c, d\}$, $B = \{c, d, e\}$, and $C = \{d, e, f, g\}$.

$$A \cap (B \cup C) = \{a, b, c, d\} \cap (\{c, d, e\} \cup \{d, e, f, g\})$$
$$= \{a, b, c, d\} \cap \{c, d, e, f, g\}$$
$$= \{c, d\}$$
$$(A \cap B) \cup C = (\{a, b, c, d\} \cap \{c, d, e\}) \cup \{d, e, f, g\}$$
$$= \{c, d\} \cup \{d, e, f, g\}$$
$$= \{c, d, e, f, g\}.$$

In this case, $A \cap (B \cup C) \neq (A \cap B) \cup C$. We have found what is
counterexample   called a **counterexample** in mathematics, that is, an example that illustrates that a general statement is not always true. One counterexample is enough to make a conjecture false. Thus, in general, $A \cap (B \cup C) \neq (A \cap B) \cup C$. (Drawing Venn diagrams to show that $A \cap (B \cup C) \neq (A \cap B) \cup C$ and $A \cup (B \cap C) \neq (A \cup B) \cap C$ is left as an exercise.)

To discover an expression that is equal to $A \cap (B \cup C)$, consider the Venn diagram for $A \cap (B \cup C)$ shown by the shaded region in Figure 2-11.

According to the figure, two regions, $A \cap C$ and $A \cap B$, are parts (subsets) of the shaded region. The union of these two regions is the entire shaded region of the figure. Thus, this shaded region can be identified as $(A \cap C) \cup (A \cap B)$. Consequently, $A \cap (B \cup C) = (A \cap B) \cup (A \cap C)$. A similar approach illustrates that $A \cup (B \cap C) = (A \cup B) \cap (A \cup C)$. These properties that relate intersection and union are called

distributive properties   **distributive properties.**

FIGURE 2-11

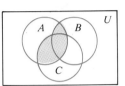

Property

For all sets A, B, and C,
(1) Distributive Property of Set Intersection over Union.
$$A \cap (B \cup C) = (A \cap B) \cup (A \cap C)$$
(2) Distributive Property of Set Union over Intersection.
$$A \cup (B \cap C) = (A \cup B) \cap (A \cup C)$$

Example 2-15

If $A = \{a, b, c\}$, $B = \{b, c, d\}$, and $C = \{d, e, f, g\}$, verify the distributive property of intersection over union for these sets.

Solution

$$
\begin{aligned}
A \cap (B \cup C) &= \{a, b, c\} \cap (\{b, c, d\} \cup \{d, e, f, g\}) \\
&= \{a, b, c\} \cap \{b, c, d, e, f, g\} \\
&= \{b, c\}
\end{aligned}
$$

$$
\begin{aligned}
(A \cap B) \cup (A \cap C) &= (\{a, b, c\} \cap \{b, c, d\}) \cup (\{a, b, c\} \cap \{d, e, f, g\}) \\
&= \{b, c\} \cup \varnothing \\
&= \{b, c\}
\end{aligned}
$$

Thus, $A \cap (B \cup C) = (A \cap B) \cup (A \cap C)$.

The following properties of set operations can also be verified.

1. *Identity Properties.* For every set A and the universe U,
    (a) $A \cap U = U \cap A = A$ U is the Identity for Set Intersection.
    (b) $A \cup \varnothing = \varnothing \cup A = A$ $\varnothing$ is the Identity for Set Union.
2. *Complement Properties.* For every set A and the universe U,
    (a) $\overline{U} = \varnothing$ (b) $\overline{\varnothing} = U$ (c) $A \cap \overline{A} = \varnothing$
    (d) $A \cup \overline{A} = U$ (e) $\overline{\overline{A}} = A$

PROBLEM SET 2-3

1. Is it true that $A \cup (B \cap C) = (A \cup B) \cap C$? Investigate by trying examples and using Venn diagrams.
2. Use Venn diagrams to verify the associative property of union; that is, show $A \cup (B \cup C) = (A \cup B) \cup C$.
3. Draw Venn diagrams for $A \cap (B \cup C)$ and $(A \cap B) \cup C$. What do you conclude?
4. Use Venn diagrams to investigate the truth of the distributive property of union over intersection; that is, investigate $A \cup (B \cap C) = (A \cup B) \cap (A \cup C)$.
5. Decide whether each of the following is true.
   (a) $\overline{A} \cup B = B \cup \overline{A}$ (b) $\overline{A \cup B} = \overline{A} \cup \overline{B}$ (c) $(\overline{A} \cup B) \cap C = \overline{A} \cup (B \cap C)$
6. Investigate the following properties of the set difference operation.
   (a) Is it commutative, that is, does $A - B = B - A$?
   (b) Is it associative, that is, does $A - (B - C) = (A - B) - C$?
   (c) Does the distributive property of set difference over union hold, that is, does $A - (B \cup C) = (A - B) \cup (A - C)$?
7. Suppose $U = \{e, q, u, a, l, i, t, y\}$, $A = \{l, i, t, e\}$, $B = \{t, i, e\}$, and $C = \{q, u, e\}$. Decide whether the following pairs of sets are equal.
   (a) $A \cap B$ and $B \cap A$ (b) $A \cup B$ and $B \cup A$
   (c) $A \cup (B \cup C)$ and $(A \cup B) \cup C$ (d) $A \cup \varnothing$ and A
   (e) $(A \cap A)$ and $(A \cap \varnothing)$ (f) $\overline{\overline{C}}$ and C
8. The equations $\overline{A \cup B} = \overline{A} \cap \overline{B}$ and $\overline{A \cap B} = \overline{A} \cup \overline{B}$ are referred to as *DeMorgan's laws* in honor of the famous British mathematician who first discovered them. Use Venn diagrams to show each of the following.
   (a) $\overline{A \cup B} = \overline{A} \cap \overline{B}$ (b) $\overline{A \cap B} = \overline{A} \cup \overline{B}$
   (c) Verify (a) and (b) for specific sets A and B.
9. If $A \cap B = A \cup B$, how are A and B related?

2-4 COMPARING SETS

Primitive people kept track of things by *matching* even before they learned to count. For example, they dropped a stone in a container for each animal leaving a pen in the morning and then removed a stone as each animal returned at night. A person could easily tell whether the same number of animals, fewer animals, or, sometimes, more animals returned at night than left in the morning. This idea of matching is a basic concept in mathematics. In the lower elementary grades, students match items such as frogs with lily pads or flowers with stems. No counting is involved in these examples, yet its foundations are being formed.

one-to-one correspondence

Consider the sets of basketball players {Tom, Dick, Harry, Mary} and of numbered shirts {1, 2, 3, 4}. To show that each player receives a numbered shirt, we pair the elements of the two sets. Such a pairing is called **one-to-one correspondence.** One way to exhibit a one-to-one correspondence is to use double-headed arrows as follows.

Tom, Dick, Harry, Mary
$\updownarrow$ $\updownarrow$ $\updownarrow$ $\updownarrow$
1,   2,   3,   4

An equivalent notation is: Tom $\leftrightarrow$ 1, Dick $\leftrightarrow$ 2, Harry $\leftrightarrow$ 3, Mary $\leftrightarrow$ 4.

DEFINITION

> Two sets A and B are said to be in *one-to-one correspondence* (or matched) if and only if the elements of A and B can be paired so that for each element of A there is exactly one element of B, and for each element of B there is exactly one element of A.

Example 2-16

Let $C = \{a, b, c\}$, $D = \{1, 2, 3\}$, and establish a one-to-one correspondence between C and D.

Solution

One possible one-to-one correspondence is $a \leftrightarrow 1$, $b \leftrightarrow 2$, and $c \leftrightarrow 3$.

Other possible one-to-one correspondences exist between the sets C and D in Example 2-16. There are several schemes for exhibiting them. In this case, the double arrow approach is useful. For example, all six possible one-to-one correspondences for Example 2-16 can be listed as follows

$a \leftrightarrow 1$	$a \leftrightarrow 2$	$a \leftrightarrow 3$
$b \leftrightarrow 2$	$b \leftrightarrow 1$	$b \leftrightarrow 1$
$c \leftrightarrow 3$	$c \leftrightarrow 3$	$c \leftrightarrow 2$

$a \leftrightarrow 1$	$a \leftrightarrow 2$	$a \leftrightarrow 3$
$b \leftrightarrow 3$	$b \leftrightarrow 3$	$b \leftrightarrow 2$
$c \leftrightarrow 2$	$c \leftrightarrow 1$	$c \leftrightarrow 1$

Suppose $A = \{$cat, dog, fish$\}$ and $B = \{$Mary, Angela, John, Bob$\}$. In any attempted one-to-one correspondence between A and B, there is a member of

B that is not paired with any element of *A*. This is true regardless of how the elements are paired. The following is one example.

{cat,   dog,   fish}
 ↕   ↕   ↕
{Mary, Angela, John, Bob}

In this case, we say that *A* has fewer members than *B*.

When two sets *A* and *B* are compared, one of three possible conditions exists.

A has as many elements as *B* and can be put in one-to-one correspondence with *B*.

A has fewer elements than *B*.

A has more elements than *B*.

These comparisons can be made without counting. In fact, children who do not know how to count can often tell which set contains more elements. Suppose *C* is the set of all children in the school, and *S* is the set of all seats in the school gymnasium. By pairing, you can determine, without counting, whether or not the sets match each other, whether one has fewer members than the other, or whether one has more elements than the other.

Suppose a room contains 20 chairs, and one student is sitting in each chair with no one standing. We say that there is a one-to-one correspondence between the set of chairs and the set of students in the room. We also say that equivalent sets the set of chairs and the set of students are **equivalent.**

DEFINITION

> Two sets *A* and *B* are said to be **equivalent,** written *A* ~ *B*, if and only if there exists a one-to-one correspondence between the sets.

The term equivalent should not be confused with equal. The difference should be made clear by the following example.

Example 2-17

Let $A = \{1, 2, 3, 4, 5\}$,
   $B = \{a, b, c\}$,
   $C = \{x, y, z\}$, and
   $D = \{b, a, c\}$.
Compare the sets using the terms *equal* and *equivalent*.

Solution
| Sets A and B are not equivalent ($A \nsim B$) and not equal ($A \neq B$).
Sets A and C are not equivalent ($A \nsim C$) and not equal ($A \neq C$).
Sets A and D are not equivalent ($A \nsim D$) and not equal ($A \neq D$).
Sets B and C are equivalent ($B \sim C$) but not equal ($B \neq C$).
Sets B and D are equivalent ($B \sim D$) and equal ($B = D$).
Sets C and D are equivalent ($C \sim D$) but not equal ($C \neq D$).

Remark
| Notice that if two sets are equal, they are equivalent. If two sets are equivalent, they are not necessarily equal.

Consider the five sets $\{a, b\}$, $\{1, 2\}$, $\{x, y\}$, $\{b, a\}$, and $\{*, \#\}$. How are these sets related? They are equivalent to each other. In fact, they are equivalent in a special way. Another way of saying this is that they share the property of "twoness." In mathematics, we say that these sets have the same cardinal
cardinal number number, namely 2. The **cardinal number** of a set X, denoted by $n(X)$, indicates the number of elements in the set X. If $D = \{a, b, c\}$, we say that the cardinal number of D is 3 and write $n(D) = 3$.

Note that if A is equivalent to B, then A and B have the same cardinal number; that is, $n(A) = n(B)$. Also, if $n(A) = n(B)$, the two sets are equivalent but not necessarily equal. Furthermore, if $A = B$, then $A \sim B$ and $n(A) = n(B)$.

In Section 2-2, we mentioned finite and infinite sets. To make these notions more precise, we notice that if A is any finite set and B is any proper subset of A, then B is not equivalent to A, written $B \nsim A$, since B has fewer elements than A. For example, if $A = \{a, b, c, d\}$ and $B = \{a, b, c\}$, then $B \subset A$ and $B \nsim A$. Neither can A be put into one-to-one correspondence with *any* other proper subset of itself.

The situation is different for infinite sets. Consider, for example, $N = \{1, 2, 3, 4, 5, \ldots\}$ and $E = \{2, 4, 6, 8, 10, \ldots\}$. Notice that $E \subset N$. There is a natural matching between the two sets.

$$N = \{1, 2, 3, 4, \ 5, \ \ldots, \ n, \ \ldots\}$$
$$\updownarrow \updownarrow \updownarrow \updownarrow \ \updownarrow \qquad\quad \updownarrow$$
$$E = \{2, 4, 6, 8, 10, \ \ldots, 2n, \ \ldots\}$$

Thus, the two sets can be placed in one-to-one correspondence. For every $n \in N$, there corresponds $2n \in E$; and for every $m \in E$, there corresponds $m/2 \in N$. It may seem strange that the sets are equivalent even though one set is a proper subset of the other. This happens only when both sets are
infinite **infinite.**

DEFINITION	A set A is **infinite** if and only if it can be put into one-to-one correspondence with a proper subset of itself.

Remark | All other sets are **finite.** Note that the empty set is a finite set.

Example 2-18 | Let $T = \{3, 6, 9, 12, 15, \ldots\}$. Show that T is an infinite set.

Solution | T is infinite if we can establish a one-to-one correspondence between T and a proper subset of T. One method follows. (Add 3 to each element of T.)

$$T = \{3, 6, 9, 12, 15, \ldots, \quad 3n, \quad \ldots\}$$
$$\updownarrow \updownarrow \updownarrow \updownarrow \updownarrow \qquad\qquad \updownarrow$$
$$N = \{6, 9, 12, 15, 18, \ldots, 3n + 3, \ldots\}$$

PROBLEM SET 2-4

1. Which of the following pairs of sets can be placed in one-to-one correspondence?
   (a) $\{1, 2, 3, 4, 5\}$ and $\{m, n, o, p, q\}$
   (b) $\{m, a, t, h\}$ and $\{f, u, n\}$
   (c) $\{a, b, c, d, e, f, \ldots, m\}$ and $\{1, 2, 3, 4, 5, 6, \ldots, 13\}$
   (d) $\{x \mid x$ is a letter in the word "mathematics"$\}$ and $\{1, 2, 3, 4, \ldots, 11\}$
   (e) $\{o, \triangle\}$ and $\{2\}$
2. Show all possible one-to-one correspondences between the sets A and B if $A = \{1, 2\}$ and $B = \{a, b\}$.
3. How many different one-to-one correspondences are there between two sets with four elements each? Between two sets with five elements each? Between two sets with n elements each?
4. Classify the following sets as finite or infinite.
   (a) $\{1, 2, 3, 4, \ldots, 999, 1000\}$
   (b) $\{x \mid x$ is a sixth-grade student in the state of New York on January 20, 1981.$\}$
   (c) $\{1, 4, 7, 10, 13, 16, \ldots\}$
   (d) $\{x \mid x$ is the number of seconds in 1 000 000 years$\}$
5. Use the definition of an infinite set in this section to show that the following sets are infinite.
   (a) $\{1, 3, 5, 7, 9, \ldots\}$ (b) $\{100, 101, 102, 103, \ldots\}$
6. Classify each of the following statements as true or false.
   (a) If $A \sim B$, then $B \sim A$.   (b) If $A \sim B$ and $B \sim C$, then $A \sim C$.
   (c) If $A = B$, then $A \sim B$.   (d) $\varnothing \sim \varnothing$.

ordinal
numbers

7. Cardinal numbers answer the question "how many?" **Ordinal numbers** are used to describe the relative position an element can occupy in an ordered set rather than the number of elements in

the set. For example, we might say that Carla sits in the *fourth* row and she is reading page 87 of this book. These are examples of ordinal numbers rather than cardinal numbers because they refer to position or order. Ordinal numbers answering the question "which one?" Indicate whether a cardinal number or an ordinal number is used in each of the following cases.

(a) The book has 562 pages.

(b) Christmas falls on December 25.

(c) Turn to page 125.

(d) She paid $15 for the book.

(e) Our class will take four tests and we just finished the first one.

BRAIN TEASER

Only 10 rooms were vacant in the Village Hotel. Eleven men went into the hotel at the same time, each wanting a separate room. The clerk, settling the argument, said: "I'll tell you what I'll do. I'll put two men in Room 1 with the understanding that I will come back and get one of them a few minutes later." The men agreed to this. The clerk continued: "I will put the rest of you men in rooms as follows:

the 3rd man in Room 2, the 4th man in Room 3, the 5th man in Room 4, the 6th man in Room 5, the 7th man in Room 6, the 8th man in Room 7, the 9th man in Room 8, and the 10th man in Room 9."
Then the clerk went back and got the extra man he had left in Room 1 and put him in Room 10. Everybody was happy. What is wrong with this plan?

2-5 CARTESIAN PRODUCTS AND RELATIONS

Cartesian product

There are many different ways that a third set can be created from two given sets. Two ways are by forming union of sets and intersection of sets. Another way to produce a set from two given sets is by forming the **Cartesian product.** This new way involves pairing the elements of one set with the elements of the other. For example, suppose a person has three pairs of pants, $P = \{$blue, white, green$\}$, and two shirts, $S = \{$blue, red$\}$. How many different pant-and-shirt combinations does the person have? The possible combinations follow with the color of pants listed first, and the color of shirt listed second.

blue–blue   white–blue   green–blue
blue–red   white–red   green–red

Six combinations are possible. The combination of pants and shirts forms a set of all possible pairs in which the first member of the pair is an element of set P, and the second member is an element of set S. The set of all possible combinations can be recorded as follows.

{(blue, blue), (blue, red), (white, blue), (white, red), (green, blue), (green, red)}

Because the first component in each pair represents pants and the second component in each pair represents shirts, the order in which the components are written is important. Thus, (green, blue) represents green pants and a blue shirt, whereas (blue, green) would represent blue pants and green shirt. Therefore, the two pairs represent different outfits. Because the order in each **ordered pairs**   pair is important, the pairs are called **ordered pairs.** The positions that the ordered pairs occupy within the set of outfits is immaterial since each ordered **components**   pair is an element of the set. Only the order of the **components** within each pair is significant.

    An ordered pair (x, y) is formed by choosing x from one set and y from another set in such a way that x is designated as the first component and y is designated as the second component. By definition, $(x, y) = (m, n)$ if and only if $x = m$ and $y = n$. Thus, (green, blue) $\neq$ (blue, green), although {green, blue} = {blue, green}.

    A set consisting of ordered pairs such as the ones in the pants-and-shirt example is called the Cartesian product of the two original sets, the set of pants and the set of shirts.

DEFINITION

> For any sets A and B, the **Cartesian product** of A and B, written $A \times B$, is the set of all ordered pairs such that the first element of each pair is an element of A and the second element of each pair is an element of B.

Remark

Using set notation, $A \times B = \{(x, y) \mid x \in A \text{ and } y \in B\}$. $A \times B$ is commonly read as "A cross B." Be careful not to say "A times B." You multiply numbers, but you take Cartesian products of sets.

Example 2-19

If $A = \{a, b, c\}$ and $B = \{1, 2, 3\}$, find each of the following.

(a) $A \times B$ (b) $B \times A$ (c) $A \times A$

Solution

(a) $A \times B = \{(a, 1), (a, 2), (a, 3), (b, 1), (b, 2), (b, 3), (c, 1), (c, 2), (c, 3)\}$

(b) $B \times A = \{(1, a), (1, b), (1, c), (2, a), (2, b), (2, c), (3, a), (3, b), (3, c)\}$

(c) $A \times A = \{(a, a), (a, b), (a, c), (b, a), (b, b), (b, c), (c, a), (c, b), (c, c)\}$

It is possible to form a Cartesian product involving the null set. Suppose $A = \{1, 2\}$. Since there are no elements in $\varnothing$, no ordered pairs (x, y) with $x \in A$ and $y \in \varnothing$ are possible and, therefore, $A \times \varnothing = \varnothing$. This is true for all sets A. Similarly, $\varnothing \times A = \varnothing$ for all sets A.

relation

A subset of a Cartesian product is called a **relation.** Before formally examining this mathematical concept, let us examine nonmathematical relations. The word "relations" brings to mind members of a family—parents, brothers, sisters, grandfathers, aunts, and so on. If we say Billy is the brother of Jimmy, "is the brother of" expresses the relation between Billy and Jimmy.

Other familiar relations occur in everyday life. For example, 543–8975 is the telephone number of Rick. "Is the telephone number of" expresses the relation between the number and Rick. Other examples of relations include the following.

"is the daughter of"   "is the hometown of"
"is the same color as"   "is the author of"
"sits in the same row as"   "is the social security number of"

Examples of relations in mathematics are as follows.

"is less than"   "is three more than"
"is parallel to"   "is the area of"

To illustrate relations, a diagram like Figure 2-12 is useful.

FIGURE 2-12

Suppose that each point in Figure 2-12 represents a child on a playground, the letters represent their names, and an arrow going from I to J means that I "is the sister of" J.

If all sister relationships are indicated in Figure 2-12, can you tell which of the children are boys and which are girls? Try to answer this question before reading further.

The information in Figure 2-12 indicates that A, C, D, F, G, and I are definitely girls and that B and J are definitely boys. Why? It also indicates that H and E have no sisters on the playground, but it does not indicate the gender of H and E.

Another way to exhibit the relation "is a sister of" is by using the same set twice with arrows as in Figure 2-13. Still another way to show the relation "is a sister of" is to write the relation A is a sister of B as an ordered pair (A, B). Notice that (B, A) means that B is a sister of A. Using this method, the relation "is a sister of" can be described for the children on the playground as the set $\{(A, B), (A, C), (A, D), (C, A), (C, B), (C, D), (D, A), (D, B), (D, C), (F, G), (G, F), (I, J)\}$.

FIGURE 2-13

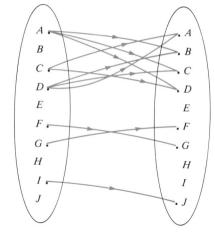

Next, try these ideas with Figure 2-14, but let the arrows represent "is less than." The relation could also be shown by using two sets with the arrows given as in Figure 2-15.

FIGURE 2-14

FIGURE 2-15

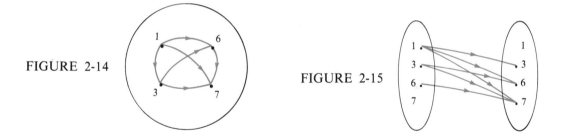

Ordered pairs also can be used to describe the relation. The relation "is less than" on the set $\{1, 3, 6, 7\}$ would appear as

$$\{(1, 3), (1, 6), (1, 7), (3, 6), (3, 7), (6, 7)\}$$

Example 2-20   The pairs (Helena, Montana), (Denver, Colorado), (Springfield, Illinois), (Juneau, Alaska) are included in some relation. Give a rule that describes the relation.

Solution   The ordered pair (x, y) indicates that x "is the capital of" y.
　　Should (California, Sacramento), (Denver, Wisconsin), or (Denver, Helena) be included using the rule described in this example?

Notice that a relation is a pairing of elements of two sets according to some criterion. In Example 2-20, the first components of the ordered pairs are state capitals; the second components are states of the United States. Each ordered pair in the example is an element of the Cartesian product $A \times B$ of the two sets: A is the set of state capitals, and B is the set of states in the United States. Notice that not all the possible ordered pairs in $A \times B$ are in the relation in Example 2-20.

DEFINITION

> Given any two sets A and B, a **relation** from A to B is a subset of $A \times B$; that is, if R is a relation, then $R \subseteq A \times B$.

In the definition, the phrase "from A to B" means that the first components in the ordered pairs are elements of A and the second components are elements of B. If $A = B$, we say that the **relation is on A.**
　　The following is an example of a game called "guess my rule." The game is one way a special kind of relation, called a **function,** is often introduced in elementary school.

relation on A

function

When Tom said 2, Noah said 5. When Dick said 4, Noah said 7. When Mary said 10, Noah said 13. When Liz said 6, what did Noah say? What is Noah's rule?

The answer to the first question is 9, and the rule is: take the original number and add 3; that is, for any number n, Noah's answer is $n + 3$.

Example 2-21   Guess the teacher's rule for the following responses.

(a)	You	Teacher	(b)	You	Teacher	(c)	You	Teacher
	1	3		2	5		2	0
	0	0		3	7		4	0
	4	12		5	11		7	1
	10	30		10	21		21	1

Solution

(a) The teacher's rule could be: multiply the given number n by 3; that is, $n \cdot 3$.

(b) The teacher's rule could be: double the original number n and add 1; that is, $2n + 1$.

(c) The teacher's rule could be: if the number n is even, answer 0; if the number is odd, answer 1.

Another way to prepare students for the formal idea of a function is by using a "function machine." The machine, such as the one in Figure 2-16, consists of an input unit where items are entered, a processing unit, and an output unit where results are obtained. The function machine is similar to actual vending machines with which many children are familiar.

With a function machine, for any input element x, there is an output element denoted by $f(x)$, read "f of x" or a "function of x." A function machine is a machine that associates **exactly one output with each input** according to some rule. That is, if you enter some number x as input and obtain some number $f(x)$ as output, then *every* time you enter that same x as input, you will obtain that same $f(x)$ as output.

x

↓

Input

Function machine

Output

$f(x)$

FIGURE 2-16

Example 2-22

Consider the following function machine.

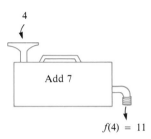

4

↓

Add 7

$f(4) = 11$

What will happen if the numbers 0, 3, 6, and 10 are entered?

Solution

$f(0) = 7, f(3) = 10, f(6) = 13, f(10) = 17$. This can be recorded in terms of ordered pairs as: (0, 7), (3, 10), (6, 13), (10, 17).

Remark

The rule associated with this function machine can be denoted as $f(x) = x + 7$. To obtain the ordered pairs listed above, the values 0, 3, 6 and 10 were substituted in this equation.

Example 2-23

If $f(x) = 4x - 2$, find (a) $f(1)$, (b) $f(3)$, and (c) $f(10)$.

Solution

(a) $f(1) = 4(1) - 2 = 4 - 2 = 2$
(b) $f(3) = 4(3) - 2 = 12 - 2 = 10$
(c) $f(10) = 4(10) - 2 = 40 - 2 = 38$

DEFINITION

A **function** from A to B is a relation from A to B in which each element of A is paired with one **and only one** element of B.

---

domain, range

The set of all first components, all the elements of A, is called the **domain.** The set of the second components, a subset of B, is called the **range.** In terms of a function machine, the domain is the set of all possible inputs. The range is the set of all outputs.

Example 2-24

Suppose a given machine is a doubling machine; that is, for any given input, it will produce its double as output. If the domain is the set of natural numbers, describe the range.

Solution

The range is the set of all even natural numbers (all multiples of two).

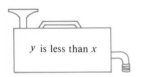
y is less than x

Are all input–output machines function machines? Consider the following machine. For any natural number input, x, the machine on the left outputs a number y, that is less than x.

If, for example, you input the number 10, the machine may output 9 since 9 is less than 10. If you input 10 again, the machine may output 3, since 3 is less than 10. This clearly violates the definition of a function, since 10 can be paired with more than one element. The machine is not a function machine.

An example of a function machine from Addison-Wesley, *Mathematics in Our World,* 1978, Grade 6, is given on page 61. Can you solve the problems?

Find the Rule

For each **input,** this math machine uses a **rule** to give a special **output** and prints an input-output card.

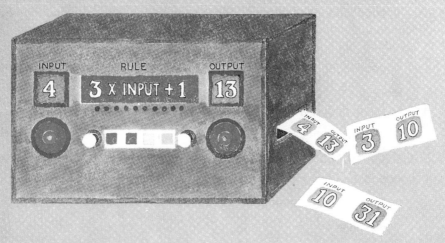

What was the rule for each of these sets of cards?

1.

input	output
2	4

input	output
3	9

input	output
4	16

2.

input	output
5.98	6

input	output
3.47	3

input	output
9.50	10

3.

input	output
△	1

input	output
▭	2

input	output
⬠	3

4. Play a math-machine game. Make up a rule and give examples of the input-output cards for the rule. See if a friend can guess your rule.

Some relations are not functions. Consider the relations described in Figure 2-17. Do they illustrate functions?

FIGURE 2-17

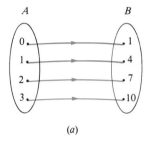 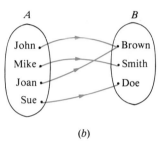

(a)   (b)

In Figure 2-17(a), for every element belonging to the domain A, there is one and only one element belonging to B. Thus, this relation is a function from A to B. A diagram, then, shows a function from A to B if there is one and only one arrow leaving each element of the domain pointing to an element of B. Figure 2-17(b) also illustrates a function since there is only one arrow leaving each element in A. It does not matter that an element of set B, Brown, has two arrows pointing to it.

Example 2-25

Which, if any, of the following three diagrams exhibits a function from A to B?

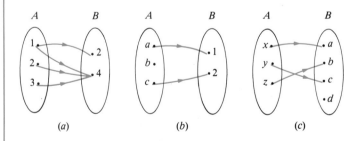

(a)   (b)   (c)

Solution

(a)   This diagram does not define a function from A to B since the element 1 is paired both with 2 and 4.

(b)   This diagram does not define a function from A to B since the element b is not paired with any element of B. (It is a function from a subset of A to B).

(c)   This diagram does define a function from A to B since there is one and only one arrow leaving each element of A. The fact that d, an element of B, is not paired with any element in the domain does not violate the definition.

Consider the relation $\{(a, b), (b, c), (c, d), (d, e)\}$. Since each first component of the ordered pairs is associated with one and only one second component, this relation is a function from the set $\{a, b, c, d\}$ of the first components to the set $\{b, c, d, e\}$ of the second components.

Example 2-26 | Determine whether the following relations are functions from the set of first components to the set of second components.
(a) $\{(1, 2), (2, 5), (3, 7), (1, 4), (4, 8)\}$
(b) $\{(1, 2), (2, 2), (3, 2), (4, 2)\}$

Solution | (a) This is not a function since the first component, 1, is associated with two different second components, namely 2 and 4.
(b) This is a function from $\{1, 2, 3, 4\}$ to $\{2\}$, since each first component is associated with exactly one second component. The fact that the second component, 2, is associated with more than one first component does not matter.

PROBLEM SET 2-5

1. Let $A = \{x, y\}$, $B = \{a, b, c\}$, and $C = \{0\}$. Find each of the following.
    (a) $A \times B$ (b) $C \times B$ (c) $B \times A$
    (d) $B \times \varnothing$ (e) $C \times C$ (f) $\varnothing \times C$
    (g) $(A \times C) \cup (B \times C)$ (h) $(A \cup B) \times C$ (i) $A \times (B \cap C)$
    (j) $(A \times B) \cap (A \times C)$

2. For each of the following, the Cartesian product, $C \times D$, is given by the following sets. Find C and D.
    (a) $\{(a, b), (a, c), (a, d), (a, e)\}$
    (b) $\{(1, 1), (1, 2), (1, 3), (2, 1), (2, 2), (2, 3)\}$
    (c) $\{(0, 1), (0, 0), (1, 1), (1, 0)\}$

3. Answer each of the following.
    (a) If A has 3 elements and B has 1 element, how many elements are in $A \times B$?
    (b) If A has 3 elements and B has 2 elements, how many elements are in $A \times B$?
    (c) If A has 3 elements and B has 3 elements, how many elements are in $A \times B$?
    (d) If A has 5 elements and B has 4 elements, how many elements are in $A \times B$?
    (e) If A has m elements and B has n elements, how many elements are in $A \times B$?
    (f) If A has m elements, B has n elements, and C has p elements, how many elements are in $(A \times B) \times C$?

4. If $A = \{1, 2, 3\}$, $B = \{0\}$, and $C = \varnothing$, find the number of elements in each of the following.
    (a) $A \times B$ (b) $A \times C$ (c) $B \times C$

5. If the number of elements in set B is 3 and the number of elements in $(A \cup B) \times B$ is 24, what is the number of elements in A if $A \cap B = \varnothing$?

6. If $A \times B = B \times A$, $A \neq \varnothing$, and $B \neq \varnothing$, does $A = B$?

7. Suppose you can choose one piece of fruit from the set {apple, orange, banana} and one piece of candy from the set {sucker, jawbreaker, candy kiss, licorice}. How many different combinations could you choose?

8. If there are 6 teams in the Alpha league and 5 teams in the Beta league, and if each team from one league plays each team from the other league exactly once, how many games are played?

9. José has 4 pairs of slacks, 5 shirts, and 3 sweaters. From how many different combinations can he choose if he chooses a pair of slacks, a shirt, and a sweater each time?

10. (a) Is the operation of forming Cartesian products commutative?
    (b) Is the operation of forming Cartesian products associative?

11. Each of the following gives pairs that are included in some relation. Give a rule or phrase that could describe each relation and list two more pairs that could be included in the relation.
    (a) $(1, 1), (2, 4), (3, 9), (4, 16)$
    (b) (Blondie, Dagwood), (Martha, George), (Rosalyn, Jimmy), (Flo, Andy), (Scarlett, Rhett)
    (c) $(a, A), (b, B), (c, C), (d, D)$
    (d) (3 candies, 10¢), (6 candies, 20¢)

12. Let $X = \{a, b, c\}$ and $Y = \{m, n\}$, and suppose X and Y represent two sets of students. The students in X point to the shorter students in Y. The following diagrams list two possibilities. Tell as much as you can about the students in each diagram.

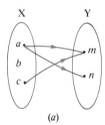   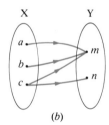

(a)   (b)

13. For each of the following, guess a teacher's rule.

(a) You	Teacher	(b) You	Teacher	(c) You	Teacher
3	8	0	1	6	42
4	11	3	10	0	0
5	14	5	26	8	72
10	29	8	65	2	6

14. Following are five relations from the set $\{1, 2, 3\}$ to the set $\{a, b, c, d\}$. Which are functions? (A diagram may help.) If the relation is not a function, tell why it is not.
    (a) $\{(1, a), (2, b), (3, c), (1, d)\}$
    (b) $\{(1, c), (3, d)\}$
    (c) $\{1, a), (2, b), (3, a)\}$
    (d) $\{(1, a), (1, b), (1, c)\}$

15. State the domain and range for each function in Problem 14.

16. Does the following diagram define a function from A to B? Why or why not?

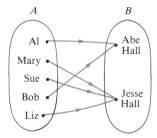

17. If $g(x) = 3x + 5$, find (a) $g(0)$, (b) $g(2)$, (c) $g(10)$, and (d) $g(a)$.
18. The domain of a function f is $\{1, 10, 11\}$. If $f(x) = 4x + 1$, what is the range of f?
19. Draw a diagram of a function with domain $\{1, 2, 3, 4, 5\}$ and range $\{a, b\}$. (There are many possibilities.)
20. Tell which of the following are functions and why.

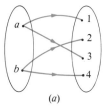

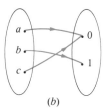

(a)   (b)

*2-6 PROPERTIES OF RELATIONS

Figure 2-18 represents a set of children in a small group. They have drawn all possible arrows representing the relation: "has the same first letter in his or her name as." Notice that the children were very careful to observe that each child in the group has the same first initial as himself or herself. Three properties of relations are illustrated in Figure 2-18.

FIGURE 2-18

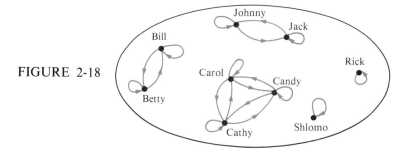

Property | **The Reflexive Property**   A relation R on a set X is reflexive if and only if, for every element $a \in X$, a is related to a. That is, for every $a \in X$, $(a, a) \in R$.

In terms of the diagram, there is a loop at every point. For example, Rick has the same first initial as himself, namely R. A relation such as "is taller than" is not reflexive because people cannot be taller than themselves.

Property | **The Symmetric Property**   A relation R on a set X is symmetric if and only if, for all elements a and b in X, whenever a is related to b, then b also is related to a. That is, if $(a, b) \in R$, then $(b, a) \in R$.

In terms of the diagram, every pair of points that has an arrow headed one direction also has a return arrow.

For example, if Bill has the same first initial as Betty, then Betty has the same first initial as Bill. A relation such as "is a brother of" is not symmetric since Dick can be the brother of Jane, but Jane is not a brother of Dick.

Property | **The Transitive Property**   A relation R on a set X is transitive if and only if, for all elements a, b, and c of X, whenever a is related to b and b is related to c, then a is related to c. That is, if $(a, b) \in R$ and $(b, c) \in R$, then $(a, c) \in R$.

Remark | a, b, and c do not have to be different. Three symbols are used to allow for difference.

In terms of the diagram in Figure 2-18, every connected portion satisfies the transitive property. For example, if Carol has the same first initial as Candy, and Candy has the same first initial as Cathy, then Carol has the same first initial as Cathy. A relation such as "is the father of" is not transitive since, if Tom Jones is the father of Tom Jones, Jr. and Tom Jones, Jr. is the father of Joe Jones, then Tom Jones is not the father of Joe Jones. He is instead the grandfather.

The relation "is the same color as" is reflexive, symmetric, and transitive. The common relation "is equal to" also satisfies all three properties. In general, relations that satisfy all three properties are called **equivalence relations** | **equivalence relations.**

DEFINITION | An **equivalence relation** is any relation R that satisfies the reflexive, symmetric, and transitive properties.

Example 2-27

If $X = \{\{1\}, \{1, 2\}, \{1, 2, 3\}, \{2, 4\}, \{2, 4, 5\}, \{6\}\}$, draw a diagram where the points represent subsets, illustrating the relation "is a subset of" on the set X, and indicate which properties are satisfied.

Solution

The diagram might be like Figure 2-19. This relation is reflexive, since every element of X is a subset of itself. (Notice that there is a loop at every point.) The relation is not symmetric since $\{2, 4\} \subseteq \{2, 4, 5\}$ but $\{2, 4, 5\} \not\subseteq \{2, 4\}$. (Notice that there is an arrow connecting the two sets but no return arrow.) Since this relation is not symmetric on the set X, it is not an equivalence relation. However, it is transitive.

FIGURE 2-19

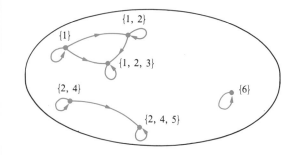

Example 2-28

Tell whether or not the following relations are reflexive, symmetric, or transitive on the set of all people.
(a) "is older than"
(b) "sits in the same row as"
(c) "is heavier than"

Solution

The solution is given in the form of a table.

Relation	Reflexive	Symmetric	Transitive
(a) "is older than"	No	No	Yes
(b) "sits in the same row as"	Yes	Yes	Yes
(c) "is heavier than"	No	No	Yes

Note that "sits in the same row as" is an equivalence relation.

Example 2-29

Are the following relations equivalence relations?
(a) $R = \{(1, 1) (1, 2) (2, 2), (2, 1)\}$
(b) $R = \{(a, a) (a, c), (c, b), (a, b), (b, a), (b, c), (b, b) (c, c)\}$

Solution (a) It is reflexive, symmetric, and transitive; hence, it is an equivalence relation.

(b) A diagram for this relation follows.

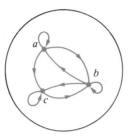

Notice that there is an arrow from a to c but not from c to a. Thus, the symmetric property fails. In terms of ordered pairs, $(a, c) \in R$ but $(c, a) \notin R$. Since the symmetric property does not hold, R is not an equivalence relation.

Suppose P is the set consisting of all persons attending Mu University and consider the relation "is the same sex as." This relation is an equivalence relation. The relation partitions the persons at Mu University into two classes, females and males. Any equivalence relation defined on a set has the effect of

equivalence classes partitioning the set into disjoint subsets, called **equivalence classes.** In this example, the class of females can be described as the set of all students who are the same sex as Jane, a student at M.U., and the set can be called Jane's equivalence class. This class also can be called Mary's equivalence class as long as Mary is a student at M.U. An equivalence class can be named after any of its members.

When elementary children sort objects, putting all the red objects in one pile, the blue objects in another pile, and the white in another pile, they are forming equivalence classes using the relation "is the same color as." A principal in an elementary school with grades one through six uses the relation "is in the same grade as" to sort the children into six equivalence classes—the six grades in the school.

PROBLEM SET 2-6

1. Tell whether each of the following is reflexive, symmetric, or transitive on the set of all people. Which are equivalence relations?
    (a) "is a parent of"
    (b) "is the same age as"
    (c) "has the same last name as"
    (d) "is a brother or sister of"
    (e) "is the same height as"
    (f) "is married to"

2. Tell whether each of the following is reflexive, symmetric, or transitive on the set of subsets of a nonempty set. Which are equivalence relations?
   (a) "is equal to"   (b) "is a proper subset of"   (c) "is not equal to"
3. Tell whether or not each of the following relations is reflexive, symmetric, or transitive.
   (a) $\{(a, a), (a, b), (a, c), (b, b), (b, c), (c, c)\}$
   (b) $\{(1, 1), (1, 2), (2, 1)\}$
   (c) $\{(1, 1), (1, 2), (2, 1), (2, 2)\}$
4. If $S = \{5, 7, 10, 13, 14, 30\}$ and a relation on S is defined by the following diagram, what properties does this relation have?

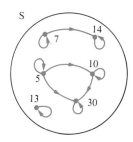

5. Consider the set S such that $S = \{$Abe, George, Laura, Ben, Sue, Betty, Dax, Zachary, Doug, Mike, Mary, Carolyn, Aza$\}$. Identify the equivalence classes formed by each of the following relations.
   (a) "has the same first letter in his or her name as"
   (b) "has the same last letter in his or her name as"
   (c) "has the same number of letters in his or her name as"
6. Give an example of a relation that is reflexive and symmetric but not transitive.

SOLUTION TO THE PRELIMINARY PROBLEM

Understanding the Problem

Three sportcasters made the following picks for Sunday's football games:

Howie: Cowboys, Steelers, Vikings, Bills
Frank: Steelers, Packers, Cowboys, Redskins
Dandy: Redskins, Vikings, Jets, Cowboys

The only team not picked that is playing Sunday is the Giants. Thus, 8 teams will play Sunday in 4 games. The problem is to determine which teams will play which other teams based on this information.

Devising a Plan

At first glance, it may appear that there is not enough information to solve this problem, but recording the information in a Venn diagram may provide the insight we need. A Venn diagram with circles H, F, D for each of the pickers is shown in Figure 2-20. The three circles divide the universal set into

FIGURE 2-20

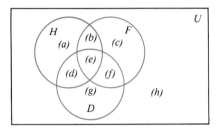

8 disjoint regions: (a), (b), (c), (d), (e), (f), (g), (h). Each sportscaster picked the Cowboys to win. Since this was the only team that all three picked to win, region (e) consists only of the Cowboys. We can place the Giants in region (h) since none of the three picked the Giants. Howie and Frank both picked the Steelers, so now the Steelers belong in region (b). Howie and Dandy both picked the Vikings, so the Vikings belong in region (d). Frank and Dandy both picked the Redskins, so they belong in region (f). This leaves region (a) for the Bills, region (c) for the Packers, and region (g) for the Jets. This information is given in Figure 2-21. To complete the problem, we must now determine which teams will play each other.

FIGURE 2-21

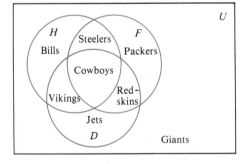

Carrying Out the Plan

From Figure 2-21, we know the Cowboys will not play the Steelers, Bills, or Vikings since Howie picked all these teams as winners. Likewise, the Cowboys will not play the Packers or the Redskins since Frank picked all these teams as winners. Similarly, the Cowboys will not play the Jets since Dandy picked both the Cowboys and Jets as winners. This leaves the Cowboys with only one possible opponent, namely the Giants.

Next, we can determine which team the Vikings will play. Since the Vikings are picked by both Howie and Dandy, their opponent must be outside circles H and D. This means that the Vikings will play the Packers. In a similar manner, we can deduce that the Steelers will play the Jets, and the Redskins will play the Bills.

Looking Back

The four games on Sunday will be:

> Cowboys versus Giants
> Vikings versus Packers
> Steelers versus Jets
> Redskins versus Bills

Each team has an opponent and there are no contradictions in the given information. Problems of this type can also be generated from other events, such as baseball, basketball, or even dating, where some type of pairing is used.

QUESTIONS FROM THE CLASSROOM

1. A student argues that $\{\varnothing\}$ is the proper notation for the empty set. What is your response?
2. A student does not believe that the empty set is a subset of every set. What is your response?
3. A student asks if $A = \{a, b, c\}$ and $B = \{b, c, d\}$, why isn't it true that $A \cup B = \{a, b, c, b, c, d\}$? What is your response?
4. A student asks, "How can I tell if a set is infinite?" What is your response?
5. A student asks, "Are any two infinite sets equivalent?" What is your response?
6. A student claims that a finite set of numbers is any set that has a largest element. Do you agree?
7. A student claims that the complement bar can be broken over the operation of intersection; that is, $\overline{A \cap B} = \overline{A} \cap \overline{B}$. What is your response?
8. A student claims that $\overline{A} \cap B$ includes all elements that are not in A. What is your response?
9. A student asks whether a formula and a function are the same. What is your response?
10. A student asks whether all functions are relations. What is your reply?
11. A student states that either $A \subseteq B$ or $B \subseteq A$. Is the student correct?

CHAPTER OUTLINE

I. Set definitions and notations
  A. A **set** can be described as any collection of objects.
  B. Sets should be **well defined;** that is, it is possible to tell whether or not an object belongs to the set.
  C. An **element** is any member of the set, for example, $a \in \{a, b\}$.
  D. A set is **infinite** if and only if it can be put in a one-to-one correspondence with a proper subset of itself. All other sets are **finite.**
  E. Sets can be specified by using either the **roster method** or **set-builder notation.**
  F. The **empty set,** written $\varnothing$, contains no elements.
  G. The **universal set** contains all the elements being discussed.
II. Relationships between sets
  A. Two sets are **equal** if and only if they have exactly the same elements.
  B. Two sets A and B are in **one-to-one correspondence** if and only if each element of A can be paired with exactly one element of B and each element of B can be paired with exactly one element of A.
  C. Two sets are **equivalent** if and only if their elements can be placed into one-to-one correspondence (written $A \sim B$).
  D. Set A is a **subset** of B if and only if every element of A is an element of B (written $A \subseteq B$).
  E. Set A is a **proper subset** of B if and only if every element of A is an element of B and there is at least one element of B that is not in A (written $A \subset B$).
  F. The **union** of two sets A and B is the set of all elements in A, in B or in both A and B (written $A \cup B$).
  G. The **intersection** of two sets A and B

is the set of all elements belonging to both A and B (written $A \cap B$).
  H. The **complement** of a set A is the set consisting of the elements of the universal set not in A (written $\overline{A}$).
  I. The **complement of set A relative to set B** (set difference) is the set of all elements in B that are not in A (written $B - A$).
  J. The **Cartesian product** of sets A and B is the set of all ordered pairs such that the first element of each pair is an element of A and the second element of each pair is an element of B (written $A \times B$).
  K. **Venn diagrams** are useful in determining relationships between sets.
III. Properties of set operations
  For all sets A, B, C, and the universal set U, the following properties hold.
  A. $A \cap B = B \cap A$: Commutative property of set intersection
  B. $A \cup B = B \cup A$: Commutative property of set union
  C. $(A \cap B) \cap C = A \cap (B \cap C)$: Associative property of set intersection
  D. $(A \cup B) \cup C = A \cup (B \cup C)$: Associative property of set union
  E. $A \cap (B \cup C) = (A \cap B) \cup (A \cap C)$: Distributive property of set intersection over union
  F. $A \cup (B \cap C) = (A \cup B) \cap (A \cup C)$: Distributive property of set union over intersection
  G. $A \cap U = U \cap A = A$: U is the identity for set intersection
  H. $A \cup \varnothing = \varnothing \cup A = A$: $\varnothing$ is the identity for set union
IV. Relations and functions
  A. A **relation** R from set A to set B is a subset of $A \times B$; that is, if R is a relation, then $R \subseteq A \times B$.
  B. A **function** from set A to set B is a re-

lation from A to B in which each element of A is paired with one and only one element of B.
1. The set of all first components of a function, all the elements of A, is called the **domain** of the function.
2. The set of all second components of a function, a subset of B, is called the **range** of the function.
C. An **equivalence relation** is a relation that is reflexive, symmetric, and transitive.

1. A relation R on a set X is **reflexive** if and only if for every element $a \in X$, a is related to a.
2. A relation R on a set X is **symmetric** if and only if for all elements a and b in X, whenever a is related to b, then b is related to a.
3. A relation R on a set X is **transitive** if and only if for all elements a, b, c of X, whenever a is related to b and b is related to c, then a is related to c.

CHAPTER TEST

1. Write the set of the first five letters of the English alphabet using each of the following.
   (a) the roster method
   (b) set-builder notation
2. List all the subsets of $\{m, a, t, h\}$.
3. Let $U = \{x \mid x$ is a person living in Montana$\}$
   $A = \{x \mid x$ is a person 30 years or older$\}$
   $B = \{x \mid x$ is a person less than 30 years old$\}$
   $C = \{x \mid x$ is a person who owns a gun$\}$
   Describe in words each of the following.
   (a) $\overline{A}$ (b) $A \cap C$ (c) $A \cup B$ (d) $\overline{C}$ (e) $\overline{A \cap C}$
4. Let $U = \{u, n, i, v, e, r, s, a, l\}$,
   $A = \{r, a, v, e\}$, $C = \{l, i, n, e\}$,
   $B = \{a, r, e\}$, $D = \{s, a, l, e\}$.
   Find each of the following.
   (a) $A \cup B$ (b) $C \cap D$
   (c) $\overline{D}$ (d) $A \cap \overline{D}$
   (e) $\overline{B \cup C}$ (f) $(B \cup C) \cap D$
   (g) $(\overline{A} \cup B) \cap (C \cap \overline{D})$ (h) $(C \cap D) \cap A$
   (i) $n(\overline{C})$ (j) $n(C \times D)$
5. Indicate the following sets by shading.

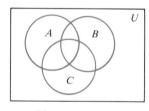

(a) $A \cap (B \cup C)$

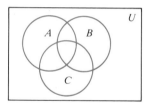

(b) $\overline{A \cup B} \cap C$

6. Let $A = \{s, e, t\}$ and $B = \{i, d, e, a\}$. Find each of the following.
   (A) $B \times A$ (b) $A \times A$ (c) $n(A \times \varnothing)$ (d) $n(B - A)$
7. If $C = \{e, q, u, a, l, s\}$, how many proper subsets does C have?
8. Show one possible one-to-one correspondence between sets D and E if $D = \{t, h, e\}$ and $E = \{e, n, d\}$. How many different one-to-one correspondences between sets D and E are possible?
9. Use a Venn diagram to determine whether $A \cap (B \cup C) = (A \cap B) \cup C$ for all sets A, B, and C.
10. Describe, using symbols, the shaded portion in each of the following.

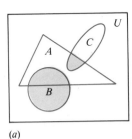

(a)

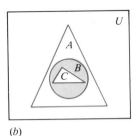

(b)

11. Which of the following relations are functions from the set of first components to the set of second components?
   (a) $\{(a, b), (c, d), (e, a), (f, g)\}$
   (b) $\{(a, b), (a, c), (b, b), (b, c)\}$
   (c) $\{(a, b), (b, a)\}$
12. Determine which of the reflexive, symmetric, and transitive properties hold for each of the following on the set of all people. Which, if any, are equivalence relations?
   (a) "lives on the same street as"   (b) "jumps higher than"
13. Given the following function rules and the domains, find the associated ranges.
   (a) $f(x) = x + 3$ domain $= \{0, 1, 2, 3\}$
   (b) $f(x) = 3x - 1$ domain $= \{5, 10, 15, 20\}$
   (c) $f(x) = x^2$ domain $= \{0, 1, 2, 3, 4\}$
   (d) $f(x) = x^2 + 3x + 5$ domain $= \{0, 1, 2\}$
14. If $A = \{1, 2, 3\}$, $B = \{2, 3, 4, 5\}$, and $C = \{3, 4, 5, 6, 7\}$, illustrate the associative property of intersection of sets. Using sets A and B, illustrate the commutative property of union of sets.
15. Classify each of the following as true or false. If false, tell why.
   (a) For all sets A and B, either $A \subseteq B$ or $B \subseteq A$.
   (b) The empty set is a proper subset of every set.
   (c) For all sets A and B, if $A \sim B$, then $A = B$.
   (d) The set $\{5, 10, 15, 20, \ldots\}$ is a finite set.
   (e) No set is equivalent to a proper subset of itself.
   (f) If A is an infinite set and $B \subseteq A$, then B also is an infinite set.
   (g) For all finite sets A and B, if $A \cap B \neq \varnothing$, then $n(A \cup B) \neq n(A) + n(B)$.
   (h) If A and B are sets such that $A \cap B = \varnothing$, then $A = \varnothing$ or $B = \varnothing$.
   (i) $\varnothing \in \varnothing$
   (j) If A and B are sets such that $A \times B = \varnothing$, then $A = \varnothing$ or $B = \varnothing$.
16. In a student survey, it was found that 16 students liked history, 19 liked English, 18 liked mathematics, 8 liked mathematics and English, 5 liked history and English, 7 liked history

and mathematics, 3 liked all three subjects, and every student liked at least one of the subjects. Draw a Venn diagram describing this information and answer the following questions.

(a) How many students were in the survey?

(b) How many students liked only mathematics?

(c) How many students liked English and mathematics but not history?

SELECTED BIBLIOGRAPHY

Brieske, T. "Functions, Mappings, and Mapping Diagrams." *The Mathematics Teacher,* **66** (May 1973): 463–468.

Bruni, J., and H. Silverman. "Using Classification to Interpret Consumer Information." *The Arithmetic Teacher,* **24** (January 1977): 4–12.

Coltharp, F. "Mathematical Aspects of the Attribute Games." *The Arithmetic Teacher,* **21** (March 1974): 246–251.

Cruikshank, D. "Sorting, Classifying and Logic." *The Arithmetic Teacher,* **21** (November 1974): 588–598.

Geddes, D., and S. Lipsey. "The Hazards of Sets." *The Mathematics Teacher,* **62** (October 1969): 454.

Gilbert, R. "Hey Mister! It's Upside Down!" *The Arithmetic Teacher,* **25** (December 1977): 18–19.

Lettieri, F. "Meet the Zorkies: A New Attribute Material." *The Arithmetic Teacher,* **26** (September 1978): 36–39.

Liedtke, W. "Experiences with Blocks in Kindergarten," *The Arithmetic Teacher,* **22** (May 1975): 406–412.

Liedtke, W. "Rational Counting." *The Arithmetic Teacher,* **26** (October 1978): 20–26.

National Council of Teachers of Mathematics. *Topics in Mathematics for Elementary School Teachers.* Booklet Number 1. Sets. 1964.

Papy, F. *Graphs and The Child.* New Rochelle, N.Y., Cuisenaire Company of America, Inc., 1970.

Papy, F., *Mathematics and The Child.* New Rochelle, N.Y., Cuisenaire Company of America Inc., 1971.

Peterson, J., and G. Dolson. "Property Games." *The Arithmetic Teacher,* **24** (January 1977): 36–38.

Schoen, "Some Difficulty in the Language of Sets." *The Arithmetic Teacher,* **21** (March 1974): 236–237.

Silverman, H. "Teacher Made Materials for Teaching Numbers and Counting." *The Arithmetic Teacher,* **19** (October 1972): 431–433.

Vance, J. "The Large-Blue-Triangle: A Matter of Logic." *The Arithmetic Teacher,* **22** (March 1975): 237–240.

Vilenkin, N. *Stories about Sets.* New York and London, Academic Press, 1969.

Numeration Systems and Whole Numbers

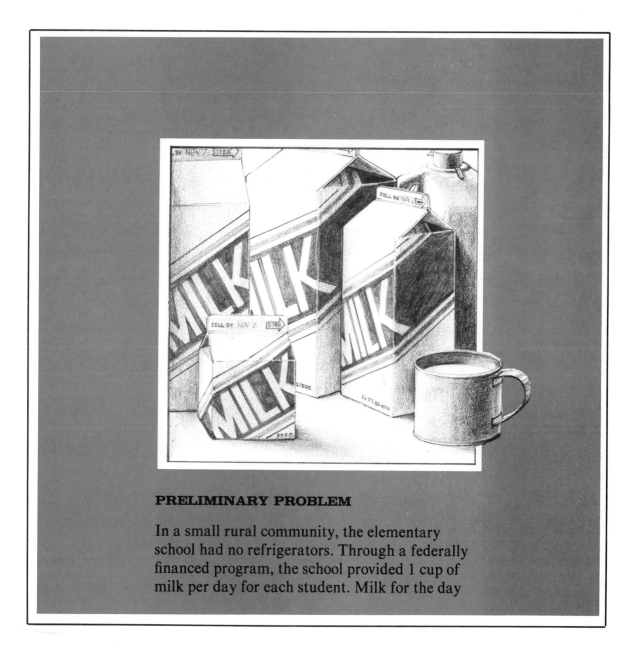

PRELIMINARY PROBLEM

In a small rural community, the elementary school had no refrigerators. Through a federally financed program, the school provided 1 cup of milk per day for each student. Milk for the day was purchased at the local store each morning. The milk was available in gallons, half-gallons, quarts, pints, or cups, and the larger containers were better buys. If 1 gallon, 1 quart, and 1 pint of milk were purchased on Tuesday, how many students were at school that day? On Wednesday, 31 students were at school. How much milk was purchased on Wednesday to make the best buy?

INTRODUCTION

The earliest numerals were strokes drawn on a wall. They represented animals such as mammoths and deer, and each stroke represented one animal. Since that time, numerals have changed extensively. Figure 3-1 shows some changes leading to our present-day Hindu–Arabic system. Even today there are variations in the Hindu-Arabic symbols used around the world. For example, Arabs use 0 for 5 and . for 0.

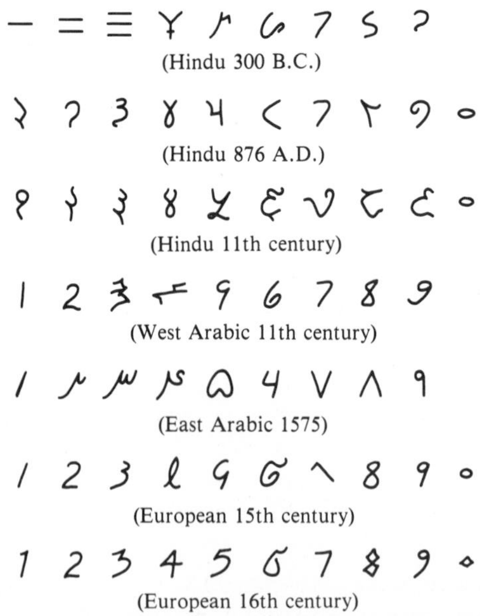

$$- = \equiv \Upsilon \; \digamma \; 6 \; 7 \; S \; ?$$
(Hindu 300 B.C.)

$$\text{१} \; ? \; 3 \; 8 \; 4 \; < \; 7 \; \Gamma \; 9 \; \circ$$
(Hindu 876 A.D.)

$$? \; \gamma \; ? \; 8 \; \Upsilon \; \varepsilon \; \upsilon \; \varsigma \; \varsigma \; \circ$$
(Hindu 11th century)

FIGURE 3-1
$$1 \; 2 \; ? \; \digamma \; 9 \; 6 \; 7 \; 8 \; 9$$
(West Arabic 11th century)

$$/ \; \digamma \; \mu \; \digamma \; \bigcirc \; 4 \; \vee \; \wedge \; 9$$
(East Arabic 1575)

$$1 \; 2 \; 3 \; \ell \; 9 \; 6 \; \wedge \; 8 \; 9 \; \circ$$
(European 15th century)

$$1 \; 2 \; 3 \; 4 \; 5 \; 6 \; 7 \; 8 \; 9 \; \circ$$
(European 16th century)

As you can see, different symbols can be used to represent the same quantity. For example, 3 and III both represent the quantity we call three. **numeral**   The symbols 3 and III are called numerals. Strictly speaking, a **numeral** is a number   written symbol used to represent a quantity or number. A **number** is an abstract concept used to describe quantity. You can see a numeral but not a number. In this text, we distinguish between number and numeral only if the distinction clarifies a concept.

3-1   NUMERATION SYSTEMS

numeration systems   Many civilizations developed **numeration systems**—logically structured methods of denoting numbers. Egyptian numerical hieroglyphics belong to one such system. Remnants of this system, dating back to the thirty-fourth century B.C., have been found on shards of pottery and on the Ahmes papyrus. The preserved hieroglyphs indicate that the system had the symbols shown in Table 3-1.

TABLE 3-1

Egyptian Numeral	Description	Hindu–Arabic Face Value
I	vertical staff	1
∩	heel bone	10
9	scroll	100
ꝉ	lotus flower	1000
ℓ	pointing finger	10 000
ꙮ	polliwog or burbot	100 000
𓀎	astonished man	1 000 000

additive property   The Egyptian system employs the **additive property.** The value of a number is the sum of the value of the numerals. For example,

ꙮ	represents	100 000	
999	represents	300	$(100 + 100 + 100)$
∩∩	represents	20	$(10 + 10)$
II	represents	2	$(1 + 1)$
ꙮ999∩∩II	represents	100 322	

In the Egyptian system, 100 322 could also be written as 999∩∩ꙮII. The order of the numerals makes no difference.

     The Babylonian system was developed at about the same time as the Egyptian system. Records of the Babylonian system have been preserved for centuries because the Babylonians used clay tablets that were more durable than the Egyptians' papyrus since the tablets were indented with a stylus and baked in the sun. The Babylonian system uses the symbols given in Table 3-2.

TABLE 3-2

Babylonian Numerals	Hindu–Arabic Face Value
▼	1
<	10

The Babylonian numerals for 1 through 59 are created via the additive property. For example, ≪▼▼ represents 22. Numbers greater than 59 are based on repeated groupings of sixty, much as we use groupings of ten today. For example, ▼▼ ≪<▼▼ represents 2 · 60 + 22 or 142. The space indicates that ▼▼ represents 2 · 60 rather than 2. Numerals to the left of a second space have a value 60 · 60 times their face value, and so on.

≪ ▼ represents 20 · 60 + 1 or 1201

<▼ <▼ ▼ represents 11 · 60 · 60 + 11 · 60 + 1 or
11 · 60^2 + 11 · 60 + 1 or 40 261

▼ <▼ <▼ ▼ represents 1 · 60 · 60 · 60 + 11 · 60 · 60 + 11 · 60 + 1 or
1 · 60^3 + 11 · 60^2 + 11 · 60 + 1 or 256 261

The notion of exponents simplifies the writing of 60 · 60 · 60 as 60^3.

DEFINITION

> If a is any number and n is any natural number, then a^n is defined by the following equation.
>
> $$a^n = \underbrace{a \cdot a \cdot a \cdot \ldots \cdot a}_{n \text{ terms}}$$

*n*th power of *a*
exponent
base

a^n is called the ***n*th power of *a*;** n is called the **exponent;** a is called the **base.** The definition can be extended as follows: If $a \neq 0$ and $n = 0$, then $a^0 = 1$. (The definitions and properties of exponents are discussed in detail in Chapter 6.)

In the Babylonian system, the value of a numeral is determined not only by the values of each symbol but also by the placement of the symbols. The placement of the symbols determines the particular powers of 60. In general,

place value
a numeration system has **place value** if the placement of the symbols in a

numeral determines the powers of a base by which the value of the symbols is multiplied to determine the value of the number.

The Roman numeration system remains in use today. Roman numerals appear on cornerstones, on the opening pages of books, and on the faces of clocks. The basic Roman numerals are pictured in Table 3-3.

TABLE 3-3

Roman Numeral	Hindu–Arabic Equivalent
I	1
V	5
X	10
L	50
C	100
D	500
M	1000

Roman symbols can be combined using the additive property. The additive property applies to Roman numerals listed in decreasing order from left to right. For example, MDCLXVI represents 1000 + 500 + 100 + 50 + 10 + 5 + 1 = 1666, CCCXXVIII represents 328, and VI represents 6. However, if the numerals are not listed in decreasing order from left to right, then the **subtractive property** applies. For example, I is less than V, so if it is to the left of V, it is subtracted. Thus, IV has a value of 5 − 1 or 4, and XC represents 100 − 10 or 90. The only pairings of symbols based on the subtractive property which are allowed are given in Table 3-4. Be careful. Some extensions of the subtractive property could lead to ambiguous results. For example, IXC could be 91 or 89. By custom, 91 is written XCI, and 89 is written LXXXIX. In general, only one smaller symbol can be to the left of a larger symbol, and the pair must be one of those listed in Table 3-4.

subtractive property

TABLE 3-4

Roman Numeral	Hindu–Arabic Equivalent
IV	5 − 1 or 4
IX	10 − 1 or 9
XL	50 − 10 or 40
XC	100 − 10 or 90
CD	500 − 100 or 400
CM	1000 − 100 or 900

multiplicative property

The Romans adopted the use of bars to write large numbers. The use of bars is based on the **multiplicative property.** A bar over a symbol or symbols indicates that the value is multiplied by 1000. For example, $\overline{V}$ represents 5 · 1000 or 5000, and $\overline{CDX}$ represents 410 · 1000 or 410 000. To indicate even greater numbers, more bars appear. The number of bars indicates the power of 1000 to be used as the multiplier. Thus, $\overline{\overline{V}}$ represents 5 · 1000^2 or 5 000 000; $\overline{\overline{\overline{CXI}}}$ represents 111 · 1000^3 or 111 000 000 000; $\overline{CXI}$ represents 110 · 1000 + 1 or 110 001.

The properties of numeration systems illustrated in this section are not definitive, but several of them are used in the Hindu–Arabic system. The Hindu–Arabic numeration system we use today has ten basic symbols, called

digits

digits: 0, 1, 2, 3, 4, 5, 6, 7, 8, 9. The system uses place value. The value of a digit in a given numeral depends on the placement of the digit with respect to other digits in the numeral. Each place in a Hindu–Arabic numeral repre-

decimal system

sents a power of 10. Thus, the system is called a **decimal system** after the Latin word *decem* for ten. The value of a numeral is determined by multiplying each digit times its place value and finding the sum of these products.

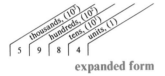

expanded form

In the numeral 5984, the 5 represents five 1000's or 5 · 10^3; the 9 represents nine 100's or 9 · 10^2; the 8 represents eight 10's or 8 · 10; the 4 represents four units or 4 · 1. Hence, 5984 = 5 · 10^3 + 9 · 10^2 + 8 · 10 + 4. This representation is called the **expanded form** of the number.

A special feature of the Hindu–Arabic system is a place-holding symbol, 0. It represents the absence of a power of 10. For example, in 403, the 0 indicates that there are *no* tens. None of the other three systems—Egyptian, Babylonian, or Roman—had this feature.

PROBLEM SET 3-1

1. Complete the following chart, which compares symbols for numbers in different numeration systems.

	Hindu-Arabic	Babylonian	Egyptian	Roman
(a)	3672			
(b)		⟨ ▼▼		
(c)			𐎅99∩∩|||	
(d)				MDCLXVII

2. For each of the following, tell which numeral represents the greater number and why.
    (a) $\overline{MCDXXIV}$ and $\overline{\overline{MCDXXIV}}$ (b) 4632 and 46 032
    (c) ⟨▼▼   and ⟨ ▼▼   (d) 999∩∩|| and

3. For each of the following, name both the succeeding and preceding numerals (one more and one less).
   (a) MCMXLIX   (b) $\overline{\text{MI}}$ (c) CMXCIX   (d) << <▼   (e) 𝆯99

4. For each of the following systems, discuss how you might add 245 and 989.
   (a) Babylonian   (b) Egyptian   (c) Roman

5. For each of the following decimal numerals, give the place value of the underlined digit.
   (a) 827 3<u>6</u>7   (b) 8 421 00<u>0</u>
   (c) 97 9<u>9</u>8   (d) <u>8</u>10 485
   (e) 1 <u>6</u> 450   (f) a <u>b</u> c d e f g

6. The following are numerals written using expanded form. Rewrite each as it is normally seen.
   (a) $3 \cdot 10^6 + 4 \cdot 10^3 + 5$ (b) $2 \cdot 10^4 + 1$
   (c) $3 \cdot 10^3 + 5 \cdot 10^2 + 6 \cdot 10$ (d) $9 \cdot 10^6 + 9 \cdot 10 + 9$

7. Discuss the advantages and disadvantages of each of the numeration systems named in this section.

8. Do Problems 1, 3, 4, and 5 appearing in Appendix II.

3-2 ADDING AND ORDERING WHOLE NUMBERS

Because numbers from the set of natural numbers {1, 2, 3, 4, . . .} are used to count, they are also called the set of counting numbers. Zero is not a counting number; it is a place holder. The set {0, 1, 2, 3, 4, . . .} or *W* is called the set of

whole numbers   **whole numbers.**

The concept of addition of whole numbers is normally introduced to children using the notion of "combining." Suppose Jane has 4 pencils in one pile and 3 pencils in another. If she combines the two groups of pencils into one pile, how many pencils are in the combined pile? The solution is shown in Figure 3-2. Addition of whole numbers is used to describe the situation. The combined set of pencils is the union of the set of 4 pencils and the set of 3 pencils. Thus, the notion of *combining* two groups can be expressed mathematically as the union of two disjoint sets.

FIGURE 3-2

4   3   4 + 3

DEFINITION

> Let A and B be two disjoint sets. If $n(A) = a$ and $n(B) = b$, then $a + b = n(A \cup B)$.

Remark | The numbers a and b are called the **addends;** $a + b$ is called the **sum.**

This carefully worded definition actually says how addition of numbers is related to union of sets. The importance of A and B being disjoint is explored in the problem set.

In elementary school classrooms, a number line can be used as a model for whole numbers. Any line marked with two fundamental points, one representing 0 and the other representing 1, can be turned into a number line. For example, on a horizontal line, choose an arbitrary point and label the point 0. Then choose any other point on the line to the right of the point labeled 0, and label this point 1. The points representing 0 and 1 mark the ends of a **unit segment.** Other points are marked and labeled as shown in Figure 3-3. Any two consecutive points in Figure 3-3 mark the ends of a segment which has the same length as the unit segment.

unit segment

FIGURE 3-3

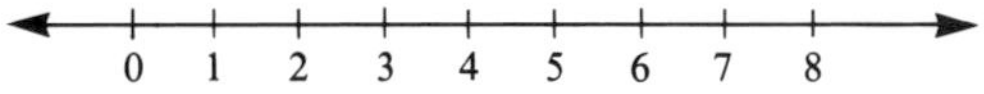

```
◄──┼──┼──┼──┼──┼──┼──┼──┼──┼──►
   0  1  2  3  4  5  6  7  8
```

Any given number can be represented by a directed arrow of a given length. For example, Figure 3-4 shows several directed arrows that represent 2. Using directed arrows on the number line, it is possible to model addition

FIGURE 3-4

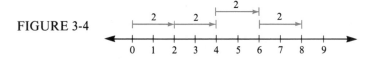

problems. For example, the sum $4 + 3$ is shown in Figure 3-5. Arrows representing the addends, 4 and 3, are combined into one arrow representing the sum.

FIGURE 3-5

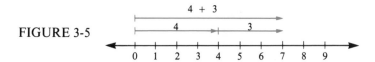

greater than
less than

The number line can also be used to describe **greater than** and **less than.** For example, notice that 7 is to the right of 4 on the number line. We say, "seven is greater than four," and we write $7 > 4$. Since 7 is to the right of 4, there is a number that can be added to 4 to get 7, namely, 3. Thus, $7 > 4$ since $7 = 4 + 3$.

DEFINITION

> For any whole numbers a and b, a is **greater than** b, written $a > b$, if and only if there exists a natural number k such that $a = b + k$.

greater than or equal to,
less than or equal to

The expression $a > b$ can be read from left to right or from right to left. From right to left, it reads "b is less than a," and this can be written as $b < a$. For example, 7 is greater than 3 implies that 3 is less than 7. Sometimes equality is combined with the inequalities greater than and less than to give **greater than or equal to** or **less than or equal to** relations, denoted by $\geq$ and $\leq$. (Note that $5 \geq 3$ and $3 \geq 3$ are both true statements.)

Have you ever heard children arguing over who has the most? "I have a million!" "I have a million one!" "Well, I have a million three!" The children's remarks show that intuitively they understand the definition of inequality. Also, the remarks indicate that there is no greatest whole number. In addition, the children's remarks suggest the following property.

Property

Closure Property of Addition of Whole Numbers   If a and b are any whole numbers, then $a + b$ is a unique whole number.

closed under addition

We say that the set of whole numbers is **closed under addition.** The closure property can be extended to any finite sum of whole numbers. For example, if a, b, c, and d are whole numbers, then $a + b + c + d$ is a unique whole number.

Figure 3-6 shows two additions. Pictured above the number line is $3 + 5$, and below the number line is $5 + 3$. The sums are exactly the same. The numbers can be added in either order without affecting the sum.

FIGURE 3-6

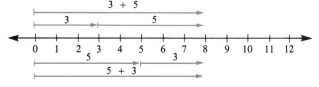

Property | **Commutative Property of Addition of Whole Numbers** If a and b are any whole numbers, then $a + b = b + a$.

commutative under addition

This property is abbreviated in this book as CPA. The set of whole numbers is said to be **commutative under addition.** Table 3-5 shows that the existence of the commutative property for addition of whole numbers reduces the number of single-digit addition facts to be learned from 100 to 55.

TABLE 3-5

BRAIN TEASER

Place the numbers 1 through 11 in the circles shown so that the sums are the same in each direction.

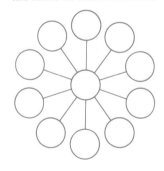

+	0	1	2	3	4	5	6	7	8	9
0	0	1	2	3	4	5	6	7	8	9
1		2	3	4	5	6	7	8	9	10
2			4	5	6	7	8	9	10	11
3				6	7	8	9	10	11	12
4					8	9	10	11	12	13
5						10	11	12	13	14
6		Commutative					12	13	14	15
7		property						14	15	16
8		gives these							16	17
9										18

An addition problem like $2 + 3 + 4$ can be completed in several ways. One student might first find $2 + 3$ and then add $5 + 4$. Using parentheses to indicate this method, we write $(2 + 3) + 4 = 5 + 4 = 9$. Another way to complete the problem is first to add 3 and 4 to get 7 and then to add 2 and 7. Again, the solution is 9.

$$(2 + 3) + 4 = 2 + (3 + 4)$$

This example illustrates a more general property described as follows.

Property | **Associative Property of Addition of Whole Numbers** If a, b, and c are any whole numbers, then $(a + b) + c = a + (b + c)$.

associative under addition

This property is abbreviated APA. The set of whole numbers is said to be **associative under addition.** Usually, when several terms are added, the parentheses are omitted because the grouping does not alter the result. We simply write $a + b + c$.

Another property of addition of whole numbers is seen when one addend is 0. In Figure 3-7, set A has 5 blocks and set B has 0 blocks. The union of sets A and B has only 5 blocks.

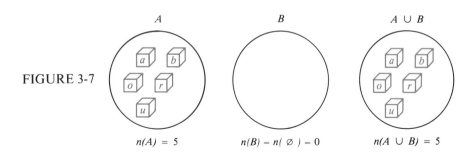

FIGURE 3-7

$n(A) = 5$ $n(B) = n(\varnothing) = 0$ $n(A \cup B) = 5$

This example illustrates yet another general property as follows.

Property | **Identity Property of Addition for Whole Numbers**   There is a unique whole number 0 such that for any whole number a, $a + 0 = 0 + a = a$.

additive identity

This property is abbreviated IPA. The number 0 is called the **additive identity** for whole numbers. With the identity property of addition, the number of basic addition facts in Table 3-5 is reduced from 55 to 45.

PROBLEM SET 3-2

1. Use a number line to explain why $5 < 7$ and why $6 > 3$.
2. Explain why $5 < 7$ and why $6 > 3$ by finding the natural numbers k such that
   (a) $5 + k = 7$ (b) $6 = 3 + k$
3. In the definition of "greater than," can the natural number k be replaced by the whole number k? Why or why not?
4. Give an example to show why, in the definition of addition, sets A and B must be disjoint.
5. Use the number line model to illustrate $6 + 3 = 9$.
6. For each of the following, indicate which whole numbers will make the statements true.
   (a) $2 + \square = 7$ (b) $\square + 4 = 6$
   (c) $3 + \square \le 5$ (d) $\square + 6 \ge 9$
7. Tell whether or not the following sets are closed under addition. Why or why not?
   (a) $A = \{0, 1\}$ (b) $B = \{0\}$
   (c) $N = \{1, 2, 3, 4, 5, \ldots\}$ (d) $E = \{0, 2, 4, 6, 8, \ldots\}$
   (e) $R = \{1, 3, 5, 7, \ldots\}$ (f) $T = \{0, 3, 6, 9, 12, \ldots\}$
8. Each of the following is an example of one of the properties of addition of whole numbers. Identify the property illustrated.
   (a) $7 + 0 = 7$ (b) $6 + 3 = 3 + 6$
   (c) $(6 + 3) + 5 = 6 + (3 + 5)$ (d) $(6 + 3) + 5 = (3 + 6) + 5$
   (e) $12 + 0 = 12$ (f) If $q, r, s \in W$, $(q + r) + s = q + (r + s)$
9. For each of the following, use the underlined expressions to illustrate that English expressions are not always commutative.
   (a) Siamese <u>cat show</u>   (b) <u>Going to school</u> I saw the kids.

10. For each of the following, use the three words to illustrate that English expressions are not always associative.
    (a) dog house broken
    (b) short story writer

★11. Suppose the following addition table came from another planet. On the back of the table are notes stating that the commutative and associative properties, and the zero identity property, hold. Complete the table.

+	0	1	2	3	4	5	6
0	0	1	2				
1	1	2	3				
2	2		4				
3		4	5	6	10	11	12
4					11		
5						13	14
6							15

 12. Do problems 7, 8, and 12 appearing in Appendix II.

LABORATORY ACTIVITY Construct a number line on an adding machine tape. Using the same units, construct a box 5 units wide. Cut slits in each end of the box and insert the tape. Figure 3-8 shows how the model illustrates $7 + 5 = 12$. Write an equation to describe the mathematical function illustrated. Use this model to investigate $a + 5$, where a is any whole number.

FIGURE 3-8

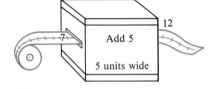

3-3 MULTIPLICATION OF WHOLE NUMBERS

Soon after elementary students have mastered the addition facts, they begin the study of multiplication.

Example 3-1

Looking at her empty classroom before the first bell, a mathematics teacher noticed that there were 6 rows of chairs with 4 chairs in each row. When the bell rang, each chair was occupied by a student. How many students were present?

Solution

A strategy here is to reduce the problem to one that we know how to solve. In this case, the problem can be rewritten as an addition problem. Since each chair is occupied, there are 6 rows of students with 4 students in each row for a total of

$$\underbrace{4 + 4 + 4 + 4 + 4 + 4}_{\text{six 4's}} = 24$$

Example 3-1 illustrates the need for a shorthand method of writing repeated additions. We use the notation 6×4 or $6 \cdot 4$ to mean six 4's are added. Multiplication can be described as repeated addition, and it can be denoted symbolically as follows.

For any natural numbers n and a,

$$n \cdot a = \underbrace{a + a + \cdots + a}_{n \text{ terms}}$$

Multiplication of whole numbers can be modeled on a number line. For example, the number line model for $5 \cdot 4$ is shown in Figure 3-9.

FIGURE 3-9

The following example suggests another model for multiplication of whole numbers.

Example 3-2

At the health food bar, one can order a soyburger on dark or light bread with any one of the following: mustard, mayonnaise, or horseradish. How many different soyburgers can a waiter call out to the cook?

Solution

Understanding the Problem

The problem asks for the number of combinations of bread and condiments.

Devising a Plan

One strategy is to list all possibilities in an organized manner. The tree diagram in Figure 3-10 shows such a list. To solve the problem, simply count the items under "What the Cook Hears."

FIGURE 3-10

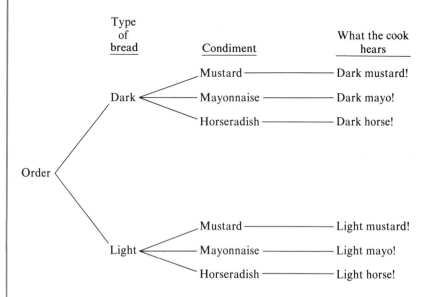

Carrying Out the Plan

There are six ways the order can be placed by the waiter.

Looking Back

Figure 3-10 illustrates the Cartesian product of sets {dark, light} and {mustard, mayo, horse}. Denoting A = {dark, light} and B = {mustard, mayo, horse}, then $n(A) = 2$, $n(B) = 3$, and $2 \cdot 3 = n(A \times B)$.

Example 3-2 illustrates the following definition of multiplication of whole numbers.

DEFINITION

> For finite sets A and B, if $n(A) = a$ and $n(B) = b$, then $a \cdot b = n(A \times B)$.

Remark | $a \cdot b$ is called the **product** of a and b. a is called the **multiplier,** and b is called the **multiplicand.**

As with addition, multiplication on the set of whole numbers is closed, commutative, and associative

Property | **Closure Property of Multiplication of Whole Numbers**   For any whole numbers a and b, $a \cdot b$ is a unique whole number.

Property | **Commutative Property of Multiplication of Whole Numbers**   For any whole numbers a and b, $a \cdot b = b \cdot a$.

Property | **Associative Property of Multiplication of Whole Numbers**   For any whole numbers a, b, and c, $(a \cdot b) \cdot c = a \cdot (b \cdot c)$.

The commutative property of multiplication will be abbreviated CPM. Figure 3-11 illustrates that $3 \cdot 5 = 5 \cdot 3$.

Using the commutative property of multiplication reduces the number of multiplication facts students must learn from 100 to 55. This is illustrated in Table 3-6.

$3 \cdot 5 = 15$

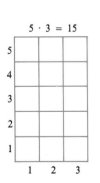

$5 \cdot 3 = 15$

FIGURE 3-11

TABLE 3-6

×	0	1	2	3	4	5	6	7	8	9
0	0									
1	0	1				Commutative				
2	0	2	4			Property				
3	0	3	6	9		gives these				
4	0	4	8	12	16					
5	0	5	10	15	20	25				
6	0	6	12	18	24	30	36			
7	0	7	14	21	28	35	42	49		
8	0	8	16	24	32	40	48	56	64	
9	0	9	18	27	36	45	54	63	72	81

The associative property of multiplication of whole numbers is abbreviated as APM. It can be illustrated as follows. Suppose $a = 3$, $b = 5$, and $c = 4$. Compare $3 \cdot (5 \cdot 4)$ and $(3 \cdot 5) \cdot 4$. First, $5 \cdot 4$ can be illustrated with 20 cubes as shown in Figure 3-12(a), and $3 \cdot (5 \cdot 4)$ is seen in Figure 3-12(b) so that $3 \cdot (5 \cdot 4) = 60$ in Figure 3-12(c).

FIGURE 3-12

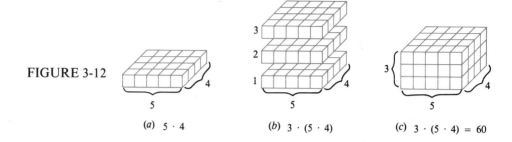

(a) 5 · 4   (b) 3 · (5 · 4)   (c) 3 · (5 · 4) = 60

In Figure 3-13, the cubes are combined in a different way to show (3 · 5) · 4. In Figures 3-12 and 3-13, the final number of cubes is 60. Thus, 3 · (5 · 4) = (3 · 5) · 4.

FIGURE 3-13

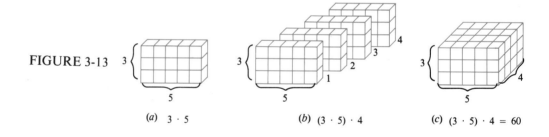

(a) 3 · 5   (b) (3 · 5) · 4   (c) (3 · 5) · 4 = 60

To examine other properties of multiplication of whole numbers, consider Table 3-6. The first column contains all zeros. To see why this is true, consider 6 · 0. Using repeated addition, $6 \cdot 0 = 0 + 0 + 0 + 0 + 0 + 0 = 0$. This idea can be stated as follows.

Property | **Zero Multiplication Property of Whole Numbers**   For any whole number $a, a \cdot 0 = 0 = 0 \cdot a$.

The zero multiplication property can also be verified using the definition of multiplication in terms of Cartesian products. Let A be any set such that $n(A) = a$. Then $a \cdot 0 = n(A \times \varnothing) = n(\varnothing) = 0$.

The second column of a multiplication chart matches the outside column. This is true since, for example, $6 \cdot 1 = 1 + 1 + 1 + 1 + 1 + 1 = 6$, and $3 \cdot 1 = 1 + 1 + 1 = 3$. In general, for any whole number a,

$$a \cdot 1 = \underbrace{1 + 1 + 1 + \cdots + 1}_{a \text{ terms}} = a$$

Thus, $a \cdot 1 = a$. Also, by the commutative property of multiplication, $1 \cdot a = a$, and 1 is called the **multiplicative identity** for whole numbers.

multiplicative identity

Property | **Identity Property of Multiplication of Whole Numbers**   There is a unique whole number 1 such that for any whole number a, $a \cdot 1 = 1 \cdot a = a$.

The identity property of multiplication is abbreviated IPM.

The next property that we investigate involves the use of both addition and multiplication. For example, in Figure 3-14, $5 \cdot (3 + 4) = (5 \cdot 3) + (5 \cdot 4)$. The properties of addition and multiplication also can be used to justify this result.

FIGURE 3-14

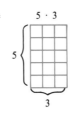
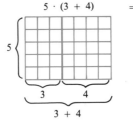

$$5 \cdot (3 + 4) = 5 \cdot 3 + 5 \cdot 4$$

$5 \cdot (3 + 4) = \underbrace{(3 + 4) + (3 + 4) + (3 + 4) + (3 + 4) + (3 + 4)}_{5 \text{ times}}$ Multiplication is repeated addition.

$= (3 + 3 + 3 + 3 + 3) + (4 + 4 + 4 + 4 + 4)$ Commutative and associative properties of addition.

$= 5 \cdot 3 + 5 \cdot 4$ Multiplication is repeated addition.

$5 \cdot (3 + 4) = 5 \cdot 3 + 5 \cdot 4$ Transitive property of equality.

distributive property of multiplication over addition

This example illustrates the **distributive property of multiplication over addition** for whole numbers, which is stated in general as follows.

Property | **Distributive Property of Multiplication over Addition for Whole Numbers**   For any whole numbers a, b, and c,

$$a \cdot (b + c) = a \cdot b + a \cdot c$$

This property is abbreviated as DPM/A. Using the commutative property of multiplication, the distributive property of multiplication over addition can be rewritten as $(b + c) \cdot a = b \cdot a + c \cdot a$. The distributive property can be generalized to any finite number of terms. For example, $a \cdot (b + c + d) = a \cdot b + a \cdot c + a \cdot d$.

Example 3-3   Rename each of the following using the distributive property.

(a) $3 \cdot (x + y)$ (b) $(x + 1) \cdot x$
(c) $3 \cdot (2x + y + 3)$ (d) $a \cdot x + a \cdot y$
(e) $a \cdot x + a$ (f) $(x + 2) \cdot 5 + (x + 2) \cdot a$

Solution   (a) $3 \cdot (x + y) = 3 \cdot x + 3 \cdot y = 3x + 3y$
(b) $(x + 1) \cdot x = x \cdot x + 1 \cdot x = x^2 + x$
(c) $3 \cdot (2x + y + 3) = 3 \cdot (2x) + 3 \cdot y + 3 \cdot 3 = (3 \cdot 2) \cdot x + 3 \cdot y + 9 = 6x + 3y + 9$
(d) $a \cdot x + a \cdot y = a \cdot (x + y) = a(x + y)$
(e) $a \cdot x + a = a \cdot x + a \cdot 1 = a \cdot (x + 1) = a(x + 1)$
(f) $(x + 2) \cdot 5 + (x + 2) \cdot a = (x + 2) \cdot (5 + a) = (x + 2)(5 + a)$

Remark   Where there is no ambiguity, we omit the multiplication dot and, for example, write $3x$ rather than $3 \cdot x$. Furthermore, an expression such as $2 \cdot (a \cdot b)$ can be written as $2ab$.

Example 3-4   Using the distributive property, simplify $(a + b)^2$.

Solution   By the definition of exponents, $(a + b)^2 = (a + b)(a + b)$. Consider the first term, $(a + b)$, as a single whole number and apply the distributive property.

$$
\begin{aligned}
(a + b)(a + b) &= (a + b) \cdot a + (a + b) \cdot b & &\text{DPM/A} \\
&= (a \cdot a + b \cdot a) + (a \cdot b + b \cdot b) & &\text{DPM/A} \\
&= (a^2 + b \cdot a) + (a \cdot b + b^2) & &\text{Definition of exponents} \\
&= a^2 + (b \cdot a + a \cdot b) + b^2 & &\text{APA} \\
&= a^2 + (a \cdot b + a \cdot b) + b^2 & &\text{CPM} \\
&= a^2 + 1(ab) + 1(ab) + b^2 & &\text{IPM} \\
&= a^2 + (1 + 1)(ab) + b^2 & &\text{DPM/A} \\
&= a^2 + 2ab + b^2 & &\text{Addition table} \\
& & &(1 + 1 = 2)
\end{aligned}
$$

Difficulties involving the order of operations sometimes arise. For example, many students will treat $2 + 3 \cdot 6$ as $(2 + 3) \cdot 6$, while others will treat it as $2 + (3 \cdot 6)$. In the first case, the value is 30. In the second case, the value is 20. In order to avoid confusion, mathematicians agree that when no parentheses are present, multiplications are performed *before* additions. Thus, $2 + 3 \cdot 6 = 2 + 18 = 20$.

PROBLEM SET 3-3

1. Use the number line model to illustrate why $3 \cdot 5 = 15$.
2. For each of the following, find the whole numbers that make the equations true.
   (a) $2 \cdot \square = 10$ (b) $\square \cdot 3 = 21$
   (c) $3 \cdot \square = 15$ (d) $\square \cdot 4 = 12$
3. Each ticket to the band concert costs $2.00. How much do 8 tickets cost?
4. Tell whether or not the following sets are closed under multiplication.
   (a) $\{0, 1\}$ (b) $\{0\}$
   (c) $\{2, 4, 6, 8, 10, \ldots\}$ (d) $\{1, 3, 5, 7, 9, \ldots\}$
   (e) $\{1, 4, 7, 10, 13, 16, \ldots\}$
5. Use the distributive property to describe how you might find the product $8 \cdot 3$ if you know only the addition table and the two and six multiplication facts.
6. Each of the following illustrates a property of multiplication, addition, or the distributive property of multiplication over addition of whole numbers. Tell which.
   (a) $3 \cdot 2 = 2 \cdot 3$ (b) $3(2 \cdot 4) = (3 \cdot 2)4$
   (c) $3(2 + 3) = 3(3 + 2)$ (d) $8 \cdot 0 = 0$
   (e) $1 \cdot 8 = 8$ (f) $6(3 + 5) = (3 + 5)6$
   (g) $6(3 + 5) = 6 \cdot 3 + 6 \cdot 5$ (h) $(3 + 5)6 = 3 \cdot 6 + 5 \cdot 6$
   (i) $1(a + b) = a + b$ (j) $(a + b)0 = 0$
7. Rename each of the following using the distributive property.
   (a) $3(100 + 1)$ (b) $(3 + 1)(4 + 2)$ (c) $(a + b)(c + d)$
   (d) $3(x + y + 5)$ (e) $\square(\triangle + \star)$ (f) $(x + y)(x + y + z)$
   ★(g) $(x + y + z)^2$
8. For each of the following, find the whole numbers that make the equations true, if possible.
   (a) $3 \square = 15$ (b) $18 = 6 + 3 \square$ (c) $\square \cdot \square = 25$
   (d) $5(\square + \triangle) = 5 \cdot 3 + 5 \cdot 4$ (e) $\square (5 + 6) = \square 5 + \square 6$
9. Rename each of the following using the distributive property.
   (a) $2x + 3x$ (b) $x + 5x + 8x$ (c) $2(x + 1) + 3(x + 1)$
   (d) $ab + a$ (e) $mb + mc + m$ (f) $2(x + 3) + x(x + 3)$
10. Perform each of the following computations.
    (a) $2 \cdot 3 + 5$ (b) $2(3 + 5)$ (c) $2 \cdot 3 + 2 \cdot 5$ (d) $3 + 2 \cdot 5$
11. Does the distributive property of addition over multiplication of whole numbers hold, that is, for any whole numbers a, b, and c, is it true that
    $$a + (bc) = (a + b)(a + c)$$
    If not, for what values of a, b, and c is the property true?
12. The generalized distributive property for three terms states that for any whole numbers a, b, c, and d, $a(b + c + d) = ab + ac + ad$. Justify this property using the distributive property for two terms.
13. The FOIL method is often used as a shortcut to multiply expressions like $(m + n)(x + y)$.

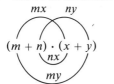

$$= mx + my + nx + ny$$

    where F stands for product of the *first* terms, mx
           O stands for product of the *outer* terms, my
           I stands for product of the *inner* terms, nx
           L stands for product of the *last* terms, ny

> (a)   Use the FOIL method on each of the following.
> $(a + b)(a + b)$
> $(50 + 8)(20 + 6)$
> (b)   Use the distributive property to show why the FOIL method works.
> 14.   Do problems 42, 43, 44, and 59 appearing in Appendix II.

3-4 ALGORITHMS FOR ADDITION AND MULTIPLICATION

algorithm

An **algorithm** (named for the Arabian mathematician, Al-Khowarizmi) is a step-by-step procedure used to accomplish a mathematical operation. It is valuable for every prospective elementary teacher to know more than one algorithm to do operations. Not all students learn in the same manner, and the shortest, most efficient algorithms may not be the best for every individual. Not only should teachers know alternative algorithms, but they also should know why each algorithm works. Single-digit addition and multiplication facts, the properties of addition and multiplication, and the meaning of place value are prerequisites for understanding algorithms.

Addition Algorithms

The use of concrete teaching aids, such as multibase blocks, helps provide insight into the creation of algorithms for addition. A set of multibase blocks, shown in Figure 3-15, consists of "units," "longs," "flats," and "blocks,"

FIGURE 3-15

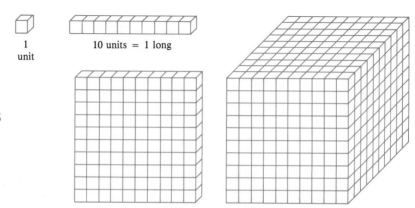

1 unit

10 units = 1 long

100 units = 1 flat

1000 units = 1 block

representing 1, 10, 100, and 1000, respectively. Note that there is no block for 10 000. Why?

　　Students trade blocks by regrouping; that is, they take a set of multibase blocks representing a number and trade them until they have the fewest possible pieces representing the same number.

Example 3-5　Suppose you have 58 units and want to trade them. What is the fewest number of pieces you can receive in exchange?

Solution　The units can be grouped into tens to form longs. Five sets of 10 units each can be traded for five longs. Thus, 58 units can be traded for 5 longs and 8 units. In terms of numbers, this is analogous to rewriting 58 as $5 \cdot 10 + 8$. You cannot receive flats or blocks. The fewest number of pieces you can receive is 13.

Example 3-6　Suppose you have 11 flats, 17 longs, and 16 units. What is the fewest number of pieces you can receive in exchange?

Solution　The 16 units can be traded for 1 long and 6 units.

11 flats	17 longs	~~16 units~~
	1 long	6 units
11 flats	18 longs	6 units

(16 units = 1 long and 6 units)

(after the first trade)

The 18 longs can be traded for 1 flat and 8 longs.

11 flats	~~18 longs~~	6 units
1 flat	8 longs	
12 flats	8 longs	6 units

(18 longs = 1 flat and 8 longs)

(after the second trade)

The 12 flats can be traded for 1 block and 2 flats.

	~~12 flats~~	8 longs	6 units
1 block	2 flats		
1 block	2 flats	8 longs	6 units

(12 flats = 1 block and 2 flats)

(after the third trade)

　　The fewest number of pieces is $1 + 2 + 8 + 6$ or 17; that is, 1 block, 2 flats, 8 longs, and 6 units. In terms of numbers, this is analogous to rewriting $11 \cdot 10^2 + 17 \cdot 10 + 16$ as $1 \cdot 10^3 + 2 \cdot 10^2 + 8 \cdot 10 + 6$, which implies that there are 1286 units.

　　The sample on page 98 from *Heath Mathematics*, 1979, Grade 4 illustrates how multibase blocks can be used to introduce the concepts involved in addition. Study how regrouping is introduced.

Adding with regrouping

In this example, 10 ones are regrouped for 1 ten.

Step 1. Add ones.   **Step 2.** Regroup.   **Step 3.** Add tens.

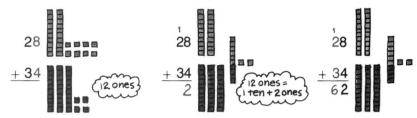

In this example, 10 tens are regrouped for 1 hundred.

Step 1. Add ones.   **Step 2.** Add tens.

Here 10 tens are regrouped for 1 hundred.

Step 1. Add ones.   **Step 2.** Add tens and regroup.   **Step 3.** Add hundreds.

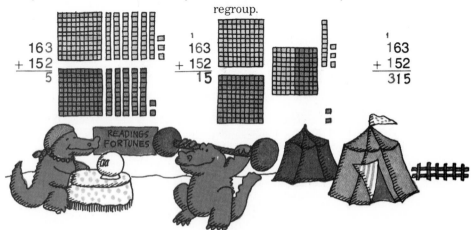

Several examples of addition algorithms are now demonstrated. When a simple computation involving single-digit addition or multiplication is performed, we refer to addition or multiplication tables, such as Tables 3-5 and 3-6 as the reason. In each example, version (a) shows the detailed justification for the computation, while versions (b) and (c) are condensed forms of (a).

Example 3-7

Solution

Compute $14 + 3$.

(a) $\begin{aligned} 14 + 3 &= (1 \cdot 10 + 4) + 3 \\ &= 1 \cdot 10 + (4 + 3) \\ &= 1 \cdot 10 + 7 \\ &= 17 \end{aligned}$
    Place value
    APA
    Addition table $(4 + 3)$
    Place value

(b)
$$
\begin{array}{r}
14 = 1 \cdot 10 + 4 \\
+3 = + 3 \\
\hline
1 \cdot 10 + 7 = 17
\end{array}
$$

(c)
$$
\begin{array}{r}
14 \\
+3 \\
\hline
17
\end{array}
$$

Example 3-8

Solution

Compute $27 + 68$.

(a) $\begin{aligned} 27 + 68 &= (2 \cdot 10 + 7) + (6 \cdot 10 + 8) \\ &= 2 \cdot 10 + (7 + 6 \cdot 10) + 8 \\ &= 2 \cdot 10 + (6 \cdot 10 + 7) + 8 \\ &= (2 \cdot 10 + 6 \cdot 10) + (7 + 8) \\ &= (2 \cdot 10 + 6 \cdot 10) + 15 \\ &= (2 \cdot 10 + 6 \cdot 10) + (1 \cdot 10 + 5) \\ &= (2 \cdot 10 + 6 \cdot 10 + 1 \cdot 10) + 5 \\ &= (2 + 6 + 1) \cdot 10 + 5 \\ &= 9 \cdot 10 + 5 \\ \\ &= 95 \end{aligned}$
    Place value
    APA
    CPA
    APA
    Addition table $(7 + 8)$
    Place value
    APA
    DPM/A
    Addition table $(2 + 6 + 1)$
    Place value

(b)
$$
\begin{array}{r}
27 = 2 \cdot 10 + 7 \\
+68 = 6 \cdot 10 + 8 \\
\hline
8 \cdot 10 + 15 \\
1 \cdot 10 + 5 \\
\hline
9 \cdot 10 + 5 = 95
\end{array}
$$

$\left.\begin{array}{l} 8 \cdot 10 + 15 \\ 1 \cdot 10 + 5 \end{array}\right\}$ Regroup 15 as $1 \cdot 10 + 5$

(c)   27
        +68
         15    $(7 + 8)$
       +80 $(20 + 60)$
         95

The conventional algorithm for computing $27 + 68$ is as follows.

①
27
+68
9⑤   The circled numbers represent the 15.

The 9 represents $9 \cdot 10$, which is obtained from $1 \cdot 10 + 2 \cdot 10 + 6 \cdot 10$.

scratch addition   An alternative algorithm for addition, called **scratch addition,** is shown for $87 + 65 + 49$.

(a) 8   7   (a)   Add the numbers in the units place starting
     6   $\cancel{5}_2$ at the top. When the sum is 10 or more, record
     4   9   this sum by scratching a line through the last
                         number added and writing the number of units
                         next to the scratched number. For example,
                         since $7 + 5 = 12$, the "scratch" repre-
                         sents 10 and the 2 written down repre-
                         sents the units.

(b) 8   7   (b)   Continue adding the units. When the addition
     6   $\cancel{5}_2$ again results in a sum of 10 or more, repeat
     4   $\cancel{9}^2_1$ the process described in (a); $2 + 9 = 11$.

        2
(c) 8   7   (c)   When the first column of additions is completed,
     6   $\cancel{5}_2$ write the number of units, 1, below the addition
     4   $\cancel{9}^2_1$ line. Count the number of scratches, 2, and
        1   record this above the second column.

         2
(d) $\cancel{8}_0$ 7   (d)   Repeat the procedure for each successive
         6   $\cancel{5}_2$ · column.
       $\cancel{4}_0$ $\cancel{9}^2_1$
     2   0   1

Example 3-9   Compute the following additions using the scratch algorithm.

(a) 296   (b) 1369
     840   4813
      27   5879
             6183

Solution   (a)

$$
\begin{array}{ccc}
\overset{1}{2} & \overset{1}{\cancel{9}}_0 & 6 \\
\cancel{8}_1 & 4 & 0 \\
 & 2 & \cancel{7}_3 \\
\hline
1 \quad 1 & 6 & 3
\end{array}
$$

(b)

$$
\begin{array}{cccc}
\overset{2}{1} & \overset{2}{3} & \overset{2}{6} & 9 \\
4 & \cancel{8}_3 & 1 & \cancel{3}_2 \\
\cancel{3}_2 & \cancel{8}_1 & \cancel{7}_6 & \cancel{9}_1 \\
6 & 1 & \cancel{8}_4 & 3 \\
\hline
1 \quad 8 & 2 & 4 & 4
\end{array}
$$

Multiplication Algorithms

The distributive property of multiplication over addition of whole numbers is vital to the development of multiplication algorithms. Consider the product $10 \cdot 49$.

$$
\begin{aligned}
10 \cdot 49 &= 10 \cdot (4 \cdot 10 + 9) & &\text{Place value} \\
&= 10 \cdot (4 \cdot 10) + 10 \cdot 9 & &\text{DPM/A} \\
&= 10 \cdot (10 \cdot 4) + 10 \cdot 9 & &\text{CPM} \\
&= (10 \cdot 10) \cdot 4 + 10 \cdot 9 & &\text{APM} \\
&= 10^2 \cdot 4 + 10 \cdot 9 & &\text{Definition of exponents} \\
&= 4 \cdot 10^2 + 9 \cdot 10 & &\text{CPM} \\
&= 4 \cdot 10^2 + 9 \cdot 10 + 0 & &\text{IPA} \\
&= 490 & &\text{Place value}
\end{aligned}
$$

The preceding example illustrates that multiplication by 10 results in annexing a zero to the multiplicand. It can be shown that multiplication by 10^2 results in annexing two zeros, and, in general, *multiplication by 10^n where n is a natural number results in annexing n zeros to the multiplicand.*

When multiplying powers of 10, an extension of the definition of exponents is used. For example, $10^2 \cdot 10^1 = (10 \cdot 10) \cdot 10 = 10^3$. Observe that $10^3 = 10^{2+1}$. In general, where a is a natural number, m and n are whole numbers, $a^m \cdot a^n$ is given by the following.

$$
a^m \cdot a^n = \underbrace{(a \cdot a \cdot a \cdot \ldots \cdot a)}_{m \text{ terms}} \underbrace{(a \cdot a \cdot a \cdot \ldots \cdot a)}_{n \text{ terms}}
$$

$$
= \underbrace{a \cdot a \cdot a \cdot \ldots \cdot a}_{m + n \text{ terms}} = a^{m+n}
$$

Consequently $a^m \cdot a^n = a^{m+n}$.

Example 3-10   Multiply:

(a) $10^5 \cdot 36$ (b) $10^3 \cdot 279$ (c) $10^{13} \cdot 10^8$

Solution   (a) $10^5 \cdot 36 = 3\,600\,000$ (b) $10^3 \cdot 279 = 279\,000$
(c) $10^{13} \cdot 10^8 = 10^{13+8} = 10^{21}$

The following examples demonstrate an algorithm for multiplication of whole numbers where the multiplier is a number other than a power of 10. Various algorithms are given in each example.

Example 3-11   Compute $3 \cdot 12$.

Solution   (a) $3 \cdot 12 = 3(1 \cdot 10 + 2)$ Place value
$= 3 \cdot (1 \cdot 10) + 3 \cdot 2$ DPM/A
$= (3 \cdot 1) \cdot 10 + 3 \cdot 2$ APM
$= 3 \cdot 10 + 3 \cdot 2$ IPM
$= 3 \cdot 10 + 6$ Multiplication table $(3 \cdot 2)$
$= 36$ Place value

(b) $12 = 1 \cdot 10 + 2$ (c) 12
$\underline{\times 3 =}\underline{\times 3}$ $\underline{\times 3}$
$3 \cdot 10 + 6 = 36$ $6\ |(3 \cdot 2)$
$\underline{30}\ |(3 \cdot 10)$
36

You should supply the reasons for each step in Example 3-12(a).

Example 3-12   Compute $6 \cdot 411$.

Solution   (a) $6 \cdot 411 = 6(4 \cdot 10^2 + 1 \cdot 10 + 1)$
$= 6 \cdot (4 \cdot 10^2) + 6 \cdot (1 \cdot 10) + 6 \cdot 1$
$= (6 \cdot 4) \cdot 10^2 + (6 \cdot 1) \cdot 10 + 6 \cdot 1$
$= (24) \cdot 10^2 + 6 \cdot 10 + 6$
$= (2 \cdot 10 + 4) \cdot 10^2 + 6 \cdot 10 + 6$
$= (2 \cdot 10) \cdot 10^2 + 4 \cdot 10^2 + 6 \cdot 10 + 6$
$= 2 \cdot (10 \cdot 10^2) + 4 \cdot 10^2 + 6 \cdot 10 + 6$
$= 2 \cdot 10^3 + 4 \cdot 10^2 + 6 \cdot 10 + 6$
$= 2466$

(c) 411
$\underline{\times 6}$

(b) $411 = 4 \cdot 10^2 + 1 \cdot 10 + 1$
$\underline{\times 6 =}\underline{\times 6}$
$\underline{24 \cdot 10^2 + 6 \cdot 10 + 6}\Big\}\,\text{Regroup } 24 \cdot 10^2$
$2 \cdot 10^3 + 4 \cdot 10^2$
$\overline{2 \cdot 10^3 + 4 \cdot 10^2 + 6 \cdot 10 + 6} = 2466$

$6\ |\ (6 \cdot 1)$
$60\ |\ (6 \cdot 10)$
$2400\ |\ (6 \cdot 400)$
$\overline{2466}$

Now, consider a problem with a two-digit multiplier.

Example 3-13 | Compute $27 \cdot 68$.

Solution | The horizontal steps for this computation are not completely written out with each reason. In (a), the algorithms for multiplication by one-digit and by powers of 10 are used. In (b), the product is found by use of the distributive property more than once. Further steps in the development of the traditional algorithm are seen in (c) and (d). Part (c) has all the products of part (b) illustrated vertically, while part (d) combines the addends as seen in part (a).

(a) $27 \cdot 68 = (2 \cdot 10 + 7) \cdot 68$
$= [(2 \cdot 10) \cdot 68] + (7 \cdot 68)$
$= 2 \cdot (10 \cdot 68) + 7 \cdot 68$
$= 2 \cdot (68 \cdot 10) + 7 \cdot 68$
$= (2 \cdot 68) \cdot 10 + 7 \cdot 68$
$= 136 \cdot 10 + 476$
$= 1360 + 476$
$= 1836$

(b) $27 \cdot 68 = (20 + 7)(60 + 8)$
$= [(20 + 7) \cdot 60] + [(20 + 7) \cdot 8]$
$= 20 \cdot 60 + 7 \cdot 60 + 20 \cdot 8 + 7 \cdot 8$
$= 1200 + 420 + 160 + 56$
$= 1836$

(c)
```
      68
     ×27
     ───
      56 │ (7 · 8)
     420 │ (7 · 60)
     160 │ (20 · 8)
    1200 │ (20 · 60)
    ────
    1836
```

(d)
```
      68
     ×27
     ───
     476 │ (56 + 420)
    1360 │ (1200 + 160)
    ────
    1836
```

Finally, 68×27 is computed using the conventional algorithm, where 136 is indented to represent 1360.

```
      68
     ×27
     ───
     476
    136
    ────
    1836
```

An alternative to the conventional algorithm for multiplying 68 and 27 follows. It is called **lattice multiplication.** (The reasons why lattice multiplication works are left as an exercise.)

lattice multiplication

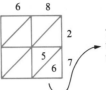

This computation is 7 · 8. The tens go above the diagonal and the units below. Continue this procedure for all the blocks.

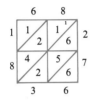

Once the multiplication is complete, add along the diagonals. It is necessary in this example to "carry" 1 to the hundreds.

PROBLEM SET 3-4

1. Perform the following addition using both the scratch and conventional algorithms.

    3789
    9296
    +6843

2. Explain why the scratch addition algorithm works.

3. An addition algorithm from an elementary text follows. Explain why it works.

    $$\begin{array}{r|l} 2 & 7 \\ +6 & 8 \\ \hline 1 & 5 \\ 8 & \\ \hline 9 & 5 \end{array}$$

4. Perform the following multiplication using both the conventional and lattice multiplication algorithms.

    728
    ×94

5. Explain why the lattice multiplication algorithm works.

6. Use the distributive property to explain why 386 · 10 000 = 3 860 000.

7. Fill in the missing numbers for each of the following.

    (a)   4_6   (b)   327
           ×783   +9_1
           ‾‾‾‾‾‾   ‾‾‾‾‾‾
            1_78   _308
           3408
            982
           ‾‾‾‾‾‾
           3335_8

8. Simplify each of the following using properties of exponents.

    (a). $5^7 \cdot 5^{12}$ (b) $6^{10} \cdot 6^2 \cdot 6^3$
    (c). $10^{296} \cdot 10^{17}$ (d) $2^7 \cdot 10^5 \cdot 5^7$

9. The following chart gives water usage for one person for one day.

Use	Average Amount
Taking bath	110 L (liters)
Taking shower	75 L
Flushing toilet	22 L
Washing hands, face	7 L
Getting a drink	1 L
Brushing teeth	1 L
Doing dishes (one meal)	30 L
Cooking (one meal)	18 L

(a) Use the chart to calculate how much water you use each day.
(b) The average American uses approximately 200 L of water per day. Are you average?
(c) If there are 215 000 000 people in the United States, approximately how much water is used in the United States per day?

10. How many seconds are in a day? A week? A year?

11. The following geometric model illustrates the algorithm for 25 · 36 given on the right.

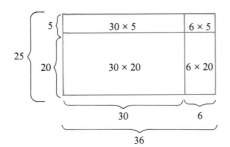

$$\begin{array}{r} 25 \\ \times 36 \\ \hline 30 \\ 120 \\ 150 \\ 600 \\ \hline 900 \end{array} \begin{array}{l} (6 \cdot 5) \\ (6 \cdot 20) \\ (30 \cdot 5) \\ (30 \cdot 20) \end{array}$$

Draw similar geometric models to illustrate each of the following problems.
(a) 6 · 23   (b) 38 · 54   (c) 112 · 23

12. In a certain book, 2981 digits were used to print the page numbers. How many pages are in the book?

13. Consider the following.

$$\begin{array}{r} 476 \\ \times 293 \\ \hline 952 \\ 4284 \\ 1428 \\ \hline 139468 \end{array} \begin{array}{l} (2 \cdot 476) \\ (9 \cdot 476) \\ (3 \cdot 476) \end{array}$$

(a) Show that by using the conventional algorithm, the answer is correct.
(b) Explain why the algorithm works.
(c) Try the method to multiply 84 × 363.

★14.   The Russian peasant algorithm for multiplying 27 × 68 follows.

	Halves	Doubles	
	→ 27	× 68	
Halve 27 (Disregard remainders)	→ 13	136	Double 68
Halve 13	6	272	Double 136
Halve 6	→ 3	544	Double 272
Halve 3	→ 1	1088	Double 544

In the "Halves" column, choose the odd numbers. In the "Doubles" column, choose the numbers paired with the odds from the "Halves" column. Add the circled numbers.

```
  68
 136
 544
1088
────
1836 (This is the product 27 · 68)
```

Try this algorithm for 17 · 63. For an explanation of why the Russian peasant algorithm works, read "Understanding the Russian Peasant" (Reardin, 1973).

★15.   Show that, in general $a^x + a^y \neq a^{x+y}$, where a, x, and y are whole numbers.

 16.   Do problems 13, 14, 15, 19, 20, 21, 29, 30, 45, 46, 48, 49, 50, 51, 52, 53, 58, and 64 appearing in Appendix II.

BRAIN TEASER

For each of the following, replace the letters with digits in such a way that the computation is correct. A single letter may represent only one digit.

(a)
```
  SEND
+ MORE
──────
 MONEY
```

(b)
```
 LYNDON
    × B
────────
JOHNSON
```

LABORATORY ACTIVITY

1.   Finger multiplication has long been popular in many parts of the world. Multiplication of single digits by 9 is very simple using the following steps.

(a)   Place your hands next to each other as shown below.

(b)   To multiply 2 by 9, bend down the second finger from the left. The remaining fingers show the product.

Second finger bent

(c)   Similarly, to multiply 3 by 9, we would bend down the third finger from the left. The remaining fingers would show the product 3 × 9 = 27. Try this procedure with other multiplications by 9.

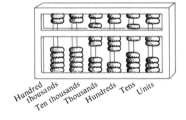

Hundred thousands, Ten thousands, Thousands, Hundreds, Tens, Units

2. The Chinese abacus, *suan pan,* is still in use today. A bar separates two sets of bead counters. Each counter above the bar represents five times the counter below the bar. Numbers are illustrated by moving the counter toward the bar. The number 7362 is pictured at the left. Practice demonstrating numbers and adding on the *suan pan.*

3. "Napier's bones" were a set of multiplication tables, originally constructed on bones or ivory. The method for using them is similar to lattice multiplication. Find 4 × 1783 on the bones below.

Index	1	7	8	3
1	1	7	8	3
2	2	1/4	1/6	6
3	3	2/1	2/4	9
4	4	2/8	3/2	1/2
5	5	3/5	4/0	1/5
6	6	4/2	4/8	1/8
7	7	4/9	5/6	2/1
8	8	5/6	6/4	2/4
9	9	6/3	7/2	2/7

For further reference see Jones, 1954.

3-5 WHOLE NUMBER SUBTRACTION AND DIVISION

In the preceding cartoon, Peppermint Patty reacts to the next operation on whole numbers. This operation is subtraction, and it is directly related to addition as is seen in the following situation.

Juan's Books

Betty took these.

Juan had 13 mathematics books. Betty came and took 12 of them. How many did Juan have left? The illustration at the left pictures the Juan–Betty situation.

As seen in the diagram, Juan had 1 book left. Consequently, 13 "take away" 12 is 1, or $13 - 12 = 1$. This illustrates subtraction as a take-away process. Notice that the number being subtracted, 12, is less than or equal to the beginning number, 13. The example shows that $13 - 12 = 1$. In terms of addition, this can be written as $12 + 1 = 13$. Each subtraction can be thought of as an addition in which one of the addends is unknown. For example, $13 - 12$ is a number c such that $12 + c = 13$. We say that subtraction "undoes" addition or that subtraction is the inverse of addition.

DEFINITION

For any whole numbers a and b, $a - b$ is the unique whole number c such that $c + b = a$.

Remark

The notation $a - b$ is read "a subtract b" or "a minus b." The number a is called the **minuend**; b is called the **subtrahend**; c is called the **difference**.

For $a - b$ to be meaningful for whole numbers, b must be less than or equal to a. Consider the difference $3 - 5$. Using the definition of subtraction, $3 - 5 = c$ means $c + 5 = 3$. Since there is no whole number c that satisfies the equation, the solution for $3 - 5$ cannot be found in the set of whole numbers. This means that the set of whole numbers is *not* closed under subtraction. Showing that the set of whole numbers does not have the commutative, associative, or identity properties under subtraction is left as an exercise.

Subtraction of whole numbers can be illustrated on a number line. For example, $5 - 3$ is shown in Figure 3-16. Observe that from 0, an arrow points 5 units to the right. Because the operation is subtraction, the second arrow points 3 units to the left.

FIGURE 3-16

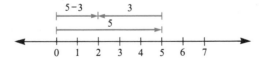

An alternate way to find $5 - 3$ is to determine what number must be added to 3 to obtain the sum 5. This is illustrated in Figure 3-17 and is referred to as the "missing-addend" approach.

FIGURE 3-17

The missing-addend approach to subtraction considers subtraction as the inverse of addition. Multiplication also has an inverse operation called division. Division is illustrated in the following example.

Example 3-14   Benny Crocker baked 18 cookies. He decided to give an equal number of cookies to each of his three best friends, Bob, Charlie, and Dean. How many did each friend receive?

Solution   If we use the strategy of drawing a picture, we see that we can divide (or partition) the 18 cookies into three sets with an equal number of cookies in each set. Figure 3-18 shows that each friend received 6 cookies.

FIGURE 3-18
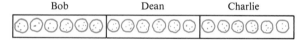

The solution, 6, in Example 3-14, can be designated by $18 \div 3$. In terms of multiplication, this can be rewritten as $6 \cdot 3 = 18$. In fact, any division problem can be defined in terms of multiplication.

DEFINITION

> For any whole numbers a and b with $b \neq 0$, $a \div b$ is the unique whole number c such that $b \cdot c = a$.

Remark   The notation $a \div b = c$ is read "a divided by b is equal to c." The number a is called the **dividend,** b is called the **divisor,** and c is called the **quotient.**

Note that $a \div b$ can also be written as a/b or $b\overline{\smash{)}a}$.

Example 3-15   Compute each of the following.

   (a) $15 \div 5$ (b) $24 \div 6$ (c) $3 \div 1$

Solution

(a) $15 \div 5 = 3$ because $5 \cdot 3 = 15$
(b) $24 \div 6 = 4$ because $6 \cdot 4 = 24$
(c) $3 \div 1 = 3$ because $1 \cdot 3 = 3$

Observe that division "undoes" multiplication, or division is the inverse of multiplication. The relationship between division and multiplication is shown in the following portion of a student page from *Holt School Mathematics*, 1974, Grade 6.

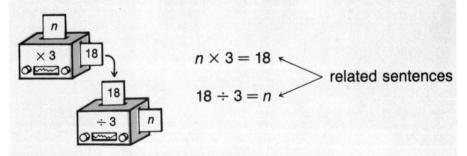

Multiplication and division are **opposite** operations. One operation undoes the other.

$n \times 3 = 18$
$18 \div 3 = n$

related sentences

Related sentences have the same solution.

Just as subtraction of whole numbers is not always meaningful, division of whole numbers is not always meaningful. For example, to find $5 \div 3$, look for a whole number c such that

$3 \cdot c = 5$

There is no whole number c that satisfies this equation. Thus, $5 \div 3$ has no meaning in the set of whole numbers. Thus, the set of whole numbers is not closed under division. (Other properties of division on the set of whole numbers are investigated in the exercises.)

It is not always easy to tell by looking that a division is meaningful on the set of whole numbers. Consider $383 \div 57$. To find a solution to this division, we need to find a number c such that $57 \cdot c = 383$. Table 3-7 shows several products of whole numbers times 57. Since 383 is between 342 and 399, there is no whole number c such that $57 \cdot c = 383$.

TABLE 3-7

$57 \cdot 1$	$57 \cdot 2$	$57 \cdot 3$	$57 \cdot 4$	$57 \cdot 5$	$57 \cdot 6$	$57 \cdot 7$
57	114	171	228	285	342	399

In the real world, if 383 apples were to be divided among 57 students, then the division would have a solution; each student would receive 6 apples, and 41 apples would remain. The number 41 is called the **remainder.** Thus, 383 contains six 57's with a remainder of 41. Observe that the remainder is a whole number less than 57. The concept illustrated is called the **division algorithm.**

remainder

division algorithm

The Division Algorithm

Given any whole numbers a and b with $b \neq 0$, there exist whole numbers q (quotient) and r (remainder) such that

$$a = b \cdot q + r \text{ with } 0 \leq r < b$$

Remark | The quotient q is the greatest whole number of b's in a.

Example 3-16 | Find whole numbers q and r such that $16 = 3q + r$ with $0 \leq r < 3$.

Solution | $16 = 15 + 1 = 3 \cdot 5 + 1$. Thus, $q = 5$ and $r = 1$.

Remark | Note that $16 = 3 \cdot 4 + 4$ is not the correct form of the division algorithm because 4 cannot be the remainder since it is greater than 3.

The two whole numbers 0 and 1 deserve special attention with respect to division of whole numbers. Try finding the values of the following three expressions.

(a) $3 \div 0$ (b) $0 \div 3$ (c) $0 \div 0$

Consider the following explanations.

(a) By definition, $3 \div 0 = c$ if $0 \cdot c = 3$. Since the zero property of multiplication states that $0 \cdot c = 0$ for any whole number c, there is no whole number c such that $0 \cdot c = 3$. Thus, $3 \div 0$ is undefined.
(b) By definition, $0 \div 3 = c$ if $3 \cdot c = 0$. The zero property of multiplication states that any number times 0 is 0. Since $3 \cdot 0 = 0$, then $c = 0$ and $0 \div 3 = 0$. Note that $c = 0$ is the only number that satisfies $3 \cdot c = 0$.

(c)   By definition, $0 \div 0 = c$ if there is a unique whole number c such that $0 \cdot c = 0$. Notice that for *any* c, $0 \cdot c = 0$. According to the definition of division, c must be unique. Since there is *no* unique number c such that $0 \cdot c = 0$, we say that $0 \div 0$ is indeterminate or undefined.

Division involving 0 may be summarized as follows.
Let n be any natural number, then

(1) $n \div 0$ is undefined.
(2) $0 \div n = 0$.
(3) $0 \div 0$ is indeterminate or undefined.

Recall that $n \cdot 1 = n$ for any whole number n. Thus, by the definition of division, $n \div 1 = n$. For example, $3 \div 1 = 3$, $1 \div 1 = 1$, and $0 \div 1 = 0$.

PROBLEM SET 3-5

1.   For each of the following, find the whole numbers to make the statements true, if possible.
   (a) $8 - 5 = \square$ (b) $8 - \square = 5$ (c) $\square - 4 = 9$ (d) $a - 0 = \square$
   (e) $a - \square = a$ (f) $\square - 3 \le 6$ (g) $\square - 3 > 6$
2.   Jill lost 7 pounds while Jack lost only 3. How much more weight did Jill lose than Jack?
3.   Rewrite each of the following subtraction problems as addition problems.
   (a) $x - 119 = 213$ (b) $213 - x = 119$ (c) $213 - 119 = x$
4.   Use a number line to illustrate each of the following subtractions.
   (a) $11 - 3$ (b) $8 - 4$
5.   One model for subtraction is the comparison model. It is based on the concept of one-to-one correspondence. Suppose, for example, Noah has 5 balloons and Betty has 3. How many more balloons does Noah have than Betty? To solve the problem, notice that there is a one-to-one correspondence between Betty's balloons and a subset of Noah's balloons. To answer the question, simply count the number of Noah's balloons not paired with Betty's. How is the comparison model related to the "take-away" model?

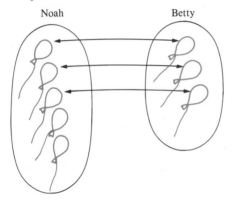
Noah   Betty

6. Show that in general, each of the following is false for the set of whole numbers.
   (a) $a - b = b - a$ (b) $(a - b) - c = a - (b - c)$ (c) $a - 0 = 0 - a = a$
7. For each of the following, determine possible whole numbers a, b, and c for which the statement is true.
   (a) $a - b = b - a$ (b) $(a - b) - c = a - (b - c)$
   (c) $a - 0 = 0 - a = a$ (d) $a(b - c) = ab - ac$
8. For each of the following, find the whole numbers to make the statement true, if possible.
   (a) $18 \div 3 = \square$ (b) $\square \div 76 = 0$ (c) $28 \div \square = 7$
9. Rewrite each of the following division problems as multiplication problems.
   (a) $40 \div 8 = 5$ (b) $326 \div 2 = x$
   (c) $48 \div x = 16$ (d) $x \div 5 = 17$
   (e) $a \div b = c$ (f) $(48 - 36) \div 6 = x$
10. Show that, in general, each of the following is false if a, b, and c are whole numbers.
    (a) $a \div b = b \div a$ (b) $(a \div b) \div c = a \div (b \div c)$
    (c) $a \div (b + c) = (a \div b) + (a \div c)$
11. For each of the following, name all whole numbers, a, b, and c for which the statement is true.
    (a) $a \div b = b \div a$ (b) $(a \div b)b = a$
    (c) $(ab) \div b = a$ (d) $(a \div b)b = (ab) \div b$
12. Use the definition of division to justify that for any whole numbers a and b, where $b \neq 0$, $(ab) \div b = a$.
13. Because the Jones' water meter was stuck, they were billed the same amount for water each month for 5 months. If they paid $160, what was the monthly bill?
14. If Charlie drove 200 km in 4 hours at a constant speed, at what speed was he traveling?
15. There were 17 sandwiches for 7 people on a picnic. How many whole sandwiches were there for each person if they were divided equally?
16. If it takes 1 minute per cut, how long will it take to cut a 10-ft log into 10 equal pieces?
17. For each of the following, name all the possible pairs of replacements for $\square$ and $\triangle$.
    (a) $34 = \square \cdot 8 + \triangle$ (b) $\triangle = 4 \cdot 16 + 2$ (c) $28 = \square \cdot \triangle + 3$
★18. Suppose $A \subseteq B$. If $n(A) = a$ and $n(B) = b$, then $b - a$ could be defined as $n(B - A)$. Choose two sets, A and B, and illustrate this definition.
19. Do problems 39 and 72 appearing in Appendix II.

3-6 ALGORITHMS FOR SUBTRACTION AND DIVISION

Subtraction Algorithms

As with addition, the use of multibase blocks can provide a concrete model for subtraction. The student page on page 114 taken from *Heath Mathematics*, 1979, grade 4 shows how the blocks can be used to demonstrate regrouping for subtraction.

The examples using multibase blocks lead to the conventional algorithm for subtraction.

Subtracting with regrouping

In this example, 1 ten is regrouped for 10 ones.

Step 1. Not enough ones.   **Step 2.** Regroup 1 ten for 10 ones.   **Step 3.** Subtract.

```
  5 4          ⁴ ¹⁴          ⁴ ¹⁴
- 2 9          5̷ 4̷          5̷ 4̷
             - 2 9        - 2 9
                            2 5
```

Here 1 hundred is regrouped for 10 tens.

Step 1. Subtract ones.

```
  426
- 152
    4
```

Step 2. Not enough tens. Regroup 1 hundred for 10 tens.

```
  ³ ¹²
  4̷ 2̷ 6
- 1 5 2
      4
```

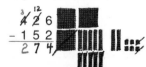

Step 3. Subtract tens.

```
  ³ ¹²
  4̷ 2̷ 6
- 1 5 2
    7 4
```

Step 4. Subtract hundreds.

```
  ³ ¹²
  4̷ 2̷ 6
- 1 5 2
  2 7 4
```

60

Example 3-17

Subtract

$$428$$
$$-153$$

Solution

$$
\begin{array}{r}
4 \cdot 10^2 + 2 \cdot 10 + 8 \ = \ \ \ \ 3 \cdot 10^2 + 12 \cdot 10 + 8 \\
-(1 \cdot 10^2 + 5 \cdot 10 + 3) = -(1 \cdot 10^2 + \ \ 5 \cdot 10 + 3) \\
\hline
2 \cdot 10^2 + \ \ 7 \cdot 10 + 5 \ = 275
\end{array}
$$

In the units place $8 - 3 = 5$. In order to subtract $5 \cdot 10$ from $2 \cdot 10$ in the tens place, $4 \cdot 10^2$ is renamed as $(3 + 1) \cdot 10^2$ or $3 \cdot 10^2 + 10 \cdot 10$. Then, $10 \cdot 10 + 2 \cdot 10 = 12 \cdot 10$. So, $4 \cdot 10^2 + 2 \cdot 10 + 8$ is renamed as $3 \cdot 10^2 + 12 \cdot 10 + 8$.

The conventional algorithm summarizes the method.

$$
\begin{array}{r}
{}^3\!\!\not{4} \ \ {}^1 2 \ \ 8 \\
- \ 1 \ \ \ 5 \ \ \ 3 \\
\hline
2 \ \ \ 7 \ \ \ 5
\end{array}
$$

The subtraction in Example 3-17 can be checked by using the definition of subtraction: $428 - 153 = 275$ if and only if $275 + 153 = 428$.

The "cashier's algorithm" for subtraction is closely related to the formal definition of subtraction; that is, $a - b = c$ if and only if $b + c = a$. An example of the cashier's algorithm follows.

Example 3-18

Noah owed $11 for his groceries. He used a $50 check to pay the bill. While handing Noah the change, the cashier said: "$11, $12, $13, $14, $15, $20, $30, $50. Thank you. Have a good day." How much change did Noah receive?

Solution

Table 3-8 shows what the cashier said and how much money Noah received each time. Since $11 plus $1 is $12, Noah must have received $1 when the cashier said $12. The same reasoning follows for $13, $14, and so on. Thus, the total amount of change that Noah received is given by

$$1 + \$1 + \$1 + \$1 + \$5 + \$10 + \$20 = \$39$$

In other words, $50 - \$11 = \$39$ because $39 + \$11 = \$50$.

TABLE 3-8

What the cashier said	$11	$12	$13	$14	$15	$20	$30	$50
Amount of money Noah received each time	0	$1	$1	$1	$1	$5	$10	$20

Division Algorithms

One algorithm for division uses repeated subtraction. This concept is illustrated in Example 3-19.

Example 3-19

The Milltown Bank's computer malfunctioned in the following way. One week, it automatically subtracted $24 from an account each time a check was presented for payment, regardless of the amount of the check. If Maria's account contained $114 on Monday and $18 on Friday, how many checks were presented for payment?

Solution

This problem can be solved by using the strategy of building a model to act as the computer did. A model of the computer's printout is as follows.

Balance on Monday	$114
Check 1 presented	−24
	90
Check 2 presented	−24
	66
Check 3 presented	−24
	42
Check 4 presented	−24
Balance Friday	$ 18

The model shows that 4 checks were presented for payment because 24 is subtracted 4 times.

A looking back activity leads to an alternate solution to Example 3-19. Since there was $114 in the account on Monday and $18 on Friday, $114 − $18 or $96 was paid out of the account. If each check presented resulted in an automatic disbursal of $24, the question becomes: What is $96 \div 24$? The solution is 4, since $4 \cdot 24 = 96$.

Division by repeated subtractions can be accomplished in a variety of ways. In the following, notice that the number of 4's subtracted varies. Which of the methods is most efficient?

(1)

$$4\overline{)28}$$

−4	1 four
24	
−4	1 four
20	
−4	1 four
16	
−4	1 four
12	
−4	1 four
8	
−4	1 four
4	
−4	1 four
0	7 fours

(2)

$$4\overline{)28}$$

−8	2 fours
20	
−4	1 four
16	
−16	4 fours
0	7 fours

(3) $4\overline{)28}$
$\quad \underline{-20}$ 5 fours
$\quad\quad 8$
$\quad \underline{-8}$ 2 fours
$\quad\quad 0$ 7 fours

(4) $4\overline{)28}$
$\quad \underline{-28}$ 7 fours
$\quad\quad 0$

Elementary students able to complete problems using method (4) are ready to attempt a problem like $4\overline{)946}$ using powers of 10 and their multiples. Two methods are shown below.

(1) $4\overline{)946}$
$\quad \underline{-400}$ 100 fours
$\quad\quad 546$
$\quad \underline{-400}$ 100 fours
$\quad\quad 146$
$\quad \underline{-40}$ 10 fours
$\quad\quad 106$
$\quad \underline{-40}$ 10 fours
$\quad\quad 66$
$\quad \underline{-40}$ 10 fours
$\quad\quad 26$
$\quad \underline{-24}$ 6 fours
$\quad\quad 2$ 236 fours

(2) $4\overline{)946}$
$\quad \underline{-800}$ 200 fours
$\quad\quad 146$
$\quad \underline{-120}$ 30 fours
$\quad\quad 26$
$\quad \underline{-24}$ 6 fours
$\quad\quad 2$ 236 fours

Observe that method (2) is more efficient than method (1). Efficiency comes with practice. The advent of the calculator has diminished the need for efficiency with long division. Thus, simply understanding the repeated subtraction algorithm may be sufficient for some students.

Recall that in defining division, we used an example that partitioned 18 cookies into three equal groups. Suppose we try to partition 376 into groups of 29; that is, divide 376 by 29. There are at least 10 groups of 29, or 290, in 376 as shown in (1). In fact, with 10 groups of 29, there are still 86 left. Next, partition 86 into groups of 29. There are two groups of 29 with 28 left over, as shown in (2). Hence, there are 10 + 2, or 12, groups of 29 in 376 with 28 left over.

(1) $\quad\quad 10$
$29\overline{)376}$
$\quad\quad 290$
$\quad\quad\quad 86$

(2) $\quad\quad\quad 2$
$\quad\quad\quad 10$
$29\overline{)376}$
$\quad\quad 290$
$\quad\quad\quad 86$
$\quad\quad\quad 58$
$\quad\quad\quad 28$

(3) $\quad\quad 12$
$29\overline{)376}$
$\quad\quad 29$
$\quad\quad 86$
$\quad\quad 58$
$\quad\quad 28$

The conventional division algorithm for whole numbers is illustrated in method (3). It represents the most efficient form of repeated subtraction.

(Also, it involves estimation techniques.) The sample from *Scott, Foresman Mathematics,* 1980, Grade 5 shows how division usually is taught today.

Two-Digit Divisors, Zeros in the Quotient

A. All 73 rooms in the Ridgeland Hotel were decorated for a total cost of $59,057. What was the average cost for each room?

Find 59,057 ÷ 73.

$$73)\overline{59057} \mathbf{57}$$
$$-584$$

How many 73s in 590?
THINK How many 7s in 59? *8*
Write 8 above the 0.

Multiply. 8 × 73 = 584

Subtract and compare.

$$\begin{array}{r} 8 \\ 73)\overline{59057} \\ -584 \end{array}$$

Bring down the 5.

How many 73s in 65? *0*
Write 0 above the 5.

$$\begin{array}{r} 80 \\ 73)\overline{59057} \\ -584 \end{array}$$

Bring down the 7.

How many 73s in 657?
THINK How many 7s in 65? *9*
Write 9 above the 7.

Multiply. 9 × 73 = 657

Subtract and compare.

There are no more digits to bring down. The remainder is 0.

The average cost for each room was $809.

Example 3-20 | Divide 32) 463.

Solution | The repeated subtraction method is shown on the left and the conventional algorithm is shown on the right.

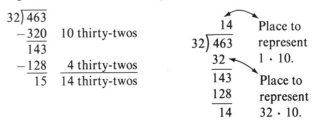

The division algorithm verifies the solution, 463 = 14 · 32 + 15.

PROBLEM SET 3-6

1. Perform each subtraction using both the conventional and the cashier's algorithms. Verify your answers by using the definition of subtraction.
   (a)   436   (b)   1001
       −79   −99
2. Perform each division using both the repeated subtraction and conventional algorithms. Verify your answers by using the division algorithm.
   (a) 8) 623   (b) 36) 298   (c) 391) 4001
3. Explain the place value meaning of the circled numbers for each of the following.

    (a)   ⑦
         ₁ ₁
        Ɫ Ɫ Ɫ 6
        −7 2 9
        ─────
         7 5 7

    (b)   77
         27) 2095
             189
            ────
            ⑳5
            18 9
            ────
             1 6

4. The Earth is approximately 149 600 000 km from the sun. If a rocket travels at the rate of 1500 km/hr, how many days will it take to reach the sun if it follows a direct path from the earth?
5. Tom's diet allows only 1500 calories per day. For breakfast, Tom had skim milk (90 calories), a waffle with no syrup (120 calories), and a banana (119 calories). For lunch, he had ½ cup of salad (185 calories) with mayonnaise (110 calories), tea (0 calories), and then he blew it with pecan pie (570 calories). Can he have dinner? Can he have a steak (250 calories), a salad with no mayonnaise, and tea?
6. A year on Saturn is 10 759 Earth-days, while a year on Mercury is only 88 Earth-days. About how many times longer is a Saturn-year than a Mercury-year?

7. If the astronauts from Apollo X traveled 720 km in 1 minute at re-entry, how far did they travel in 1 second?

8. The Wright brothers flew approximately 50 m in 10 seconds. How far did they fly in 1 second?

9. Consider the following subtraction algorithm, called "the equal additions" algorithm.

$$836 = \quad 8 \cdot 10^2 + 3 \cdot 10 + 6$$
$$-584 = -(5 \cdot 10^2 + 8 \cdot 10 + 4)$$

In order to subtract $8 \cdot 10$ from $3 \cdot 10$, add ten 10's to the minuend and $1 \cdot 10^2$ (or ten 10's) to the subtrahend. Thus,

$$8 \cdot 10^2 + 3 \cdot 10 + 6$$
$$-(5 \cdot 10^2 + 8 \cdot 10 + 4)$$

becomes

$$8 \cdot 10^2 + 13 \cdot 10 + 6$$
$$-(6 \cdot 10^2 + \quad 8 \cdot 10 + 4)$$
$$\overline{\quad 2 \cdot 10^2 + \quad 5 \cdot 10 + 2} \ = 252$$

Notice that the problem is changed, but 252 is the answer to the original problem. Will this algorithm work in general? Why or why not?

10. Do problems 31, 33, 34, 35, 40, 41, 66, 68, 69, 70, 71, 73, 75, and 76 appearing in Appendix II.

3-7 OTHER NUMBER BASES

The Babylonian numeration system was based on 60, and the Hindu–Arabic or decimal system is based on 10. There are many other numeration systems with different number bases. For example, the Mayans' numeration system used base twenty, and the digital computer uses base two.

Mathematical historians believe that one reason the majority of the world uses the base ten system, with ten digits 0 through 9, is that most people have 10 fingers. When you count with two hands and reach the last finger, you begin using two-digit numbers. Suppose you have only one hand. The digits available for counting are 0, 1, 2, 3, 4. Thus, in the "one-hand system," you count 1, 2, 3, 4, 10, where 10 represents 1 hand and no fingers. One hand is 5 fingers, so the one-hand system is a base five system. (Recall that in base ten, 10 represents 1 ten and no units.)

In the one-hand, or base five system, counting is in groups of five, rather than ten. In Figure 3-19, x's are grouped into tens in (*a*) and fives, or hands, in (*b*). In (*a*), the grouping shows 1 set of ten *x*'s and 9 other *x*'s. This is written as 19_{ten}, or just 19.

FIGURE 3-19

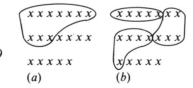

(*a*) (*b*)

In (*b*), the grouping shows 3 groups of five *x*'s (hands) and 4 other *x*'s. This is written as 34_{five}. Thus, $19_{ten} = 34_{five}$. We write the small "five" below the numeral as a reminder that the number is written in base five. Counting in base five proceeds as shown in Figure 3-20.

FIGURE 3-20

Base Five Symbol	Base Five Grouping	One-Hand System
0_{five}		0 fingers
1_{five}	x	1 fingers
2_{five}	xx	2 fingers
3_{five}	xxx	3 fingers
4_{five}	xxxx	4 fingers
10_{five}	(xxxxx)	1 hand and 0 fingers
11_{five}	(xxxxx) x	1 hand and 1 fingers
12_{five}	(xxxxx) xx	1 hand and 2 fingers
13_{five}	(xxxxx) xxx	1 hand and 3 fingers
14_{five}	(xxxxx) xxxx	1 hand and 4 fingers
20_{five}	(xxxxx) (xxxxx)	2 hands
21_{five}	(xxxxx) (xxxxx) x	2 hands and 1 finger

What number follows 44_{five}? There are no more two-digit numbers in the system after 44_{five}. The number represents the maximum of 4 hands and 4 fingers. In base ten the same situation occurs at 99. We use 100 to represent ten tens or "one hundred." In the one-hand system, we need a symbol to represent 1 group of five hands, or five fives. To continue the analogy with base ten, we use 100_{five} to represent 1 group of five hands (or five fives), no groups of five, and no units. To distinguish from "one hundred" in base ten, the name for 100_{five} is "one-zero-zero base five." The number 100_{ten} means $(1 \cdot 10^2 + 0 \cdot 10^1 + 0)_{ten}$, whereas the number 100_{five} means $(1 \cdot 10^2 + 0 \cdot 10^1 + 0)_{five}$.

The value of a number is determined by its base. The base ten value of 100_{five} could be computed as follows.

$$100_{five} = (1 \cdot 10^2 + 0 \cdot 10^1 + 0)_{five} = (1 \cdot 5^2 + 0 \cdot 5^1 + 0)_{ten} = 25_{ten}$$

This illustration shows a method of converting a number in any base to base ten; namely, use powers of the base value and write the number as an expanded base ten number.

Example 3-21

Convert each of the following to base ten: (a) 34412_{five}, (b) 1002_{five}.

Solution

(a) $\begin{aligned} 34412_{five} &= (3 \cdot 5^4 + 4 \cdot 5^3 + 4 \cdot 5^2 + 1 \cdot 5 + 2)_{ten} \\ &= (3 \cdot 625 + 4 \cdot 125 + 4 \cdot 25 + 5 + 2)_{ten} \\ &= (1875 + 500 + 100 + 5 + 2)_{ten} \\ &= 2482_{ten} \end{aligned}$

(b) $\begin{aligned} 1002_{five} &= (1 \cdot 5^3 + 0 \cdot 5^2 + 0 \cdot 5 + 2)_{ten} \\ &= (1 \cdot 125 + 0 + 0 + 2)_{ten} \\ &= (125 + 2)_{ten} \\ &= 127_{ten} \end{aligned}$

Example 3-21 also suggests a method for changing a base ten number to a base five number. Notice that the conversion involves powers of five. To convert 824_{ten} to base five, divide by the powers of five:—5^1 or 5, 5^2 or 25, 5^3 or 125, 5^4 or 625, 5^5 or 3125, and so on. For example, the greatest power of 5 contained in 824 is 5^4 or 625. There is $1 \cdot 5^4$ with 199 left over. Thus,

$$824 = 1 \cdot 5^4 + 199$$

The greatest power of 5 contained in 199 is 5^3. There is $1 \cdot 5^3$ with 74 left over in 199. Thus,

$$824 = 1 \cdot 5^4 + 1 \cdot 5^3 + 74$$

The greatest power of 5 contained in 74 is 5^2. There are $2 \cdot 5^2$ with 24 left over in 74.

$$824 = 1 \cdot 5^4 + 1 \cdot 5^3 + 2 \cdot 5^2 + 24$$

Finally, the greatest power of 5 in 24 is 5^1. There are $4 \cdot 5^1$ with 4 left in 24, and there are 4 ones in 4. Thus,

$$824 = 1 \cdot 5^4 + 1 \cdot 5^3 + 2 \cdot 5^2 + 4 \cdot 5 + 4 = 11244_{five}$$

Thus changing from base ten to base five can be accomplished by dividing by successive powers of five. A shorthand method for illustrating this conversion follows.

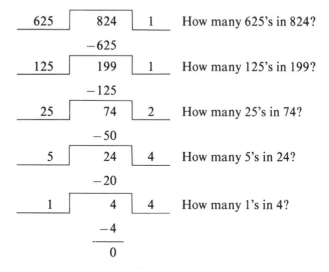

Again, $824 = 11244_{\text{five}}$.

Historians tell of early tribes that used base two. Some Australian tribes still count as follows: one, two, two and one, two twos, two twos and one, and so on. Perhaps early tribes used base two because it is the simplest number base since there are only two digits, 0 and 1. When counting in base two, multidigit numbers are reached rapidly as shown in Figure 3-21.

Base Two	Base Two Grouping	Base Ten Name
1_{two}	x	1
10_{two}	⊗	2
11_{two}	⊗ x	3
100_{two}	⊗ ⊗	4
101_{two}	⊗ ⊗ x	5
110_{two}	⊗ ⊗ ⊗	6
111_{two}	⊗ ⊗ ⊗ x	7
1000_{two}	⊗ ⊗ ⊗ ⊗	8

FIGURE 3-21

The conversions from base two to base ten, and vice versa, may be accomplished in a manner similar to base five conversions.

Example 3-22 | Convert 10111_{two} to base ten.

Solution | $$10111_{two} = (1 \cdot 2^4 + 0 \cdot 2^3 + 1 \cdot 2^2 + 1 \cdot 2^1 + 1)_{ten}$$
$$= (16 + 0 + 4 + 2 + 1)_{ten}$$
$$= 23_{ten}$$

Example 3-23 | Convert 27_{ten} to base two.

Solution |

16	27	1	How many 16's in 27?
	-16		
8	11	1	How many 8's in 11?
	-8		
4	3	0	How many 4's in 3?
	-0		
2	3	1	How many 2's in 3?
	-2		
1	1	1	How many 1's in 1?
	-1		
	0		

Thus, 27_{ten} is equivalent to 11011_{two}.

Another commonly used number base system is base twelve, known popularly as the "dozens" system. Eggs are bought by the dozens, and pencils are bought by the gross (a dozen dozens). In base twelve, there are twelve digits, just as there are ten digits in base ten, five digits in base five, and two digits in base two. In base twelve, new symbols are needed to represent the following groups of x's.

$$\overbrace{x\,x\,x\,x\,x\,x\,x\,x\,x\,x}^{10\ x\text{'s}} \quad \text{and} \quad \overbrace{x\,x\,x\,x\,x\,x\,x\,x\,x\,x\,x}^{11\ x\text{'s}}$$

The new symbols chosen are T and E, respectively, so that the base twelve digits are 0, 1, 2, 3, 4, 5, 6, 7, 8, 9, T, E. Thus, in base twelve you count "1, 2, 3, 4, 5, 6, 7, 8, 9, T, E, 10, 11, 12, ..., 17, 18, 19, $1T$, $1E$, 20, 21, 22, ..., 28, 29, $2T$, $2E$, 30, ..." Notice that T_{twelve} is another way of writing 10_{ten} and E_{twelve} is another way of writing 11_{ten}. Also $10_{twelve} = 12_{ten}$.

Example 3-24 | Convert $E2T_{\text{twelve}}$ to base ten.

Solution | $\begin{aligned} E2T_{\text{twelve}} &= (11 \cdot 12^2 + 2 \cdot 12^1 + 10)_{\text{ten}} \\ &= (11 \cdot 144 + 24 + 10)_{\text{ten}} \\ &= (1584 + 24 + 10)_{\text{ten}} \\ &= 1618_{\text{ten}} \end{aligned}$

Example 3-25 | Convert 1277_{ten} to base twelve.

Solution |

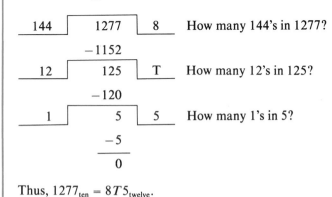

Thus, $1277_{\text{ten}} = 8T5_{\text{twelve}}$.

PROBLEM SET 3-7

1. Write the first fifteen counting numbers for each of the following bases.
    (a) base two   (b) base three   (c) base four   (d) base eight
2. Group the x's below to write the number of x's in bases five, three, and eight.

    (a) $x\,x\,x\,x$ (b) $x\,x\,x\,x\,x$
      $x\,x\,x\,x$ $x\,x\,x\,x\,x$
      $x\,x\,x$ $x\,x\,x\,x$

3. How many different digits are needed for base twenty?
4. Find the numbers preceding and succeeding each of the following.
    (a) $EE0_{\text{twelve}}$ (b) 100000_{two} (c) 555_{six}
    (d) 100_{seven} (e) 1000_{five}
5. Convert each of the following base ten numbers to numbers in the indicated bases.
    (a) 432 to base five   (b) 1963 to base twelve
    (c) 404 to base four   (d) 37 to base two
    (e) $3 \cdot 10^4 + 2 \cdot 10^2 + 4$ to base five   (f) $4 \cdot 10^4 + 3 \cdot 10^2$ to base twelve
    (g) $9 \cdot 12^5 + 11 \cdot 12$ to base twelve
6. Write each of the following numbers in base ten.
    (a) 432_{five} (b) 101101_{two} (c) $92E_{\text{twelve}}$ (d) TOE_{twelve}
    (e) 111_{twelve} (f) 346_{seven} (g) 551_{six}

7. For each of the following, find b.
    (a) $b2_{seven} = 44_{ten}$ (b) $5b2_{twelve} = 734_{ten}$ (c) $23_{ten} = 25_b$
8. A bookstore ordered 11 gross, 6 dozen, 6 pencils. Express the number of pencils in base ten.
9. George was cooking an elaborate meal for Thanksgiving. He could only cook one thing at a time in his microwave oven. His turkey takes 75 minutes; the pumpkin pie takes 18 minutes; rolls take 45 seconds; and a cup of coffee takes 30 seconds to heat. How much time did he need to cook the meal?
10. What are the advantages and disadvantages of bases two and twelve over base ten?
11. An inspector of weights and measures has a special set of weights used to check the accuracy of scales. Various weights are placed on a scale to check accuracy of any amount from 1 ounce through 15 ounces. What is the least number of weights that the inspector needs? What weights are needed to check the accuracy of scales from 1 ounce through 15 ounces? From 1 through 31 ounces?
12. Anna's bank contains only pennies, nickels, and quarters. What is the fewest number of coins she could trade for 117 pennies? If she trades 2 quarters, 4 nickels, and 3 pennies for pennies, how many pennies will she have?

16 8 4 2 1

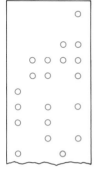

LABORATORY ACTIVITY

1. Messages can be coded on paper tape using base two. A hole in the tape represents 1, while a space represents 0. The value of each hole depends upon its position, from left to right, 16, 8, 4, 2, 1 (all powers of 2). Using base two, letters of the alphabet may be coded according to their position in the alphabet. For example, G is the seventh letter. Since $7 = 1 \cdot 4 + 1 \cdot 2 + 1$, the holes appear as they do at the left.
    (a) Decode the message on the left.
    (b) Write your name on a tape using base two.
2. The following number game uses base two arithmetic.

Card A		Card B		Card C		Card D		Card E	
16	24	8	24	4	20	2	18	1	17
17	25	9	25	5	21	3	19	3	19
18	26	10	26	6	22	6	22	5	21
19	27	11	27	7	23	7	23	7	23
20	28	12	28	12	28	10	26	9	25
21	29	13	29	13	29	11	27	11	27
22	30	14	30	14	30	14	30	13	29
23	31	15	31	15	31	15	31	15	31

Suppose a person's age appears on cards A, C, and D. Then, the person is 22. Can you discover how this works and why?

3-8 COMPUTATIONS IN DIFFERENT BASES

One reason for studying computations in different number bases is to enhance your understanding of base ten computations. Another reason is to put you, as a prospective teacher, in somewhat the same role as a child studying arithmetic. We hope that by studying bases other than ten, you will better understand the problems that the children encounter learning place value and computational skills.

Recall that before studying algorithms in base ten, you had to assume a knowledge of the basic addition and multiplication facts. The same is true for other bases.

Addition in Different Bases

A table of basic addition facts for base five can be developed using the number line or other models similar to the whole number models. We urge you to construct your own table without copying the one in Table 3-9. We use the facts from Table 3-9 in Example 3-26 to show that the algorithms for base five are comparable to those in base ten.

TABLE 3-9

+	0	1	2	3	4
0	0	1	2	3	4
1	1	2	3	4	10
2	2	3	4	10	11
3	3	4	10	11	12
4	4	10	11	12	13

Addition Table (Base Five)

Example 3-26

Add:

(a) 42_{five}
     $+2_{five}$

(b) 234_{five}
     $+41_{five}$

Solution

Each problem is solved in two ways, the second using the more conventional algorithm.

(a) $42_{five} = (4 \cdot 10 + 2)_{five}$
     $+2_{five} = + 2)_{five}$
     $ (4 \cdot 10 + 4)_{five} = 44_{five}$

     42_{five}
     $+2_{five}$
     44_{five}

(b) 234_{five} = $(2 \cdot 10^2 + 3 \cdot 10 + 4)_{\text{five}}$
     $+41_{\text{five}}$ $+(4 \cdot 10 + 1)_{\text{five}}$
     _____
     $(2 \cdot 10^2 + \cancel{12 \cdot 10} + 10)_{\text{five}}$
     $(1 \cdot 10^2 \qquad\quad + 2 \cdot 10)_{\text{five}}$ $\Big\}$ Regroup $12 \cdot 10$
     _____
     $3 \cdot 10^2 \qquad\quad + 3 \cdot 10 \quad = 330_{\text{five}}$

$\overset{1\,1}{234}_{\text{five}}$
$+41_{\text{five}}$
_____
330_{five}

Example 3-27   Add:

(a) 101_{two} (b) $E2T_{\text{twelve}}$
     111_{two} 389_{twelve}
     110_{two} $2T0_{\text{twelve}}$
     _____   _____

Solution   (a) $\overset{1\,1}{101}_{\text{two}}$ (b) $\overset{1\,1}{E2T}_{\text{twelve}}$
                     111_{two} 389_{twelve}
                     110_{two} $2T0_{\text{twelve}}$
                     _____   _____
                     10010_{two} 1597_{twelve}

Subtraction in Different Bases

The subtraction facts for a particular base can be derived from the addition facts table by using the definition of subtraction. For example, to find $(12 - 4)_{\text{five}}$, recall that $(12 - 4)_{\text{five}} = c_{\text{five}}$ if and only if $(c + 4)_{\text{five}} = 12_{\text{five}}$. From Table 3-9, $c = 3_{\text{five}}$. More involved subtraction problems can be performed using the same ideas developed for base ten.

Example 3-28   Subtract:

(a) 43_{five} (b) 32_{five} (c) 432_{five}
      -12_{five} -14_{five} -344_{five}
      _____   _____   _____

Solution   Each problem is solved in two ways, the second being the more conventional algorithm.

(a) 43_{five} = $(4 \cdot 10 + 3)_{\text{five}}$
      -12_{five} = $-(1 \cdot 10 + 2)_{\text{five}}$
      _____
                       $(3 \cdot 10 + 1)_{\text{five}} = 31_{\text{five}}$

43_{five}
-12_{five}
_____
31_{five}

(b) $32_{\text{five}} = \quad (3 \cdot 10 + 2)_{\text{five}} = \quad (2 \cdot 10 + 12)_{\text{five}}$ 32_{five}
        $-14_{\text{five}} = -(1 \cdot 10 + 4)_{\text{five}} = -(1 \cdot 10 + 4)_{\text{five}}$ -14_{five}
        $\phantom{32_{\text{five}} = (3 \cdot 10 + 2)_{\text{five}} = }\quad (1 \cdot 10 + 3)_{\text{five}} = 13_{\text{five}}$ 13_{five}

(c) $432_{\text{five}} = \quad (4 \cdot 10^2 + 3 \cdot 10 + 2)_{\text{five}}$
        $-344_{\text{five}} = -(3 \cdot 10^2 + 4 \cdot 10 + 4)_{\text{five}}$

        $\phantom{432_{\text{five}}} = \quad (3 \cdot 10^2 + 12 \cdot 10 + 12)_{\text{five}}$ 432_{five}
        $\phantom{432_{\text{five}}} = -(3 \cdot 10^2 + 4 \cdot 10 + 4)_{\text{five}}$ -344_{five}
        $\phantom{432_{\text{five}} = (3 \cdot 10^2 + 12)}\quad (3 \cdot 10 + 3)_{\text{five}} = 33_{\text{five}}$ 33_{five}

Subtraction examples using bases two and twelve follow.

Example 3-29 | Subtract:
(a) 1010_{two} (b) $2E3_{\text{twelve}}$
        -111_{two} $-1T9_{\text{twelve}}$

Solution | (a) 1010_{two} (b) $2E3_{\text{twelve}}$
        -111_{two} $-1T9_{\text{twelve}}$
        $\overline{11_{\text{two}}}$ $\overline{106_{\text{twelve}}}$

Multiplication in Different Bases

As with addition and subtraction, the basic facts of multiplication must be learned before algorithms can be used. The multiplication table for base five is given in Table 3-10. It can be derived by using repeated addition. (A number line may be helpful, too.)

TABLE 3-10

×	0	1	2	3	4
0	0	0	0	0	0
1	0	1	2	3	4
2	0	2	4	11	13
3	0	3	11	14	22
4	0	4	13	22	31

Multiplication Table (Base Five)

The multiplications in the following examples involve the distributive property. The algorithms here are analogous to those used in base ten.

Example 3-30

Multiply:

$$43_{\text{five}}$$
$$\times 23_{\text{five}}$$

Solution

The partial products are shown on the left and the shorthand version is shown on the right.

$$
\begin{array}{r}
43_{\text{five}} \\
\times 23_{\text{five}} \\
\hline
14 \\
220 \\
110 \\
1300 \\
\hline
2144_{\text{five}}
\end{array}
\quad
\begin{array}{l}
(3 \times 3)_{\text{five}} \\
(3 \times 40)_{\text{five}} \\
(20 \times 3)_{\text{five}} \\
(20 \times 40)_{\text{five}}
\end{array}
\qquad
\begin{array}{r}
43_{\text{five}} \\
\times 23_{\text{five}} \\
\hline
234 \\
141 \\
\hline
2144_{\text{five}}
\end{array}
\quad
\begin{array}{l}
(14 + 220)_{\text{five}} \\
(110 + 1300)_{\text{five}}
\end{array}
$$

Example 3-31

Multiply:

(a) 101_{two} (b) $E29_{\text{twelve}}$
         $\times 11_{\text{two}}$ $\times T3_{\text{twelve}}$

Solution

(a) 101_{two} (b) $E29_{\text{twelve}}$
         $\times 11_{\text{two}}$ $\times T3_{\text{twelve}}$

$$
\begin{array}{r}
101 \\
101 \\
\hline
1111_{\text{two}}
\end{array}
\qquad
\begin{array}{r}
2983 \\
9436 \\
\hline
97123_{\text{twelve}}
\end{array}
$$

Division in Different Bases

Division in different bases can be performed using the multiplication facts and the definition of division. For example, $(22 \div 3)_{\text{five}} = c$ if and only if $(c \cdot 3 = 22)_{\text{five}}$. From Table 3-10, we see that $c = 4_{\text{five}}$. As with base ten, computing multidigit divisions efficiently in different bases requires practice.

Example 3-32

Divide:

$$43_{\text{five}} \overline{)\,3241_{\text{five}}}$$

The repeated subtraction method is used on the left, and the conventional algorithm is used on the right.

Solution

$$43_{five} \overline{)\, 3241_{five}}$$

$$
\begin{array}{r}
43_{five} \overline{)\, 3241_{five}} \\
-430 \quad (10 \cdot 43)_{five} \\
\overline{2311} \\
-430 \quad (10 \cdot 43)_{five} \\
\overline{1331} \\
-430 \quad (10 \cdot 43)_{five} \\
\overline{401} \\
-141 \quad (2 \cdot 43)_{five} \\
\overline{210} \\
141 \quad (2 \cdot 43)_{five} \\
\overline{14\ R} \quad (34 \cdot 43)_{five}
\end{array}
$$

$$
\begin{array}{r}
34_{five} \\
43_{five} \overline{)\, 3241_{five}} \\
-234 \\
\overline{401} \\
-332 \\
\overline{14\ R}
\end{array}
$$

Thus, $3241_{five} \div 43_{five} = 34_{five}$ with remainder 14_{five}.

Base two division is much simpler than base five division, because the partial quotients are either 1 or 0.

Example 3-33

Divide:

$$101_{two} \overline{)\, 110110_{two}}$$

Solution

$$
\begin{array}{r}
1010_{two} \\
101_{two} \overline{)\, 110110_{two}} \\
-101 \\
\overline{111} \\
-101 \\
\overline{100\ R}
\end{array}
$$

PROBLEM SET 3-8

1. Perform each of the following operations using the bases shown:
   (a) $(43_{five}) \cdot (23_{five})$ (b) $(43_{five}) + (23_{five})$
   (c) $(432_{five}) \div (23_{five})$ (d) $(42_{five}) - (23_{five})$
   (e) $(110_{two}) - (11_{two})$ (f) $(E29_{twelve}) + (ET9_{twelve})$
2. Construct addition and multiplication tables for base eight.
3. Perform each of the following operations.

   (a)   3 hours 36 minutes 58 seconds   (b)   5 hours 36 minutes 38 seconds
          + 5 hours 56 minutes 27 seconds   − 3 hours 56 minutes 58 seconds

4. Perform each of the following operations (2 cups = 1 pint, 2 pints = 1 quart).

   (a)   1 quart 1 pint 1 cup   (b)   1 quart 1 cup
          +   1 pint 1 cup   − 1 pint 1 cup

5. For what possible bases are each of the following computations correct?

(a) $\begin{array}{r} 213 \\ +308 \\ \hline 522 \end{array}$ (b) $\begin{array}{r} 322 \\ -233 \\ \hline 23 \end{array}$ (c) $\begin{array}{r} 213 \\ \times 32 \\ \hline 430 \\ 1043 \\ \hline 11300 \end{array}$ (d) $\begin{array}{r} 101 \\ 11\overline{)1111} \\ -11 \\ \hline 11 \\ -11 \\ \hline 0\ R \end{array}$

SOLUTION TO THE PRELIMINARY PROBLEM

Understanding the Problem

A rural elementary school provided 1 cup of milk for each student each day. Milk was cheaper when bought in large quantities, but the exact amount had to be bought each day. Milk could be bought in gallons, half-gallons, quarts, pints, and cups. If 1 gallon, 1 quart, and 1 pint were bought, how many students were present on Tuesday? If there were 31 students present on Wednesday, how much milk was purchased?

Devising a Plan

There is one other bit of information required before a solution is found. Each child is to have 1 cup of milk per day, but the quantities to be bought are not only cups but also pints, quarts, half-gallons, and gallons. We need the following information:

1 pint = 2 cups
1 quart = 2 pints = 2 · (2 cups) = 4 cups
1 half-gallon = 2 quarts = 2 · (4 cups) = 8 cups
1 gallon = 2 half-gallons = 2 · (8 cups) = 16 cups

A table is helpful in solving the first problem. The fact that 1 gallon, 1 quart, and 1 pint was bought is recorded in Table 3-11 along with the equivalent number of cups.

TABLE 3-11

Amount Bought	1 gallon	0 half-gallons	1 quart	1 pint	0 cups
No. of Cups in Quantity	1 · (16 cups)	0 · (8 cups)	1 · (4 cups)	1 · 2 (cups)	0 · (1 cup)

Carrying Out the Plan

The total number of cups bought on Tuesday is $16 + 0 + 4 + 2 + 0 = 22$. Since each student receives 1 cup, there were 22 students present.

To determine what combinations of containers of milk must be bought for 31 students, we use the number of cups in each quantity. Thirty-one students require 31 cups of milk. Since 1 gallon = 16 cups, then 31 cups = 1 gallon + 15 cups. Since 1 half-gallon = 8 cups, then 31 cups = 1 gallon + 1 half-gallon + 7 cups. Since 1 quart equals 4 cups, 31 cups = 1 gallon + 1 half-gallon + 1 quart + 3 cups. Since 1 pint equals 2 cups, 31 cups = 1 gallon + 1 half-gallon + 1 quart + 1 pint + 1 cup. Therefore, 31 cups is equivalent to 1 gallon, 1 half-gallon, 1 quart, 1 pint, and 1 cup.

Looking Back

Questions like those in this problem can be modeled in the base two number system. To understand the problem, we looked back at powers of 2 to determine the number of cups in each of the quantities that could be purchased. In the base two setting, the first question of converting 1 gallon, 0 half-gallons, 1 quart, 1 pint, and 0 cups to cups becomes a question of converting 10110_{two} to base ten. The second question becomes one of converting 31_{ten} to base two.

QUESTIONS FROM THE CLASSROOM

1. A student asks, "Does $2 \cdot (3 \cdot 4)$ equal $(2 \cdot 3) \cdot (2 \cdot 4)$?" Is there a distributive property of multiplication over multiplication?
2. Since $39 + 41 = 40 + 40$, is it true that $39 \cdot 41 = 40 \cdot 40$?
3. The division algorithm, $a = bq + r$, holds for $a > b$. Is this true when $a < b$?
4. A student asks if 5 times 4 is the same as 5 multiplied by 4. How do you respond?
5. Can we define $0 \div 0$ as 1? Why or why not?
6. A student divides as follows:

$$
\begin{array}{r}
15 \\
6{\overline{\smash{\big)}\,36}} \\
\underline{6} \\
30 \\
\underline{30}
\end{array}
$$

How do you help?
7. When using Roman numerals, a student asks whether or not it is correct to write $\overline{\text{II}}$, as well as MI, for 1001. How do you respond?

8.   A student says that $(x + 7) \div 7 = x + 1$. What is that student doing wrong?
9.   A student says $x \div x$ always is 1. Is the student correct?
10. What is the difference in the expressions $(2^3)^2$ and $2^{(3^2)}$?
11. A student asks if division on the set of whole numbers is distributive over subtraction. How do you respond?
12. A student says that 0 is the identity for subtraction. How do you respond?
13. A student asks if zero is the same as nothing. What is your answer?

CHAPTER OUTLINE

I. Numeration systems
   A.   Studying numeration systems, including those with bases other than ten, provides insight into the Hindu-Arabic system (base ten) of numbers.
   B.   Properties of numeration systems give basic structure to the systems.
     1.   Additive property
     2.   Place value property
     3.   Subtractive property
     4.   Multiplicative property

II. Exponents
   A.   For any whole number a and any natural number n,

$$a^n = \underbrace{a \cdot a \cdot a \cdot \ldots \cdot a,}_{n \text{ terms}}$$

     where a is the **base,** and n is the **exponent.**
   B.   For any natural number a with whole numbers m and n, $a^m \cdot a^n = a^{m+n}$.
   C.   For any number $a \in W, a \neq 0, a^0 = 1$.

III. Whole numbers
   A.   The set of whole numbers W is $\{0, 1, 2, 3, \ldots\}$.
   B.   The basic operations for whole numbers are addition, subtraction, multiplication, and division.
     1.   Addition: If $n(A) = a$ and $n(B) = b$, where $A \cap B = \varnothing$, then $a + b = n(A \cup B)$. The numbers a and b are **addends,** and $a + b$ is the **sum.**

     2.   Subtraction: If a and b are any whole numbers, then $a - b$ is the unique whole number c such that $b + c = a$. The number a is the **minuend;** b is the **subtrahend;** and c is the **difference.**
     3.   Multiplication: If a and b are any whole numbers, then $a \cdot b =$

$$\underbrace{b + b + b + \cdots + b}_{a \text{ terms}}$$

     a is the multiplier, b is the multiplicand, and $a \cdot b$ the product.
     4.   Multiplication: If A and B are sets such that $n(A) = a$ and $n(B) = b$, then $a \cdot b = n(A \times B)$.
     5.   Division: If a and b are any whole numbers with $b \neq 0$, $a \div b$ is the unique whole number c such that $b \cdot c = a$. The number a is the **dividend;** b is the **divisor;** and c is the **quotient.**
     6.   Division Algorithm: Given any whole numbers a and b with $b \neq 0$, there exist unique whole numbers q and r such that $a = b \cdot q + r$ with $0 \leq r < b$.
   C.   Properties of addition and multiplications of whole numbers
     1.   Closure: If $a, b \in W$, then $a + b \in W$ and $a \cdot b \in W$.
     2.   Commutative: If $a, b \in W$, then $a + b = b + a$ and $a \cdot b = b \cdot a$.

3. Associative: If $a, b, c \in W$, then $(a + b) + c = a + (b + c)$ and $a \cdot (b \cdot c) = (a \cdot b) \cdot c$.
4. Identity: 0 is the unique identity element for addition of whole numbers; 1 is the unique identity element for multiplication.
5. Distributive property of multiplication over addition. If $a, b, c \in W$, then $a \cdot (b + c) = a \cdot b + a \cdot c$.

D. Summary of properties for whole numbers

	Addition	Subtraction	Multiplication	Division
Closure	Yes	No	Yes	No
Associative	Yes	No	Yes	No
Commutative	Yes	No	Yes	No
Identity	Yes	No	Yes	No

E. Relations on whole numbers
1. $a < b$ if and only if there is a natural number c such that $a + c = b$.
2. $a > b$ if and only if there is a natural number c such that $a = b + c$.

CHAPTER TEST

1. Convert each of the following to base ten.
   (a) $\overline{\text{CDXLIV}}$ (b) 432_{five} (c) ETO_{twelve} (d) 1011_{two} (e) 4136_{seven}
2. Convert each of the following base ten numbers to numbers in the indicated system.
   (a) 999 to Roman (b) 346_{ten} to base five (c) 1728_{ten} to base twelve
   (d) 27_{ten} to base two (e) 928_{ten} to base nine
3. Simplify each of the following, if possible. Write your answers in exponential form, a^b.
   (a) $3^4 \cdot 3^7 \cdot 3^6$ (b) $2^{10} \cdot 2^{11}$ (c) $3^4 + 2 \cdot 3^4$
4. For each of the following, identify the properties of the operation(s) for whole numbers illustrated.
   (a) $3 \cdot (a + b) = 3 \cdot a + 3 \cdot b$
   (b) $2 + a = a + 2$
   (c) $16 \cdot 1 = 1 \cdot 16 = 16$
   (d) $6 \cdot (12 + 3) = 6 \cdot 12 + 6 \cdot 3$
   (e) $3 \cdot (a \cdot 2) = 3 \cdot (2 \cdot a)$
   (f) $3 \cdot (2 \cdot a) = (3 \cdot 2) \cdot a$
5. Using the definitions of less than or greater than, prove that each of the following inequalities is true.
   (a) $3 < 13$ (b) $12 > 9$
6. Explain why the product of $1000 \cdot 483$, namely 483 000, has 0 for the hundreds, tens, and units digits.
7. Use both the scratch and traditional algorithms to perform each of the following.

   (a) $\begin{array}{r} 316 \\ 712 \\ +91 \\ \hline \end{array}$ (b) $\begin{array}{r} 316_{\text{twelve}} \\ 712_{\text{twelve}} \\ +913_{\text{twelve}} \\ \hline \end{array}$

8. Use both the traditional and lattice multiplication algorithms to perform each of the following:

   (a) $\begin{array}{r} 613 \\ \times 98 \\ \hline \end{array}$ (b) $\begin{array}{r} 216_{\text{eight}} \\ \times 54_{\text{eight}} \\ \hline \end{array}$

9. Use both the repeated subtraction and the conventional algorithms to perform each of the following.
   (a) $912\overline{)4803}$ (b) $11\overline{)1011}$

10. Use the division algorithm to check your answers in Problem 9.

11. For each of the following base ten numbers, tell the place value for each of the circled digits.
    (a) 4③2   (b) ③432   (c) 19③24

12. For each of the following, find all possible whole number replacements that make the following true statements.
    (a) $4 \cdot \square - 36 < 27$ (b) $398 = \square \cdot 37 + 28$
    (c) $\square \cdot (3 + 4) = \square \cdot 3 + \square \cdot 4$ (d) $42 - \square \geq 16$

13. Use the number line to perform each of the following operations.
    (a) $27 - 15$ (b) $17 + 2$

14. Use the distributive property to rename each of the following.
    (a) $3a + 7a + 5a$ (b) $3x^2 + 7x^2 - 5x^2$
    (c) $x(a + b + y)$ (d) $(x + 5)3 + (x + 5)y$

15. For each of the following, decide which operations apply and then solve the problems.
    (a) Mary had 5 apples, 14 oranges, and 6 raisins. How many fruits did she have?
    (b) Carlos had 32 apricots and 4 friends. If he wished to give each friend an equal number of apricots, how many did each receive?
    (c) Joe had 6 books, each with 12 chapters. How many chapters were there in all?
    (d) Jerry paid $24 for a shirt with a $50 bill. How much change did he receive?

SELECTED BIBLIOGRAPHY

Anderson, A. L. "Why the Continuing Resistance to the Use of Counting Sticks?" *The Arithmetic Teacher*, **25** (March 1978): 18.

Arnsdorf, E. E. "A Game for Reviewing Basic Facts of Arithmetic." *The Arithmetic Teacher*, **19** (November 1972): 589–590.

Ballew, D. "Numeration Systems with Unusual Bases." *The Mathematics Teacher*, **67** (May 1974): 413–414.

Bachrach, B. "Using Money to Clarify the Decomposition Subtraction Algorithm." *The Arithmetic Teacher*, **33** (April 1976): 244–246.

Balin, F. "Finger Multiplication." *Arithmetic Teacher*, **26** (March 1979): 34–37.

Bergamini, D. *Mathematics* (Life Science Library Series). New York: Time, Inc., 1967. (Time Life Books, Time and Life Bldg., Rockefeller Center, New York, NY 10020.)

Bolduc, E. J., Jr. "Genaille Division Sticks." *Arithmetic Teacher*, **28** (January 1979): 12–13.

Boykin, W. E. "The Russian–Peasant Algorithm: Rediscovery and Extension." *The Arithmetic Teacher*, **20** (January 1973): 29–32.

Bradford, J. W. "Methods and Materials for Learning Subtraction." *The Arithmetic Teacher*, **25** (February 1978): 19–21.

Broadbent, F. W. " 'Contig': A Game to Practice and Sharpen Skills and Facts in the Four Fundamental Operations." *The Arithmetic Teacher*, **19** (May 1972): 388–390.

Cacha, F. B. "Understanding Multiplication and Division of Multidigit Numbers." *The Arithmetic Teacher*, **19** (May 1972): 349–354.

Cleminson, R. A. "Developing the Subtraction Algorithm." *The Arithmetic Teacher*, **20** (December 1973): 634–638.

Davidson, P., G. Galton and A. Fair. *Chip Trading Activities*, Fort Collins, Colo.: Scott Resources, Inc., 1972. (Scott Resources, Inc., P.O. Box 2121, Fort Collins, CO 80522.)

Davidson, P., G. Galton and A. Fair. *Student Activity Cards for Cuisenaire Rods*. New Rochelle, N.Y.: Cuisenaire Company of America, Inc., 1971. (Cuisenaire Company of America, Inc., 12 Church St., New Rochelle, NY 10805.)

Ellison, A. "The Binary Adders: A Flow Chart for the Addition of Binary Numbers." *The Mathematics Teacher*, **66** (February 1973): 131–134.

Encyclopaedia Britannica Publications, Ltd. *Mathex*. Montreal, Canada, 1970. (Encylopaedia Britannica Publications, Ltd., 2 Bloor St. W., Suite 1100, Toronto, Ontario, Canada M4W 3J1).

Fishback, S. "Times Without Tears." *The Arithmetic Teacher,* 21 (March 1974): 200–201.

Gladstone, D., and J. Gladstone. *Mathematics Involvement Program.* Chicago: Science Research Associates, 1971. (Science Research Associates, 259 E. Erie St., Chicago, IL 60611.)

Granito, D. "Number Patterns and the Addition Operation." *The Arithmetic Teacher,* 23 (October 1976): 432–434.

Hall, D. E., and C. T. Hall. "The Odometer in the Addition Algorithm." *The Arithmetic Teacher,* 24 (January 1977): 18–21.

Johnson, P. B. "Finding the Missing Addend, or Checkbook Subtraction." *The Arithmetic Teacher,* 19 (November 1972): 540–542.

Jones, P. "Tangible Arithmetic, I—Napier's and Genaille's Rods." *The Mathematics Teacher,* 48 (November 1954): 482–487.

Keller, R. W. "A Discovery Approach with Ancient Numeration Systems." *The Arithmetic Teacher,* 19 (November 1972): 543–544.

King, I. "Giving Meaning to the Addition Algorithm." *The Arithmetic Teacher,* 19 (May 1972): 345–348.

Lee, J. W. "Changing Bases by Direct Computation." *The Mathematics Teacher,* 65 (December 1972): 752–753.

Leutzinger, L. P., and G. Nelson. "Let's Do It: Using Addition Facts to Learn Subtraction Facts." *Arithmetic Teacher,* 27 (December 1979): 8–13.

Logan, H. L. "Renaming with a Money Model." *Arithmetic Teacher,* 26 (September 1978): 23–24.

Marcy, S., and J. Marcy. *Mathimagination, Books A–F.* Palo Alto, Calif.: Creative Publications, Inc., 1973. (Creative Publications, Inc., P.O. Box 10328, Palo Alto, CA 94303.)

Menninger, K. *Number Words and Number Symbols.* Cambridge, Mass.: Massachusetts Institute of Technology Press, 1969. (Massachusetts Institute of Technology Press, 28 Carleton St., Cambridge, MA 02142.)

Merriell, D. "Nim and Natural Numbers." *The Mathematics Teacher,* 64 (April 1971). 342–344.

Morgenstern, F. B., and M. Pincus. "Reading Big Numbers." *The Arithmetic Teacher,* 19 (November 1972): 569–570.

Murray, P. J. "Addition Practice Through Partitioning of Sets of Numbers." *The Arithmetic Teacher,* 23 (October 1976): 430–431.

Pagni, D. L. "Magic Squares: Would You Believe . . . ?" *The Arithmetic Teacher,* 21 (May 1974): 439–441.

Pincus, M. "A Fifth Grade's Revision of our Number System." *The Arithmetic Teacher,* 19 (March 1972): 197–199.

Reardin, C. R., Jr. "Understanding the Russian Peasant." *The Arithmetic Teacher,* 20 (January 1973): 33–35.

Rucker, W., and C. Dilley. *Math Card Games.* Palo Alto, Calif.: Creative Publications, Inc., 1974. (Creative Publications, Inc., P.O. Box 10328, Palo Alto, CA 94303.)

Schreiner, N. B. *More Games and Aids for Teaching Math.* Palos Verdes Estates, Calif.: Touch and See Educational Resources, 1973. (Touch and See Educational Resources, P.O. Box 794, Palos Verdes Estates, CA 90274.)

Schultz, J. E. "Using a Calculator to Do Arithmetic in Bases Other than Ten," *Arithmetic Teacher,* 26 (September 1978): 25–27.

Seymour, D., M. Laycock, B. Larsen, R. Heller, and V. Holmberg. *Aftermath, Volumes 1–4.* Palo Alto, Calif.: Creative Publications, Inc., 1971. (Creative Publications, Inc., P.O. Box 10328, Palo Alto, CA 94303.)

Shokoohi, G-H. "Manipulative Devices for Teaching Place Value." *Arithmetic Teacher,* 25 (March 1978): 49–51.

Smeltzer, D. *Man and Number.* London: A. and C. Black, Ltd., 1970. (A. and C. Black, Ltd., 35 Bedford Row, London, WC1R 4JH, England).

Smith, K. J. "Inventing a Numeration System." *The Arithmetic Teacher,* 20 (November 1973): 550–553.

Thompson, C. and J. Babcock. "A Successful Strategy for Teaching Missing Addends." *Arithmetic Teacher,* 26 (December 1978): 38–41.

Unenge, J. "Introducing the Binary System in Grades Four to Six." *The Arithmetic Teacher,* 20 (March 1973): 182–183.

Wenner, W. J. "Compound Subtraction—An Easier Way." *The Arithmetic Teacher,* 25 (January 1978): 33–34.

Wheatley, C. L., and G. H. Wheatley. "How Shall We Teach Column Addition? Some Evidence." *The Arithmetic Teacher,* 25 (January 1978): 18–19.

Willcott, R. E., M. A. Spikell, and C. E. Greenes. *Multibase Activities, Base 10.* Palo Alto, Calif.: Creative Publications, Inc., 1974. (Creative Publications, Inc., P.O. Box 10328, Palo Alto, Calif. 94303.)

Wolfers, E. P. "The Original Counting Systems of Papua and New Guinea." *The Arithmetic Teacher,* 18 (February 1971): 77–83.

Zweng, M. J. "The Fourth Operation Is Not Fundamental." *The Arithmetic Teacher,* 19 (December 1972): 623–627.

The Integers

PRELIMINARY PROBLEM

Mary, a ten-year old calculator genius,
announced a discovery to her classmates one day.
She said, "I have found a special five-digit
number I call *abcde*. If I enter 1 and then the

a	b	c	d	e	1

number on my calculator and then multiply by 3, the result is the number with 1 on the end!"
Mary's discovery is shown in the figure at left.
Can you find her number?

INTRODUCTION

Hindus were reputedly among the first to use negative numbers to represent amounts of money owed. For centuries, mathematicians resisted the negative number concept, and as late as the seventeenth century, negative numbers were referred to as "fictitious" or "false." By their very creation, negative numbers are not fictitious. Morris Kline (1976) describes the situation well.

> The history of mathematics illustrates the rather significant observation that it is more difficult to get a truth accepted than to discover it. The mathematician to whom "number" meant whole numbers and fractions found it hard to accept negative numbers as true numbers. They [sic], too, failed to realize for centuries that mathematical concepts are man-made abstractions which can be introduced at will if they can serve useful purposes.

The following cartoon suggests that the use of negative numbers is still resisted.

© 1957 United Feature Syndicate, Inc.

Negative numbers are useful for recording everyday events. For example, a temperature that is five degrees below zero Celsius can be written as ⁻5°C. The surface of the Dead Sea, the lowest point on Earth, is 1292 feet below sea level, which can be written as ⁻1292 feet. The balance of a bank account overdrawn by $100 can be written as ⁻$100. These are only a few possible uses of negative numbers. Negative numbers are indispensable in algebra and, consequently, in many applications of mathematics.

4-1 INTEGERS AND THE OPERATIONS OF ADDITION AND SUBTRACTION

The need for negative numbers arises because subtraction cannot always be performed with whole numbers. An operation like $0 - 3$ is not defined within the system of whole numbers. Using the definition of subtraction of whole numbers, $0 - 3 = x$ if and only if $x + 3 = 0$. This equation does not have a solution in the set of whole numbers. In order to solve the equation, a new number, $^-3$, is created such that $^-3 + 3 = 0$. In general, to solve for x in equations of the form $x + n = 0$ and $n + x = 0$, where $n \in N$, a set of new numbers is created. For each n, there is a unique new number, ^-n, called the additive inverse of n, such that $^-n + n = 0 = n + {}^-n$. This new set of numbers, $\{^-1, ^-2, ^-3, ^-4, ^-5, \ldots\}$, is called the set of negative integers. The union of the set $\{^-1, ^-2, ^-3, ^-4, ^-5, \ldots\}$ and the set of whole numbers, $\{0, 1, 2, 3, \ldots\}$, is **integers** called the set of **integers.** The set of integers is denoted by I and is listed as follows:

$$I = \{\ldots, ^-5, ^-4, ^-3, ^-2, ^-1, 0, 1, 2, 3, 4, 5, \ldots\}$$

The set of natural numbers, $\{1, 2, 3, 4, \ldots\}$, is called the set of positive integers. *Zero is neither negative nor positive.* Thus, the set of all integers can be partitioned into three disjoint subsets: positive integers, $\{0\}$, and negative integers.

Unfortunately, the symbol "$-$" is used to indicate both subtraction and negative integers. To reduce confusion between the uses of this symbol, it is customary initially to use a raised minus sign for negative numbers, as in $^-5$, in contrast to the ordinary minus sign for subtraction, as in $7 - 5$. To emphasize that an integer is positive, some people use a raised plus sign, as in $^+3$. In this text, we use the plus sign for addition only and write $^+3$ simply as 3.

The integers, like whole numbers, can be illustrated using a number line. One familiar number line that includes integers appears on a thermometer as in Figure 4-1. Customarily, number lines are drawn horizontally. One such example is shown in Figure 4-2. The position of the negative integers can be described as mirror images of the positive integers, assuming the mirror is placed at 0 perpendicular to the number line. For example, the mirror image of 5 is $^-5$, and the mirror image of 0 is 0.

Similarly, the positive integers can be described as mirror images of the negative integers. For example, 4 is the mirror image of $^-4$. The mathemati- **additive inverse** cal term for "mirror image of" is **additive inverse** or "opposite." Thus, the

FIGURE 4-1

FIGURE 4-2

-5 -4 -3 -2 -1   0   1   2   3   4   5

opposite of 4 is denoted by ⁻4, and the opposite of ⁻4 can be denoted as ⁻(⁻4) or 4. In general, additive inverses are defined in the following way.

DEFINITION

> If n is an integer, then the unique integer $⁻n$ is called the **additive inverse** of n or the **opposite** of n. Likewise, n is called the additive inverse of $⁻n$ or the opposite of $⁻n$.

Example 4-1

Find the additive inverse of each of the following integers.

(a) 3   (b) ⁻5   (c) 0   (d) ⁻a

Solution

(a) ⁻3   (b) 5   (c) 0   (d) a

Example 4-2

For each of the following, find the value of $⁻x$.

(a) $x = 3$ (b) $x = ⁻5$ (c) $x = 0$

Solution

(a) $⁻x = ⁻3$ (b) $⁻x = ⁻(⁻5) = 5$ (c) $⁻x = ⁻0 = 0$

Notice that $⁻x$ does not necessarily represent a negative integer. For example, the value of $⁻x$ in (b) of Example 4-2 is 5.

The number line can also be used to determine the distance between two given points. For example, the points ⁻2 and 3 are 5 units apart as shown in Figure 4-3.

FIGURE 4-3

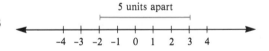

5 units apart

absolute value   Distance is always a positive number or zero. The distance between an integer and 0 is called the **absolute value** of the integer. Thus, the absolute value of ⁻3 is 3. We write this as $|⁻3| = 3$. (A more formal definition of absolute value is given in Problem 15 of Problem Set 4-1.)

Example 4-3

Evaluate each of the following.

(a) $|20|$ (b) $|⁻5|$ (c) $|0|$
(d) $|n|$ if n is a positive integer   (e) $|⁻n|$ if n is a positive integer

Solution | (a) $|20| = 20$ (b) $|^-5| = 5$ (c) $|0| = 0$
(d) $|n| = n$ (e) $|^-n| = n$

Addition of Integers

Addition of integers, like addition of whole numbers, can be illustrated on a number line. Consider the following example.

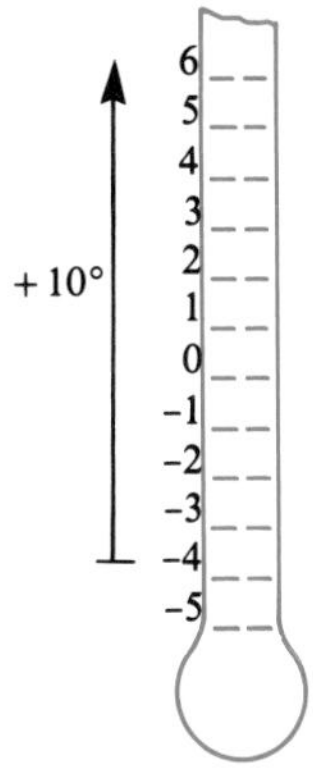

Example 4-4 | The temperature was $^-4°C$. In an hour, it rose 10°C. What is the new temperature?

Solution | Figure 4-4 shows that the new temperature is 6°C. The picture shows that $^-4 + 10 = 6$.

+10°

FIGURE 4-4

On a horizontal number line, picture a positive integer as an arrow pointing to the right and a negative integer as an arrow pointing to the left. For example, $^-3$ can be pictured using any of the arrows in Figure 4-5.

FIGURE 4-5

Figure 4-6 shows how to perform $8 + ^-5$ on a number line. Place the starting end of the arrow representing the second number, $^-5$, at the point of the arrow representing the first number, 8. An arrow from 0 to the tip of the second arrow represents the sum of the two integers. Notice that the representation of $8 + ^-5$ is the same as that of $8 - 5$.

FIGURE 4-6

Example 4-5 | Find $^-5 + 3$.

Solution | The number line in this example shows that $^-5 + 3 = ^-2$.

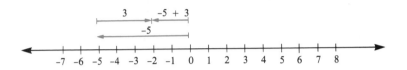

BRAIN TEASER

If the digits 1 through 9 are written in order, it is possible to place plus and minus signs between the numbers, or no operation symbol at all, to obtain a total of 100. For example,

$1 + 2 + 3 + {}^-4 + 5 + 6 + 78 + 9 = 100$

Can you obtain a total of 100 using fewer plus or minus signs than in the given example? Notice that digits, like 7 and 8, may be combined.

Addition of integers also can be illustrated by a gain-and-loss model.

(a) If a person gains $10 on one investment and loses $4 on another, the net profit is $10 − $4 = $6. Interpreting a gain of $10 as positive 10 and a loss of $4 as negative 4, the net profit can be written as $10 + {}^-4$. Thus, $10 + {}^-4 = 10 − 4 = 6$.

(b) A certain stock dropped 10 points on Monday and then dropped an additional 15 points on Tuesday. Think about the total loss in points as ${}^-10 + {}^-15$. Since the total loss is 25 points, ${}^-10 + {}^-15 = {}^-25$.

(c) If a stock dropped 10 points and then gained 10 points, the net gain is 0. Thus, ${}^-10 + 10 = 0$.

(d) A certain stock gained 10 points and then dropped 25 points. Think of the total loss in points as $10 + {}^-25$. Since the total loss is 15 points, $10 + {}^-25 = {}^-15$. Since $25 − 10 = 15$, we see that $10 + {}^-25 = {}^-(25 − 10)$.

Results of the gain-and-loss model can be generalized as follows.

DEFINITION

> For any whole numbers m and n,
> (a) If $m > n$, then $m + {}^-n = {}^-n + m = m − n$.
> (b) For all m and n, ${}^-m + {}^-n = {}^-(m + n)$.
> (c) For all n, ${}^-n + n = n + {}^-n = 0$.
> (d) If $m < n$, then $m + {}^-n = {}^-n + m = {}^-(n − m)$.

Example 4-6

Find each of the following sums.

(a) $9 + {}^-4$ (b) ${}^-5 + {}^-8$ (c) ${}^-5 + 5$
(d) $3 + {}^-10$ (e) ${}^-10 + 3$ (f) $5 + {}^-7$

Solution

(a) $9 + {}^-4 = 9 − 4 = 5$ (b) ${}^-5 + {}^-8 = {}^-(5 + 8) = {}^-13$
(c) ${}^-5 + 5 = 0$ (d) $3 + {}^-10 = {}^-(10 − 3) = {}^-7$
(e) ${}^-10 + 3 = {}^-(10 − 3) = {}^-7$ (f) $5 + {}^-7 = {}^-(7 − 5) = {}^-2$

Subtraction of Integers

For the set of whole numbers, the difference $a - b$ is defined as the unique whole number c such that $c + b = a$. Subtraction of integers is defined in an analogous way.

DEFINITION

> If a and b are integers, then $a - b$ is the unique integer c such that $c + b = a$.

Example 4-7

Using the definition of subtraction, find each of the following.

(a) $3 - 10$ (b) $^-2 - 10$

Solution

(a) Let $3 - 10 = c$. Then $c + 10 = 3$, and hence, $c = ^-7$. Therefore, $3 - 10 = ^-7$.

(b) Let $^-2 - 10 = c$. Then $c + 10 = ^-2$ and hence, $c = ^-12$. Therefore, $^-2 - 10 = ^-12$.

By knowing the addition facts for whole numbers, it is possible to solve subtraction problems involving integers. Since $3 + (^-10) = ^-7$ and from Example 4-7(a), $3 - 10 = ^-7$, then $3 - 10 = 3 + (^-10)$. Similarly, $^-2 - 10 = ^-2 + (^-10)$.

theorem

The following **theorem**—that is, statement that can be logically deduced from the basic properties—shows how addition of integers and subtraction of integers are related. (The proof of the theorem is left as an exercise in Problem Set 4-3.)

THEOREM 4-1

> For any two integers a and b, $a - b = a + ^-b$.

Example 4-8

Change each subtraction problem into an addition problem to find the following.

(a) $2 - 8$ (b) $2 - (^-8)$

Solution

(a) $2 - 8 = 2 + ^-8 = ^-6$ (b) $2 - (^-8) = 2 + ^-(^-8) = 2 + 8 = 10$

PROBLEM SET 4-1

1. Find the additive inverses for each of the following integers. Write your answer in the simplest possible form.
   (a) 2 (b) $^-5$ (c) m (d) 0 (e) ^-m (f) $a + b$

2. Simplify each of the following.
   (a) $^-(^-2)$ (b) $^-(^-m)$ (c) $^-0$

3. Add.
   (a) $10 + ^-3$ (b) $10 + ^-12$ (c) $10 + ^-10$ (d) $^-10 + 10$
   (e) $^-2 + ^-8$ (f) $(^-2 + ^-3) + 7$ (g) $^-2 + (^-3 + 7)$

4. Demonstrate each addition on a number line.
   (a) $5 + ^-3$ (b) $^-2 + 3$ (c) $^-3 + 2$ (d) $^-3 + ^-2$
   (e) $(2 + ^-4) + ^-3$

5. Write an addition fact corresponding to each of the following sentences, and then answer the question.
   (a) A certain stock fell 17 points and the following day gained 10 points. What was the net change in the stock's worth?
   (b) The temperature was $^-10°C$, and then it rose 8°C. What is the new temperature?
   (c) The plane was at 5000 feet and dropped 100 feet. What is the new altitude of the plane?
   (d) A visitor in a Las Vegas casino lost $200, won $100, and then lost $50. What was the change in the gambler's net worth?
   (e) In four downs, the football team lost 2 yards, gained 7 yards, gained 0 yards, and lost 8 yards. What was the total gain or loss?

6. On January 1, Jane's bank balance was $300. During the month, she wrote checks for $45, $55, $165, $35, and $100 and made deposits of $75, $25, and $400.
   (a) If a check is represented by a negative integer and a deposit by a positive integer, express Jane's transactions as a sum of positive and negative integers.
   (b) What was the balance in Jane's account at the end of the month?

7. Evaluate each of the following.
   (a) $|^-5|$ (b) $|10|$ (c) $|2 + ^-5|$ (d) $|^-3 + ^-4|$ (e) $^-|^-5|$

8. For each of the following, solve for x where x is an integer.
   (a) $x + 3 = 0$ (b) $x + ^-10 = 1$ (c) $^-x = 5$ (d) $|x| = 3$
   (e) $|^-x| = 3$ (f) $|x| = ^-3$

9. Evaluate each of the following using the definition of subtraction.
   (a) $2 - 11$ (b) $^-3 - 7$ (c) $5 - (^-8)$ (d) $0 - 4$

10. Use addition to compute each of the following.
    (a) $3 - 15$ (b) $^-2 - 5$ (c) $^-3 - (^-15)$ (d) $0 - 4$

11. Perform each of the following.
    (a) $^-2 + (3 - 10)$ (b) $[8 - (^-5)] - 10$
    (c) $(^-2 - 7) + 10$ (d) $^-2 - (7 + 10)$

12. Solve for x where x is an integer.
    (a) $x - 3 = ^-5$ (b) $x + (3 - 10) = 0$
    (c) $x - 3 = ^-3$ (d) $x - x = 0$

13. Consider the expressions $(x + y) - (z + w)$ and $(x - z) + (y - w)$.
    (a) Are the expressions equal for $x = 30$, $y = 4$, $z = 10$, and $w = 7$?
    (b) Are the expressions equal if $x = ^-4$, $y = 5$, $z = ^-9$, and $w = 7$?

14. Let W stand for the set of whole numbers, I the set of integers, I^+ the set of positive integers, and I^- the set of negative integers. Find each of the following.
  (a) $W \cup I$ (b) $W \cap I$ (c) $I^+ \cup I^-$ (d) $I^+ \cap I^-$
  (e) $W - I$ (f) $I - W$ (g) $W - I^+$ (h) $W - I^-$

★15. The following is a definition for the absolute value of an integer x.

  If x is a positive integer or 0, then $|x| = x$.
  If x is a negative integer, then $|x| = {}^-x$.

  Use the definition to evaluate each of the following.
  (a) $|5|$ (b) $|{}^-5|$ (c) $|0|$ (d) ${}^-|{}^-7|$

16. Do problems 83 and 84 appearing in Appendix II.

4-2 MULTIPLICATION AND DIVISION OF INTEGERS

One way to define multiplication of whole numbers is by repeated addition. In some cases this interpretation carries over to the multiplication of integers. Consider, for instance, $3 \cdot ({}^-4)$. This product can be thought of as the sum of ${}^-4 + {}^-4 + {}^-4$ which equals ${}^-12$. Since ${}^-12$ can be written as ${}^-(3 \cdot 4)$, it follows that $3 \cdot ({}^-4) = {}^-(3 \cdot 4)$. Thus, if n and m are whole numbers, we can interpret $n \cdot ({}^-m)$ as follows.

$$n \cdot ({}^-m) = \underbrace{{}^-m + {}^-m + {}^-m + \cdots + {}^-m}_{n \text{ terms}} = {}^-(n \cdot m)$$

Next, consider a product like $({}^-4) \cdot 3$. It is meaningless to say that there are ${}^-4$ threes in a sum. However, if the commutative property holds for multiplication of integers, then $({}^-4) \cdot 3 = 3 \cdot ({}^-4) = {}^-12$. Thus, multiplication of integers can be defined in the following way.

DEFINITION

> For any whole numbers n and m, $n \cdot ({}^-m) = ({}^-m) \cdot n = {}^-(n \cdot m)$.

Example 4-9   Find each of the following products.

  (a) $3 \cdot ({}^-15)$ (b) $({}^-5) \cdot 7$
  (c) $0 \cdot ({}^-3)$ (d) $0 \cdot ({}^-n), n \in W$

Solution   (a) $3 \cdot ({}^-15) = {}^-(3 \cdot 15) = {}^-45$ (b) $({}^-5) \cdot 7 = {}^-(5 \cdot 7) = {}^-35$
  (c) $0 \cdot ({}^-3) = {}^-(0 \cdot 3) = 0$ (d) $0 \cdot ({}^-n) = {}^-(0 \cdot n) = 0$

Products such as $(^-3)(^-4)$ are usually introduced with patterns. Find the missing products for the following equations by observing a pattern among the first four answers.

$$3(^-4) = {}^-12$$
$$2(^-4) = {}^-8$$
$$1(^-4) = {}^-4$$
$$0(^-4) = 0$$
$$(^-1)(^-4) =$$
$$(^-2)(^-4) =$$
$$(^-3)(^-4) =$$

Notice that each number on the right is 4 greater than the preceding product. It seems reasonable to continue the pattern as follows.

$$3(^-4) = {}^-12$$
$$2(^-4) = {}^-8$$
$$1(^-4) = {}^-4$$
$$0(^-4) = 0$$
$$(^-1)(^-4) = 4$$
$$(^-2)(^-4) = 8$$
$$(^-3)(^-4) = 12$$

The textbook page reproduced on page 149 from *Growth in Mathematics,* Harcourt, Brace, Jovanovich, 1978, Grade 7, shows the use of patterns to teach products of integers.

Remember, patterns can be misleading, so it is important to study many examples and consider possible exceptions. However, in this case, patterns lead to a true conjecture concerning the multiplication of two negative integers.

Another, more formal, approach uses the uniqueness property of additive inverses for showing that $(^-3)(^-4) = 3 \cdot 4$. If $(^-3)(^-4)$ and $3 \cdot 4$ are both the additive inverses of the same number, then $(^-3)(^-4) = 3 \cdot 4$. Now, $3 \cdot 4$ is the additive inverse of $^-(3 \cdot 4)$. The following reasoning shows that $(^-3)(^-4)$ is also the additive inverse of $^-(3 \cdot 4)$ by showing that $(^-3)(^-4) + {}^-(3 \cdot 4) = 0$. The argument assumes that the distributive property of multiplication over addition and the multiplication property of zero hold for integers.

$$(^-3)(^-4) + {}^-(3 \cdot 4) = (^-3)(^-4) + (^-3)4 \qquad \text{Definition of } (^-3)4$$
$$= (^-3)(^-4 + 4) \qquad \text{DPM/A}$$
$$= {}^-3 \cdot 0 \qquad \text{Additive inverse property}$$
$$= 0 \qquad \text{Multiplication property of zero}$$
$$(^-3)(^-4) + {}^-(3 \cdot 4) = 0 \qquad \text{Transitive property of equality}$$

Multiplying with Unlike Signs

Look for a pattern.

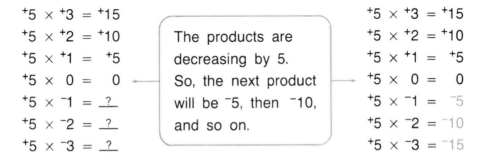

$$^+5 \times {}^+3 = {}^+15$$
$$^+5 \times {}^+2 = {}^+10$$
$$^+5 \times {}^+1 = {}^+5$$
$$^+5 \times 0 = 0$$
$$^+5 \times {}^-1 = \underline{}$$
$$^+5 \times {}^-2 = \underline{}$$
$$^+5 \times {}^-3 = \underline{}$$

The products are decreasing by 5. So, the next product will be ⁻5, then ⁻10, and so on.

$$^+5 \times {}^+3 = {}^+15$$
$$^+5 \times {}^+2 = {}^+10$$
$$^+5 \times {}^+1 = {}^+5$$
$$^+5 \times 0 = 0$$
$$^+5 \times {}^-1 = {}^-5$$
$$^+5 \times {}^-2 = {}^-10$$
$$^+5 \times {}^-3 = {}^-15$$

The product of two integers that have unlike signs is negative.

Solve: ⁻4 × ⁺6 = *n.*

The signs are unlike.
The product is negative.

⁻4 × ⁺6 = ⁻24

Multiply: 4 × 6 = 24.

Thus, $(^-3)(^-4)$ and $3 \cdot 4$ are both additive inverses of $^-(3 \cdot 4)$ and so $(^-3)(^-4) = 3 \cdot 4$. The preceding discussion motivates the following theorem.

THEOREM 4-2

If m and n are any whole numbers, then $(^-m)(^-n) = mn$.

We have motivated this result through two approaches. The last approach, which uses the distributive property of multiplication over addition and the fact that each integer has a unique additive inverse, is mathematically superior to the pattern approach. The general case when m and n are any integers is proved in the next section.

Division

On the set of whole numbers, $a \div b$ where $b \neq 0$, is defined to be the unique whole number c such that $a = bc$. If such a whole number c does not exist, then $a \div b$ is undefined. Division in the set of integers is defined analogously.

DEFINITION

If a and b are any integers with $b \neq 0$, then $a \div b$ is the unique integer c such that $a = bc$.

Example 4-10

Use the definition of division to evaluate each of the following.

(a) $12 \div (^-4)$ (b) $^-12 \div 4$ (c) $^-12 \div (^-4)$

Solution

(a)   Let $12 \div (^-4) = c$. Then, $12 = ^-4c$, and consequently, $c = ^-3$. Thus, $12 \div (^-4) = ^-3$.

(b)   Let $^-12 \div 4 = c$. Then, $^-12 = 4c$, and therefore, $c = ^-3$. Thus, $^-12 \div 4 = ^-3$.

(c)   Let $^-12 \div (^-4) = c$. Then $^-12 = ^-4c$, and consequently, $c = 3$. Thus, $^-12 \div (^-4) = 3$.

Example 4-10 suggests that, if it exists, the quotient of two negative integers is a positive integer and, if it exists, the quotient of a positive and a negative integer, or a negative and a positive integer, is negative.

A model illustrating the operations on integers is given in the Postman

Stories in the Teaching Ideas section following Problem Set 4-2. Students may find reading the Postman Stories helpful in doing the problems.

PROBLEM SET 4-2

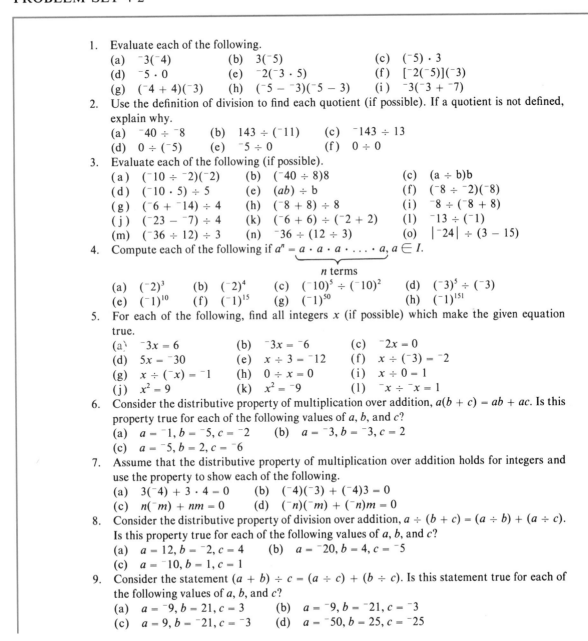

1. Evaluate each of the following.
    (a) $^-3(^-4)$ (b) $3(^-5)$ (c) $(^-5) \cdot 3$
    (d) $^-5 \cdot 0$ (e) $^-2(^-3 \cdot 5)$ (f) $[^-2(^-5)](^-3)$
    (g) $(^-4 + 4)(^-3)$ (h) $(^-5 - {^-3})(^-5 - 3)$ (i) $^-3(^-3 + {^-7})$

2. Use the definition of division to find each quotient (if possible). If a quotient is not defined, explain why.
    (a) $^-40 \div {^-8}$ (b) $143 \div (^-11)$ (c) $^-143 \div 13$
    (d) $0 \div (^-5)$ (e) $^-5 \div 0$ (f) $0 \div 0$

3. Evaluate each of the following (if possible).
    (a) $(^-10 \div {^-2})(^-2)$ (b) $(^-40 \div 8)8$ (c) $(a \div b)b$
    (d) $(^-10 \cdot 5) \div 5$ (e) $(ab) \div b$ (f) $(^-8 \div {^-2})(^-8)$
    (g) $(^-6 + {^-14}) \div 4$ (h) $(^-8 + 8) \div 8$ (i) $^-8 \div (^-8 + 8)$
    (j) $(^-23 - {^-7}) \div 4$ (k) $(^-6 + 6) \div (^-2 + 2)$ (l) $^-13 \div (^-1)$
    (m) $(^-36 \div 12) \div 3$ (n) $^-36 \div (12 \div 3)$ (o) $|^-24| \div (3 - 15)$

4. Compute each of the following if $a^n = \underbrace{a \cdot a \cdot a \cdot \ldots \cdot a}_{n \text{ terms}}, a \in I.$
    (a) $(^-2)^3$ (b) $(^-2)^4$ (c) $(^-10)^5 \div (^-10)^2$ (d) $(^-3)^5 \div (^-3)$
    (e) $(^-1)^{10}$ (f) $(^-1)^{15}$ (g) $(^-1)^{50}$ (h) $(^-1)^{151}$

5. For each of the following, find all integers x (if possible) which make the given equation true.
    (a) $^-3x = 6$ (b) $^-3x = {^-6}$ (c) $^-2x = 0$
    (d) $5x = {^-30}$ (e) $x \div 3 = {^-12}$ (f) $x \div (^-3) = {^-2}$
    (g) $x \div (^-x) = {^-1}$ (h) $0 \div x = 0$ (i) $x \div 0 = 1$
    (j) $x^2 = 9$ (k) $x^2 = {^-9}$ (l) $^-x \div {^-x} = 1$

6. Consider the distributive property of multiplication over addition, $a(b + c) = ab + ac$. Is this property true for each of the following values of a, b, and c?
    (a) $a = {^-1}, b = {^-5}, c = {^-2}$ (b) $a = {^-3}, b = {^-3}, c = 2$
    (c) $a = {^-5}, b = 2, c = {^-6}$

7. Assume that the distributive property of multiplication over addition holds for integers and use the property to show each of the following.
    (a) $3(^-4) + 3 \cdot 4 = 0$ (b) $(^-4)(^-3) + (^-4)3 = 0$
    (c) $n(^-m) + nm = 0$ (d) $(^-n)(^-m) + (^-n)m = 0$

8. Consider the distributive property of division over addition, $a \div (b + c) = (a \div b) + (a \div c)$. Is this property true for each of the following values of a, b, and c?
    (a) $a = 12, b = {^-2}, c = 4$ (b) $a = {^-20}, b = 4, c = {^-5}$
    (c) $a = {^-10}, b = 1, c = 1$

9. Consider the statement $(a + b) \div c = (a \div c) + (b \div c)$. Is this statement true for each of the following values of a, b, and c?
    (a) $a = {^-9}, b = 21, c = 3$ (b) $a = {^-9}, b = {^-21}, c = {^-3}$
    (c) $a = 9, b = {^-21}, c = {^-3}$ (d) $a = {^-50}, b = 25, c = {^-25}$

10. Use patterns to show that $(^-1)(^-1) = 1$.
11. The temperature has been rising 6° each hour. If the temperature is 9°C now, what was it four hours ago?

12. Do Problems 77, 78, 79, 80, 81, 82, and 84 appearing in Appendix II.

TEACHING IDEAS

Postman Stories

BRAIN TEASER

Express each of the numbers from 1 through 10 using four 4's and any operations. For example, $1 = 44 \div 44$ or $1 = (4 \div 4)^{44}$ or $1 = {}^-4 + 4 + (4 \div 4)$.

A model for operations on integers was introduced in the Madison Project (Davis, 1967) in the form of Postman Stories. Our Postman Stories take place during summer vacation and involve three main characters: the postman, an absent-minded mathematics professor, and her 13-year-old son who likes to do calculations mentally. The postman behaves in a peculiar way. He delivers the mail at random (not necessarily to the right person) but remembers to whom each letter was addressed. The postman eventually comes back and picks up the mail he has misdelivered and gives it to the right person. The professor always keeps a day-to-day account of her funds. She never reads the addresses on the delivered mail or the names on the checks or bills. However, she reads the amount on each check or bill, tells her son the amount, and adjusts her record of funds accordingly. The math professor denotes bills by negative integers such as $^-3$, $^-10$, and $^-45$, and checks by positive integers such as 3, 10, and 50. The following are examples of different mail deliveries and their recordings.

1. On Friday, the postman brought a check for $15 and a check for $68. As a result, the boy calculated a gain of $83. The professor wrote $15 + 68 = 83$ and believed she was $83 richer.
2. On Monday, the postman brought a check for $45 and a bill for $25. The boy calculated a gain of $20. The professor wrote $45 + {}^-25 = 20$ and believed she was $20 richer.
3. On Tuesday, the postman brought a check for $10 and a bill for $15. The boy recorded a loss of $5. The professor wrote $10 + {}^-15 = {}^-5$ and believed she was $5 poorer.
4. On Wednesday, the postman brought a check for $50 and took away the check for $68, which was intended for someone else. The boy calculated a loss of $18. The professor wrote $50 - 68 = {}^-18$ and believed she was $18 poorer.
5. On Thursday, the postman brought a bill for $12 and took away the $10 check delivered Tuesday. The boy calculated a loss of $22. The professor wrote $^-12 - 10 = {}^-22$ and believed she was $22 poorer.

6. On Friday, the postman brought a bill for $10 and took away the bill for $12. The boy figured out that the bill for $10 decreased the funds by $10, while taking away the $12 bill increased the funds by $12. He calculated the net as $2. The professor wrote $^{-}10 - (^{-}12) = 2$ and believed she was $2 richer.

7. On the next Monday, the postman took away the bill for $25. The boy computed a gain of $25. The professor wrote $^{-}(^{-}25) = 25$ and believed she was $25 richer.

8. On Tuesday, the postman took away two checks for $10 each delivered several weeks ago. The boy computed that the funds are decreased by $20. The professor wrote $^{-}2 \cdot 10 = ^{-}20$ and believed she was poorer by $20. (Notice that in this product $^{-}2$ indicates the number of letters taken away, while 10 indicates the amount of each check.)

9. On Wednesday, the postman took away two old bills for $15 each. The boy calculated that his mother was $30 richer. The professor recorded the transaction as $(^{-}2)(^{-}15) = 30$. (The product $(^{-}2)(^{-}15)$ indicates that two pieces of mail were taken away, each containing a bill for $15.)

Additional models portraying operations of integers can be found in Kindle, 1976 and Peterson, 1972.

4-3 THE SYSTEM OF INTEGERS—A SUMMARY WITH PROOFS

This section looks at integers from a more formal point of view. It assumes some basic properties of integers and deduces others.

DEFINITION

The **system of integers** consists of the set of integers $\{\ldots, ^{-}3, ^{-}2, ^{-}1, 0, 1, 2, 3, \ldots\}$ or I, along with the operations of addition and multiplication, which for any integers a, b, c satisfy the following properties.

Closure Properties $a + b$ is a unique integer; ab is a unique integer.
Commutative Properties $a + b = b + a$; $ab = ba$.
Associative Properties $(a + b) + c = a + (b + c)$; $(ab)c = a(bc)$.
Identity Elements   There are unique integers 0 and 1 such that for all integers, a, $0 + a = a + 0 = a$; $1 \cdot a = a \cdot 1 = a$.
Additive Inverse   For every integer a, there exists a unique integer b such that $a + b = b + a = 0$. The integer, b, is called the additive inverse of a (also the opposite of a) and is denoted by ^{-}a.
Distributive Property of Multiplication over Addition $a(b + c) = ab + ac$ and $(b + c)a = ba + ca$.

The following properties of equality, which were discussed in Chapter 2, also hold for integers.

Property

For any integers a, b, and c,
Reflexive Property $a = a$.
Symmetric Property   If $a = b$, then $b = a$.
Transitive Property   If $a = b$ and $b = c$, then $a = c$.

Property

The Addition Property of Equality   For any integers a, b, and c, if $a = b$, then $a + c = b + c$.

According to the addition property of equality, it is possible to add the same integer to both sides of an equation without affecting the equality.

Property

The Multiplication Property of Equality   For any integers a, b, and c, if $a = b$, then $ac = bc$.

According to the multiplication property of equality, it is possible to multiply both sides of an equation by the same integer without affecting the equality. Multiplication of both sides by zero is rarely used.

In mathematical expressions, it is valid to substitute a number for its **substitution property**   equal. This property is referred to as the **substitution property.** Examples of substitution follow.

(a)   If $a + b = c + d$ and $d = 5$, then $a + b = c + 5$.
(b)   If $a + b = c + d$, if $b = e$, and if $d = f$, then $a + e = c + f$.
(c)   If $x = 2$, then $3x = 3 \cdot 2 = 6$.
(d)   Since $^-2(^-3) = 6$, it is possible to write $6 = 10 + {^-4}$ as $^-2(^-3) = 10 + {^-4}$.

The process of logically justifying a theorem from basic properties is **proof**   called a **proof.** Once a theorem is proved, it may be used to prove other theorems. There are many different ways to write proofs. A standard method utilized in many secondary school textbooks is the two-column format with statements on the left and reasons on the right. Other forms include paragraph proofs that have reasons integrated with statements, and proofs by contradiction. A variety of forms of proof are used in this text. To illustrate the nature of mathematical proof, we give proofs of some of the theorems and leave the proofs of others as exercises.

The addition property of equality was formulated as follows. For any integers, a, b, and c, if $a = b$, then $a + c = b + c$. A new statement results from reversing the order of the *if* and *then* parts of this addition property. This new statement is called the **converse** of the original statement. In the case of the addition property, the converse is a true statement. However, in general, the converse of a true statement may not be true. The converses for both the addition property and the multiplication property follow.

converse

THEOREM 4-3

The Cancellation Properties for Addition and Multiplication
(a)   For any integers a, b, and c, if $a + c = b + c$, then $a = b$.
(b)   For any integers a, b, and c, with $c \neq 0$, if $ac = bc$, then $a = b$.

Before beginning a proof of Theorem 4-3(a) consider the second step of problem solving, devising a plan or strategy. Assume that the statement $a + c = b + c$ is true. Since the goal of the proof is to show $a = b$, c must be eliminated from each side of the equation $a + c = b + c$. This can be achieved by adding ^-c to each side of the equation.

Proof

	Statement	*Reason*
(1)	$a + c = b + c$	Given
(2)	$(a + c) + {}^-c = (b + c) + {}^-c$	Addition property of equality
(3)	$a + (c + {}^-c) = b + (c + {}^-c)$	Associative property of addition
(4)	$a + 0 = b + 0$	Additive inverse property
(5)	$a = b$	Identity property for addition

The proof of Theorem 4-3(b) is left as an exercise.

In previous sections, we investigated how to find the opposite of an integer, how to add integers, and how to multiply integers. These results are stated formally in Theorem 4-4.

THEOREM 4-4

For all integers a and b,
(a) $^-(^-a) = a$
(b) $^-a + {}^-b = {}^-(a + b)$
(c) $(^-a)b = {}^-(ab)$
(d) $(^-a)(^-b) = ab$

The proofs of parts (a) and (b) are left as problems; proofs for parts (c) and (d) follow.

Strategy for part (c).   To prove $(^-a)b = {}^-(ab)$, we show that $(^-a)b$ and $^-(ab)$ are the additive inverses of the same integer. Since each integer has a unique additive inverse, it will follow that $(^-a)b = {}^-(ab)$. Since $ab + {}^-(ab) = 0$, show that $(^-a)b$ also is the additive inverse of ab by showing that $ab + (^-a)b = 0$.

Proof   Using the distributive property of multiplication over addition, the definition of the additive inverse, and the multiplication property of zero, the following holds.

$$(^-a)b + ab = (^-a + a)b = 0 \cdot b = 0$$

Consequently, $(^-a)b + ab = 0$, and thus, $(^-a)b$ is the additive inverse of ab. Since $^-(ab)$ is also the additive inverse of ab, the uniqueness of the additive inverse implies that $(^-a)b = {}^-(ab)$.

Strategy for part (d).   To prove that $(^-a)(^-b) = ab$, show that $(^-a)(^-b)$ and ab are additive inverses of the same integer. The integer ab is the additive inverse of $^-(ab)$. By part (c) of Theorem 4-4, $^-(ab) = (^-a)b$, and therefore, ab is the additive inverse of $(^-a)b$. Next, show that $(^-a)(^-b)$ is also the additive inverse of $(^-a)b$; that is, $(^-a)(^-b) + (^-a)b = 0$.

Proof   It follows from part (c) of Theorem 4-4 that ab is the additive inverse of $(^-a)b$. Using the distributive property of multiplication over addition, the definition of the additive inverse, and the multiplicative property of 0, the following holds.

$$(^-a)(^-b) + (^-a)b = (^-a)(^-b + b) = (^-a) \cdot 0 = 0$$

Consequently, $(^-a)(^-b) + (^-a)b = 0$, and thus, $(^-a)(^-b)$ is the additive inverse of $(^-a)b$. The fact that ab and $(^-a)(^-b)$ are both additive inverses of $(^-a)b$ implies that $(^-a)(^-b) = ab$.

In Theorem 4-4(c), if $a = b$, then $(^-b)b = {}^-(b \cdot b) = {}^-(b^2)$. We write $^-(b^2)$ as $^-b^2$. Thus, $^-(3^2) = {}^-3^2 = {}^-9$. On the other hand, $(^-b)^2 = (^-b)(^-b) = b^2$. Hence, $^-b^2 \neq (^-b)^2$.

An expression like $3 - 15 - 8$ is ambiguous unless there is agreement about the order in which subtractions are performed. Mathematicians agree that $3 - 15 - 8$ means $(3 - 15) - 8$; that is, the subtractions in $3 - 15 - 8$ are performed in the order of their appearance from left to right. Similarly, $3 - 4 + 5$ means $(3 - 4) + 5$ and not $3 - (4 + 5)$. Thus, $(a - b) - c$ may be written without parentheses as $a - b - c$.

Finding an equivalent expression for $a - (b - c)$ without parentheses can be completed as follows. (The reasons should be supplied by the reader.)

$$\begin{aligned} a - (b - c) &= a + {}^-(b - c) \\ &= a + {}^-(b + {}^-c) \\ &= a + ({}^-b + {}^-({}^-c)) \\ &= a + ({}^-b + c) \\ &= (a + {}^-b) + c \\ &= (a - b) + c \\ &= a - b + c \end{aligned}$$

Hence, $a - (b - c) = a - b + c$.

Notice that in the process of showing $a - (b - c) = a - b + c$, it was necessary to show that ${}^-(b - c) = {}^-b + c$. Since ${}^-b + c = c + {}^-b = c - b$, we have ${}^-(b - c) = c - b$; that is, $b - c$ and $c - b$ are additive inverses of each other.

Example 4-11

Compute or simplify each of the following.

(a) $2 - 5 - 5$ (b) $2 - (5 - x)$ (c) $3 - 7 + 3$
(d) $3 - (7 + 3)$ (e) $5 - (x - 3)$ (f) ${}^-(x - y) - y$

Solution

(a) $2 - 5 - 5 = {}^-3 - 5 = {}^-8$
(b) $2 - (5 - x) = 2 - 5 + x = {}^-3 + x$
(c) $3 - 7 + 3 = {}^-4 + 3 = {}^-1$
(d) $3 - (7 + 3) = 3 - 10 = {}^-7$
(e) $5 - (x - 3) = 5 - x + 3 = 8 - x$
(f) ${}^-(x - y) - y = ({}^-x + y) - y = {}^-x + (y - y) = {}^-x$

Recall that when addition and multiplication appear in a problem without parentheses, multiplication is done first. When addition, subtraction, multiplication, and division appear without parentheses, multiplications and divisions are done first in the order of their appearance from left to right and then additions and subtractions in the order of their appearance from left to right. Any arithmetic appearing inside parentheses must be done first.

Example 4-12

Evaluate

(a) $2 - 5 \cdot 4 + 1$ (b) $(2 - 5) \cdot 4 + 1$ (c) $2 - 3 \cdot 4 + 5 \cdot 2 - 1 + 5$

Solution

(a) $2 - 5 \cdot 4 + 1 = 2 - 20 + 1 = {}^-18 + 1 = {}^-17$
(b) $(2 - 5) \cdot 4 + 1 = {}^-3 \cdot 4 + 1 = {}^-12 + 1 = {}^-11$
(c) $2 - 3 \cdot 4 + 5 \cdot 2 - 1 + 5 = 2 - 12 + 10 - 1 + 5 = 4$

| Remark | Problems like Example 4-12 should be examined by students so that they later realize that $2 - 5x + 1$ is *not* equal to $^-3x + 1$. |

The distributive property of multiplication over addition can be used to develop the distributive property of multiplication over subtraction as follows.

$$a(b - c) = a(b + {}^-c)$$
$$= ab + a({}^-c)$$
$$= ab + {}^-(ac)$$
$$= ab - ac$$

Consequently, $a(b - c) = ab - ac$.

Similarly, it can be shown that $(b - c)a = ba - ca$.

| Property | **Distributive Property of Multiplication over Subtraction**   For any integers a, b, and c, |

$$a(b - c) = ab - ac$$
$$(b - c)a = ba - ca$$

| Example 4-13 | Use the distributive properties of multiplication over addition and subtraction to simplify each of the following. |

(a) $({}^-3)(x - 2)$ (b) $(a + b)(a - b)$

| Solution | (a) $({}^-3)(x - 2) = ({}^-3)x - ({}^-3)(2) = {}^-3x - ({}^-6) = {}^-3x + 6$ |

(b) $(a + b)(a - b) = (a + b)a - (a + b)b$
$$= (a^2 + ba) - (ab + b^2)$$
$$= a^2 + ab - ab - b^2$$
$$= a^2 - b^2$$

Thus, $(a + b)(a - b) = a^2 - b^2$

The result $(a + b)(a - b) = a^2 - b^2$ in Example 4-13(b) generally is called **difference of squares**   the **difference of squares** formula.

| Example 4-14 | Perform each of the following operations using the difference of squares formula. |

(a) $22 \cdot 18$ (b) $(4 + b)(4 - b)$ (c) $({}^-4 + b)({}^-4 - b)$

| Solution | (a) $22 \cdot 18 = (20 + 2)(20 - 2) = 20^2 - 2^2 = 400 - 4 = 396$ |

(b) $(4 + b)(4 - b) = 4^2 - b^2 = 16 - b^2$
(c) $({}^-4 + b)({}^-4 - b) = ({}^-4)^2 - b^2 = 16 - b^2$

Both the difference of squares formula and the distributive properties of multiplication over addition and subtraction can be used for factoring.

Example 4-15 Factor each of the following.

(a) $x^2 - 9$ (b) $(x + y)^2 - z^2$ (c) $^-3x + 5xy$ (d) $3x - 6$

Solution

(a) $x^2 - 9 = x^2 - 3^2 = (x + 3)(x - 3)$
(b) $(x + y)^2 - z^2 = (x + y + z)(x + y - z)$
(c) $^-3x + 5xy = x(^-3 + 5y)$
(d) $3x - 6 = 3(x - 2)$

BRAIN TEASER

Find the product
$(x - a)(x - b)(x - c) \cdots (x - z)$
if $a, \cdots, z$ are integers.

PROBLEM SET 4-3

1. Compute each of the following.
    (a) $^-2 + 3 \cdot 5 - 1$ (b) $10 - 3 \cdot 7 - 4(^-2) + 3$ (c) $10 - 3 - 12$
    (d) $10 - (3 - 12)$ (e) $(^-3)^2$ (f) $^-3^2$
    (g) $^-5^2 + 3(^-2)^2$ (h) $^-2^3$ (i) $(^-2)^3$
    (j) $^-2^4$ (k) $(^-2)^4$
2. If x is an integer and $x \neq 0$, which of the following are always positive and which are always negative?
    (a) $^-x^2$ (b) x^2 (c) $(^-x)^2$ (d) $^-x^3$ (e) $(^-x)^3$
    (f) $^-x^4$ (g) $(^-x)^4$ (h) x^4 (i) x (j) ^-x
3. Which of the expressions in Problem 2 are always equal to each other?
4. Simplify each of the following expressions.
    (a) $(^-x)(^-y)$ (b) $^-2x(^-y)$ (c) $^-(x + y) + x + y$ (d) $^-1 \cdot x$
    (e) $x - 2(^-y)$ (f) $a - (a - b)$ (g) $y - (y - x)$ (h) $^-(x - y) + x$
5. Multiply each of the following.
    (a) $^-2(x - 1)$ (b) $^-2(x - y)$ (c) $x(x - y)$
    (d) $^-x(x - y)$ (e) $^-2(x + y - z)$ (f) $^-x(x - y - 3)$
    (g) $(^-5 - x)(5 + x)$ (h) $(x - y - 1)(x + y + 1)$ (i) $(^-x^2 + 2)(x^2 - 1)$
6. Use the difference of squares formula to perform each of the following, if possible.
    (a) $52 \cdot 48$ (b) $(5 - 100)(5 + 100)$
    (c) $(^-x - y)(^-x + y)$ (d) $(2 + 3x)(2 - 3x)$
    (e) $(x - 1)(1 + x)$ (f) $213^2 - 13^2$

7. Can $(^-x - y)(x + y)$ be multiplied by using the difference of squares formula? Explain why or why not.

8. Factor each of the following expressions, and then simplify, if possible:
   - (a) $3x + 5x$
   - (b) $ax + 2x$
   - (c) $xy + x$
   - (d) $ax - 2x$
   - (e) $x^2 + xy$
   - (f) $3x - 4x + 7x$
   - (g) $3xy + 2x - xz$
   - (h) $3x^2 + xy - x$
   - (i) $abc + ab - a$
   - (j) $(a + b)(c + 1) - (a + b)$
   - (k) $16 - a^2$
   - (l) $x^2 - 9y^2$
   - (m) $4x^2 - 25y^2$
   - (n) $(x^2 - y^2) + x + y$

9. Perform each of the following operations.
   - (a) $(x + y)^2$
   - (b) $(x - y)^2$

10. Is it true that $(x - y)^2 = x^2 - y^2$? Why or why not?

★11. Prove that for any integers a and b, $a - b = a + (^-b)$.

★12. Prove part (b) of Theorem 4-3.

★13. Prove the first two parts of Theorem 4-4.

★14. Use the properties of the system of integers to prove that if a is an integer, then $a \cdot 0 = 0$.

4-4   SOLVING EQUATIONS AND INEQUALITIES

Before we consider the algebra of solving equations and inequalities, we have to develop additional properties of inequalities for integers. As with whole numbers, "greater than" and "less than" relations can be defined for integers.

DEFINITION

For any integers a and b, a is greater than b, written $a > b$, if and only if there exists a positive integer k such that $a = b + k$. Also, b is less than a, written $b < a$, if and only if $a > b$.

By the definition of "greater than," $a > b$ if and only if there exists a positive integer k such that $a = b + k$. By the definition of subtraction, $a = b + k$ if and only if $a - b = k$. Thus, since k is positive, $a - b > 0$.

THEOREM 4-5

For any two integers a and b, $a > b$ if and only if $a - b > 0$.

Remark   It follows from Theorem 4-5 that $a < b$ if and only if $a - b < 0$.

The following table compares the properties of the inequality relations with the properties of the equality relation. Assume that a, b, and c represent integers.

Property	Equality	Inequality
Reflexive	$a = a$	—
Symmetric	$a = b$ implies $b = a$	—
Transitive	$a = b$ and $b = c$ implies $a = c$	$a > b$ and $b > c$ implies $a > c$
		$a < b$ and $b < c$ implies $a < c$
Addition	$a = b$ implies $a + c = b + c$	$a > b$ implies $a + c > b + c$
		$a < b$ implies $a + c < b + c$
Multiplication	$a = b$ implies $ac = bc$	$a > b$ and $c > 0$ implies $ac > bc$
		$a > b$ and $c < 0$ implies $ac < bc$
		$a < b$ and $c > 0$ implies $ac < bc$
		$a < b$ and $c < 0$ implies $ac > bc$

Remark | It is possible to combine properties of equality and inequality using the $\geq$ or $\leq$ symbols.

The reflexive property does not hold for inequality. For example, $5 > 5$ is false. Also, the symmetric property does not hold for inequality. For example, while $6 > 2$ is true, $2 > 6$ is false. One way to demonstrate the transitive property for inequality is with temperature. If the temperature in Aberdeen is higher than the temperature in Barstow, and if the temperature in Barstow is higher than the temperature in Cranston, then the temperature in Aberdeen is higher than the temperature in Cranston. In other words, $a > b$ and $b > c$ implies $a > c$.

Examples for the addition property of "greater than" follow.

$5 > 2$ implies $5 + 10 > 2 + 10$
$^-2 > {}^-5$ implies $^-2 + 2 > {}^-5 + 2$
$x > 3$ implies $x + 2 > 3 + 2$
$x - 3 > 5$ implies $x - 3 + 3 > 5 + 3$

It is important to observe that when both sides of an inequality are multiplied by a positive integer, the direction of inequality is preserved, but if both sides of an inequality are multiplied by a negative integer, the direction of inequality is reversed. Consider the following examples.

$5 > 3$ implies $5 \cdot 2 > 3 \cdot 2$, but $5 \cdot ({}^-2) < 3 \cdot ({}^-2)$
$^-3 > {}^-5$ implies $({}^-3)2 > ({}^-5)2$, but $({}^-3)({}^-2) < ({}^-5)({}^-2)$
$x > 3$ implies $2x > 2 \cdot 3$, but $^-2x < {}^-2 \cdot 3$

Properties for subtraction and division of inequalities follow from the addition and multiplication properties of inequality.

THEOREM 4-6

> If a, b, and c are any integers, then
>
> (a) $a > b$ implies $a - c > b - c$
> (b) $a > b$ and $c > 0$ implies $a \div c > b \div c$, provided the divisions are defined
> (c) $a > b$ and $c < 0$ implies $a \div c < b \div c$, provided that the divisions are defined

The proof of Theorem 4-6 is left as an exercise.

Example 4-16

Justify each of the following.
(a) $^{-}2 > {}^{-}5$ implies $^{-}7 > {}^{-}10$
(b) $10 > 6$ implies $5 > 3$
(c) $10 > 6$ implies $^{-}5 < {}^{-}3$

Solution

(a)   By the subtraction property of inequality, $^{-}2 > {}^{-}5$ implies $^{-}2 - 5 > {}^{-}5 - 5$; that is, $^{-}7 > {}^{-}10$.
(b)   By the division property of inequality , $10 > 6$ implies $10 \div 2 > 6 \div 2$; that is, $5 > 3$.
(c)   By the division property of inequality, $10 > 6$ implies $10 \div {}^{-}2 < 6 \div {}^{-}2$; that is, $^{-}5 < {}^{-}3$.

algebra

The study of **algebra** concerns itself with operations on numbers and other elements often represented by symbols. Finding solutions to equations and inequalities is one part of algebra.

Solving an equation or inequality means finding the set of all possible values of the variable for which the equation or inequality is true. This set is

  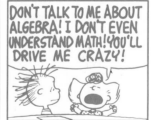 

solution set | called the **solution set.** For example, suppose a is an integer such that $4a > 12$. By Theorem 4-6, divide both sides of the inequality by 4. Thus, $(4a) \div 4 > 12 \div 4$ or $a > 3$. Since a is an integer, the solution set to $4a > 12$ is $\{4, 5, 6, 7, \ldots\}$.

Example 4-17 | Solve each of the following for x, where x is an integer.

    (a) $x + 4 = {}^-6$ (b) $x + 4 > {}^-6$

Solution | (a)

$$
\begin{aligned}
x + 4 &= {}^-6 \\
(x + 4) + {}^-4 &= {}^-6 + {}^-4 \\
x &= {}^-10
\end{aligned}
$$

The solution set is $\{{}^-10\}$.

(b)

$$
\begin{aligned}
x + 4 &> {}^-6 \\
(x + 4) + {}^-4 &> {}^-6 + {}^-4 \\
x &> {}^-10
\end{aligned}
$$

The solution set is $\{{}^-9, {}^-8, {}^-7, \ldots\}$.

It is not necessary to show every detail when solving an equation or inequality. Notice that in Example 4-17(a) we omitted the details between $(x + 4) + {}^-4 = {}^-6 + {}^-4$ and $x = {}^-10$.

Example 4-18 | Solve each of the following for x, where x is an integer.

    (a) ${}^-x - 5 = 8$ (b) ${}^-x - 5 \geq 8$
    (c) ${}^-2x + 3 = {}^-11$ (d) ${}^-2x + 3 > {}^-11$

Solution | (a)

$$
\begin{aligned}
{}^-x - 5 &= 8 \\
({}^-x - 5) + 5 &= 8 + 5 \\
{}^-x &= 13 \\
({}^-x)({}^-1) &= 13({}^-1) \\
x &= {}^-13
\end{aligned}
$$

(b)

$$
\begin{aligned}
{}^-x - 5 &\geq 8 \\
({}^-x - 5) + 5 &\geq 8 + 5 \\
{}^-x &\geq 13 \\
({}^-x)({}^-1) &\leq 13({}^-1) \\
x &\leq {}^-13
\end{aligned}
$$

(c)

$$
\begin{aligned}
{}^-2x + 3 &= {}^-11 \\
({}^-2x + 3) + {}^-3 &= {}^-11 + {}^-3 \\
{}^-2x &= {}^-14 \\
({}^-2x) \div {}^-2 &= {}^-14 \div {}^-2 \\
x &= 7
\end{aligned}
$$

(d)
$$^-2x + 3 > ^-11$$
$$(^-2x + 3) + ^-3 > ^-11 + ^-3$$
$$^-2x > ^-14$$
$$(^-2x) \div ^-2 < (^-14) \div ^-2$$
$$x < 7$$

BRAIN TEASER

The following is an argument showing that an ant weighs as much as an elephant. What is wrong?

Let e be the weight of the elephant and a the weight of the ant. Let $e - a = d$. Consequently, $e = a + d$. Multiply each side of $e = a + d$ by $e - a$.

Then simplify.

$$e(e - a) = (a + d)(e - a)$$
$$e^2 - ea = ae + de - a^2 - da$$
$$e^2 - ea - de = ae - a^2 - da$$
$$e(e - a - d) = a(e - a - d)$$
$$e = a$$

Thus, the weight of the elephant equals the weight of the ant.

PROBLEM SET 4-4

1. Write each of the following lists of numbers in increasing order.
    (a) $^-13, ^-20, ^-5, 0, 4, ^-3$ (b) $^-5, ^-6, 5, 6, 0$
    (c) $^-20, ^-15, ^-100, 0, ^-13$ (d) $13, ^-2, ^-3, 5$
2. Use Theorem 4-5 to show that each of the following is true.
    (a) $^-3 > ^-5$ (b) $^-6 < 0$
    (c) $^-8 > ^-10$ (d) $^-5 < 4$
3. Solve each of the following if x is an integer.
    (a) $x + 3 = ^-15$ (b) $x + 3 > ^-15$
    (c) $3 - x = ^-15$ (d) $^-x + 3 > ^-15$
    (e) $^-x - 3 = 15$ (f) $^-x - 3 \geq 15$
    (g) $3x + 5 = ^-16$ (h) $3x + 5 < ^-16$
    (i) $^-3x + 5 = 11$ (j) $^-3x + 5 \leq 11$
    (k) $5x - 3 = 7x - 1$ (l) $5x - 3 > 7x - 1$
    (m) $3(x + 5) = ^-4(x + 5) + 21$ (n) $^-5(x + 3) > 0$
4. Solve the following if x is an integer.
    (a) $x^2 = 16$ (b) $^-x^2 = 16$
    (c) $x^3 = 27$ (d) $x^3 = ^-27$
    (e) $|x| = 5$ (f) $|x| = ^-3$
    (g) $|x| > ^-5$ (h) $|x| \leq 0$
5. Which of the following are true for all possible integer values of x?
    (a) $3(x + 1) = 3x + 3$ (b) $x - 3 = 3 - x$
    (c) $x + 3 = 3 + x$ (d) $2(x - 1) + 2 = 3x - x$
    (e) $x^2 + 1 > 0$ (f) $3x > 4x - x$

6. Solve each of the following if x is an integer.
   (a) $(x + 5)^2 = 64$ (b) $(x + 5)^3 = 27$
   (c) $|x + 1| = 10$ (d) $|x^2 + 1| = 10$
   (e) $|x| > 0$ (f) $|x| = x$

7. For each of the following, which elements of the given set, if any, satisfy the equation or inequality?
   (a) $x^3 + x^2 = 2x, \{1, \,^-1, \,^-2, 0\}$
   (b) $3x - 3 = 24, \{^-9, 9\}$
   (c) $^-x \geq 5, \{6, \,^-6, 7, \,^-7, 2\}$
   (d) $x^2 < 16, \{^-4, \,^-3, \,^-2, \,^-1, 0, 1, 2, 3, 4\}$

8. Solve each of the following equations. Check your answers by substituting in the given equation. Assume x, y, and z represent integers.
   (a) $^-2x + \,^-11 = 3x + 4$ (b) $5(^-x + 1) = 5$
   (c) $^-3y + 4 = y$ (d) $^-3(z - 1) = 8z + 3$

★9. (a) Prove the transitive property of "greater than."
   (b) Prove the addition property of "greater than."
   (c) Prove the multiplication properties of "greater than."

★10. Prove Theorem 4-6.

★11. (a) Is it always true that for any integers x and y, $x^2 + y^2 \geq 2xy$? Prove your answer.
   (b) For which integers x and y is $x^2 + y^2 = 2xy$?

★12. If $0 < a < b$ where a and b are integers, prove that $a^2 < b^2$.

★13. If $a < b$ where a and b are integers, is it always true that $a^2 < b^2$?

★14. If $a < b$ where a and b are integers, prove that $c - b < c - a$, if c is an integer.

★15. For each of the following, find all integers x such that the statement is true.
   (a) $x + 1 < 3$ and $^-x + 1 < 5$ (b) $2x < \,^-6$ or $1 + x < 0$

4-5 SOLVING WORD PROBLEMS

Algebra can be used to solve many kinds of word problems. To understand word problems, first identify what is given and what is to be found. Devising a plan involves assigning letters to the unknown quantities and translating the information in the problem into a model involving equations or inequalities. Carrying out the plan means solving the equations or inequalities. Looking back to check the solution and to be sure the original problem is answered is the final step.

Example 4-19 | David is thinking of a number. If he multiplies that number by $^-3$ and then adds 6, he has $^-4$ times his original number. What is David's original number?

Solution

Understanding the Problem

The problem asks for a number. The number times ⁻3, plus 6 equals ⁻4 times the number.

Devising a Plan

Let *n* represent David's number. Now, translate the information from the problem into mathematical symbols and solve the resulting equation.

Information	*Mathematical Translation*
David is thinking of a number	n
He multiplies that number by ⁻3	^-3n
Adds 6	$^-3n + 6$
He has (⁻4) times his original number	$^-3n + 6 = (^-4)n$

Carrying Out the Plan

Solve the equation.

$$^-3n + 6 = ^-4n$$
$$4n + {^-3n} + 6 = 4n + {^-4n}$$
$$n + 6 = 0$$
$$n = {^-6}$$

Looking Back

The number David thought about is ⁻6. To check that ⁻6 is the correct solution, follow the written information using ⁻6 as David's number. The number, ⁻6 times ⁻3 is 18. Next, 18 plus 6 is 24. Also, ⁻4 times the number, ⁻6, is 24. So the answer is correct.

Example 4-20

Beans that cost 75¢ per pound are mixed with beans that cost 95¢ per pound to produce a 20-pound mixture that costs 80¢ per pound. How many pounds of each type of beans are used?

Solution

Understanding the Problem

The problem asks for the number of pounds of each type of beans used to make an 80¢ per pound mixture, from 75¢ per pound and 95¢ per pound beans. The final mixture weighs 20 pounds.

Devising a Plan

Let x stand for the number of pounds of 75¢ beans. Let y stand for the number of pounds of 95¢ beans. Next, translate the information from the problem into mathematical statements.

Since there are 20 pounds in the blend, we have $x + y = 20$. The remaining information tells us about the cost per pound of each type of beans. To produce an equation using this information, notice that the value of the 75¢ beans plus the value of the 95¢ beans equals the value of the 20-pound mixture of beans.

cost of 75¢ beans plus cost of 95¢ beans $=$ cost of mixture
$$75x + 95y = 80 \cdot 20$$

The two equations obtained are as follows.

$$x + y = 20 \qquad 75x + 95y = 80 \cdot 20$$

Since we know how to solve equations with one unknown, try to combine these two equations into one equation with one unknown. This can be achieved by solving one of the equations for y and then substituting the expression for y in the other equation. Since $x + y = 20$ implies $y = 20 - x$, substitute $20 - x$ for y in the second equation and solve for x. Use the value of x obtained to find the value of y.

Carrying Out the Plan

$$75x + 95(20 - x) = 80 \cdot 20$$
$$75x + 1900 - 95x = 1600$$
$$^-20x + 1900 = 1600$$
$$^-20x = {^-}300$$
$$x = 15$$

Since $y = 20 - x$, $y = 20 - 15 = 5$. Thus, 15 pounds of the 75¢ beans and 5 pounds of the 95¢ beans are used in the blend.

Looking Back

The reader should check these answers in the original problem.

Example 4-21 In a certain factory, machine A produces three times as many bolts as machine B. Machine C produces 13 more bolts than machine A. If the total production is 4997 bolts per day, how many bolts does each machine produce in a day?

Solution | **Understanding the Problem**

The problem asks for the number of bolts machine A, machine B, and machine C produce in 1 day. The problem gives information that compares the production of A to B and of C to A.

Devising a Plan

Let a, b, and c be the number of bolts produced by machines A, B, and C, respectively. Translate the given problem into equations as follows.

machine A produces 3 times as many bolts as B: $a = 3b$
machine C produces 13 more bolts than A: $c = a + 13$
total production is 4997: $a + b + c = 4997$

In order to reduce the number of variables, substitute $3b$ for a in the second and third equations.

$c = a + 13$ becomes $c = 3b + 13$
$a + b + c = 4997$ becomes $3b + b + c = 4997$

Then, make an equation in one variable, b, by substituting $3b + 13$ for c in the equation $3b + b + c = 4997$. Solve for c. Then find a and b.

Carrying Out the Plan

$$3b + b + 3b + 13 = 4997$$
$$7b + 13 = 4997$$
$$7b = 4984$$
$$b = 712$$

Thus $a = 3b = 3 \cdot 712 = 2136$. Also, $c = a + 13 = 2136 + 13 = 2149$.

Machine A produces 2136 bolts, machine B produces 712 bolts, and machine C produces 2149 bolts.

Looking Back

To check the answers, follow the original information using $a = 2136$, $b = 712$, and $c = 2149$. The information in the first sentence, "machine A produces three times as many bolts as machine B" checks, since $2136 = 3 \cdot 712$. The second sentence, "Machine C produces 13 more bolts than machine A" is true since $2149 = 13 + 2136$. The information in the last sentence, "the total production was 4997 bolts" checks, since $2136 + 712 + 2149 = 4997$.

Part of the Looking Back stage of Chapter 1 involved looking for alternate solutions. An alternate solution to Example 4-21 is as follows. Let x be the number of bolts produced by machine B. Then, express the number of bolts that machines A and C produce in terms of x.

Information	*Mathematical Translation*
The number of items that machine B produces	x
machine A produces three times as many items as machine B	$3x$
machine C produces 13 more items than machine A	$3x + 13$
The total production is 4997	$x + 3x + (3x + 13) = 4997$

Solve the equation.

$$x + 3x + (3x + 13) = 4997$$
$$7x + 13 = 4997$$
$$7x = 4984$$
$$x = 712$$

Hence, machine B produces 712 bolts. Machine A produces 2136 bolts, since $3x = 3 \cdot 712 = 2136$. Machine C produces 2149 bolts since $3x + 13 = 2136 + 13 = 2149$.

If we had let x be the number of bolts that machine A produces, the problem would have been more complicated to solve since machine B then produces $x \div 3$ bolts.

Word problems appear throughout the elementary mathematics curriculum. The sample on page 170 was taken from *Macmillan Mathematics*, 1978, Grade 7. Can you work through the page?

PROBLEM SET 4-5

1. Five times a number is equal to ⁻95. What is the number?
2. If you multiply a number by ⁻6 and then add 20 to the product, the result is 50. What is the number?
3. David has three times as much money as Rick. Together, they have $400. How much does each have?

Applications

You can use an equation with one variable to find a number that satisfies a **condition**.

The sum of a number and 3 is 10. Find the number.

Restate: the number plus 3 equals 10.

Write an equation: $n + 3 = 10$

Solve: $n + 3 = 10$ $\rightarrow$ n = ▨   Solution: ▨

Check with the original statement.
"The sum of 7 and 3 is 10" is a true statement.
The number is 7.

When 8 is subtracted from 6 times a number the difference is 46. Find the number.

Restate: 6 times the number minus 8 equals 46.

Write an equation: $6n - 8 = 46$

Solve: $6n - 8 = 46$ $\rightarrow$ $6n = 54$ $\rightarrow$ $n = $ ▨   Solution: ■

Check with the original statement.
"When 8 is subtracted from 6 times 9 the difference is 46" is
a true statement.
$(6 \times 9) - 8 = 54 - 8 = 46$ The number is 9.

Elena is paid $3 per hour at her after-school job.
How many hours must she work in order to pay back $16 she
owes her sister and have $50 left for herself?

Restate: Amount earned minus $16 she owes equals $50

          3 times the number of hours minus 16 equals 50

Write an equation: $3h - 16 = 50$

Solve: $3h - 16 = 50$ $\rightarrow$ $3h = 66$ $\rightarrow$ $h = $ ■   Solution: ■

Check: Amount earned = $3 \times 22 = $ ■
          $66 - $16 = 50 is a true number statement.
          She must work ■ hours.

Language of Algebra

4. Ran is 4 years older than Nureet. Six years ago Ran was twice as old as Nureet. How old are they now?
5. Factory *A* produces twice as many cars per day as factory *B*. Factory *C* produces 300 cars more per day than factory *A*. If the total production in the three factories is 7300 cars per day, how many cars per day are produced in each factory?
6. Tea that costs 60¢ per pound is mixed with tea that costs 45¢ per pound to produce a 100-pound blend that costs 51¢ per pound. How much of each kind of tea is used?
7. For a certain event, 812 tickets were sold totaling $1912. If students paid $2 per ticket and nonstudents paid $3 per ticket, how many student tickets were sold?
8. The sum of three consecutive integers is 237. Find the three integers.
9. The sum of three consecutive even integers is 240. Find the three integers.
10. The sum of two numbers is 21. The first number is twice the second number. Find the numbers.
11. A man left an estate of $64,000 to three children. The eldest child received three times as much as the youngest. The middle child received $14,000 more than the youngest. How much did each child receive?

SOLUTION TO THE PRELIMINARY PROBLEM

Understanding the Problem

Mary found a five-digit number called *abcde*, so that three times the display 1*abcde* gives the display *abcde*1 on the calculator. It will help us to understand the problem if we guess any five-digit number and see if our guess is correct. Suppose we guess 34 578. With 1 after it, it becomes 345 781. With 1 before it, it becomes 134 578. Since $3 \cdot 134\,578 \neq 345\,781$, our guess is incorrect.

Devising a Plan

We know that three times 1*abcde* is *abcde*1. This can be translated to an equation by letting the unknown number on the display *abcde* be n and using place value. Note that 1*abcde* means $1 \cdot 10^5 + n$, or $100\,000 + n$ and *abcde*1 means $n \cdot 10 + 1$, or $10n + 1$. Thus, Mary's computation tells us that

$$3(100\,000 + n) = 10n + 1$$

Now all that is necessary to solve the problem is to solve this equation for n.

Carrying Out the Plan

We use properties of equality to solve the equation for n as shown:

$$3(100\,000 + n) = 10n + 1$$
$$300\,000 + 3n = 10n + 1$$
$$299\,999 = 7n$$
$$42\,857 = n$$

Consequently, the five-digit number is 42 857.

Looking Back

To check the answer, we compute $3 \cdot 142\,857 = 428\,571$ and see that the solution is correct. Similar problems can be investigated by asking analogous questions for six-, seven-, or eight-digit numbers. Another generalization is to find a five-digit number, n, such that $k(100\,000 + n) = 10n + 1$, where k is different from 3.

QUESTIONS FROM THE CLASSROOM

1. A student argues that $(^-1)(^-1) = 1$, since $^-(^-1) = 1$. What is your response?
2. A fourth-grade student devised the following subtraction algorithm for subtracting $84 - 27$.

Four minus seven equals negative three.

$$\begin{array}{r} 84 \\ -27 \\ \hline ^-3 \end{array}$$

Eighty minus twenty equals sixty.

$$\begin{array}{r} 84 \\ -27 \\ \hline ^-3 \\ 60 \end{array}$$

Sixty plus $^-3$ equals 57.

$$\begin{array}{r} 84 \\ -27 \\ \hline ^-3 \\ 60 \\ \hline 57 \end{array}$$

Thus, the answer is 57. What is your response as a teacher?

3. A seventh-grade student does not believe that $^-5 < ^-2$. He argues that a debt of $5 is greater than a debt of $2. How do you respond?

4. An eighth-grade student claims she can prove that subtraction of integers is commutative. She points out that if a and b are integers, then $a - b = a + ^-b$. Since addition is commutative, so is subtraction. What is your response?

5. A student claims that if $x \neq 0$, then $|x| = ^-x$ is never true since absolute value is always positive. What is your response?

6. A student claims that since $(a \cdot b)^2 = a^2 \cdot b^2$, it must also be true that $(a + b)^2 = a^2 + b^2$. How do you respond?

7. A student solves $1 - 2x > x - 5$, where x is an integer, and reports the solution as $x < 2$. She asks if it is possible to check the answer in a way similar to the method of substitution for equations. What is your response?

8. A student computes $^-8 - 2(^-3)$ by writing $^-10(^-3) = 30$. How would you help this student?

9. A student says that his father showed him a very simple method for dealing with expressions like $^-(a - b + 1)$ and $x - (2x - 3)$. The rule is: If there is a negative sign before the parentheses, change the signs of the expressions inside the parentheses. Thus, $^-(a - b + 1) = a + b - 1$ and $x - (2x - 3) = x - 2x + 3$. What is your response?

10. A student solving word problems always checks her solutions by substituting in equations rather than following the written information. Is this an accurate check for the word problem?

CHAPTER OUTLINE

I. Basic concepts of integers
   A. The set of **integers**, I, is $\{\ldots, ^-3, ^-2, ^-1, 0, 1, 2, 3, \ldots\}$.
   B. The distance from any integer to 0 is called the **absolute value** of the integer. The absolute value of an integer x is denoted $|x|$.
   C. Operations with integers
      1. **Addition:** If $m, n \in W$
         (a) If $m > n$, then $m + ^-n = ^-n + m = m - n$.
         (b) For all m and n, $^-m + ^-n = ^-(m + n)$.
         (c) For all n, $^-n + n = n + ^-n = 0$.
         (d) If $m < n$, then $m + ^-n = ^-n + m = ^-(n - m)$.
      2. **Subtraction:** If a and b are any integers, then $a - b$ is the unique integer c such that $c + b = a$. All subtractions can be written in

terms of addition using the property $a - b = a + ^-b$.

      3. **Multiplication:** For any integers n and m, $n(^-m) = (^-m)n = ^-(nm)$ and $(^-m)(^-n) = mn$.

      4. **Division:** If a and b are any integers with $b \neq 0$, then $a \div b$, is the unique integer c such that $a = bc$.

      5. **Order of operations:** When addition and multiplication appear in a problem without parentheses, multiplication is done first. When addition, subtraction, multiplication and division appear without parentheses, multiplication and divisions are done first in the order of their appearance from left to right and then additions and subtractions in the order of their appearance from

left to right. Any arithmetic in parentheses is done first.

II. The system of integers

A. The **system of integers** consists of the set of integers $I = \{\ldots, ^-3, ^-2, ^-1, 0, 1, 2, 3, \ldots\}$, along with the operations of addition and multiplication, which, for any integers a, b, c, satisfy the following properties as shown.

Property	$+$	$\times$
closure	yes	yes
commutative	yes	yes
associative	yes	yes
identity	yes, 0	yes, 1
inverse	yes	no
Distributive Property of Multiplication over Addition		

B. **Addition property of equality:** For any integers a, b, c, if $a = b$, then $a + c = b + c$.

C. **Multiplication property of equality:** For any integers a, b, c, if $a = b$, then $ac = bc$.

D. **Substitution property:** Any number may be substituted for its equal.

E. **Cancellation properties for addition and multiplication:**
(a) For any integers a, b, and c, if $a + c = b + c$, then $a = b$.
(b) For any integers a, b, and c, if $c \neq 0$ and $ac = bc$, then $a = b$.

F. For all integers a, b, and c:
1. $^-(^-a) = a$
2. $a - (b - c) = a - b + c$
3. $(a + b)(a - b) = a^2 - b^2$ (Difference of squares formula)

III. Inequalities

A. $a > b$ if and only if there exists a positive integer k such that $a = b + k$. $b < a$ if and only if $a > b$.

B. Let a and b be any two integers. Then, $a > b$ if and only if $a - b > 0$.

C. Properties of inequalities
1. **Addition property:** If $a > b$ and c is any integer, then $a + c > b + c$.
2. **Multiplication properties:**
(a) If $a > b$ and $c > 0$, then $ac > bc$.
(b) If $a > b$ and $c < 0$, then $ac < bc$.

IV. Solving word problems

A. The solution to word problems involves each of the following.
1. **Understanding the problem:** Identify what is given and what is to be found.
2. **Devising a plan:** Assign letters to the unknown quantities and translate the data into equations or inequalities.
3. **Carrying out the plan:** Solve the equations or inequalities.
4. **Looking back:** Check and interpret the solution in terms of the situation given in the problem.

CHAPTER TEST

1. Find the additive inverse of each of the following.
   (a) 3   (b) ^-a (c) 0   (d) $x + y$ (e) $^-x + y$
2. Perform each of the following operations:
   (a) $(^-2 + {}^-8) + 3$ (b) $^-2 - (^-5) + 5$
   (c) $^-3(^-2) + 2$ (d) $^-3(^-5 + 5)$
   (e) $^-40 \div (^-5)$ (f) $(^-25 \div 5)(^-3)$

3. For each of the following, find all integer values of x (if there are any) that make the given equation true.
   (a) $^-x + 3 = 0$ (b) $^-2x = 10$
   (c) $0 \div (^-x) = 0$ (d) $^-x \div 0 = ^-1$
   (e) $3x - 1 = ^-124$ (f) $^-2x + 3x = x$

4. (a) Use a pattern approach to show that $(^-2)(^-3) = 6$.
   (b) Using the properties of the system of integers and the fact that $(^-a)b = ^-(ab)$, show that $(^-a)(^-b) = ab$.

5. (a) Show that $(x - y)(x + y) = x^2 - y^2$.
   (b) Use the result in part (a) to compute $(^-2 - x)(^-2 + x)$.

6. Simplify each of the following expressions.
   (a) ^-1x (b) $(^-1)(x - y)$
   (c) $2x - (1 - x)$ (d) $(^-x)^2 + x^2$
   (e) $(^-x)^3 + x^3$ (f) $(^-3 - x)(3 + x)$

7. Factor each of the following expressions and then simplify, if possible.
   (a) $x - 3x$ (b) $x^2 + x$
   (c) $5 + 5x$ (d) $(x - y)(x + 1) - (x - y)$

8. Solve each of the following for x, if x is an integer:
   (a) $^-3x + 7 = ^-x + 11$ (b) $|x| = 5$
   (c) $^-2x + 1 < 0$ (d) $^-2(^-3x + 7) < ^-2(^-x + 11)$

9. A certain college has 5715 undergraduates. There are 115 more seniors than juniors. The number of sophomores is twice the number of seniors, and the number of freshmen is twice the number of juniors. How many freshmen, sophomores, juniors, and seniors attend the college?

10. Classify each of the following as true or false (all letters represent integers.)
    (a) $|x|$ always is positive.
    (b) For all x and y, $|x + y| = |x| + |y|$.
    (c) If $a < ^-b$, then $a < 0$.
    (d) For all x and y, $(x - y)^2 = (y - x)^2$.
    (e) $(^-a)(^-b)$ is the additive inverse of ab.

11. If the temperature was $^-16°C$ and it rose by $9°C$, what is the new temperature?

12. Find a counterexample to disprove each of the properties on the set of integers.
    (a) Commutative property of division
    (b) Associative property of subtraction
    (c) Closure property for division
    (d) Distributive property of division over subtraction

13. Twice Molly's weight added to 50 pounds is equal to 78 pounds. Find Molly's weight.

SELECTED BIBLIOGRAPHY

Brumfiel, C. "An Introduction to Negative Integers." *The Mathematics Teacher*, **49**(November 1956):531–534.

Davis, R. B. (The Madison Project) *Explorations in Mathematics: A Text for Teachers.* Reading, Mass.: Addison-Wesley, 1967, 54–91.

Entwhistle, A. "Subtracting Signed Numbers." *The Mathematics Teacher*, **48**(March 1955):1975–1976.

Grady, M. "A Manipulative Aid for Adding and Subtracting Integers." *The Arithmetic Teacher*, **26**(November, 1978):40.

Jacobs, H. R. *Algebra,* San Francisco: W. H. Freeman, 1979.

Jencks, S. M., and D. M. Peck. "Hot and Cold Cubes." *The Arithmetic Teacher,* **24**(January 1977):70–71.

Kilhefner, D. Z. "Equation Hangman." *Arithmetic Teacher,* **27**(January, 1979):46–47.

Kindle, G. E. "Droopy, The Number Line, and Multiplication of Integers." *The Arithmetic Teacher,* **23**(December 1976):647–650.

Kline, M. *Mathematics for Liberal Arts,* Reading, Mass.: Addison-Wesley, 1967, pp. 74–75.

Kruase, E. F. *Mathematics for Elementary Teachers,* Englewood Cliffs, N.J.: Prentice-Hall, 1978.

Morrow, L. J. "Flow Charts for Equation Solving and Maintenance of Skills." *The Mathematics Teacher,* **66**(October 1973):499–506.

National Council of Teachers of Mathematics. *More Topics in Mathematics for Elementary School Teachers.* Thirtieth Yearbook, 1968.

National Council of Teachers of Mathematics, "The System of Integers." booklet number 9. *Topics in Mathematics for Elementary School Teachers,* 1968.

Peterson, J. C. "Fourteen Different Strategies for Multiplication of Integers, or Why $(^-1)(^-1) =$

$^+1$," *The Arithmetic Teacher,* **19**(May 1972):396–403..

Pratt, E. M. "A Teaching Aid for Signed Numbers." *The Arithmetic Teacher,* **13**(November 1966):589–590.

Rheins, J. J., and G. B. Rheins. "The Additive Inverse in Elementary Algebra." *The Mathematics Teacher,* **54**(November 1961):538–539.

Richardson, L. I. "The Role of Strategies for Teaching Pupils to Solve Verbal Problems." *The Arithmetic Teacher,* **22**(May 1975):414–421.

Schultz, J. E. *Mathematics for Elementary School Teachers,* Columbus, Ohio: Charles E. Merrill Publishing Co., 1977.

Sconyers, J. M. "Something New on Number Lines." *The Mathematics Teacher,* **67**(March 1974):253–254.

Uth, C. "Teaching Aid for Developing $(a + b)(a - b)$." *The Mathematics Teacher,* **48**(April 1955):247–249.

Williams, K. C. "The Three Faces of $(-)$." *The Mathematics Teacher,* **55**(December 1962):668–669.

Zweng, M. J. "One Point of View: The Problem of Solving Story Problems." *The Arithmetic Teacher,* **27**(September 1979):2.

Number Theory

PRELIMINARY PROBLEM

A woman with a basket of eggs finds that if she removes the eggs from the basket either two, three, four, five, or six at a time, there is always one egg left. However, if she removes the eggs seven at a time, there are no eggs left. If the basket holds up to 500 eggs, how many eggs does the woman have?

INTRODUCTION

Number theory deals primarily with properties of natural numbers. It is associated with names like Pythagoras (500 B.C.), Euclid (300 B.C.), and Diophantus (300 A.D.). Number theory began to flourish in the seventeenth century with the work of the lawyer Pierre de Fermat (1601–1665), referred to as the father of number theory. His extensive mathematical notes on the margins of his copy of Diophantus' *Arithmetica* included a conjecture now known as Fermat's Last Theorem. Next to a problem about finding squares that are sums of two squares (for example, $5^2 = 3^2 + 4^2$ and $13^2 = 12^2 + 5^2$), Fermat wrote,

> On the other hand, it is impossible for a cube to be the sum of two cubes, a fourth power to be the sum of two fourth powers, or, in general, for any number that is a power greater than the second to be the sum of two like powers. I have discovered a truly marvelous demonstration of this proposition that this margin is too narrow to contain.

No one has been able to prove or disprove the conjecture. It remains one of the most prominent unsolved problems of mathematics.

Many of the great mathematicians of the last three centuries were attracted to the theory of numbers. Among them Leonhard Euler (1707–1783), whose name is associated with almost every branch of mathematics, and Karl Friedrich Gauss (1777–1855), who was perhaps the greatest mathematician of all time. Gauss referred to the theory of numbers as the "Queen of Mathematics."

Topics from number theory that appear in elementary school curricula include prime numbers, prime factorization, greatest common divisor, least common multiple, and divisibility tests.

5-1   DIVISIBILITY

In a division problem involving integers a, b, and c, when $a \div b = c$, we say
divides   that a is divisible by b, or b **divides** a, written $b \mid a$. Similarly, we say that b is a

factor, multiple **factor** of a, and a is a **multiple** of b. The following true statements show how the preceding concepts are used.

3 is a factor of 12
12 is a multiple of 3
12 is divisible by 3
3 divides 12
$3 \mid 12$

To indicate that 12 is not divisible by 5, or 5 does not divide 12, we write $5 \nmid 12$.

DEFINITION

If a and b are any integers with $b \neq 0$, then b divides a, written $b \mid a$, if and only if there is a unique integer c such that $a = cb$.

Remark │ Do not confuse $b \mid a$ with b/a, which is interpreted as $b \div a$.

Example 5-1 │ Classify each of the following as true or false. Explain your answer.

(a) $^-3 \mid 12$ (b) $0 \mid 3$ (c) $3 \mid 0$ (d) $8 \nmid 2$
(e)   For all integers a, $1 \mid a$ (f)   For all integers a, $^-1 \mid a$
(g) $0 \mid 0$

Solution │ (a) $^-3 \mid 12$ is true since $12 = 4(^-3)$.
(b) $0 \mid 3$ is false since there is no integer c such that $3 = c \cdot 0$.
(c) $3 \mid 0$ is true since $0 = 0 \cdot 3$.
(d) $8 \nmid 2$ is true since there is no integer c such that $2 = c \cdot 8$.
(e) $1 \mid a$ is true for all integers a, since $a = a \cdot 1$.
(f) $^-1 \mid a$ is true for all integers a, since $a = (^-a)(^-1)$.
(g) $0 \mid 0$ is false because there is no unique integer c such that $0 = c \cdot 0$.

We now investigate some properties of divisibility for two integers. Consider two bags of apples, each of which contains a certain number of apples that can be equally divided among three students. If all the apples are put in one large bag, it is still possible to divide the apples equally among the three students. Consequently, if the number of apples in the first bag is a, and the number of apples in the second bag is b, then we can record the preceding discussion as: $3 \mid a$ and $3 \mid b$ implies $3 \mid (a + b)$. If the number of apples in one bag cannot be divided among three students, then the total number of apples cannot be equally divided among three students. That is, if $3 \mid a$ and $3 \nmid b$, then $3 \nmid (a + b)$.

THEOREM 5-1

For any integers a, b, and d with $d \neq 0$,

(a)   If $d \mid a$ and $d \mid b$, then $d \mid (a + b)$.
(b)   If $d \mid a$ and $d \nmid b$, then $d \nmid (a + b)$.

Since subtraction is defined in terms of addition, a similar theorem holds for subtraction.

THEOREM 5-2

For any integers a, b, and d with $d \neq 0$,

(a)   If $d \mid a$ and $d \mid b$, then $d \mid (a - b)$.
(b)   If $d \mid a$ and $d \nmid b$, then $d \nmid (a - b)$.

The proofs of most theorems in this section are left as exercises.

Suppose two integers, a and b, are equal. Substituting a for b in part (a) of Theorem 5-1, we have if $d \mid a$ and $d \mid a$, then $d \mid (a + a)$. Thus, if $d \mid a$, then $d \mid 2a$. Now, $d \mid a$ and $d \mid 2a$ imply that $d \mid (a + 2a)$, which can be written as $d \mid 3a$. Continuing in this way, it is possible to show that if d divides a, then d divides any positive multiple of a. That is, $d \mid a$ implies $d \mid ka$, where k is a positive integer. It can be shown that this statement is also true when k is a negative integer.

THEOREM 5-3

For any integers a and d with $d \neq 0$, if $d \mid a$ and k is any integer, then $d \mid ka$.

Example 5-2

Use Theorem 5-3 to tell whether each of the following is true or false,

(a) $5 \mid 70$ (b) $5 \mid 1000$

Solution

Because $10 = 5 \cdot 2$, $5 \mid 10$. Thus, by Theorem 5-3, $5 \mid k \cdot 10$, where k is any integer.

(a)   If $k = 7$, then $5 \mid 7 \cdot 10$ and $5 \mid 70$ is true.
(b)   If $k = 10^2$, then $5 \mid 10^2 \cdot 10$, that is $5 \mid 10^3$ and $5 \mid 1000$ is true.

Another property of divisibility is based on factoring. Since $21 = 7 \cdot 3$, 3 is a factor of 21. Since $105 = 5 \cdot 21$, 21 is a factor of 105. Consequently, $105 = 5 \cdot 7 \cdot 3$, and 3 is a factor of 105. In general, if a is a factor of b and b is a factor of c, then a is a factor of c. This is summarized in the following theorem.

THEOREM 5-4

> For any integers a, b, and c, with $a \neq 0$, and $b \neq 0$, if $a \mid b$ and $b \mid c$, then $a \mid c$.

Remark   Theorem 5-4 says that the relation "divides" is transitive.

Example 5-3   Classify each of the following as true or false where x, y, and z are integers. If a statement is true, prove it. If a statement is false, exhibit a counter-example.

(a)   If $3 \mid x$ and $3 \mid y$, then $3 \mid xy$.
(b)   If $3 \mid (x + y)$, then $3 \mid x$ and $3 \mid y$.
(c)   If $9 \nmid a$, then $3 \nmid a$.

Solution

(a)   True. By Theorem 5-3, if $3 \mid x$, then for any integer k, $3 \mid kx$. If $k = y$, then $3 \mid yx$ or $3 \mid xy$. (Notice that $3 \mid xy$ regardless of whether $3 \mid y$ or $3 \nmid y$.)
(b)   False. For example, $3 \mid (7 + 2)$ but $3 \nmid 7$ and $3 \nmid 2$. [How does this compare with Theorem 5-1, part (a)?]
(c)   False. For example, $9 \nmid 21$, but $3 \mid 21$.

Divisibility Tests

The properties of divisibility are helpful in determining whether one number is divisible by another. For example, to determine if 187 is divisible by 17 without performing the actual division, first find a number close to 187 known to be divisible by 17. The number 170 is divisible by 17. Now, $187 = 170 + 17$. Since both 170 and 17 are divisible by 17, it follows that their sum, 187, is divisible by 17.

Similar procedures can be used to investigate divisibility by 2. Consider the number 358 whose expanded form is $3 \cdot 10^2 + 5 \cdot 10 + 8$. Since $2 \mid 10$, then $2 \mid 10^2$ and $2 \mid 5 \cdot 10$. Likewise, $2 \mid 10^2$ implies that $2 \mid 3 \cdot 10^2$. Hence, $2 \mid (3 \cdot 10^2 + 5 \cdot 10)$. Now, since $358 = (3 \cdot 10^2 + 5 \cdot 10) + 8$ and $2 \mid 8$, it follows that the sum $[(3 \cdot 10^2 + 5 \cdot 10) + 8]$ is divisible by 2; that is, $2 \mid 358$. In general, the following divisibility test holds.

| Divisibility Test for 2 | A number is divisible by 2 if and only if the units digit of the number is divisible by 2. |

There are similar tests for divisibility by 5 and 10. The tests follow from the fact that the only positive integers that divide 10, other than 1 and 2, are 5 and 10.

| Divisibility Test for 5 | A number is divisible by 5 if and only if the units digit of the number is divisible by 5; that is, the units digit is 0 or 5. |

| Divisibility Test for 10 | A number is divisible by 10 if and only if the units digit is divisible by 10; that is, the units digit is 0. |

Other one-digit numbers that divide powers of 10 are 4 and 8. To develop a divisibility rule for 4, consider any four-digit number n such that $n = a \cdot 10^3 + b \cdot 10^2 + c \cdot 10 + d$. The first step is to write the given number as a sum of two numbers, one of which is as great as possible and divisible by 4. Notice that $4 \nmid 10$ but $4 \mid 10^2$. Consequently, $4 \mid 10 \cdot 10^2$; that is, $4 \mid 10^3$. Now, $4 \mid 10^2$ implies $4 \mid b \cdot 10^2$, and $4 \mid 10^3$ implies $4 \mid a \cdot 10^3$. Finally, $4 \mid a \cdot 10^3$ and $4 \mid b \cdot 10^2$ imply $4 \mid (a \cdot 10^3 + b \cdot 10^2)$. Since $4 \mid (a \cdot 10^3 + b \cdot 10^2)$, the divisibility of $a \cdot 10^3 + b \cdot 10^2 + c \cdot 10 + d$ by 4 depends upon the divisibility of $(c \cdot 10 + d)$ by 4. If $4 \mid (c \cdot 10 + d)$, then 4 divides the given number, n. If $4 \nmid (c \cdot 10 + d)$, then 4 does not divide the given number n. Notice that $c \cdot 10 + d$ is the number represented by the last two digits in the given number, n.

| Divisibility Test for 4 | A number is divisible by 4 if and only if the last two digits of the number represent a number divisible by 4. |

To investigate divisibility by 8, note that the least positive power of 10 divisible by 8 is 10^3. Consequently, all integral powers of 10 greater than 10^3 are divisible by 8. Hence, the following is a divisibility test for 8.

| Divisibility Test for 8 | A number is divisible by 8 if and only if the last three digits of the number represent a number divisible by 8. |

Example 5-4

(a) Determine whether or not 97 128 is divisible by 2, 4, and 8.
(b) Determine whether or not 83 026 is divisible by 2, 4, and 8.

Solution

(a) $2 \mid 97\ 128$ since $2 \mid 8$.   (b) $2 \mid 83\ 026$ since $2 \mid 6$.
       $4 \mid 97\ 128$ since $4 \mid 28$. $4 \nmid 83\ 026$ since $4 \nmid 26$.
       $8 \mid 97\ 128$ since $8 \mid 128$. $8 \nmid 83\ 026$ since $8 \nmid 026$.

Next we consider a divisibility test for 3. We illustrate the procedure on the number 5721; that is, $5 \cdot 10^3 + 7 \cdot 10^2 + 2 \cdot 10 + 1$. No power of 10 is divisible by 3, but there are numbers close to powers of 10 that are divisible by 3. The numbers 9, 99, 999, and so on are such numbers. Although it is not yet possible to determine whether 5721, or $5 \cdot 10^3 + 7 \cdot 10^2 + 2 \cdot 10 + 1$ is divisible by 3, the number $5 \cdot 999 + 7 \cdot 99 + 2 \cdot 9$ is close to 5721 and is divisible by 3. (Why?) Next, look for a number, x, to make the following equation true.

$$5721 = 5 \cdot 10^3 + 7 \cdot 10^2 + 2 \cdot 10 + 1 = (5 \cdot 999 + 7 \cdot 99 + 2 \cdot 9) + x$$

What must be added to $5 \cdot 999$ to obtain $5 \cdot 10^3$? Since $5 \cdot 10^3 = 5 \cdot 1000 = 5(999 + 1) = 5 \cdot 999 + 5 \cdot 1$, the answer is 5. Similarly, $7 \cdot 10^2 = 7 \cdot 100 = 7(99 + 1) = 7 \cdot 99 + 7 \cdot 1$, and $2 \cdot 10 = 2 \cdot (9 + 1) = 2 \cdot 9 + 2 \cdot 1$. Thus, the number x is $5 \cdot 1 + 7 \cdot 1 + 2 \cdot 1 + 1$ or $5 + 7 + 2 + 1$. Consequently

$$5721 = 5 \cdot 10^3 + 7 \cdot 10^2 + 2 \cdot 10 + 1$$
$$= (5 \cdot 999 + 7 \cdot 99 + 2 \cdot 9) + (5 + 7 + 2 + 1)$$

Since the sum in the first set of parentheses is divisible by 3, the divisibility of 5721 by 3 depends upon the sum in the second set of parentheses. In this case, $5 + 7 + 2 + 1 = 15$ and $3 \,|\, 15$. Thus, $3 \,|\, [(5 \cdot 999 + 7 \cdot 99 + 2 \cdot 9) + (5 + 7 + 2 + 1)]$, that is, $3 \,|\, 5721$. Thus, to test 5721 for divisibility by 3, simply test $5 + 7 + 2 + 1$. Notice that $5 + 7 + 2 + 1$ is the sum of the digits of 5721. The example suggests the following test for divisibility by 3.

Divisibility Test for 3 | A number is divisible by 3 if and only if the sum of its digits is divisible by 3.

The argument used to demonstrate that $3 \,|\, 5721$ can be used to prove the divisibility by 3 test for an integer with any number of digits and in particular for any four-digit number n such that $n = a \cdot 10^3 + b \cdot 10^2 + c \cdot 10 + d$. Even though $a \cdot 10^3 + b \cdot 10^2 + c \cdot 10 + d$ is not necessarily divisible by 3, the number $a \cdot 999 + b \cdot 99 + c \cdot 9$ is close to n and *is* divisible by 3.

$$a \cdot 10^3 = a \cdot 1000 = a(999 + 1) = a \cdot 999 + a \cdot 1$$

$$b \cdot 10^2 = b \cdot 100 = b(99 + 1) = b \cdot 99 + b \cdot 1$$

$$c \cdot 10^1 = c \cdot 10 = c(9 + 1) = c \cdot 9 + c \cdot 1$$

Thus, $n = a \cdot 10^3 + b \cdot 10^2 + c \cdot 10 + d = (a \cdot 999 + b \cdot 99 + c \cdot 9) + (a + b + c + d)$. Since $3 \,|\, 9$, $3 \,|\, 99$, and $3 \,|\, 999$, it follows that $3 \,|\, (a \cdot 999 + b \cdot 99 + c \cdot 9)$. If $3 \,|\, (a + b + c + d)$, then $3 \,|\, [(a \cdot 999 + b \cdot 99 + c \cdot 9) + (a + b + c + d)]$, that is, $3 \,|\, n$. If, on the other hand, $3 \nmid (a + b + c + d)$, it follows that $3 \nmid n$.

Since $9 \,|\, 9$, $9 \,|\, 99$, $9 \,|\, 999$, and so on, a test similar to that for divisibility by 3 applies to divisibility by 9.

Divisibility Test for 9

A number is divisible by 9 if and only if the sum of the digits of the number is divisible by 9.

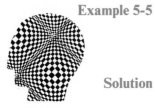

Example 5-5

Use divisibility tests to determine whether or not each of the following numbers is divisible by 3 and divisible by 9.

(a)   1002   (b)   14 238

Solution

(a)   Since $1 + 0 + 0 + 2 = 3$ and $3\,|\,3$ but $9 \nmid 3$, it follows that $3\,|\,1002$, but $9 \nmid 1002$.

(b)   Since $1 + 4 + 2 + 3 + 8 = 18$ and $3\,|\,18$, it follows that $3\,|\,14\ 238$. Since $9\,|\,18$, it follows that $9\,|\,14\ 238$.

BRAIN TEASER

After a sixth-grade teacher finished explaining the divisibility rule by 4, Judy, one of the better students, declared that she had an easier test. Add the last digit to twice the preceding digit of the tested number and check the new number for divisibility by 4. According to Judy's rule, to test 7192 for divisibility by 4, form the number $2 + 2 \cdot 9$ or 20. Since 20 is divisible by 4, so is 7192. To test 84 786 for divisibility by 4 using Judy's rule, form the number $6 + 2 \cdot 8$ or 22. Since 22 is not divisible by 4, neither is 84 786. Prove that Judy's rule works for any four-digit number.

To develop a test for divisibility by 11, consider a five-digit number n such that $n = a \cdot 10^4 + b \cdot 10^3 + c \cdot 10^2 + d \cdot 10 + e$. Since 11 does not divide any power of 10, look for numbers close to powers of 10 that are divisible by 11.

Since $11\,|\,11$, we have $11\,|\,(10^1 + 1)$, and thus, $11\,|\,10(10^1 + 1)$, or $11\,|\,(10^2 + 10)$. Now, $11\,|\,(10^2 + 10)$ and $11\,|\,11$ imply $11\,|\,(10^2 + 10 - 11)$ or $11\,|\,(10^2 - 1)$. Similarly, $11\,|\,(10^2 - 1)$ implies $11\,|\,10(10^2 - 1)$ or $11\,|\,(10^3 - 10)$. Now, $11\,|\,(10^3 - 10)$ and $11\,|\,11$ imply $11\,|\,(10^3 - 10 + 11)$ or $11\,|\,(10^3 + 1)$. Similarly, $11\,|\,(10^4 - 1)$.

Even though $a \cdot 10^4 + b \cdot 10^3 + c \cdot 10^2 + d \cdot 10 + e$ is not necessarily divisible by 11, the number $a(10^4 - 1) + b(10^3 + 1) + c(10^2 - 1) + d(10 + 1)$ is divisible by 11. Next, look for a number, x, to make the equation below true.

$$a \cdot 10^4 + b \cdot 10^3 + c \cdot 10^2 + d \cdot 10 + e$$
$$= a\,(10^4 - 1) + b\,(10^3 + 1) + c\,(10^2 - 1) + d(10 + 1) + x$$

It is left as an exercise to show that x is $a - b + c - d + e$. Thus, n is divisible by 11 if and only if $11\,|\,(a - b + c - d + e)$, or $11\,|\,[(a + c + e) - (b + d)]$. In general, the following test applies for divisibility by 11.

Divisibility Test for 11

A number is divisible by 11 if and only if the sum of the digits in the odd-powered positions minus the sum of the digits in the even-powered positions is divisible by 11.

Example 5-6

Test each of the following numbers for divisibility by 11.

(a)   964 194   (b)   7 803 569

Solution   (a) $4 + 1 + 6 - (9 + 4 + 9) =\ ^-11$. Since $11 \mid\ ^-11$, $11 \mid 964\ 194$.
             (b) $9 + 5 + 0 + 7 - (6 + 3 + 8) = 4$. Since $11 \nmid 4$, $11 \nmid 7\ 803\ 569$.

PROBLEM SET 5-1

1. Classify each of the following as true or false.
    (a)   6 is a factor of 30   (b)   6 is a divisor of 30   (c) $6 \mid 30$
    (d)   30 is divisible by 6   (e)   30 is a multiple of 6   (f)   6 is a multiple of 30
2. Use part (a) of Theorem 5-1 to complete each of the following sentences. Assume a, b, and d are integers with $d \neq 0$. Simplify your answers, if possible.
    (a)   If $7 \mid 14$ and $7 \mid 21$, then _____.
    (b)   If $d \mid (213 - 57)$ and $d \mid 57$, then _____.
    (c)   If $d \mid (a - b)$ and $d \mid b$, then _____.
3. For each of the following, state the theorems that justify the given statements assuming a, b, and c are integers. If a statement cannot be justified by one of the theorems in this section, answer "none."
    (a) $4 \mid 20$ implies $4 \mid 113 \cdot 20$.
    (b) $4 \mid 100$ and $4 \nmid 13$ imply $4 \nmid (100 + 13)$.
    (c) $4 \mid 100$ and $4 \nmid 13$ imply $4 \nmid 1300$.
    (d) $3 \mid (a + b)$ and $3 \nmid c$ imply $3 \nmid (a + b + c)$.
    (e) $3 \mid a$ implies $3 \mid a^2$.
4. Classify each of the following as true or false assuming a, b, c, and d are integers with $d \neq 0$. If a statement is true, justify it; if it is false, give a counterexample.
    (a)   If $d \mid (a + b)$, then $d \mid a$ and $d \mid b$.   (b)   If $d \mid (a + b)$, then $d \mid a$ or $d \mid b$.
    (c)   If $d \mid a$ and $d \mid b$, then $d \mid ab$.   (d)   If $d \mid ab$, then $d \mid a$ or $d \mid b$.
    (e)   If $ab \mid c$, $a \neq 0$, and $b \neq 0$, then $a \mid c$ and $b \mid c$.   (f) $1 \mid a$
    (g) $d \mid 0$
5. Prove or disprove the following where a, b, d are integers and $d \neq 0$.
    (a)   If $d \mid a$ and $d \mid b$, then $d \mid (13a + 21b)$.
    (b)   If $d \mid a$ and $d \mid b$, then for all integers m and n, $d \mid (ma + nb)$.
6. For each of the following devise a test for divisibility by the given number.
    (a)   16   (b)   25
7. Classify each of the following as true or false.
    (a)   If every digit of a number is divisible by 3, the number itself is divisible by 3.
    (b)   If a number is divisible by 3, then every digit of the number is divisible by 3.
    (c)   A number is divisible by 3 if and only if every digit of the number is divisible by 3.
    (d)   If a number is divisible by 6, then it is divisible by 2 and by 3.
    (e)   If a number is divisible by 2 and 3, then it is divisible by 6.
    (f)   If a number is divisible by 2 and 4, then it is divisible by 8.
    (g)   If a number is divisible by 8, then it is divisible by 2 and 4.
8. Devise divisibility tests for 6, 12, and 15.
9. The following is a test for divisibility by 7. A number is divisible by 7 if and only if the difference between the number represented by crossing out the last digit and the number that

is twice the last digit is divisible by 7. For example, to test 2198 for divisibility by 7, repeat the test as many times as necessary.

7 | 2198 if and only if 7 | (219 − 2 · 8), that is, if and only if 7 | 203

Now, 7 | 203 if and only if 7 | (20 − 2 · 3); that is, if and only if 7 | 14. But, 7 | 14 is true, and hence, 7 | 2198.
Test each of the following numbers for divisibility by 7:
    (a)   805   (b)   6405   (c)   2002   (d)   20 002

10. Test each of the following numbers for divisibility by 2, 3, 4, 5, 6, 7, 8, 9, 10, 11, 12, and 15.
    (a)   746 988   (b)   81 342   (c)   15 810   (d)   183 324
    (e)   901 815   (f)   4 201 012   (g)   1001   (h)   10 001

11. Answer each of the following and justify your answer.
    (a)   If a number is not divisible by 5, can it be divisible by 10?
    (b)   If a number is not divisibly by 10, can it be divisible by 5?

12. Fill each blank with the greatest digit that makes the statement true.
    (a)   3 | 74_   (b)   9 | 83_45   (c)   11 | 6_55

13. A number in which each digit except 0 appears exactly three times is divisible by 3. For example, 777 555 222 and 414 143 313 are divisible by 3. Explain why this statement is true.

14. The following is another method for testing divisiblity by 3. To test whether 279 017 152 is divisible by 3, cross out 2 and 7, since their sum, 9, is divisible by 3. Then, cross out 9 and 0, since each is divisible by 3. Next, we cross out 1, 7, and 1, since their sum, 9, is divisible by 3. The remaining digits are 5 and 2. Their sum is 5 + 2, or 7, which is not divisible by 3. Thus, 279 017 152 is not divisible by 3. Try this test with other numbers, and explain why the procedure always works.

15. Complete the details of the proof for divisibility by 11.

★16. Prove each of the following.
    (a)   Theorem 5-1   (b)   Theorem 5-2   (c)   Theorem 5-3   (d)   Theorem 5-4

★17. Prove the test for divisibility by 9 for any five-digit number.

★18. Prove the test for divisibility by 2 for any number n, such that

$$n = a_k 10^k + a_{k-1} 10^{k-1} + \cdots + a_3 10^3 + a_2 10^2 + a_1 10 + a_0.$$

19. Do Problems 10, 43, 44, 74, 93, and 94 appearing in Appendix II.

5-2 PRIME AND COMPOSITE NUMBERS

prime numbers

composites

Some numbers like 7 and 13 have exactly two distinct positive factors, namely, 1 and themselves. Such numbers are called **prime numbers** or **primes.** Numbers like 6 and 10 that have a positive factor other than 1 and themselves are called **composites.** The number 1 has only one positive factor and, therefore, is neither prime nor composite. (Problem 12 in Problem Set 5-2 is concerned with why the number 1 is not included among the prime numbers.) The first ten primes are 2, 3, 5, 7, 11, 13, 17, 19, 23, and 29.

Example 5-7 | Show that each of the following numbers is composite.

(a)　1564　　(b)　2781　　(c)　1001

Solution | (a)　Since $2\,|\,4$, 1564 is divisible by 2.
(b)　Since $3\,|\,(2 + 7 + 8 + 1)$, 2781 is divisible by 3.
(c)　Since $11\,|\,[(1 + 0) - (0 + 1)]$, 1001 is divisible by 11.

Composite numbers can be expressed as a product of two or more lesser whole numbers. For example, $18 = 2 \cdot 9$, or $18 = 3 \cdot 6$, or $18 = 2 \cdot 3 \cdot 3$. Each **factorization** expression of 18 as a product of factors is called a **factorization.** A factoriza-**prime factorization** tion containing only prime numbers is called **prime factorization.** To find the prime factorization of a given composite number, first rewrite the number as a product of two smaller numbers. Continue the process, factoring the lesser numbers until it is impossible to factor anymore, that is, until all factors are primes. For example, consider 260.

$$260 = 26 \cdot 10 = 2 \cdot 13 \cdot 2 \cdot 5 = 2 \cdot 2 \cdot 5 \cdot 13 = 2^2 \cdot 5 \cdot 13$$

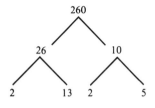

The procedure for finding the prime factorization of a number can be **FIGURE 5-1　factor tree** organized using a model called a **factor tree.** A factor tree is demonstrated in Figure 5-1. Notice that the last branches of the tree display the prime factors of 260.

The factorization of 260, or any other composite number, can be started in different ways. A second way for factoring 260 is shown in Figure 5-2. The two trees produced the same prime factorization, except for the order in which the primes appear in the products. In general, the prime factorization of a number is unique. The Fundamental Theorem of Arithmetic, sometimes called the Unique Factorization Theorem, states this fact.

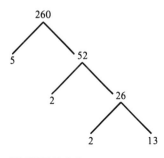

FIGURE 5-2

THEOREM 5-5 | **Fundamental Theorem of Arithmetic**　Each composite number has one and only one prime factorization.

Normally, the primes in the prime factorization of a number are listed in increasing order from left to right. If a prime appears in a product more than once, exponential notation is used. Thus, $13 \cdot 2 \cdot 2 \cdot 2 \cdot 5 \cdot 5 \cdot 5 \cdot 7$ is customarily written $2^3 \cdot 5^3 \cdot 7 \cdot 13$.

In determining the factorization of a number such as 8127, observe that $9\,|\,8127$. Thus, $9k = 8127$. Since $9k = 8127$, then k is a factor of 8127 and $k = 8127/9$. Theorem 5-6 states the general case.

THEOREM 5-6   If d is a factor of n, where $n \neq 0$ and $d \neq 0$, then n/d is a factor of n.

Remark   Sometimes $n/d = d$. For example, 7 is a factor of 49 and so is $49/7$.

To determine if a number n is composite, use Theorem 5-6. Suppose p is the *smallest* prime factor of the number n. If n is prime, then $p = n$, but if n is composite, then $p \leq n/p$. Thus, $p^2 \leq n$. This idea is summarized by the following theorem.

THEOREM 5-7   If n is composite, then n has a prime factor p such that $p^2 \leq n$.

Using Theorem 5-7, it is possible to determine whether a given number is prime or composite. Consider, for example, the number 109. If 109 is composite, it must have a prime divisor p such that $p^2 \leq 109$. Now, the primes whose squares do not exceed 109, are 2, 3, 5, and 7. Checking for divisibility by these primes reveals that $2 \nmid 109$, $3 \nmid 109$, $5 \nmid 109$, and $7 \nmid 109$. Hence, 109 is prime. The argument used leads to the following theorem.

THEOREM 5-8   If n is an integer greater than 1 such that n is not divisible by any prime p such that $p^2 \leq n$, then n is a prime.

Example 5-8   Is 397 composite or prime?

Solution   The possible primes, p, such that $p^2 \leq 397$, are 2, 3, 5, 7, 11, 13, 17, and 19. Since $2 \nmid 397$, $3 \nmid 397$, $5 \nmid 397$, $7 \nmid 397$, $11 \nmid 397$, $13 \nmid 397$, $17 \nmid 397$, and $19 \nmid 397$, the number 397 is prime.

One way to find all the primes less than a given number is to use the Sieve of Eratosthenes, named after the Greek mathematician Eratosthenes (200 B.C.). If all the natural numbers greater than 1 are considered (or placed in the sieve), the numbers that are not prime are methodically crossed out (or drop through the holes of the sieve). The remaining numbers are prime. The procedure is presented here from *Heath Mathematics,* 1979, Grade 6. We leave it as an exercise to work through the student page and to explain why, after crossing out all the multiples of 2, 3, 5, and 7, the remaining numbers in the sieve are primes.

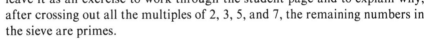

CHAPTER CHALLENGE

Eratosthenes, an ancient Greek mathematician, invented a way to find prime numbers. It is called the Sieve of Eratosthenes.

Follow these steps to make your own sieve.

1. Make a number table as shown.

2. Cross off all multiples of 2 except 2.

3. 3 is the next number that is not crossed off. Cross off all multiples of 3 except 3.

4. What is the next number that is not crossed off? Cross off all multiples of that number except the number itself.

5. Repeat step 4 until no more numbers can be crossed off. The numbers not crossed off are prime numbers.

	2	3	4	5	6	7	8	9	10
11	12	13	14	15	16	17	18	19	20
21	22	23	24	25	26	27	28	29	30
31	32	33	34	35	36	37	38	39	40
41	42	43	44	45	46	47	48	49	50
51	52	53	54	55	56	57	58	59	60
61	62	63	64	65	66	67	68	69	70
71	72	73	74	75	76	77	78	79	80
81	82	83	84	85	86	87	88	89	90
91	92	93	94	95	96	97	98	99	100

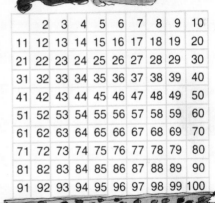

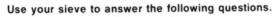

Use your sieve to answer the following questions.

6. What is the greatest prime number that is less than 100?

7. How many prime numbers are less than 100?

8. **Twin primes** are prime numbers that have a difference of 2. List the twin primes that are less than 100.

More about Primes

There are infinitely many whole numbers, infinitely many odd numbers, and infinitely many even numbers. Are there infinitely many primes? Since prime numbers do not appear in any known pattern, the answer to this question is not obvious. Euclid was first to prove that there are infinitely many primes (see Problem Set 5-2, problem 17).

For centuries, mathematicians have looked for a formula that produces only primes, but no one has ever found one. One such attempt resulted in the expression $n^2 - n + 41$, where n is a whole number. Substituting 0, 1, 2, 3, and so on up to 40 for n in the expression always results in a prime number. However, substituting 41 for n gives $41^2 - 41 + 41$ or 41^2, a composite number.

Mersenne primes   Prime numbers of the form $2^p - 1$, where p is a prime, are called **Mersenne primes** after the French mathematician Marin Mersenne (1588–1648). One of the largest known primes, which is a Mersenne prime, was discovered at the University of Illinois. It has 3376 digits and can be written in the form $2^{11\,213} - 1$. To realize just how great this number is, note that 2^{64} grains of wheat is more wheat than has ever been produced in the history of the world. The University of Illinois advertised the discovery on its postal meter (Figure 5-3).

FIGURE 5-3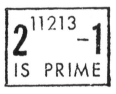

Until recently, the largest known prime was $2^{19\,937} - 1$, found in 1971 by Bryant Tuckerman of IBM. However, in 1978, two high school students, Laura Nickel and Curt Noll, from Hayward, California found a larger prime, namely, $2^{23\,209} - 1$. Other primes have been discovered recently with a computer.

There are many interesting problems concerning primes. Christian Goldbach (1690–1764) asserted that: "Every even number greater than 2 is **Goldbach's Conjecture**   the sum of two primes." This statement is known as **Goldbach's Conjecture.** For example, $4 = 2 + 2$, $6 = 3 + 3$, $8 = 3 + 5$, $10 = 3 + 7$, $12 = 5 + 7$, and $14 = 3 + 11$. In spite of the simplicity of the statement, no one knows for sure whether or not the statement is true.

PROBLEM SET 5-2

1. Use a factor tree to find the prime factorization for each of the following.
   (a) 504   (b) 2475   (c) 11 250
2. Which of the following numbers are primes?
   (a) 149   (b) 923   (c) 433
3. What is the greatest prime you must consider to test whether or not 5669 is prime?
4. Explain why, in the Sieve of Eratosthenes on page 189, after crossing out all the multiples of 2, 3, 5, and 7, the remaining numbers are primes.
5. Use the Sieve of Eratosthenes to find all primes less than 200.
6. (a) Find a composite number different from 41^2 that is of the form $n^2 - n + 41$.
   ★(b) Prove that there are infinitely many composite numbers of the form $n^2 - n + 41$.
7. Find the least number divisible by each natural number less than or equal to 12.
8. The primes 2 and 3 are consecutive integers. Is there another pair of consecutive integers both of which are prime? Justify your answer.

twin primes 9. The prime numbers 11 and 13 are called **twin primes** because they differ by 2. Find all the twin primes less than 200. (The existence of infinitely many twin primes has not been proved.)

10. (a) Use the Fundamental Theorem of Arithmetic to justify that if $2|n$ and $3|n$, then $6|n$.
    (b) Is it always true that if $a|n$ and $b|n$, then $ab|n^2$? Either prove the statement or give a counterexample.
11. (a) Is it always true that if $3|ab$, then $3|a$ or $3|b$?
    (b) Is it always true that if $4|ab$, then $4|a$ or $4|b$?
12. Show that if 1 were considered a prime, every number would have more than one prime factorization.
13. Denoting $3 \cdot 2 \cdot 1$ by 3!, $4 \cdot 3 \cdot 2 \cdot 1$ by 4! and, in general, $n \cdot (n - 1) \cdot \ldots \cdot 3 \cdot 2 \cdot 1$ by n!, show each of the following.
    (a) $5! + 2$, $5! + 3$, $5! + 4$, $5! + 5$ is a sequence of four consecutive composite numbers.
    (b) $11! + 2$, $11! + 3$, $11! + 4$, $\ldots$, $11! + 11$ is a sequence of 10 consecutive composite numbers.
★14. Use the ideas from Problem 13 to write each of the following.
    (a) A sequence of 20 consecutive composite numbers
    (b) A sequence of n consecutive composite numbers
15. (a) Find all the positive divisors of 2^8.
    (b) Find all the positive divisors of 3^5.
    (c) How many positive divisors does $2^8 \cdot 3^5$ have?
    ★(d) If p and q are primes, how many divisors does $p^k q^m$ have?
★16. If $d_1, d_2, d_3, \ldots, d_k$ are all the positive divisors of n and are written in an increasing order, then
    (i) n/d_1, n/d_2, n/d_3, $\ldots$, n/d_k are all the positive divisors of n written in a decreasing order.
    (ii) $(d_1 d_2 d_3 \ldots d_k)^2 = n^k$
    (a) Illustrate the assertions (i) and (ii) if $n = 12$.
    (b) Prove assertions (i) and (ii).
★17. Complete the details for the following proof, which shows that there are infinitely many prime numbers.

If the number of primes is finite, then there is a greatest prime denoted by p. Consider the product of all the primes, $2 \cdot 3 \cdot 5 \cdot \ldots \cdot p$, and let $N = (2 \cdot 3 \cdot 5 \cdot \ldots \cdot p) + 1$. Since $N > p$, where p is the greatest prime, N is composite. Since N is composite, there is a prime, q, among the primes $2, 3, 5, \ldots, p$ such that $q \mid N$. However, none of the primes $2, 3, 5, \ldots, p$ divides N. (Why?)

Consequently, $q \nmid N$, which is a contradiction. Thus, the assumption that there are finitely many primes is false and the set of primes must be infinite.

18. Do Problems 47, 88, 89, and 96 appearing in Appendix II.

BRAIN TEASER

Consider the factorization of numbers in the set, E, of even counting numbers, $\{2, 4, 6, 8, 10, \ldots\}$. In this set, there are numbers that cannot be written as products of other numbers in the set. For example, 6 is not a product of two other elements of the set ($6 = 2 \cdot 3$, but 3 is not in E). A number in E that cannot be written as a product of other numbers in E is called an E-prime. A number in E that can be written as a product of numbers in E is called an E-composite.

(a) List the first 10 E-primes.

(b) Find an even number whose E-prime factorization is not unique, that is, an even number that can be factored into a product of E-primes in more than one way.

(c) Find a test for determining whether or not an even number is an E-prime.

5-3   GREATEST COMMON DIVISOR AND LEAST COMMON MULTIPLE

greatest common divisor (GCD)

The **greatest common divisor (GCD)** of two numbers is the greatest divisor or factor that the two numbers have in common. To find the GCD of two given numbers, first find the set of all the positive divisors of the first and second numbers, then find the set of all the common divisors, and, finally, pick the greatest element in that set. For example, to find the GCD of 20 and 32, denote the sets of the divisors of 20 and 32 by D_{20} and D_{32}, respectively.

$D_{20} = \{1, 2, 4, 5, 10, 20\}$

$D_{32} = \{1, 2, 4, 8, 16, 32\}$

The set of all common positive divisors of 20 and 32 is as follows.

$$D_{20} \cap D_{32} = \{1, 2, 4\}$$

Since the greatest number in the set of common positive divisors is 4, the GCD of 20 and 32 is 4, written GCD$(20, 32) = 4$.

The method for finding the GCD of two numbers just described, called the *intersection of sets method,* is rather time consuming and tedious if the numbers have many divisors. Another, more efficient, method involves finding the prime factorization of each number. To find the GCD$(180, 168)$, first notice that $180 = 2 \cdot 2 \cdot 3 \cdot 3 \cdot 5$ and $168 = 2 \cdot 2 \cdot 2 \cdot 3 \cdot 7$. Place these two numbers in such a way that the common prime factors correspond.

$$180 = 2 \cdot 2 \cdot 3 \cdot 3 \cdot 5$$
$$\updownarrow \quad \updownarrow \qquad \updownarrow$$
$$168 = 2 \cdot 2 \cdot 2 \cdot 3 \cdot 7$$

The greatest common factor is $2 \cdot 2 \cdot 3$, that is, GCD$(180, 168) = 2 \cdot 2 \cdot 3 = 12$. Notice that $180 = 2^2 \cdot 3^2 \cdot 5$, $168 = 2^3 \cdot 3 \cdot 7$, and GCD$(180, 168) = 2^2 \cdot 3$. Thus, to find the GCD of numbers, first find the prime factorizations of the given numbers, then take each of the primes that are common factors of the given numbers. The GCD is the product of these primes, each raised to the lowest power of that prime that occurs in either of the prime factorizations.

Example 5-9	Find each of the following.

    (a) GCD$(108, 72)$
    (b) GCD(x, y) if $x = 2^3 \cdot 7^2 \cdot 11 \cdot 13$ and $y = 2 \cdot 7^3 \cdot 13 \cdot 17$.
    (c) GCD(x, y, z) if $z = 2^2 \cdot 7$, using x and y from part (b).

Solution

    (a) Since $108 = 2^2 \cdot 3^3$ and $72 = 2^3 \cdot 3^2$, it follows that GCD$(108, 72) = 2^2 \cdot 3^2 = 36$.
    (b) GCD$(x, y) = 2 \cdot 7^2 \cdot 13 = 1274$.
    (c) Since $x = 2^3 \cdot 7^2 \cdot 11 \cdot 13$, $y = 2 \cdot 7^3 \cdot 13 \cdot 17$, and $z = 2^2 \cdot 7$, then GCD$(x, y, z) = 2 \cdot 7 = 14$. Notice that GCD$(x, y, z)$ also can be obtained by finding the GCD of z and 1274, and the answer from part (b).

If the prime factorization technique is applied to finding GCD$(4, 9)$, the result is that 4 and 9 have no common prime factors. Consequently, 1 is the only common divisor, so GCD$(4, 9) = 1$. Numbers such as 4 and 9 whose **relatively prime**   GCD is 1 are called **relatively prime**.

Some numbers are hard to factor. For these numbers a third method, **Euclidean Algorithm**   called the **Euclidean Algorithm,** is more efficient for finding the GCD. Consider GCD$(975, 105)$. According to the division algorithm (Chapter 3) $975 = 9 \cdot 105 + 30$. Every common divisor of 975 and 105 must also be a divisor of 30 since $30 = 975 - 9 \cdot 105$. Thus, every common divisor of 975 and 105 is also a divisor of 105 and 30. Conversely, every common divisor of 30 and 105 must be a divisor of 975. Consequently, the set of all common divisors of 975 and 105 equals the set of all common divisors of 105 and 30. Since the sets of common divisors are equal, the greatest elements from each set must be equal. Thus, $GCD(975, 105) = GCD(105, 30)$. Since 30 is the remainder when 975 is divided by 105, the procedure outlined above illustrates the following theorem.

THEOREM 5-9

> If a and b are any whole numbers and $a \geq b$, then $GCD(a, b) = GCD(b, r)$, where r is the remainder when a is divided by b.

The Euclidean Algorithm is the procedure of finding the GCD of two numbers a and b using the idea of Theorem 5-9. The method consists of performing successive divisions. For example, to find GCD (1804, 328), first perform the following division.

$$\begin{array}{r} 5 \\ 328 \overline{)\ 1804} \\ \underline{1640} \\ 164 \end{array}$$

Thus, $1804 = 5 \cdot 328 + 164$ and, by Theorem 5-9, GCD (1804, 328) = GCD (328, 164). Apply Theorem 5-9 again, performing the following division.

$$\begin{array}{r} 2 \\ 164 \overline{)\ 328} \\ \underline{328} \\ 0 \end{array}$$

Therefore, $328 = 2 \cdot 164 + 0$, and hence, GCD (328, 164) = GCD (164, 0) = 164. Consequently, GCD (1804, 328) = 164. Notice that in performing the divisions, the values of the remainders decrease. Eventually, one of the remainders must be 0 and the algorithm stops because, for any positive integer a, GCD $(a, 0) = a$.

Example 5-10

Use the Euclidean Algorithm to find GCD (10 764, 2300).

Solution

$$\begin{array}{r} 4 \\ 2300 \overline{)\ 10764} \\ \underline{9200} \\ 1564 \end{array}$$

$$\begin{array}{r} 1 \\ 1564\overline{)2300} \\ \underline{1564} \\ 736 \end{array}$$

$$\begin{array}{r} 2 \\ 736\overline{)1564} \\ \underline{1472} \\ 92 \end{array}$$

$$\begin{array}{r} 8 \\ 92\overline{)736} \\ \underline{736} \\ 0 \end{array}$$

Since the last nonzero remainder is 92, GCD (10 764, 2300) = 92.

Remark   The procedure for the Euclidean Algorithm can be stopped at any step at which the GCD is obvious.

Another useful number theory concept is least common multiple. This concept is useful for determining the least common denominator of two fractions. The **least common multiple (LCM)** of two natural numbers is the least positive multiple that the two numbers have in common. To find the LCM of two given natural numbers, first find the set of all positive multiples of both the first and second numbers, then find the set of all common multiples of both numbers, and, finally, pick the least element in that set. For example, to find the LCM of 8 and 12, denote the sets of positive multiples of 8 and 12 by M_8 and M_{12}, respectively.

least common multiple (LCM)

$M_8 = \{8, 16, 24, 32, 40, 48, 56, 64, 72, \dots\}$

$M_{12} = \{12, 24, 36, 48, 60, 72, 84, 96, 108, \dots\}$

The set of common multiples is as follows.

$M_8 \cap M_{12} = \{24, 48, 72, \dots\}$

Since the least number in $M_8 \cap M_{12}$ is 24, the LCM of 8 and 12 is 24, written LCM (8, 12) = 24.

The method for finding the LCM of two numbers described above is often lengthy, especially for finding the LCM of three or more natural numbers. Another, more efficient method for finding the LCM of several numbers involves prime factorization. For example, to find LCM(40, 12), first find the prime factorizations of 40 and 12, namely $2^3 \cdot 5$ and $2^2 \cdot 3$, respectively. Next, let $m = \text{LCM}(40, 12)$. Since m is a multiple of 40, it must contain both 2^3 and 5 as factors. Also, since m is a multiple of 12, it must contain 2^2 and 3 as factors. Since 2^3 is a multiple of 2^2, then $m = 2^3 \cdot 5 \cdot 3 = 120$. In general, to find the LCM of two natural numbers, first find the prime factorization of each number. Then take each of the primes that are factors of *either* of the given numbers. The LCM is the product of these primes, each raised to the largest power of that prime that occurs in either of the prime factorizations.

Example 5-11   Find the LCM of 2520 and 10 530.

Solution

$$2520 = 2^3 \cdot 3^2 \cdot 5 \cdot 7$$
$$10\ 530 = 2 \cdot 3^4 \cdot 5 \cdot 13$$
$$\text{LCM}(2520, 10\ 530) = 2^3 \cdot 3^4 \cdot 5 \cdot 7 \cdot 13$$

The similarity between the prime factorization algorithms for GCD and LCM suggests a connection. Consider the GCD and LCM of 6 and 9. Since $6 = 2 \cdot 3$ and $9 = 3^2$, it follows that GCD $(6, 9) = 3$ and LCM$(6, 9) = 18$. Notice that GCD $(6, 9) \cdot$ LCM $(6, 9) = 3 \cdot 18 = 54$. Observe that 54 is also the product of the original numbers 6 and 9. In general, for any two natural numbers a and b, the connection between their GCD and LCM is given by the following theorem.

THEOREM 5-10

For any two natural numbers a and b,

$$\text{GCD}(a, b) \cdot \text{LCM}(a, b) = ab$$

This result is useful for finding the LCM of two numbers, the prime factorization of which is not easy to find, because the GCD can be found by the Euclidean Algorithm, and the product can be found by simple multiplication.

Example 5-12   Find LCM$(731, 952)$.

Solution   By the Euclidean Algorithm, GCD $(731, 952) = 17$. By Theorem 5-10, $17 \cdot$ LCM$(731, 952) = 731 \cdot 952$. Consequently, LCM$(731, 952) = (731 \cdot 952)/17 = 40\ 936$.

It is possible to find the LCM for three or more numbers. For example, to find LCM$(12, 18, 120)$, use a method similar to the one for two numbers.

$$12 = 2^2 \cdot 3$$
$$108 = 2^2 \cdot 3^3$$
$$120 = 2^3 \cdot 3 \cdot 5$$

BRAIN TEASER

A friend tells you that his house number had three digits. If you subtract 7 from it, the result is divisible by 7. If you subtract 8 from it, the result is divisible by 8, and if you subtract 9, the result is divisible by 9. What is the number?

Consequently, $LCM(12, 18, 120) = 2^3 \cdot 3^3 \cdot 5 = 1080$.

Another procedure for finding the LCM of several natural numbers involves division by primes. For example, to find $LCM(12, 75, 120)$, start with the least prime that divides at least one of the given numbers and divide as follows.

$$2\lfloor \underline{12, 75, 120} \\ 6, 75, 60$$

Since 2 does not divide 75, simply bring down the 75. In order to obtain the LCM using this procedure, the division process is continued until the row of answers consists of relatively prime numbers.

$$2\lfloor \underline{12, 75, 120} \\ 2\lfloor \underline{6, 75, 60} \\ 2\lfloor \underline{3, 75, 30} \\ 3\lfloor \underline{3, 75, 15} \\ 5\lfloor \underline{1, 25, 5} \\ 1, 5, 1$$

Thus, $LCM(12, 75, 120) = 2 \cdot 2 \cdot 2 \cdot 3 \cdot 5 \cdot 1 \cdot 5 \cdot 1 = 2^3 \cdot 3 \cdot 5^2 = 600$.

PROBLEM SET 5-3

1. Find the GCD and the LCM for each of the following using the intersection of sets method.
   (a) 18 and 10   (b) 24 and 36   (c) 8, 24, and 52
2. Find the GCD and the LCM for each of the following using the prime factorization method.
   (a) 132 and 504   (b) 65 and 1690   (c) 900, 96, and 630
3. Find the GCD for each of the following using the Euclidean Algorithm.
   (a) 220 and 2924   (b) 14 595 and 10 856   (c) 122 368 and 123 152
4. Find the LCM for each of the following using any method.
   (a) 24 and 36   (b) 72 and 90 and 96   (c) 90 and 105 and 315
5. Find the LCM for each of the following pairs of numbers using Theorem 5-10 and the answers from Problem 3.
   (a) 220 and 2924   (b) 14 595 and 10 856   (c) 122 368 and 123 152
6. Find each of the following by using any method.
   (a) GCD(56, 72)   (b) GCD(84, 92)   (c) GCD(1804, 328)
   (d) LCM(56, 72)   (e) LCM(24, 82)   (f) LCM(963, 657)
7. (a) Find the GCD for each of the following pairs of numbers:
        50 and 51,   189 and 190,   278 and 279.
   (b) Make a conjecture based on your answers for part (a).
   ★(c) Prove or disprove your conjecture.
8. Assume a and b are any natural numbers, and answer each of the following.
   (a) If $GCD(a, b) = 1$, find $LCM(a, b)$.
   (b) Find $GCD(a, a)$ and $LCM(a, a)$.

      (c)   Find $GCD(a^2, a)$ and $LCM(a^2, a)$.

      (d)   If $a \mid b$, find $GCD(a, b)$ and $LCM(a, b)$.

      (e)   If a and b are two different primes, find $GCD(a, b)$ and $LCM\ (a, b)$.

      (f)   What is the relationship between a and b if $GCD(a, b) = a$?

      (g)   What is the relationship between a and b if $LCM(a, b) = a$?

  9.   Classify each of the following as true or false. Justify your answers.

      (a)   If $GCD(a, b) = 1$, then a and b cannot be both even.

      (b)   If $GCD(a, b) = 2$, then both a and b are even.

      (c)   If a and b are even, then $GCD(a, b) = 2$.

      (d)   For all natural numbers a and b, $LCM(a, b) \mid GCD(a, b)$.

      (e)   For all natural numbers a and b, $LCM(a, b) \mid ab$.

10.   Find $GCD(120, 75, 105)$ using the Euclidean Algorithm applied to two numbers at a time.

11.   Is it true that $GCD(a, b, c) \cdot LCM(a, b, c) = abc$? Justify your answer.

12.   Two bike riders ride around a circular path. The first rider completes one round in 12 minutes and the second rider completes it in 18 minutes. If they both start at the same place and the same time, after how many minutes will they meet again at the starting place?

13.   A pie is divided into 12 equal pieces, and another pie of the same size is divided into 9 equal pieces. If the pies are to be divided so that they each have the same number of the same size pieces, how many pieces will be in each pie?

14.   (a)   Show that 97 219 988 751 and 4 are relatively prime.

      (b)   Show that 181 345 913 and 11 are relatively prime.

      (c)   Show that 181 345 913 and 33 are relatively prime.

15.   (a)   Find all the numbers less than 13 that are relatively prime to 13.

      (b)   Suppose p is a prime; find all the numbers less than p that are relatively prime to p.

   ★(c)   If p is a prime, how many numbers exist that are less than p^2 and relatively prime to p?

16.   Find all natural numbers x such that $GCD(25, x) = 1$ and $1 \le x \le 25$.

17.   If $GCD(a, b) = 1$, what can be said about $GCD(a^2, b^2)$? Justify your answer.

18.   (a)   Make a conjecture about a relationship between $GCD(a, b)$ and $GCD(a, a + b)$ where a and b are natural numbers.

   ★(b)   Prove or disprove your conjecture in part (a).

 19.   Do problems 90, 91, and 92 appearing in Appendix II.

*5-4   CLOCK AND MODULAR ARITHMETIC

The book *Disquisitiones Arithmeticae* is among Gauss' great mathematical works. Many problems that had been attacked without success by other mathematicians were solved by Gauss for the first time in this book. In his book Gauss introduced a new topic, the theory of congruences, which very rapidly gained general acceptance and has since become a foundation for number theory. The basics of the theory of congruences can be understood in elementary school and can provide enrichment for students.

FIGURE 5-4

One type of enrichment activity involving congruences uses arithmetic of a 12-hour clock. For example, if it is 9 o'clock, what time will it be 8 hours later? It is possible to determine on the clock in Figure 5-4 that 8 hours after 9 o'clock is 5 o'clock. We record this as $9 \oplus 8 = 5$, where $\oplus$ denotes clock addition.

The answer, $9 \oplus 8 = 5$, can also be obtained by performing the regular addition $9 + 8 = 17$ and then subtracting 12 (or by dividing 17 by 12 and taking the remainder). Thus, whenever the sum of two digits on a 12-hour clock under regular addition exceeds 12, add the numbers in the regular way and then subtract 12 to obtain the answer for clock addition.

It is possible to perform other operations on the clock. For example, $2 \ominus 9$ on the clock, where $\ominus$ denotes clock subtraction, could be interpreted as the time 9 hours before 2 o'clock. Counting backward (counterclockwise) 9 units from 2 reveals that $2 \ominus 9 = 5$. If subtraction on the clock is defined in terms of addition, we have $2 \ominus 9 = x$, if and only if $2 = 9 \oplus x$. Consequently, $x = 5$.

Example 5-13

Perform each of the following computations on a 12-hour clock.

(a) $8 \oplus 8$ (b) $4 \ominus 12$ (c) $4 \ominus 4$

Solution

(a) $8 + 8 - 12 = 4$. Hence, $8 \oplus 8 = 4$.
(b) $4 \ominus 12 = 4$, since by counting forward or backward 12 hours, you arrive at the original position.
(c) $4 \ominus 4 = 12$. This should be clear by looking at the clock, but it can also be found using the definition of subtraction in terms of addition.

As with whole numbers, clock multiplication can be defined as repeated addition. For example, $2 \otimes 8 = 8 \oplus 8 = 4$, where $\otimes$ denotes clock multiplication. Similarly, $3 \otimes 5 = (5 \oplus 5) \oplus 5 = 10 \oplus 5 = 3$. As with whole numbers, clock division can be defined in terms of multiplication. For example, $8 \oslash 5 = x$, where $\oslash$ denotes clock division, if and only if $8 = 5 \otimes x$, for some x in the set $\{1, 2, 3, \ldots, 12\}$. Since $5 \otimes 4 = 8, 8 \oslash 5 = 4$.

Example 5-14

Perform the following operations on a 12-hour clock, if possible.

(a) $3 \otimes 11$ (b) $2 \oslash 7$ (c) $3 \oslash 2$ (d) $5 \oslash 12$

Solution

(a) $3 \otimes 11 = 11 \oplus 11 \oplus 11 = 10 \oplus 11 = 9$.
(b) $2 \oslash 7 = x$ if and only if $2 = 7 \otimes x$. Consequently, $x = 2$.
(c) $3 \oslash 2 = x$ if and only if $3 = 2 \otimes x$. Multiplying each of the numbers $1, 2, 3, 4, \ldots, 12$ by 2, shows that none of the multiplications yield 3.

Thus, the equation $3 = 2 \otimes x$ has no solution, and consequently, $3 \ominus 2$ is undefined.

(d) $5 \ominus 12 = x$ if and only if $5 = 12 \otimes x$. However, $12 \otimes x = 12$ for every x in the set $\{1, 2, 3, \ldots, 12\}$. Thus, $5 = 12 \otimes x$ has no solution on the clock, and, therefore, $5 \ominus 12$ is undefined.

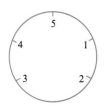

FIGURE 5-5

On a 12-hour clock, addition, subtraction, and multiplication can be performed for any two numbers but, as shown in Example 5-14, not all divisions can be performed. Division by 12, the additive identity, on a 12-hour clock can either never be performed or is not meaningful, since it does not yield a unique answer. However, there are clocks on which all divisions can be performed, except by the corresponding additive identities. One such clock is a 5-hour clock shown in Figure 5-5.

On this clock, $3 \oplus 4 = 2$, $2 \ominus 3 = 4$, $2 \otimes 4 = 3$, and $3 \oslash 4 = 2$. Since adding 5 to any number yields the original number, 5 is the additive identity for this 5-hour clock. Consequently, you might suspect that division by 5 is not possible on a 5-hour clock. To determine which divisions are possible, consider Table 5-1, a multiplication table for 5-hour clock arithmetic.

TABLE 5-1

$\otimes$	1	2	3	4	5
1	1	2	3	4	5
2	2	4	1	3	5
3	3	1	4	2	5
4	4	3	2	1	5
5	5	5	5	5	5

To find $1 \oslash 2$, write $1 \oslash 2 = x$, which is equivalent to $1 = 2 \otimes x$. The second row of the table shows that $2 \otimes 1 = 2$, $2 \otimes 2 = 4$, $2 \otimes 3 = 1$, $2 \otimes 4 = 3$, and $2 \otimes 5 = 5$. The solution of $1 = 2 \otimes x$ is $x = 3$, and hence, $1 \oslash 2 = 3$. The information given in the second row of the table can be used to determine the following divisions.

$2 \oslash 2 = 1$ since $2 = 2 \otimes 1$
$3 \oslash 2 = 4$ since $3 = 2 \otimes 4$
$4 \oslash 2 = 2$ since $4 = 2 \otimes 2$
$5 \oslash 2 = 5$ since $5 = 2 \otimes 5$

According to the table, division by 2 is always possible since every element occurs in the second row. Similarly, division by all other numbers, except 5, is always possible. In the problem set, you will be asked to perform arithmetic on different clocks and investigate for which clocks all computations, including division by numbers different from the additive identity, can be performed.

Many of the concepts for clock arithmetic can be used to work problems involving a calendar. Look at the calendar at the left. Notice that the five Sundays have dates 1, 8, 15, 22, and 29. Any two of these dates for Sunday differ by a multiple of 7. The same property is true for any other day of the week. If the second day of the month falls on Monday, then 7 days later the day will be Monday again. In fact, it will be Monday after any multiple of 7 days. For example, the second and thirtieth days fall on the same day since $30 - 2 = 28$ and 28 is a multiple of 7. We say that 30 is congruent to 2, modulo 7, and write $30 \equiv 2(\bmod\ 7)$. We need not restrict ourselves to the number 7. Since 18 and 6 differ by a multiple of 12, we write $18 \equiv 6(\bmod\ 12)$. This leads to the following definition.

April

S	M	T	W	T	F	S
1	2	3	4	5	6	7
8	9	10	11	12	13	14
15	16	17	18	19	20	21
22	23	24	25	26	27	28
29	30					

DEFINITION

> For integers a and b, **a is congruent to b modulo m,** written $a \equiv b(\bmod\ m)$, if and only if a and b differ by a multiple of m, where m is a positive integer greater than 1.

Example 5-15

Tell why each of the following is true.

(a) $23 \equiv 3(\bmod\ 10)$
(b) $23 \equiv 3(\bmod\ 4)$
(c) $23 \not\equiv 3(\bmod\ 7)$
(d) $10 \equiv {}^-1(\bmod\ 11)$

Solution

(a) $23 \equiv 3(\bmod\ 10)$, since $23 - 3$ is a multiple of 10.
(b) $23 \equiv 3(\bmod\ 4)$, since $23 - 3$ is a multiple of 4.
(c) $23 \not\equiv 3(\bmod\ 7)$, since $23 - 3$ is not a multiple of 7.
(d) $10 \equiv {}^-1(\bmod\ 11)$, since $10 - ({}^-1) = 11$ is a multiple of 11.

Example 5-16

Find all integers, x, such that $x \equiv 1(\bmod\ 10)$.

Solution

$x \equiv 1(\bmod\ 10)$, if and only if $x - 1 = 10k$, where k is any integer. Consequently, $x = 10k + 1$. Letting $k = 0, 1, 2, 3, \ldots$ yields the sequence 1, 11, 21, 31, 41, $\ldots$ Also, letting $k = {}^-1, {}^-2, {}^-3, {}^-4, \ldots$ yields the negative integers ${}^-9, {}^-19, {}^-29, {}^-39, \ldots$ The two sequences can be combined to give the following solution set.

$$\{\ldots, {}^-39, {}^-29, {}^-19, {}^-9, 1, 11, 21, 31, 41, 51, \ldots\}$$

In Example 5-16, the positive integers obtained 1, 11, 21, 31, 41, 51, . . , all differ from each other by a multiple of 10 and, hence, are congruent to each other modulo 10. Notice that each of the numbers 1, 11, 21, 31, 41, 51, . . . has a remainder of 1 when divided by 10. In general, two whole numbers are congruent modulo m if and only if their remainders, upon division by m, are the same. (This generalization can be extended to integers if the division algorithm includes division of integers.)

Many properties of equality carry over to congruence.

Property

For all integers a, b, and c,
(1) $a \equiv a (\text{mod } m)$
(2)   If $a \equiv b (\text{mod } m)$, then $b \equiv a (\text{mod } m)$.
(3)   If $a \equiv b (\text{mod } m)$, and $b \equiv c (\text{mod } m)$, then $a \equiv c (\text{mod } m)$.
(4)   If $a \equiv b (\text{mod } m)$, then $a + c \equiv b + c (\text{mod } m)$.
(5)   If $a \equiv b (\text{mod } m)$, then $ac \equiv bc (\text{mod } m)$.
(6)   If $a \equiv b (\text{mod } m)$ and $c \equiv d (\text{mod } m)$, then $ac \equiv bd (\text{mod } m)$.
(7)   If $a \equiv b (\text{mod } m)$ and k is a natural number, then $a^k \equiv b^k (\text{mod } m)$.

With the help of these properties, it is possible to solve many problems. For example, to find the remainder when 2^{96} is divided by 7, find a number less than 2^{96} that has the same remainder upon division by 7; that is, find a lesser number congruent to 2^{96} modulo 7. Since $2^3 = 8$ then $2^3 \equiv 1 (\text{mod } 7)$, and consequently, $(2^3)^{32} \equiv (1)^{32} (\text{mod } 7)$, or $2^{96} \equiv 1 (\text{mod } 7)$. Thus, 2^{96} gives remainder 1 when divided by 7.

Example 5-17

Find the remainder when 3^{100} is divided by 5.

Solution

$3^2 \equiv 4 (\text{mod } 5)$
$3^3 \equiv 3 \cdot 4 \equiv 2 (\text{mod } 5)$
$3^3 \equiv 2 (\text{mod } 5)$
$3^4 \equiv 3 \cdot 2 \equiv 1 (\text{mod } 5)$
$3^4 \equiv 1 (\text{mod } 5)$
$(3^4)^{25} \equiv (1)^{25} (\text{mod } 5)$

Therefore $3^{100} \equiv 1 (\text{mod } 5)$. It follows that 3^{100} and 1 have the same remainder when divided by 5. Thus, 3^{100} has remainder 1 when divided by 5.

PROBLEM SET 5-4

1. Perform each of the following operations on a 12-hour clock, if possible.
    (a) $7 \oplus 8$ (b) $4 \oplus 10$ (c) $3 \ominus 9$ (d) $4 \ominus 8$
    (e) $3 \otimes 9$ (f) $4 \otimes 4$ (g) $1 \ominus 3$ (h) $2 \oplus 5$

2. Perform each of the following operations on a 5-hour clock.
    (a) $3 \oplus 4$ (b) $3 \oplus 6$ (c) $3 \otimes 4$ (d) $1 \otimes 4$
    (e) $3 \otimes 4$ (f) $2 \otimes 3$ (g) $3 \ominus 4$ (h) $1 \ominus 4$
3. (a) Construct an addition table for a 7-hour clock.
    (b) Using the addition table in (a), find $5 \ominus 6$ and $2 \ominus 5$.
    (c) Using the addition table in (a), show that subtraction can always be performed on a 7-hour clock.
4. (a) Construct a multiplication table for a 7-hour clock.
    (b) Use the multiplication table in (a) to find $3 \oslash 5$ and $4 \oslash 6$.
    (c) Use the multiplication table to find whether division by numbers different from 7 is always possible.
5. (a) Construct the multiplication tables for 3-, 4-, 6-, and 11-hour clocks.
    (b) On which of the clocks in part (a) can divisions by numbers other than the additive identity always be performed?
    (c) How do the multiplication tables of clocks for which division can always be performed (except by an additive identity) differ from the multiplication tables of clocks for which division is not always meaningful?
6. On a 12-hour clock, the additive inverse of m is a number x such that $m \oplus x = 12$. Denote the additive inverse of m by ^-m and find each of the following.
    (a) additive inverse of 2   (b) additive inverse of 3   (c) $(^-2) \oplus {}^-3$
    (d) $^-(2 \oplus 3)$ (e) $^-2 \ominus (^-3)$ (f) $(^-2) \otimes (^-3)$
7. If September 3 falls on Monday, on what day of the week will it fall the next year, if next year is a leap year?
8. Show that each of the following statements is true.
    (a) $81 \equiv 1 \pmod 8$ (b) $81 \equiv 1 \pmod{10}$ (c) $1000 \equiv {}^-1 \pmod{13}$
    (d) $10^{84} \equiv 1 \pmod 9$ (e) $10^{100} \equiv 1 \pmod{11}$ (f) $937 \equiv 37 \pmod{100}$
9. Fill in each blank in such a way that the answer is nonnegative and the least possible number.
    (a) $29 \equiv$ _____ $\pmod 5$ (b) $3498 \equiv$ _____ $\pmod 3$
    (c) $3498 \equiv$ _____ $\pmod{11}$ (d) $^-23 \equiv$ _____ $\pmod{10}$
10. Show that $a \equiv 0 \pmod m$, if and only if $m \mid a$.
11. Translate each of the following statements into the language of congruences.
    (a) $8 \mid 24$ (b) $3 \mid {}^-90$ (c) Any nonzero integer n divides itself.
12. (a) Find all x such that $x \equiv 0 \pmod 2$.
    (b) Find all x such that $x \equiv 1 \pmod 2$.
    (c) Find all x such that $x \equiv 3 \pmod 5$.
13. Find the remainders for each of the following.
    (a) 5^{100} is divided by 6   (b) 5^{101} is divided by 6   (c) 10^{99} is divided by 11
★14. (a) Find a negative integer value for x such that $10^3 \equiv x \pmod{13}$ and $|x|$ is the least possible.
    (b) Find the remainder when 10^{99} is divided by 13.
★15. Use the fact that $100 \equiv 0 \pmod 4$ to find and prove a test for divisibility by 4.
★16. Use congruences to find and prove a divisibility test by 5, 8, 10, and 25.
★17. (a) Show that, in general, the cancellation property for multiplication does not hold for congruences; that is, show that $ac \equiv bc \pmod m$ does not always imply $a \equiv b \pmod m$.
    (b) Show that, in general, $a^k \equiv b^k \pmod m$ does not imply $a \equiv b \pmod m$.
★18. Prove each of the properties of congruences mentioned in this section.

SOLUTION TO THE PRELIMINARY PROBLEM

Understanding the Problem

When a woman removes eggs from the basket two, three, four, five, or six at a time, there is always one egg left. That means that if the number of eggs is divided by 2, 3, 4, 5, or 6, the remainder is always 1. We also know that when she removes the eggs seven at a time, there are no eggs left; that is, the number of eggs is a multiple of 7. Finally, we know that the basket holds up to 500 eggs. We have to find the number of eggs in the basket.

Devising a Plan

One way to solve the problem is to write all the multiples of 7 between 7 and 500 and check which ones have a remainder of 1 when divided by 2, 3, 4, 5, or 6. Since this method is tedious, we look for a different approach. Let the number of eggs be n. Then if n is divided by 2, the remainder is 1. Consequently, $n - 1$ will be divisible by 2. Similarly, 3, 4, 5, and 6 divide $n - 1$.

Since 2 and 3 divide $n - 1$, the primes 2 and 3 appear in the prime factorization of $n - 1$. Note that $4 \mid (n - 1)$ implies that $2 \mid (n - 1)$, and hence, from the information $2 \mid (n - 1)$ and $4 \mid (n - 1)$, we can only conclude that 2^2 appears in the prime factorization of $n - 1$. Since $5 \mid (n - 1)$, 5 appears in the prime factorization of $n - 1$. The fact that $6 \mid (n - 1)$ does not provide any new information, since it only implies that 2 and 3 are prime factors of $n - 1$, which we already know. Now $n - 1$ may also have other prime factors. Denoting the product of these prime factors by k, we have $n - 1 = 2^2 \cdot 3 \cdot 5 \cdot k = 60k$, where k is some natural number and therefore $n = 60k + 1$. We now find all possible values for n in the form $60k + 1$ less than 500 and determine which ones are divisible by 7.

Carrying Out the Plan

Since $n = 60k + 1$ and k is any natural number, we substitute $k = 1, 2, 3$, and so on, to obtain the following possible values for n that are less than 500:

61, 121, 181, 241, 301, 361, 421, 481

Among these values, only 301 is divisible by 7, and hence, 301 is the only possible answer to the problem.

Looking Back

In the preceding situation, we still have to test eight numbers for divisibility by 7. Is it possible to further reduce the computations? We know that $n = 60k + 1$ and that the possible values for k are $k = 1, 2, 3, 4, 5, 6, 7, 8$. We also know that $7 \mid n$; that is, $7 \mid (60k + 1)$. The problem is to find for which of the above values of k, $7 \mid (60k + 1)$. The question would have been easier to answer if instead of $60k + 1$, we had a smaller number. We know that the multiple of k closest to $60k$ that is divisible by 7 is $56k$. Since $7 \mid (60k + 1)$ and $7 \mid 56k$, we conclude that $7 \mid (60k + 1 - 56k)$; that is, $7 \mid (4k + 1)$. We now see that $7 \mid (60k + 1)$, if and only if $7 \mid (4k + 1)$. The only value of k between 1 and 8 that makes $4k + 1$ divisible by 7 is 5. Consequently, $7 \mid (60 \cdot 5 + 1)$, and 301 is the solution to the problem.

QUESTIONS FROM THE CLASSROOM

1. A student claims that $a \mid a$ and $a \mid a$ implies $a \mid (a - a)$, and hence, $a \mid 0$. Is she correct?
2. A student argues that $0 \mid 0$, since $0 = k \cdot 0$ for any integer k. How do you respond?
3. A student writes, "If $d \nmid a$ and $d \nmid b$, then $d \nmid (a + b)$." How do you respond?
4. A seventh-grade teacher just completed a unit on divisibility rules. One of the better students asks why divisibility by numbers other than 3 and 9 cannot be tested by dividing the sum of the digits by the tested number. How should the teacher respond?
5. A student claims that a number with an even number of digits is divisible by 7, if and only if each of the numbers formed by pairing the digits into groups of two is divisible by 7. For example, 49 562 107 is divisible by 7, since each of the numbers 49, 56, 21, and 07 is divisible by 7. Is this true?
6. A sixth-grade student argues that there are infinitely many primes, since "there is no end to numbers." How do you respond?
7. A student claims that a number is divisible by 21 if and only if it is divisible by 3 and by 7, and, in general, a number is divisible by $a \cdot b$ if and only if it is divisible by a and by b. What is your response?
8. A student claims that there are no integers x and y that make the equation $12x - 9y = 7$ true. How do you respond?
9. A student claims that the greatest common divisor of two numbers is always less than their least common multiple. Is he correct?

CHAPTER OUTLINE

I. Divisibility
   A. If a and b are any integers with $b \neq 0$, then b divides a, denoted $b \mid a$,

   if and only if there is a unique integer c such that $a = cb$.
   B. The following are basic divisibility

theorems for integers a, b, and d with $d \neq 0$.

1. If $d\,|\,a$ and $d\,|\,b$, then $d\,|\,(a + b)$.
2. If $d\,|\,a$ and $d \nmid b$, then $d \nmid (a + b)$.
3. If $d\,|\,a$ and $d\,|\,b$, then $d\,|\,(a - b)$.
4. If $d\,|\,a$ and $d \nmid b$, then $d \nmid (a - b)$.
5. If $d\,|\,a$ and k is any integer, then $d\,|\,ka$

C. Divisibility tests
1. A number is divisible by 2, 5, or 10 if and only if the units digit of the number is divisible by 2, 5, or 10, respectively.
2. A number is divisible by 4 if and only if the last two digits of the number represent a number divisible by 4.
3. A number is divisible by 8 if and only if the last three digits of the number represent a number divisible by 8.
4. A number is divisible by 3 or by 9 if and only if the sum of its digits is divisible by 3 or 9, respectively.
5. A number is divisible by 11 if and only if the sum of the digits in the odd-powered positions minus the sum of the digits in the even-powered positions is divisible by 11.

II. Prime and composite numbers
A. Integers that have exactly two positive divisors, namely, 1 and themselves, are called **primes.** Integers greater than 1 that are not primes are called **composites.**
B. The Fundamental Theorem of Arithmetic: Every composite number has one and only one prime factorization.
C. Criterion for determining if a given number n is prime: If n is not divisible by any prime p such that $p^2 \leq n$, then n is prime.

III. Greatest common divisor and least common multiple
A. The **greatest common divisor (GCD)** of two or more natural numbers is the greatest divisor, or factor, that the numbers have in common.
B. The **least common multiple (LCM)** of two or more natural numbers is the least positive multiple that the numbers have in common.
C. The Euclidean Algorithm. If a and b are whole numbers and $a \geq b$, then $GCD(a, b) = GCD(b, r)$, where r is the remainder when a is divided by b. The procedure of finding the GCD of two numbers a and b by using the above result repeatedly is called the *Euclidean Algorithm.*
D. $GCD(a, b) \cdot LCM(a, b) = ab$.

IV. Clock and modular arithmetic
A. For any integers a and b, *a is congruent to b modulo m* if and only if a and b differ by a multiple of m, where m is a positive integer greater than 1.
B. Two integers are congruent modulo m if and only if their remainders upon division by m are the same.

CHAPTER TEST

1. Classify each of the following as true or false.
   (a) $8\,|\,4$ (b) $0\,|\,4$ (c) $4\,|\,0$
   (d) If a number is divisible by 4 and by 6, then it is divisible by 24.
   (e) If a number is not divisible by 12, then it is not divisible by 3.

2. Classify each of the following as true or false. If false, show a counterexample.
   (a) If $7 \mid x$ and $7 \nmid y$, then $7 \nmid xy$.
   (b) If $d \nmid (a + b)$, then $d \nmid a$, and $d \nmid b$.
   (c) If $16 \mid 10^4$, then $16 \mid 10^6$.
   (d) If $d \mid (a + b)$ and $d \nmid a$, then $d \nmid b$.
   (e) If $d \mid (x + y)$ and $d \mid x$, then $d \mid y$.
   (f) If $4 \nmid x$ and $4 \nmid y$, then $4 \nmid xy$.
3. Test each of the following numbers for divisibility by 2, 3, 4, 5, 6, 7, 8, 9, and 11.
   (a) 83 160   (b) 83 193
4. Assume that 10 007 is prime. Without actually dividing 10 024 by 17, prove that 10 024 is not divisible by 17.
5. Prove the test for divisibility by 9 using a three-digit number n such that $n = a \cdot 10^2 + b \cdot 10 + c$.
6. Determine whether each of the following numbers are prime or composite.
   (a) 143   (b) 223
7. How can you tell if a number is divisible by 24? Check 4152 for divisibility by 24.
8. Find the GCD for each of the following:
   (a) 24 and 52   (b) 5767 and 4453
9. Find the LCM for each of the following.
   (a) $2^3 \cdot 5^2 \cdot 7^3$ and $2 \cdot 5^3 \cdot 7^2 \cdot 13$, and $2^4 \cdot 5 \cdot 7^4 \cdot 29$
   (b) 278 and 279

SELECTED BIBLIOGRAPHY

Avital, S. "The Plight and Might of Number Seven," *The Arithmetic Teacher*, **25**(Feburary 1978):22–24.

Brown, S. *Some Prime Comparisons*. National Council of Teachers of Mathematics, 1978.

Burton, G. M., and J. D. Knifong. "Definitions for Prime Numbers." *The Arithmetic Teacher*, **27**(February 1980):44–47.

Duncan, D. R., and B. H. Litwiller. "A Pattern in Number Theory: Example Generalization Proof." *The Mathematics Teacher*, **64**(November 1971):661–664.

Engle, J. A. "A Rediscovered Test for Divisibility by Eleven." *The Mathematics Teacher*, **69**(December 1976):669.

Gullen, G. III. "The Smallest Prime Factor of a Natural Number." *The Mathematics Teacher*, **67**(April 1974):329–332.

Henry, B. "Modulo 7 Arithmetic—A Perfect Example of Field Properties." *The Mathematics Teacher*, **65**(October 1972):525–528.

Henry, L. L. "Another Look at Least Common Multiple and Greatest Common Factor." *The Arithmetic Teacher*, **25**(March 1978):52–53.

Hoffer, A. R. "What You Always Wanted to Know about Six But Have Been Afraid to Ask." *The Arithmetic Teacher*, **20**(March 1973):173–180.

Johnson, P. E. "Understanding the Check of Nines." *The Arithmetic Teacher*, **26**(November 1978):54–55.

Kennedy, R. E. "Divisibility for Integers Ending in 1, 3, 7, or 9." *The Mathematics Teacher*, **64**(February 1971):137–138.

Lappan, G., and M. J. Winter. "Prime Factorizations." *The Arithmetic Teacher*, **27**(March 1980):24–27.

Long, C. F. "A Simpler '7' Divisibility Rule." *The Mathematics Teacher*, **64**(May 1971):473–475.

Mann, N., III. "Modulo Systems: One More Step." *The Mathematics Teacher*, **65**(March 1972):207–209.

Ore, O. *Invitation to Number Theory*. New York: Random House, The L. W. Singer Company New Mathematical Library, 1967.

Parkerson, E. "Patterns in Divisibility." *The Arithmetic Teacher*, **25**(January 1978):58.

Prielipp, R. W. "Perfect Numbers, Abundant Numbers, and Deficient Numbers." *The Mathematics Teacher,* **63**(December 1970):692–696.

Rockwell, C. H. "Another 'Sieve' for Prime Numbers." *The Arithmetic Teacher,* **20**(November 1973):603–605.

Roy, S. P. "LCM and GCF in the Hundred Chart." *The Arithmetic Teacher* **26**(December 1978):53.

Scheuer, D. W., Jr. "All-Star GCF." *The Arithmetic Teacher,* **26**(November 1978):34–35.

Sherzer, L. "A Simplified Presentation for Finding the LCM and the GCF." *The Arithmetic Teacher,* **21**(May 1974):415–416.

Singer, R. "Modular Arithmetic and Divisibility Criteria." *The Mathematics Teacher,* **63**(December 1970):653–656.

Smith, L. T. "A General Test of Divisibility." *The Mathematics Teacher,* **71**(November 1978):668–669.

Stock, M. E. "On What Day Were You Born?" *The Mathematics Teacher,* **65**(January 1972):73–75.

Swafford, J., and R. McGinty. "Story Numbers." *The Arithmetic Teacher.* **26**(October 1978):16–17.

Thomson, M. *Number Theory.* Reading, Mass.: Addison-Wesley, (Mathematics Methods Program), 1976.

Tucker, B. F. "The Division Algorithm." *The Arithmetic Teacher,* **20**(December 1973):639–646.

White, P. A. "An Application of Clock Arithmetic." *The Mathematics Teacher,* **66**(November 1973):645–647.

Yazbak, N. "Some Unusual Tests of Divisibility." *The Mathematics Teacher,* **69**(December 1976):669.

Numbers: Rational and Irrational

6

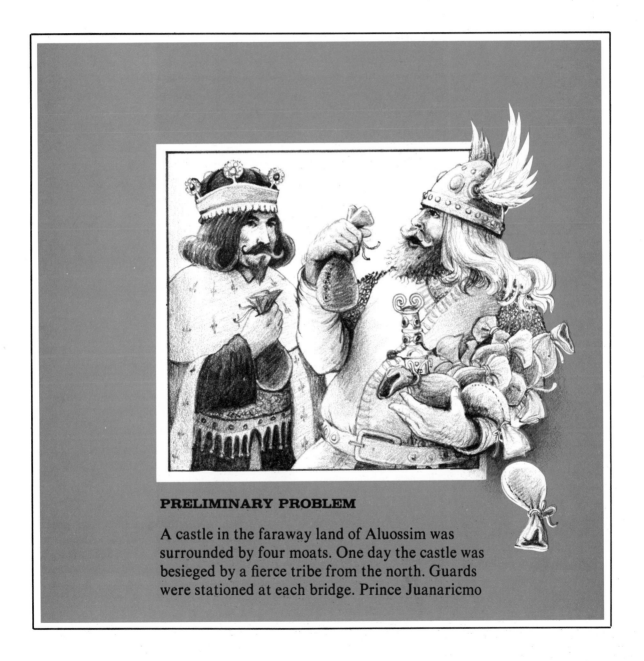

PRELIMINARY PROBLEM

A castle in the faraway land of Aluossim was surrounded by four moats. One day the castle was besieged by a fierce tribe from the north. Guards were stationed at each bridge. Prince Juanaricmo was allowed to take a number of bags of gold from the castle as he went into exile. However, the guard at the first bridge demanded half the prince's bags of gold plus one more bag. Prince Juanaricmo met this demand and proceeded to the next bridge. The guard at the second, third, and fourth bridges made identical demands, all of which the prince met. When the prince finally crossed all of the bridges, he had a single bag of gold left. How many bags did he start with?

6-1   THE SET OF RATIONAL NUMBERS

The early Egyptian numeration system had symbols for fractions with numerators of 1. For example, one-third was ⌒, and one-tenth was . Fractions, other than unit fractions (fractions with numerators of 1), were expressed as a sum of two different unit fractions, for example, seven-twelfths was one-third plus one-fourth.

Table 6-1 shows how fractions are used in several different ways.

TABLE 6-1

Use	Example
Division problem or solution to a multiplication problem	The solution to $2x = 3$ is $3/2$.
Partition or part of a whole	Joe received one-half of Mary's salary each month for alimony.
Ratio	The ratio of Republicans to Democrats in the Senate is three to five.
Element of a mathematical system	The number ⁻2/3 is a rational number.

(a)

(b)

0   1

(c)

FIGURE 6-1

rational numbers

Figure 6-1 illustrates the use of fractions as a part of a whole. For example, in Figure 6-1(a), one part out of three congruent parts, or ⅓ of the rectangle, is shaded. In Figure 6-1(b), three circles out of five circles, or ⅗ of the circles are shaded. In Figure 6-1(c), two parts out of three parts, or ⅔ of the unit segment, are shaded.

Numbers represented by fractions such as ⅓, ⅗, and ⅔ belong to the set of **rational numbers.**

DEFINITION

> A rational number is a number that may be represented by $\frac{a}{b}$, where a and b are integers and $b \neq 0$.

numerator

In the rational number $\frac{a}{b}$, a is called the **numerator** and b is called the

denominator

denominator. The rational number $\frac{a}{b}$ may also be represented as a/b or as $a \div b$. The set of rational numbers, denoted by Q, can be written as follows.

$$Q = \left\{ \frac{a}{b} \,\middle|\, a \text{ and } b \text{ are integers and } b \neq 0 \right\}$$

Every integer a can be written as $a/1$. Thus, the set of integers is a subset of the set of rational numbers. Also, the set of rational numbers is a subset of a much larger set of numbers of the form a/b, called fractions, where a and b are not necessarily integers. We will use the term *fractions* to mean rational numbers whenever there is no ambiguity.

In Figure 6-2(a), one of three congruent parts, or $\frac{1}{3}$, is shaded. Also, in Figure 6-2(a) two of the six congruent parts, or $\frac{2}{6}$, are shaded. Thus, both $\frac{1}{3}$ and $\frac{2}{6}$ represent exactly the same shaded portion. Although $\frac{1}{3}$ and $\frac{2}{6}$ do not look alike, they represent the same rational number. Strictly speaking, $\frac{1}{3}$ and

(a)

equivalent

$\frac{2}{6}$ are **equivalent** rational numbers. However, in most applications we call them equal and write $\frac{1}{3} = \frac{2}{6}$.

Figure 6-2(b) shows the rectangle subdivided into twelve parts, with four parts shaded. Thus, $\frac{1}{3}$ is equivalent to $\frac{4}{12}$, or $\frac{1}{3} = \frac{4}{12}$. Similarly, we could

(b)

illustrate that $\frac{1}{3} = \frac{2}{6} = \frac{4}{12} = \frac{8}{24}\ldots$. In other words, there are infinitely many rational numbers that are equivalent to $\frac{1}{3}$.

The Fundamental Law of Fractions shows how to obtain equivalent fractions.

FIGURE 6-2

Property

Fundamental Law of Fractions   For any rational number a/b and any integer $c \neq 0$, $a/b = ac/bc$.

Example 6-1

Find a value for x so that $x/210 = 12/42$.

Solution

By the Fundamental Law of Fractions, $12/42 = 12c/42c$, where c is an integer such that $c \neq 0$. Let $42c = 210$. Then, $c = 5$. Thus,

$$\frac{12}{42} = \frac{12 \cdot 5}{42 \cdot 5} = \frac{60}{210}$$

Hence, $x = 60$.

Example 6-2 | Find the set, S, of all rational numbers, each of whose elements is equal to $\frac{3}{5}$.

Solution | $$\frac{3}{5} = \frac{3 \cdot 2}{5 \cdot 2} = \frac{3 \cdot 3}{5 \cdot 3} = \frac{3 \cdot 4}{5 \cdot 4} = \frac{3 \cdot 5}{5 \cdot 5} = \cdots$$

Also,

$$\frac{3}{5} = \frac{3(^-1)}{5(^-1)} = \frac{3(^-2)}{5(^-2)} = \frac{3(^-3)}{5(^-3)} = \cdots$$

So,

$$S = \left\{ \frac{a}{b} \,\middle|\, \frac{a}{b} = \frac{3c}{5c} \text{ where } c \text{ is an integer and } c \neq 0 \right\}.$$

In Example 6-2, the fraction $\frac{3}{5}$ is called the simplest form of each of the rational numbers in set S. (In elementary texts, a fraction in simplest form is called a fraction in **lowest terms.**)

lowest terms

Both $\frac{6}{9}$ and $\frac{2}{3}$ are equivalent to $\frac{12}{18}$. Which is the simplest form?

$$\frac{12}{18} = \frac{2 \cdot 6}{2 \cdot 9} = \frac{6}{9} \qquad \text{but} \qquad \frac{6}{9} = \frac{2 \cdot 3}{3 \cdot 3} = \frac{2}{3}$$

reduced form
simplest form

The fraction $\frac{6}{9}$ is a **reduced form** of $\frac{12}{18}$, but $\frac{2}{3}$ is the simplest form of $\frac{12}{18}$. In general, a/b is the **simplest form** of a fraction if and only if a and b are relatively prime; that is, no whole number other than 1 divides both a and b. To find a reduced form of $\frac{12}{18}$, divide both 12 and 18 by any positive common divisor of 12 and 18 other than 1. To find the simplest form of $\frac{12}{18}$, divide both 12 and 18 by their greatest common divisor (GCD).

Example 6-3 | Reduce $\frac{45}{60}$ to its simplest form.

Solution | Since GCD $(45, 60) = 15$, then

$$\frac{45}{60} = \frac{3 \cdot 15}{4 \cdot 15} = \frac{3}{4}$$

Two fractions, $\frac{12}{42}$ and $\frac{10}{35}$, can be shown to be equal by several methods.

1. Reduce both fractions to the same simplest form.

$$\frac{12}{42} = \frac{2^2 \cdot 3}{2 \cdot 3 \cdot 7} = \frac{2}{7} \quad \text{and} \quad \frac{10}{35} = \frac{5 \cdot 2}{5 \cdot 7} = \frac{2}{7}$$

Thus,

$$\frac{12}{42} = \frac{10}{35}$$

2. Rewrite both fractions with the same least common denominator. Since the LCM (42, 35) = 210, then

$$\frac{12}{42} = \frac{60}{210} \quad \text{and} \quad \frac{10}{35} = \frac{60}{210}$$

Thus,

$$\frac{12}{42} = \frac{10}{35}$$

3. Rewrite both fractions with a common denominator (not necessarily the least). A common multiple of 42 and 35 may be found by finding the product 42 · 35 or 1470. Now,

$$\frac{12}{42} = \frac{420}{1470} \quad \text{and} \quad \frac{10}{35} = \frac{420}{1470}$$

Hence,

$$\frac{12}{42} = \frac{10}{35}$$

The third method suggests a general algorithm for determining if two fractions, a/b and c/d, are equal. Rewrite both fractions with common denominator, bd. That is, $a/b = ad/bd$ and $c/d = cb/bd$. Since the denominators are the same, $ad/bd = cb/bd$ if and only if $ad = cb$. For example, $^{24}/_{36} = ^6/_9$ because $9 \cdot 24 = 216 = 36 \cdot 6$. In general, the following property results.

Property | Two fractions, a/b and c/d, are equal if and only if $ad = bc$.

PROBLEM SET 6-1

1. Write a sentence illustrating $^7/_8$ used in each of the following ways.
   - (a) As a division problem
   - (b) As a part of a whole
   - (c) As a ratio
   - (d) As an element of a mathematical system

2. For each of the following, write a fraction to represent the shaded portion.

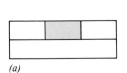

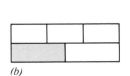

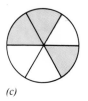

(a)   *(b)*   *(c)*   *(d)*

3. For each of the following, write three fractions equal to the given rational number.

   (a) $\dfrac{2}{9}$ (b) $\dfrac{^-2}{5}$ (c) $\dfrac{0}{3}$ (d) $\dfrac{a}{2}$

4. Find the simplest form for each of the following rational numbers.

   (a) $\dfrac{156}{93}$ (b) $\dfrac{27}{45}$ (c) $\dfrac{14x^2y}{63xy^2}$ (d) $\dfrac{^-65}{91}$

   (e) $\dfrac{a^2 + ab}{a + b}$ (f) $\dfrac{6629}{70\,395}$ (g) $\dfrac{0}{68}$ (h) $\dfrac{a}{a}$

5. Determine if the following pairs are equal by writing each in simplest form.

   (a) $\dfrac{3}{8}$ and $\dfrac{375}{1000}$ (b) $\dfrac{18}{54}$ and $\dfrac{23}{69}$

   (c) $\dfrac{6}{10}$ and $\dfrac{600}{1000}$ (d) $\dfrac{17}{27}$ and $\dfrac{25}{45}$

   (e) $\dfrac{24}{36}$ and $\dfrac{6}{9}$ (f) $\dfrac{^-7}{49}$ and $\dfrac{^-14}{98}$

6. Determine if the following pairs are equal by changing both to the same denominator.

   (a) $\dfrac{10}{16}$ and $\dfrac{12}{18}$ (b) $\dfrac{3}{12}$ and $\dfrac{41}{154}$

   (c) $\dfrac{3}{12}$ and $\dfrac{36}{144}$ (d) $\dfrac{^-21}{86}$ and $\dfrac{^-51}{215}$

   (e) $\dfrac{6}{10}$ and $\dfrac{6000}{10\,000}$ (f) $\dfrac{2}{75}$ and $\dfrac{8}{300}$

7. Determine if the following pairs are equal.

   (a) $\dfrac{^-3}{8}$ and $\dfrac{3}{^-8}$ (b) $\dfrac{0}{962}$ and $\dfrac{0}{17}$

   (c) $\dfrac{^-a}{b}$ and $\dfrac{a}{^-b}$ (d) $\dfrac{138}{492}$ and $\dfrac{124}{481}$

(e) $\dfrac{a}{3a + b}$ and $\dfrac{b}{3 + b}$ (f) $\dfrac{x}{y}$ and $\dfrac{y}{x}$

8. (a) If $a/c = b/c$, what must be true?
    (b) If $a/b = a/c$, what must be true?
9. Prove that each integer can be written as a rational number.
10. Let W be the set of whole numbers, I be the set of integers, and Q be the set of rational numbers. Classify each of the following as true or false.
    (a) $W \subseteq Q$ (b) $(I \cup W) \subset Q$
    (c) If Q is the universal set, $\overline{I} = W$.   (d) $Q \cap I = W$
    (e) $Q \cap W = W$

11. Do Problem 99 appearing in Appendix II.

LABORATORY ACTIVITY

1. This activity gives a model for showing equal fractions. Draw and cut out a rectangle. Label one end of the rectangle 0 and the other end 1 as shown in the figure.

0   1

Fold the rectangle in two parts matching the ends. Label the fold $\frac{1}{2}$ and the ends $\frac{0}{2}$ and $\frac{2}{2}$. Fold the folded paper again matching the ends. Label the folds $\frac{1}{4}$, $\frac{2}{4}$, $\frac{3}{4}$, as shown in the figure. Label the ends $\frac{0}{4}$ and $\frac{4}{4}$.

$\frac{0}{4}$	$\frac{1}{4}$	$\frac{2}{4}$	$\frac{3}{4}$	$\frac{4}{4}$
$\frac{0}{2}$		$\frac{1}{2}$		$\frac{2}{2}$
0				1

Unfold the paper. Then, fold it into three equal parts. Label the ends and the folds $\frac{0}{3}$, $\frac{1}{3}$, $\frac{2}{3}$, and $\frac{3}{3}$. Fold the newly folded rectangle in two equal parts labeling the ends and folds $\frac{0}{6}$, $\frac{1}{6}$, $\frac{2}{6}$, $\frac{3}{6}$, $\frac{4}{6}$, $\frac{5}{6}$, and $\frac{6}{6}$. On your own, label the eighths and twelfths.

2. Use a sheet of graph paper to make a 10×10 grid. Demonstrate $\frac{1}{2}$, $\frac{1}{4}$, $\frac{1}{5}$, $\frac{1}{10}$, and $\frac{1}{20}$ on the grid. Use the grid to determine the sum of $\frac{1}{2}$ and $\frac{1}{4}$.

6-2   ADDITION AND SUBTRACTION OF RATIONAL NUMBERS

As with whole numbers and integers, we use the number line model to motivate the definitions of addition and subtraction of rational numbers. Most elementary textbooks use rational numbers whose numerators and denominators are natural numbers. We will do the same. However, the definitions developed hold for all rational numbers: positive, negative, and zero.

Consider the sum $1/5 + 2/5$. Both $1/5$ and $2/5$ can be pictured as arrows on the number line (in the same way as whole numbers and integers). The sum can be represented using a single arrow, as shown in Figure 6-3. The

FIGURE 6-3

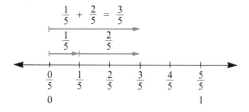

number line model shows that $1/5 + 2/5 = (1+2)/5$ or $3/5$. In a similar manner, we can find the sum of any two rational numbers, a/b and c/b, where the denominators are the same. *If a/b and c/b are rational numbers, then*

$$\frac{a}{b} + \frac{c}{b} = \frac{a + c}{b}$$

Example 6-4   Find each sum.

(a) $\dfrac{4}{6} + \dfrac{5}{6}$ (b) $\dfrac{5}{18} + \dfrac{11}{18}$

Solution   (a) $\dfrac{4}{6} + \dfrac{5}{6} = \dfrac{4 + 5}{6} = \dfrac{9}{6}$ (b) $\dfrac{5}{18} + \dfrac{11}{18} = \dfrac{5 + 11}{18} = \dfrac{16}{18}$

To find the sum of fractions with unlike denominators such as $\frac{1}{2} + \frac{1}{3}$, first rewrite each fraction with the same denominator (using the methods in Section 6-1). Then, add.

$$\frac{1}{2} = \frac{1 \cdot 3}{2 \cdot 3} = \frac{3}{6} \qquad \text{and} \qquad \frac{1}{3} = \frac{1 \cdot 2}{3 \cdot 2} = \frac{2}{6}$$

Now, $1/2 + 1/3 = 3/6 + 2/6 = (3+2)/6 = 5/6$. This example is pictured on the number line in Figure 6-4.

FIGURE 6-4

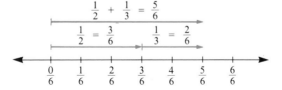

Often, when adding fractions, it is convenient to find the least common denominator of the given fractions. This is done by finding the least common multiple (LCM) of the denominators as shown in the following example.

Example 6-5

Find

$$\frac{2}{15} + \frac{4}{21}.$$

Solution

The LCM(15, 21) = $3 \cdot 5 \cdot 7$ = 105. Consequently,

$$\frac{2}{15} = \frac{2 \cdot 7}{3 \cdot 5 \cdot 7} = \frac{14}{105} \quad \text{and} \quad \frac{4}{21} = \frac{4 \cdot 5}{3 \cdot 7 \cdot 5} = \frac{20}{105}$$

Hence,

$$\frac{2}{15} + \frac{4}{21} = \frac{14}{105} + \frac{20}{105} = \frac{34}{105}$$

Another way to find the sum $\frac{2}{15} + \frac{4}{21}$ is to find any common denominator, not necessarily the least one. For example, $15 \cdot 21$, or 315, is certainly a common denominator, and the calculation is as follows.

$$\frac{2}{15} + \frac{4}{21} = \frac{2 \cdot 21}{15 \cdot 21} + \frac{4 \cdot 15}{21 \cdot 15} = \frac{42}{315} + \frac{60}{315} = \frac{42 + 60}{315} = \frac{102}{315} = \frac{34}{105}$$

In general, this leads to the following definition.

DEFINITION

Addition of Rational Numbers If a/b and c/d are any two rational numbers, then

$$\frac{a}{b} + \frac{c}{d} = \frac{ad + bc}{bd}$$

Example 6-6 Find

$$\frac{2}{^-3} + \frac{1}{5}.$$

Solution

$$\frac{2}{^-3} + \frac{1}{5} = \frac{(2)(5) + (^-3)(1)}{(^-3)(5)} = \frac{10 + ^-3}{^-15} = \frac{7}{^-15}$$

Since $7/^-15 = 7(^-1)/^-15(^-1) = ^-7/15$, then $7/^-15 = ^-7/15$. Although $7/^-15$ is an acceptable answer, $^-7/15$ is the preferred form for the answer.

mixed number   The sum of an integer and a rational number usually is written as a **mixed number.** Thus, $1 + \frac{3}{4}$ is usually written $1\frac{3}{4}$. Because

$$1 + \frac{3}{4} = \frac{1}{1} + \frac{3}{4} = \frac{1 \cdot 4 + 1 \cdot 3}{1 \cdot 4} = \frac{4 + 3}{4} = \frac{7}{4}$$

improper fraction   it follows that $1\frac{3}{4} = \frac{7}{4}$. A fraction of the form a/b, where $0 < b \leq a$, is called
proper fraction   an **improper fraction.** A fraction a/b, where $0 \leq a < b$ is called a **proper fraction.** For example, $\frac{7}{4}$ and $\frac{4}{4}$ are improper fractions and $\frac{4}{7}$ is a proper fraction.

Example 6-7 Change $4\frac{1}{3}$ to an improper fraction.

Solution

$$4\frac{1}{3} = 4 + \frac{1}{3} = \frac{4}{1} + \frac{1}{3} = \frac{4 \cdot 3 + 1 \cdot 1}{1 \cdot 3} = \frac{12 + 1}{3} = \frac{13}{3}$$

Example 6-8 Change $\frac{29}{5}$ to a mixed number.

Solution By the Division Algorithm, $29 = 5 \cdot 5 + 4$. Thus,

$$\frac{29}{5} = \frac{5 \cdot 5 + 4}{5} = \frac{5 \cdot 5}{5} + \frac{4}{5} = 5 + \frac{4}{5} = 5\frac{4}{5}$$

Conventionally, in elementary schools, problems like Example 6-8 are solved using divison.

$$\begin{array}{r} 5 \\ 5\overline{)29} \\ \underline{25} \\ 4 \end{array}$$

Hence, $\frac{29}{5} = 5 + \frac{4}{5} = 5\frac{4}{5}$.

Example 6-9 | Find

$$2\frac{4}{5} + 3\frac{5}{6}.$$

Solution | The problem is solved in two ways for comparison.

$$2\frac{4}{5} + 3\frac{5}{6} = \frac{14}{5} + \frac{23}{6}$$

$$= \frac{14\cdot 6 + 5\cdot 23}{5\cdot 6}$$

$$= \frac{84 + 115}{30}$$

$$= \frac{199}{30}$$

$$= 6\frac{19}{30}$$

$$2\frac{4}{5} = 2\frac{24}{30}$$

$$+3\frac{5}{6} = +3\frac{25}{30}$$

$$5\frac{49}{30}$$

But

$$\frac{49}{30} = 1\frac{19}{30}$$

so

$$5\frac{49}{30} = 5 + \frac{49}{30} = 5 + 1\frac{19}{30} = 6\frac{19}{30}$$

As with integers, rational numbers have the following properties under addition.

Properties | **Closure Property of Addition**   If a/b and c/d are any rational numbers, then $a/b + c/d$ is a rational number.

Commutative Property of Addition   If a/b and c/d are rational numbers, then $a/b + c/d = c/d + a/b$.

Associative Property of Addition   If a/b, c/d, and e/f are rational numbers, then $(a/b + c/d) + e/f = a/b + (c/d + e/f)$.

Additive Identity   The number 0 is the unique number such that for every rational number a/b, $0 + a/b = a/b = a/b + 0$.

Remark | The number 0 may be written as $0/n$, where n is any nonzero integer.

Property

Additive Inverse   For any rational number $\frac{a}{b}$, $-\frac{a}{b}$ $\left(\text{the opposite of } \frac{a}{b}\right)$ is the unique rational number having the property that $\frac{a}{b} + \left(-\frac{a}{b}\right) = 0 = \left(-\frac{a}{b}\right) + \frac{a}{b}$.

Another form of $-\frac{a}{b}$ can be found by considering the sum $\frac{a}{b} + \frac{^-a}{b}$

$$\frac{a}{b} + \frac{^-a}{b} = \frac{a + {}^-a}{b} = \frac{0}{b} = 0$$

Thus, $-\frac{a}{b}$ and $\frac{^-a}{b}$ are both additive inverses of $\frac{a}{b}$ and, since the additive inverse is unique, then $-\frac{a}{b} = \frac{^-a}{b}$. Also, since $\frac{^-a}{b} = \frac{a}{^-b}$, then $-\frac{a}{b} = \frac{a}{^-b}$.

Example 6-10

Find the additive inverses for each of the following.

(a) $\frac{3}{5}$ (b) $\frac{^-5}{11}$ (c) $4\frac{1}{2}$

Solution

(a) $\frac{^-3}{5}$ or $-\frac{3}{5}$ (b) $-\left(\frac{^-5}{11}\right)$ or $\frac{5}{11}$ (c) $^-4\frac{1}{2}$

Properties of the additive inverse for rational numbers are analogous to those of the additive inverse for integers as shown in Table 6-2.

TABLE 6-2   Properties of Additive Inverse

Integers		Rational Numbers	
1. $^-(^-a) = a$		1. $-\left(-\frac{a}{b}\right) = \frac{a}{b}$	
2. $^-(a + b) = {}^-a + {}^-b$		2. $-\left(\frac{a}{b} + \frac{c}{d}\right) = \frac{^-a}{b} + \frac{^-c}{d}$	

The set of rational numbers also has the addition property of equality similar to the set of integers.

Property

Addition Property of Equality   If a/b and c/d are any rational numbers such that $a/b = c/d$, and if e/f is any rational number, then

$$\frac{a}{b} + \frac{e}{f} = \frac{c}{d} + \frac{e}{f}$$

Subtraction for rational numbers is defined in terms of addition.

DEFINITION   **Subtraction of Rational Numbers**   If a/b and c/d are any rational numbers, then $a/b - c/d = e/f$ if and only if $a/b = c/d + e/f$.

If a/b and c/d are any rational numbers, then $\dfrac{a}{b} - \dfrac{c}{d} = \dfrac{a}{b} + \dfrac{^{-}c}{d}$

and using the definition of addition of rational numbers, the following results.

$$\frac{a}{b} - \frac{c}{d} = \frac{ad - bc}{bd}$$

Example 6-11   Find each difference.

(a) $\dfrac{5}{8} - \dfrac{1}{3}$ (b) $5\dfrac{1}{3} - 2\dfrac{3}{4}$

Solution   (a) $\dfrac{5}{8} - \dfrac{1}{3} = \dfrac{5 \cdot 3 - 8 \cdot 1}{8 \cdot 3} = \dfrac{15 - 8}{24} = \dfrac{7}{24}$

(b)   Two methods of solution are given.

$5\dfrac{1}{3} - 2\dfrac{3}{4} = \dfrac{16}{3} - \dfrac{11}{4}$

$= \dfrac{16 \cdot 4 - 3 \cdot 11}{3 \cdot 4}$

$= \dfrac{64 - 33}{12}$

$= \dfrac{31}{12}$ or $2\dfrac{7}{12}$

$5\dfrac{1}{3} = 5\dfrac{4}{12} = 4 + 1\dfrac{4}{12} = 4\dfrac{16}{12}$

$-2\dfrac{3}{4} = -2\dfrac{9}{12} = -2\dfrac{9}{12} \quad = -2\dfrac{9}{12}$

$\underline{\qquad}\quad 2\dfrac{7}{12}$

PROBLEM SET 6-2

1. Use a number line to find $\frac{1}{5} + \frac{2}{3}$.
2. Perform the following computations using the least common denominator method.

(a) $\dfrac{3}{16} + \dfrac{7}{^{-}8}$ (b) $\dfrac{4}{12} - \dfrac{2}{3}$ (c) $\dfrac{5}{6} + \dfrac{^{-}4}{9} + \dfrac{2}{3}$ (d) $\dfrac{2}{21} - \dfrac{3}{14}$

3. Use the definition of addition to find each of the following sums of rational numbers.

    (a) $\dfrac{6}{5} + \dfrac{^{-}11}{4}$ (b) $\dfrac{4}{5} + \dfrac{6}{7}$

    (c) $\dfrac{^{-}7}{8} + \dfrac{2}{5}$ (d) $\dfrac{5}{x} + \dfrac{^{-}3}{y}$

4. Add the following rational numbers. Write your answers in the simplest form

    (a) $\dfrac{6}{7} + \dfrac{3}{14}$ (b) $\dfrac{^{-}2}{3} + \dfrac{^{-}4}{7} + \dfrac{3}{21}$

    (c) $\dfrac{^{-}3}{2x} + \dfrac{3}{2y} + \dfrac{^{-}1}{4xy}$ (d) $\dfrac{^{-}3}{2x^2y} + \dfrac{5}{6xy^2} + \dfrac{7}{x^2}$

5. Change each of the following improper fractions to mixed numbers.

    (a) $\dfrac{56}{3}$ (b) $\dfrac{14}{5}$

    (c) $-\dfrac{293}{100}$ (d) $-\dfrac{47}{8}$

6. Change each of the following mixed numbers to improper fractions.

    (a) $6\dfrac{3}{4}$ (b) $7\dfrac{1}{2}$

    (c) $^{-}3\dfrac{5}{8}$ (d) $^{-}4\dfrac{2}{3}$

7. Compute the following.

    (a) $2\dfrac{1}{3} - 1\dfrac{3}{4}$ (b) $2\dfrac{1}{3} + 1\dfrac{3}{4}$ (c) $3\dfrac{5}{6} - 2\dfrac{1}{8}$

    (d) $\dfrac{5}{6} + 2\dfrac{1}{8}$ (e) $^{-}4\dfrac{1}{2} - 3\dfrac{1}{6}$ (f) $^{-}4\dfrac{3}{4} + 2\dfrac{5}{6}$

8. Joe lives $\frac{4}{10}$ mile from the university, and Mary lives $\frac{1}{6}$ mile away. How much further from school does Joe live than Mary?

9. A clerk sold three pieces of ribbon. One piece was $\frac{1}{3}$ yard long, another piece was $\frac{3}{4}$ yard long, and the third was $\frac{1}{2}$ yard long. What was the total length of ribbon sold?

10. What, if anything, is wrong with each of the following?

    (a) $2 = \dfrac{6}{3} = \dfrac{3+3}{3} = \dfrac{3}{3} + 3 = 1 + 3 = 4$

    (b) $1 = \dfrac{4}{2+2} = \dfrac{4}{2} + \dfrac{4}{2} = 2 + 2 = 4$

    (c) $\dfrac{ab + c}{a} = \dfrac{\not{a}b + c}{\not{a}} = b + c$

(d) $\dfrac{a^2 - b^2}{a - b} = \dfrac{a \cdot \cancel{a} - b \cdot \cancel{b}}{\cancel{a} - \cancel{b}} = a - b$

(e) $\dfrac{a + c}{b + c} = \dfrac{a + \cancel{c}}{b + \cancel{c}} = \dfrac{a}{b}$

11. Do each of the following properties hold for subtraction of rational numbers?
   (a) Closure   (b) Commutative   (c) Associative
   (d) Identity   (e) Inverse   (f) Subtraction property of equality

12. Perform the indicated operations on the following rational numbers. Write your answers in simplest form.

   (a) $\dfrac{d}{bc} - \dfrac{a}{bc}$ (b) $\dfrac{d}{b} + \dfrac{a}{bc}$ (c) $\dfrac{7}{a - b} + \dfrac{5}{a + b}$

   (d) $\dfrac{a^2 b}{c} - \dfrac{bc}{ad}$ (e) $\dfrac{a}{a - b} + \dfrac{b}{a + b}$ (f) $\dfrac{a}{a^2 - b^2} - \dfrac{b}{a - b}$

13. Prove each of the following properties of rational numbers.
   (a) Closure property of addition   (b) Commutative property of addition
   (c) Addition property of equality   ★(d) Associative property of addition

14. Do Problems 101, 102, and 103 appearing in Appendix II.

6-3 MULTIPLICATION AND DIVISION OF RATIONAL NUMBERS

BRAIN TEASER

When Professor Sum was asked by Mr. Little how many students were in his classes, he answered, "One-half of them study languages only, one-third of them study French, one-seventh of them study physics only, and there are twenty who do not study at all." How many students does Professor Sum have?

To motivate the definition of multiplication of rational numbers, we interpret $\frac{1}{4} \cdot \frac{1}{3}$ as $\frac{1}{4}$ of $\frac{1}{3}$ and use a rectangular diagram. Suppose the entire rectangular region in Figure 6-5(a) represents one unit. The shaded section represents $\frac{1}{3}$ of the rectangle. Figure 6-5(b) shows the rectangle further separated into four congruent parts with $\frac{1}{4}$ of these parts shaded. The cross-hatched portion represents $\frac{1}{4}$ of $\frac{1}{3}$, and is one-twelfth of the entire one-unit region. Thus, we interpret $\frac{1}{4} \cdot \frac{1}{3}$ as $\frac{1}{12}$.

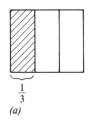

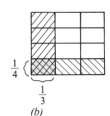

FIGURE 6-5

Figure 6-6(a) shows a one-unit rectangle separated into fifths, with ⅖ shaded. Figure 6-6(b) shows the rectangle further separated into thirds with ⅔ shaded. The crosshatched portion represents four parts out of fifteen, or ⁴⁄₁₅ of the rectangle. Thus,

$$\frac{2}{3} \cdot \frac{2}{5} = \frac{4}{15} = \frac{2 \cdot 2}{3 \cdot 5}.$$

FIGURE 6-6

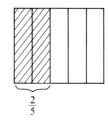

(a)   (b)

DEFINITION

If a/b and c/d are any rational numbers, then $a/b \cdot c/d = (a \cdot c)/(b \cdot d)$.

Example 6-12

Find each of the following products.

(a) $\frac{5}{6} \cdot \frac{7}{11}$ (b) $6 \cdot \frac{1}{5}$ (c) $2\frac{1}{3} \cdot 3\frac{1}{5}$

Solution

(a) $\frac{5}{6} \cdot \frac{7}{11} = \frac{5 \cdot 7}{6 \cdot 11} = \frac{35}{66}$

(b) $6 \cdot \frac{1}{5} = \frac{6}{1} \cdot \frac{1}{5} = \frac{6 \cdot 1}{1 \cdot 5} = \frac{6}{5}$

(c) $2\frac{1}{3} \cdot 3\frac{1}{5} = \frac{7}{3} \cdot \frac{16}{5} = \frac{7 \cdot 16}{3 \cdot 5} = \frac{112}{15} = 7\frac{7}{15}$

Rational numbers have the following properties under multiplication.

Properties

Closure Property of Multiplication   If $\frac{a}{b}$ and $\frac{c}{d}$ are any rational numbers, then $\frac{a}{b} \cdot \frac{c}{d}$ is a rational number.

Commutative Property of Multiplication   If $\frac{a}{b}$ and $\frac{c}{d}$ are any rational numbers, then $\frac{a}{b} \cdot \frac{c}{d} = \frac{c}{d} \cdot \frac{a}{b}$.

Associative Property of Multiplication   If $\frac{a}{b}$, $\frac{c}{d}$, and $\frac{e}{f}$ are any rational numbers, then $\left(\frac{a}{b} \cdot \frac{c}{d}\right) \cdot \frac{e}{f} = \frac{a}{b} \cdot \left(\frac{c}{d} \cdot \frac{e}{f}\right)$.

Multiplicative Identity   The number 1 is the unique number such that for every rational number $\frac{a}{b}$, $1 \cdot \left(\frac{a}{b}\right) = \left(\frac{a}{b}\right) \cdot 1 = \frac{a}{b}$.

Remark | The number 1 may be written as $\frac{n}{n}$, where n is any nonzero integer.

Property | **Multiplicative Inverse**   For any nonzero rational number $\frac{a}{b}$, $\frac{b}{a}$ is the unique rational number such that $\frac{a}{b} \cdot \frac{b}{a} = 1 = \frac{b}{a} \cdot \frac{a}{b}$. The multiplicative

reciprocal | inverse of $\frac{a}{b}$ is also called the **reciprocal** of $\frac{a}{b}$.

Finally, the rational numbers satisfy the distributive property of multiplication over addition.

Property | **Distributive Property of Multiplication over Addition**   If $\frac{a}{b}$, $\frac{c}{d}$, and $\frac{e}{f}$ are any rational numbers, then $\frac{a}{b}\left(\frac{c}{d} + \frac{e}{f}\right) = \left(\frac{a}{b} \cdot \frac{c}{d}\right) + \left(\frac{a}{b} \cdot \frac{e}{f}\right)$.

Verifications of these properties are left as exercises.

Example 6-13 | Find the multiplicative inverse of each of the following rational numbers.

(a) $\frac{2}{3}$ (b) $\frac{^-2}{5}$ (c) 4 (d) 0 (e) $\frac{x}{y}$, where $x \neq 0$

Solution | (a) $\frac{3}{2}$ (b) $\frac{5}{^-2}$, which can be written as $\frac{^-5}{2}$

(c) Since $4 = \frac{4}{1}$, then the multiplicative inverse is $\frac{1}{4}$.

(d) Even though $0 = \frac{0}{1}$, $\frac{1}{0}$ is undefined, so there is no multiplicative inverse of 0.

(e) $\frac{y}{x}$

Additional properties for multiplication on the set of rational numbers are the following.

Properties

Multiplication Property of Equality   If $\dfrac{a}{b}$ and $\dfrac{c}{d}$ are any rational numbers such that $\dfrac{a}{b} = \dfrac{c}{d}$ and $\dfrac{e}{f}$ is any rational number, then $\dfrac{a}{b} \cdot \dfrac{e}{f} = \dfrac{c}{d} \cdot \dfrac{e}{f}$.

Multiplication Property for Zero   If $\dfrac{a}{b}$ is any rational number, then

$$\frac{a}{b} \cdot 0 = 0 \cdot \frac{a}{b} = 0.$$

Example 6-14

Solve for x, where x is a rational number.

(a) $\dfrac{3}{2}x = \dfrac{3}{4}$

(b) $\dfrac{2}{3}x - \dfrac{1}{5} = \dfrac{3}{4}$

Solution

(a)
$$\frac{3}{2}x = \frac{3}{4}$$

$$\frac{2}{3} \cdot \frac{3}{2}x = \frac{2}{3} \cdot \frac{3}{4}$$

$$x = \frac{6}{12} \text{ or } \frac{1}{2}$$

(b)
$$\frac{2}{3}x - \frac{1}{5} = \frac{3}{4}$$

$$\frac{2}{3}x - \frac{1}{5} + \frac{1}{5} = \frac{3}{4} + \frac{1}{5}$$

$$\frac{2}{3}x = \frac{19}{20}$$

$$\frac{3}{2} \cdot \frac{2}{3}x = \frac{3}{2} \cdot \frac{19}{20}$$

$$x = \frac{57}{40}$$

Remark

$\dfrac{3}{2}x$ is a multiplication that can be treated as $\dfrac{3}{2} \cdot \dfrac{x}{1}$ or $\dfrac{3 \cdot x}{2 \cdot 1} = \dfrac{3x}{2}$.

Hence, $\dfrac{3}{2}x = \dfrac{3x}{2}$.

Division for rational numbers is defined as follows.

DEFINITION

If $\dfrac{a}{b}$ and $\dfrac{c}{d}$ are any rational numbers and $\dfrac{c}{d}$ is not zero, then $\dfrac{a}{b} \div \dfrac{c}{d} = \dfrac{e}{f}$ if and only if $\dfrac{e}{f}$ is the unique rational number such that $\dfrac{c}{d} \cdot \dfrac{e}{f} = \dfrac{a}{b}$.

Remark | In the definition of division, c/d is not zero because, as with integers, division by zero is impossible. Also, notice that $c/d \neq 0$ implies that $c \neq 0$.

To find an algorithm for rational number division, examine the following.

Example 6-15 | Find $1 \div \frac{2}{3}$.

Solution | By definition $1 \div \frac{2}{3} = x$ if and only if $\frac{2}{3} \cdot x = 1$. Since $\frac{2}{3}$ and x must be multiplicative inverses of each other, $x = \frac{3}{2}$. Thus, $1 \div \frac{2}{3} = \frac{3}{2}$.

Example 6-16 | Find $\frac{2}{3} \div \frac{5}{7}$.

Solution | Let $\frac{2}{3} \div \frac{5}{7} = x$. Then $\frac{5}{7} \cdot x = \frac{2}{3}$. To solve for x, multiply both sides of the equation by the reciprocal of $\frac{5}{7}$, namely, $\frac{7}{5}$. Thus,

$$\frac{7}{5}\left(\frac{5}{7}x\right) = \frac{7}{5} \cdot \frac{2}{3}.$$

Hence,

$$x = \frac{7}{5} \cdot \frac{2}{3} = \frac{14}{15}.$$

The procedures in Examples 6-15 and 6-16 suggest using an extension of the Fundamental Law of Fractions, $a/b = ac/bc$, where a, b, and c are all fractions.

$$\frac{2}{3} \div \frac{5}{7} = \frac{\frac{2}{3}}{\frac{5}{7}} = \frac{\frac{2}{3} \cdot \frac{7}{5}}{\frac{5}{7} \cdot \frac{7}{5}} = \frac{\frac{2}{3} \cdot \frac{7}{5}}{1} = \frac{2}{3} \cdot \frac{7}{5}$$

Thus,

$$\frac{2}{3} \div \frac{5}{7} = \frac{2}{3} \cdot \frac{7}{5}.$$

The preceding equations illustrate the standard algorithm, invert and multiply, taught to elementary school students.

$$\frac{a}{b} \div \frac{c}{d} = \frac{a}{b} \cdot \frac{d}{c}$$

Examples of this algorithm are seen on page 228 on the elementary textbook page from Addison-Wesley Series, *Mathematics in Our World,* 1978, Grade 6.

Dividing fractional numbers

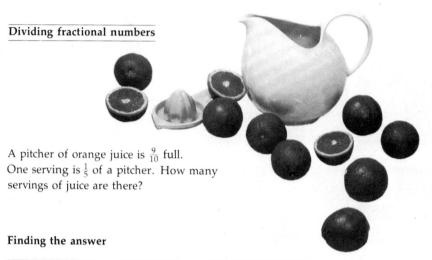

A pitcher of orange juice is $\frac{9}{10}$ full.
One serving is $\frac{1}{5}$ of a pitcher. How many
servings of juice are there?

Finding the answer

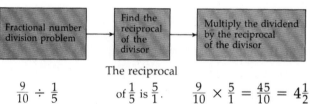

| Fractional number division problem | → | Find the reciprocal of the divisor | → | Multiply the dividend by the reciprocal of the divisor |

$$\frac{9}{10} \div \frac{1}{5}$$

The reciprocal of $\frac{1}{5}$ is $\frac{5}{1}$.

$$\frac{9}{10} \times \frac{5}{1} = \frac{45}{10} = 4\frac{1}{2}$$

There are $4\frac{1}{2}$ servings of juice.

Other examples

$$\frac{2}{3} \div \frac{3}{4} = \frac{2}{3} \times \frac{4}{3} = \frac{8}{9}$$

$$\frac{3}{4} \div \frac{3}{5} = \frac{3}{4} \times \frac{5}{3} = \frac{15}{12} = 1\frac{1}{4}$$

$$\frac{2}{3} \div 5 = \frac{2}{3} \div \frac{5}{1} = \frac{2}{3} \times \frac{1}{5} = \frac{2}{15}$$

$$4 \div \frac{3}{8} = \frac{4}{1} \times \frac{8}{3} = \frac{32}{3} = 10\frac{2}{3}$$

Find the quotients.

1. $\frac{2}{3} \div \frac{1}{2}$ 2. $\frac{1}{2} \div \frac{1}{4}$ 3. $\frac{1}{2} \div \frac{4}{5}$ 4. $\frac{3}{4} \div \frac{1}{10}$ 5. $\frac{3}{4} \div \frac{1}{2}$

6. $\frac{3}{5} \div \frac{3}{4}$ 7. $\frac{5}{6} \div \frac{2}{3}$ 8. $\frac{9}{10} \div \frac{2}{5}$ 9. $\frac{7}{8} \div \frac{1}{2}$ 10. $\frac{1}{3} \div \frac{2}{3}$

11. $\frac{1}{5} \div \frac{1}{2}$ 12. $\frac{3}{10} \div \frac{3}{4}$ 13. $\frac{3}{4} \div \frac{1}{8}$ 14. $\frac{3}{2} \div \frac{3}{4}$ 15. $\frac{3}{8} \div \frac{9}{10}$

Example 6-17 | Perform the following divisions.

(a) $\dfrac{^-5}{6} \div \dfrac{^-3}{8}$ (b) $5\dfrac{1}{6} \div 4\dfrac{2}{3}$

Solution | (a) $\dfrac{^-5}{6} \div \dfrac{^-3}{8} = \dfrac{^-5}{6} \cdot \dfrac{8}{^-3} = \dfrac{^-40}{^-18} = \dfrac{20}{9}$

(b) $5\dfrac{1}{6} \div 4\dfrac{2}{3} = \dfrac{31}{6} \div \dfrac{14}{3} = \dfrac{31}{6} \cdot \dfrac{3}{14} = \dfrac{93}{84} = \dfrac{31}{28}$ or $1\dfrac{3}{28}$

PROBLEM SET 6-3

1. In the following figures, a unit rectangle is used to illustrate the product of two fractions. Name the fractions and their product.

(a)

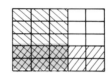

(b)

2. Use a rectangular region to illustrate each of the following products.

(a) $\dfrac{3}{4} \cdot \dfrac{1}{3}$ (b) $\dfrac{1}{5} \cdot \dfrac{2}{3}$

3. Find each product of rational numbers. Write your answers in simplest form.

(a) $\dfrac{10}{9} \cdot \dfrac{27}{40}$ (b) $\dfrac{^-3}{5} \cdot \dfrac{^-15}{24}$ (c) $\dfrac{49}{65} \cdot \dfrac{26}{98}$

(d) $\dfrac{a}{b} \cdot \dfrac{b^2}{a^2}$ (e) $\dfrac{2a}{3b} \cdot \dfrac{^-5ab}{2ab}$ (f) $\dfrac{xy}{z} \cdot \dfrac{z^2a}{x^3y^2}$

4. Find each product. Write your answers as mixed numbers.

(a) $2\dfrac{1}{3} \cdot 3\dfrac{3}{4}$ (b) $^-5\dfrac{1}{6} \cdot 4\dfrac{1}{2}$

(c) $\dfrac{22}{7} \cdot 4\dfrac{2}{3}$ (d) $\dfrac{^-5}{2} \cdot 2\dfrac{1}{2}$

5. Use the distributive property to find each product.

(a) $4\dfrac{1}{2} \cdot 2\dfrac{1}{3}$ $\left[Hint: \left(4 + \dfrac{1}{2}\right) \cdot \left(2 + \dfrac{1}{3}\right).\right]$ (b) $3\dfrac{1}{3} \cdot 2\dfrac{1}{2}$

6. Find the multiplicative inverse for each of the following.

(a) $\dfrac{^-1}{3}$ (b) $\dfrac{3}{5}$ (c) $\dfrac{14}{7}$

(d) $3\dfrac{1}{3}$ (e) $\dfrac{x}{y}$, if $x \neq 0$ and $y \neq 0$ (f) $^-7$

7. Perform each of the following divisions using the invert-and-multiply method. Write your answers in simplest form.

(a) $3 \div \dfrac{1}{9}$ (b) $\dfrac{2}{3} \div \dfrac{7}{12}$ (c) $\dfrac{^-3}{4} \div \dfrac{7}{8}$ (d) $\dfrac{x}{y} \div \dfrac{x^2}{y^2}$, where $x, y \neq 0$

8. Express each of the following as a fraction in simplest form.

(a) $\dfrac{\frac{3}{16}}{\frac{4}{9}}$ (b) $\dfrac{\frac{3}{16}}{\frac{9}{4}}$ (c) $\dfrac{\frac{8}{7}}{\frac{3}{4}}$ (d) $\dfrac{\frac{1}{4}+\frac{3}{2}}{\frac{5}{6}+\frac{-7}{8}}$

9. Solve each of the following for x, where x is a rational number.

(a) $\dfrac{1}{3}x = \dfrac{7}{8}$ (b) $\dfrac{2}{5} \cdot \dfrac{3}{6} = x$ (c) $\dfrac{1}{5} = \dfrac{7}{3} \cdot x$

(d) $x \div \dfrac{3}{4} = \dfrac{5}{8}$ (e) $\dfrac{2}{3}\left(\dfrac{1}{2}x - 7\right) = \dfrac{3}{4}x$ (f) $2\dfrac{1}{3}x + 7 = 3\dfrac{1}{4}$

10. Find two consecutive integers, x and $x + 1$, such that one-half of the greater integer exceeds one-third of the lesser integer by 9.

11. The sum of the ages of a father and his son is 75 years. Five years later the son's age is one-fourth of the father's age. Find their ages.

12. Peppermint Patty is frustrated with the following problem. Help her solve it.

© 1979 United Feature Syndicate, Inc.

13. Skip A. Little was absent one-fourth of the school year. If there are 180 days in the school year, how many days was he absent?

14. Di Paloma University had a faculty reduction and lost one-fifth of its faculty. If there were 320 faculty members left after the reduction, how many members were there originally?

15. Ten minutes is what part of an hour? Of a week?

16. Show that the following properties do *not* hold for division of rational numbers.
    (a) Commutative   (b) Associative   (c) Identity   (d) Inverse
★17. If Sherwin can paint the house in 2 days working by himself, and William can paint the house in 4 days by himself, how many days would it take Sherwin and William working together?
★18. If Mary and Carter can paint a house in 5 hours, while Mary alone can do the same job in 8 hours, how long will it take Carter working alone?
★19. Prove the following properties of rational numbers.
    (a) Closure for multiplication
    (b) Commutative for addition
    (c) Associative for multiplication
    (d) Multiplication property of zero
    (e) Distributive property of multiplication over addition

20. Do Problems 100 and 104 appearing in Appendix II.

BRAIN TEASER

A woman's will decreed that her cats would be shared among her three daughters as follows: ½ of the cats to the eldest daughter, ⅓ of the cats to the middle daughter, and ⅑ of the cats to the youngest daughter. Since the woman had 17 cats, the daughters decided that they could not carry out their mother's wishes. The judge who held the will agreed to lend the daughters a cat so they could share the cats as their mother wished. Now, ½ of 18 is 9; ⅓ of 18 is 6; and ⅑ of 18 is 2. Since 9 + 6 + 2 = 17, the daughters were able to divide the 17 cats and return the borrowed cat. They obviously did not need the extra cat to carry out the mother's will, but they could not divide 17 into halves, thirds, and ninths. Has the woman's will really been followed?

6-4 SOME PROPERTIES OF RATIONAL NUMBERS

Ordering of Rational Numbers

The greater than and less than relations for rational numbers are defined in such a way that the definitions of these relations for integers are still true.

Thus, if $\frac{a}{b}$ and $\frac{c}{d}$ are rational numbers, then $\frac{a}{b} > \frac{c}{d}$ if and only if there is a positive rational number k such that $\dfrac{c}{d} + k = \dfrac{a}{b}$. Since $\dfrac{c}{d} + k = \dfrac{a}{b}$, then

$\dfrac{a}{b} - \dfrac{c}{d} = k$. Consequently, since $k > 0$, $\dfrac{a}{b} > \dfrac{c}{d}$ if and only if $\dfrac{a}{b} - \dfrac{c}{d} > 0$.

This criterion for the greater than relation can be further simplified by noticing that if $\dfrac{a}{b} - \dfrac{c}{d} > 0$, then $\dfrac{ad - bc}{bd} > 0$. Suppose the denominators b and d are positive. Then $bd > 0$. It follows that $ad - bc > 0$ and, finally, that $ad > bc$.

Property | For any rational numbers $\dfrac{a}{b}$ and $\dfrac{c}{d}$, with b and d positive integers, $\dfrac{a}{b} > \dfrac{c}{d}$ if and only if $ad > bc$. Similarly, $\dfrac{a}{b} < \dfrac{c}{d}$ if and only if $ad < bc$.

Example 6-18 | Prove that the following order relations are true.

(a) $\dfrac{8}{9} > \dfrac{16}{19}$ (b) $\dfrac{^-7}{8} < \dfrac{14}{15}$ (c) $\dfrac{1}{^-4} < \dfrac{2}{11}$

Solution | (a) $\dfrac{8}{9} > \dfrac{16}{19}$ since $8 \cdot 19 > 9 \cdot 16$, or $152 > 144$.

(b) $\dfrac{^-7}{8} < \dfrac{14}{15}$ since $^-7 \cdot 15 < 8 \cdot 14$, or $^-105 < 112$.

(c) $\dfrac{1}{^-4} < \dfrac{2}{11}$ because $\dfrac{1}{^-4} = \dfrac{^-1}{4}$ and $\dfrac{^-1}{4} < \dfrac{2}{11}$,

since $(^-1) \cdot 11 < 4 \cdot 2$, or $^-11 < 8$.

The proofs of the following properties of the greater than relation on rational numbers are similar to those involving integers and are left as exercises.

THEOREM 6-1 | **Transitive Property of Greater Than**   For any rational numbers $\dfrac{a}{b}, \dfrac{c}{d}$,

and $\dfrac{e}{f}$, if $\dfrac{a}{b} > \dfrac{c}{d}$ and $\dfrac{c}{d} > \dfrac{e}{f}$, then $\dfrac{a}{b} > \dfrac{e}{f}$.

THEOREM 6-2 | **Addition Property of Greater Than**   For any rational numbers $\dfrac{a}{b}, \dfrac{c}{d}$,

and $\dfrac{e}{f}$, if $\dfrac{a}{b} > \dfrac{c}{d}$ then $\dfrac{a}{b} + \dfrac{e}{f} > \dfrac{c}{d} + \dfrac{e}{f}$.

THEOREM 6-3

> **Multiplication Property of Greater Than** For any rational numbers
>
> $\frac{a}{b}, \frac{c}{d},$ and $\frac{e}{f},$
>
> (a) If $\frac{a}{b} > \frac{c}{d}$ and $\frac{e}{f} > 0,$ then $\frac{a}{b} \cdot \frac{e}{f} > \frac{c}{d} \cdot \frac{e}{f}.$
>
> (b) If $\frac{a}{b} > \frac{c}{d}$ and $\frac{e}{f} < 0,$ then $\frac{a}{b} \cdot \frac{e}{f} < \frac{c}{d} \cdot \frac{e}{f}.$

Similar properties hold for $<$, $\leq$, and $\geq$.

Example 6-19

Solve for x, where x is a rational number.

(a) $\frac{3}{2}x < \frac{3}{4}$ (b) $\frac{1}{4}x + \frac{1}{5} \geq \frac{2}{3}x - \frac{1}{7}$

Solution

(a) $\frac{3}{2}x < \frac{3}{4}$

$$\left(\frac{2}{3}\right)\left(\frac{3}{2}x\right) < \left(\frac{2}{3}\right)\left(\frac{3}{4}\right)$$

$$x < \frac{6}{12} \text{ or } x < \frac{1}{2}$$

(b) $\qquad \frac{1}{4}x + \frac{1}{5} \geq \frac{2}{3}x - \frac{1}{7}$

$$\frac{1}{4}x + \frac{1}{5} + \frac{^-1}{5} \geq \frac{2}{3}x - \frac{1}{7} + \frac{^-1}{5}$$

$$\frac{1}{4}x \geq \frac{2}{3}x - \frac{12}{35}$$

$$\frac{^-2}{3}x + \frac{1}{4}x \geq \frac{^-2}{3}x + \frac{2}{3}x - \frac{12}{35}$$

$$\left(\frac{^-2}{3} + \frac{1}{4}\right)x \geq \frac{^-12}{35}$$

$$\frac{^-5}{12}x \geq \frac{^-12}{35}$$

$$\left(\frac{^-12}{5}\right)\left(\frac{^-5}{12}x\right) \leq \left(\frac{^-12}{5}\right)\left(\frac{^-12}{35}\right)$$

$$x \leq \frac{144}{175}$$

Often there is more than one way to solve an inequality. Two alternate methods for solving the second inequality in Example 6-19 follow.

1. First, add the fractions on each side of the inequality. Then, solve the resulting inequality.

$$\frac{1}{4}x + \frac{1}{5} \geq \frac{2}{3}x - \frac{1}{7}$$

$$\frac{5x + 4}{20} \geq \frac{14x - 3}{21}$$

$$21(5x + 4) \geq 20(14x - 3)$$

$$105x + 84 \geq 280x - 60$$

$$^-175x \geq ^-144$$

$$\left(\frac{^-1}{175}\right)(^-175x) \leq \left(\frac{^-1}{175}\right)(^-144)$$

$$x \leq \frac{144}{175}$$

2. First, multiply both sides of the inequality by the LCM of the denominators. (This gives an inequality that does not involve fractions.) Then, solve the resulting inequality.

$$\frac{1}{4}x + \frac{1}{5} \geq \frac{2}{3}x - \frac{1}{7}$$

$$420\left(\frac{1}{4}x + \frac{1}{5}\right) \geq 420\left(\frac{2}{3}x - \frac{1}{7}\right)$$

$$105x + 84 \geq 280x - 60$$

$$^-175x \geq ^-144$$

$$x \leq \frac{144}{175}$$

Denseness Property

denseness property   The set of rational numbers has a very special property called the **denseness property.** Neither the set of whole numbers nor the set of integers has this property. Given any two rational numbers a/b and c/d, there is another rational number *between* these two. Also, between a/b and the new rational number, there is another rational number. Continuing this process shows that between any two rational numbers, a/b and c/d, there are infinitely many other rational numbers. Consider for example, 1/2 and 2/3. First, rewrite the fractions with the least common denominator, that is, as 3/6 and 4/6. Since there is no whole number between the numerators, 3 and 4, next, find two fractions equal to 1/2 and 2/3 with greater denominators. For example, 1/2 = 6/12 and 2/3 = 8/12, and 7/12 is between the two fractions 6/12 and 8/12. So, 7/12 is between 1/2 and 2/3.

Another way to find a rational number between two given rationals, a/b and c/d, is to find the average of the two numbers. For example, the average of 1/2 and 2/3 is 1/2 (1/2 + 2/3), or 7/12. The proof that the average of two given rational numbers always is between them is left as an exercise.

Ratio and Proportion

One of the primary uses of fractions is as ratios. For example, there may be a two-to-three ratio of Democrats to Republicans on a certain legislative committee, a friend may be given a speeding ticket for driving 63 miles per hour, or eggs are 98¢ per dozen. Each of these illustrates a **ratio,** or a quotient. A 1 to 2 ratio of males to females means that the number of males is 1/2 the number of females. The ratio 1 to 2 can be written as 1/2 or 1:2. In general, a ratio is denoted by a/b, or a:b, where $b \neq 0$.

ratio

Example 6-20   There were 7 males and 12 females in the Dew Drop Inn on Monday evening. In the Game Room next door, there were 14 males and 24 females.

(a)   Express the number of males to females in the Inn as a ratio.
(b)   Express the number of males to females in the Game Room as a ratio.

Solution   (a)   The ratio is 7/12.   (b)   The ratio is 14/24.

The ratios 7/12 and 14/24 in Example 6-20 are said to be proportional to one another. In general, two ratios are **proportional** if and only if the fractions representing them are equal. Two equal ratios are said to form a **proportion.** For rational numbers, $a/b = c/d$ if and only if $ad = bc$. Thus, $a/b = c/d$ is a proportion if and only if $ad = bc$. For example, 14/24 = 7/12 is a proportion, since $14 \cdot 12 = 24 \cdot 7$.

proportion

Frequently, one term in a proportion is missing, as in $3/8 = x/16$. Finding x requires solving an equation. The definition of equality of rational numbers can be used to solve such an equation.

$$\frac{3}{8} = \frac{x}{16}$$

$$3 \cdot 16 = 8 \cdot x$$

$$48 = 8 \cdot x$$

$$6 = x$$

Example 6-21   If there should be 3 calculators for every 4 students in an elementary class, how many calculators are needed for 44 students?

Solution   Set up a table (Table 6-3). The ratio of calculators to students should always be the same.

TABLE 6-3

Number of Calculators	3	x
Number of Students	4	44

$$\frac{3}{4} = \frac{x}{44}$$

$$3 \cdot 44 = 4 \cdot x$$

$$132 = 4x$$

$$33 = x$$

Thus, 33 calculators are needed.

Example 6-22   Suppose a car travels 50 km/hr.

(a)   How far will it travel in $3\frac{1}{2}$ hours?
(b)   How long will it take the car to travel 1300 km?

Solution   (a)   Again, set up a table (Table 6-4).

TABLE 6-4

Distance (km)	50	x
Number of Hours	1	$3\frac{1}{2}$

$$\frac{50}{1} = \frac{x}{3\frac{1}{2}}$$

$$50(3\frac{1}{2}) = 1 \cdot x$$

$$175 = x$$

Therefore, the distance traveled in 3½ hours is 175 km.

TABLE 6-5   (b)

Distance (km)	50	1300
Number of Hours	1	x

$$\frac{50}{1} = \frac{1300}{x}$$

$$50x = 1300$$

$$x = 26$$

Thus, to travel 1300 km requires 26 hr.

Consider the proportion $15/30 = 3/6$. Since the ratios in the proportion are equal fractions and equal fractions have equal reciprocals, then $30/15 = 6/3$.

THEOREM 6-4

> For any rational numbers a/b and c/d with $a \neq 0$ and $c \neq 0$, $a/b = c/d$ if and only if $b/a = d/c$.

Using the properties of rational numbers, $15/30 = 3/6$ if and only if $15 \cdot 6 = 30 \cdot 3$. Also, $15/3 = 30/6$ if and only if $15 \cdot 6 = 3 \cdot 30$. Hence $15/30 = 3/6$ if and if $15/3 = 30/6$. This result is generalized in the following theorem.

THEOREM 6-5

> For any rational numbers a/b and c/d with $c \neq 0$, $a/b = c/d$ if and only if $a/c = b/d$.

PROBLEM SET 6-4

1. For each of the following pairs of fractions, replace the comma with the correct symbol $(<, =, >)$ to make a true statement.

   (a) $\frac{7}{8}, \frac{5}{6}$ (b) $2\frac{4}{5}, 2\frac{3}{6}$ (c) $\frac{^-7}{8}, \frac{^-4}{5}$

   (d) $\frac{1}{^-7}, \frac{1}{^-8}$ (e) $\frac{2}{5}, \frac{4}{10}$ (f) $\frac{0}{7}, \frac{0}{17}$

2. Arrange each of the following in decreasing order.

   (a) $\dfrac{11}{22}$, $\dfrac{11}{16}$, $\dfrac{11}{13}$ (b) $\dfrac{33}{16}$, $\dfrac{23}{12}$, 3 (c) $\dfrac{^-1}{5}$, $\dfrac{^-19}{36}$, $\dfrac{^-17}{30}$

3. Find the solution sets for each of the following, where x is a rational number.

   (a) $\dfrac{2}{3}x - \dfrac{7}{8} \le \dfrac{1}{4}$ (b) $\dfrac{1}{5}x - 7 \ge \dfrac{2}{3}$

   (c) $x - \dfrac{1}{3} < \dfrac{2}{3}x + \dfrac{4}{5}$ (d) $5 - \dfrac{2}{3}x \le \dfrac{1}{4}x - \dfrac{7}{8}$

4. For each of the following, find two rational numbers between the given fractions.

   (a) $\dfrac{3}{7}$ and $\dfrac{4}{7}$ (b) $\dfrac{^-7}{9}$ and $\dfrac{^-8}{9}$

   (c) $\dfrac{5}{6}$ and $\dfrac{83}{100}$ (d) $\dfrac{^-1}{3}$ and $\dfrac{3}{4}$

5. (a) If $b < 0$ and $d > 0$, is it true that $a/b > c/d$ if and only if $ad > bc$? Explain your answer.

   (b) If $b < 0$ and $d < 0$, is it true that $a/b > c/d$ if and only if $ad > bc$? Explain your answer.

6. The difference between one-fifth of a certain number and one-ninth of the number is less than 4. Find all possible rational numbers that satisfy this sentence.

7. Twice the number of pupils in a certain class is less than three times the number minus 39. Four times the number plus 20 is greater than 5 times the number minus 21. Find the number of pupils in the class.

8. (a) Explain why the set of whole numbers does not have the denseness property.

   (b) Explain why the set of integers does not have the denseness property.

9. If there are eighteen poodles and twelve cocker spaniels in a dog show, what is the ratio of poodles to cockers?

10. If a 4-ounce can of pepper costs 98¢, what is the cost per ounce?

11. If a new car is 8 feet long and 4½ feet high, what is the ratio of length to height?

12. Solve for x in each proportion.

   (a) $\dfrac{12}{x} = \dfrac{18}{45}$ (b) $\dfrac{x}{7} = \dfrac{^-10}{21}$

   (c) $\dfrac{5}{7} = \dfrac{3x}{98}$ (d) $3\dfrac{1}{2}$ is to 5 as x is to 15

13. There are five adult drivers for each teenage driver in Aluossim. If there are 12 345 adult drivers in Aluossim, how many teenage drivers are there?

14. If three grapefruits sell for 79¢, how much do eighteen grapefruits cost?

15. On a map, ⅓ inch represents 5 miles. If New York and Aluossim are 18 inches apart on the map, what is the actual distance between them?

16. Prove: For any rational numbers a/b and c/d, if $a/b = c/d$ where $a \ne 0$ and $c \ne 0$, then $b/a = d/c$.

17.   (a)   In Room A of the University Center there are one man and two women; in Room B there are two men and four women; and in Room C there are five men and ten women. If all the people in Rooms B and C go to Room A, what will be the ratio of men to women in Room A?

   ★(b)   Prove the following generalization of the proportions used in part (a).

$$\text{If } \frac{a}{b} = \frac{c}{d} = \frac{e}{f}, \text{ then } \frac{a}{b} = \frac{c}{d} = \frac{e}{f} = \frac{a+c+e}{b+d+f}.$$

18.   (a)   Prove that if

$$\frac{a}{b} = \frac{c}{d}, \text{ then } \frac{a+b}{b} = \frac{c+d}{d}. \left(\textit{Hint: } \frac{a}{b} + 1 = \frac{c}{d} + 1. \right)$$

   ★(b)   Prove that if

$$\frac{a}{b} = \frac{c}{d}, \text{ then } \frac{a-b}{a+b} = \frac{c-d}{c+d}.$$

★19.   Prove: (a)   Theorem 6-1   (b)   Theorem 6-2   (c)   Theorem 6-3

★20.   If

$$0 < \frac{a}{b} < \frac{c}{d}, \text{ prove that } 0 < \frac{a}{b} < \frac{1}{2}\left(\frac{a}{b} + \frac{c}{d} \right) < \frac{c}{d}.$$

6-5   EXPONENTS REVISITED

Recall that for whole numbers a, m, and n, with $a \neq 0$, the following properties hold.

1. $a^m = \underbrace{a \cdot a \cdot a \cdot \ldots \cdot a}_{m \text{ terms}}$

2. $a^m \cdot a^n = a^{m+n}$

3. $a^0 = 1$ where $a \neq 0$

BRAIN TEASER

Find the exact time between 2 o'clock and 3 o'clock when the hands of a clock coincide.

Notice that Property (3) is consistent with Property (2). If $m = 0$, then $a^m \cdot a^n = a^{m+n}$ becomes $a^0 \cdot a^n = a^{0+n} = a^n$ and 1 is the only number that, upon multiplying by a^n, gives a^n. The above notions can be extended for rational number values of a. For example,

$$\left(\frac{2}{3} \right)^4 = \frac{2}{3} \cdot \frac{2}{3} \cdot \frac{2}{3} \cdot \frac{2}{3};$$

$$\left(\frac{2}{3} \right)^2 \cdot \left(\frac{2}{3} \right)^3 = \left(\frac{2}{3} \cdot \frac{2}{3} \right) \cdot \left(\frac{2}{3} \cdot \frac{2}{3} \cdot \frac{2}{3} \right) = \left(\frac{2}{3} \right)^{2+3} = \left(\frac{2}{3} \right)^5; \text{ and } \left(\frac{2}{3} \right)^0 = 1.$$

Exponents can also be extended to negative integers. Consider the following pattern.

$10^3 = 10 \cdot 10 \cdot 10$
$10^2 = 10 \cdot 10$
$10^1 = 10$
$10^0 = 1$

Notice that as the exponents decrease by one, the products on the right are divided by 10. Thus, the pattern might be continued as follows.

$$10^{-1} = \frac{1}{10} = \frac{1}{10^1}$$

$$10^{-2} = \frac{1}{10} \cdot \frac{1}{10} = \frac{1}{10^2}$$

$$10^{-3} = \frac{1}{10^2} \cdot \frac{1}{10} = \frac{1}{10^3}$$

If the pattern is extended, then we would predict that $10^{-n} = 1/10^n$. This is true and in general, for any nonzero number, a, $a^{-n} = 1/a^n$.

Another explanation for the definition of a^{-n} is as follows. If the property $a^m \cdot a^n = a^{m+n}$ is to hold for all integer exponents, then $a^{-n} \cdot a^n = a^{-n+n} = a^0 = 1$. Thus, a^{-n} is the multiplicative inverse of a^n, and, consequently, $a^{-n} = 1/a^n$.

Consider whether the property, $a^m \cdot a^n = a^{m+n}$, can be extended to include all powers of a, where the exponents are integers. For example, is it true that $2^4 \cdot 2^{-3} = 2^{4+^-3} = 2^1$? The definitions of 2^{-3} and the properties of nonnegative exponents assure that this is true.

$$2^4 \cdot 2^{-3} = 2^4 \cdot \frac{1}{2^3} = \frac{2^4}{2^3} = \frac{2^1 \cdot 2^3}{2^3} = 2^1$$

Also, $2^{-4} \cdot 2^{-3} = 2^{-4+^-3} = 2^{-7}$ by the following derivation.

$$2^{-4} \cdot 2^{-3} = \frac{1}{2^4} \cdot \frac{1}{2^3} = \frac{1 \cdot 1}{2^4 \cdot 2^3} = \frac{1}{2^{4+3}} = \frac{1}{2^7} = 2^{-7}$$

In general, with integer exponents the following property holds.

Property | For any nonzero rational number a and any integers m and n, $a^m \cdot a^n = a^{m+n}$.

Other properties of exponents can be developed using the notions of rational numbers. Consider the following.

$$\frac{2^5}{2^3} = \frac{2^3 \cdot 2^2}{2^3} = 2^2 = 2^{5-3}$$

Thus, for any rational number a such that $a \neq 0$ and for integers m and n such that $m > n$, $a^m/a^n = a^{m-n}$. Now, consider the case when $m < n$. For example, $2^5/2^8$. If the property $a^m/a^n = a^{m-n}$ is to hold, then $2^5/2^8 = 2^{5-8} = 2^{-3}$. This is true by the following argument.

$$\frac{2^5}{2^8} = \frac{2^5}{2^5 \cdot 2^3} = \frac{1}{2^3} = 2^{-3}$$

Since the same procedure applies if $m = n$, the following property holds.

Property | For any rational number a such that $a \neq 0$ and for any integers m and n, $a^m/a^n = a^{m-n}$.

Suppose a is a nonzero rational number and m and n are positive integers.

$$(a^m)^n = \underbrace{a^m \cdot a^m \cdot a^m \cdot \ldots \cdot a^m}_{n \text{ terms}} = a^{\overbrace{m+m+\cdots+m}^{n \text{ terms}}} = a^{nm}$$

Thus, $(a^m)^n = a^{mn}$. For example, $(2^3)^4 = 2^{3 \cdot 4} = 2^{12}$.

Does this property hold for negative integer exponents? For example, does $(2^3)^{-4} = 2^{(3)(-4)} = 2^{-12}$? The answer is yes, because $(2^3)^{-4} = 1/(2^3)^4 = 1/2^{12} = 2^{-12}$. Also, $(2^{-3})^4 = (1/2^3)^4 = 1/2^3 \cdot 1/2^3 \cdot 1/2^3 \cdot 1/2^3 = 1^4/(2^3)^4 = 1/2^{12} = 2^{-12}$.

Property | For any rational number $a \neq 0$ and integers m and n, $(a^m)^n = a^{mn}$.

Using the definitions and properties developed, additional properties can be derived. Notice, for example, that

$$\left(\frac{2}{3}\right)^4 = \frac{2}{3} \cdot \frac{2}{3} \cdot \frac{2}{3} \cdot \frac{2}{3} = \frac{2 \cdot 2 \cdot 2 \cdot 2}{3 \cdot 3 \cdot 3 \cdot 3} = \frac{2^4}{3^4}$$

Property | For any nonzero rational number a/b and any integer m, $(a/b)^m = a^m/b^m$.

Also, $(2 \cdot 3)^{-3} = 1/(2 \cdot 3)^3 = 1/(2^3 \cdot 3^3) = (1/2^3) \cdot (1/3^3) = 2^{-3} \cdot 3^{-3}$, and in general, it is true that $(a \cdot b)^m = a^m \cdot b^m$ if a and b are rational numbers and m is an integer.

The definitions and properties of exponents are summarized in the following list.

1. $a^m = \underbrace{a \cdot a \cdot a \cdot \ldots \cdot a}_{m \text{ terms}}$, where m is a positive integer

2. $a^0 = 1$, where $a \neq 0$

3. $a^{-m} = \dfrac{1}{a^m}$, where $a \neq 0$

4. $a^m \cdot a^n = a^{m+n}$

5. $\dfrac{a^m}{a^n} = a^{m-n}$, where $a \neq 0$

6. $(a^m)^n = a^{mn}$

7. $\left(\dfrac{a}{b}\right)^m = \dfrac{a^m}{b^m}$, where $b \neq 0$

8. $(ab)^m = a^m \cdot b^m$

Observe that all the properties of exponents refer to powers with either the same base or the same exponent. Hence, to evaluate expressions using exponents where different bases or powers are used, perform all the computations or rewrite the expressions using either the same base or exponent if possible. For example, $27^4/81^3$ can be rewritten as $27^4/81^3 = (3^3)^4/(3^4)^3 = 3^{12}/3^{12} = 1$.

Example 6-23   Write each of the following in the simplest form using positive exponents in the final answer.

(a) $16^2 \cdot 8^{-3}$ (b) $20^2 \div 2^4$

(c) $(3x)^3 + 2y^2x^0 + 5y^2 + x^2 \cdot x$, where $x \neq 0$

Solution   (a) $16^2 \cdot 8^{-3} = (2^4)^2 \cdot (2^3)^{-3} = 2^{8+{-9}} = 28 + {-9} = 2^{-1} = 1/2$
(b) $20^2/2^4 = (2^2 \cdot 5)^2/2^4 = (2^4 \cdot 5^2)/2^4 = 5^2$
(c) $(3x)^3 + 2y^2x^0 + 5y^2 + x^2 \cdot x = 27x^3 + 2y^2 \cdot 1 + 5y^2 + x^3 = (27x^3 + x^3) + (2y^2 + 5y^2) = 28x^3 + 7y^2$

PROBLEM SET 6-5

1. Write each of the following in the simplest form with positive exponents in the final answer.

(a) $3^{-7} \cdot 3^{-6}$ (b) $3^7 \cdot 3^6$ (c) $5^{15} \div 5^4$ (d) $5^{15} \div 5^{-4}$

(e) $(^-5)^{-2}$ (f) $\dfrac{a^2}{a^{-3}}$, where $a \neq 0$ (g) $\dfrac{a}{a^{-1}}$, where $a \neq 0$

2. Write each of the following in the simplest form using positive exponents in the final answer.

   (a) $\left(\dfrac{1}{2}\right)^3 \cdot \left(\dfrac{1}{2}\right)^7$ (b) $\left(\dfrac{1}{2}\right)^9 \div \left(\dfrac{1}{2}\right)^6$ (c) $\left(\dfrac{2}{3}\right)^5 \cdot \left(\dfrac{4}{9}\right)^2$

   (d) $\left(\dfrac{3}{5}\right)^7 \div \left(\dfrac{3}{5}\right)^7$ (e) $\left(\dfrac{3}{5}\right)^{-7} \div \left(\dfrac{5}{3}\right)^4$ (f) $\left[\left(\dfrac{5}{6}\right)^7\right]^3$

3. If a and b are rational numbers with $a \neq 0$ and $b \neq 0$, m and n are integers, which of the following are true and which are false? Justify your answer.

   (a) $a^m \cdot b^n = (ab)^{m+n}$ (b) $a^m \cdot b^n = (ab)^{mn}$

   (c) $a^m \cdot b^m = (ab)^{2m}$ (d) $a^0 = 0$

   (e) $(a + b)^m = a^m + b^m$ (f) $(a + b)^{-m} = \dfrac{1}{a^m} + \dfrac{1}{b^m}$

   (g) $a^{mn} = a^m \cdot a^n$ (h) $\left(\dfrac{a}{b}\right)^{-n} = \left(\dfrac{b}{a}\right)^n$

4. Solve for the integer n in each of the following.
   (a) $2^n = 32$ (b) $n^2 = 36$ (c) $2^n \cdot 2^7 = 2^5$
   (d) $2^n \cdot 2^7 = 8$ (e) $(2 + n)^2 = 2^2 + n^2$ (f) $3^n = 27^5$

5. A human has approximately 25 trillion $(25 \cdot 10^{12})$ red blood cells, each with an average radius of $4 \cdot 10^{-3}$ millimeters. If these cells were placed end-to-end in a line, how long would the line be in millimeters? If 1 kilometer is 10^6 millimeters, how long will the line be in kilometers?

6. Solve each of the following inequalities for x, where x is an integer.
   (a) $3^x \leq 81$ (b) $4^x < 8$
   (c) $3^{2x} > 27$ (d) $2^x > 1$

7. Rewrite the following expressions using positive exponents and expressing all fractions in the simplest form.

   (a) $x^{-1} - x$ (b) $x^2 - y^{-2}$

   (c) $y^{-3} + y^3$ (d) $2x^2 + (2x)^2 + 2^2 x$

   (e) $\dfrac{3a - b}{(3a - b)^{-1}}$ (f) $(2x)^2 + (4a)^3 + a^2 \cdot 3a + 4x^2$

   (g) $(x^{-2} + 3y^{-1})^{-1}$

6-6   DECIMALS AND DECIMAL OPERATIONS

Historians have not determined when or where decimal notation was invented. Such notation has been found in documents from ancient China, medieval Arabia, and Renaissance Europe. In 1585, Simon Stevin published a pamphlet, *La Thiende* ("The Tenth"), and a book, *La Disme* ("The Decimal"), in which he presented an account of decimals and their usage.

Stevin's notation was not exactly like ours is today, but his work established the place of decimals in mathematics.

decimal point

Decimal numbers like 4.2, 0.234, and 562.681, include a dot called a **decimal point.** The digits to the left of the decimal point form the integer part of the decimal. The digits to the right represent the sum of a set of rational numbers whose numerators are the given digits and whose denominators are successive powers of ten starting with 10^1. For example, 562.681 represents $562 + 6/10^1 + 8/10^2 + 1/10^3 = 562 + 6/10 + 8/100 + 1/1000$ or $562 \; ^{681}/_{1000}$. The decimal 562.681 is read "five hundred sixty-two and six hundred eighty-one thousandths." The decimal point is read as "and." Table 6-6 shows other examples.

TABLE 6-6

Decimal	Meaning	Fraction
5.3	$5 + \dfrac{3}{10}$	$5\dfrac{3}{10}$ or $\dfrac{53}{10}$
0.02	$0 + \dfrac{0}{10} + \dfrac{2}{100}$	$\dfrac{2}{100}$
0.58	$0 + \dfrac{5}{10} + \dfrac{8}{100}$	$\dfrac{58}{100}$
2.0103	$2 + \dfrac{0}{10} + \dfrac{1}{100} + \dfrac{0}{1000} + \dfrac{3}{10\,000}$	$2\dfrac{103}{10\,000}$ or $\dfrac{20\,103}{10\,000}$
-3.6	$-\left(3 + \dfrac{6}{10}\right)$	$-3\dfrac{6}{10}$ or $-\dfrac{36}{10}$

Each place to the right of a decimal point may be named by its power of 10. For example, the places of 12.6184325 can be named as shown in Table 6-7. Every decimal also can be written in expanded form, using place value and negative exponents. For example, 12.6184325 is written $1 \cdot 10^1 + 2 \cdot 10^0 + 6 \cdot 10^{-1} + 1 \cdot 10^{-2} + 8 \cdot 10^{-3} + 4 \cdot 10^{-4} + 3 \cdot 10^{-5} + 2 \cdot 10^{-6} + 5 \cdot 10^{-7}$. However, to avoid negative exponents, most elementary texts use fractional notation. For example, $12.61843 = 1 \cdot 10^1 + 2 \cdot 10^0 + 6/10 +$

1/100 + 8/1000 + 4/10 000 + 3/100 000. Both forms are acceptable, and we use them interchangeably.

TABLE 6-7

1	2	.	6	1	8	4	3	2	5
Tens	Units	And	Tenths	Hundredths	Thousandths	Ten-thousandths	Hundred-thousandths	Millionths	Ten-millionths

Example 6-24 shows how to convert rational numbers whose denominators are powers of 10 to a decimal.

Example 6-24

Convert each of the following to decimals.

(a) $\dfrac{8}{10}$ (b) $\dfrac{56}{100}$ (c) $\dfrac{326}{10}$ (d) $\dfrac{235}{10\ 000}$

Solution

(a) $\dfrac{8}{10} = 0.8$

(b) $\dfrac{56}{100} = \dfrac{5 \cdot 10 + 6}{10^2} = \dfrac{5 \cdot 10}{10^2} + \dfrac{6}{10^2} = \dfrac{5}{10} + \dfrac{6}{10^2} = 0.56$

(c) $\dfrac{326}{10} = \dfrac{3 \cdot 10^2 + 2 \cdot 10 + 6}{10} = \dfrac{3 \cdot 10^2}{10} + \dfrac{2 \cdot 10}{10} + \dfrac{6}{10}$

$= 3 \cdot 10 + 2 + \dfrac{6}{10} = 32.6$

(d) $\dfrac{235}{10\ 000} = \dfrac{2 \cdot 10^2 + 3 \cdot 10 + 5}{10^4} = \dfrac{2 \cdot 10^2}{10^4} + \dfrac{3 \cdot 10}{10^4} + \dfrac{5}{10^4}$

$= \dfrac{2}{10^2} + \dfrac{3}{10^3} + \dfrac{5}{10^4} = 0.0235$

Example 6-24 suggests the following algorithm for expressing rational numbers, whose denominators are powers of 10, as decimals.

To express a rational number whose denominator is a power of 10 as a decimal, place the decimal point so that the number of digits to the right of the decimal point is the same as the exponent of the power of 10 in the denominator.

For example, $3/10^3 = 0.003$; $32/10^4 = 0.0032$; $52/10 = 5.2$.

In some cases, where the denominator is not a power of 10, a rational number can be rewritten so that the new denominator is a power of 10. For example, $3/5 = (3 \cdot 2)/(5 \cdot 2) = 6/10 = 0.6$. The reason for multiplying by 2 is apparent by observing that $10^n = (2 \cdot 5)^n = 2^n \cdot 5^n$. Thus, in order for the denominator of a rational number to be 10^n, the prime factorization of the denominator must be $2^n \cdot 5^n$.

Example 6-25   Express each of the following rational numbers as decimals.

(a) $\dfrac{7}{2^6}$ (b) $\dfrac{1}{2^3 \cdot 5^4}$

(c) $\dfrac{1}{5^3}$ (d) $\dfrac{7}{250}$

Solution   (a) $\dfrac{7}{2^6} = \dfrac{7 \cdot 5^6}{2^6 \cdot 5^6} = \dfrac{7 \cdot 15\,625}{(2 \cdot 5)^6} = \dfrac{109\,375}{10^6} = 0.109375$

(b) $\dfrac{1}{2^3 \cdot 5^4} = \dfrac{1 \cdot 2^1}{2^3 \cdot 5^4 \cdot 2^1} = \dfrac{2}{2^4 \cdot 5^4} = \dfrac{2}{(2 \cdot 5)^4} = \dfrac{2}{10^4} = 0.0002$

(c) $\dfrac{1}{5^3} = \dfrac{1 \cdot 2^3}{5^3 \cdot 2^3} = \dfrac{8}{(5 \cdot 2)^3} = \dfrac{8}{10^3} = 0.008$

(d) $\dfrac{7}{250} = \dfrac{7}{2 \cdot 5^3} = \dfrac{7 \cdot 2^2}{(2 \cdot 5^3)2^2} = \dfrac{28}{(2 \cdot 5)^3} = \dfrac{28}{10^3} = 0.028$

terminating decimals   The solutions in Example 6-25 are illustrations of **terminating decimals;** that is, decimals that can be written with only a finite number of places to the right of the decimal point.

In an attempt to rewrite 2/11 as a terminating decimal using the method in Example 6-25, first try to find a number b such that the following holds.

$$\frac{2}{11} = \frac{2b}{11b}, \text{ where } 11b \text{ is a power of } 10$$

By the Fundamental Theorem of Arithmetic (discussed in Chapter 5), the only prime factors of a power of 10 are 2 and 5. Thus, $11b$ cannot be a power of 10, since 11 is not a prime factor of 10. Therefore, there is no whole number b that will satisfy $2/11 = 2b/11b$, where $11b$ is a power of 10. A similar argument using the Fundamental Theorem of Arithmetic holds in general.

A rational number in simplest form, a/b, can be written as a terminating decimal if and only if the prime factorization of the denominator contains no primes other than 2 or 5.

Example 6-26 | Which of the following fractions can be written as terminating decimals?

(a) $\dfrac{7}{8}$ (b) $\dfrac{6}{125}$

(c) $\dfrac{21}{28}$ (d) $\dfrac{37}{768}$

Solution |
(a) $7/8 = 7/2^3$. Since the denominator is 2^3, $7/8$ can be written as a terminating decimal, namely, 0.875.
(b) $6/125 = 6/5^3$. Since the denominator is 5^3, $6/125$ can be written as a terminating decimal, namely, 0.048.
(c) $21/28 = 21/(2^2 \cdot 7) = 3/2^2$. Since the denominator of the fraction in simplest form is 2^2, then $21/28$ can be written as a terminating decimal, namely, 0.75.
(d) $37/768 = 37/(2^8 \cdot 3)$. Since this fraction is in simplest form and the denominator contains a factor of 3, $37/768$ cannot be written as a terminating decimal.

Remark | To determine whether or not a rational number a/b can be represented as a terminating decimal, consider the prime factorization of the denominator *only if* the fraction is in simplest form.

Decimal Operations

Consider the sum 3.26 + 14.7. Expressing these decimals as fractions gives the following.

$$3.26 + 14.7 = \left(3 + \frac{2}{10} + \frac{6}{100}\right) + \left(14 + \frac{7}{10}\right)$$

$$= (3 + 14) + \left(\frac{2}{10} + \frac{7}{10}\right) + \left(\frac{6}{100}\right)$$

$$= 17 + \frac{9}{10} + \frac{6}{100}$$

$$= 17.96$$

This addition, using fractions, was accomplished by grouping the tenths and hundredths and adding. This same grouping is accomplished by lining up the decimal points and adding as is done with whole numbers.

$$\begin{array}{r} 3.26 \\ +14.7 \\ \hline 17.96 \end{array}$$

Subtraction of terminating decimals also can be accomplished by lining up the decimal points. The argument that this is true is left as an exercise.

Example 6-27 | Compute each of the following.

(a)   14.36 + 5.2 + 0.036
(b)   17.013 − 2.98
(c)   17.01 − 2.938

Solution |

(a)
$$\begin{array}{r} 14.360 \\ 5.200 \\ +\ 0.036 \\ \hline 19.596 \end{array}$$

(b)
$$\begin{array}{r} 17.013 \\ -\ 2.980 \\ \hline 14.033 \end{array}$$

(c)
$$\begin{array}{r} 17.010 \\ -\ 2.938 \\ \hline 14.072 \end{array}$$

Remark | In Example 6-27, zeros are included for the missing place values. This does not change the problems. For example, $17.01 = 17 + 0/10 + 1/100 = 17 + 0/10 + 1/100 + 0/1000 = 17.010$.

Algorithms for multiplication of terminating decimals can be found by multiplying the corresponding fractions, each in the form a/b. Consider the product $(4.62)(2.4)$.

$$(4.62)(2.4) = \frac{462}{100} \cdot \frac{24}{10} = \frac{462}{10^2} \cdot \frac{24}{10^1}$$

$$= \frac{462 \cdot 24}{10^2 \cdot 10^1}$$

$$= \frac{11\ 088}{10^3}$$

$$= 11.088$$

The answer is obtained by multiplying the whole numbers 462 and 24 and then dividing the result by 10^3. In other words, the multiplication can be accomplished by first ignoring the decimal points in the product $(4.62)(2.4)$ and, then, positioning the decimal point in the answer three places to the left.

In general, if there are n digits to the right of the decimal point in one number and m digits to the right of the decimal point in a second number, multiply the two numbers ignoring the decimals and then place the decimal point so that there are $m + n$ digits to the right of the decimal point in the product.

Example 6-28

Compute each of the following.

(a) (6.2)(14.3) (b) (0.02)(0.013) (c) (1000)(3.6)

Solution

(a)
```
   1 4.3   (1 digit after the decimal point)
  × 6.2    (1 digit after the decimal point)
  -----
   2 8 6
  8 5 8
  -------
  8 8.6 6  (2 digits after the decimal point)
```

(b)
```
    0.0 1 3
  × 0.0 2
  ---------
  0.0 0 0 2 6
```

(c)
```
        3.6
  × 1 0 0 0
  ---------
  3 6 0 0.0
```

Remark

Example 6-28(c) suggests that multiplication by 10^n where n is a positive integer results in moving the decimal point in the multiplicand n places to the right.

Division of terminating decimals is based upon division of fractions. Consider the following examples.

$$4.9 \div 0.07 = \frac{49}{10} \div \frac{7}{100} = \frac{49}{10} \cdot \frac{100}{7} = \frac{4900}{70} = 70$$

$$2.5664 \div 3.2 = \frac{25\ 664}{10\ 000} \div \frac{32}{10} = \frac{25\ 664}{10\ 000} \cdot \frac{10}{32} = \frac{256\ 640}{320\ 000} = \frac{802}{1000} = 0.802$$

In both examples, the decimals were converted to fractions, the divisions performed, and then the decimal point placed in the quotient. Consider the division, $2 \div 4$. There are no decimal points and, hence, no apparent reason to follow the procedure just described. However, in elementary school textbooks, $2 \div 4$ is normally computed using the following algorithm.

$$
\begin{array}{r}
.5 \\
4\overline{)2.0} \\
\underline{2\,0}
\end{array}
$$

This algorithm does not reflect the earlier procedure that makes use of fractions since there are no obvious decimal points in 2 and 4 and thus no reason to introduce fractions. However, in the algorithm, the computation requires consideration of $2 \div 4$. The justification for the algorithm is as follows.

$$2 \div 4 = \frac{2}{4} = \frac{2 \cdot 10}{4 \cdot 10} = \frac{20}{4 \cdot 10} = \frac{20}{4} \cdot \frac{1}{10} = 5 \cdot \frac{1}{10} = 0.5$$

The procedure used on $2 \div 4$ can be extended to handle all divisions involving decimals. For example, $2.56 \div 3.2$ can be rewritten as $25.6 \div 32$ because

$$\frac{2.56}{3.2} = \frac{(2.56)10}{(3.2)10} = \frac{25.6}{32}$$

Then the algorithm developed for $2 \div 4$ works as follows.

$$
\begin{array}{r}
.8 \\
32\overline{)2\,5.6} \\
\underline{2\,5\,6}
\end{array}
$$

Notice that to use the algorithm for $2.56 \div 3.2$, the problem is first rewritten so the divisor, 3.2, becomes a whole number. To do this, multiply 3.2 by a power of 10. Then, to keep the fractions equal, multiply the dividend, 2.56, by the same power of 10. This moves the decimal points the same number of places. Usually arrows are drawn in the division to show where the decimal point should be after multiplying by the power of 10.

$$
\begin{array}{r}
.8 \\
3.2\overline{)2.5\,6} \\
\underline{2\,5\,6}
\end{array}
$$

Example 6-29	Compute each of the following.
	(a) $13.169 \div 0.13$ (b) $13.1 \div 1000$

Solution   (a)
$$
\begin{array}{r}
1\ 0\ 1.3 \\
0.1\ 3\overline{)1\ 3.1\ 6\ 9} \\
1\ 3 \\
\hline
1\ 6 \\
1\ 3 \\
\hline
3\ 9 \\
3\ 9 \\
\hline
\end{array}
$$

(b)
$$
\begin{array}{r}
.0\ 1\ 3\ 1 \\
1\ 0\ 0\ 0\overline{)1\ 3.1\ 0\ 0\ 0} \\
1\ 0\ 0\ 0 \\
\hline
3\ 1\ 0\ 0 \\
3\ 0\ 0\ 0 \\
\hline
1\ 0\ 0\ 0 \\
1\ 0\ 0\ 0 \\
\hline
\end{array}
$$

PROBLEM SET 6-6

1. Write each of the following in expanded form.
    (a) 0.023   (b) 206.06   (c) 312.0103   (d) 0.000132
2. Rewrite each of the following as decimals.
    (a) $4 \cdot 10^3 + 3 \cdot 10^2 + 5 \cdot 10 + 6 + 7 \cdot 10^{-1} + 8 \cdot 10^{-2}$
    (b) $4 \cdot 10^3 + 6 \cdot 10^{-1} + 8 \cdot 10^{-3}$
3. Write each of the following as numerals.
    (a) Five hundred thirty-six and seventy-six ten-thousandths
    (b) Three and eight thousandths
    (c) Four hundred thirty-six millionths
    (d) Five million and two tenths
4. Write each of the following terminating decimals as fractions.
    (a) 0.436   (b) 25.16   (c) $^-$316.027
    (d) 28.1902   (e) $^-$4.3   (f) $^-$62.01
5. Determine which of the following represent terminating decimals, without performing the actual divisions.

    (a) $\dfrac{4}{5}$ (b) $\dfrac{61}{2^2 \cdot 5}$ (c) $\dfrac{3}{6}$

    (d) $\dfrac{1}{2^{15}}$ (e) $\dfrac{36}{5^5}$ (f) $\dfrac{133}{625}$

    (g) $\dfrac{1}{3}$ (h) $\dfrac{2}{35}$ (i) $\dfrac{1}{13}$

6. Where possible, write each of the numbers in Problem 5 as terminating decimals.
7. Compute each of the following.
    (a) $36.812 + 0.43 + 1.96$ (b) $200.01 + 32.007 + {}^-1.32$
    (c) $200.01 - 32.007$ (d) $^-4.612 - 386.0193$
    (e) $(3.61)(0.413)$ (f) $(0.0123)(4.681)$
    (g) $(^-2.6)(4)$ (h) $10.7663 \div 2.3$
    (i) $0.006384 \div (^-1.6)$

8. Calculate the following by converting each decimal to a fraction, performing the computation and then converting the fraction answer to a decimal.
   (a) 13.62 + 4.082   (b) 12.62 − 4.082   (c) (1.36)(0.02)
   (d) (1.36) ÷ (0.02)

9. Multiply each of the following by (i) 10, (ii) 1000, (iii) 10^8.
   (a) 4.63   (b) 0.04   (c) 46.3   (d) 463.0
   (e) 0.00463   (f) 0.0000000463   (g) 0.79   (h) 6.2

10. Explain why $10^3(0.abcd) = abc.d$.

11. Explain why subtraction of terminating decimals can be accomplished by lining up the decimal points and subtracting as if the numbers were whole numbers (or integers).

12. If 0.896 inch of rain fell during 7 hours, what was the average amount of rain per hour?

13. If the average for common stocks rose 8.395 points during 5 days of trading, what was the average gain per day?

14. If Moose went to the store and bought a chair for $17.95, a lawn rake for $13.59, a spade for $14.86, a lawn mower for $179.98, and two six-packs for $2.43 each, what was the bill?

15. If the rainfall was 1.9 inches in March and 2.7 inches in April, how much more rain was there in April than March?

16. At 60° Fahrenheit, 1 quart of water weighs 2.082 pounds. One cubic foot of water is 29.922 quarts. What is the weight of a cubic foot of water?

★17. Given any reduced rational a/b with $0 < a < b$, where b is of the form $2^m \cdot 5^n$ (m and n are whole numbers), determine a relationship between m and/or n and the number of digits in the terminating decimal.

 18. Do Problems 105, 106, 110, 111, 125, 126, and 128 appearing in Appendix II.

6-7 MORE ABOUT DECIMALS AND THEIR PROPERTIES

The division processes described in the previous section can be used to develop a procedure for converting any rational number to a decimal. Recall that 7/8 can be written as a terminating decimal since the denominator $8 = 2^3$.

```
      .875
   8) 7.000
      6 4
      ───
       60
       56
       ──
        40
        40
        ──
```

BRAIN TEASER

Arrange four 7's using any operations and decimal points needed to obtain a value of 100.

In a similar way, nonterminating decimals can be obtained for other rational numbers. For example, to find a decimal representation for 2/11, consider the following division.

$$
\begin{array}{r}
.18 \\
11\overline{)2.00} \\
\underline{1\ 1} \\
90 \\
\underline{88} \\
2
\end{array}
$$

Notice that the remainder of 2 is exactly the same as the dividend and hence, the original division repeats. Thus, the answer to the problem is 0.181818. . . .

repeating decimal
repetend Observe that 0.18181818 . . . has a block of two repeating digits. A decimal of this type is called a **repeating decimal,** and the repeating block of digits is called the **repetend.** The repeating decimal is written as $0.\overline{18}$, where the bar (called the vinculum) indicates that the block of digits underneath is repeated endlessly.

Example 6-30   Convert 1/7 to a decimal.

Solution

$$
\begin{array}{r}
.142857 \\
7\overline{)1.000000} \\
\underline{7} \\
30 \\
\underline{28} \\
20 \\
\underline{14} \\
60 \\
\underline{56} \\
40 \\
\underline{35} \\
50 \\
\underline{49} \\
1
\end{array}
$$

Since the remainder of 1 is the same as the dividend, the division repeats and, thus, $1/7 = 0.\overline{142857}$.

In Example 6-30, the remainders obtained in the division are 3, 2, 6, 4, 5, and 1. These are all the possible nonzero remainders that can be obtained when dividing by 7. (If the remainder of 0 had been obtained, the decimal would terminate.) If a/b is any rational number in simplest form and it does not represent a terminating decimal, then the possible remainders upon division by b are 1, 2, 3, 4, . . . , $b - 1$. After b divisions, there are b remainders, which cannot *all* be different, since there are only $b - 1$ possible different remainders. Thus, after b divisions, at least one remainder appears twice. When this happens, a block of at most $b - 1$ digits in the quotient repeats. Therefore, *a rational number may always be represented either as a terminating decimal or as a repeating decimal.*

Converting Repeating Decimals to Fractions

Consider the repeating decimal, $0.\overline{5}$ or $0.555\ldots$. To write $0.\overline{5}$ in the form a/b, it would be natural to try the same method used with terminating decimals, for example, $0.55 = 55/10^2 = 55/100$. However, the repeating decimal has infinitely many places, and hence, there is no single power of 10 that can be placed in the denominator. Let $n = 0.\overline{5}$. Since $10(0.555\ldots) = 5.555\ldots = 5.\overline{5}$, then, $10n = 5.\overline{5}$. Now, subtract as below to obtain an equation whose solution is in the form a/b.

$$
\begin{array}{r}
10n = 5.\overline{5} \\
-n = -0.\overline{5} \\
\hline
9n = 5
\end{array}
$$

$$n = \frac{5}{9}$$

Thus, $0.\overline{5} = 5/9$. This result can be checked by performing the division $5 \div 9$. Notice that by performing the subtraction above, an equation containing only rational numbers results. (The repeating blocks "cancel" each other.)

Suppose a decimal has a repetend of more than one digit, such as $0.\overline{235}$. In order to write it in the form a/b, it is reasonable to multiply by 10^3, since there is a three-digit repetend. Let $n = 0.\overline{235}$. Then,

$$
\begin{array}{r}
1000n = 235.\overline{235} \\
-n = -0.\overline{235} \\
\hline
999n = 235
\end{array}
$$

$$n = \frac{235}{999}$$

Hence, $0.\overline{235} = 235/999$.

Notice that $0.\overline{5}$ repeats in blocks of one digit, and to write it in the form a/b, we first multiply by 10^1; $0.\overline{235}$ repeats in blocks of three digits, and we first multiply by 10^3. In general, if the repetend is immediately to the right of the decimal point, first multiply by 10^n, where n is the number of digits in the repetend.

Now, suppose the repeating block is not immediately after the decimal point. For example, let $n = 2.3\overline{45}$. To rewrite this problem in a form where the decimal point immediately precedes the repeating block, multiply by 10.

$10n = 23.\overline{45}$

Now use the procedure for the repetend immediately to the right of the decimal point. Since $10n = 23.\overline{45}$, then $100(10n) = 2345.\overline{45}$. Thus,

$$1000n = 2345.\overline{45}$$
$$-10n = -23.\overline{45}$$
$$990n = 2322$$

$$n = \frac{2322}{990} \quad \text{or} \quad \frac{774}{330}$$

Hence, $2.3\overline{45} = 2322/990$ or $774/330$.

Since rational numbers can be written as either terminating or repeating decimals and vice versa, decimals of this type have all the properties of rational numbers. The properties of rational numbers that hold for all operations are summarized in Table 6-8. Since the denseness property holds for the set of rational numbers (between any two rational numbers there is another rational number), it also holds for the set of all repeating or terminating decimals.

TABLE 6-8   Properties of Operations of Rational Numbers

Property	+	×	−	÷
Closure	Yes	Yes	Yes	Yes (except for division by 0)
Commutative	Yes	Yes	No	No
Associative	Yes	Yes	No	No
Identity	Yes	Yes	No	No
Inverse	Yes	Yes (except for 0)	No	No
The distributive property of multiplication over addition holds.				

One way to order two decimals is to convert both to fractions and then compare the fractions. To compare terminating decimals such as 3.869 and 3.87, rewrite the decimals so that there are exactly the same number of digits after the decimal points, namely 3.869 and 3.870. Now, since $3870/1000 > 3869/1000$, $3.870 > 3.869$. This procedure can be accomplished without the use of fractions simply by writing the decimals one under the other, lining up the decimal points as follows.

3.870
3.869

The digits are the same in the units and tenths places. Since the digit in the hundredths place of 3.870 is larger than the hundredths digit in 3.869, then 3.870 > 3.869. This procedure will work for all terminating decimals.

To compare nonterminating decimals such as $1.\overline{3478}$ and $1.34\overline{7821}$ without converting them to fractions, first write the decimals, one under the other, in their equivalent form without the bar, and line up the decimal points.

1.34783478 . . .
1.34782178 . . .

Notice that the first four digits after the decimal points are the same in each of the numbers. Since the digit in the hundred-thousandths place of the top number is 3, which is greater than the digit 2 in the hundred-thousandths place of the bottom number, $1.\overline{3478}$ is greater than $1.34\overline{7821}$.

Example 6-31	Find a rational number in decimal form between $0.\overline{35}$ and $0.\overline{351}$.
Solution	First line up the decimals.

0.353535 . . .
0.351351 . . .

To find a decimal between these two, observe that starting from the left, the first place that the two numbers differ is the thousandths place. Clearly, one decimal between these two is 0.352. However, there are infinitely many others.

PROBLEM SET 6-7

1. Find the decimal representation for each of the following.

   (a) $\dfrac{4}{9}$ (b) $\dfrac{2}{7}$ (c) $\dfrac{3}{11}$ (d) $\dfrac{1}{15}$

   (e) $\dfrac{2}{75}$ (f) $\dfrac{1}{99}$ (g) $\dfrac{5}{6}$ (h) $\dfrac{1}{13}$

2. Convert each of the following repeating decimals to fractions.
   (a) $2.4\overline{5}$ (b) $2.\overline{45}$ (c) $2.4\overline{54}$ (d) $0.2\overline{45}$
   (e) $0.02\overline{45}$ (f) $24.\overline{54}$ (g) $0.\overline{4}$ (h) $0.\overline{6}$
   (i) $0.\overline{55}$ (j) $0.\overline{34}$ (k) $^-2.\overline{34}$ (l) $^-0.0\overline{2}$

3. Order each of the following sets of decimals from greatest to least.
    (a) $\{3.2, 3.\overline{22}, 3.\overline{23}, 3.2\overline{3}, 3.23\}$ (b) $\{^-1.454, ^-1.45\overline{4}, ^-1.45, ^-1.4\overline{54}, ^-1.\overline{454}\}$
4. Find a decimal between each of the following pairs of decimals.
    (a) 3.2 and 3.3   (b) 462.24 and 462.25   (c) $462.2\overline{4}$ and $462.\overline{24}$
    (d) 0.003 and 0.03
5. (a) Find a rational number in the form a/b for $0.\overline{9}$.
    (b) $0.\overline{9}$ is either less than 1, greater than 1, or equal to 1. Argue that both $0.\overline{9} < 1$ and $0.\overline{9} >$ 1 are impossible.
    (c) Use the fact that $1/3 = 0.\overline{3}$ and multiply both sides of the equation by 3 to show that $0.\overline{9}$ = 1.
    ★(d) Read "Persuasive Arguments: .9999 · · · · = 1" by Lucien T. Hall, Jr. in *The Mathematics Teacher,* December 1971, pp. 749–750.
6. Suppose $a = 0.\overline{32}$ and $b = 0.\overline{123}$.
    (a) Find $a + b$ by adding from left to right. How many digits are in the repetend of the sum?
    (b) Find $a + b$ if $a = 1.2\overline{34}$ and $b = 0.1\overline{234}$. Is the answer a rational number? How many digits are in the repetend?
7. Find the decimal half-way between the two given decimals.
    (a) 3.2 and 3.3   (b) 462.24 and 462.25   (c) 0.0003 and 0.03
    ★(d) $462.2\overline{4}$ and $462.\overline{24}$
8. Do Problems 97 and 98 appearing in Appendix II.

6-8   PERCENTS, ROUNDING, AND SCIENTIFIC NOTATION

Percents

percent   A common ratio in everyday usage is **percent.** The word *percent* comes from the Latin phrase *per centum,* which may be translated as per hundred. For example, a bank that pays 6 percent interest on a savings account pays $6 for each $100 on the account. In other words, the bank pays 6/100 of whatever amount is in the account. A percent is the numerator of a fraction in which the denominator is 100. We use the symbol % to indicate percent and write 15% for 15/100.

     Any ratio such as 3/5 can be expressed as a percent by finding the number x such that $3/5 = x/100$.

$$3 \cdot 100 = 5x$$
$$300 = 5x$$
$$60 = x$$

Thus, $3/5 = 60/100 = 60\%$.

Example 6-32

Express each of the following as percents.

(a) $\dfrac{4}{5}$ (b) $\dfrac{1}{11}$

Solution

(a) $\dfrac{4}{5} = \dfrac{x}{100}$

$5 \cdot x = 4 \cdot 100$

$5x = 400$

$x = 80$

Hence,

$$\dfrac{4}{5} = \dfrac{80}{100} = 80\%.$$

(b) $\dfrac{1}{11} = \dfrac{x}{100}$

$1 \cdot 100 = 11 \cdot x$

$100 = 11x$

$\dfrac{100}{11} = x$

Hence,

$$\dfrac{1}{11} = \dfrac{\dfrac{100}{11}}{100} = \dfrac{100}{11}\% \text{ or } 9\dfrac{1}{11}\%.$$

To express a decimal such as 3.02 as a percent, consider the proportion

$$\dfrac{3.02}{1} = \dfrac{x}{100}$$

$(3.02)(100) = 1 \cdot x$

$302 = x$

Hence, $3.02 = 302/100 = 302\%$. In general, to express a decimal as a percent, move the decimal point two places to the right and annex the % symbol.

Example 6-33

Express each of the following as percents.

(a)   21.6   (b)   0.060   (c) $\dfrac{3}{4}$ (d) $\dfrac{1}{3}$

Solution

(a) $21.6 = 2160\%$ (b) $0.060 = 6.0\%$

(c) $\dfrac{3}{4} = 0.75 = 75\%$ (d) $\dfrac{1}{3} = 0.\overline{3} = 33.\overline{3}\%$

Because percent is the numerator of a fraction in which the denominator is 100, percents can be converted into decimals by simply moving the decimal point two places to the left and dropping the % symbol.

Example 6-34   Convert each of the following percents to decimals.

(a)   5%   (b)   6.3%   (c)   250%   (d) $\dfrac{1}{4}\%$ (e) $\dfrac{1}{3}\%$

Solution

(a) $5\% = \dfrac{5}{100} = 0.05$

(b) $6.3\% = \dfrac{6.3}{100} = 0.063$

(c) $250\% = \dfrac{250}{100} = 2.50$

(d) $\dfrac{1}{4}\% = \dfrac{\frac{1}{4}}{100} = \dfrac{1}{4} \cdot \dfrac{1}{100} = 0.25 \cdot \dfrac{1}{100} = 0.0025$

(e) $\dfrac{1}{3}\% = \dfrac{\frac{1}{3}}{100} = \dfrac{1}{3} \cdot \dfrac{1}{100} = 0.\overline{3} \cdot \dfrac{1}{100} = 0.00\overline{3}$

Remark   The algorithm for converting a percent to a decimal by moving the decimal point two places to the left and dropping the % symbol is somewhat misleading. For example, in part (d) above, rarely is a decimal written as $0.00\frac{1}{4}$, which would be obtained using the algorithm.

Percent problems can be solved using either ratios or decimals. Applications using percents usually involve finding a percent of a number, finding a number when a percent of that number is known, or finding what percent one number is of another number.

Example 6-35   Find 5% of 700.

Solution | 5% of 700 means 5/100 · 700, which equals 35. Thus, 5% of 700 is 35.

Alternate solution

5% of 700 means 0.05 · 700 = 35.00. Thus, 5% of 700 is 35.

Example 6-36 | If $800 is deposited in a savings account paying 6% interest per year, find the interest paid at the end of a year.

Solution | Interest in dollars = 6% of 800

$$= 0.06 \cdot 800$$

$$= 48.00$$

Thus, $48 is the interest paid at the end of the year.

Example 6-37 | Forty-two percent of the parents of the school children in the Paxson School District are employed at Di Paloma University. If the number of parents employed by D.P.U. is 168, how many parents are in the school district?

Solution | Let n = the total number of parents in the district

$$168 = 42\% \text{ of } n$$

$$168 = 0.42 \cdot n$$

$$\frac{168}{0.42} = n$$

$$400 = n$$

Thus, there are 400 parents in the school district.

Example 6-38 | If Joe Smart has 45 correct answers on an 80 question test, what percent of his answers are correct?

Solution | Let n = the percent of correct answers

$$45 = n\% \text{ of } 80$$

$$45 = \frac{n}{100} \cdot 80$$

$$\frac{45}{80} = \frac{n}{100}$$

$$0.5625 = \frac{n}{100}$$

$$56.25 = n$$

Thus, Joe had 56.25% of his answers correct.

Additional problems involving percents are found on page 262 from Addison-Wesley, *Mathematics in Our World,* Grade 6, 1978.

Rounding

BRAIN TEASER

The crust of a certain pumpkin pie is 25% of the pie. By what percent should the amount of crust be reduced in order to make it constitute 20% of the pie?

Frequently, it is not necessary to know the exact numerical answer to a question. For example, if we ask a person's age, we usually are not interested in an exact answer. Also, we do not know exactly how far it is to the moon or how many people live in New York City. However, we do know approximately how old we are, and we can find that it is approximately 239 000 miles to the moon and that there are approximately 7 772 000 people who live in New York City.

In order to approximate numbers, we adopt the following rules for "rounding."

1. To round a whole number to a given place value, find the place value and then examine the digit to its right. If the digit to the right is 5 or greater, then replace all digits to the right by zeros and increase the given place value by 1. If the digit to the right is less than 5, then replace all digits to the right of the given place value by zeros.
2. To round a decimal less than 1 to a given place value or to a fixed number of decimal places, find the place value and then examine the digit to its right. If the digit to the right is 5 or greater, then drop all digits to the right and increase the given place value by 1. If the digit to the right is less than 5, then drop all the digits to the right of the given place value.

Remark   To round a number like 216.38 to a place value greater than or equal to 1, use rule 1. To round to a place value less than 1, use rule 2.

To symbolize approximations, we use $\doteq$. In some books, $\approx$ is used.

Example 6-39   Round each of the following numbers.

(a) 7.456 to the nearest hundredth
(b) 7.456 to the nearest tenth

Finding interest

Banks and savings companies pay their customers **interest** on the money deposited in savings accounts. If a bank pays 5% per year interest, how much interest would it pay on $145 deposited in an account for one year?

Finding the answer

Rate of interest × Amount of savings = Interest

$$5\% \quad \times \quad \$145 \quad = \quad n$$

$$\begin{array}{r} \$\ 145 \\ \times\ 0.05 \\ \hline \$\ 7.25 \end{array}$$

The interest on $145 for one year at a rate of 5% per year is $7.25.

Find the interest for one year on the following amounts.

1. Amount of savings: $500
   Rate of interest: 4%
   Interest: ▓

2. Amount of savings: $250
   Rate of interest: 4.5%
   Interest: ▓

3. Amount of savings: $2000
   Rate of interest: 5%
   Interest: ▓

4. Amount of savings: $3500
   Rate of interest: 6%
   Interest: ▓

(c)   7.456 to the nearest unit
(d)   7456 to the nearest thousand
(e)   745 to the nearest ten
(f)   74.56 to the nearest ten

Solution

(a) $7.456 \doteq 7.46$ (b) $7.456 \doteq 7.5$ (c) $7.456 \doteq 7$
(d) $7456 \doteq 7000$ (e) $745 \doteq 750$ (f) $74.56 \doteq 70$

Rounded numbers usually are used for estimating answers to computations. For example, if we computed $(16.23)(4.08)$ and obtained an answer of 662.184, then by rounding 16.23 to 16 and 4.08 to 4, a quick check of $16 \cdot 4 = 64$ shows that there must be an error in the answer.

Scientific Notation

scientific notation

In disciplines such as chemistry, microbiology, and physics, where either very large or very small numbers are used, a scientific notation is used to help handle such numbers. In **scientific notation,** a number is written as the product of a number between 1 and 10, and a power of 10. For example, "the sun is 93 000 000 miles from earth" is expressed as "the sun is $9.3 \cdot 10^7$ miles from earth." A micrometer, a metric unit of measure that is 0.000001 meter, is written as $1 \cdot 10^{-6}$ meter.

Example 6-40

Write each of the following in scientific notation.

(a)   413 682 000   (b)   0.0000231

Solution

(a) $413\ 682\ 000 = 4.13682 \cdot 10^8$ (b) $0.0000231 = 2.31 \cdot 10^{-5}$

Example 6-41

Convert each of the following to standard numerals.

(a) $6.84 \cdot 10^{-5}$ (b) $3.12 \cdot 10^7$

Solution

(a) $6.84 \cdot 10^{-5} = 6.84 \cdot (1/10^5) = 0.0000684$
(b) $3.12 \cdot 10^7 = 31\ 200\ 000$

PROBLEM SET 6-8

1.   Express each of the following as percents.

(a)   7.89   (b)   0.032   (c)   193.1   (d)   0.2

(e) $\dfrac{5}{6}$ (f) $\dfrac{3}{20}$ (g) $\dfrac{1}{75}$ (h) $\dfrac{40}{7}$

2. Convert each of the following percents to decimals.

   (a)   16%   (b) $4\frac{1}{2}\%$ (c) $\frac{1}{5}\%$ (d) $\frac{2}{7}\%$

3. Answer each of the following.
   (a)   Find 6% of 34.   (b)   17 is what percent of 34?
   (c)   18 is 30% of what number?

4. Marc had 84 boxes of Cub Scout candy to sell. He sold 75% of the boxes. How many did he sell?

5. Gail was making $16 000 a year and received a 6% raise. How much does she make now?

6. Gail received a 7% raise last year. If her salary is now $15 515, what was her salary last year?

7. Joe sold 180 newspapers out of 200. Bill sold 85% of his 260 newspapers. Ran sold 212 newspapers, 80% of the ones he had.
   (a)   Who sold the most newspapers? How many?
   (b)   Who sold the greatest percent of his newspapers? What percent?
   (c)   Who started with the greatest number of newspapers? How many?

8. Interest, I, equals the principal, P, multiplied by the rate, r, and the time, t. That is, $I = Prt$.
   (a)   A loan of $2000 is made for 1 year at a rate of 6% per year. How much is the interest owed at the end of the year?
   (b)   Solve for r in the preceding formula.

9. A bank pays 6% yearly interest on money left in a savings account for a year. If you put $100 in an account on January 1, 1980, what is the earliest date your account would contain at least $200, assuming that you made no additional deposits or withdrawals?

10. In a savings plan, 5% interest is paid every 6 months. If the account had $500 on January 1, 1980 and interest was paid July 1 and January 1, how much is in the savings account on January 1, 1982, assuming there were no withdrawals?

11. Work all the problems on the student page in this section.

12. If a dress that normally sells for $35 is on sale for $28, what is the "percent off"? (This could be called a **percent of decrease,** or a discount.)

13. Mort bought his house in 1975 for $29 000. It was recently appraised at $55 000. What is the **percent of increase** in value?

14. Round each of the following numbers as specified.
    (a)   203.651 to the nearest hundred   (b)   203.651 to the nearest ten
    (c)   203.651 to the nearest unit   (d)   203.651 to the nearest tenth
    (e)   203.651 to the nearest hundredth

15. Express each of the following numbers in scientific notation.
    (a)   3325   (b)   46.32   (c)   0.00013   (d)   930 146

16. Convert each of the following numbers to standard numerals.
    (a) $3.2 \cdot 10^{-9}$ (b) $3.2 \cdot 10^{9}$ (c) $4.2 \cdot 10^{-1}$ (d) $6.2 \cdot 10^{5}$

17. Do Problems 107, 113–124, 127, and 129 appearing in Appendix II.

6-9 REAL NUMBERS

Are there any decimals that neither terminate or repeat? Consider the characteristics that such decimals must have.

1. There must be an infinite number of nonzero digits to the right of the decimal point.
2. There cannot be a repeating block of digits (a repetend).

Does a decimal like 0.1432865 . . . have these characteristcs? Since the decimal is infinite, the first characteristic is satisfied. However, without more information, there is no way to tell whether there is a repeating block of digits in the decimal.

There are several ways to construct a nonterminating, nonrepeating decimal. Perhaps the simplest is to devise a pattern of infinite digits in such a way that there will definitely be no repeated block. Consider the number 0.1010010001. . . . If the pattern shown continues, the next groups of digits are four zeros followed by 1, five zeros followed by 1, etc. It is possible to describe a *pattern* for this decimal, but there is no repeating block of digits. Since this decimal is nonterminating and nonrepeating, it cannot represent a

irrational numbers   rational number. Numbers that are not rational are called **irrational numbers.**

In the early twentieth century, it was proved that the number that is the

pi   ratio of the circumference of a circle to its diameter, symbolized by π (**pi**), is irrational. Traditionally, in schools we use $^{22}\!/_{7}$, or 3.14, or 3.14159 for π. These are only rational approximations of π. The value of π has been computed to thousands of decimal places with no apparent pattern.

Other irrational numbers occur in the study of area. For example, to find the area of a square, we use the formula $A = s^2$, where A is the area and s is the length of a side of the square. If a side of a square is 3 cm long, then the area of the square is 9 cm^2 (square centimeters). Conversely, we can use the formula to find the length of a side, given the area. If the area of a square is

square root   25 cm^2, then $s^2 = 25$, so $s = 5$ or -5. Each of these solutions is called a **square root** of 25. However, because lengths are always nonnegative, 5 is the only possible solution. The positive solution of $s^2 = 25$, namely, 5, is called the

principal square root   **principal square root** of 25 and is denoted $\sqrt{25}$. Similarly, the principal square root of 2 is denoted $\sqrt{2}$.

DEFINITION

> If a is any whole number, the **principal square root** of a is the nonnegative number b such that $b \cdot b = b^2 = a$.

The principal square root of a is denoted by $\sqrt{a}$, where the symbol $\sqrt{}$ is called

radical sign, radicand   a **radical sign** and a is called the **radicand**.

Example 6-42   Find the principal square root of the following.

(a)   36   (b)   144

Solution   (a) $\sqrt{36} = 6$ because $6 \cdot 6 = 36$.
(b) $\sqrt{144} = 12$ because $12 \cdot 12 = 144$.

Some square roots are rational. For example $\sqrt{25}$ is 5, a rational number. Other square roots, like $\sqrt{2}$, are irrational. Since $1^2 = 1$ and $2^2 = 4$, there is no whole number s such that $s^2 = 2$. Is there a rational number a/b such that $(a/b)^2 = 2$? If we assume there is such a rational number, then the following must be true.

$$\left(\frac{a}{b}\right)^2 = 2$$

$$\frac{a^2}{b^2} = 2$$

$$a^2 = 2b^2$$

Since $a^2 = 2b^2$, the Fundamental Theorem of Arithmetic says that the prime factorizations of a^2 and $2b^2$ are the same. In particular, the prime 2 appears the same number of times in the prime factorization of a^2 as it does in the factorization of $2b^2$. Since $b^2 = b \cdot b$, then no matter how many times 2 appears in the prime factorization of b, it appears twice as many times in $b \cdot b$. In $2b^2$, another factor of 2 is introduced resulting in an odd number of 2's in the prime factorization of $2b^2$ and hence of a^2. But 2 cannot appear both an odd number of times and an even number of times in the same prime factorization. We have a contradiction. This contradiction could have been caused only by the assumption that $\sqrt{2}$ is a rational number. Consequently $\sqrt{2}$ must be an irrational number.

Can $3\sqrt{2}$ be written in the form a/b, where a/b is rational? Suppose $a/b = 3\sqrt{2}$. Thus,

$$\frac{1}{3} \cdot \frac{a}{b} = \frac{1}{3}(3\sqrt{2})$$

$$\frac{a}{3b} = \sqrt{2}$$

Now $a/3b$ is a rational number, and $\sqrt{2}$ is an irrational number, which is a contradiction. Therefore, $3\sqrt{2}$ cannot be a rational number and, hence, is an irrational number. In a similar fashion, we could show that $m\sqrt{2}$ is an irrational number, where m is any rational number except 0.

Example 6-43 Prove that $2 + \sqrt{2}$ is an irrational number.

Solution Suppose $2 + \sqrt{2} = a/b$, where a/b is a rational number.

Then,

$$\sqrt{2} = \frac{a}{b} - 2$$

$$\sqrt{2} = \frac{a - 2b}{b}$$

But $(a - 2b)/b$ is a rational number, and this is a contradiction since $\sqrt{2}$ is an irrational number. Thus, $2 + \sqrt{2}$ is an irrational number.

Remark In a similar manner, we could prove $m + n\sqrt{2}$ is an irrational number for all rational numbers m and n except $n = 0$.

Many irrational numbers can be interpreted geometrically. For example, a point can be found to represent $\sqrt{2}$ on a number line by using the Pythagorean Theorem. That is, if a and b are the lengths of the shorter sides (legs) of a right triangle and c the length of the longer side (hypotenuse), then $a^2 + b^2 = c^2$, as shown in Figure 6-7.

FIGURE 6-7

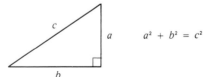

Figure 6-8 shows a segment one unit long constructed perpendicular to a number line at point P. Thus, two sides of the triangle shown are one unit long. By the Pythagorean Theorem, $1^2 + 1^2 = c^2$. Thus, $c^2 = 2$, and $c = \sqrt{2}$.

FIGURE 6-8

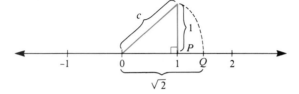

Since $\sqrt{2}$ is the length of the hypotenuse, there must be some point Q on the number line such that the distance from zero to Q is $\sqrt{2}$. Similarly, other square roots can be constructed as shown in Figure 6-9 and corresponding points found on the number line.

FIGURE 6-9

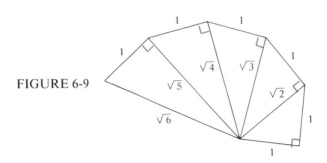

Irrational numbers can be approximated by "squeezing" them between two rational numbers. For example, $1 < \sqrt{2} < 2$ because $1^2 = 1$, $(\sqrt{2})^2 = 2$, and $2^2 = 4$. Similarly, $1.4 < \sqrt{2} < 1.5$ because $1.4^2 = 1.96$ and $1.5^2 = 2.25$. Also, $1.41 < \sqrt{2} < 1.42$ because $1.41^2 = 1.9881$ and $1.42^2 = 2.0164$. The continued process of squeezing results in as accurate an approximation of $\sqrt{2}$ as we wish. (A calculator is a definite aid in using this procedure.)

Newton's method
A different algorithm for approximating square roots is called **Newton's method**. (It also is called the guess-and-average method.) If we make any guess G_1 for $\sqrt{2}$, it can be proved that $\sqrt{2}$ is always between G_1 and $2/G_1$. (The proof is left as an exercise.) Using G_1 and $2/G_1$, compute a second guess, G_2, the average, $(1/2)(G_1 + 2/G_1)$. The second guess G_2 is a more accurate approximation to $\sqrt{2}$ than is G_1. Continue the process. Suppose $G_1 = 1.4$, then $2/G_1 = 2/1.4 \doteq 1.42$. Then, $\frac{1}{2}(1.4 + 1.42) = 1.41 = G_2$. Now, $2/G_2 = 2/1.41 \doteq 1.418$. So, $G_3 = 1/2(1.41 + 1.418) = 1.414$, and so on. In general, to approximate $\sqrt{n}$ for any number n, the following steps may be used.

1. Guess an approximate square root of n; that is, $G_1 \doteq \sqrt{n}$. It does not matter whether the guess is too large or too small, but the closer the guess, the fewer the steps, it takes to reach a given accuracy.
2. Divide: n/G_1.
3. Average G_1 and n/G_1. Call the average G_2. Then, $G_2 = 1/2[G_1 + (n/G_1)]$.
4. Using G_2 as the new guess, repeat the process.

The System of Real Numbers

real numbers
The set of all decimals—terminating, repeating, and nonterminating nonrepeating—comprises the set of **real numbers**. In other words, the set of real numbers is the union of both the set of rational numbers and the set of irrational numbers. The concept of fractions can now be extended to include all numbers of the form a/b where a and b are real numbers with $b \neq 0$, for example, $\sqrt{3}/5$. Further extensions of fractions are beyond the scope of this

text. Addition, subtraction, multiplication, and division are defined on the set of real numbers in such a way that all the properties of these operations on rationals still hold. The properties are summarized below for addition and multiplication.

Properties

Closure Properties   For real numbers a and b, $a + b$ and $a \cdot b$ are real numbers.

Commutative Properties   For real numbers a and b, $a + b = b + a$ and $a \cdot b = b \cdot a$.

Associative Properties   For real numbers a, b, and c, $a + (b + c) = (a + b) + c$ and $a \cdot (b \cdot c) = (a \cdot b) \cdot c$.

Identity Properties   The number 0 is the unique additive identity and 1 is the unique multiplicative identity such that for any real number a, $0 + a = a = a + 0$ and $1 \cdot a = a = a \cdot 1$.

Inverse Properties   (1) For every real number a, ^-a is its unique additive inverse; that is, $a + {}^-a = 0 = {}^-a + a$. (2) For every nonzero real number, $1/a$ is its unique multiplicative inverse; that is, $a \cdot (1/a) = 1 = (1/a) \cdot a$.

Distributive Property of Multiplication over Addition   For real numbers a, b, and c, $a \cdot (b + c) = a \cdot b + a \cdot c$.

In addition, the set of real numbers has the denseness property and the properties of equality and inequality similar to those for rational numbers. Using these properties, real number equations and inequalities can be solved. Also, since the real numbers can be placed in a one-to-one correspondence with the points on a line, the solution sets of real number equations and inequalities can be graphed on a number line.

Example 6-44

Solve each of the following and exhibit the solution on a number line.

(a) $x - 3 \leq \sqrt{2} + {}^-2$ (b) $\dfrac{3x^2}{2} - 4 = 5$

Solution

(a) $x - 3 \leq \sqrt{2} + {}^-2$
$ x \leq \sqrt{2} + 1$

Thus, the solution set is $\{x \mid x \leq \sqrt{2} + 1$, where x is a real number$\}$ and it is shown in Figure 6-10.

FIGURE 6-10

(b) $\dfrac{3x^2}{2} - 4 = 5$

$$\dfrac{3x^2}{2} = 9$$

$$3x^2 = 18$$

$$x^2 = 6$$

$$x = \sqrt{6} \text{ or } x = {}^-\sqrt{6}$$

Hence, the solution set is $\{\sqrt{6}, {}^-\sqrt{6}\}$ and it is shown in Figure 6-11.

FIGURE 6-11

$$-3 \quad -\sqrt{6} \;\; -2 \qquad -1 \qquad 0 \qquad 1 \qquad 2 \;\; \sqrt{6} \quad 3$$

PROBLEM SET 6-9

1. Without using a radical sign, write an irrational number all of whose digits are 2's and 3's.
2. Arrange the following real numbers in order from least to greatest.
   $0.78, 0.\overline{7}, 0.\overline{78}, 0.788, 0.7\overline{8}, 0.7\overline{88}, 0.77, 0.787787778\ldots$
3. Which of the following represent irrational numbers?
   (a) $\sqrt{51}$ (b) $\sqrt{64}$ (c) $\sqrt{324}$
   (d) $\sqrt{325}$ (e) $2 + 3\sqrt{2}$ (f) $\sqrt{2} \div 5$
4. Find the square roots for each of the following, if possible.
   (a) 225   (b) 251   (c) 169
   (d) 512   (e) $^-81$ (f) 625
5. Find the approximate square roots for each of the following to the nearest hundredth by (i) the squeezing method and (ii) Newton's method.
   (a) 17   (b) 7   (c) 21
   (d) 0.0120   (e) 20.3   (f) 1.64
6. Classify each of the following as true or false. If false, give a counterexample.
   (a) The sum of any rational number and any irrational number is a rational number.
   (b) The sum of any two irrational numbers is an irrational number.
   (c) The product of any two irrational numbers is an irrational number.
   (d) The difference of any two irrational numbers is an irrational number.
7. Is it true that $\sqrt{a + b} = \sqrt{a} + \sqrt{b}$? Either prove the statement or give a counterexample.
8. Solve each of the following for real numbers and graph the solution set on a number line.

   (a) $5x - 1 \le \dfrac{7}{2}x + 3$ (b) $4 + 3x \ge \sqrt{5} - 7x$ (c) $\dfrac{2}{3}x + \sqrt{3} \le {}^-5x$

   (d) $(2x - 1)^2 = 4$ (e) $|x| \ge 7$ (f) $|x| \le 3$

★ 9. Prove: $\sqrt{3}$ is irrational.
★ 10. Prove: If p is a prime number, then $\sqrt{p}$ is an irrational number.

★ 11.   (a)   For what whole numbers m is $\sqrt{m}$ a rational number?
  ★★(b)   Prove your answer in part 11(a).
★ 12.   (a)   Show that $0.5 + 1/0.5 \geq 2$.
  ★★(b)   Prove that any positive real number x plus its reciprocal $1/x$ is greater than or equal to 2.
13.   Do Problem 132 appearing in Appendix II.

*6-10 RADICALS AND RATIONAL EXPONENTS

*n*th root

index

The positive solution to $x^2 = 5$ is $\sqrt{5}$. Similarly, the solution to $x^3 = 5$ can be denoted as $\sqrt[3]{5}$. In general, the positive solution to $x^n = 5$ is $\sqrt[n]{5}$ and is called the **nth root** of 5. The numeral n is called the **index**. Note that in the expression $\sqrt{5}$, the index 2 is understood and is not expressed.

In general, the positive solution to $x^n = b$, where b is nonnegative, is $\sqrt[n]{b}$. Substituting $\sqrt[n]{b}$ for x in the equation $x^n = b$ gives the following.

$$(\sqrt[n]{b})^n = b$$

If b is negative, $\sqrt[n]{b}$ cannot always be defined. For example, if $\sqrt[4]{-16} = x$, then $x^4 = {}^-16$. Since any real number raised to the fourth power is positive, there is no real number solution to $x^4 = {}^-16$ and, therefore, $\sqrt[4]{-16}$ cannot be a real number. Similarly, it is not possible to find *any* even root of a negative number. However, the value $^-2$ satisfies the equation $x^3 = {}^-8$. Hence $\sqrt[3]{-8} = {}^-2$. In general, the odd root of a negative number is a negative number.

Now, consider an expression like $4^{1/2}$. What does it mean? By extending the properties of exponents previously developed for integer exponents, it must be that $4^{1/2} \cdot 4^{1/2} = 4^{1/2+1/2} = 4^1$. This implies that $(4^{1/2})^2 = 4$, or $4^{1/2}$ is a square root of 4. The number $4^{1/2}$ is assumed to be the principal square root of 4; that is, $4^{1/2} = \sqrt{4}$. In general, if x is a nonnegative real number, then $x^{1/2} = \sqrt{x}$. Similarly, $(x^{1/3})^3 = x^{(1/3)\cdot3} = x^1$, and $x^{1/3} = \sqrt[3]{x}$. This discussion leads to the following definition.

DEFINITION

> For any real number x and any positive integer n, $x^{1/n} = \sqrt[n]{x}$, where $\sqrt[n]{x}$ is meaningful.

Also since $(x^m)^{1/n} = \sqrt[n]{x^m}$ and if $(x^m)^{1/n} = x^{m/n}$, it follows that $x^{m/n} = \sqrt[n]{x^m}$.

Example 6-45 Write each of the following in radical form.

(a) $16^{1/4}$ (b) $32^{1/6}$ (c) $(^-8)^{1/3}$ (d) $64^{3/2}$

Solution (a) $16^{1/4} = \sqrt[4]{16}$ (b) $32^{1/6} = \sqrt[6]{32}$
(c) $(^-8)^{1/3} = \sqrt[3]{^-8}$ (d) $64^{3/2} = \sqrt{64^3}$

The properties of integer exponents also hold for rational exponents. These properties are equivalent to the corresponding properties of radicals. For example, let r and s be any rational numbers, x and y be any real numbers, and n be any integer such that $r = 1/n$.

(a) $(xy)^r = x^r \cdot y^r$ implies $(xy)^{1/n} = x^{1/n}y^{1/n}$ and $\sqrt[n]{xy} = \sqrt[n]{x} \sqrt[n]{y}$.
(b) $(x/y)^r = x^r/y^r$ implies $(x/y)^{1/n} = x^{1/n}/y^{1/n}$ and $\sqrt[n]{x/y} = \sqrt[n]{x}/\sqrt[n]{y}$.
(c) $(x^r)^s = x^{rs}$ implies $(x^{1/n})^s = x^{s/n}$ and hence, $(\sqrt[n]{x})^s = \sqrt[n]{x^s}$.

The preceding properties can be used to simplify the square roots of many numbers. For example, $\sqrt{96} = \sqrt{16 \cdot 6} = \sqrt{16} \sqrt{6} = 4\sqrt{6}$. When $\sqrt{96}$ is written as $4\sqrt{6}$, it is said to be in simplest form. In general, to simplify nth roots, factor out as many nth powers as possible. For example, $\sqrt{32} = \sqrt{4 \cdot 8} = 2\sqrt{8}$. Hence, $2\sqrt{8}$ is a simplified form, but not the simplest form. The simplest form of $\sqrt{32}$ is $4\sqrt{2}$.

Example 6-46 Write each of the following in simplest form.
(a) $\sqrt{200}$ (b) $\sqrt{75}$ (c) $\sqrt[3]{240}$ (d) $\sqrt{3} \cdot \sqrt{15}$
(e) $\sqrt[3]{81} \cdot \sqrt[3]{32}$

Solution (a) $\sqrt{200} = \sqrt{100 \cdot 2} = \sqrt{100} \sqrt{2} = 10\sqrt{2}$
(b) $\sqrt{75} = \sqrt{25 \cdot 3} = \sqrt{25} \sqrt{3} = 5\sqrt{3}$
(c) $\sqrt[3]{240} = \sqrt[3]{8 \cdot 30} = \sqrt[3]{8} \sqrt[3]{30} = 2\sqrt[3]{30}$
(d) $\sqrt{3} \cdot \sqrt{15} = \sqrt{3 \cdot 15} = \sqrt{45} = \sqrt{9 \cdot 5} = \sqrt{9} \cdot \sqrt{5} = 3\sqrt{5}$
(e) $\sqrt[3]{81} \cdot \sqrt[3]{32} = \sqrt[3]{81 \cdot 32} = \sqrt[3]{3^4 \cdot 2^5} = \sqrt[3]{3^3 \cdot 2^3 \cdot 3 \cdot 2^2}$
$= \sqrt[3]{3^3 \cdot 2^3} \cdot \sqrt[3]{3 \cdot 2^2} = 6\sqrt[3]{12}$

Some expressions in the form $\sqrt{x} + \sqrt{y}$ can be simplified. For example,

$$\sqrt{24} + \sqrt{54} = \sqrt{4 \cdot 6} + \sqrt{9 \cdot 6}$$
$$= \sqrt{4} \sqrt{6} + \sqrt{9} \sqrt{6}$$
$$= 2\sqrt{6} + 3\sqrt{6}$$
$$= (2 + 3)\sqrt{6}$$
$$= 5\sqrt{6}$$

Be careful. Notice that $\sqrt{9} + \sqrt{4} = 3 + 2 = 5$, but $\sqrt{9 + 4} = \sqrt{13}$. Thus, $\sqrt{9} + \sqrt{4} \neq \sqrt{9 + 4}$, and, in general, $\sqrt{x} + \sqrt{y} \neq \sqrt{x + y}$.

Example 6-47

Write each expression in simplest form.

(a) $\sqrt{20} + \sqrt{45} - \sqrt{80}$ (b) $\sqrt{12} + \sqrt{13}$ (c) $\sqrt{49x} + \sqrt{4x}$

Solution

(a) $\sqrt{20} + \sqrt{45} - \sqrt{80} = 2\sqrt{5} + 3\sqrt{5} - 4\sqrt{5} = \sqrt{5}$
(b) $\sqrt{12} + \sqrt{13} = 2\sqrt{3} + \sqrt{13}$
(c) $\sqrt{49x} + \sqrt{4x} = 7\sqrt{x} + 2\sqrt{x} = 9\sqrt{x}$

PROBLEM SET 6-10

1. Write each of the following square roots in simplest form.

    (a) $\sqrt{180}$ (b) $\sqrt{529}$ (c) $\sqrt{363}$

    (d) $\sqrt{252}$ (e) $\sqrt{\dfrac{169}{196}}$ (f) $\sqrt{\dfrac{49}{196}}$

2. Write each of the following in simplest form.

    (a) $\sqrt[3]{-27}$ (b) $\sqrt[5]{96}$ (c) $\sqrt[5]{32}$
    (d) $\sqrt[3]{250}$ (e) $\sqrt[5]{-243}$ (f) $\sqrt[4]{64}$

3. Write each of the following expressions in simplest form.

    (a) $2\sqrt{3} + 3\sqrt{2} + \sqrt{180}$ (b) $\sqrt[3]{4} \cdot \sqrt[3]{10}$

    (c) $(2\sqrt{3} + 3\sqrt{2})^2$ (d) $\sqrt{6} \div \sqrt{12}$

    (e) $5\sqrt{72} + 2\sqrt{50} - \sqrt{288} - \sqrt{242}$ (f) $\sqrt{\dfrac{8}{7}} \div \sqrt{\dfrac{4}{21}}$

4. In the following cartoon, Woodstock illustrates the technique for rationalizing fractions (removing the radical symbol from the denominator of a fraction).

Use the technique demonstrated in the cartoon to rationalize the denominators for each of the following.

(a) $\dfrac{2}{\sqrt{3}}$ (b) $\dfrac{7\sqrt{2}}{\sqrt{5}}$ (c) $\dfrac{5\sqrt{5}}{\sqrt{18}}$ (d) $\dfrac{1}{\sqrt{3}}$ (e) $\dfrac{2}{\sqrt{2}}$ (f) $\dfrac{3}{\sqrt{8}}$

5. Rewrite each of the following in simplest form.

(a) $16^{1/2}$ (b) $16^{-1/2}$ (c) $27^{2/3}$ (d) $27^{-2/3}$

(e) $64^{5/6}$ (f) $32^{2/5}$ (g) $3^{1/2} \cdot 3^{3/2}$ (h) $8^{3/2} \cdot 4^{1/4}$

(i) $\dfrac{(32)^{-2/5}}{\left(\dfrac{1}{16}\right)^{-3/2}}$ (j) $(10^{1/3} \cdot 10^{-1/6})^6$ (k) $9^{2/3} \cdot 27^{2/9}$

6. Does $\sqrt{x^2 + y^2} = x + y$? Explain your answer.
7. The following exponential function approximates the number of bacteria after t hours: $E(t) = 2^{10} \cdot 16^t$.
   (a) What is the initial number of bacteria, that is, when $t = 0$?
   (b) After $\frac{1}{4}$ hour, how many bacteria are there?
   (c) After $\frac{1}{2}$ hour, how many bacteria are there?
8. Solve for x, where x is a rational number.

(a) $3^x = 81$ (b) $4^x = 8$ (c) $128^{-x} = 16$ (d) $\left(\dfrac{4}{9}\right)^{3x} = \dfrac{32}{243}$

SOLUTION TO THE PRELIMINARY PROBLEM

Understanding the Problem

Prince Juanaricmo was in a castle surrounded by four moats. When the castle was besieged, guards were placed at each of the four bridges across the moats. When the prince was allowed to leave with a number of bags of gold, the guards at each bridge made the same demand. "Give me half of your bags of gold plus one more." When the prince had crossed the last bridge, he had only one bag left. We are to find how many bags he started with.

Devising a Plan

We can solve this problem by setting up an equation that satisfies the conditions of the problem. We write an algebraic expression for the number of bags of gold the prince had after crossing the first bridge. Using this expression, we write a similar expression for the number of bags of gold he had after crossing the second bridge, and so on. Then we set the expression representing the number of bags that the prince had after crossing the final bridge equal to 1. The solution to the resulting equation is the answer to the problem.

Carrying Out the Plan

Let n be the number of bags of gold with which the prince started. We summarize what happened at each bridge in Table 6-9.

TABLE 6-9

	Number of Bags Each Guard Took	Number of Bags the Prince Had After Crossing
First Bridge	$\frac{1}{2}n + 1$	$n - \left(\frac{1}{2}n + 1\right) = \frac{1}{2}n - 1$
Second Bridge	$\frac{1}{2}\left(\frac{1}{2}n - 1\right) + 1 = \frac{1}{4}n + \frac{1}{2}$	$\frac{1}{2}n - 1 - \left(\frac{1}{4}n + \frac{1}{2}\right) = \frac{1}{4}n - \frac{3}{2}$
Third Bridge	$\frac{1}{2}\left(\frac{1}{4}n - \frac{3}{2}\right) + 1 = \frac{1}{8}n + \frac{1}{4}$	$\frac{1}{4}n - \frac{3}{2} - \left(\frac{1}{8}n + \frac{1}{4}\right) = \frac{1}{8}n - \frac{7}{4}$
Fourth Bridge	$\frac{1}{2}\left(\frac{1}{8}n - \frac{7}{4}\right) + 1 = \frac{1}{16}n + \frac{1}{8}$	$\frac{1}{8}n - \frac{7}{4} - \left(\frac{1}{16}n + \frac{1}{8}\right) = \frac{1}{16}n - \frac{15}{8}$

Since the prince had only one bag left after crossing the fourth bridge, we have

$$\frac{1}{16}n - \frac{15}{8} = 1$$

$$\frac{1}{16}n = 1 + \frac{15}{8}$$

$$\frac{1}{16}n = \frac{23}{8}$$

$$n = \frac{23}{8} \cdot 16$$

$$n = 46$$

Looking Back

Another way of finding the solution is "working backwards." In the preceding solution, observe that after crossing each bridge, the prince was left with half the number of bags he had previously minus one additional bag of gold. To determine the number he had prior to crossing the bridge, we can use the inverse operations; that is, add 1 and multiply by 2. The prince had one bag left after crossing the fourth bridge. He must have had two before he gave the guard the extra bag. Finally he must have had four bags before he gave the guard at the fourth bridge any bags. The entire procedure can be summarized in Table 6-10.

TABLE 6-10

Bridge	Bags After Crossing	Bags Before Guard Given Extra	Bags Prior to Crossing
Fourth	1	2	4
Third	4	5	10
Second	10	11	22
First	22	23	46

QUESTIONS FROM THE CLASSROOM

1. A student wrote the solution set to the equation $x/7 - 2 < -3$ as $\{-8, -9, -10, -11, \ldots\}$. Is she correct?
2. A student reduced the fraction $(m + n)/(p + n)$ to m/p. Is that student correct?
3. A student asks if the reason we "invert and multiply" when dividing fractions is because division is the inverse of multiplication. Is this argument valid? Explain your answer.
4. When working on the problem of simplifying $\frac{3}{4} \cdot \frac{1}{2} \cdot \frac{2}{3}$, a student did the following.

$$\frac{3}{4} \cdot \frac{1}{2} \cdot \frac{2}{3} = \left(\frac{3 \cdot 1}{4 \cdot 2}\right)\left(\frac{3 \cdot 2}{4 \cdot 3}\right) = \frac{3}{8} \cdot \frac{6}{12} = \frac{18}{96}$$

What was his error?
5. A student asks, "If the ratio of boys to girls in the class is 2/3, and 4 boys and 6 girls join the class, then the new ratio is $(2 + 4)/(3 + 6)$, or 6/9. Since $2/3 + 4/6 = (2 + 4)/(3 + 6)$, can all fractions be added in the same way?
6. Is 0/6 in simplest form? Why or why not?
7. A student argues that $0.\overline{9} \neq 1$. How do you respond?
8. A student says that $3\frac{1}{4}\% = 0.03 + 0.25 = 0.28$. What is her error, if any?
9. Why is $\sqrt{25} \neq -5$?
10. A student says, "I know another way to express $\sqrt{n^2}$. It is $|n|$." Is he correct?

11. A student says that taking one-half of a number is the same as dividing the number by one-half. Is this correct?
12. A student claims that $\sqrt{(^-5)^2} = -5$ because $\sqrt{a^2} = a$. Is she correct?
13. Another student says that $\sqrt{(^-5)^2} = [(^-5)^2]^{1/2} = (^-5)^{2/2} = (^-5)^1 = ^-5$. Is this correct?
14. A student claims that the equation $\sqrt{^-x} = 3$ has no solution since the square root of a negative number does not exist. Why is this argument wrong?
15. A student multiplies $(6.5)(8.5)$ to obtain the following

    $$
    \begin{array}{r}
    8.5 \\
    \times 6.5 \\
    \hline
    4\,2\,5 \\
    5\,1\,0 \\
    \hline
    5\,5.2\,5
    \end{array}
    $$

    However, when he multiplies $8\frac{1}{2} \cdot 6\frac{1}{2}$, he obtains the following.

    $$
    \begin{array}{r}
    8\frac{1}{2} \\
    \times 6\frac{1}{2} \\
    \hline
    4\frac{1}{4} \\
    48 \\
    \hline
    52\frac{1}{4}
    \end{array}
    \qquad
    \begin{array}{c}
    \left(\frac{1}{2} \cdot 8\frac{1}{2}\right) \\
    (6 \cdot 8)
    \end{array}
    $$

    How is this possible?
16. A student writes, $15/53 < 1/3$ since $3 \cdot 15 < 53 \cdot 1$. Another student writes $\dfrac{1\!\!\!/5}{5\!\!\!/3} = \dfrac{1}{3}$. Where is the fallacy?
17. On a test, a student wrote the following.

    $$\frac{x}{7} - 2 < ^-3$$

    $$\frac{x}{7} < -1$$

    $$x > ^-7$$

    What is his error?

CHAPTER OUTLINE

I. Rational numbers
  A. Numbers of the form a/b, where a and b are integers and $b \neq 0$, are called **rational numbers.**
  B. Uses of rational numbers include the following.
    1. As a division problem or the solution to a multiplication problem

2.   As a partition or part of a whole

3.   As a ratio

4.   As an element of a mathematical system

C.   Two rational numbers, a/b and c/d, are equal if and only if $ad = bc$.

D.   If $\gcd(a, b) = 1$, then a/b is said to be in **simplest form.**

E.   If $a > b$, then a/b is called an **improper fraction.**

F.   If $a \leq b$, then a/b is called a **proper fraction.**

II.   Operations on rational numbers

A. $\dfrac{a}{b} + \dfrac{c}{b} = \dfrac{a + c}{b}$

B. $\dfrac{a}{b} + \dfrac{c}{d} = \dfrac{ad + bc}{bd}$

C. $\dfrac{a}{b} - \dfrac{c}{d} = \dfrac{ad - bc}{bd}$

D. $\dfrac{a}{b} \cdot \dfrac{c}{d} = \dfrac{ac}{bd}$

E. $\dfrac{a}{b} \div \dfrac{c}{d} = \dfrac{a}{b} \cdot \dfrac{d}{c} = \dfrac{ad}{bc}$, where $c \neq 0$

III.   Properties of rational and real numbers

A.

	Addition	Subtraction	Multiplication	Division
Closure	Yes	Yes	Yes	Yes, except for division by 0
Commutative	Yes	No	Yes	No
Associative	Yes	No	Yes	No
Identity	Yes	No	Yes	No
Inverse	Yes	No	Yes, except 0	No

B.   **Distributive property of multiplication over addition** for real numbers x, y, and z: $x(y + z) = xy + xz$.

C.   **Denseness property:** Between any two real numbers, there is another real number. This property also holds for rational numbers and irrational numbers.

IV.   Ratio and proportion

A.   A quotient, $a \div b$, is a **ratio.**

B.   A **proportion** is an equation of two ratios.

C.   Properties of proportions

1.   If $a/b = c/d$, then $b/a = d/c$, where $a \neq 0$ and $c \neq 0$.

2.   If $a/b = c/d$, then $a/c = b/d$, where $c \neq 0$.

D.   **Percent** means "per hundred." Percent is symbolized as $x\%$ and $x\% = x/100$.

E.   A percent can be written as a decimal.

V.   Exponents and radicals

A. $a^m = \underbrace{a \cdot a \cdot a \cdot \ldots \cdot a}_{m \text{ terms}}$, where m is a positive integer

B.   Properties of exponents and radicals

1. $a^0 = 1$, where $a \neq 0$

2. $a^{-n} = 1/a^n$, where $a \neq 0$ and n is any rational number

3. $a^m \cdot a^n = a^{m+n}$

4. $(a^m)^n = a^{mn}$

5. $(ab)^m = a^m b^m$

6. $\left(\dfrac{a}{b}\right)^m = \dfrac{a^m}{b^m}$

7. $\dfrac{a^m}{a^n} = a^{m-n}$

8. $a^{m/n} = \sqrt[n]{a^m} = (\sqrt[n]{a})^m$

9. $\sqrt[n]{ab} = \sqrt[n]{a}\ \sqrt[n]{b}$

10. $\sqrt[n]{\dfrac{a}{b}} = \dfrac{\sqrt[n]{a}}{\sqrt[n]{b}}$

VI.   Decimals

A.   Every rational number can be represented as a terminating or repeating decimal.

B.   A rational number a/b, whose denominator is of the form $2^m \cdot 5^n$, where m and n are whole numbers can be expressed as a **terminating decimal.**

C. A **repeating decimal** is a decimal with a block of digits, called the **repetend,** repeated infinitely many times.
D. A number is in **scientific notation** if it is written as the product of a number between 1 and 10 and a power of 10.
E. An **irrational number** is represented by a nonterminating, nonrepeating decimal.

VII. Real numbers
A. The set of **real numbers** is the set of all decimals, namely, the union of the set of rational and the set of irrational numbers.
B. If a is any whole number, then the principal square root of a, denoted by $\sqrt{a}$, is the nonnegative number b such that $b \cdot b = b^2 = a$.

CHAPTER TEST

1. For each of the following, draw a diagram illustrating the fraction.

    (a) $\dfrac{3}{4}$ (b) $\dfrac{2}{3}$

2. Write three rational numbers equal to ⅚.

3. Reduce each of the following rational numbers to simplest form.

    (a) $\dfrac{24}{28}$ (b) $\dfrac{ax^2}{bx}$ (c) $\dfrac{0}{17}$

    (d) $\dfrac{45}{81}$ (e) $\dfrac{b^2 + bx}{b + x}$ (f) $\dfrac{16}{216}$

4. Place $>$, $<$, or $=$ between each of the following pairs to make true sentences.

    (a) $\dfrac{6}{10}$ and $\dfrac{120}{200}$ (b) $0.\overline{33}$ and $\dfrac{1}{30}$

    (c) $0.\overline{35}$ and $0.3\overline{5}$ (d) $\sqrt{2}$ and 1.4

5. Perform each of the following computations.

    (a) $\dfrac{5}{6} + \dfrac{4}{15}$ (b) $\dfrac{4}{25} - \dfrac{3}{35}$ (c) $\dfrac{5}{6} \cdot \dfrac{12}{13}$

    (d) $\dfrac{5}{6} \div \dfrac{12}{15}$ (e) $\left(5\dfrac{1}{6} + 7\dfrac{1}{3}\right) \div 2\dfrac{1}{4}$ (f) $0.26 + 3.193 + 42.001$

    (g) $0.26 \cdot 3.19$ (h) $3.194 \div 0.26$ (to nearest tenth)   (i) $42.001 - 3.19$

    (j) $5\dfrac{3}{4} + 9.612$

6. Find the additive and multiplicative inverses for each of the following:

    (a) 3 (b) $3\dfrac{1}{7}$ (c) 0.23 (d) $\dfrac{5}{6}$ (e) $-\dfrac{3}{4}$

7. Simplify each of the following. Write your answer in a/b form, where a and b are integers, and $b \neq 0$.

   (a) $\dfrac{\dfrac{1}{2} - \dfrac{3}{4}}{\dfrac{5}{6} - \dfrac{7}{8}}$ (b) $\dfrac{\dfrac{3}{4} \cdot \dfrac{5}{6}}{\dfrac{1}{2}}$

8. Solve each of the following for x, where x is a real number.

   (a) $\dfrac{1}{4}x - \dfrac{3}{5} \leq \dfrac{1}{2}(3 - 2x)$ (b) $x\sqrt{2} - 3 = 5x\sqrt{2}$

   (c) $0.2x - 0.75 \geq \dfrac{1}{2}(x - 3.5)$ (d) $\dfrac{5}{6} = \dfrac{4 - x}{3}$

   (e) $23\%(x) = 4600$ (f) 10 is x percent of 50

   (g) 17 is 50% of x (h) $0.\overline{3} + x = 1$

   (i) $0.\overline{9} + x = 1$

9. Justify the algorithm for addition of the decimals $8.34 + 23.6$.
10. Justify the invert-and-multiply algorithm for division of rational numbers.
11. Answer each of the following.
    (a) 6 is what percent of 24?   (b) What is 320% of 60?
    (c) 17 is 30% of what number?
12. Change each of the following to percents.

    (a) $\dfrac{1}{8}$ (b) $\dfrac{3}{40}$ (c) 6.27   (d) 0.0123

13. Change each of the following percents to decimals.
    (a) 60%   (b) (2/3)%   (c) 100%
14. If the ratio of boys to girls in Mr. Good's class is 3 to 5 and the ratio of boys to girls in Ms. Garcia's is the same and you know that there are 15 girls in her class, how many boys are in her class?
15. Answer each of the following and explain your answers.
    (a) Is the set of irrational numbers closed under addition?
    (b) Is the set of irrational numbers closed under subtraction?
    (c) Is the set of irrational numbers closed under multiplication?
    (d) Is the set of irrational numbers closed under division?
16. Convert each of the following rational numbers to the form a/b.
    (a) 0.26   (b) 312.4   (c) $0.2\overline{3}$ (d) $0.\overline{23}$
17. Convert each of the following fractions to decimals that either terminate or repeat.

    (a) $\dfrac{2}{25}$ (b) $\dfrac{3}{48}$ (c) $\dfrac{1}{13}$ (d) $\dfrac{2}{23}$

18. Find an approximation for $\sqrt{23}$ correct to three decimal places.
19. Rewrite each of the following in scientific notation.
    (a) 426 000   (b) 0.00000237

20. Classify each of the following as rational or irrational.

 (a) $2.191199119991199991119\ldots$ (b) $\dfrac{1}{\sqrt{2}}$ (c) $\dfrac{4}{9}$

 (d) $0.0011001100110011\ldots$

 (e) $0.001100011000011\ldots$

21. Find the simplest form for each of the following.

 (a) $\sqrt{242}$ (b) $\sqrt{288}$ (c) $\sqrt{360}$ (d) $\sqrt[3]{162}$

22. Write each of the following in simplest form with nonnegative exponents in the final answer.

 (a) $\left(\dfrac{1}{2}\right)^4\left(\dfrac{1}{2}\right)^7$ (b) $5^{-16} \div 5^4$ (c) $\left[\left(\dfrac{2}{3}\right)^7\right]^{-4}$ (d) $3^{16} \cdot 3^2$

SELECTED BIBLIOGRAPHY

Allison, J. F. "A Picture of the Rational Numbers: Dense but Not Complete." *The Mathematics Teacher,* **65**(January 1972):87–89.

Arnold, W. R. "Reinforce Division by Learning Ratios." *The Arithmetic Teacher,* **21**(May 1974):393–395.

Ballew, H. "Of Fractions, Fractional Numerals, and Fractional Numbers." *The Arithmetic Teacher,* **21**(May 1974):442–444.

Bell, K. M., and D. D. Rucker. "An Algorithm for Reducing Fractions." *The Arithmetic Teacher,* **21**(April 1974):299–300.

Brown, C. N. "Fractions on Grid Paper." *The Arithmetic Teacher,* **27**(January 1979):8–10.

Brown, G. W., and L. B. Kinney. "Let's Teach Them about Ratio." *The Mathematics Teacher,* **66**(April 1973):352–355.

Bruni, J. V., and H. J. Silverman. "Let's Do It: Using Rectangles and Squares to Develop Fraction Concepts." *The Arithmetic Teacher,* **24**(February 1977):96–102.

Carlisle, E. "Fractions and Popsicle Sticks." *The Arithmetic Teacher,* **27**(February 1980):50–51.

Cohen, L. S. "The Board Stretcher: A Model to Introduce Factors, Primes, Composites, and Multiplication by a Fraction." *The Arithmetic Teacher,* **20**(December 1973):649–656.

Cole, B. L., and H. S. Weissenfluh. "An Analysis of Teaching Percentages." *The Arithmetic Teacher,* **21**(March 1974):226–228.

Dana, M. E., and M. M. Lindquist. "Let's Do It: From Halves to Hundredths." *The Arithmetic Teacher,* **26**(November 1978):4–8.

Feinberg, M. M. "Is It Necessary to Invert?" *The Arithmetic Teacher,* **27**(January 1980):50–52.

Firl, D. H. "Fractions, Decimals and Their Futures." *The Arithmetic Teacher,* **24**(March 1977):238–240.

Green, G. F., Jr. "A Model for Teaching Multiplication of Fractional Numbers." *The Arithmetic Teacher,* **20**(January 1973):5–9.

Haris, V. C. "On Proofs of the Irrationality of $\sqrt{2}$." *The Mathematics Teacher,* **64**(January 1971):19–21.

Hilferty, M. R. "Some Convenient Fractions for Work with Repeating Decimals." *The Mathematics Teacher,* **65**(March 1972):240–241.

Hutchinson, M. R. "Investigating the Nature of Periodic Decimals." *The Mathematics Teacher,* **65**(April 1972):325–327.

Jacobs, J. E., and E. B. Herbert. "Making 2 Seem "Real."" *The Arithmetic Teacher,* **21**(February 1974):133–136.

Manchester, M. "Decimal Expansions of Rational Numbers." *The Mathematics Teacher,* **65**(December 1972):698–702.

Martin, D. S. "Jigsaw Mathematics." *The Arithmetic Teacher,* **23**(February 1976):111.

Mielke, P. T. "Rational Points on the Number Line." *The Mathematics Teacher,* **63**(October 1970):475–479.

Miller, A. "Teaching the Concept of ½ in the Primary Grades." *The Arithmetic Teacher,* **25**(March 1978):57–58.

Moulton, J. P. "A Working Model for Rational Numbers." *The Arithmetic Teacher,* **22**(April 1975):328–332.

Ness, H. M., Jr. "Another Look at Fractions." *The Arithmetic Teacher,* **20**(January 1973):10–12.

Payne, J. N. "One Point of View: Sense and Nonsense about Fractions and Decimals." *The Arithmetic Teacher,* **27**(January 1980):4–7.

Prielipp, R. W. "Decimals." *The Arithmetic Teacher*, **23**(April 1976):285–288.

Robidoux, D., and N. Montefusco. "An Easy Way to Change Repeating Decimals to Fractions—Nick's Method." *The Arithmetic Teacher*, **24**(January 1977):81–82.

Schmalz, R. "A Visual Approach to Decimals." *The Arithmetic Teacher*, **25**(May 1978):22–25.

Sherzer, L. "Adding Fractions Using the Definition of Addition of Rational Numbers and the Euclidean Algorithm." *The Arithmetic Teacher*, **20**(January 1973):27–28.

Shookoohi, G-H. "Readiness of Eight-Year-Old Children to Understand the Division of Fractions." *The Arithmetic Teacher*, **27**(March 1980):40–43.

Wassmansdorf, M. "Reducing Fractions Can Be Easy, Maybe Even Fun." *The Arithmetic Teacher*, **21**(February 1974):99–102.

Probability

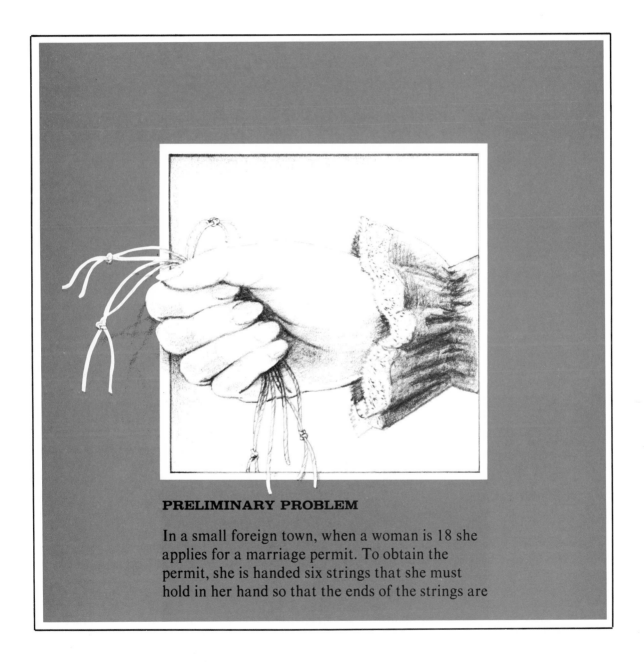

PRELIMINARY PROBLEM

In a small foreign town, when a woman is 18 she applies for a marriage permit. To obtain the permit, she is handed six strings that she must hold in her hand so that the ends of the strings are exposed. On one side, the ends (top or bottom) are picked randomly, two at a time, and tied forming three separate knots. The same procedure is then repeated for the other set of string ends forming three more knots. If the tied strings form one closed ring, the woman obtains the permit. If not, she must wait until her next birthday to reapply for a permit. What is the probability that she will obtain a marriage permit on her first try?

INTRODUCTION

Blaise Pascal and Pierre de Fermat are generally recognized as the founders of probability theory. Pascal and Fermat became involved with Chevalier de Meré, a professional gambler, who realized that mathematics could be profitably applied to his profession. Since Chevalier had a limited knowledge of mathematics, he sent some dice problems to Pascal in 1653. Pascal in turn corresponded with Fermat. The correspondence between Pascal and Fermat led to the development of probability theory.

Concepts of probability appear frequently in daily life. For example,

"My chances of passing a probability test are very good."
"The Cowboys will probably win the Superbowl."

The following cartoon suggests one use of probability.

Children, as well as adults, use the basics of probability when they play games with dice, cards, and spinners. Children's natural interest in playing

games provides a high level of motivation to study probability. Although spinner, card, and dice games are helpful for developing intuitive ideas of chance, there is no guarantee that the ideas of probability are a part of every child's background. For example, if children are asked if some numbers are harder to roll on a die than others, many will respond yes.

7-1 HOW PROBABILITIES ARE FOUND

One of the simplest games of chance is coin tossing. Assuming that a fair coin cannot land on its edge, there are only two distinct and equally likely outcomes possible, heads (H) and tails (T). Activities such as coin tossing and throwing a die are called **experiments.** The set of all possible outcomes for an experiment is called a **sample space** or **outcome set.** In the case of a single coin toss, the sample space, S, is given by $S = \{H, T\}$.

experiments

sample space, outcome set

Example 7-1 Write the sample space, S, for rolling a single die.

Solution $S = \{1, 2, 3, 4, 5, 6\}$.

Example 7-2 Write the sample space, S, for spinning the spinner in Figure 7-1.

FIGURE 7-1

Solution $S = \{Blue, Red, Yellow, White\}$.

Example 7-3 Suppose a coin is tossed and then tossed again. Write the sample space for the experiment.

Solution Let HT represent a head followed by a tail, TH represent a tail followed by a head, and so on. Then, the sample space is $\{HH, HT, TH, TT\}$.

Example 7-4 List the sample space for an experiment consisting of tossing a coin and then rolling a die.

Solution | Indicate the results of coin tossing as {H, T} and the results of rolling a die as {1, 2, 3, 4, 5, 6}. The sample space for tossing a coin and then rolling a die is given by the following.

$S = \{$H1, H2, H3, H4, H5, H6, T1, T2, T3, T4, T5, T6$\}$

event | Any subset of a sample space is called an **event.** For example, the set of all even-numbered rolls of a die is a subset of all possible rolls of a die. The set of all even-numbered rolls is an event.

Example 7-5 | Suppose an experiment is to draw one slip of paper from a jar containing twelve slips of paper, each with a month of the year written on it. Find each of the following.
(a) The sample space, S, for the experiment.
(b) The event, A, consisting of outcomes from drawing a slip having a month beginning with J.
(c) The event, B, consisting of outcomes from drawing a slip having the name of a month that has exactly 4 letters.
(d) The event, C, consisting of outcomes from drawing a slip having a month that begins with M or N.

Solution | (a) $S = \{$January, February, March, April, May, June, July, August, September, October, November, December$\}$
(b) $A = \{$January, June, July$\}$
(c) $B = \{$June, July$\}$
(d) $C = \{$March, May, November$\}$

Example 7-6 | Two spinners are shown in Figure 7-2. Suppose an experiment is to spin X and then spin Y. Find each of the following.
(a) The sample space, S, for the experiment.
(b) The event, A, consisting of outcomes from spinning an even number followed by an even number.
(c) The event, B, consisting of outcomes from spinning at least one 2.
(d) The event, C, consisting of outcomes from spinning exactly one 2.

FIGURE 7-2 |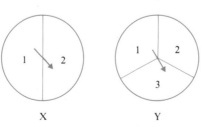

X   Y

Solution

(a) The sample space for this experiment can be described using ordered pairs. The first component in each pair is the result of the first spin, and the second component is the result of the second spin.

$$S = \{(1, 1), (1, 2), (1, 3), (2, 1), (2, 2), (2, 3)\}$$

(b) $A = \{(2, 2)\}$
(c) $B = \{(1, 2), (2, 1), (2, 2), (2, 3)\}$
(d) $C = \{(1, 2), (2, 1), (2, 3)\}$

Suppose a fair coin is tossed 40 times with the following result.

HTTHT HHHHH TTTHH HTTTH TTHTH TTHHT THTHT TTHTT

Observe the following.

$$\frac{\text{number of heads}}{\text{number of trials}} = \frac{18}{40}$$

Heads resulted in approximately $\frac{1}{2}$ of the tosses. The number of heads cannot be accurately predicted when a coin is tossed a few times. However, when the coin is tossed many times, heads appear in approximately $\frac{1}{2}$ of the tosses. For this reason, we say the probability of a head is $\frac{1}{2}$ and write $P(H) = \frac{1}{2}$. Another argument is that since a fair coin is symmetric and has two sides, each side should appear roughly half of the time in long strings of tosses, and hence,

$$P(H) = P(T) = \frac{1}{2}$$

If a fair die with sample space given by $S = \{1, 2, 3, 4, 5, 6\}$ is rolled many times, each outcome will appear about $\frac{1}{6}$ of the time. Hence, we assign to each outcome a probability of $\frac{1}{6}$ and write, for example, $P(4) = \frac{1}{6}$ for the probability of tossing a 4. Since there are 6 sides to a die, the symmetry of the die suggests in a long string of tosses that any side will appear $\frac{1}{6}$ of the time.

Coin tossing and throwing a die are examples of experiments with **equally likely outcomes**; that is, one outcome is as likely to occur as another. Probability is defined in terms of equally likely events.

DEFINITION

> If all outcomes of an experiment are equally likely, the probability of an event, A, from sample space, S, is given by $P(A) = n(A)/n(S)$.

Remark

Recall that $n(A)$ means "the number of elements in A" and $n(S)$ means "the number of elements in S."

It is important to remember that the preceding definition applies only to equally likely outcomes. Applying the definition to outcomes that are not equally likely leads to incorrect conclusions. For example, one might reason that if a die is tossed, then either a 6 appears or it does not. Thus, there are two possible outcomes, and the probability of rolling a 6 is $\frac{1}{2}$. It is correct to say that "6" and "no 6" are two possible outcomes, but these outcomes are not equally likely. There are five numbers on the die that are not equal to 6. Thus, the probability that a "6" appears is $\frac{1}{6}$, whereas the probability that "no 6" appears is $\frac{5}{6}$.

impossible event

An event such as rolling a 7 on a single roll of a normal die is called an **impossible event.** Since no face has 7 spots, there are 0 elements in the event, and therefore $P(7) = \frac{0}{6} = 0$. An event is an impossible event if and only if it has a probability of 0. For example, consider the event consisting of rolling a number less than 7 on a single roll of a die. Since every face of the die has less than 7 spots, $P(\text{number less than } 7) = \frac{6}{6} = 1$. An event that has probability 1

certain event

is called a **certain event.**

No event has a probability greater than 1 since the number of ways the outcome of an event occurs cannot be greater than the total number of outcomes in the sample space. Likewise, no event has a probability less than 0. Consequently, if A is any event, then the following inequality holds: $0 \leq P(A) \leq 1$.

Example 7-7

A golf bag contains two red tees, four blue tees, and five white tees. What is the probability of the event, A, that a tee drawn at random is red? The phrase "at random" means each of the tees has an equal chance of being drawn.

Solution

Since the bag contains a total of $2 + 4 + 5$ or 11 tees, and since two tees are red, $P(A) = 2/11$.

complements

The notation $\overline{A}$ designates the event "not A." Events A and $\overline{A}$ are said to be **complements** of each other, since $A \cup \overline{A} = S$ and $A \cap \overline{A} = \phi$. In the golf bag example, $\overline{A}$ is the set of all possible outcomes for *not* drawing a red tee. Thus, $P(\overline{A}) = 9/11$ and $P(A) + P(\overline{A}) = 1$. This is true for complements in general and, therefore,

$$P(A) = 1 - P(\overline{A})$$

This formula enables you to find the probability of an event if the probability of its complement is known. Sometimes it is easier to calculate $P(\overline{A})$ than it is to calculate $P(A)$.

Example 7-8

One number is selected at random from the numbers in the set S given by $S = \{1, 2, 3, 4, \ldots, 24, 25\}$. List the elements in each event given below and calculate each probability.

(a) The event, A, consisting of outcomes from drawing an even number.

(b) The event, B, consisting of outcomes from drawing a number less than 10 and greater than 20.

(c) The event, C, consisting of outcomes from drawing a prime number.

(d) The event, D, consisting of outcomes from drawing a number that is not prime.

(e) The event, E, consisting of outcomes from drawing a number that is both even and prime.

Solution

In this experiment, $n(S) = 25$.

(a) $A = \{2, 4, 6, 8, 10, 12, 14, 16, 18, 20, 22, 24\}$, so $n(A) = 12$. Thus, $P(A) = n(A)/n(S) = 12/25$.

(b) $B = \varnothing$, so $n(B) = 0$. Thus, $P(B) = 0/25 = 0$.

(c) $C = \{2, 3, 5, 7, 11, 13, 17, 19, 23\}$, so $n(C) = 9$. Thus, $P(C) = n(C)/n(S) = 9/25$.

(d) $D = \{1, 4, 6, 8, 9, 10, 12, 14, 15, 16, 18, 20, 21, 22, 24, 25\}$, so $n(D) = 16$. Thus, $P(D) = 16/25$. Notice that D is the same as "not C." Thus, $P(D) = 1 - P(C) = 1 - 9/25 = 16/25$.

(e) $E = \{2\}$, so $n(E) = 1$. Thus, $P(E) = n(E)/n(S) = 1/25$.

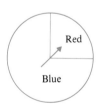

FIGURE 7-3

experimental probability

The sample space for spinning the spinner in Figure 7-3 is given by $S = \{\text{Red, Blue}\}$. The definition of probability based on equally likely outcomes does not hold for the outcomes of spinning this spinner. The outcome, Blue, is more likely to occur than the outcome, Red. (If the spinner were spun 100 times, it seems reasonable to guess that about 1/4 of the outcomes or 25 outcomes, would be Red and about 3/4 of the outcomes, or 75 outcomes, would be Blue.)

Another experiment that does not have equally likely outcomes is tossing a thumbtack. The thumbtack can land on its top, ($\perp$), or on its side, ($\curlywedge$). If a thumbtack is tossed 30 times and it lands on its top 25 times, we say the **experimental probability** of the tack landing on its top is 25/30 or 5/6. (If it lands on its top 20 times, then the experimental probability is 20/30 or 2/3.) Based on the experimental probability of 5/6, if the thumbtack is tossed 60 times for another experiment, then it probably would land on its top about $(5/6) \cdot 60$ or 50 times.

The sample on page 290 from *Scott, Foresman Mathematics,* 1980, Grade 5 shows how probability is introduced with a problem-solving approach.

Problem Solving: Probability

READ   About how many spins can you expect to stop on green if you make 15 spins?

DECIDE $\frac{1}{3}$ of the spinner is green. You can expect about $\frac{1}{3}$ of your spins to stop on green.

If you make 15 spins, you can expect about $\frac{1}{3}$ of 15 spins to stop on green.

SOLVE

$$\frac{1}{3} \times 15$$

$$\frac{1}{3} \times \frac{15}{1} = \frac{15}{3} = 5$$

ANSWER   About 5 spins

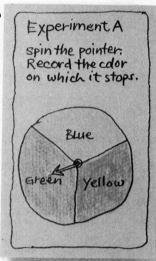

Experiment A
spin the pointer.
Record the color
on which it stops.

Blue Green Yellow

In Experiment B, the penny can land either heads or tails. You can expect it to be tails 1 out of 2 times, or $\frac{1}{2}$ of the time.

About how many times can you expect the penny to be tails if you drop it into the bottle

1. 6 times?   2. 10 times?   3. 12 times?

4. 20 times?   5. 24 times?   6. 50 times?

Experiment B
Drop a penny into
a clear bottle.
Record how it lands,
heads or tails.

PROBLEM SET 7-1

1. Write the sample space for each of the following experiments.
    (a) Draw one letter from a jar containing single letters m, a, t, h.
    (b) Spin the spinner once.   (c) Spin the spinner once.

    (d) Spin the spinner in (b) once. Then spin the spinner in (c) once.
    (e) Toss a penny, a nickel, and a quarter.
    (f) Spin the spinner in (c) once. Then roll a die.
    (g) Spin the spinner in (b) twice.
2. An experiment consists of selecting the last digit of various telephone numbers. Assume that each of the 10 digits is equally likely to appear as a last digit. List each of the following.
    (a) The sample space
    (b) The event consisting of outcomes that the digit is less than 5
    (c) The event consisting of outcomes that the digit is odd
    (d) The event consisting of outcomes that the digit is not 2
3. Find the probability of each of the events (b)–(d) listed in problem 2.
4. A card is selected from an ordinary bridge deck consisting of 52 cards. Find the probabilities for each of the following.
    (a) A red card   (b) A face card
    (c) A red card or a ten   (d) A queen
    (e) Not a queen   (f) A face card or a club
    (g) A face card and a club (h) Not a face card and not a club
5. A drawer contains six black socks, four brown socks, and two green socks. Suppose one sock is drawn from the drawer, and it is equally likely that any one of the socks is drawn. Find the probabilities for each of the following.
    (a) The sock is brown   (b) The sock is either black or green
    (c) The sock is red   (d) The sock is not black
6. What, if anything, is wrong with each of the following statements?
    (a) If the probability that a person drinks is 54/100 and the probability that a person smokes is 45/100, then the probability that a person drinks or smokes is 54/100 + 45/100 or 99/100.
    (b) The probability that the Steelers will win the Superbowl is 3/4 and the probability that they will lose is 1/5.
    (c) Since there are 50 states, the probability of being born in Montana is 1/50.
7. If each letter of the alphabet is written on a separate piece of paper and placed in a box and then one piece of paper is drawn at random, what is the probability that the paper has a vowel written on it? What is the probability that the paper has a consonant written on it?

8. The questions below refer to a very popular dice game, craps, in which a player rolls two dice.
   (a) Rolling a sum of 7 or 11 on the first roll of the dice is a win. What is the probability of winning on the first roll?
   (b) Rolling a sum of 2, 3, or 12 on the first roll of the dice is a loss. What is the probability of losing on the first roll?
   (c) Rolling a sum of 4, 5, 6, 8, 9, or 10 on the first roll is neither a win nor a loss. What is the probability of neither winning nor losing on the first roll?
   (d) After rolling a sum of 4, 5, 6, 8, 9, or 10, a player must roll the same sum again before rolling a sum of 7. Which sum 4, 5, 6, 8, 9, or 10 has the highest probability of occurring again?
   (e) What is the probability of rolling a sum of 1 on any roll of the dice?
   (f) What is the probability of rolling a sum less than 13 on any roll of the dice?
   (g) If the two dice are rolled 60 times, approximately how many sums of 7 can be expected?

9. The probability of spinning an odd number on a spinner is 7/8. Out of 240 spins, how many outcomes can be expected to be odd numbers?

10. A roulette wheel has 38 slots around the rim. The first 36 slots are numbered from 1 to 36. Half of these 36 slots are red and the other half are black. The remaining 2 slots are numbered 0 and 00 and are colored green. As the roulette wheel is spun in one direction, a small ivory ball is rolled along the rim in the opposite direction. The ball has an equally likely chance of falling into any one of the 38 slots. Find each of the following.
   (a) The probability the ball lands in a black slot
   (b) The probability the ball lands on 0 or 00
   (c) The probability the ball does not land on a number from 1 through 12
   (d) The probability the ball lands on odd number or a green slot

11. If the roulette wheel in problem 10 is spun 190 times, about how many times can we expect the ball to land on 0 or 00?

LABORATORY ACTIVITY

1. Suppose a paper cup is tossed in the air. The different ways it can land are shown below.

Top   Bottom   Side

Toss a cup 30 times and record each result. From this information, calculate the experimental probability of each outcome. Do the outcomes appear to be equally likely? Based on experimental probabilities, how many times would you predict the cup land on its side if tossed 200 times?

2. Toss a coin 30 times and record the results. From this information, calculate the experimental probability of tossing a head. Does the experimental result agree with the expected theoretical probability of 1/2?

BRAIN TEASER

A game called WIN is played with a set of nonstandard dice whose faces are shown flattened out. The game is played with two players. Each player chooses one die and the players roll the dice at the same time. The player with the greater number showing on his die wins the game. If you were to play WIN, would you choose your die first or second? Why? Can you find a strategy for maximizing your chances of winning the game? (The game of WIN was suggested by Joseph Smyth of Santa Rosa Junior College.)

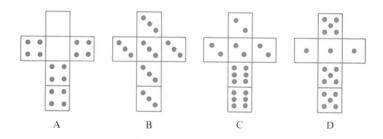

A   B   C   D

7-2 USING TREE DIAGRAMS IN PROBABILITY

tree diagram

A very useful way of describing the results of tossing a coin is with a **tree diagram** as shown in Figure 7-4. The outcomes are H and T, and the probability of each is 1/2.

FIGURE 7-4

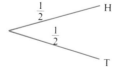

Notice that each outcome in the experiment has a separate branch and the probability of each event is listed on the branches.

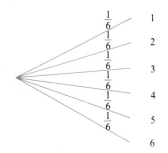

A tree diagram for rolling a fair die is given in Figure 7-5.

The box in Figure 7-6 has one black ball and three white balls. Suppose one ball is drawn at random from the box; that is no one of the four balls is preferred. Thus, the probability of any one particular ball being drawn is 1/4. Since there are three indistinguishable white balls and one black ball, the probability of drawing a white ball is 3/4, and the probability of drawing a black ball is 1/4. The sample space for the experiment is {○, ●}. A tree diagram for this experiment is given in Figure 7-7. Notice that the sum of the probabilities of the branches coming from a single point equals one.

FIGURE 7-5

FIGURE 7-6

FIGURE 7-7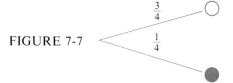

one-stage experiments
two-stage experiments
multistage experiments

The previous experiments are examples of **one-stage experiments,** experiments that are over after one step. Next consider several **two-stage experiments** and then some **multistage experiments.**

The box in Figure 7-8 contains one black and two white balls. A ball is drawn at random and its color recorded. The ball is then *replaced* and a second ball is drawn and its color recorded. The sample space for this experiment is given by $S = \{●●, ●○, ○●, ○○\}$. Figure 7-9 shows a tree diagram for this two-stage experiment.

FIGURE 7-8

FIGURE 7-9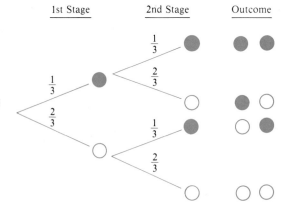

One path along the tree corresponds to each outcome. What probability should be assigned to each outcome? Consider the path for the outcome ●○. In the first stage, the probability of obtaining a black ball is 1/3. Then the probability of obtaining a white ball in the second stage (second draw) is 2/3. Thus, we expect to obtain a black ball on the first draw 1/3 of the time and then draw a white ball 2/3 of those times that we obtained a black ball; that is, 2/3 of 1/3 or 2/3 · 1/3. Observe that this product may be obtained by multiplying the probabilities along the branches used for the path leading to ●○; that is, 1/3 · 2/3 or 2/9. The probabilities shown in Table 7-1 are obtained by following the paths leading to each of the four outcomes and by multiplying the probabilities along the paths.

TABLE 7-1

Outcome	●●	●○	○●	○○
Probability	$\frac{1}{3} \cdot \frac{1}{3}$ or $\frac{1}{9}$	$\frac{1}{3} \cdot \frac{2}{3}$ or $\frac{2}{9}$	$\frac{2}{3} \cdot \frac{1}{3}$ or $\frac{2}{9}$	$\frac{2}{3} \cdot \frac{2}{3}$ or $\frac{4}{9}$

For all multistage experiments, the probability of the outcome along any path is equal to the product of all the probabilities along the branches of the path. The sum of the probabilities on branches from any point always equals one.

Look at the box pictured in Figure 7-8 again. This time, suppose two balls are drawn one by one without replacement. A tree diagram for this experiment, along with the set of possible outcomes, is shown in Figure 7-10. Notice that the denominators of the fractions along the second branch are all two. Since the draws are made without replacement, there are only 2 balls remaining for the second draw.

FIGURE 7-10

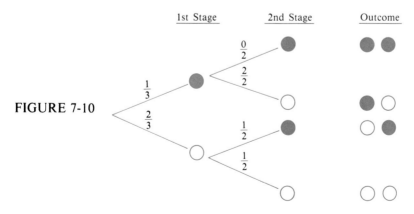

The probabilities for each outcome of the experiment are given in Table 7-2.

TABLE 7-2

Outcome	●●	●○	○●	○○
Probability	$\frac{1}{3} \cdot \frac{0}{2}$ or 0	$\frac{1}{3} \cdot \frac{2}{2}$ or $\frac{2}{6}$	$\frac{2}{3} \cdot \frac{1}{2}$ or $\frac{2}{6}$	$\frac{2}{3} \cdot \frac{1}{2}$ or $\frac{2}{6}$

Table 7-2 can be used to find the probabilities of various events. Consider the event, A, consisting of the outcomes for drawing exactly one black ball in the two draws. This event is given by $A = \{●○, ○●\}$. Since the outcome ●○ appears 2/6 of the time, and the outcome ○● appears 2/6 of the time, then either ●○ or ○● will appear 4/6 of the time. Thus, $P(A) = 2/6 + 2/6 = 4/6$.

The event, B, consisting of outcomes for drawing *at least* one black ball could be recorded as $B = \{●○, ○●, ●●\}$. Since $P(●○) = 2/6$, $P(○●) = 2/6$, and $P(●●) = 0$, $P(B) = 2/6 + 2/6 + 0 = 4/6$. Since $\overline{B} = \{○○\}$ and $P(\overline{B}) = 2/6$, the probability of B could have been computed as follows: $P(B) = 1 - P(\overline{B}) = 1 - 2/6 = 4/6$.

Example 7-9

Consider the two boxes in Figure 7-11.

FIGURE 7-11

#1   #2

A ball is drawn from box 1, and then a ball is drawn from box 2. Use a tree diagram to find the probability of obtaining at most one white ball.

Solution

Let A be the event of drawing at most one white ball, then $A = \{●●, ●○, ○●\}$. To find the probabilities of each of the outcomes in A and their sum, draw a tree diagram for the experiment as in Figure 7-12.

FIGURE 7-12

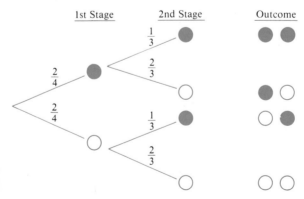

The probabilities for each outcome are given in Table 7-3.

TABLE 7-3

Outcome	●●	●○	○●	○○
Probability	$\frac{2}{4} \cdot \frac{1}{3}$ or $\frac{2}{12}$	$\frac{2}{4} \cdot \frac{2}{3}$ or $\frac{4}{12}$	$\frac{2}{4} \cdot \frac{1}{3}$ or $\frac{2}{12}$	$\frac{2}{4} \cdot \frac{2}{3}$ or $\frac{4}{12}$

Thus, $P(A) = P(●●) + P(●○) + P(○●) = 2/12 + 4/12 + 2/12 = 8/12$ or $2/3$.

Remark

The solution can also be found using the complement of A. Since the complement of A is $\overline{A} = \{○○\}$, then

$$P(A) = 1 - P(\overline{A}) = 1 - \frac{4}{12} = \frac{8}{12} \text{ or } \frac{2}{3}$$

PROBABILITY

FIGURE 7-13

Figure 7-13 shows a box with 11 letters. An example of a four-stage experiment is to draw four letters from the box one by one *without replacement*. The probability of the outcome BABY may be found by using just one branch of a much larger tree diagram. Since the entire tree is not needed to find this probability only the portion required to complete the problem is pictured in Figure 7-14. Notice that, since the experiment is performed without replacement, each successive denominator decreases by one,

FIGURE 7-14

$$\frac{2}{11} \qquad \frac{1}{10} \qquad \frac{1}{9} \qquad \frac{1}{8}$$
——B———A———B———Y

Thus $P(\text{BABY}) = (2/11) \cdot (1/10) \cdot (1/9) \cdot (1/8)$ or $2/7920$.

Suppose four letters are drawn one by one from the box in Figure 7-13 and replaced after each drawing. In this case the branch needed to find $P(\text{BABY})$ is pictured in Figure 7-15.

FIGURE 7-15

$$\frac{2}{11} \qquad \frac{:1}{11} \qquad \frac{2}{11} \qquad \frac{1}{11}$$
——B———A———B———Y

Thus, $P(\text{BABY}) = (2/11) \cdot (1/11) \cdot (2/11) \cdot (1/11)$ or $4/14\,641$.

Example 7-10 | Consider the three boxes in Figure 7-16.

FIGURE 7-16

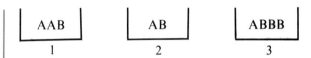

AAB	AB	ABBB
1	2	3

A letter is drawn from box 1 and placed in box 2. Then a letter is drawn from box 2 and placed in box 3. Finally, a letter is drawn from box 3. What is the probability that the letter drawn from box 3 is *B*?

Solution

A tree diagram and outcomes for this experiment follow.

1st Stage	2nd Stage	3rd Stage	Outcome

$$\frac{2}{3} \quad A \quad \frac{2}{3} \quad A \quad \frac{2}{5} \quad A \quad AAA$$

$$\frac{3}{5} \quad B \quad AAB$$

$$\frac{1}{3} \quad B \quad \frac{1}{5} \quad A \quad ABA$$

$$\frac{4}{5} \quad B \quad ABB$$

$$\frac{1}{3} \quad B \quad \frac{1}{3} \quad A \quad \frac{2}{5} \quad A \quad BAA$$

$$\frac{3}{5} \quad B \quad BAB$$

$$\frac{2}{3} \quad B \quad \frac{1}{5} \quad A \quad BBA$$

$$\frac{4}{5} \quad B \quad BBB$$

To find the probability that a *B* is drawn from box 3, add the probabilities for *AAB* and *ABB* and *BAB* and *BBB*.

$$P(AAB) = \frac{2}{3} \cdot \frac{2}{3} \cdot \frac{3}{5} = \frac{12}{45}$$

$$P(ABB) = \frac{2}{3} \cdot \frac{1}{3} \cdot \frac{4}{5} = \frac{8}{45}$$

$$P(BAB) = \frac{1}{3} \cdot \frac{1}{3} \cdot \frac{3}{5} = \frac{3}{45}$$

$$P(BBB) = \frac{1}{3} \cdot \frac{2}{3} \cdot \frac{4}{5} = \frac{8}{45}$$

Thus, the probability of obtaining a *B* in this experiment is $12/45 + 8/45 + 3/45 + 8/45 = 31/45$.

We now summarize the ideas in this section for a general case. Suppose an experiment has a sample space given by $S = \{s_1, s_2, s_3, \ldots, s_n\}$ and suppose the probability of each outcome is given in Table 7-4.

TABLE 7-4

Outcome	s_1	s_2	s_3	$\cdots$	s_n
Probability	p_1	p_2	p_3	$\cdots$	p_n

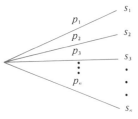

FIGURE 7-17

By definition, the probabilities are nonnegative and each is greater than or equal to zero and less than or equal to one. The sum of the probabilities, $p_1 + p_2 + p_3 + \cdots + p_n$, equals one. If A is some event, say $A = \{s_2, s_3\}$, then $P(A)$ equals the sum of the probabilities of all the outcomes in A; that is, $P(A) = p_2 + p_3$. Also, $P(A) = 1 - P(\overline{A})$. A tree diagram for the general experiment is given in Figure 7-17.

Tree diagrams are presented in some elementary school text books. Page 300 is taken from the *Macmillan Mathematics*, 1978, Grade 6. Work through the problems.

PROBLEM SET 7-2

1. A box contains the six letters shown below. What is the probability of the outcome DAN if three letters are drawn one by one (a) with replacement and (b) without replacement?

    RANDOM

2. Three boxes with letters are shown below.

    MATH   AND   HISTORY
      1   2   2

    Answer each of the following questions about the boxes.
    (a) One letter is drawn at random from each box and the results are recorded in order. What is the probability that the outcome is HAT?
    (b) From box 1, three letters are drawn one by one without replacement and recorded in order. What is the probability the outcome is HAT?
    (c) From box 1, three letters are drawn one by one with replacement and recorded in order. What is the probability the outcome is HAT?
    (d) If a box is chosen at random and then a letter is drawn at random from the box, what is the probability the outcome is A?
3. A box contains the 11 letters shown below. The letters are drawn one by one without replacement and the results recorded in order. Find the probability of the outcome MISSIS-SIPPI.

exercises

This tree diagram shows what happens when you toss 3 coins many times.

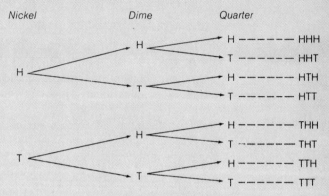

Nickel	Dime	Quarter
	H	H ‒ ‒ ‒ ‒ ‒ ‒ HHH
		T ‒ ‒ ‒ ‒ ‒ ‒ HHT
H	T	H ‒ ‒ ‒ ‒ ‒ ‒ HTH
		T ‒ ‒ ‒ ‒ ‒ ‒ HTT
	H	H ‒ ‒ ‒ ‒ ‒ ‒ THH
		T ‒ ‒ ‒ ‒ ‒ ‒ THT
T	T	H ‒ ‒ ‒ ‒ ‒ ‒ TTH
		T ‒ ‒ ‒ ‒ ‒ ‒ TTT

1. How many different ways can the coins land?

2. P (HHH) = ▧   **3.** P (HHT) = ▧

4. P (HTH) = ▧   **5.** P (HTT) = ▧

6. P (HTT or TTH or THT) = ▧

7. P (exactly one coin is heads) = ▧

8. P (at least one tail) = ▧

9. P (4 heads) = ▧

10. P (HHH or TTT) = ▧

11. If these 3 coins were tossed 800 times, about how many of these times would be all tails? About how many times would there be at least one tail?

Upside-down answers   1. 8   6. $\frac{3}{8}$

Probability

MIIIIPPSSSS

4. An executive committee consisted of ten members—four women and six men. Three members were selected at random to be sent to a meeting in Hawaii. A blindfolded woman drew three of the ten names from a hat. All three names drawn were women. If the woman who drew the names was honest, what was the probability of such luck?

5. Two boxes with letters follow. Choose a box and draw three letters at random one by one without replacement. If the outcome is SOS, you win a prize. Which box should you choose?

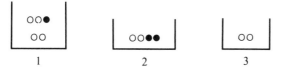

SOS

1

SOSSOS

2

6. Answer the question in problem 5 if the letters are drawn with replacement.

7. Three boxes containing balls are shown below. Draw a ball from box 1 and place it in box 2. Then draw a ball from box 2 and put it in box 3. Finally, draw a ball from box 3. What is the probability that the last ball, drawn from box 3, is white?

1

2

3

8. What is the probability that the last ball drawn in problem 7 is black?

9. Carolyn will win a large prize if she wins two tennis games in a row out of three games. She is to play alternately against Billie and Bobby. She may choose to play Billie-Bobby-Billie or Bobby-Billie-Bobby. She wins against Billie with probability of 1/2 and against Bobby with probability of 4/5. Which alternative should she choose and why?

10. Two boxes with black and white balls are shown below. A ball is drawn at random from box 1, and then a ball is drawn at random from box 2 and the colors recorded in order.

1

2

Find each of the following.
(a) The probability of two white balls
(b) The probability of at least one black ball
(c) The probability of at most one black ball
(d) The probability of ●○ or ○●

11. A penny, nickel, dime, and quarter are tossed. What is the probability of at least three heads?

12. Assume the probability that a child born is a boy is 1/2. What is the probability that if a family is going to have four children that they will have all boys?

13. The number of symbols on each of the three dials of a standard slot machine is shown in the following table.

Symbol	Dial 1	Dial 2	Dial 3
Bar	1	3	1
Bell	1	3	3
Plum	5	1	5
Orange	3	6	7
Cherry	7	7	0
Lemon	3	0	4
Total	20	20	20

Find the probability for each of the following.
(a) three plums   (b) three oranges   (c) three lemons   (d) no plums

14. If a person takes a five-question true-or-false test, what is the probability that the score is 100% if the person guesses on every question?

15. In a drawer there are ten blue socks and twelve black socks. Suppose it is dark and you choose three socks. What is the probability that you will choose a matching pair?

BRAIN TEASER

Suppose *n* people are in a room. Two people bet that at least two of the people in the room have a birthday on the same date during the year (for example, October 14). Assume that a person is as likely to be born on one day as another and ignore leap years. How many people must be in the room before the bet is even? (If *n* = 366, it is a sure bet.) Poll your class to see if two people have the same birthday. Use this information to find an experimental answer. Then find a theoretical solution. A calculator is very helpful for the computations.

LABORATORY ACTIVITY   The following experiment is adapted from *Activities in Mathematics, Probability* (Glenview, Ill.: Scott Foresman, 1971).

A grasshopper is placed on the track below at the start, S. Each section of the track, labeled with letters, is one hop long.

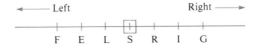

The grasshopper is as likely to jump right as left for any one hop. It takes three hops at a time. For example, the grasshopper may jump as follows.

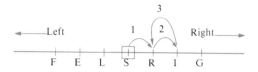

This outcome is recorded as RIR and the final stopping point is R. The grasshopper always starts at S.

Mary and Larry decide on the following game. Mary gets one point if, after three hops, the grasshopper ends up at either L or R. Larry gets one point if, after 3 hops, the grasshopper ends up at F, E, S, I, or G. Do you think the game is fair?

The three hops can be simulated by tossing a coin three times. Heads represents one hop to the right. Tails represents one hop to the left. Play the game 32 times and find the experimental probability of the grasshopper landing on each particular letter.

Draw a tree diagram for this experiment that shows all possible outcomes. Use the tree diagram to find the probabilities of Mary winning the game and of Larry winning the game. Compare these to your experimental probabilities.

7-3 ODDS AND MATHEMATICAL EXPECTATION

odds

People often speak about the *odds in favor* of or the *odds against* a particular team in an athletic contest, or the **odds** of having a baby boy or a baby girl. For example, a newspaper article may say that the odds in favor of a boxer winning his next match are 5 to 1.

To study odds, consider rolling a die. If a die is rolled, then $P(4) = 1/6$ and $P(\text{not } 4) = 5/6$. The odds in favor of rolling a 4 in one toss are defined as $1/6 \div 5/6$ or 1 to 5. Formally, odds are defined as follows.

DEFINITION

The **odds in favor** of an event A, where $P(A)$ is the probability that A occurs and $P(\overline{A})$ is the probability that A does not occur, are given by the following.

$$\frac{P(A)}{P(\overline{A})} \quad \text{or} \quad \frac{P(A)}{1 - P(A)}$$

The **odds against** an event A are given by the following.

$$\frac{P(\overline{A})}{P(A)} \quad \text{or} \quad \frac{1 - P(A)}{P(A)}$$

Thus, the odds against tossing a 4 on one throw of a die are $(5/6)/(1/6) = 5/1$ or 5 to 1.

Notice that in calculating odds, the denominators of the probabilities divide out. Thus, alternate definitions for odds in case of equally likely outcomes are as follows.

$$\text{odds in favor} = \frac{\text{number of favorable outcomes}}{\text{number of unfavorable outcomes}}$$

$$\text{odds against} = \frac{\text{number of unfavorable outcomes}}{\text{number of favorable outcomes}}$$

When rolling a die, the number of favorable ways of rolling a four in one throw of a die is 1, and the number of unfavorable ways is 5. Thus, the odds in favor of rolling a four are 1 to 5.

Example 7-11

For each of the following, find the odds in favor of the event occurring.
(a)   Rolling a number less than 5 on a die
(b)   Tossing a head on a fair coin
(c)   Drawing an ace from an ordinary 52-card deck
(d)   Drawing a heart from an ordinary 52-card deck

Solution

(a)   Since the probability of rolling a number less than 5 is 4/6 and the probability of rolling a number not less than 5 is 2/6, the odds in favor of rolling a number less than 5 are $(4/6) \div (2/6)$ or 4 to 2.
(b)   Since $P(H) = 1/2$ and $P(\overline{H}) = 1/2$, the odds in favor of getting a head are $(1/2) \div (1/2)$ or 1 to 1.
(c)   Since the probability of drawing an ace is 4/52 and the probability of not drawing an ace is 48/52, the odds in favor of drawing an ace are $(4/52) \div (48/52)$ or 4 to 48. The odds 4 to 48 are the same as 1 to 12.
(d)   Since the probability of drawing a heart is 13/52 or 1/4 and the probability of not drawing a heart is 39/52 or 3/4, the odds in favor of drawing a heart are $(13/52) \div (39/52) = 13/39$ or 13 to 39. This could be expressed as 1 to 3.

Given the probability of an event, it is possible to find the odds in favor of, (or against) the event. Conversely, given the odds in favor of (or against) an event, it is possible to find the probability of the event. For example, if the odds in favor of an event are 5 to 1, then the following proportion holds.

$$\frac{\text{number of favorable outcomes}}{\text{number of unfavorable outcomes}} = \frac{5}{1}$$

The probability of the event is obtained using properties of ratios.

$$\frac{\text{number of favorable outcomes}}{\text{number of all outcomes (favorable and unfavorable)}} = \frac{5}{5+1} = \frac{5}{6}$$

Remark | Note that the probability 5/6 is a ratio. The exact number of favorable outcomes and the exact total number of all outcomes is not necessarily known.

Example 7-12 | In the following cartoon Snoopy is told that the odds are 1000 to 1 that he will end up with a broken arm if he touches Linus' blanket. What is the probability of this event, E?

© 1974 United Feature Syndicate, Inc.

Solution | $P(E) = \dfrac{\text{number of favorable outcomes}}{\text{total number of outcomes}} = \dfrac{1000}{1001}$

An important concept related to probability is *mathematical expectation*. Suppose Jane has won an $800 oven on a television game show. She has a choice of keeping the oven or trading it for a prize behind one of three doors.

Behind one of the doors is a $2400 vacation prize, behind another is a $1200 living room set, and behind the third is $90 worth of peanuts. Should she trade her $800 for what is behind one of the doors? Each door has a probability of 1/3 of being chosen. In addition, a payoff is associated with each door. To determine how much Jane could expect to win if the experiment were repeated a large number of times, multiply the probability of choosing a door by the payoff behind the door as shown in Table 7-5.

TABLE 7-5

Probability	Payoff	Product
1/3	$2400	$ 800
1/3	$1200	$ 400
1/3	$ 90	$ 30
		$1230

mathematical expectation
expected value

The total of the products, $1230, is called the **mathematical expectation** or **expected value** of the experiment. The expected value is a kind of average of winnings for the long run. If Jane were allowed to repeat the game a large number of times, she could expect to win an average of $1230 per game. Since $1230 is greater than $800, the value of the oven, Jane should probably try her luck with the doors. Of course, since Jane has only one try, she may lose. Mathematical expectation can be used to predict the average result of an experiment when it is repeated many times, but expectation cannot be used to determine the outcome of a single experiment.

DEFINITION

If, in an experiment, the possible outcomes are numbers $a_1, a_2, \ldots, a_n$, respectively, occurring with probabilities $p_1, p_2, \ldots, p_n$, then the **mathematical expectation** (expected value), E, is given by the following equation.

$$E = a_1 \cdot p_1 + a_2 \cdot p_2 + a_3 \cdot p_3 + \cdots + a_n \cdot p_n$$

Suppose Mega-Mouth Toothpaste Company is giving away $20 000 in a contest. To win the contest, a person must send in a postcard with his or her name on it (no purchase of toothpaste is necessary). Suppose the company expects to receive one million postcards. Is it worth the time and expense of a postcard and postage to enter the contest? The expected value is one-millionth of $20 000; that is, $E = (1/1\ 000\ 000) \cdot (20\ 000/1) = 2/100 = 0.02$. The game is worthwhile if the expected value equals the cost of playing the game. Since the cost of the postcard and postage exceeds $0.02, the contest is not worthwhile (unless you feel very lucky).

Example 7-13

Consider the spinner in Figure 7-18 with the payoff for each region written on the spinner. Should the owner of this spinner expect to make money over an extended period of time if the charge is $2.00 per spin?

Solution

If the spinner is fair, then the following probabilities can be assigned to each region.

$$P(\$1.00) = \frac{1}{2}, \qquad P(\$2.00) = \frac{1}{4}, \qquad P(\$3.00) = \frac{1}{8}, \qquad P(\$4.00) = \frac{1}{8}$$

The expected value is given by $E = (1/2)1 + (1/4)2 + (1/8)3 + (1/8)4 = 1.875$ or about 1.88. Since the owner can expect to pay out about $1.88 per spin, and $1.88 is less than the $2.00 charge, the owner should make a profit on the spinner if it is used many times.

FIGURE 7-18

fair game

The game in Example 7-13 is not a **fair game.** A game is considered fair if the net winnings are $0; that is, the expected value of the game equals the price of playing the game.

Example 7-14

Lori spends $1.00 for one ticket in a raffle with a $100 prize. If 200 tickets are sold, is $1.00 a fair price to pay for the ticket?

Solution

The probability of winning $100 is 1/200. Thus, $E = (1/200)100$ or 0.50. Since $1.00 is greater than $0.50, $1.00 is not a fair price. If the raffle is repeated many times, Lori can expect to lose $0.50 per raffle.

PROBLEM SET 7-3

1. What are the odds in favor of drawing a face card from an ordinary deck of playing cards? What are the odds against drawing a face card?
2. On a single roll of a pair of dice, what are the odds against rolling a sum of 7?
3. Assume the probability of a boy being born is 1/2. If a family plans to have four children what are the odds against having all boys?
4. Diane tossed a coin nine times and got nine tails. Assume Diane's coin is fair, and answer each of the following questions.
   (a) What is the probability of tossing a tail on the tenth toss?
   (b) What is the probability of tossing ten more tails in a row?
   (c) What are the odds against tossing ten more tails in a row?

5. If the odds against Sam winning his first prize fight are 3 to 5, what is the probability he will win the fight?
6. What are the odds in favor of tossing at least two heads if a fair coin is tossed three times?
7. Suppose a player pays $1.00 to roll a die once. The player wins $3.00 if the roll is 6, otherwise the player loses the $1.00. Is this a fair game? If not, what payoff would make the game fair?
8. A game involves tossing two coins. A player wins $1.00 if both tosses result in heads. What should you pay to play this game in order to make it a fair game?
9. Suppose a player rolls a fair die and receives the number of dollars equal to the number of spots showing on the die. What is the expected value?
10. A punchout card contains 500 spaces. One particular space pays $1000, five other spaces each pay $100, and the other spaces pay nothing. If a player chooses one space, what is the expected value of the game?
11. The following chart shows the probabilities assigned by Stu to the number of hours spent on homework on a given night.

Hours	1	2	3	4	5	6
Probability	0.15	0.20	0.40	0.10	0.05	0.10

If Stu's friend Stella calls and asks how long his homework will take, what would you expect his answer to be based on this table?
12. Suppose five quarters, five dimes, five nickels, and ten pennies are in a box. One coin is selected at random. What is the expected value of this experiment?

7-4   METHODS OF COUNTING

Tree diagrams can be used to list possible outcomes of experiments. For example, the tree diagram in Figure 7-19 lists the different ways three different flavors of ice cream, chocolate (c), vanilla (v), and strawberry (s), can be arranged on a cone.

FIGURE 7-19

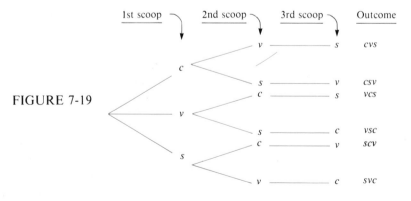

The tree starts out with three branches in the first stage, representing the three possibilities for the first scoop. For each outcome in the first stage, there are two possibilities at the second stage. Hence, there are $3 \cdot 2$ possibilities at the second stage. Then, for each outcome in the second stage, there is only one possibility at the third stage. Consequently, there are $3 \cdot 2 \cdot 1$ or 6 different arrangements.

Now, consider a double-dip ice cream cone for which there are ten flavors of ice cream and six flavors of sherbet. How many different double-dip cones can be made with ice cream on the bottom and sherbet on the top? Since for each of the ten ice cream flavors there are six flavors of sherbet, the number of all possible double dip cones is $\underbrace{6 + 6 + 6 + \cdots + 6}_{10 \text{ terms}}$ or $10 \cdot 6 = 60$. A tree diagram could be used to verify the result. The counting argument used to find the number of possible double-dip cones is an example of the Fundamental Counting Principle.

Property | **Fundamental Counting Principle** If event M can occur in m ways and, after it has occurred, event N can occur in n ways, then event M followed by event N can occur in $m \cdot n$ ways.

Remark | The Fundamental Counting Principle can be extended to any number of events.

Example 7-15 | Solve each of the following.

(a) If a man owns seven shirts and six pairs of pants, how many different shirt–pant combinations are possible?

(b) Sally is taking a five-item true-or-false test. If she guesses at every item, how many different patterns of answers are possible?

(c) Suppose eight horses are entered in a race. In how many different ways can the winning horses finish? Count win, place, and show.

Solution | (a) Since a shirt can be chosen in seven ways and a pair of pants can be chosen in six ways, there are $7 \cdot 6$ or 42 shirt–pant combinations.

(b) Since there are two ways to answer question 1 on the test, two ways to answer question 2, and so on, there are $2 \cdot 2 \cdot 2 \cdot 2 \cdot 2$ or 32 different possible patterns of answers.

(c) There are eight possible winners, leaving seven possible places, and six possible shows. Thus, there are $8 \cdot 7 \cdot 6$ or 336 ways in which the win, place, and show horses can finish the race.

Example 7-16 | If automobile license plates consist of two letters followed by four digits, what is the total number of different license plates possible if numbers and letters may be repeated?

Solution | There are 26 · 26 · 10 · 10 · 10 · 10 or 6 760 000 different license plates possible.

Now consider how many ways the owner of an ice cream parlor can display ten ice cream flavors in a row along the front of the display case. The first position can be filled in ten ways, the second position in nine ways, the third position in eight ways and so on. Thus, by the Fundamental Counting Principle there are 10 · 9 · 8 · 7 · 6 · 5 · 4 · 3 · 2 · 1 or 3 628 800 ways to display the flavors. If there were 16 flavors, there would be 16 · 15 · 14 · 13 · ... · 3 · 2 · 1 ways to arrange them. In general, if there are n containers with n positions, then the number of ways to arrange the containers in a row is the product of all the natural numbers less than or equal to n. This expression is

n factorial | called n **factorial** and is denoted by $n!$

$$8! = 8 \cdot 7 \cdot 6 \cdot 5 \cdot 4 \cdot 3 \cdot 2 \cdot 1$$

$$n! = n \cdot (n - 1) \cdot (n - 2) \cdot \ldots \cdot 3 \cdot 2 \cdot 1$$

Using factorial notation is helpful in counting and probability problems. Practice problems with factorials are included in Problem Set 7-4.

The ice cream cone arrangements discussed previously were in a definite order. A scoop of chocolate ice cream on top of a scoop of vanilla is a different arrangement than a scoop of vanilla on top of chocolate. An

permutation | arrangement of things in a definite order is called a **permutation.**

Consider the set of people in a small club, {Al, Betty, Carl, Dan}. In how many ways can they elect a president and a secretary? Order is important for counting the possibilities. Thus, this is a permutation problem. Since there are four ways of choosing a president and then three ways of choosing a secretary, by the Fundamental Counting Principle, there are 4 · 3 or 12 ways of choosing a president and secretary. Note that an Al-Betty choice is different from a Betty-Al choice.

Example 7-17 | A baseball team has nine players. Find the number of ways a baseball coach can arrange the batting order.

Solution | Here order is important, and this is a permutation problem. Since there are nine ways to choose the first batter, eight ways to choose the second batter, and so on, there are 9 · 8 · 7 · ... · 2 · 1 = 9! or 362 880 ways of arranging the batting order.

Example 7-18 | Find the number of ways of choosing three letters from the alphabet if none of the letters can be repeated.

Solution | Since order is important, this is a permutation problem. There are 26 ways of choosing the first letter, 25 ways of choosing the second letter, and 24 ways of choosing the third letter, hence, there are 26 · 25 · 24 or 15 600 ways of choosing the three letters.

Reconsider the club, {Al, Betty, Carl, Dan}. Suppose a two-person committee is selected with no chair. In this case, order is not important. In other words, an Al–Betty choice is the same as a Betty–Al choice. An arrangement of things in which the order does not make any difference is
combination | called a **combination.** A comparison of the results of electing a president and secretary for the club and the results of simply selecting a two-person committee are shown in Figure 7-20. From Figure 7-20, the number of permutations divided by 2 is the number of combinations, (4 · 3)/2 or 6.

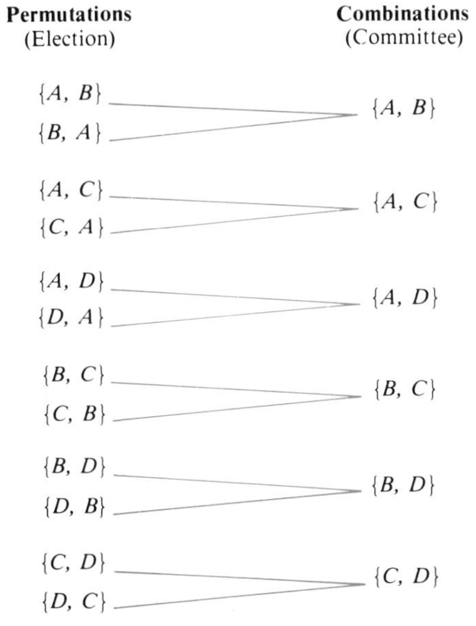

Permutations
(Election)

Combinations
(Committee)

{A, B}
{B, A}

{A, B}

{A, C}
{C, A}

{A, C}

FIGURE 7-20 {A, D}
{D, A}

{A, D}

{B, C}
{C, B}

{B, C}

{B, D}
{D, B}

{B, D}

{C, D}
{D, C}

{C, D}

In how many ways can a committee of three people be selected from the club {Al, Betty, Carl, Dan}? To solve this problem, first solve the simpler problem of finding the number of three-person committees assuming that a president, vice president and secretary are chosen. A partial list of possibilities for both problems is shown in Figure 7-21.

There are 3! or 6 times as many permutations as there are combinations. By the Fundamental Counting Principle, the number of permutations is 4 · 3 · 2 or 24. The number of combinations is (4 · 3 · 2)/3! or 4. The number of

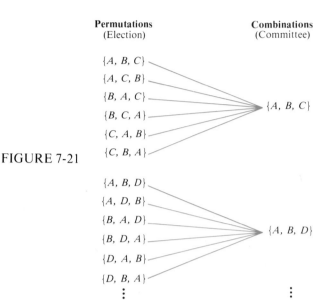

FIGURE 7-21

permutations is divided by 3! since each committee choice can be arranged 3! ways. In general, use the following rule to count combinations.

To find the number of combinations possible in a counting problem, first use the Fundamental Counting Principle to find the number of permutations and then divide by the number of ways in which each choice can be arranged.

Example 7-19

A book-of-the month club offers three free books from a list of 42 books. How many combinations are possible?

Solution

By the Fundamental Counting Principle, there are $42 \cdot 41 \cdot 40$ ways to choose the three free books in order. The number of ways the three choices of books can be arranged is 3! or 6. Therefore, the number of combinations possible for three books is $(42 \cdot 41 \cdot 40)/3!$ or 11 480.

Example 7-20

At the beginning of the second quarter of the Mathematics for Elementary Teachers class, each of the 25 students shook hands with each of the other students exactly once. How many handshakes took place?

Solution

Since the handshake between persons A and B is the same as between persons B and A, order is not important in this problem. This is a problem of choosing combinations of 25 people two at a time. Thus, there are $(25 \cdot 24)/2!$ or 300 different handshakes. (Compare this example with the Preliminary Problem in Chapter 1.)

PROBLEM SET 7-4

1. The eighth-grade class at a grade school has 16 girls and 14 boys. How many different possible boy–girl dates can be arranged?
2. How many different three-digit numbers can be formed from the digits 1, 2, 3, 4, 5, 6, 7? Each digit can be used only once.
3. If a coin is tossed five times, in how many different ways can the sequence of heads and tails appear?
4. The telephone prefix for a university is 243. The prefix is followed by four digits. How many telephones are possible before a new prefix is needed?
5. Radio stations in the United States have call letters that begin with either K or W. Some have a total of three letters, while others have four letters. How many sets of three-letter call letters are possible? How many sets of four-letter call letters are possible?
6. Carlin's Pizza House offers 3 kinds of salads, 15 kinds of pizza, and 4 kinds of desserts. How many different three-course meals can be ordered?
7. Decide whether each of the following are true or false.

    (a) $6! = 6 \cdot 5!$ (b) $3! + 3! = 6!$

    (c) $\dfrac{6!}{3!} = 2!$ (d) $\dfrac{6!}{3} = 2!$

    (e) $\dfrac{6!}{5!} = 6$ (f) $\dfrac{6!}{4!2!} = 15$

    (g) $n!(n + 1) = (n + 1)!$

8. How many ways can the letters in the word SCRAMBLE be rearranged?
9. How many two-person committees can be formed from a group of six people?
10. Explain the difference between a permutation and a combination.
11. Assume a class has 30 members.
    (a) In how many ways can a president, vice-president, and secretary be selected?
    (b) How many committees of three persons can be chosen?
12. A basketball coach was criticized in the newspaper for not trying out every combination of players. If the team roster has twelve players, how many five-player combinations are possible?
13. Solve the problem posed in the following cartoon. (AAUGHH! is not an acceptable answer.)

14. A five-volume numbered set of books is placed randomly on a shelf. What is the probability that the books will be numbered in the correct order from left to right?

15. Take ten points in a plane, no three on a line. How many straight lines can be drawn if each line is drawn through a pair of points?

★16. A committee of three people is selected at random from a set consisting of seven Americans, five Frenchpeople, and three Englishpeople.
    (a) What is the probability that the committee consists of all Americans?
    (b) What is the probability that the committee has no Americans?

★17. In how many ways can five couples be seated in a row of ten chairs if no couple is separated?

★18. From a group of six girls and nine boys, how many five-member committees can be formed involving three boys and two girls?

★19. Solve the following problem for Peppermint Patty.

© 1974 United Feature Syndicate, Inc.

 20. Do Problem 63 appearing in Appendix II.

BRAIN TEASER FOR TENNIS PLAYERS

Jane has two tennis serves, a hard serve and a soft serve. Her hard serve has a 50% chance of being good. If her hard serve is good, then she has an 80% chance of winning the point. Her soft serve has a 90% chance of being good. If her soft serve is good, she has a 50% chance of winning the point.

(a) What is the probability that Jane wins the point if she serves hard and then, if necessary, soft?

(b) What is the probability that Jane wins the point if she serves her first serve hard and then, if necessary, her second serve hard?

SOLUTION TO THE
PRELIMINARY PROBLEM

Understanding the Problem

To obtain a marriage permit in a certain town, a woman is handed six strings which she holds in her hand so that the ends of each string are exposed on the top and bottom of her hand. On one side (top or bottom), the strings are picked randomly, two at a time, and tied, forming three separate knots. The same procedure is repeated on the other side, forming three more separate knots. If one closed ring consisting of the six strings exists when the strings are released, she obtains the permit. The problem is to determine the probability that one closed ring will be formed. (One closed ring means that all six pieces are joined end-to-end to form one and only one ring.)

Devising a Plan

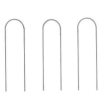

FIGURE 7-22

Figure 7-22 shows what happens when one set of ends of the strings are tied in pairs. Notice that no matter in what order those ends are tied, the result appears as in the figure.

  Then the other ends are tied in a three-stage experiment. If we pick any string in the first stage, then there are five choices for its mate. Four of these choices are favorable choices for forming a ring. Thus, the probability of forming a favorable first tie is 4/5. Figure 7-23 shows a favorable tie at the first stage.

FIGURE 7-23

  For any one of the remaining four strings, there are three choices for its mate. Two of these choices are favorable ones. Thus, the probability of forming a favorable second tie is 2/3. Figure 7-24 shows a favorable tie at the second stage.

  Now two ends remain. Since nothing can go wrong at the third stage, the probability of making a favorable tie is 1. If we use the probabilities completed at each stage and a single branch of a tree diagram, we can calculate the probability for performing three successful ties in a row and hence the probability of forming one closed ring.

FIGURE 7-24

Carrying Out the Plan

If we let S represent a successful tie at each stage, then the branch of the tree with which we are concerned is shown in Figure 7-25.

FIGURE 7-25

1st Stage	2nd Stage	3rd Stage
$\frac{4}{5}$ ——— S	$\frac{2}{3}$ ——— S	$\frac{1}{1}$ ——— S

Thus, the probability of forming one ring is

$$P(\text{ring}) = \frac{4}{5} \cdot \frac{2}{3} \cdot \frac{1}{1} = \frac{8}{15} = 0.5\overline{3}$$

Looking Back

The probability of a woman obtaining a marriage permit in any given year is 8/15. The fact that this result is larger than 1/2 is surprising to most people. A class might simulate this problem with strings to see how the experimental probability compares with the theoretical probability of 8/15.

Related problems that could be attempted are:

1. If a woman fails to get a ring 10 years in a row, she must remain single. What is the probability of such a streak of bad (good) luck?
2. If the number of strings were reduced to three and the rule was that an upper end must be tied to a lower end, what is the probability of a single ring?
3. If the number of strings were three but an upper end could be tied to either an upper or lower end, what is the probability of a single ring?
4. What is the probability of forming three rings in the original problem?
5. What is the probability of forming two rings in the original problem?

QUESTIONS FROM THE CLASSROOM

1. A student claims that if a fair coin is tossed and a head appears five times in a row, then according to the law of averages, the probability of a tail on the next toss is greater than the probability of a head. What is your reply?
2. A student observes the spinner below and claims that the color red has the highest probability of appearing since there are two red areas on the spinner. What is your reply?

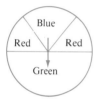

3. A student tosses a coin three times and tails appears each time. The student concludes that the coin is not fair. What is your response?
4. An experiment consists of tossing a coin twice. The student reasons that there are three

possible outcomes: two heads, one head and one tail, or two tails. Thus, $P(\text{HH}) = 1/3$. What is your reply?

5. A student finds an expression for determining the number of permutations of n things taken r at a time, namely, $n!/(n - r)!$. Explain why this formula works.

6. The student in problem 5 also finds a formula for finding the number of combinations of n things taken r at a time, namely, $n!/[(n - r)!r!]$. Explain why this formula works.

CHAPTER OUTLINE

I. Probability

A. If all outcomes of an experiment are equally likely, the **probability** of an event, A, from sample space, S, is given by

$$P(A) = \frac{n(A)}{n(S)}$$

B. A **sample space** is the set of all possible outcomes of an experiment.

C. An **event** is a subset of a sample space.

D. Outcomes are **equally likely** if each outcome is as likely to occur as another.

E. An **impossible event** is an event with a probability of zero. An impossible event can never occur.

F. A **certain event** is an event with a probability of one. A certain event is sure to happen.

G. The probability of the **complement of an event** is given by $P(\overline{A}) = 1 - P(A)$, where A is the event and $\overline{A}$ is its complement.

II. Odds

A. The **odds in favor** of an event A are given by

$$\frac{P(A)}{1 - P(A)}$$

B. The **odds against** an event A are given by

$$\frac{1 - P(A)}{P(A)}$$

III. Mathematical expectation

A. If, in an experiment, the possible outcomes are numbers $a_1, a_2, \ldots, a_n$, respectively, occurring with probabilities $p_1, p_2, \ldots, p_n$, then the **mathematical expectation,** E, is defined as

$$E = a_1 \cdot p_1 + a_2 \cdot p_2 + a_3 \cdot p_3 + \cdots + a_n \cdot p_n$$

IV. Counting principles

A. **Fundamental Counting Principle** If an event M can occur in m ways and, after it has occurred, event N can occur in n ways, then event M followed by event N can occur in $m \cdot n$ ways.

B. **Permutations** are arrangements in which order is important.

C. **Combinations** are arrangements in which order is *not* important.

D. To find the number of combinations possible, first use the Fundamental Counting Principle to find the number of permutations and then divide by the number of ways in which each choice can be arranged.

E. The expression $n!$, called n **factorial,** represents the product of all the natural numbers less than or equal to n.

CHAPTER TEST

1. Suppose the names of the days of the week are placed in a box and one name is drawn at random.
    (a) List the sample space for this experiment.
    (b) List the event consisting of outcomes that the day drawn starts with the letter T.
    (c) What is the probability of drawing a day that starts with T?

2. Complete each of the following.
    (a) If A is an impossible event, then $P(A) = $ _____ .
    (b) If A is a certain event, then $P(A) = $ _____ .
    (c) If A is any event, then _____ $\leq P(A) \leq$ _____ .
    (d) If A is any event, then $P(\overline{A}) = $ _____ .

3. A box contains three red balls, five black balls, and four white balls. Suppose one ball is drawn at random. Find the probability for each of the following events.
    (a) A black ball is drawn.
    (b) A black or a white ball is drawn.
    (c) Neither a red nor a white ball is drawn.
    (d) A red ball is not drawn.
    (e) A black ball and a white ball are drawn.
    (f) A black or white or red ball is drawn.

4. One card is selected at random from an ordinary set of 52 cards. Find the probability for each of the following events.
    (a) A club is drawn.   (b) A spade and a 5 are drawn.
    (c) A heart or a face card are drawn.   (d) A jack is not drawn.

5. A box contains five black balls and four white balls. If three balls are drawn one by one, find the probability that they are all white if the draws are made as follows.
    (a) With replacement   (b) Without replacement

6. Suppose a three-stage rocket is launched into orbit. The probability for failure at stage one is $1/10$, at stage two is $1/5$, and at stage three is $1/3$. What is the probability for a successful flight?

7. Consider the two boxes pictured below. If a letter is drawn from box 1 and placed in box 2, and then a letter is drawn from box 2, what is the probability that the letter is an L?

$$\boxed{\text{LINUS}} \qquad \boxed{\text{LUCY}}$$
$$\qquad 1 \qquad\qquad\qquad 2$$

8. Consider the following two-stage experiment using the boxes below. First, select a box at random and then select a letter at random from the box. What is the probability of drawing an A?

$$\boxed{\text{MY}} \qquad \boxed{\text{DEAR}} \qquad \boxed{\text{AUNT}} \qquad \boxed{\text{SALLY}}$$
$$\quad 1 \qquad\qquad 2 \qquad\qquad\quad 3 \qquad\qquad\quad 4$$

9. Consider the boxes below. Draw a ball from box 1 and put it in box 2. Then draw a ball from box 2 and put it into box 3. Finally, draw a ball from box 3. Construct a tree diagram for this experiment and calculate the probability that the last ball chosen is black.

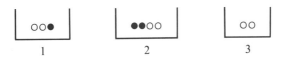

1   2   3

10. What are the odds in favor of drawing a jack when one card is drawn from an ordinary deck of playing cards?

11. A die is rolled once. What are the odds against rolling a prime number?

12. If the odds in favor of a certain event are 3 to 5, what is the probability the event will occur?

13. A game consists of rolling two dice. Rolling double 1's pays $7.20. Rolling double 6's pays $3.60. Any other roll pays nothing. What is the expected value for this game?

14. A total of 3000 tickets have been sold for a drawing. If one ticket is drawn for a single prize of $1000, what is a fair price for a ticket?

15. How many four-digit numbers can be formed if the first digit cannot be zero and the last digit must be two?

16. A club consists of ten members. In how many different ways can a group of three people be selected to go on a European trip?

17. In how many ways can the names of four candidates be listed on a ballot for an election?

18. Compute 100!/98!. (Look for short cuts!)

19. Find the number of different ways that four flags can be run up a flag pole, one above the other, if ten different flags are available.

20. Five women live together in an apartment. Two of the women have blue eyes. If two of the women are chosen at random, what is the probability that they both have blue eyes?

SELECTED BIBLIOGRAPHY

Billstein, R. "A Fun Way to Introduce Probability." *The Arithmetic Teacher*, **24**(January 1977):39–42.

Burns, M. "Ideas." *The Arithmetic Teacher*, **21**(December 1974):686–694.

Choate, S. "Activities in Applying Probability Ideas." *Arithmetic Teacher*, **26**(February 1979):40–42.

Coltharp, F. "Mathematical Aspects of the Attribute Games." *The Arithmetic Teacher*, **21**(March 1974):250–262.

Corbet, J., and Milton, J. "Who Killed the Cook?" *Arithmetic Teacher*, **71**(April 1978):263–266.

Elements of Mathematics. Book 0: Intuitive Background, Chapter 8, "An Introduction to Probability." St. Ann, Mo.: Central Midwestern Regional Education Laboratory, Inc. 1971.

Enman, V. "Probability in the Intermediate Grades." *Arithmetic Teacher*, **26**(February 1979):38–39.

Fielker, D. *Towards Probability*. Cambridge: Cambridge University Press, 1971.

Higgins, J. "Probability with Marbles and a Juice Container." *The Arithmetic Teacher*, **20**(March 1973):165–166.

Jacobs, H. *Mathematics: A Human Endeavor*, Chapters 7 and 8. San Francisco: W. H. Freeman, 1970.

Johnson, D., et al. *Activities in Mathematics. First Course, Probability*. Glenview, Ill.: Scott, Foresman and Co., 1971.

Jones, G. "A Case For Probability." *Arithmetic Teacher*, **26**(February 1979):37, 57.

Lai, T. "Bingo and the Law of Equal Ignorance." *The Arithmetic Teacher*, **24**(January 1977):83–84.

Niman, J., and Postman, R. "Probability on the Geoboard." *The Arithmetic Teacher,* **20**(March 1973):167–170.

Nuffield Mathematics Project. *Probability and Statistics.* New York: John Wiley, 1969.

Piaget, J., and Inhelder, B. *The Origin of the Idea of Chance in Children.* London: Routledge and Kegan, 1975.

Reeves, C. "Volleyball and Probability." *The Mathematics Teacher,* **71**(October 1978):595–596.

Rudd, D. "A Problem in Probability." *The Mathematics Teacher,* **67**(February 1974):180–181.

School Mathematics Study Group. *Probability for Intermediate Grades.* Stanford, Calif.: Stanford University Press, 1966.

School Mathematics Study Group. *Probability for Primary Grades.* Stanford, Calif.: Stanford University Press, 1966.

Souviney, R. "Quantifying Chance." *The Arithmetic Teacher,* **67**(February 1973):166–168.

Stone, J. "Place Value and Probability (with Promptings from Pascal)." *Arithmetic Teacher,* **27**(March 1980):47–49.

Varga, T. "Logic and Probability in the Lower Grades." *Educational Studies in Mathematics.* **4**(1972):346–357.

Watson, J. "A Current Event for the Mathematics Classroom." *The Mathematics Teacher,* **71**(November 1978):658–663.

Webb, L., and McKay J. "Making Inferences from Marbles and Coffee Cans." *Arithmetic Teacher,* **26**(September 1978):33–35.

Statistics

PRELIMINARY PROBLEM

Lacking time to record his students' homework grades, Mr. Van Gruff asked them to keep track of their own grades. A few days later, Mr. Van

Gruff asked the students to report their grades. One of the students, Eddy, had lost his papers but remembered the grades on four of the six assignments—100, 82, 74, and 60. Also, according to Eddy, the mean average of all six papers was 69, and the other two papers had identical grades. What were the grades on Eddy's other two homework papers?

INTRODUCTION

For a long time the word *statistics* referred to numerical information about state or political territories. The word itself comes from the Latin *statisticus* meaning "of the state." Statistics as we know it today took several centuries and many great minds to develop. John Graunt (1620–1674) was one of the first people to record his work in the area of statistics. He studied birth and death records in various cities and discovered that more boys were born than girls. He also found that since men were more subject to death from occupational accidents, diseases, and war, the number of men and women at the age of marriage was about equal. Graunt's work on the predictability of deaths via mortality tables led to the development of ideas used by life insurance companies today.

descriptive statistics   This chapter is concerned with **descriptive statistics,** the science of organizing and summarizing numerical data. Newspapers, magazines, radio, and television all use descriptive statistics to inform and persuade us on certain courses of action. Governments and organizations use statistics to make decisions that directly affect our lives. Statistics are both used and abused. Do you know when and how, or are you like Charlie Brown?

© 1974 United Feature Syndicate, Inc.

8-1 GETTING THE PICTURE

It is often said that one picture is worth a thousand words. Pictures are an important part of statistics. They take many forms—circle graphs, line graphs, bar graphs, histograms, or frequency polygons. These pictures are used to display data and make data more understandable.

Suppose, for example, that Dan offers the following deal. He rolls a die. If any number other than 6 appears, he pays $5. If a 6 appears, you pay him $5. With a fair die, the probability of Dan's winning is 1/6. Thus, it is not likely that Dan will win unless the die is loaded, or 6 appears more often than normally expected. The following data show the results of 60 rolls with Dan's die.

1	6	6	2	6	3	6	6	4	6
6	2	6	6	4	5	6	6	1	6
1	6	6	5	6	6	4	6	5	6
6	5	6	2	4	2	5	6	3	4
3	6	1	6	3	6	6	1	6	6
6	4	6	3	6	3	6	4	6	5

raw data

frequency table

These numbers are referred to as **raw data** and are arranged in order of occurrence. The raw data become more meaningful when they are summarized in a **frequency table** as shown in Table 8-1.

TABLE 8-1

Number	Tally	Frequency
1	ⵗⵗⵗⵗⵗ	5
2	‖‖‖‖	4
3	ⵗⵗⵗⵗⵗ ‖	6
4	ⵗⵗⵗⵗⵗ ‖‖	7
5	ⵗⵗⵗⵗⵗ ‖	6
6	ⵗⵗⵗⵗⵗ ⵗⵗⵗⵗⵗ ⵗⵗⵗⵗⵗ ⵗⵗⵗⵗⵗ ⵗⵗⵗⵗⵗ ⵗⵗⵗⵗⵗ ‖‖	32
	Total	60

According to the frequency table, 6 appears many more times than could be expected from a fair die. (If the die were fair, the number of 6's should be close to $1/6 \cdot 60$ or 10.)

histogram   Figure 8-1 shows a **histogram** that gives a good picture of the results from throwing Dan's die. A histogram is made up of contiguous (touching) rectangles comparing various frequencies. The numbers on the die are shown on the horizontal axis. The numbers along the vertical axis give the scale for the frequency. The frequencies of the numbers on the die are shown by vertical bars. The bars are all the same width. The higher the bar, the greater the frequency.

FIGURE 8-1

bar graph   A histogram is a particular kind of **bar graph.** A typical bar graph showing the height in centimeters of five students is given in Figure 8-2. This bar graph is not a histogram because of the spaces between the bars.

          The break in the vertical axis, denoted by a squiggle, indicates that part of the scale has been omitted. Therefore, the scale is not accurate from 0 to 130. The height of each bar represents the height in centimeters of each student named on the horizontal axis. Each space between the bars is usually one-half the width of the bars.

FIGURE 8-2

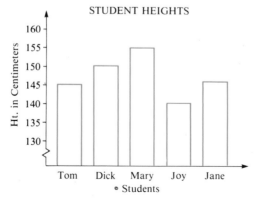

frequency polygon
line graph

Another graphic form for presenting the data from a frequency table is a **frequency polygon** or **line graph**. A frequency polygon can be plotted from a frequency table, or it can be constructed from a histogram by connecting the midpoints of the top of each of the bars with line segments. Figure 8-3(a) shows the frequency polygon (line graph) for the data from Table 8-1. Figure 8-3(b) shows how to obtain the same frequency polygon from the histogram (Figure 8-1).

FIGURE 8-3

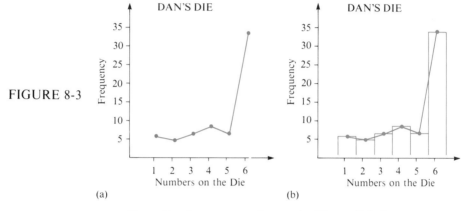

(a)   (b)

From the frequency polygons in Figure 8-3, it may appear that it is possible to find the frequency of any number between 1 and 6. For example, a frequency corresponding to 2.5 is approximately 6, but 2.5 does not appear on a roll of a die. Thus, for this particular case, a frequency polygon is misleading, and the histogram is a more meaningful graph.

Figure 8-4 shows a table and a line graph comparing temperatures during a 9-hour period from 8:00 A.M. to 5:00 P.M. at 1-hour intervals. In this example all values are meaningful, because there is a temperature at all

Time	Temperature (°C)
8:00 A.M.	0
9:00	2
10:00	4
11:00	5
12:00	8
1:00	7
2:00	6
3:00	6
4:00	5
5:00 P.M.	5

TEMPERATURES
8:00 AM–5:00 PM

FIGURE 8-4   A.M.   Hour   P.M.

times. The graph shows that temperatures increased from 8 A.M. to 12 P.M. and decreased from 12 P.M. to 5 P.M. The graph can be used to estimate temperatures at other times. For example, at 11:30 A.M. the temperature might have been 6°C.

pictograph   Examples of a bar graph and a type of graph called a **pictograph** illustrated below are taken from *Scott, Foresman Mathematics,* 1980, Grade 4.

This bar graph shows the number of talent-show tickets Mary sold each day last week.

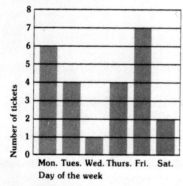

On which day did Mary sell

13. the most tickets?

14. the fewest tickets?

On which days did Mary sell

15. more than 5 tickets?

16. fewer than 4 tickets?

17. the same number of tickets?

How many tickets did Mary sell

18. Monday?

19. Thursday?

20. Wednesday and Saturday?

21. all week?

This pictograph shows how many kilograms of newspapers Anthony collected for each of the last 6 months.

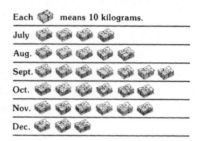

During what month were the

22. most kilograms collected?

23. fewest kilograms collected?

How many kilograms of newspapers were collected during

24. August?

25. October?

26. December?

27. September?

28. Give the total number of kilograms of newspapers collected in September, October, and November.

*29. How many kilograms of newspapers were collected in all?

The greater the amount of data, the more difficult it becomes to construct a frequency table for individual items. In cases with much data, the data are grouped. For example, consider the following 50 grades.

52	56	25	56	68	73	66	64	56	100
20	39	9	50	98	54	54	40	50	96
36	44	18	97	100	65	21	60	44	54
92	49	37	94	72	88	89	35	59	34
48	32	15	53	84	72	88	16	52	60

A frequency table for these data would represent 39 different scores. A better "quick" picture of the data can be obtained by grouping the data into **classes.** For example, the classes can be arranged in intervals of ten: 1–10, 11–20, 21–30, 31–40, and so on. Each class is assigned two class limits. For the first class, the lower limit is 1 and the upper limit is 10. The **grouped frequency table** for intervals of length ten is given in Table 8-2.

classes

grouped frequency table

TABLE 8-2

Classes	Tally	Frequency
1–10	|	1
11–20	||||	4
21–30	||	2
31–40	⳾ ||	7
41–50	⳾ |	6
51–60	⳾ ⳾ ||	12
61–70	||||	4
71–80	|||	3
81–90	||||	4
91–100	⳾ ||	7

The grouped frequency table is concise, but some information is lost by the grouping. For example, although 12 scores fall in the interval 51–60, the table does not show the particular scores in the interval. The greater the interval, the greater the amount of information lost (possibly beyond the usable point). The choice of the interval size may vary, but as a general rule, the number of intervals should be between 6 and 15. No matter what interval size is used, the same interval size must be used for each class throughout the table. Classes should be chosen to accommodate *all* the data, and each item should fit into only one class; that is, the classes should not overlap.

A bar graph can be used to display the data from a grouped frequency table. A bar graph for the data in Table 8-2 is shown in Figure 8-5.

FIGURE 8-5

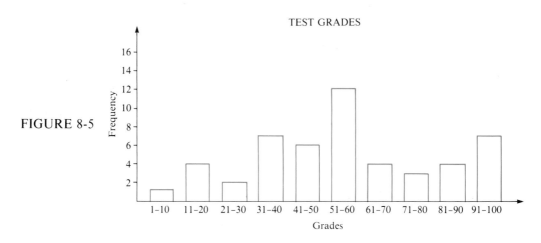

circle graph
pie chart

Another type of graph used to represent data is the **circle graph** or **pie chart.** A circle graph consists of a circular region partitioned into disjoint sections, with each section representing a part or percentage of the whole. A circle graph shows how parts are related to the whole. This type of picture usually is used when money is involved and various distributions of dollars are to be displayed.

Suppose two college roommates, Larry and Moe, kept a record of their expenses and at the end of the quarter made Table 8-3 based on their records. Figure 8-6 shows a circle graph with the data. A circle has a total of 360 degrees, written 360°. Thus, 360° represents the total expenses for the month. Since food is 30% of the total expenses, 30% of 360° is devoted to food. Thus, 0.30(360°) or 108° is devoted to food expense. In the same way, 0.25(360°) or 90° is devoted to rent. The remaining sections are computed in a similar manner. (A protractor is used to construct circle graphs.)

Expenses Last Quarter

TABLE 8-3

Item	Percentage of Total
Food	30
Rent	25
Clothing	10
Books	10
Entertainment	15
Other	10

FIGURE 8-6

Example 8-1

Construct a circle graph for the following data obtained by tossing Dan's loaded die 60 times.

Number	Frequency
1	5
2	4
3	6
4	7
5	6
6	$\frac{32}{60}$

Solution

Since 5/60 of the tosses result in the number 1, then (5/60) · 360° or 30° of the circle graph are devoted to the number 1. Likewise, (4/60) · 360° or 24° are devoted to the number 2, 36° are devoted to the number 3, 42° are devoted to 4, 36° are devoted to 5, and 192° are devoted to 6. A circle graph of this information appears in Figure 8-7.

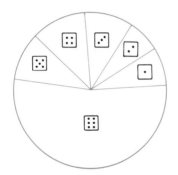

FIGURE 8-7

An example of a circle graph from Harcourt, Brace, Jovanovich *Growth in Mathematics,* 1978, Grade 6 is given on page 330. Find the angle measures for each percent.

Just as graphs can be used to accurately display data, they can also be used to distort data or exaggerate certain pieces of information. A frequency polygon, histogram, or bar graph can be altered by changing the scale of the graph. For example, consider the data for the number of graduates from Community College for the years 1977 to 1981.

Year	1977	1978	1979	1980	1981
Number of Graduates	140	180	200	210	160

Circle Graphs

Circle graphs are often used to show per cents.
This circle graph shows the way some
families spend the money they earn.

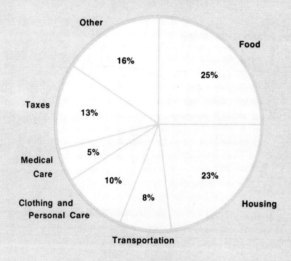

Suppose a family's yearly income is $12,000.
According to the circle graph, this is how the money is spent.
(Example: Food is 25% of $12,000, or $3000.)

Food	Housing	Transportation	Clothing and Personal Care	Medical Care	Taxes	Other
$3000	$2760	$960	$1200	$600	$1560	$1920

Find how these incomes are spent according to the graph.

1. $8000
2. $9000
3. $10,000
4. $15,000
5. $9500
6. $11,500
7. $14,500
8. $16,500

Enrichment

The two graphs in Figure 8-8 represent the same data, but different scales are used in each. The statistics presented are the same, but do these two graphs convey the same psychological message? Notice that the years on the horizontal axis of the graph are spread out and the numbers on the vertical axis are condensed. Both of these changes minimize the variability of the data. A college administrator probably would use graph (b) to convince people that the college was not in serious enrollment trouble.

NO. OF GRADUATES OF COMMUNITY COLLEGE

FIGURE 8-8

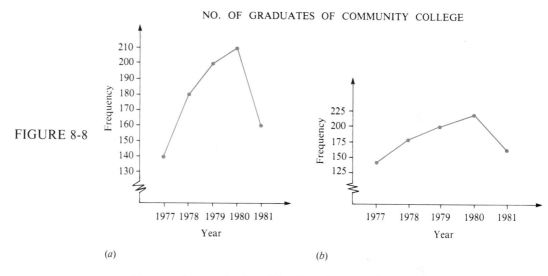

(a)   (b)

Bar graphs can also be misleading. Suppose, for example, the number of boxes of cereal sold by Sugar Plops last year was two million and the number of boxes of cereal sold by Korn Krisp was eight million. The Korn Krisp executives prepared the bar graph in Figure 8-9 to demonstrate the data. The Sugar Plop people objected. Do you see why?

The graph in Figure 8-9 clearly distorts the data, since the bar for Korn Krisp is four times as high and four times as wide as the bar for Sugar Plops.

FIGURE 8-9

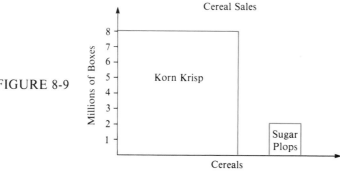

Thus, the area representing Korn Krisp is sixteen times larger than the area representing Sugar Plops, rather than four times larger as indicated by the original data. Other examples of distorted data are given in the problem set.

PROBLEM SET 8-1

1. The following figure shows a bar graph for the rainfall in centimeters during the last school year. Answer each of the following questions.
    (a)   Which month had the greatest rainfall and how much did it have?
    (b)   What were the amounts of rainfall in October, December, and January?

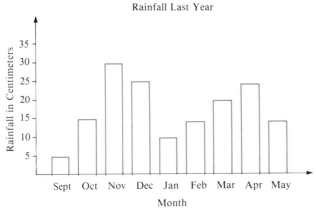

2. The following data represent total car sales for Johnson's car lot from January through June. Draw a bar graph for this data.

Month	Jan.	Feb.	March	April	May	June
Number of Cars Sold	90	86	92	96	90	100

3. A list of presidents with the number of children for each follows.

    1. Washington, 0
    2. J. Adams, 5
    3. Jefferson, 6
    4. Madison, 0
    5. Monroe, 2
    6. J. Q. Adams, 4
    7. Jackson, 0
    8. Van Buren, 4
    9. W. H. Harrison, 10
    10. Tyler, 14
    11. Polk, 0
    12. Taylor, 6

    13. Fillmore, 2
    14. Pierce, 3
    15. Buchanan, 0
    16. Lincoln, 4
    17. A. Johnson, 5
    18. Grant, 4
    19. Hayes, 8
    20. Garfield, 7
    21. Arthur, 3
    22. Cleveland, 5
    23. B. Harrison, 3
    24. McKinley, 2

    25. T. Roosevelt, 6
    26. Taft, 3
    27. Wilson, 3
    28. Harding, 0
    29. Coolidge, 2
    30. Hoover, 2
    31. F. D. Roosevelt, 6
    32. Truman, 1
    33. Eisenhower, 2
    34. Kennedy, 3
    35. L. B. Johnson, 2
    36. Nixon, 2

    37. Ford, 4
    38. Carter, 3

(a) Make a frequency table for these data.

(b) What is the most frequent number of children?

4. Five coins are tossed 64 times. A distribution for the number of heads that appear follows.

Number of Heads	0	1	2	3	4	5
Frequency	2	10	20	20	10	2

(a) Draw a histogram for these data.

(b) Draw a frequency polygon for these data.

5. The grade distribution for the final examination for the Mathematics for Elementary Teachers course follows.

Grade	Frequency
A	4
B	10
C	37
D	8
F	1

(a) Draw a bar graph for these data.

(b) Draw a circle graph for these data.

6. The following are the amounts (rounded to the nearest dollar) paid by 25 students for textbooks during the fall term.

35	42	33	48	45	42	50	39	41	37	37	16	23
49	62	60	58	53	62	30	50	39	51	40	23	

(a) Construct a grouped frequency table for these data, starting the first class at $10.00 with intervals of $5.00 each.

(b) Draw a histogram for the data.

(c) Draw a frequency polygon for the data.

7. Suppose the following circle graphs are used to illustrate the fact that the number of elementary teaching majors at teacher's colleges has doubled from 1970 to 1980, while the percentage of male elementary teaching majors has stayed the same. What is misleading about the way the graphs are constructed?

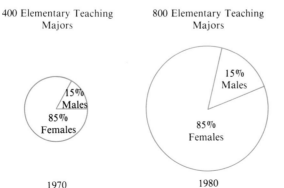

400 Elementary Teaching Majors	800 Elementary Teaching Majors

1970   1980

8. What is wrong with the following line graph?

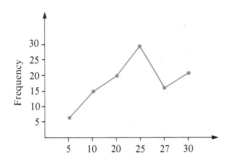

9. Give an example of a situation in which a circle graph would be preferable to a bar graph or line graph.
10. Give an example of a situation in which a line graph would be preferable to a bar graph.
11. The following graphs give the temperatures for a certain day. Which graph is more helpful for guessing the temperature at 10:00 A.M.? Why?

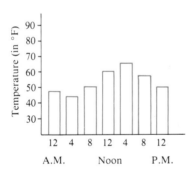 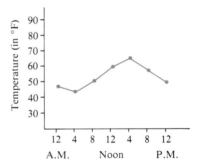

12. Work through the Scott, Foresman, Grade 4 student page given on page 326.

LABORATORY ACTIVITY

1. Collect examples of graphs from newspapers, magazines, reports, and so on. Can you find any examples where the choice of a scale has distorted the data?

2. Examine some current textbooks for grades 1 through 8. Answer each of the following questions.

    (a) At what grade level do you find various types of graphs being introduced?
    (b) What kinds of data are graphed by the elementary students?

(c) What suggestions are given to the students to aid them in constructing graphs?

8-2 ON THE AVERAGE—MEASURES OF CENTRAL TENDENCY

average

It is often easier to look at tables or graphs than to study large quantities of raw data. Another way to study raw data is to determine a single number that represents the data. This single number is called an **average.** The word "average" is often used loosely, and in many cases, it is not clear what is meant.

The average salary at the university is $20 100.
The average family has 2.3 children.
The average grade for the first test was 72.

Consider the following set of data for three teachers, each of whom claims that, "on the average," his or her class scored better than the other two classes.

Mr. Smith: 62, 94, 95, 98, 98
Mr. Jones: 62, 62, 98, 99, 100
Ms. Leed: 40, 62, 85, 99, 99

All these teachers are correct in their assertions. Each one has used a different average. There are five different averages in general use: the arithmetic mean, the median, the mode, the geometric mean, and the harmonic mean. We will discuss only the arithmetic mean, the median, and the mode.

arithmetic mean

The most commonly used average is the **arithmetic mean,** which we simply call the **mean.** To find the mean of the scores for each of the three teachers just mentioned, find the sum of the scores in each case and divide by 5, the number of scores.

$$\text{Mean (Smith): } \frac{62 + 94 + 95 + 98 + 98}{5} = \frac{447}{5} = 89.4$$

$$\text{Mean (Jones): } \frac{62 + 62 + 98 + 99 + 100}{5} = \frac{421}{5} = 84.2$$

$$\text{Mean (Leed): } \frac{40 + 62 + 85 + 99 + 99}{5} = \frac{385}{5} = 77$$

Thus, using the mean as the average, Mr. Smith's class scored better "on the average" than the other two classes. In general, the mean is defined as follows.

DEFINITION

> The **mean** of the numbers $x_1, x_2, \ldots, x_n$, denoted by $\bar{x}$, is given by
>
> $$\bar{x} = \frac{x_1 + x_2 + x_3 + \ldots + x_n}{n}$$

median

The value exactly in the middle of an ordered distribution is called the **median.** To find the median for the teachers' scores, arrange each of their scores in increasing order and pick the middle score. Intuitively, half the scores are greater than the median and half are less.

Median (Smith): 62, 94, 95, 98, 98   median = 95
Median (Jones): 62, 62, 98, 99, 100   median = 98
Median (Leed):   40, 62, 85, 99, 99   median = 85

Thus, using the median, Mr. Jones' class scored better "on the average" than the other two classes.

With an odd number of scores, as in the preceding case, the median is the middle score. With an even number of scores, the median is defined as the mean of the middle two numbers; that is, to find the median, add the middle two numbers and divide by 2. For example, the median of the following scores is $(70 + 74)/2$ or 72.

64, 68, 70, 74, 82, 90

In general, to find the median for a set of n numbers, proceed as follows.

1.   Arrange the numbers in order from least to greatest.
2.   (a)   If n is odd, the median is the middle number.
     (b)   If n is even, the median is the arithmetic mean of the two middle numbers.

mode

The **mode** of a set of data is the number(s) that appear most frequently. Not every distribution has a mode, and some distributions may have more than one mode. For example, the set of scores 64, 79, 80, 82, 90 has no mode

bimodal

(or five modes). The set of scores 64, 75, 75, 82, 90, 90, 98 is **bimodal** (two modes), since both 75 and 90 are modes. It is possible for a set of data to have too many modes to be useful.

For the three classes listed earlier, if the mode is used, then Ms. Leed's class has the best average.

Mode (Smith): 62, 94, 95, 98, 98   mode = 98
Mode (Jones): 62, 62, 98, 99, 100   mode = 62
Mode (Leed):   40, 62, 85, 99, 99   mode = 99

Example 8-2 | Find the (a) mean, (b) median, and (c) mode for the following collection of data:

60, 60, 70, 95, 95, 100

Solution | (a) $\bar{x} = \dfrac{60 + 60 + 70 + 95 + 95 + 100}{6} = \dfrac{480}{6} = 80.$

(b) The median is $(70 + 95)/2$ or 82.5.
(c) The set of data is bimodal and has both 60 and 95 as modes.

BRAIN TEASER

The speeds of racing cars were timed after 3 miles, $4\frac{1}{2}$ miles, and 6 miles. Freddy averaged 140 miles per hour (mph) for the first 3 miles, 168 mph for the next $1\frac{1}{2}$ miles, and 210 mph for the last $1\frac{1}{2}$ miles. What was his mean speed for the total 6-mile run?

Although the mean is the average most commonly used, it may not always be the best average to use. Suppose, for example, a company employs twenty people. The president of the company makes $200 000, the vice-president makes $75 000, and eighteen employees make $10 000 each. The mean salary for this company follows.

$$\frac{\$200\ 000 + \$75\ 000 + 18(\$10\ 000)}{20} = \frac{\$455\ 000}{20} = \$22\ 750$$

In this case, the mean salary of $22 750 is not representative, and the median or mode, which are both $10 000, would better describe the typical salary. Notice that the value of the mean is affected by extreme values.

In most cases, the value of the median is not affected by extreme values. The median, however, can be misleading. For example, suppose nine students make the following scores on a test: 30, 35, 40, 40, 92, 92, 93, 98, 99. From the median score of 92, one might possibly infer that the individuals all scored very well, yet 92 is certainly not a typical score.

The mode can be misleading in describing a set of data with very few items or many infrequently occurring items. For example, the following scores—40, 42, 50, 62, 63, 65, 98, 98—have a mode of 98, which is not a typical value.

The choice of which average to use for a particular set of data is not always an easy choice. In the example involving the three teachers, each teacher chose the average that best suited his or her needs. For clarity and honesty, the average that is used should always be specified.

PROBLEM SET 8-2

1. Calculate the mean, median, and mode for each of the following collections of data.
   (a) 2, 8, 7, 8, 5, 8, 10, 5
   (b) 10, 12, 12, 14, 20, 16, 12, 14, 11
   (c) 18, 22, 22, 17, 30, 18, 12
   (d) 82, 80, 63, 75, 92, 80, 92, 90, 80, 80
   (e) 5, 5, 5, 5, 5, 10

2. Suppose each of ten students scored 50 on a test. Find the mean, median, and mode of the test scores.

3. The mean score on a set of 20 tests is 75. What is the sum of the 20 test scores?

4. The tram at a ski area has a capacity of 50 people with a load limit of 7500 pounds. What is the mean weight of the passengers if the tram is loaded to capacity?

5. The mean for a set of 28 scores is 80. Suppose two more students take the test and score 60 and 50. What is the new mean?

6. The names and ages for each person in a family of five follow.

Name	Age
Dick	40
Jane	36
Kirk	8
Jean	6
Scott	2

   (a) What is the mean age?
   (b) Find the mean of the ages 5 years from now?
   (c) Find the mean 10 years from now?
   (d) Describe the relationships between the means found in parts (a), (b), and (c).

7. Ten alumni of a state college are chosen at random and asked their annual incomes. The incomes are $15 000, $20 000, $18 000, $28 000, $12 000, $30 000, $20 000, $14 000, $20 000, $50 000. Find the mean, median, and mode for these incomes.

8. Suppose you own a hat shop and decide to order hats in only *one* size for the coming season. To decide which size to order, you look at last year's sales figures, which are itemized according to size. Should you find the mean, median, or mode for the data?

9. A temperature of 25°C is considered ideal. In the city of Podunk, the mean temperature is 25°C. Does this mean that the temperature in Podunk is ideal? Explain.

10. Jenny averaged 70 on her quizzes during the first part of the quarter and 80 on her quizzes the second part of the quarter, yet her average for the quarter was not 75. How can this be?

11. The results of Jon's fall quarter grades follow. Find his grade point average for the term ($A = 4, B = 3, C = 2, D = 1, F = 0$).

Course	Credits	Grades
Math	5	B
English	3	A
Physics	5	C
German	3	D
Handball	1	A

12. If the mean weight of seven linemen on a football team is 230 pounds and the mean weight of the four backfield members is 190 pounds, what is the mean weight of the eleven-man team?

13. A total of 210 people stayed at the Rancho Costa Plenty over the weekend for a total cost of $67 200. What was the mean cost per person?

14. If ninety-nine people had a mean income of $12 000, how much is the mean income increased by the addition of a single income of $200 000?

15. The following table gives the annual salaries for the forty players of a certain professional football team. Find the mean annual salary for the team.

Salary	Number of Players
$18 000	2
22 000	4
26 000	4
35 000	3
38 000	12
44 000	8
50 000	4
80 000	2
150 000	1
	40

16. Write a list of scores, the mean and median of which are not equal, such that half the values are above the mean and half are below.

17. Do problems 131(a), (b), and (c) appearing in Appendix II.

8-3 MEASURES OF DISPERSION

Describing data with a single number (mean, median, mode) can be misleading. For example, would you wade across a river with an average depth (mean, median, or mode) of 40 cm? Although there may be many shallow areas, there may also be many holes that are several meters deep. It is apparent that an average, by itself, does not always give adequate information about a set of data.

Suppose Professors Abel and Babel both taught a section of a statistics course and each professor had six students. Both professors gave the same final exam. The results, along with the means for each group of scores follow.

Abel	Babel
100	70
80	70
70	60
50	60
50	60
10	40

$$\bar{x} = \frac{360}{6} = 60 \qquad \bar{x} = \frac{360}{6} = 60$$

Each set of scores has the same mean. Each median also equals 60. Although the mean and median for these two groups are the same, the two distributions of scores are very different. The first set of scores is more spread out than the second.

There are several ways to measure the spread of data. The simplest way is to subtract the least number from the greatest number. This difference is called the **range.** The range for Professor Abel's class is $100 - 10$ or 90. The range for Professor Babel's class is $70 - 40$ or 30. Although the range is easy to calculate, it has the disadvantage of being affected by extreme high and low scores. For example, the sets of scores 10, 20, 25, 30, 100 and 10, 80, 85, 90, 90, 100 both have a range of 90.

There are several ways that are better than the range to measure the spread of data. We consider the two most commonly used measures of scatter, variance and standard deviation.

The steps for calculating the **variance,** v, of n numbers are as follows:

1. Find the mean of the numbers.
2. Subtract the mean from each number.
3. Square each difference found in Step 2.
4. Find the sum of the squares in Step 3.
5. Divide by n to obtain the variance.

These five steps can be summarized for the numbers $x_1, x_2, x_3, \ldots, x_n$ as follows, where $\bar{x}$ is the mean of these numbers.

$$v = \frac{(x_1 - \bar{x})^2 + (x_2 - \bar{x})^2 + (x_3 - \bar{x})^2 + \cdots + (x_n - \bar{x})^2}{n}$$

Remark   In some textbooks, the formula for variance involves division by $n - 1$ instead of n. Division by $n - 1$ is more useful for advanced work in statistics.

The variances for the final exam data for the classes of Professors Abel and Babel are calculated as follows.

Abel

x	$x - \bar{x}$	$(x - \bar{x})^2$
100	40	1600
80	20	400
70	10	100
50	$^-10$	100
50	$^-10$	100
10	$^-50$	2500
Totals 360	0	4800

$$\bar{x} = \frac{360}{6} = 60$$

$$v = \frac{4800}{6} = 800$$

Babel

x	$x - \bar{x}$	$(x - \bar{x})^2$
70	10	100
70	10	100
60	0	0
60	0	0
60	0	0
40	‾20	400
Totals 360	0	600

$$\bar{x} = \frac{360}{6} = 60$$

$$v = \frac{600}{6} = 100$$

standard deviation

An essentially equivalent measure of spread to the variance is the **standard deviation,** s, which is the square root of the variance; that is, $s = \sqrt{v}$. The standard deviation has the same units as the original data and is particularly useful in making precise statements about the spread of the data.

The standard deviations for Professor Abel's and Professor Babel's classes are:

Abel   Babel

$s = \sqrt{800} \doteq 28.3$ $s = \sqrt{100} = 10$

The standard deviation is a large number when the values from a set of data are widely dispersed. The standard deviation is a small number (close to 0) when the data values are close together.

Example 8-3

Given the data 32, 41, 47, 53, 57, find each of the following.
(a) The range   (b) The variance   (c) The standard deviation

Solution

(a) The range is $57 - 32$ or 25.
(b) The variance, v, is computed using the information in the following table.

x	$x - \bar{x}$	$(x - \bar{x})^2$
32	‾14	196
41	‾5	25
47	1	1
53	7	49
57	11	121
Totals 230	0	392

$$\bar{x} = \frac{230}{5} = 46$$

$$v = \frac{392}{5} = 78.4$$

(c) $s = \sqrt{78.4} \doteq 8.9$

Statisticians have found the standard deviation an extremely useful measure of dispersion in analyzing data. The frequencies of many different sets of data in the real world approximate a smooth, bell-shaped curve. It is **normal curve** called a **normal curve.** In a normal curve, frequency values are distributed symmetrically about the mean. (Also, the mean, median, and mode all have the same value.) A fact that is true for such distributions is that 68% of the values lie within one standard deviation of the mean, 95% lie within two standard deviations, and 99% are within three standard deviations of the mean. This is illustrated in Figure 8-10.

FIGURE 8-10

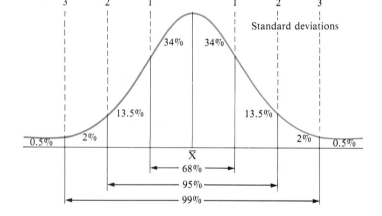

Example 8-4

A standardized test was scored, and there was a mean of 500 and a standard deviation of 100. Suppose 10 000 students took the test and their scores approximated a normal curve.

(a) How many scored between 400 and 600?
(b) How many scored between 300 and 700?
(c) How many scored between 200 and 800?

Solution

(a) Since one standard deviation on either side of the mean is from 400 to 600, about 68% of the scores fall in this interval. Thus, 0.68(10 000) or 6800 students scored between 400 and 600.
(b) About 95% of 10 000 or 9500 students scored between 300 and 700.
(c) About 99% of 10 000 or 9900 students scored between 200 and 800.

Remark

About 1% or 100 students' scores in Example 8-4 fall outside three standard deviations. About 50 of these students did very well on the test and about 50 students did very poorly.

Scores on tests can also be reported by giving a person's percentage relative to others. Suppose Tom, Dick, and Mary each took the same national test. Tom reported that he scored at the 50th percentile. Dick reported that he scored at the 5th decile. Mary reported that she scored at the 2nd quartile. They determined that they had all made the same score on the test. When Tom said he scored at the 50th percentile, he meant that 50% of the scores on the test were at or below his score and 50% were higher than his score. In general, the ***r*th percentile,** denoted by P_r, is a score such that r percent of the scores are less than or equal to P_r and $(100 - r)$ percent of the scores are higher than P_r. For example, if Sally scores at the 95th percentile, then only 5% of the people taking the same test had higher scores. There are 99 percentiles, denoted $P_1, P_2, \ldots, P_{99}$, that divide the distribution of scores into 100 intervals. Several percentiles can be determined from Figure 8-10, but a complete table of areas for a normal curve is necessary for determining all the percentiles.

rth percentile

Deciles are the points that divide a distribution into ten equally spaced sections. There are nine deciles denoted $D_1, D_2, \ldots, D_9$, and $D_1 = P_{10}, D_2 = P_{20}, \ldots, D_9 = P_{90}$. **Quartiles** are points that divide a distribution into quarters. There are three quartiles: $Q_1 = P_{25}, Q_2 = P_{50}, Q_3 = P_{75}$. Is it clear why Tom, Dick, and Mary all had the same score on the test?

deciles

quartiles

Example 8-5

The standardized test of Example 8-4 had a mean of 500 and a standard deviation of 100. The 16th percentile, P_{16}, is 400 since 400 is one standard deviation to the left of the mean and, from Figure 8-10, there is 0.5% + 2% + 13.5% or 16% of the distribution to the left of 400. Find each of the following.

(a) P_{50} (b) P_{84}

Solution

(a) Since 500 is the mean, 50% of the distribution lies to the left of 500. Thus, $P_{50} = 500$.

(b) Since 600 is one standard deviation to the right of the mean, 84% of the distribution lies to the left of 600. Thus, $P_{84} = 600$.

PROBLEM SET 8-3

1. For each of the following sets, find the range, the variance, and the standard deviation.
   (a) 5, 7, 8, 9, 1   (b) 18, 32, 17, 43, 63, 10, 35, 90, 80, 72
2. To become a night guard for a certain company, an applicant must be at least 170 cm tall. What is the standard deviation of the heights of seven applicants if their heights are 175 cm, 182 cm, 190 cm, 180 cm, 192 cm, 172 cm, 190 cm?

3. For certain workers, the mean wage is $5.00 per hour with standard deviation $0.50. If a worker is chosen at random, what is the probability that the worker's wage is between $4.50 and $5.50? Assume a normal distribution of wages.

4. What happens to the mean and standard deviation of a set of data when the same number is added to each value in the data?

5. The mean IQ score for 1500 students is 100, with a standard deviation of 15. Answer each of the following, assuming the scores are approximated by a normal curve,
   (a) How many have an IQ between 85 and 115?
   (b) How many have an IQ between 70 and 130?
   (c) How many have an IQ under 55 or over 145?
   (d) How many have an IQ over 145?

6. Sugar Plops boxes say they hold 16 oz. To make sure, the manufacturer fills the box to a mean weight of 16.1 oz with a standard deviation of 0.05 oz. If the weights have a normal curve, what percent of the boxes actually contain 16 oz or more?

7. (a) If all the numbers in a set are equal, what is the standard deviation?
   (b) If the standard deviation of a set of numbers is zero, must all the numbers in the set be equal?

8. A standardized test has a mean of 65 and a standard deviation of 12. Find (a) Q_2, (b) P_{16}, and (c) P_{84}.

★ 9. Show that the following formula for variance is equivalent to the one given in the text.

$$v = \frac{x_1^2 + x_2^2 + \cdots + x_n^2}{n} - \bar{x}^2$$

 10. Do problems 131(d) and (e) appearing in Appendix II.

LABORATORY ACTIVITY

1. Roll a pair of dice 50 times. Record the total number of spots showing on each roll.
   (a) Make a frequency chart.
   (b) Compute the mean.
   (c) Compute the standard deviation.

SOLUTION TO THE PRELIMINARY PROBLEM

Understanding the Problem

Mr. Van Gruff had his students keep track of their own grades. Eddy reported that he had scores of 100, 82, 74, and 60 on four of his six papers. He also reported that the mean average of all six papers was 69 and that he had identical scores on the missing two grades. The problem is to determine the two missing grades from this information.

Devising a Plan

Since the mean is obtained by finding the sum of the scores and then dividing by the number of scores, which is six, if we let x stand for each of the two missing grades, we have

$$69 = \frac{100 + 82 + 74 + 60 + x + x}{6}$$

To find the missing grades we solve this equation for x.

Carrying Out the Plan

We now solve the preceding equation as follows:

$$69 = \frac{100 + 82 + 74 + 60 + x + x}{6}$$

$$69 = \frac{316 + 2x}{6}$$

$$49 = x$$

Looking Back

Since the solution to the equation is $x = 49$, we conclude that each of the two missing scores was 49. The answer seems reasonable since the mean of 69 is below three of the four given scores. This can be easily checked by computing the mean of the scores 100, 82, 74, 60, 49, 49 and showing that it is indeed 69.

QUESTIONS FROM THE CLASSROOM

1. A student asks if the average income of each of ten people is $10 000 and one person gets a raise of $10 000, is the median, the mean, or the mode changed and, if so, by how much?
2. A student asks for an example of when the mode is the best average. What is your response?
3. Suppose the class takes a test and the following averages are obtained: mean, 80; median, 90, mode, 70. Tom, who scored 80, would like to know if he did better than half the class. What is your response?

4. A student asks for the advantages of presenting data in graphical form rather than in tabular form. What is your response? What are the disadvantages?

5. A student asks if it is possible to find the mode for data in a grouped frequency table. What is your response?

6. A student asks if she can make any conclusions about a set of data knowing that the mean for the data is less than the median. How do you answer?

7. A student asks if it is possible to have a standard deviation of zero. What is your answer?

8. A student asks if it is possible to score at the 100th percentile on a test. How do you answer?

9. A student reports that the average life of a pickup is around 10 years, since she read that nine out of ten pickup trucks sold in the last 10 years are still on the road. Is she correct?

CHAPTER OUTLINE

I. Descriptive statistics
  A. **Descriptive statistics** is the science of organizing and summarizing numerical data.
  B. Information can be summarized in **frequency tables.**
  C. Graphs can be used to picture data:
    1. **Histograms** or **bar graphs**
    2. **Frequency polygons** or **line graphs**
    3. **Circle graphs**
  D. Graphs can be used to distort data.

II. Averages
  A. An **average** is a single numerical figure used to represent data.
  B. The **mean** of n given numbers is the sum of the numbers divided by n.
  C. The **median** of a set of numbers is the middle number if the numbers are arranged in numerical order or, if there is no middle number, it is the mean of the two middle numbers.
  D. The **mode** of a set of numbers is the number or numbers that occur most frequently in the set.
  E. Averages can be used to misinterpret data.

III. Measures of dispersion
  A. The **range** is the difference between the greatest and least numbers in the set.
  B. The **variance** is found by subtracting the mean from each value, squaring each of these differences, finding the sum of these squares, and dividing by n, when n is the number of observations.
  C. The **standard deviation** is equal to the square root of the variance.
  D. In a **normal curve,** 68% of the numbers are within one standard deviation of the mean, 95% are within two standard deviations of the mean, and 99% are within three standard deviations of the mean.

CHAPTER TEST

1. Suppose you read that "the average family in Rattlesnake Gulch has 2.41 children." What average is being used? Explain your answer. Suppose the sentence said 2.5. Then what are the possibilities?

2. At Bug's Bar-B-Q restaurant, the average weekly wage for full-time workers is $150. If there are ten part-time employees whose average weekly salary is $50 and the total weekly payroll is $3950, how many full-time employees are there?

3. Find the mean, median, and mode for each of the following groups of data.
   (a) 10, 50, 30, 40, 10, 60, 10
   (b) 5, 8, 6, 3, 5, 4, 3, 6, 1, 9

4. Find the range, variance, and standard deviation for each set of scores in Problem 3.

5. The masses, in kilograms, of children in a certain class follow.

40	49	43	48
42	41	42	39
46	42	49	39
47	49	44	42
41	40	45	43

   (a) Make a frequency table for this data.
   (b) Draw a bar graph for the data.

6. The grades on a test for 30 students follow.

96	73	61	76	77	84
78	98	98	80	67	82
61	75	79	90	73	80
85	63	86	100	94	77
86	84	91	62	77	64

   (a) Make a grouped frequency table for these scores using four classes, starting the first class at 61.
   (b) Draw a histogram for the grouped data.
   (c) Draw a line graph for the data.

7. The budget for the Wegetem Crime Company is $2 000 000. If $600 000 is spent on bribes, $400 000 is spent for legal fees, $300 000 for bail money, $300 000 for contracts, and $400 000 for public relations, draw a circle graph to indicate how the company spent its money.

8. What, if anything, is wrong with the following bar graph?

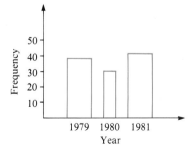

9. The mean salary of twenty-four people is $9000. How much will one additional salary of $80 000 increase the mean salary?

10. A standardized test has a mean of 600 and a standard deviation of 75. If 1000 students took the test and their scores approximated a normal curve, how many scored between 600 and 750?

11. Use the information in Problem 10, to find (a) P_{16}, (b) D_5, and (c) P_{84}.

SELECTED BIBLIOGRAPHY

Ball, J. "Finding Averages with Bar Graphs." *The Arithmetic Teacher,* **16**(October 1969):354–366.

Bruni, J. V., and H. Silverman. "Graphing as a Communication Skill." *The Arithmetic Teacher,* **22**(May 1975):354–366.

Buzitis, B., and J. Kella. *The News Math.* Seattle: The Seattle Times, 1974.

Fielker, D. *Topics from Mathematics, Statistics.* New York: Cambridge University Press, 1967.

Huff, D. and Geis, I. *How to Lie with Statistics.* New York: W. W. Norton, 1954.

Hyatt, D. "M and M's Candy: A Statistical Approach." *The Arithmetic Teacher,* **24**(January 1977):34.

Jacobson, M. "Graphing in the Primary Grades: Our Pets." *Arithmetic Teacher,* **26**(February 1979):25–26.

Johnson, D., et al. *Activities in Mathematics,* second course, *Statistics.* Glenview, Ill.: Scott, Foresman, 1971.

Joiner, B., and C. Campbell. "Some Interesting Examples for Teaching Statistics." *The Mathematics Teacher,* **68**(May 1975):364–369.

Klitz, R., and J. Hofmeister. "Statistics in the Middle School." *Arithmetic Teacher,* **26**(February 1979):35–36.

Leake, L. "Distribution of the Mean." *The Mathematics Teacher,* **64**(May 1971):441–447.

Le Blanc, J., et al. *Mathematics—Methods Program, Graphs, The Picturing of Information.* Reading, Mass.: Addison-Wesley, 1976.

Le Blanc, J., et al., *Mathematics—Methods Program, Probability, and Statistics.* Reading, Mass.: Addison-Wesley, 1976.

Mosteller, F., ed. *Statistics by Example.* Reading, Mass.: Addison-Wesley, 1973.

National Council of Teachers of Mathematics, *More Topics in Mathematics for Elementary Teachers,* Thirtieth Yearbook, Booklet 16. Washington, D.C.: National Council of Teachers of Mathematics, 1969.

Noether, G. "The Nonparametric Approach in Elementary Statistics." *The Mathematics Teacher,* **67**(February 1974):123–126.

Nuffield Mathematics Project. *Probability and Statistics.* New York: John Wiley, 1969.

Pincus, M., and F. Morgenstem. "Graphing in the Primary Grades." *The Arithmetic Teacher,* **17**(October 1970):499–501.

Shulte, A. "A Case for Statistics." *The Arithmetic Teacher,* **26**(February 1979): 24.

Smith, R. "Bar Graphs for Five Year Olds." *The Arithmetic Teacher.* **27**(October 1979):38–41.

Introductory Geometry

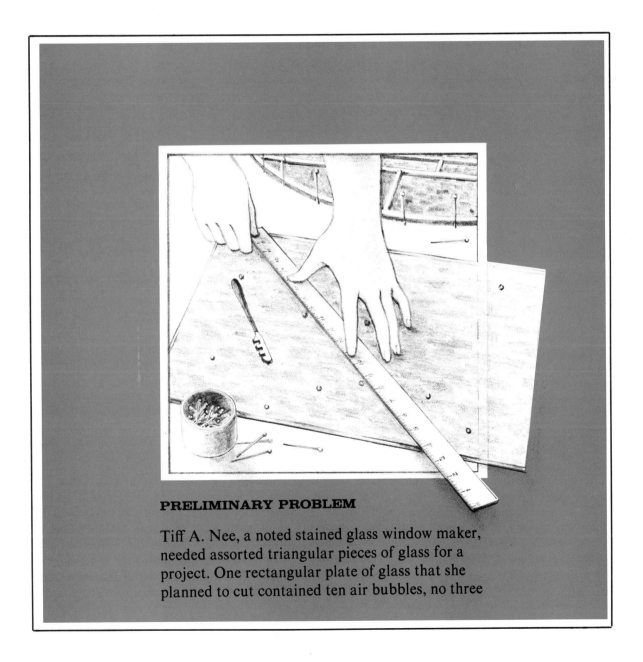

PRELIMINARY PROBLEM

Tiff A. Nee, a noted stained glass window maker, needed assorted triangular pieces of glass for a project. One rectangular plate of glass that she planned to cut contained ten air bubbles, no three

in a line, as shown in the figure on the left. To avoid having an air bubble showing in her finished project, she decided to cut triangular pieces by making the air bubbles and the corners of the plate the vertices of the triangles. How many triangular pieces did she cut?

INTRODUCTION

In Greek, the word *geometry* means "earth measure," which suggests the practical origins of geometry. A different side of geometry emerged in the first half of the sixth century B.C. Thales (640–550 B.C.), a Greek philosopher and mathematician, insisted that geometric facts be demonstrated by logical reasoning, rather than by observation and experimentation. Along with Euclid, Eudoxus, and others, Thales helped to establish geometry on an abstract, deductive level. In *The Elements,* a treatise on geometry, Euclid was probably the first to represent geometry in an organized logical fashion. He

axioms

started with a few basic assumptions called **axioms** and logically deduced other geometric information. Euclid's work so influenced the teaching of geometry that many people describe it as the subject in which "you prove theorems."

    A rigorous Euclidean geometry requires many axioms and proofs and is inappropriate for the majority of students in elementary school. In this chapter and following chapters, geometry is presented from an experimental, constructive point of view. Many properties of geometry are accepted on the basis of intuition. These properties then are used to deduce other geometric facts.

9-1   BASIC NOTIONS

point

line

The simplest of all geometric figures is a **point.** A point has no dimensions. A point is often used to describe location. We designate points by capital letters such as A and B. A **line** is a collection of points. Figure 9-1 shows a line and names two points on the line, A and B. The arrowheads on the line in Figure 9-1 indicate that the line extends indefinitely. Lines have no thickness or width. The line through the points A and B is designated as $\overleftrightarrow{AB}$ or $\overleftrightarrow{BA}$ or by any lower case letter. (In Figure 9-1, $\overleftrightarrow{AB} = \ell$.) Many lines can be drawn through a given point, but only one line exists through two points. As shown in

FIGURE 9-1

Figure 9-1, line ℓ goes through points A and B. Any other collection of points going through A and B is not a line. (In our discussions, a "line" always means "a straight line.")

Points and lines are mathematical abstractions and, in geometry, are undefined terms.

Intuitively, a line contains infinitely many points. We say that the points A and B belong to $\overleftrightarrow{AB}$ or are contained in $\overleftrightarrow{AB}$, and write $A \in \overleftrightarrow{AB}$ and $B \in \overleftrightarrow{AB}$. Points that belong to the same line are called **collinear points.** Thus, points A, B, and C in Figure 9-2 are collinear. Points B, D, and C are not collinear. If three collinear points A, B, and C are arranged as in Figure 9-2, we say that B is **between** A and C. Point D is not between B and C, since B, D, and C are not collinear. Notice that even though we have not defined *between,* precisely, it is possible to recognize which point among three points on a line is between the other two points.

collinear points

between

FIGURE 9-2

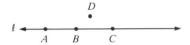

line segment

Certain subsets of a line are given separate names and symbols. A **line segment** is a subset of a line that contains two points and all the points between them. The line segment in Figure 9-3(a) is denoted by $\overline{AB}$ or $\overline{BA}$.

FIGURE 9-3

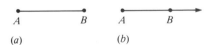

A B A B

(a)   (b)

half-lines

ray

Any point on a line separates the line into three disjoint subsets, the point itself and two **half-lines.** The point itself along with either of the half-lines is called a **ray.** Figure 9-3(b) shows a ray denoted by $\overrightarrow{AB}$ (where B is any point on the ray different from A). In $\overrightarrow{AB}$, A is the starting point and the arrowhead indicates that the direction of the ray is from A toward B. $\overrightarrow{BA}$ is the notation for a ray starting at B and extending toward A. Thus, $\overrightarrow{AB} \neq \overrightarrow{BA}$. A half line denoted by $\overset{\circ}{\overrightarrow{AB}}$ consists of all the points of $\overrightarrow{AB}$ except the starting point A.

Example 9-1

Find each of the following in Figure 9-4.

(a) $\overleftrightarrow{AD} \cap \overleftrightarrow{EC}$ (b) $\overrightarrow{AB} \cap \overrightarrow{BA}$ (c) $\overrightarrow{AB} \cup \overrightarrow{BD}$
(d) $\overleftrightarrow{AB} \cap \overleftrightarrow{BC} \cap \overleftrightarrow{AC}$ (e) $\overleftrightarrow{AB} \cap \overset{\circ}{\overrightarrow{BC}}$

FIGURE 9-4

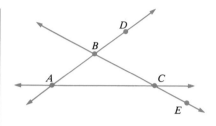

Solution

(a) $\overleftrightarrow{AD} \cap \overleftrightarrow{EC} = \{B\}$
(b) $\overrightarrow{AB} \cap \overrightarrow{BA} = \overline{AB}$
(c) $\overrightarrow{AB} \cup \overrightarrow{BD} = \overrightarrow{AD}$
(d) $\overleftrightarrow{AB} \cap \overleftrightarrow{BC} \cap \overleftrightarrow{AC} = (\overleftrightarrow{AB} \cap \overleftrightarrow{BC}) \cap \overleftrightarrow{AC} = \{B\} \cap \overleftrightarrow{AC} = \varnothing$
(e) $\overrightarrow{AB} \cap \overset{\circ}{B}\overset{\circ}{C} = \varnothing$, since $B \notin \overset{\circ}{B}\overset{\circ}{C}$

plane

Another collection of points is called a **plane.** *Plane* is another undefined term in geometry. A table top and a wall are both physical models of portions of planes. However, a plane itself is a flat surface that extends infinitely far in two directions and has no thickness. A plane contains infinitely many points as well as infinitely many lines. A plane usually is denoted by a small Greek letter such as alpha (α), beta (β), gamma (γ), and may be pictured as in

coplanar points   Figure 9-5. Points (or lines) in the same plane are called **coplanar points** (or
coplanar lines   **lines**).

FIGURE 9-5

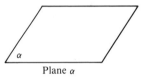

Plane α

intersecting lines

Two lines, *m* and *n,* as in Figure 9-6, are called **intersecting lines** if the intersection point, *P*, is the only point that belongs to both lines. This can be written as $m \cap n = \{P\}$. Distinct lines that can be contained in a single plane
parallel lines   and do not intersect are called **parallel lines.** The lines *r* and *s* in Figure 9-7 are parallel. We write $r \parallel s$.

FIGURE 9-6

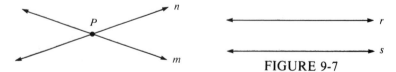

FIGURE 9-7

Two distinct lines that cannot be contained in any single plane are
skew lines   called **skew lines.** For example, the lines *p* and *q* in Figure 9-8 are skew lines.

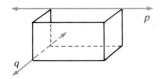

FIGURE 9-8

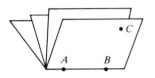

FIGURE 9-9

Note that skew lines are not parallel lines even though they do not intersect. Only intersecting lines and parallel lines are coplanar. Skew lines are noncoplanar.

Many planes can be drawn through a given point. Similarly, many planes can be drawn through any two given points. Exactly one plane can be drawn through three noncollinear points. We say that these three points determine a plane. To see this, consider $\overleftrightarrow{AB}$ in Figure 9-9 and imagine a point, C, not on that line. Imagine that one of the planes containing $\overleftrightarrow{AB}$ is rotated around $\overleftrightarrow{AB}$ like a page in a notebook, until it contains the point C. This "new" plane contains A, B, and C and may be symbolized as plane ABC. Intuitively, there should be only one plane that contains the three points A, B, and C.

There are in fact, several ways to determine a plane. The most important ones are the following:

1. Three noncollinear points determine a plane.
2. A line and a point not on the line determine a plane.
3. Two parallel lines determine a plane.
4. Two intersecting lines determine a plane.

Two planes either intersect in a line or are parallel. In Figure 9-10(a), the planes are parallel; that is, $\alpha \cap \beta = \varnothing$. In Figure 9-10(b), the planes intersect in a line, $\overleftrightarrow{AB}$; that is, $\alpha \cap \beta = \overleftrightarrow{AB}$.

FIGURE 9-10

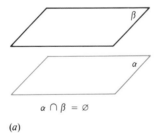

$\alpha \cap \beta = \varnothing$

(a)

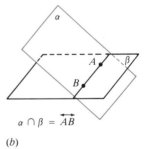

$\alpha \cap \beta = \overleftrightarrow{AB}$

(b)

The floor and ceiling of a typical room together represent parallel planes. The floor and a wall together represent intersecting planes. The edge **line of intersection** between the floor and wall represents the **line of intersection.**

A line and a plane can be related in one of three possible ways. If a line **parallel to the plane** and a plane have no points in common, we say that the line is **parallel to the plane.** If two points of a line are in the plane, then the entire line containing the points is contained in the plane. If a line shares all its points with a plane, we say the line is in the plane. If a line intersects a plane, but is not contained in the plane, it intersects the plane in only one point. The three relative positions between a line ℓ and a plane α are shown in Figure 9-11.

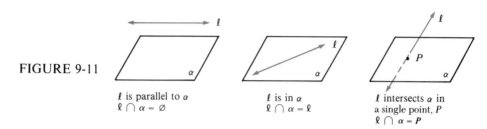

FIGURE 9-11

ℓ is parallel to α
$\ell \cap \alpha = \varnothing$

ℓ is in α
$\ell \cap \alpha = \ell$

ℓ intersects α in
a single point, P
$\ell \cap \alpha = P$

Example 9-2   Given Figure 9-12, answer each of the following.

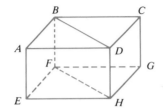

FIGURE 9-12

(a)   Name two pairs of skew lines.
(b)   Are $\overleftrightarrow{BD}$ and $\overleftrightarrow{FH}$ parallel, skew, or intersecting lines?
(c)   Are $\overleftrightarrow{BD}$ and $\overleftrightarrow{GH}$ parallel?
(d)   Find the intersection of $\overleftrightarrow{BD}$ and plane EFG.
(e)   Find the intersection of $\overleftrightarrow{BH}$ and plane DCG.

Solution   (a) $\overleftrightarrow{BC}$ and $\overleftrightarrow{DH}$, and $\overleftrightarrow{AE}$ and $\overleftrightarrow{BD}$. Others are possible.
(b) $\overleftrightarrow{BD}$ and $\overleftrightarrow{FH}$ are parallel.
(c)   No, $\overleftrightarrow{BD}$ and $\overleftrightarrow{GH}$ are skew lines.
(d)   The intersection is the empty set, since $\overleftrightarrow{BD}$ and the plane EFG have no points in common.
(e)   The intersection of $\overleftrightarrow{BH}$ and plane DCG is $\{H\}$.

Since a plane is a flat surface, it cannot contain three-dimensional
space   objects. **Space** is the set of all points in three dimensions. A point separates a
line into two half-lines and the point itself. Similarly, a line separates a plane
half-planes   into two **half-planes** and the line itself and a plane separates space into two
half-spaces   **half-spaces** and the plane itself. In Figure 9-13, ℓ separates the plane, α, into
two half-planes. The point A is in one half-plane determined by ℓ, and B is in

FIGURE 9-13

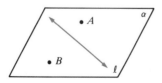

the other half-plane. The line separating the plane does not belong to either half-plane. A line and the two half-planes determined by the line are three disjoint subsets of a plane. Likewise, a plane and the two half-spaces determined by the plane are three disjoint subsets of space.

PROBLEM SET 9-1

1. Given the figure below, find each of the following.

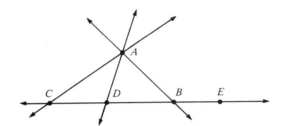

   (a) $\overleftrightarrow{AC} \cap \overleftrightarrow{BE}$ (b) $\overline{AC} \cap \overline{BE}$ (c) $\overleftrightarrow{CA} \cap \overrightarrow{EB}$ (d) $\overleftrightarrow{CA} \cap \overrightarrow{BC}$
   (e) $\overrightarrow{CB} \cup \overrightarrow{BE}$ (f) $\overrightarrow{AB} \cup \overrightarrow{AB}$ (g) $\overrightarrow{AB} \cup \overrightarrow{BA}$ (h) $\overrightarrow{AD} \cup \overrightarrow{DA}$

2. Given the line ℓ, answer the following.

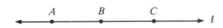

   (a) Give six other names for ℓ.　　　　　　　(b) Name three line segments on ℓ.
   (c) Name two rays on line ℓ with endpoint B.　(d) Find a simpler name for $\overrightarrow{BC} \cap \overrightarrow{CB}$.
   (e) Find a simpler name for $\overleftrightarrow{AB} \cap \overline{BC}$.　　(f) Find a simpler name for $\overrightarrow{BA} \cup \overrightarrow{BC}$.

3. Consider the following figure and answer each of the following questions.

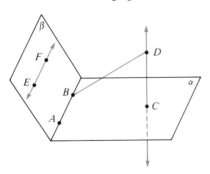

   (a) Name a pair of skew lines.
   (b) If $\overleftrightarrow{EF}$ and $\overleftrightarrow{AB}$ are parallel, what can be said about $\overleftrightarrow{EF}$ and α?

    (c) Find and name the intersections for each of the following pairs of planes.

        (i) β and α (ii) *BDC* and α (iii) *ABD* and *BDC*

    (d) Is there a single plane containing the points *E*, *F*, *B*, and *D*? Explain your answer.

4. Indicate whether each of the following statements is true or false. If false, explain why.

    (a) Two distinct planes either intersect in a line or are parallel.

    (b) If there are two points common to a line and a plane, then the entire line is in the plane.

    (c) It is always possible to find a plane through four given points in space.

    (d) If two distinct lines do not intersect, they are parallel.

    (e) The intersection of three planes may be a single point.

    (f) If two distinct lines intersect, there is one and only one plane containing the lines.

    (g) There are infinitely many planes containing two skew lines.

    (h) If each of two parallel lines is parallel to a plane, α, then the plane determined by the two parallel lines is parallel to α.

5. Suppose ℓ is a line and *A* is a point not on ℓ.

    (a) How many lines may be drawn through *A* intersecting ℓ?

    (b) How many planes contain ℓ and *A*?

6. Suppose ℓ is a line and two points, *A* and *B*, are not on ℓ. For each of the following, how many planes contain *A* and *B* and at least one point on ℓ?

    (a) $\overleftrightarrow{AB}$ and ℓ are skew lines   (b) $\overleftrightarrow{AB}$ and ℓ are not skew lines

7. (a) If two parallel planes, α and β, intersect a third plane, γ, in two lines, ℓ and *m*, are ℓ and *m* necessarily parallel? Explain your answer.

    (b) If two planes, α and β, intersect a third plane in two parallel lines, are α and β always parallel? Why?

    (c) Suppose two intersecting lines are both parallel to a plane, α. Is the plane determined by these intersecting lines parallel to α? Why?

8. Determine whether each of the following statements is true or false. If false, explain why.

    (a) If two distinct lines are parallel to a third line in space, then the two lines are parallel to each other.

    (b) If a plane, α, contains one line, ℓ, but not another line, *m*, and ℓ is parallel to *m*, then α is parallel to *m*.

    (c) A line parallel to each of two intersecting planes is parallel to the line of intersection of these planes.

9. How many rays are determined by each of the following?

    (a) Three collinear points   (b) Four collinear points

    (c) Five collinear points   (d) *n* collinear points

10. (a) How many lines are determined by three noncollinear points?

    (b) How many lines are determined by four points, no three of which are collinear?

    (c) Given five points, no three of which are collinear, draw a diagram illustrating all the lines that can be drawn through the given points. How many lines are there?

    (d) Given *n* points, no three of which are collinear, how many lines are determined by the *n* points?

11. What is the greatest number of intersection points determined by each of the following?

    (a) Three distinct lines   (b) Four distinct lines

    (c) Five distinct lines   (d) *n* distinct lines

★12. Use the statement, "There is one and only one plane containing three distinct noncollinear points," to prove each of the following.
  (a) A line and a point not on the line determine a plane.
  (b) Two intersecting lines determine a plane.
★13. Prove that if two parallel planes are intersected by a third plane, the lines of intersection are parallel.

9-2 PLANE FIGURES

angle In a plane, an **angle** is the union of two distinct rays that have a common endpoint but do not lie on the same line. Figure 9-14(a) illustrates an angle.

FIGURE 9-14

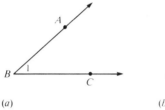
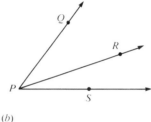

(a)   (b)

Remark | The restriction in the definition of an angle that the two rays are distinct and noncollinear is modified in a later section so that straight angles can be considered.

sides
vertex

  The rays of an angle are called the **sides** of the angle, and the common endpoint is called the **vertex** of the angle. An angle can be named by three different points, the vertex and a point on each ray, with the vertex always listed between the other two points. Thus, the angle in Figure 9-14(a) can be named as $\angle ABC$, read "angle ABC," or $\angle CBA$. When there is no confusion, it is also customary to name an angle either by its vertex or by a number. Thus, the angle in Figure 9-14(a) can be named as $\angle B$ or $\angle 1$. However, in Figure 9-14(b), there is more than one angle with vertex P, namely $\angle QPR$, $\angle RPS$, and $\angle QPS$. Thus, the notation $\angle P$ is inadequate for naming any one of the angles.

  An angle separates the plane into disjoint sets of points: the interior, the angle itself, and the exterior. The interior of the angle in Figure 9-15 is shaded.

FIGURE 9-15

adjacent angles

Two intersecting lines form four angles in the plane. In Figure 9-16, the four angles are ∢1, ∢2, ∢3, and ∢4. Angles 1 and 2 are called **adjacent angles** because they have a common vertex, a common side, and their interiors do not overlap. (Can you name three more pairs of adjacent angles?)

FIGURE 9-16

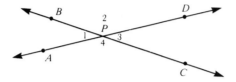

vertical angles

The nonadjacent angles formed by two intersecting lines are called **vertical angles.** In Figure 9-16, ∢1 and ∢3 are one pair of vertical angles, and ∢2 and ∢4 are another pair of vertical angles.

Other subsets of the plane that are studied in geometry are curves. A careful definition of a curve requires advanced mathematical concepts. Therefore, we intuitively describe a plane curve. A **plane curve** is a set of points in a plane that can be traced without lifting a pencil from the paper and without retracing any portion of the drawing other than single points. We use the terms *plane curve* and *curve* interchangeably. Figures 9-17(a), (b), (d), and (e) are examples of curves. Figure 9-17(c) is not a curve since it cannot be traced without lifting the pencil.

plane curve

FIGURE 9-17

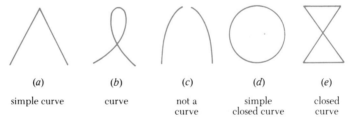

| (a) | (b) | (c) | (d) | (e) |
| simple curve | curve | not a curve | simple closed curve | closed curve |

simple curve

Figures 9-17(a) and (d) are examples of simple curves. A **simple curve** is a curve that can be traced in such a way that no point is traced more than once except the tracing may stop at the same point where it started. Figures 9-17(d) and (e) are examples of **closed curves.** A closed curve is a curve that can be traced so that the starting and stopping points are the same. Notice that Figure 9-17(d) is a **simple closed curve.**

closed curve

simple closed curve

Example 9-3

Consider Figure 9-18.

FIGURE 9-18

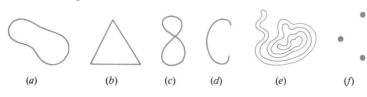

| (a) | (b) | (c) | (d) | (e) | (f) |

(a)   Which parts of Figure 9-18 represent curves?
(b)   Which represent simple curves?
(c)   Which represent closed curves?
(d)   Which represent simple closed curves?

Solution

(a)   Figures 9-18(a), (b), (c), (d), and (e) are curves.
(b)   Figures 9-18(a), (b), (d), and (e) are simple curves.
(c)   Figures 9-18(a), (b), (c), and (e) are closed curves.
(d)   Figures 9-18(a), (b), and (e) are simple closed curves.

Any simple closed curve partitions the plane into three mutually disjoint sets of points—the curve itself, the interior, and the exterior of the curve. This property of simple closed curves is known as the **Jordan curve theorem.**

Jordan curve theorem
polygonal curve

Any plane curve that is the union of line segments is called a **polygonal curve.** All the curves in Figure 9-19 are examples of polygonal curves.

FIGURE 9-19

   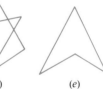

(a)   (b)   (c)   (d)   (e)

polygon

Polygonal curves, such as Figures 9-19(c) and (e) which are simple and closed, are called polygons. A **polygon** is a simple, closed polygonal curve such that no two segments with a common endpoint are collinear. The line

sides
vertex
polygonal region

segments forming a polygon are called **sides** of the polygon. A point where the two sides meet is called a **vertex.** Together, a polygon and its interior are called a **polygonal region.**

Strictly speaking, there are no angles in a polygon since an angle is composed of two rays, whereas the sides of a polygon are line segments. However, there are angles associated with a polygon. For example, in Figure 9-20, $\angle ABC$, $\angle BCA$, and $\angle CAB$ are called the three angles of polygon ABC.

FIGURE 9-20

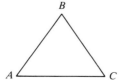

A polygon has three or more sides and is classified by the number of sides (or angles) it has. The names for many polygons have prefixes indicating *n*-gon   the number of sides (angles), as shown in Table 9-1. A polygon having *n* sides is referred to as an ***n*-gon.**

TABLE 9-1

Number of Sides	Name
3	Triangle
4	Quadrilateral
5	Pentagon
6	Hexagon
7	Heptagon
8	Octagon
9	Nonagon
10	Decagon
12	Dodecagon

diagonal   Any line segment connecting nonconsecutive vertices of a polygon is called a **diagonal.** Thus, in Figure 9-21(a) the segments $\overline{AC}, \overline{AD}, \overline{BE}, \overline{BD}$, and $\overline{CE}$ are diagonals of the given pentagon. In Figure 9-21(b) the segments $\overline{QS}$ and $\overline{PR}$ are the diagonals of the quadrilateral *PQRS*.

FIGURE 9-21

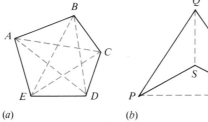

(a)   (b)

convex polygon

concave polygon

Notice that, except for their endpoints, all the diagonals of the pentagon in Figure 9-21(a) lie in the interior of the pentagon. The quadrilateral in Figure 9-21(b) has a diagonal that, except for its endpoints, lies in the exterior of the quadrilateral. A polygon having no diagonals in its exterior is called a **convex polygon,** whereas a polygon having at least one diagonal in its exterior is called a **concave polygon.** The pentagon in Figure 9-21(a) is convex, while the quadrilateral in Figure 9-21(b) is concave. Because a triangle has no diagonals, it has no diagonals in its exterior, and hence is convex. (A definition of a convex region is given in Problem 15 of Problem Set 9-2.)

Example 9-4 | · Which of the polygons in Figure 9-22 are convex and which are concave?

FIGURE 9-22

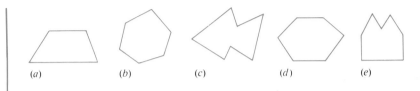

(a)   (b)   (c)   (d)   (e)

Solution | Polygons (a), (b), and (d) are convex. Polygons (c) and (e) are concave.

congruent segments

Two line segments are described as **congruent** if the two segments can be fitted exactly one on top of the other. If $\overline{AB}$ is congruent to $\overline{CD}$, we write $\overline{AB} \cong \overline{CD}$. Triangles can be classified according to congruent sides as follows.

isosceles triangle
1. An **isosceles triangle** is a triangle with at least two congruent sides.

equilateral triangle
2. An **equilateral triangle** is a triangle with all sides congruent.

scalene triangle
3. A **scalene triangle** is a triangle having no two sides congruent.

Two angles are described as congruent if the two angles can be fitted exactly one on top of the other. If $\angle A$ is congruent to $\angle B$, we write $\angle A \cong \angle B$. Polygons in which all the angles are congruent and all the sides are **regular polygons** congruent are called **regular polygons.** We say that a regular polygon is both equiangular and equilateral. A regular triangle is an equilateral triangle. A regular pentagon and a regular hexagon are illustrated in Figure 9-23. The congruent sides and congruent angles are marked.

When two lines intersect so that all the angles formed are congruent to **perpendicular lines** one another, we say that the lines are **perpendicular lines.** The four angles **right angles** formed are called **right angles.** In Figure 9-24, the two lines, m and n, are perpendicular and we write $m \perp n$. The symbol ⌐ is used to indicate right angles. Two intersecting segments, two intersecting rays, or a segment and a ray that intersect are called perpendicular if they lie on perpendicular lines. For example, in Figure 9-24, $\overline{AB} \perp \overline{BC}$, $\overrightarrow{BA} \perp \overrightarrow{BC}$, and $\overleftrightarrow{AB} \perp \overrightarrow{BC}$.

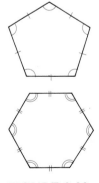

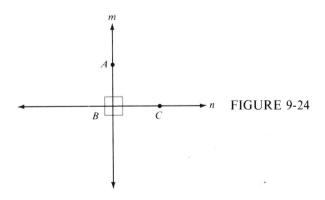

FIGURE 9-24

FIGURE 9-23

Quadrilaterals may be classified using angles and sides as follows.

parallelogram   1. A **parallelogram** is a quadrilateral in which each pair of opposite sides (nonintersecting) is parallel.

rectangle   2. A **rectangle** is a parallelogram with a right angle.

square   3. A **square** is a rectangle with all sides congruent. (A square is a **regular** quadrilateral.)

rhombus   4. A **rhombus** is a parallelogram with all sides congruent.

trapezoid   5. A **trapezoid** is a quadrilateral with exactly two sides parallel.

The quadrilaterals are pictured in Figure 9-25.

FIGURE 9-25

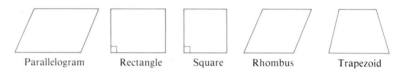

Parallelogram   Rectangle   Square   Rhombus   Trapezoid

The following section presents information needed to show that if a parallelogram has one right angle, then it has four right angles. Thus, all angles in a rectangle are right angles.

PROBLEM SET 9-2

1. Use the accompanying figure to solve each of the following.

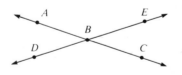

   (a) Name at least four different angles.
   (b) Find $\angle ABE \cap \angle EBC$.
   (c) Find $\angle EBA \cap \angle DBC$.
   (d) Find $\angle EBC \cap \angle CBE$.
   (e) Is is true that $\angle ABE \cup \angle EBC = \angle ABC$?

2. Draw all possible intersections of a line and an angle.

3. For each of the given figures, name which pairs of angles marked are adjacent and which are vertical?

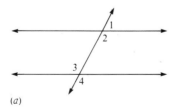

(a)

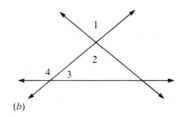

(b)

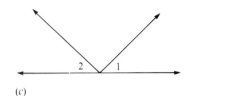

(c)

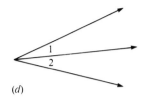

(d)

4. For each of the following, sketch a pair of angles whose intersection is given.
   (a) The empty set   (b) Exactly two points   (c) Exactly three points
   (d) Exactly four points   (e) More than four points

5. For each of the following, name which figures labeled (1)–(12) can be classified by the given term?
   (a) Curves   (b) Simple curves   (c) Simple closed curves
   (d) Polygons   (e) Convex polygons   (f) Concave polygons

(1)   (2)   (3)   (4)   (5)   (6)

(7)   (8)   (9)   (10)   (11)   (12)

6. Which of the printed capital letters of the English alphabet can be classified as follows?
   (a) Simple curves   (b) Closed curves
   (c) Simple closed curves   (d) Polygons

7. Is it possible for a polygon to have fewer than three sides? Why or why not?

8. How many diagonals can be drawn from a single vertex of an *n*-gon?

9. How many diagonals do each of the following have?
   (a) quadrilateral   (b) pentagon   (c) hexagon   (d) n-gon

10. Use the drawing below to find each of the following.
    (a) ℓ ∩ (polygon *ABCD*)
    (b) ℓ ∩ (interior of polygon *ABCD*)
    (c) ℓ ∩ (exterior of polygon *ABCD*)
    (d) ℓ ∩ $\overleftrightarrow{AC}$

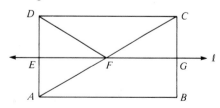

11. Find the number of triangles in each of the following figures.

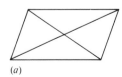

(a)   (b)

12. Identify each of the following triangles as scalene, isosceles, or equilateral.

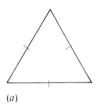   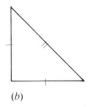   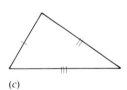

(a)   (b)   (c)

13. Tell whether each of the following is true or false. If the statement is false, explain why.
    (a) Every isosceles triangle is equilateral.
    (b) All equilateral triangles are isosceles.
    (c) All squares are rectangles.
    (d) Some rectangles are rhombi.
    (e) All parallelograms are quadrilaterals.
    (f) Every rhombus is a regular quadrilateral.
14. Use Venn diagrams to describe the relationships among the sets of all quadrilaterals (Q), parallelograms (P), trapezoids (T), rhombi, (R), rectangles (F), and squares (S).
15. A region is called convex if, for every two points in the region, a segment joining them lies completely within the region. Otherwise, the region is called concave. Which of the following regions are convex and which are concave?

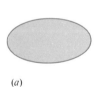

(a)   (b)   (c)   (d)

BRAIN TEASER

Given three factories, A, B, and C, as shown in the figure on the right, and three utility centers, electricity (E), gas (G), and water (W), is it possible to connect each of the three factories to each of the three utility centers without crossing lines?

A B C

E G W

LABORATORY ACTIVITY   A geoboard consists of a square array of nails driven into a board at equally spaced intervals. Students form various geometric shapes by stretching rubber bands around the nails. Geoboard exercises can be simulated by connecting dots on paper. The arrangement of nails is represented by the following figure.

Form each of the following using either geoboards or dotted paper.
(a) Scalene triangle   (b) Isosceles triangle
(c) Square   (d) Parallelogram
(e) Trapezoid   (f) Pentagon
(g) Convex hexagon   (h) Concave hexagon

9-3 MORE ABOUT ANGLES

degree   A unit commonly used for measuring angles is the **degree.** Figure 9-26 shows that $\angle BAC$ has a measure of 30 degrees, written $m(\angle BAC) = 30°$. The

protractor   measuring device pictured is called a **protractor.**

FIGURE 9-26

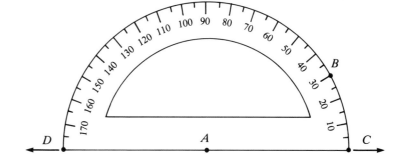

minutes   A degree is subdivided into 60 equal parts called **minutes,** and each minute is
seconds   further subdivided into 60 equal parts called **seconds.** The measurement 29 degrees, 47 minutes, 13 seconds is written 29°47′13″.

Example 9-5   (a)   In Figure 9-27, find the measure of $\angle BAC$ if $m(\angle 1) = 27°58'$ and $m(\angle 2) = 19°47'$.

FIGURE 9-27

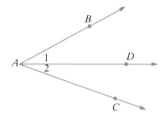

(b)   Express $21.8°$ in degrees and minutes without decimals.

Solution   (a) $m(\angle BAC) = 27° 58' + 19° 47'$
$$= (27° + 19°) + (58' + 47')$$
$$= 46° + 105'$$
$$= 46° + 1° + 45'$$
$$= 47° 45'$$

(b) $21.8° = 21° + 0.8°$. There are 60 minutes in 1 degree. Thus, $0.8° = 0.8 (60') = 48'$ and therefore, $21.8° = 21° 48'$.

Remark   In the solution of Example 9-5(a) we used the fact that $m(\angle BAC) = m(\angle 1) + m(\angle 2)$. In general, if D is in the interior of $\angle BAC$, then $m(\angle BAC) = m(\angle BAD) + m(\angle DAC)$. Also $m(\angle BAC) - m(\angle BAD) = m(\angle DAC)$.

Angles can be classified according to their measure.

acute angle   1.   If the degree measure of an angle is greater than 0° and less than 90°, the angle is called an **acute angle.**

obtuse angle   2.   If the degree measure of an angle is greater than 90° but less than 180°, the angle is called an **obtuse angle.**

right angle   3.   If the degree measure of an angle is 90°, the angle is called a **right angle.**

According to the definition of an angle as the union of two noncollinear rays, the union of two collinear rays $\overrightarrow{AC}$ and $\overrightarrow{AD}$ is not an angle. However, when D, A, and C are collinear with C between A and D, it is convenient to **straight angle**   define a **straight angle,** $\angle ACD$, as an angle with measure 180°.

supplementary angles   Two angles are called **supplementary angles** if the sum of their measures is 180°. Each is said to be a supplement of the other. Two angles are called **complementary angles**   **complementary angles** if the sum of their measures is 90°. Each is said to be a complement of the other. Figure 9-28 shows examples of supplementary and complementary angles.

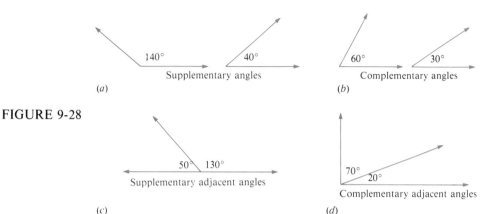

FIGURE 9-28

Supplementary angles (a)

Complementary angles (b)

Supplementary adjacent angles (c)

Complementary adjacent angles (d)

congruent angles

Intuitively, two angles are congruent if they can be fitted exactly one atop the other. More precisely, two angles are **congruent angles** if and only if they have the same measure. Using the notion of congruence, we can derive the following properties of supplementary and complementary angles.

Properties

1. Supplements of the same angle, or congruent angles, are congruent.
2. Complements of the same angle, or congruent angles, are congruent.

BRAIN TEASER

Find the sum of the measures of the angles ∡1, ∡2, ∡3, ∡4, and ∡5, in any five-pointed star like the one in the accompanying figure. What is the sum of the measures of the angles in any seven-pointed star?

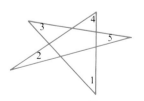

Using Property 1, it is easy to prove that vertical angles are congruent. Look at Figure 9-29. Since ℓ is a straight line, ∡1 is a supplement of ∡4. Since *m* is a straight line, ∡2 is a supplement of ∡4. Since ∡1 and ∡2 are the supplements of the same angle, ∡4, they are congruent and equal in measure. Similarly, ∡3 and ∡4 are supplements of ∡1 and, therefore, are congruent. Thus, vertical angles are congruent.

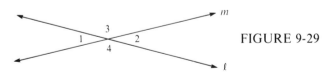

FIGURE 9-29

The property of complementary angles can also be used to deduce congruence relationships among certain angles as shown in Example 9-6.

Example 9-6

Suppose, in Figure 9-30, that ∡*APC* and ∡*BPD* are right angles. Prove that ∡1 and ∡3 are congruent.

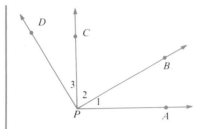

FIGURE 9-30

Solution | Since ∡*APC* is a right angle, ∡1 is a complement of ∡2. Since ∡*BPD* is a right angle, ∡3 is also a complement of ∡2. Thus, ∡1 and ∡3 are complements of the same angle and hence are congruent.

Angles are formed when a line intersects two distinct lines. Any line

transversal that intersects a pair of lines is called a **transversal** of these lines. In Figure 9-31(a), line *p* is a transversal of lines *m* and *n*. Two lines and a transversal

corresponding angles form four pairs of **corresponding angles:** ∡1 and ∡2; ∡3 and ∡4; ∡5 and

interior angles ∡7; and ∡6 and ∡8. Angles 2, 4, 5, and 6 are called **interior angles** and

exterior angles angles 1, 3, 7, and 8 are called **exterior angles.** There are two pairs of **alternate**

alternate interior angles **interior angles,** namely ∡2 and ∡5, and ∡4 and ∡6. Angles 1 and 7 and

alternate exterior angles angles 3 and 8 are pairs of **alternate exterior angles.**

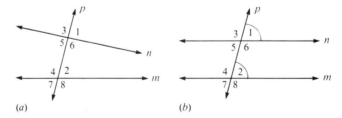

FIGURE 9-31

(a)   (b)

If corresponding angles, such as ∡1 and ∡2, are congruent as in Figure 9-31(b), it can be shown that members of each pair of corresponding angles are congruent. Also, in Figure 9-31(b), it appears that *n* and *m* are parallel. This is true. We leave it as an exercise to show that if a transversal intersecting two lines forms congruent corresponding angles, then the alternate interior or alternate exterior angles also are congruent. A summary of this discussion follows.

If any two distinct lines are cut by a transversal, a pair of corresponding angles, or alternate interior angles, or alternate exterior angles are congruent if and only if the lines are parallel.

The sum of the measures of the angles in a triangle can intuitively be shown to be 180° by using a protractor. This result can also be shown by assuming what is known in Euclidean geometry as the Parallel Postulate and using other properties of parallel lines just discussed.

Parallel Postulate | Given a line and a point, P, not on the line, there exists exactly one line through P parallel to the given line.

In Figure 9-32(a), choose any vertex of the triangle. For example, choose A. In Figure 9-32(b), if $\angle 2$, congruent to $\angle B$, is placed adjacent to $\angle 1$ as shown, then line ℓ is parallel to $\overleftrightarrow{BC}$. This is true since they are congruent alternate interior angles along transversal $\overleftrightarrow{AB}$. Since ℓ is parallel to $\overleftrightarrow{BC}$, then $\angle 3$ is congruent to $\angle C$ because they are alternate interior angles formed by transversal $\overleftrightarrow{AC}$. Consequently, $m(\angle 1) + m(\angle B) + m(\angle C) = m(\angle 1) + m(\angle 2) + m(\angle 3) = 180°$.

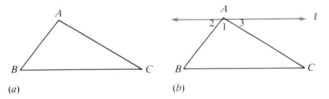

FIGURE 9-32

(a)   (b)

Hence, we have the following theorem.

THEOREM 9-1 | The sum of the measures of the angles of a triangle is 180°.

Example 9-7 | (a) In Figure 9-33(a), $m(\angle D) = 90°$ and $m(\angle E) = 25°$. Find $m(\angle A)$.
(b) In Figure 9-33(b), the measures of $\angle A$ and $\angle B$ are twice the measure of $\angle C$. Find the measures of each of the angles in the triangle.

FIGURE 9-33

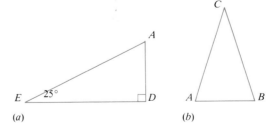

(a)   (b)

Solution

(a) The sum of the measures of the angles in a triangle is 180°. Thus, $m(\angle A) + 90° + 25° = 180°$, and consequently, $m(\angle A) = 65°$.

(b) Suppose $m(\angle C) = x$. Then $m(\angle A) = 2x$, and $m(\angle B) = 2x$. Thus, $x + 2x + 2x = 180°$. Consequently, $5x = 180°$ and $x = 36°$. Since $2x = 72°$, $m(\angle C) = 36°$, $m(\angle A) = 72°$, and $m(\angle B) = 72°$.

In Figure 9-33(a), the measure of $\angle D$ is 90°. A triangle such as triangle **right triangle** *ADE* that contains a right angle is called a **right triangle.** Similarly, a triangle **obtuse triangle** that contains an obtuse angle is called an **obtuse triangle.** A triangle in which **acute triangle** all the angles are acute is called an **acute triangle.**

Example 9-8

In Figure 9-34, assume that *m* and *n* are parallel lines cut by a transversal.

(a) In Figure 9-34(a), show that $m(\angle 2) + m(\angle 3) = 180°$.

(b) In Figure 9-34(b), show that if $\angle 4 \cong \angle 5$ and $\angle 6 \cong \angle 7$, then $m(\angle 8) = 90°$.

FIGURE 9-34

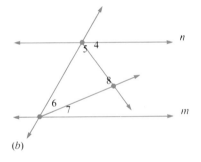

(*a*)   (*b*)

Solution

(a) $m(\angle 2) + m(\angle 1) = 180°$. Since $\angle 1$ and $\angle 3$ are corresponding angles formed by a transversal cutting parallel lines, $m(\angle 1) = m(\angle 3)$. Consequently, $m(\angle 2) + m(\angle 3) = 180°$.

(b) Let $m(\angle 4) = m(\angle 5) = x$ and $m(\angle 6) = m(\angle 7) = y$. Then by part (a), it follows that $2x + 2y = 180°$. Dividing both sides of this equation by 2, we obtain $x + y = 90°$. Since the sum of the measures of angles of a triangle is 180°, we have $x + y + m(\angle 8) = 180°$, which implies $m(\angle 8) = 90°$.

Is it possible to find the sum of the measures of the angles in any convex polygon? That is, is there a formula for finding the sum of the measures of the angles in any convex *n*-gon? We use the four problem-solving steps to find a solution.

Understanding the Problem

Given a polygon with *n* sides, we are to find a formula that will give the sum of the measures of the angles. We know that the sum of the measures of the angles in any triangle is 180°. Any formula that we develop for an *n*-gon must hold for a triangle.

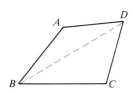

(a)

Devising a Plan

Consider several simple cases before trying to generalize the result. From any vertex of a polygon, diagonals can be drawn to form adjacent nonoverlapping triangles. For example, in the quadrilateral in Figure 9-35, the diagonal from *B* partitions the quadrilateral into two triangles. In the pentagon, the diagonals from *B* partition the pentagon into three triangles. In the hexagon, the diagonals from *B* partition the hexagon into four triangles. In general, the diagonals from a single vertex in any *n*-gon partition the *n*-gon into $(n - 2)$ triangles. This fact and the fact that the sum of the measures of the angles of a triangle is 180° can be used to solve the problem.

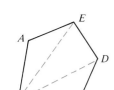

(b)

Carrying Out the Plan

Since the sum of the measures of the angles in any triangle is 180°, the sum of the measures of the angles in $(n - 2)$ triangles is $(n - 2)180°$.

Looking Back

An interesting exercise is to determine whether the formula developed and given in the following theorem holds for concave polygons. Example 9-9 is another looking-back activity.

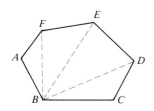

(c)

FIGURE 9-35

THEOREM 9-2	The sum of the measures of the angles of any convex *n*-gon is $(n - 2)180°$.

Example 9-9

(a) Find the measure of each angle of a regular decagon.
(b) Find the number of sides of a regular polygon, each of whose angles has a measure of 175°.

Solution   (a)   The sum of the measures of the angles in any n-gon is $(n - 2)180°$, and a decagon has ten sides. Thus, the sum of the measures of the angles of a decagon is $(10 - 2)180°$ or $1440°$. A regular decagon has ten angles, all of which are congruent, so each one has a measure of $1440°/10$ or $144°$.

(b)   Since the sum of the measures of the angles is $(n - 2)180°$ and there are n congruent angles, each angle has a measure of $(n - 2)180/n$. The measure of each angle is $175°$, and therefore, $(n - 2)180/n = 175$. Next, solve this equation.

$$\frac{(n - 2)\,180}{n} = 175$$

$$(n - 2)180 = 175n$$
$$180n - 360 = 175n$$
$$180n - 175n = 360$$
$$5n = 360$$
$$n = 72$$

Thus, the polygon has 72 sides.

PROBLEM SET 9-3

1.   Use a protractor to find the measures of each of the following angles.

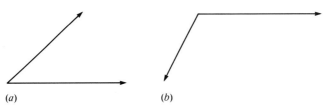

(a)   (b)

2.   If $m(\angle 1) = 50°$ in the given figure, find each of the following.
(a) $m(\angle 2)$ (b) $m(\angle 3)$ (c) $m(\angle 4)$

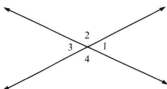

3.   Perform each of the following operations, leaving your answers in simplest form.
(a) $18°35'29'' + 22°55'61''$ (b) $93°38'14'' - 13°49'27''$

4. Express each of the following in degrees, minutes, and seconds without decimals.
   (a) 0.9°   (b) 15.13°
5. In the given figure, m and n are parallel lines and $m(\angle 4) = 60°$. Find $m(\angle 1)$, $m(\angle 2)$, $m(\angle 3)$, $m(\angle 5)$, $m(\angle 6)$, $m(\angle 7)$, and $m(\angle 8)$.

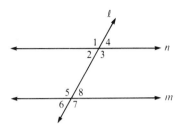

6. In the following figure, $\overleftrightarrow{DE} \parallel \overleftrightarrow{BC}$, $\overleftrightarrow{EF} \parallel \overleftrightarrow{AB}$ and $\overleftrightarrow{DF} \parallel \overleftrightarrow{AC}$. Also $m(\angle 1) = 45°$ and $m(\angle 2) = 65°$. Find:
   (a) $m(\angle 3)$ (b) $m(\angle D)$ (c) $m(\angle E)$ (d) $m(\angle F)$

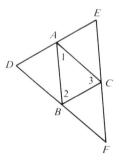

7. In each of the following cases, are m and n parallel lines? Justify your answer.

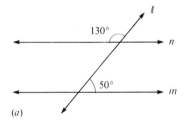

(a)

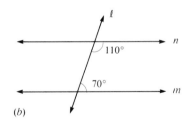

(b)

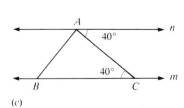

(c)

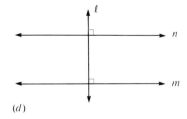

(d)

8.   Prove that two lines perpendicular to the same line are parallel.
9.   (a)   If one of the angles in a triangle is obtuse, can another angle be obtuse? Why?
     (b)   If one of the angles in a triangle is acute, can the other two angles be acute? Why?
     (c)   Can a triangle have two right angles? Why?
     (d)   If a triangle has one acute angle, is it necessarily an acute triangle? Why?
10.   Find the measure of the third angle in each of the following triangles.

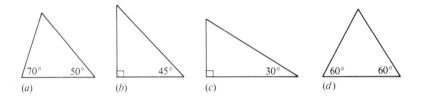

(a)   (b)   (c)   (d)

11.   (a)   Find the sum of the measures of the angles of any convex pentagon.
      (b)   Find the sum of the measures of the angles of any convex hexagon.
      (c)   How many sides does a convex polygon have if the sum of the measures of its angles is 2880°?
12.   (a)   In a regular polygon, the measure of each angle is 162°. How many sides does the polygon have?
      (b)   Find the measure of each of the angles of a regular dodecagon.
13.   (a)   Show how to find the sum of the measures of the angles of any convex pentagon by choosing any point, P, in the interior and constructing triangles as shown below.

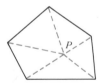

      (b)   Using the method suggested by the diagram in part (a), find the sum of the measures of the angles of any convex n-gon. Is your answer the same as the one already obtained in this section, that is, $(n - 2)180$?
14.   For the given figure, prove that $m(\angle 4) = m(\angle 1) + m(\angle 2)$.

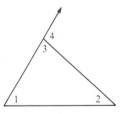

15.   Suppose polygon $ABCD$ is a parallelogram. Prove each of the following.

(a) $m(\angle A) + m(\angle B) = 180°$ (b) $m(\angle A) = m(\angle C)$ and $m(\angle B) = m(\angle D)$

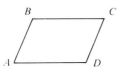

16. Use the definition of a rectangle and properties of parallel lines to show that all the angles in a rectangle are right angles.

★17. Prove that if the opposite angles in a quadrilateral are congruent, then the quadrilateral is a parallelogram.

★18. In the given figure, prove that $\overrightarrow{AD}$ and $\overrightarrow{CE}$ are parallel. (*Hint:* Draw $\overleftrightarrow{EC}$ and $\overleftrightarrow{AB}$.)

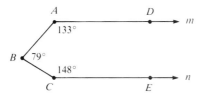

★19. For triangle ABC, $m(\angle C) = 102°$, $m(\angle 1) = m(\angle 2)$, and $m(\angle 3) = m(\angle 4)$. Find $m(\angle BPA)$.

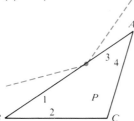

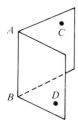

FIGURE 9-36

9-4 GEOMETRY IN THREE DIMENSIONS

Most of the concepts developed so far in this chapter have dealt with figures in a plane. Many concepts can be extended to three-dimensional space.

In a plane, an angle is the union of two distinct noncollinear rays with a common endpoint. A dihedral angle is a plane angle's three-dimensional

dihedral angle   counterpart. The **dihedral angle** shown in Figure 9-36 consists of all the points on $\overleftrightarrow{AB}$, all the points of the half-plane containing C, and all the points of the half-plane containing D.

Perpendicularity also can be extended to three dimensions. For example, in Figure 9-37, planes β and γ represent two walls of the room intersecting along line $\overleftrightarrow{AB}$. The edge, $\overleftrightarrow{AB}$, is perpendicular to the floor. Every line in the plane of the floor (plane α) passing through point A is perpendicular to $\overleftrightarrow{AB}$.

FIGURE 9-37

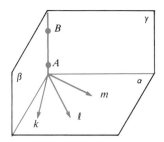

DEFINITION

> **A line and a plane are perpendicular** if and only if they intersect and the line is perpendicular to every line in the plane that passes through the point of intersection.

The plane containing one wall and the plane containing the floor of a typical room, such as α and β in Figure 9-37, are perpendicular planes. Notice that β and γ contain $\overleftrightarrow{AB}$, which is perpendicular to α. In fact, any plane containing $\overleftrightarrow{AB}$ is perpendicular to plane α.

DEFINITION

> **Two planes are perpendicular** if and only if one plane contains a line perpendicular to the other plane.

simple closed surface

A concept analogous to a simple closed curve in a plane is a **simple closed surface** in space. A simple closed surface partitions space into three sets—points outside the surface, points belonging to the surface, and points inside the surface. Simple closed surfaces have no holes and are hollow. (Simple closed surfaces can be thought of as figures that can be distorted into spheres.) For example, in Figure 9-38, parts (a), (b), and (c) are simple closed surfaces; (d) and (e) are not. A **polyhedron** is a simple closed surface formed by polygonal regions. Figures 9-38(a) and (b) are examples of polyhedra, but (c), (d), and (e) are not. The union of the points on a simple closed surface and the interior points is referred to as a **solid.**

polyhedron

solid

FIGURE 9-38

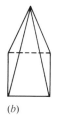
(a)
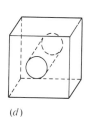
(b)
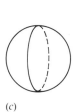
(c)
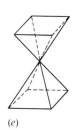
(d)
(e)

face
vertices
edges
prism

bases

Each of the polygonal regions of a polyhedron is called a **face.** The vertices of the polygonal regions are called the **vertices** of the polyhedron, and the sides of each polygonal region are called the **edges** of the polyhedron.

A **prism** is a polyhedron in which two congruent polygonal faces lie in parallel planes, and the other faces are bounded by parallelograms. Figure 9-39 shows four different prisms. The parallel faces of a prism, like the faces *ABC* and *DEF* on top and bottom of the prism in Figure 9-39(a), are called the **bases** of the prism. A prism usually is named after its bases. Thus, the prism in Figure 9-39(a) is called a triangular prism, the one in Figure 9-39(b) is a quadrilateral prism, and the prisms in Figures 9-39(c) and (d) are hexagonal prisms.

FIGURE 9-39

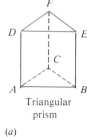
Triangular
prism
(a)

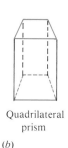
Quadrilateral
prism
(b)

Hexagonal
prism
(c)

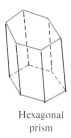
Hexagonal
prism
(d)

lateral faces

right prism
oblique prism

pyramid

base

The **lateral faces** of a prism, the faces other than the bases, are bounded by parallelograms. If the lateral faces of a prism are all bounded by rectangles, the prism is called a **right prism.** The first three prisms in Figure 9-39 are right prisms. Figure 9-39(d) is called an **oblique prism** because its lateral edges are *not* perpendicular to the bases, and, therefore, its faces are *not* bounded by rectangles.

A **pyramid** is a polyhedron determined by a simple closed polygonal region, a point not in the plane of the region, and triangular regions determined by the point and the vertices of the polygonal region. The polygonal region is called the **base** of the pyramid, and the point is called the apex   **apex.** Pyramids are classified according to their bases as shown in Figure 9-40.

FIGURE 9-40

 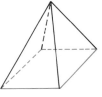 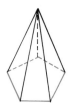

Triangular pyramid   Square pyramid   Pentagonal pyramid

convex polyhedron   A polyhedron is **convex** if and only if a segment connecting any two points in the interior of the polyhedron is itself in the interior. Figure 9-41 shows a polyhedron that is not convex.

regular polyhedron   A **regular polyhedron** is a polyhedron whose faces are congruent regular polygonal regions such that the number of edges that meet at each vertex is the same for all the vertices of the polyhedron. The ancient Greeks discovered

tetrahedron   the five regular polyhedra shown in Figure 9-42. A **tetrahedron** is formed by

cube   four congruent triangular regions; a **cube** is formed by six congruent square

octahedron   regions; an **octahedron** is formed by eight congruent triangular regions; a

dodecahedron   **dodecahedron** is formed by twelve congruent pentagonal regions; and an

icosahedron   **icosahedron** is formed by twenty congruent triangular regions. These regular

Platonic solids   polyhedra are also called the **Platonic solids,** after the Greek philosopher Plato (fourth century B.C.). Plato attached a mystical significance to the five regular polyhedra, associating them with what he believed were the four elements—Earth, Air, Fire, Water—and the Universe. Plato suggested that the smallest particles of earth have the form of a cube, those of air look like an octahedron, those of fire have a tetrahedron shape, those of water are shaped like the icosahedron, and those of the universe have the shape of a dodecahedron.

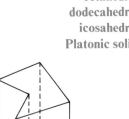

FIGURE 9-41

FIGURE 9-42   Regular tetrahedron   Cube   Regular octahedron   Regular dodecahedron   Regular icosahedron

A simple relationship between the number of faces, edges, and vertices of any polyhedron was discovered by the French mathematician and philosopher René Descartes (1596–1650) and rediscovered by the Swiss mathematician Leonhard Euler (1707–1783). Table 9-2 suggests the relationship for the number of vertices (V), edges (E), and faces (F).

TABLE 9-2

Name	V	F	E	$V + F - E$
Tetrahedron	4	4	6	2
Cube	8	6	12	2
Octahedron	6	8	12	2
Dodecahedron	20	12	30	2
Icosahedron	12	20	30	2

Euler's formula

In each case, $V + F - E = 2$. This result is known as **Euler's formula.**

A cylinder is an example of a simple closed surface that is not a polyhedron. Consider a line segment, $\overline{AB}$, and a line, ℓ, as shown in Figure 9-43. When $\overline{AB}$ moves so that it is always parallel to a given line ℓ and points A and B trace simple closed curves other than polygons, the surface generated by $\overline{AB}$ along with the simple closed curves and their interiors form a **cylinder.** The simple closed curves along with their interiors are called the **bases** of the cylinder. Three different cylinders are pictured in Figure 9-43.

cylinder
bases

FIGURE 9-43

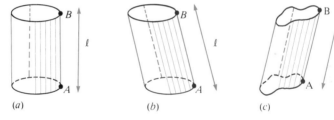

(a) (b) (c)

circular cylinder
right cylinder
oblique cylinders

If a base of a cylinder is a circular region, the cylinder is called a **circular cylinder.** If the line segment forming a cylinder is perpendicular to a base, the cylinder is called a **right cylinder.** All other cylinders are called **oblique cylinders.** The cylinder in Figure 9-43(a) is a right cylinder; the ones in Figure 9-43(b) and (c) are oblique cylinders.

cones
vertex
altitude
right circular cone

oblique circular cone

Suppose we have a simple closed curve, other than a polygon, in a plane and a point, P, not in the plane of the curve. By drawing line segments connecting each point of a simple closed curve to point P, **cones** result as in Figure 9-44. Point P is called the **vertex** of the cone. A line segment from the vertex, P, perpendicular to the base, is called the **altitude.** A **right circular cone,** such as the one in Figure 9-44(a), is a cone whose altitude intersects the base (a circular region) at the center of the circle. Figure 9-44(b) illustrates an oblique cone and Figure 9-44(c) illustrates an **oblique circular cone.**

FIGURE 9-44

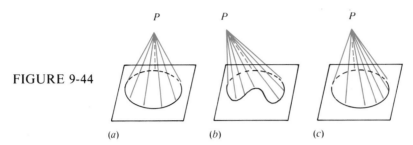

(a)   (b)   (c)

Spheres are three-dimensional analogues of circles. They will be discussed in Chapter 10.

PROBLEM SET 9-4

1. In the figure below, m is a line perpendicular to a plane, α. The intersection of m with α is C. Points A and B are in the plane, α. $D \in m$, but $D \notin \alpha$.

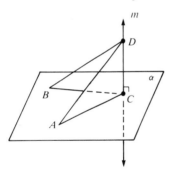

   (a) Are triangle BDC and triangle ADC right triangles? Explain your answer.

   (b) Is it possible to find a point, P, in the plane, α, so that the $\angle DPC$ is obtuse? Justify your answer.

   (c) Is the plane determined by the points A, D, and C perpendicular to plane, α? Why?

2. (a) Is it possible that a line is perpendicular to one line in a plane but is not perpendicular to the plane?

   (b) Can a line be perpendicular to two distinct lines in a plane and not be perpendicular to the plane?

   (c) If a line not in a given plane is perpendicular to two distinct lines in the plane, is the line necessarily perpendicular to the plane?

3. Identify each of the following polyhedra. If a polyhedron can be described in more than one way, give as many names as possible.

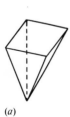 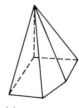 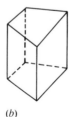

   (a)   (b)   (c)

4. For each of the following, what is the minimum number of faces possible?
    (a) Prism   (b) Pyramid   (c) Polyhedron
5. Classify each of the following as true or false.
    (a)   If the lateral faces of a prism are rectangles, it is a right prism.
    (b)   Every pyramid is a prism.
    (c)   Every pyramid is a polyhedron.
    (d)   The bases of a prism lie in perpendicular planes.
    (e)   The bases of all cones are circles.
    (f) A cylinder has only one base.
    (g)   All lateral faces of an oblique prism are rectangular regions.
    (h)   All regular polyhedra are convex.
6. Given a rectangular prism, how many possible pairs of bases does it have? Explain.
7. For each of the following, draw a prism and a pyramid having the given region as a base.
    (a) Triangle   (b) Pentagon   (c) Regular hexagon
8. Verify Euler's formula for each of the polyhedra in Problem 3.
9. Answer each of the following concerning a pyramid and a prism, each having an *n*-gon as a base.
    (a)   How many faces does it have?
    (b)   How many vertices does it have?
    (c)   How many edges does it have?
    (d)   Use your answers to parts (a), (b), and (c) to verify Euler's formula for all pyramids and all prisms.
10. Check whether Euler's formula holds for the figures given below.

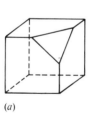   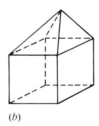   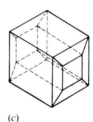

(*a*)   (*b*)   (*c*)

★11. In the cube below, $\overline{BF}$ and $\overline{AE}$ are diagonals of the upper and lower faces, respectively.

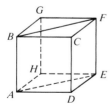

(a)   Is quadrilateral *ABFE* a parallelogram? Is it a rectangle? Explain.
(b)   Find six planes perpendicular to the plane containing square *ADEH*.
(c)   Is $\overleftrightarrow{CD}$ parallel to the plane containing the quadrilateral *ABFE*? Why?

LABORATORY ACTIVITY

1. The following are patterns for constructing the five regular polyhedra. Enlarge these patterns and fold them appropriately to construct the corresponding polyhedra.

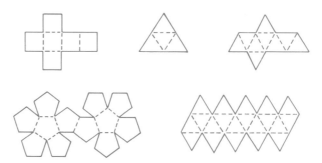

2. (a) Construct a pattern for making a square pyramid.
   (b) Construct a pattern for making a right pentagonal prism. (*Hint:* Imagine a pentagonal prism cut along one of the lateral edges.)
   (c) Construct a pattern for making a right circular cone.

*9-5   NETWORKS

A famous problem introduced by Leonhard Euler in 1735 is known as the *Königsberg Bridge Problem.* The old German city of Königsberg contained a river, two islands, and seven bridges as shown in Figure 9-45. The problem is to determine if a person can take a walk around the city in such a way that each bridge is crossed exactly once. A person can start at any land area and end at the same or a different land area. The person may visit any part of the city more than once. We designate the land areas *A*, *B*, *C*, and *D* by points and a path between land areas by a curve connecting the appropriate points.

network   The diagram in Figure 9-45 is an example of a **network.** The points are
vertices   arcs   called **vertices,** and the curves are called **arcs.** Using a network diagram, the

FIGURE 9-45

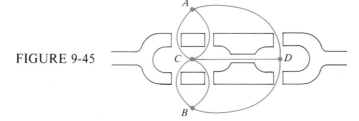

Königsberg bridge problem can be restated as follows: Is there a path through the network beginning at some vertex and ending at the same or another vertex such that each arc is traversed exactly once? A network having such a path is called **traversable;** that is, each arc is passed through exactly once.

Consider the networks in Figure 9-46. The first three networks, (a), (b), and (c), are traversable; the fourth network, (d), is not. Notice that the number of arcs meeting at each vertex in networks (a) and (c) is even. Any such vertex is called an **even vertex.** If the number of arcs meeting at a vertex is odd, it is called an **odd vertex.** In network (b), the only odd vertices are possible starting or stopping points. In network (d), which is not traversable, all the vertices are odd. If a network is traversable, each arrival at a vertex other than a starting or a stopping point requires a departure. Thus, each such vertex is even. The starting and stopping vertices in a traversable network may be even or odd as seen in Figures 9-46(a) and (b), respectively.

FIGURE 9-46

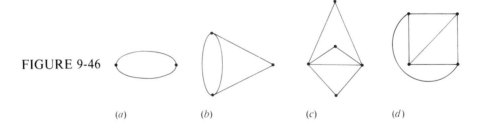

(a)   (b)   (c)   (d)

In general, networks have the following properties.

1. If a network has all even vertices, it is traversable. Any vertex can be a starting point, and the same vertex must be the stopping point.
2. If a network has two odd vertices, it is traversable. One odd vertex must be the starting point, and the other odd vertex must be the stopping point.
3. If a network has more than two odd vertices, it is not traversable.
4. There is no network with exactly one odd vertex.

Example 9-10   Which of the networks in Figure 9-47 are traversable?

FIGURE 9-47

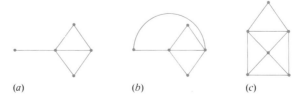

(a)   (b)   (c)

FIGURE 9-47
(con't.)

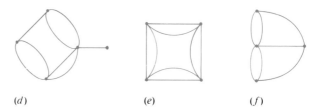

(d)   (e)   (f)

Solution | Networks (b) and (e) have all even vertices and therefore are traversable. Networks (a) and (c) have exactly two odd vertices and are traversable. Network (d) and (f) have four odd vertices and are not traversable.

Network (f) of Example 9-10 represents the Königsberg bridge problem. The network has four odd vertices, and consequently, the network is not traversable, and hence, no walk is possible to complete the problem.

Example 9-11 | Look at the floor plan of the house shown in Figure 9-48. Is it possible to go through all the rooms of the house and pass through each door only once?

FIGURE 9-48

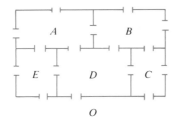

Solution | Represent the floor plan as a network. Designate the rooms and the outside as vertices and the paths through the doors as arcs.

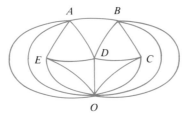

The network has more than two odd vertices, namely, A, B, D, and O. Thus, the network is not traversable, and it is impossible to go through all the rooms and pass through each door only once.

Network problems are useful in determining the most efficient routes for such tasks as mail delivery and garbage collection where it is desirable to travel along a street only once.

PROBLEM SET 9-5

1. Which of the following networks are traversable? If the network is traversable, draw an appropriate path labeling the starting and stopping vertices.

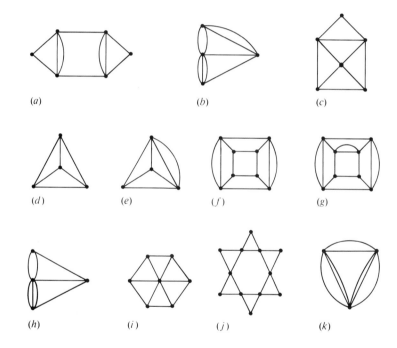

(a)   (b)   (c)

(d)   (e)   (f)   (g)

(h)   (i)   (j)   (k)

2. A city contains a river, three islands, and ten bridges as shown in the accompanying figure. Is it possible to take a walk around the city by starting at any land area and returning after visiting every part of the city and crossing each bridge exactly once? If so, show such a path both on the original figure and on the corresponding network.

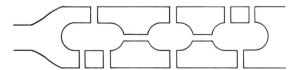

3. Use the accompanying floor plans for each of the following.
    (a) Draw a network that corresponds to each floor plan.
    (b) Determine if it is possible to pass through each room of each house by passing through each door exactly once. If possible, draw such a trip.

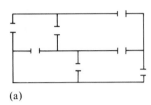

(a)

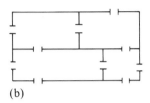

(b)

4. Can a person walk through each door once and only once and, also, go through both of the following houses with a single path? If possible, draw such a path.

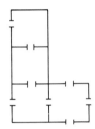

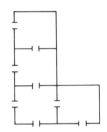

5. At a party, some people shake hands with each other. No person shakes hands more than once with the same person. A person who shakes hands with an odd number of people is called an odd fellow and a person who shakes hands with an even number of people is called an even fellow. Someone makes the statement, "At every party, regardless of how many handshakes takes place, the number of odd fellows is even."
    (a) Check the validity of the above statement for at least four different cases by drawing appropriate networks.
    (b) Is a similar statement regarding even fellows true? Why?

6. Euler's formula for polyhedra can be interpreted for networks by designating F as the number of regions in the plane, V as the number of vertices, and E as the number of arcs. For example, network (a) below separates the plane into three regions and network (b) forms only one region, the outside. For network (a), $V - E + F = 2 - 3 + 3 = 2$, and for network (b) $V - E + F = 6 - 5 + 1 = 2$. Verify Euler's formula for each of the networks in Problem 1.

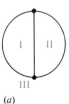

(a)

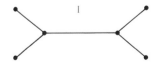

(b)

LABORATORY ACTIVITY

1. Take a strip of paper like the one shown below. Give one end a half-twist and join the ends by taping them. The surface obtained is called a Moebius strip.

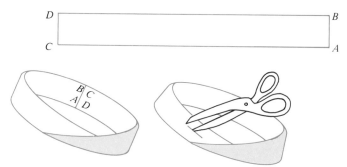

(a)   Use a pencil to shade one side of a Moebius strip. What do you discover?

(b)   Imagine cutting a Moebius strip all around, midway between the edges. What do you predict will happen? Now, do the actual cutting. What is the result?

(c)   Imagine cutting a Moebius strip one-third of the way from an edge and parallel to the edge all the way through until you return to the starting point. Predict the result. Then, actually do the cutting. Was your prediction correct?

(d)   Imagine cutting around a Moebius strip one-fourth of the way from an edge. Predict the result. Then, actually do the cutting. How does the result compare to the result of experiment (c)?

2. (a)   Take a strip of paper and give it two half-twists (one full twist). Then, join the ends together. Answer the questions in Problem 1.

(b)   Repeat the experiment in (a) using three half-twists.

(c)   Repeat the experiment in (a) using four half-twists. What do you find for odd-numbered twists? Even-numbered twists?

SOLUTION TO THE PRELIMINARY PROBLEM

Understanding the Problem

Tiff A. Nee has to cut assorted triangular pieces from a rectangular plate of glass for a project. The plate contained ten air bubbles, no three in a line. To aid in visualizing the plate, we draw a model as in Figure 9-49 and label the corners of the plate X, Y, Z, and W and the bubbles A through J. A possible way to cut the glass is illustrated with dotted lines.

Observe that in this particular model, there are twenty-two triangular

FIGURE 9-49

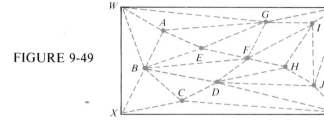

regions. There are many different ways that the bubbles and corners of the plate could be connected to produce the triangular regions. For example, instead of connecting B with W and X, we could have connected A with W and X to obtain a triangular region. Hence, in devising a solution to the problem, we must determine whether a different configuration yields a different number of triangles or whether the given constraints will always yield twenty-two triangular pieces.

Devising a Plan

The sum of the measures of the angles of all the triangles formed is 180 times the number of triangles. If we knew that sum, we could divide by 180 to find the number of triangles. What is the sum of the measures of all the angles in the triangles? Observe that in Figure 9-49 the angles of the triangles are either angles around the air bubbles or are in the corners of the rectangular plate. No matter how the triangles are drawn, the sum of the measures of the angles of the rectangle is always the same. The sum of the measures of the angles around each bubble is 360°. Since there are ten bubbles, the sum of the measures of the angles around the bubbles is $10 \cdot 360° = 3600°$. The sum of the measures of the four angles at the corners of the rectangular plate is 360°; thus, we can find the sum of the measures of the angles in the triangles.

Carrying Out the Plan

The sum of the measures of the angles in all the triangles is $3600° + 360° = 3960°$. Consequently, the number of triangles is $3960/180 = 22$, and our model gave us an accurate number.

Looking Back

The problem can be generalized to a plate of glass that is in the shape of a convex n-gon with m air bubbles. The procedure for solving the problem is similar to the one used in the original problem. The sum of the measures of the angles of the n-gon is $(n - 2)180$. The sum of the measures of the angles about the air bubbles is $360m$. Hence, the number of the triangles formed is

$$\frac{(n - 2)180 + 360m}{180} = n - 2 + 2m$$

QUESTIONS FROM THE CLASSROOM

1. A student claims that if any two planes that do not intersect are parallel, then any two lines that do not intersect should also be parallel. How do you respond?
2. A student says that it is actually impossible to measure an angle, since each angle is the union of two rays that extend infinitely and, therefore, continue forever. What is your response?
3. A student asks, if every rhombus is a parallelogram, why is a special name for a rhombus necessary? What is your reply?
4. A student asks whether a polygon whose sides are congruent is necessarily a regular polygon and whether a polygon with all angles congruent is necessarily a regular polygon. How do you answer?
5. A student thinks that a square is the only regular polygon with all right angles. She asks if this is true and if so, why. How do you answer?
6. A student says that a line is parallel to itself. How do you reply?
7. A student says that a line in the plane of the classroom ceiling cannot be parallel to a line in the plane of the classroom floor since the lines are not in the same plane. Is this student correct? Why?
8. A student says that she heard the shortest distance between any two points is a straight line. Therefore straight lines should have endpoints. What is your reply?

CHAPTER OUTLINE

I. Basic geometrical notions
   A. Properties of points, lines, and planes
      1. **Points, lines,** and **planes** are basic, but undefined, terms.
      2. Through any two points there is one and only one line.
      3. **Collinear points** are points that belong to the same line.
      4. **Parallel lines** are distinct lines in the same plane that do not intersect.
      5. **Skew lines** are two lines that do not intersect and are not contained in any single plane.
      6. A line that has no points in common with a plane is parallel to the plane.
      7. **Parallel planes** are planes that have no points in common.
      8. **Perpendicular lines** are two lines that intersect to form a right angle.
      9. A line and a plane are perpendicular if and only if they intersect and the line is perpendicular to every line in the plane that passes through the point of intersection.

10. Two planes are perpendicular if and only if one plane contains a line that is perpendicular to the other plane.

B. Plane figures
   1. A **simple closed curve** is a plane curve that can be traced so that the starting and stopping points are the same and no point other than the endpoint is traced more than once.
   2. A **polygon** is a simple closed curve that is the union of line segments such that no two segments with a common endpoint are collinear.
      (a) A **convex polygon** is a polygon with no diagonals in the exterior.
      (b) A **concave polygon** is a polygon with at least one diagonal in the exterior.
      (c) A **regular polygon** is a polygon in which all the angles are congruent and all the sides are congruent.

II. Angles
A. An **angle** is the union of two distinct noncollinear rays having a common endpoint.
   1. **Adjacent angles** are angles with a common vertex, a common side, and whose interiors do not overlap.
   2. **Vertical angles** are nonadjacent angles formed by two intersecting lines.
   3. A **right angle** has a measure of 90°.
   4. An **acute angle** is an angle whose measure is greater than 0° and less than 90°.
   5. An **obtuse angle** is an angle whose measure is greater than 90° and less than 180°.
   6. A **straight angle** has a measure of 180°.
   7. **Supplementary angles** are two angles the sum of whose measures is 180°.

   8. **Complementary angles** are two angles the sum of whose measures is 90°.
B. Two lines cut by a transversal are **parallel** if and only if either congruent corresponding angles, congruent alternate interior angles or congruent alternate exterior angles are formed.
C. The sum of the measures of the angles in a triangle is 180°.
D. The sum of the measures of the angles in a convex n-gon is $(n - 2)180°$.

III. Three dimensional figures
A. A **polyhedron** is a simple closed surface formed by polygonal regions.
B. **Euler's formula, $V + F - E = 2$,** holds for polyhedra, where V, E, and F represent the number of vertices, the number of edges, and the number of faces of a polyhedron, respectively.

*IV. Networks
A. A **network** is a collection of points called **vertices** and a collection of curves called **arcs.**
B. A vertex of a network is called an **even vertex** if the number of arcs meeting at the vertex is even. A vertex is called an **odd vertex** if the number of arcs meeting at a vertex is odd.
C. A network is called **traversable** if there is a path through the network such that each arc is passed through exactly once.
   1. If all the vertices of a network are even, then the network is traversable. Any vertex can be a starting point and the same vertex must be the stopping point.
   2. If a network has two odd vertices, it is traversable. One odd vertex must be the starting point and the other odd vertex must be the stopping point.
   3. If a network has more than two odd vertices, it is not traversable.
   4. No network has exactly one odd vertex.

CHAPTER TEST

1. (a) Give three different names for *m*.
   (b) Name two different rays on *m* with endpoint *B*.
   (c) Find a simpler name for $\overrightarrow{AB} \cap \overrightarrow{BA}$.
   (d) Find a simpler name for $\overrightarrow{AB} \cap \overleftrightarrow{BC}$.
   (e) Find a simpler name for $\overrightarrow{BA} \cap \overrightarrow{AC}$.

2. In the figure at the right, $\overleftrightarrow{PQ}$ is perpendicular to α.
   (a) Name a pair of skew lines.
   (b) Using only the letters in the figure, name as many planes as possible each perpendicular to α.
   (c) What is the intersection of the planes *APQ* and β.
   (d) Is there a single plane containing *A*, *B*, *P*, and *Q*? Explain your answer.

3. List at least three ways to determine a plane.

4. For each of the following sketch two parallelograms, if possible, that satisfy the given conditions.
   (a) Their intersection is a single point.
   (b) Their intersection is exactly two points.
   (c) Their intersection is exactly three points.
   (d) Their intersection is exactly one line segment.

5. Draw each of the following curves:
   (a) A simple closed curve   (b) A closed curve that is not simple
   (c) A concave hexagon   (d) A convex decagon

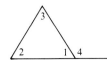

6. Prove that the measure of ∡4 on the left equals the sum of the measures of ∡2 and ∡3.

7. (a) Can a triangle have two obtuse angles? Justify your answer.
   (b) Can a parallelogram have four acute angles? Justify your answer.

8. In a certain triangle, the measure of one angle is twice the measure of the smallest angle. The measure of the third angle is seven times greater than the measure of the smallest angle. Find the measures of each of the angles in the triangle.

9. (a) Explain how to derive an expression for the sum of the measures of the angles in a convex *n*-gon.
   (b) In a certain regular polygon, the measure of each angle is 176°. How many sides does the polygon have?

10. (a) Sketch a convex polyhedron with at least ten vertices.
    (b) Count the number of vertices, edges, and faces for the polyhedron in part (a) and determine if Euler's formula holds for this polyhedron.

11. If $3x°$ and $(6x - 18)°$ are measures of corresponding angles formed by two parallel lines and a transversal, what is the value of *x*?

12. Find $6°48'59'' + 28°19'36''$. Write your answer in simplest terms.

13. In the figure on the right ℓ is parallel to *m*, and $m(∡1) = 60°$.
    Find each of the following.
    (a) $m(∡3)$
    (b) $m(∡6)$
    (c) $m(∡8)$

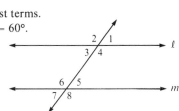

14. If a pyramid has an octagon for a base, how many lateral faces does it have?
15. If ABC is a right triangle and $m (\angle)A = 42°$, what is the measure of the other acute angle?
16. (a) Which of the following networks is traversable?
    (b) Find a corresponding path for those networks that are traversable.

     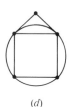

(a)   (b)   (c)   (d)

SELECTED BIBLIOGRAPHY

Alexick, H. F., and F. R. Kidder. "Why Is a Rectangle Not a Square?" *Arithmetic Teacher,* **27**(December 1979):26–27.

Anderson, H. "Griefless Graphing for the Novice." *The Mathematics Teacher,* **66**(October 1973):519–522.

Barr, S. *Experiments in Topology.* New York: Thomas Y. Crowell, 1964.

Beard, R. S. *Patterns in Space.* Palo Alto, Calif: Creative Publications, 1973.

Bright, G. W. "Using Tables to Solve Some Geometry Problems." *Arithmetic Teacher,* **25**(May 1978), 39–43.

Brydegaard, M., and J. E. Inskeep, Jr. *Readings in Geometry from the Arithmetic Teacher.* Washington, D.C.: National Council of Teachers of Mathematics, 1970.

Cohen, D. *Inquiry in Mathematics via the Geoboard, Teacher Guide.* New York: Walker Educational Book Corp., 1967.

Cundy, H. M., and A. P. Rollett. *Mathematical Models.* London: Oxford University Press, 1961.

Gilbert, E. N. "The Ways to Build a Box." *The Mathematics Teacher,* **64**(December 1971):689–695.

Golomb, S. W. *Polyominoes.* New York: Charles Scribner's Sons, 1965.

Henderson, G. L., and C. P. Collier. "Geometric Activities for Later Childhood Education." *The Arithmetic Teacher,* **20**(October 1973):444–453.

Immerzeel, G. "Geometric Activities for Early Childhood Education." *The Arithmetic Teacher,* **20**(October 1973):438–443.

Laycock, M. *Straw Polyhedra.* Palo Alto, Calif.: Creative Publications, 1970.

Lietzmann, W. *Visual Topology.* London: Chatto and Windus, 1969.

O'Daffer, P. G. and S. R. Clemens. *Geometry: an Investigative Approach.* Reading, Mass.: Addison-Wesley, 1976.

Ore, Oystein. *Graphs and Their Uses.* New York: Random House, L. W. Singer, 1963.

Phillips, J. P. "The History of the Dodecahedron." *The Mathematics Teacher,* **58**(March 1965): 248–250.

Ryan, Sister M. Kara, S.S.N.D. "Probability and the Platonic Solids." *The Mathematics Teacher,* **64**(November 1971):621–624.

Shengle, C. E. "A Look at Regular and Semi-Regular Polyhedra." *The Mathematics Teacher,* **65**(December 1972):713–718.

Toth, L. F. *Regular Figures.* Oxford: Pergamon Press, 1964.

Trigg, C. W. "Collapsible Models of Regular Octahedrons." *The Mathematics Teacher,* **65**(October 1972):530–533.

Wahl, M. Stoessel. "Marshmallows, Toothpicks, and Geodesic Domes." *Arithmetic Teacher,* **25**(December 1977):39–42.

Wenninger, M. *Polyhedron Models.* New York: Cambridge University Press, 1970.

Wenninger, M. *Polyhedron Models for the Classroom.* Washington, D.C.: National Council of Teachers of Mathematics, 1966.

Metric Measure, Constructions, and Congruence

PRELIMINARY PROBLEM

The June 1979 *National Geographic* reported that archaeologists had found a lost Virginia settlement. Among the remains was a fragment of a saucer as shown. To restore the saucer, the

archaeologists had to determine the radius of the
original saucer. How can they find the radius?

10-1   THE METRIC SYSTEM: UNITS OF LENGTH

Early attempts at measurement used hands, arms, and feet as units of
measure. These early crude measurements were eventually refined and
standardized by the English into a very complicated system, including three
types of weights: troy, avoirdupois, and apothecary. The English system of
weights and measures has been used in many countries, including the United
States. When they are faced with problems using English measures, many
people feel like Peppermint Patty does in the cartoon.

© 1974 United Feature Syndicate, Inc.

The United States, along with many other countries, is now changing to
the metric system. The metric system was first proposed by Gabriel Mouton
in France in 1670. However, not until the French Revolution in 1790 did the
French Academy of Sciences bring various groups together to develop the
new system. The academy recognized the need for a standard base unit of
linear measurement. The members chose 1/10 000 000 of the distance from
the equator to the North Pole, on a meridian through Paris, as the base unit of
meter   length and called it the **meter.** Later, the meter was redefined in terms of
krypton-86 wavelengths. The name *meter* was derived from the Greek word
metron meaning "a measure." Base units of volume and mass were derived
from the meter. For ease in computation, larger and smaller units were
created by multiplying or dividing the base units by powers of 10. Thus, the
metric system is a decimal system, just as our monetary system is a decimal
system.

The krypton-86 definition of meter is important for accuracy but not
very meaningful to everyday life. If you turn your head away from your

outstretched arm, then the distance from your nose to your fingertip is about 1 meter. Also, 1 meter is about the distance from a door knob to the floor. In fact, 1 meter is about 39 inches, slightly longer than 1 yard. (Most educators strongly recommend that the metric system be taught independently and not taught as conversions to and from the English system.)

Different units of length in the metric system are obtained by combining an appropriate prefix with the base unit. The prefixes, the multiplication factors they indicate, and their symbols are given in Table 10-1.

TABLE 10-1

Prefix	Factor	Symbol
kilo	1000 (one thousand)	k
hecto	100 (one hundred)	h
deka	10 (ten)	da
deci	0.1 (one tenth)	d
centi	0.01 (one hundredth)	c
milli	0.001 (one thousandth)	m

Remark

Hecto, deka, and deci are not common prefixes and have limited use. Kilo, hecto, and deka, which make the base unit greater, are Greek prefixes, whereas deci, centi, and milli, which decrease the base unit, are Latin prefixes.

Using the metric prefixes along with meter gives the names for different units of length. Table 10-2 gives these units along with their relationship to the meter and the symbol for each. The symbol m stands for meter. (Notice that there is no period after the m. It is a symbol rather than an abbreviation.)

TABLE 10-2

Unit	Symbol	Relationship to Basic Unit
kilometer	km	1000 meters
hectometer*	hm	100 meters
dekameter*	dam	10 meters
meter	m	base unit
decimeter*	dm	0.1 meter
centimeter	cm	0.01 meter
millimeter	mm	0.001 meter
*Not commonly used		

Each meter can be separated into ten congruent parts called decimeters. One decimeter is about the width of the hand or the length of an orange Cuisenaire rod. A decimeter can be further subdivided into ten congruent parts called centimeters. In other words, 1 cm = 0.1 dm = 0.01 m. One centimeter is about the width of your little finger, the diameter of the head of a thumbtack, or the width of a white Cuisenaire rod. A centimeter can be separated into ten congruent parts called millimeters. Thus, 1 mm = 0.1 cm = 0.01 dm = 0.001 m. One millimeter is about the thickness of a paper clip or a dime. Some estimations for a meter, a decimeter, a centimeter, and a millimeter are shown in Figure 10-1.

FIGURE 10-1

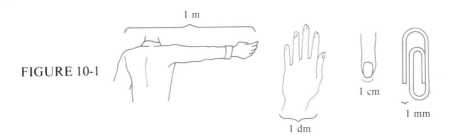

The units dekameter and hectometer represent 10 m and 100 m, respectively. One hectometer is a little more than the length of a football field. The kilometer is used for measuring long distances. One kilometer is 1000 m long. Thus, about nine football fields laid end to end together are approximately 1 km long.

Since metric units of length differ by powers of 10, the conversion from one metric unit to another is easy. As with money, simply move the decimal point to the left or right, depending on the units.

0.123 km = 1.23 hm = 12.3 dam = 123 m = 1230 dm = 12 300 cm = 123 000 mm

To convert units using the chart in Figure 10-2, count the number of steps from one unit to the other and move the decimal that many steps in the same direction.

FIGURE 10-2

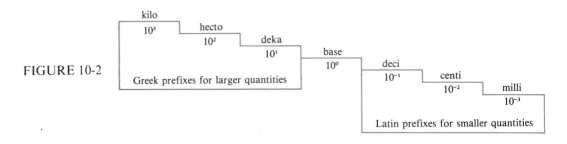

Example 10-1 | 1.4 km = ? m

Solution | Since 1 km = 1000 m, to change from kilometers to meters, multiply by 1000. Therefore, move the decimal point three places to the right. Hence, 1.4 km = 1400 m.

Example 10-2 | 285 mm = ? m

Solution | Since 1 mm = 0.001 m, to change from millimeters to meters, multiply by 0.001. In other words, move the decimal point three places to the left. Thus, 285 mm = 0.285 m.

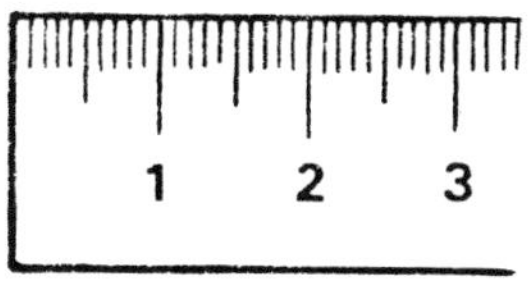

In geometry, units of length are usually used to measure distances along lines and, thus, are called linear measure. Recall that in the development of the number line (Chapter 3), we chose a point on the line to represent 0 and a second point to represent 1. If we select the points so that the distance between 0 and 1 is 1 centimeter and develop the number line accordingly, then the number line can be used to measure lengths of segments in terms of centimeters. Similarly, by making the distance between 0 and 1 an inch, a meter, a foot, and so on, we can develop other rulers for measuring lengths. Figure 10-3 shows part of a centimeter ruler.

FIGURE 10-3

The following are three basic properties of distance.

1. The distance between any two points A and B is greater than or equal to 0, written $AB \geq 0$.
2. The distance between any two points A and B is the same as the distance between B and A, written $AB = BA$.
3. For any three points A, B, and C, the distance between A and B plus the distance between B and C is greater than or equal to the distance between A and C, written $AB + BC \geq AC$.

Remark | The third property is sometimes called the **triangular inequality.** The sum
triangular inequality | of the lengths of two sides of a triangle is always greater than or equal to the length of the third side. Notice that as in Figure 10-4, the equality holds if and only if A, B, and C are collinear.

FIGURE 10-4

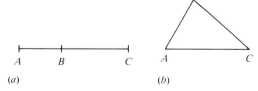

(a)   (b)

perimeter   The **perimeter** of a simple closed curve is the length of the curve; that is, the distance around the figure. If a figure is a polygon, its perimeter is the sum of the lengths of the sides.

Example 10-3   Find the perimeter P of each of the shapes in Figure 10-5.

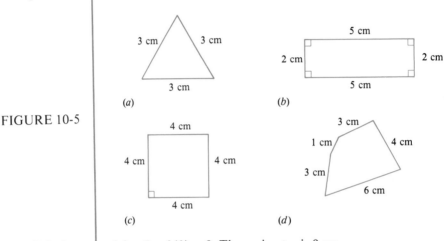

FIGURE 10-5

Solution   (a) $P = 3(3) = 9$. The perimeter is 9 cm.
(b) $P = 2(2) + 2(5) = 14$. The perimeter is 14 cm.
(c) $P = 4(4) = 16$. The perimeter is 16 cm.
(d) $P = 1 + 3 + 4 + 6 + 3 = 17$. The perimeter is 17 cm.

PROBLEM SET 10-1

1. A millimeter is the smallest distance pictured on the metric ruler in the following figure. Starting from the left end of the ruler, the distance from the end to A is 1 mm, and the distance from the end to B is 10 mm, or 1 cm. The distance from the end to J is 100 mm, 10 cm, or 1 dm.

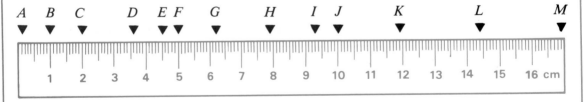

Use the ruler to answer each of the following.
(a) C points to _____ mm or _____ cm
(b) D points to _____ mm or _____ cm
(c) E points to _____ mm or _____ cm
(d) F points to _____ cm or _____ dm
(e) G points to _____ cm or _____ dm
(f) H points to _____ cm or _____ dm

(g)   *I* points to _____ dm or _____ cm
(h)   *K* points to _____ cm or _____ mm
(i)   *L* points to _____ mm or _____ cm
(j)   *M* points to _____ dm or _____ cm

2.   Draw segments that you estimate to be of the following lengths. Then, using a metric ruler, check the estimates.

    (a)   10 mm   (b)   100 mm   (c)   1 cm   (d)   10 cm   (e)   0.01 m
    (f)   15 cm   (g)   0.1 m   (h)   27 mm   (i)   23 cm   (j)   5 cm

3.   Estimate and then measure the following segment. Express the measurement in each of the following units.

    (a)   millimeters   (b)   centimeters   (c)   meters

4.   Choose an appropriate metric unit and estimate each of the following. Measure, if possible, to check the estimate.

    (a)   The length of a pencil   (b)   The diameter of a nickel
    (c)   The width of the top of a desk   (d)   The thickness of the top of a desk
    (e)   The length of this sheet of paper   (f)   The height of a door
    (g)   Your height   (h)   Your handspan

5.   Complete the following table.

Item	m	dm	cm	mm
(a) Length of a piece of paper			350	
(b) Height of a woman	1.63			
(c) Width of a film				35
(d) Length of a cigarette		1		
(e) Length of two meter sticks laid end to end				

6.   For each of the following, place a decimal point in the number to make the sentence reasonable.

    (a)   A stack of ten dimes is 1000 mm high.
    (b)   The desk is 770 m high.
    (c)   It is 100 m across the street.
    (d)   A dollar bill is 155 cm long.
    (e)   The basketball player is 1950 cm tall.
    (f)   A new piece of chalk is about 8100 cm long.
    (g)   The speed limit in town was 400 km/hr.

7.   List the following in decreasing order:

    8 cm, 38 dm, 5218 mm, 245 cm, 91 mm, 6 m, 700 mm, 52 dm

8. Complete each of the following:
   (a) 17 m + 24 dm = _____ dm
   (b) 1 m + 4 dm + 2 cm = _____ cm
   (c) 3 m + 13 dm + 3 cm = _____ cm

9. Guess the perimeter of each figure in centimeters and then check the estimates using a **ruler**.

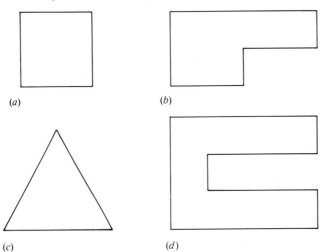

(a)   (b)

(c)   (d)

10. Complete each of the following.
   (a) 10 mm = _____ cm   (b) 17 cm = _____ m
   (c) 262 m = _____ dm   (d) 3 km = _____ m
   (e) 30 mm = _____ m   (f) 0.17 km = _____ m
   (g) 35 m = _____ cm   (h) 26 418 m = _____ km
   (i) 359 mm = _____ m   (j) 1 mm = _____ cm
   (k) 647 mm = _____ dm   (l) 1 cm = _____ dm
   (m) 5 km = _____ dam   (n) 51.3 dam = _____ hm

11. Find the perimeters of each of the following.

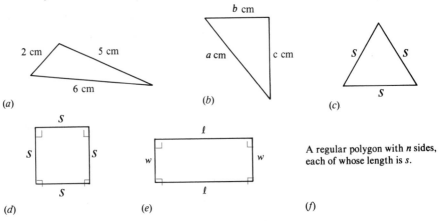

(a)

(b)

(c)

(d)

(e)

(f) A regular polygon with n sides, each of whose length is s.

LABORATORY ACTIVITY

1. Are you a square, rectangle, or an oblong? To find out, compare your height and reach (double arm). If your height and reach differ by less than 5 cm, you are a square. If your height exceeds your reach by 5 cm, you are a rectangle. If your reach exceeds your height by 5 cm, you are an oblong.
2. Do you have a perfect metric body? To find out, measure your height in centimeters and your mass in kilograms. If their difference is exactly 100, you have a perfect metric body.
3. Measure 10 meters. Count the number of paces it takes to cover 10 meters. Repeat the experiment several times

10-2 CONGRUENCE THROUGH CONSTRUCTIONS

In mathematics, the word *congruence* is used to describe objects that have exactly the same size and shape. For example, the two squares in Figure 10-6 are congruent because each has a side of measure 2 cm. We say that *ABCD* is congruent to *EFGH* and write *ABCD* ≅ *EFGH*.

Tracing is a method for determining congruence in elementary schools. For example, a tracing of one square in Figure 10-6 can be made to match exactly with a tracing of the other square.

Since any two line segments have the same shape, the only requirement for congruence is that they have the same length. Two angles are congruent if their measures are the same.

Ancient Greek mathematicians constructed geometric figures with a straightedge (no markings on it) and a collapsible compass. They thought that the use of any measuring aids weakened their mathematical arguments. Figure 10-7(a) shows a modern compass. It is used to mark off and duplicate lengths but not to measure them. The compass is also used to draw arcs or circles as in Figure 10-7(b). To draw a circle or an arc, open the compass to

2 cm

2 cm

FIGURE 10-6

FIGURE 10-7

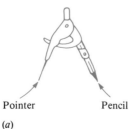

Pointer   Pencil

(a)

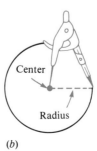

Center

Radius

(b)

circle
radius
center
arc

some width; hold the pointer in place, marking the center of the circle or arc; and then move the pencil. The figure formed will be a circle or an arc. The construction of a circle with a compass shows that a **circle** can be defined as the set of all points in a plane at a given distance, **radius,** from a given point, **center.** The notation used in this text for a circle with center C is circle C.

An **arc** of a circle is defined as the set of two points of the circle and all the points on the circle between those two points. An arc is either a part of a circle or the entire circle. Two points on a circle determine two different arcs. An arc is normally named by three letters, such as arc ACB as in Figure 10-8, to avoid this ambiguity. Arc ACB is denoted by $\overarc{ACB}$. In this notation, the first and last letters indicate the endpoints of the arc, while the middle letter indicates which of two possible arcs is intended. If there is no danger of ambiguity in a discussion, we will use two letters to name the smaller arc formed. For example, in Figure 10-8, the smaller arc will be named either

minor arc
major arc
semicircle

$\overarc{ACB}$ or $\overarc{AB}$. The smaller arc is called the **minor arc.** The larger arc, called the **major arc,** will always be named by three letters, such as $\overarc{ADB}$. If the major arc and the minor arc of a circle are the same size, each is called a **semicircle.**

There are many ways to construct a segment congruent to a given segment, $\overline{AB}$. A natural approach is to use a ruler, measure $\overline{AB}$, and then draw the congruent segment. A different way is to trace $\overline{AB}$ onto another piece of paper. A third method is to use a straightedge and compass. To copy $\overline{AB}$ on any line ℓ using a compass, first fix the compass so that the pointer is on A and the pencil is on B as in Figure 10-9(a). The compass opening represents the length of $\overline{AB}$. Then, on ℓ, choose a point C. Place the point of the compass at C and strike an arc that intersects the line as in Figure 10-9(b). Label the point of intersection of the arc and the line as D. Then, $\overline{AB} \cong \overline{CD}$.

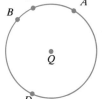

FIGURE 10-8

FIGURE 10-9

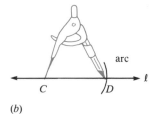

(a)   (b)

In Figure 10-10(a), circle C is given. By placing the compass point at an arbitrary point Q and opening the compass to a width equal to CR, circle Q can be constructed congruent to circle C. Thus, *two circles are congruent if their radii have the same length.*

FIGURE 10-10

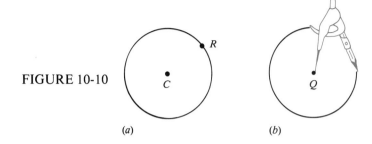

(a)   (b)

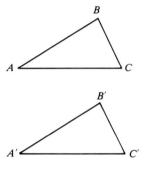

FIGURE 10-11

We use the concept of congruence for segments and angles as the basis for determining whether polygons, specifically triangles, are congruent. Attempting to construct congruent triangles provides motivation for necessary and sufficient conditions for determining congruent triangles.

Consider the two triangles shown in Figure 10-11. If triangle ABC is congruent to triangle $A'B'C'$, written $\triangle ABC \cong \triangle A'B'C'$, then the congruency establishes a one-to-one correspondence between vertices A and A', B and B', C and C' such that $\overline{AB} \cong \overline{A'B'}$, $\overline{AC} \cong \overline{A'C'}$, $\overline{BC} \cong \overline{B'C'}$, $\angle A \cong \angle A'$, $\angle B \cong \angle B'$, and $\angle C \cong \angle C'$.

The order of the letters in the symbolic congruence is important. For example, in Figure 10-12, if $\triangle ABC \cong \triangle DEF$, then vertex A corresponds to vertex D, B corresponds to E, and C corresponds to F. This correspondence identifies the congruent angles and sides of the triangles.

FIGURE 10-12

$\triangle ABC \cong \triangle DEF$

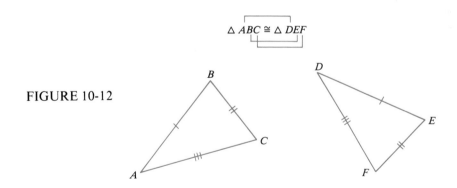

$\angle A \cong \angle D$, $\angle B \cong \angle E$, and $\angle C \cong \angle F$

$\overline{AB} \cong \overline{DE}$, $\overline{BC} \cong \overline{EF}$, and $\overline{AC} \cong \overline{DF}$

Is it necessary to use all three sides and all three angles of a $\triangle ABC$ to construct another triangle congruent to it? $\triangle ABC$ can be duplicated by copying fewer parts of the triangle. For example, using only segments of lengths *AB*, *BC*, and *AC* as shown in Figure 10-13(a), it is possible to construct a triangle congruent to △*ABC*.

FIGURE 10-13

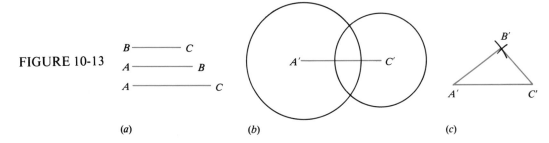

(a)   (b)   (c)

First construct $\overline{A'C'}$ so that it is congruent to $\overline{AC}$. To complete the triangle construction, the other vertex, *B′*, must be located. The distance from *A′* to *B′* is *AB*, and all points at a distance *AB* from *A′* are on a circle with center at *A′* and radius *AB*. Similarly, *B′* is on a circle with center *C′* and radius of length *BC*. Figure 10-13(b) shows the two circles. Since *B′* is on both circles, the only possible locations for *B′* are at the points where the two circles intersect. Either point is acceptable. Usually a picture of the contruction shows only one possibility, and the construction uses only arcs as pictured in Figure 10-13(c).

The construction in Figure 10-13 suggests that knowing the lengths of the three sides of a triangle is sufficient to determine the size and shape of the triangle. In other words, if three sides of one triangle are congruent to three sides of another triangle, respectively, then the triangles are congruent. This
side, side, side (SSS)   property is usually called **side, side, side** and is abbreviated SSS.

Property | **Side, Side, Side (SSS)**   If the three sides of one triangle are congruent to the three sides of a second triangle, respectively, then the triangles are congruent.

Example 10-4 | For each of the parts in Figure 10-14, use SSS to explain why the pair of triangles given is congruent.

FIGURE 10-14

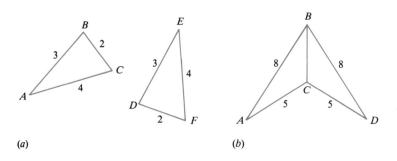

(a)   (b)

Solution

(a) $\triangle ABC \simeq \triangle EDF$ since $\overline{AB} \simeq \overline{ED}$, $\overline{BC} \simeq \overline{DF}$, and $\overline{AC} \simeq \overline{EF}$.
(b) $\triangle ABC \simeq \triangle DBC$ since $\overline{AB} \simeq \overline{DB}$, $\overline{AC} \simeq \overline{DC}$, and $\overline{BC} \simeq \overline{BC}$.

We use the SSS notion of congruent triangles to construct an angle congruent to a given angle $\measuredangle B$ by making $\measuredangle B$ a part of a triangle and then by reproducing this triangle. For example, given $\measuredangle B$, in Figure 10-15(a), draw a segment having endpoints A and C on the sides of $\measuredangle B$ to determine $\triangle ABC$.

FIGURE 10-15

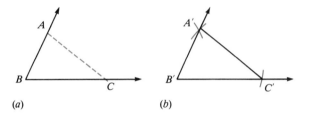

(a)   (b)

Then construct $\triangle A'B'C'$ congruent to $\triangle ABC$ using SSS as shown in Figure 10-15(b). Since congruent triangles have corresponding congruent parts, $\measuredangle B \simeq \measuredangle B'$.

A more efficient way to copy $\measuredangle B$ is as follows. First construct an isosceles triangle, $\triangle ABC$, with $\overline{AB} \simeq \overline{BC}$ by marking off any arc $\overset{\frown}{AC}$ with center B. Then, duplicate the triangle. Figure 10-16 shows the construction.

Three sides of a triangle determine the triangle. Are two sides sufficient to construct a triangle congruent to a given triangle? Two line segments are given in Figure 10-17(a). Figure 10-17(b) shows three different triangles with sides congruent to the given segments. The length of the third side depends on the measure of the angle between the other two sides. Hence, congruent triangles are not determined by two segments; it is also necessary

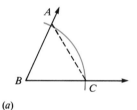

(a)

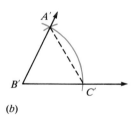

(b)

FIGURE 10-16

FIGURE 10-17

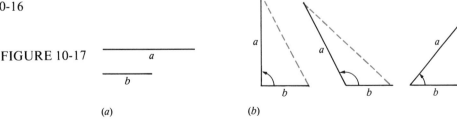

(a)   (b)

to specify the angle included between the segments. For example, Figure 10-18 shows the construction of a triangle congruent to $\triangle ABC$ using two sides $\overline{AB}$ and $\overline{AC}$ and the *included angle* $\measuredangle A$ formed by these sides. First, a

FIGURE 10-18

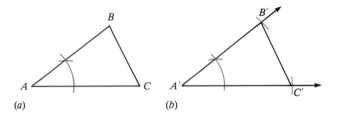

(a)   (b)

ray with an arbitrary endpoint A' is drawn, and $\overline{A'C'}$ is constructed congruent to $\overline{AC}$. Then, $\angle A'$ is constructed so that $\angle A' \simeq \angle A$, and B' is marked on the side of $\angle A'$ not containing C' so that $\overline{A'B'} \simeq \overline{AB}$. Connecting B' and C' completes $\triangle A'B'C'$ so that $\triangle A'B'C' \simeq \triangle ABC$.

Thus, two triangles are congruent if two corresponding sides and the included angle of each triangle are congruent. This property is called **side, angle, side** and is abbreviated SAS.

side, angle, side (SAS)

Property | **Side, Angle, Side (SAS)**   If two sides and the included angle of one triangle are congruent to two sides and the included angle of another triangle, respectively, then the two triangles are congruent.

Remark | When A is written between S and S, as in SAS, it is assumed to be the included angle.

Example 10-5 | For each part of Figure 10-19, use SAS to prove that the pair of triangles given is congruent.

FIGURE 10-19

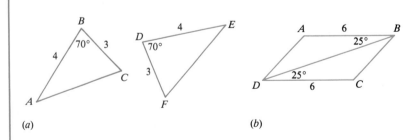

(a)   (b)

Solution | (a) $\triangle ABC \simeq \triangle EDF$ since $\overline{AB} \simeq \overline{ED}$, $\angle B \simeq \angle D$, and $\overline{BC} \simeq \overline{DF}$.
(b) $\triangle ABD \simeq \triangle CDB$ since $\overline{AB} \simeq \overline{CD}$, $\angle ABD \simeq \angle CDB$, and $\overline{DB} \simeq \overline{DB}$.

Example 10-6   Given isosceles triangle ABC with $\overline{AB} \cong \overline{AC}$ and $\overrightarrow{AD}$ the bisector of $\angle A$ as shown in Figure 10-20 use SAS to prove that $\angle B \cong \angle C$.

FIGURE 10-20

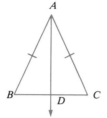

Solution   Since $\overrightarrow{AD}$ is the bisector of $\angle A$, then $\angle BAD \cong \angle CAD$. Also, $\overline{AD} \cong \overline{AD}$ and $\overline{AB} \cong \overline{AC}$, so $\triangle BAD \cong \triangle CAD$ by SAS. Therefore, $\angle B \cong \angle C$ since the angles are corresponding parts of congruent triangles.

Remark   Example 10-6 proves that the *base angles of an isosceles triangle are congruent*.

   If, in two triangles, two sides and an angle not included between these sides are congruent, respectively, the information is not sufficient to guarantee congruent triangles. For example, use $\overline{AB}$, $\overline{AC}$, and $\angle C$ of Figure 10-21(a). By making $\overline{A'C'} \cong \overline{AC}$, reproducing $\angle C$ as $\angle C'$, and finding the set of all points at a distance AB from A', it is possible to construct two noncongruent triangles as shown in Figures 10-21(b) and (c). In certain special cases, if the arc formed by the circle with center A' and radius AB intersects the side of $\angle C$ in exactly one point, only one triangle can be formed. (For what kind of triangles does this happen? For what cases is no triangle formed?)

FIGURE 10-21

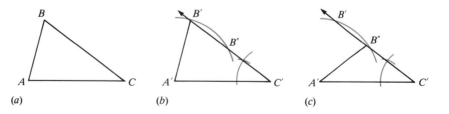

(a)   (b)   (c)

   Can a triangle be constructed congruent to a given triangle using two angles and a side? There are two possibilities, one with the side included between the angles and one with the side not between the angles. Figure 10-22 shows the construction of a triangle congruent to △*ABC* using ∡*A* and ∡*C* and the included side $\overline{AC}$. Hence, △*A′B′C′* can be constructed congruent to

angle, side, angle (ASA)   △*ABC*. This property of congruence is called **angle, side, angle** and is abbreviated ASA.

FIGURE 10-22

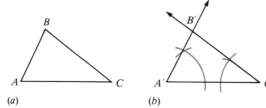

(a)   (b)

Property   **Angle, Side, Angle, (ASA)**   If two angles and the included side of one triangle are congruent to two angles and the included side of another triangle, respectively, then the triangles are congruent.

angle, angle, side (AAS)   **Angle, angle, side** (abbreviated AAS) follows directly from ASA. Since the sum of the measures of the angles in any triangle is 180°, if two angles in one triangle are congruent to two angles in another triangle, then the third angles must also be congruent. Consequently, the triangles are congruent by ASA.

Property   **Angle, Angle, Side (AAS)**   If two angles and a side of one triangle are congruent to two angles and a side of another triangle, respectively, then the triangles are congruent.

Example 10-7   Use ASA to prove that the given pairs of triangles in Figure 10-23 are congruent.

FIGURE 10-23

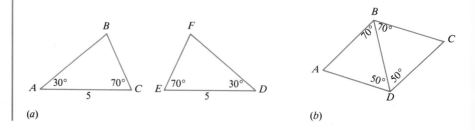

(a)   (b)

Solution

(a) $\angle A \simeq \angle D$, $\overline{AC} \simeq \overline{DE}$, and $\angle C \simeq \angle E$. Consequently, by ASA, $\triangle ABC \simeq \triangle DFE$.

(b) $\angle ABD \simeq \angle CBD$, $\overline{BD} \simeq \overline{BD}$, and $\angle ADB \simeq \angle CDB$. Consequently, by ASA, $\triangle ABD \simeq \triangle CBD$.

Example 10-8

Use AAS to prove that the given pairs of triangles in Figure 10-24 are congruent.

FIGURE 10-24

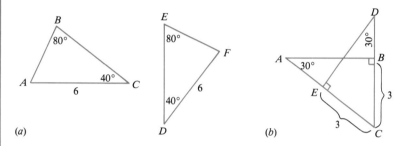

(a) (b)

Solution

(a) $\angle B \simeq \angle E$, $\angle C \simeq \angle D$, and $\overline{AC} \simeq \overline{FD}$. Consequently, by AAS, $\triangle ABC \simeq \triangle FED$.

(b) $\angle A \simeq \angle D$, $\angle ABC \simeq \angle DEC$, and $\overline{BC} \simeq \overline{EC}$. Consequently, by AAS, $\triangle ABC \simeq \triangle DEC$.

In Figure 10-25, the angles of one triangle are congruent to corresponding angles in another triangle, and the triangles are not congruent. Thus, an AAA property for congruency does not exist. (The triangles are *similar,* a concept discussed later in this chapter.)

FIGURE 10-25

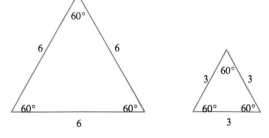

The properties of congruent triangles can be used in a variety of ways. One common use is to show that angles or segments of a given figure are congruent.

Example 10-9

Given square $ABCD$ in Figure 10-26, use congruent triangles to prove that the diagonals $\overline{AC}$ and $\overline{BD}$ are congruent.

FIGURE 10-26

Solution

By the definition of a square, $\overline{AB} \cong \overline{BC} \cong \overline{CD} \cong \overline{DA}$ and $\angle A \cong \angle B \cong \angle C \cong \angle D$ (since each is a right angle). Showing that $\triangle ADB$ and $\triangle BCA$ are congruent implies that the corresponding parts, $\overline{AC}$ and $\overline{BD}$, are congruent. In the two triangles $\overline{AD} \cong \overline{BC}$, $\overline{AB} \cong \overline{AB}$, and $\angle A \cong \angle B$. Hence, by SAS, $\triangle ADB \cong \triangle BCA$, and thus, $\overline{AC} \cong \overline{BD}$.

Example 10-10

Prove that a quadrilateral in which all sides are congruent is a rhombus.

Solution

Suppose all sides of quadrilateral $ABCD$ are congruent (Figure 10-27(a)). To prove that the figure is a rhombus, we must show that it is a parallelogram. (A rhombus is a parallelogram in which all sides are congruent.) To prove that the figure is a parallelogram, we must show that opposite sides are parallel. To prove that lines are parallel, a pair of congruent alternate interior angles, alternate exterior angles, or corresponding angles formed by a transversal are needed. Thus, to show that $\overleftrightarrow{BC}$ and $\overleftrightarrow{AD}$ are parallel, a transversal such as the diagonal $\overline{AC}$ in Figure 10-27(b) is needed. The diagonal forms $\angle 1$ and $\angle 2$, which are alternate interior angles of the lines $\overleftrightarrow{BC}$ and $\overleftrightarrow{AD}$. Are these angles congruent? Using SSS, we see that $\triangle ABC \cong \triangle ADC$, and hence, the corresponding parts of the triangles, specifically the desired angles, are congruent. It follows that $\overleftrightarrow{BC} \parallel \overleftrightarrow{AD}$. From the congruence of triangles ABC and ADC, it follows that $\angle 3 \cong \angle 4$ and hence that $\overleftrightarrow{AB} \parallel \overleftrightarrow{DC}$. (Why?) Thus, $ABCD$ is a parallelogram and hence a rhombus.

FIGURE 10-27

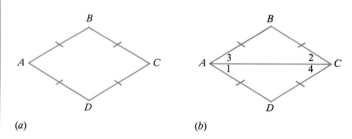

(a)   (b)

Determining congruency conditions for polygons other than triangles is not an easy task. For example, the SSS property for congruent triangles has no analogy for quadrilaterals. The quadrilaterals in Figure 10-28 are not the same shape. One way to be sure that two polygons are congruent is to know that all corresponding sides and angles of the polygons are congruent. Another way is to visualize "moving" one figure to see if it "fits" exactly on top of the other figure. The moving process is discussed in more detail in section 10-4.

FIGURE 10-28

PROBLEM SET 10-2

1. For each of the following, determine whether the given conditions are sufficient to prove that $\triangle PQR \cong \triangle MNO$. Justify your answer.
   (a) $\angle Q \cong \angle N, \angle P \cong \angle M, \overline{PQ} \cong \overline{MN}$
   (b) $\angle R \cong \angle O, \angle P \cong \angle M, \overline{QR} \cong \overline{NO}$
   (c) $\overline{PQ} \cong \overline{MN}, \overline{PR} \cong \overline{MO}, \angle N \cong \angle Q$
   (d) $\overline{PQ} \cong \overline{MN}, \overline{PR} \cong \overline{MO}, \angle P \cong \angle M$
   (e) $\overline{PQ} \cong \overline{MN}, \overline{PR} \cong \overline{MO}, \overline{QR} \cong \overline{NO}$
   (f) $\angle P \cong \angle M, \angle Q \cong \angle N, \angle R \cong \angle O$
2. For each of the following, determine whether the two triangles, (1) and (2), are congruent. Justify your answer.

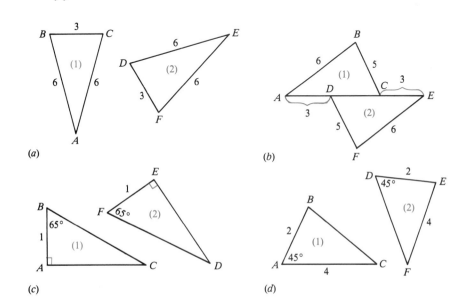

(a)

(b)

(c)

(d)

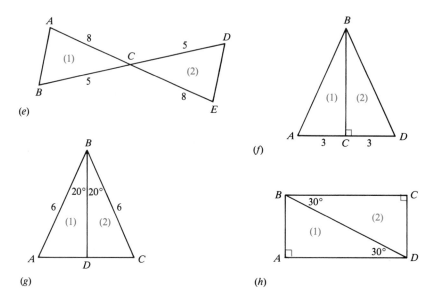

(e)

(f)

(g)

(h)

3. Using a ruler, protractor, compass, or tracing paper, construct each of the following, if possible.

(a) A segment congruent to $\overline{AB}$ and an angle congruent to $\angle CAB$

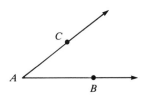

(b) A triangle with sides of lengths 2 cm, 3 cm, and 4 cm

(c) A triangle with sides of lengths 4 cm, 3 cm, and 5 cm (What kind of triangle is it?)

(d) A triangle with sides 4 cm, 5 cm, and 10 cm

(e) An equilateral triangle with sides 5 cm

(f) A triangle with sides 6 cm and 7 cm and an included angle of measure 75°

(g) A triangle with sides 6 cm and 7 cm and a nonincluded angle of measure 75°

(h) A triangle with angles 60° and 70° and an included side of 8 cm

(i) A triangle with angles 60° and 70° and nonincluded side of 8 cm on a side of the 60° angle

(j) A right triangle with one acute angle of 75° and a side of 5 cm on a side of the 75° angle

(k) A right triangle with legs 4 cm and 8 cm (The legs include the right angle.)

(l) A triangle with angles of 30°, 70°, and 80°

4. For each of the conditions in Problem 3(b)–(l) is it possible to construct two noncongruent triangles? Explain why or why not.

5. Using only a compass and straightedge, perform each of the following:
    (a) Reproduce ⊾A.

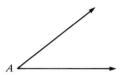

    (b) Construct an equilateral triangle with side $\overline{AB}$.

    (c) Construct a 60° angle.
    (d) Construct an isosceles triangle with ⊾A as the angle included between the two congruent sides.

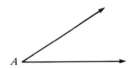

    (e) Construct ⊾C so that $m(⊾C) = m(⊾A) + m(⊾B)$.

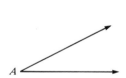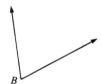

    (f) Using the angles in part (e) construct ⊾C so that $m(⊾C) = m(⊾B) - m(⊾A)$.
6. Prove that an equilateral triangle is also equiangular.
7. In the accompanying drawing, $\overrightarrow{BD}$ bisects ⊾ABC of isosceles triangle ABC with $\overline{AB} \simeq \overline{CB}$. Prove each of the following.
    (a) $\overline{AD} \simeq \overline{CD}$ (the angle bisector bisects the base).
    (b) ⊾ADB and ⊾CDB are right angles (the angle bisector is perpendicular to the base).

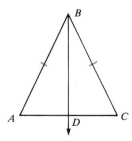

8. In the following figure, find all congruent triangles. Justify your answer. Circle O has radius OA. Circle A has radius AC. Circle B has radius BC. $\overline{BC} \simeq \overline{AC}$.

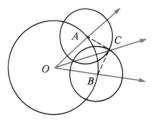

9. What information is necessary to determine each of the following?
   (a) Two squares are congruent.   (b) Two rectangles are congruent.
10. Suppose polygon $ABCD$ is any parallelogram. Use congruent triangles to prove each of the following.
   (a) $\angle A \simeq \angle C$ and $\angle B \simeq \angle D$ (opposite angles are congruent).
   (b) $\overline{BC} \simeq \overline{AD}$ and $\overline{AB} \simeq \overline{CD}$ (opposite sides are congruent).
   (c) $\overline{BF} \simeq \overline{DF}$ and $\overline{AF} \simeq \overline{CF}$ (the diagonals bisect each other).
   (d)   Prove that $\angle DAB$ and $\angle ABC$ are supplementary.

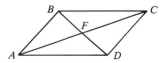

11. Suppose polygon $ABCD$ is any rectangle. Use congruent triangles to prove each of the following.
   (a) $\overline{AC}$ and $\overline{BD}$ bisect each other (the diagonals bisect each other).
   (b) $\overline{BD} \simeq \overline{AC}$ (the diagonals are congruent).

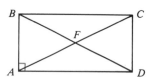

12. Suppose polygon $ABCD$ is any square. Prove that the diagonals of the square bisect each other.

13. (a)   Construct quadrilaterals having exactly one, two, and four right angles.
    (b)   Why can a convex quadrilateral not have exactly three right angles?
    (c)   Can a parallelogram have exactly two right angles?

14.   In parallelogram *ABCD* below, suppose $\overline{PQ}$ is any segment with endpoints on the parallelogram containing the intersection point, *O*, of the diagonals. Prove $\overline{OP} \cong \overline{OQ}$.

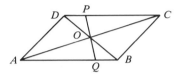

BRAIN TEASER

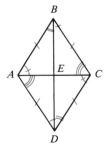

A treasure map, shown in the accompanying figure, floated ashore in a bottle. It showed Shipwreck Island where a treasure was buried. According to the directions on the map, the treasure is equidistant from two roads, one joining Bluebeard's Cove with Bottle O'Rum Inn and the other joining Long John's Bay with Bottle O'Rum Inn. Also, the treasure is equidistant from Long John's Bay and the Bottle O'Rum Inn. Can you find the treasure?

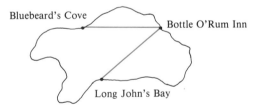

Bluebeard's Cove

Bottle O'Rum Inn

Long John's Bay

10-3   OTHER CONSTRUCTIONS

FIGURE 10-29

In the previous chapter, we defined a rhombus as a parallelogram with all sides congruent. In this section, we investigate properties of a rhombus and use these properties to do basic compass and straightedge constructions.

In the rhombus *ABCD* of Figure 10-29, diagonals $\overline{AC}$ and $\overline{BD}$ intersect at *E*. By the definition of a rhombus, $\overline{AB} \cong \overline{BC} \cong \overline{CD} \cong \overline{DA}$. In addition, since a rhombus is a parallelogram, its opposite sides are parallel and hence alternate interior angles formed along the diagonals are congruent.

It appears that $\overline{BD}$ and $\overline{AC}$ are perpendicular to each other. One way to prove that $\overline{AC} \perp \overline{BD}$ is to show that $\angle AEB$ and $\angle CEB$ are congruent and supplementary. They are supplementary since $\overleftrightarrow{AC}$ is a straight line. Are these angles corresponding parts of congruent triangles? The angles are parts of $\triangle ABE$ and $\triangle CBE$, but the given information only tells that $\overline{AB} \cong \overline{CB}$ and $\overline{BE}$ is congruent to itself. To obtain more information concerning $\triangle ABE$ and $\triangle CBE$, consider $\triangle ABD$ and $\triangle CBD$. Since $\overline{AD} \cong \overline{CD}$, $\overline{AB} \cong \overline{CB}$, and $\overline{BD}$ is congruent to itself, $\triangle ABD \cong \triangle CBD$ by SSS. Thus, $\angle ABD \cong \angle CBD$ because they are corresponding angles of congruent triangles, $\triangle ABD$ and $\triangle CBD$. As a result, $\triangle ABE \cong \triangle CBE$ by SAS. Hence, $\overline{AC} \perp \overline{BD}$. Also, $\triangle ABE \cong \triangle CBE$ implies $\overline{AE} \cong \overline{CE}$.

What else can be deduced from the rhombus in Figure 10.29? Since $\triangle ABD \cong \triangle CBD$, it follows that $\angle ADB \cong \angle CDB$. Thus, the diagonal $\overline{BD}$ bisects the angles of the rhombus at vertices B and D. Similarly, it can be shown that $\overline{AC}$ bisects the angles at A and C and that $\overline{BE} \cong \overline{DE}$.

A summary of the properties of a rhombus is given below.

Properties

1. The diagonals of a rhombus are perpendicular to each other.
2. The diagonals of a rhombus bisect each other.
3. The diagonals of a rhombus bisect the vertex angles of the rhombus.

The properties of a rhombus can be used for a variety of constructions. For example, Figure 10-30 shows the construction of a line parallel to a given line ℓ through a point P not on ℓ. First, draw any line through P that intersects ℓ, as in Figure 10-30(b). Call the point A. Then, draw an arc to locate all points that are at a distance AP from A, as shown in Figure 10-30(c). The intersection of line ℓ and the arc gives one such point, X. Complete the construction of a rhombus by locating all points at a distance AP from both P and X. The point labeled Y satisfies these conditions. Since a rhombus is also a parallelogram, the line through P and Y is parallel to ℓ.

FIGURE 10-30

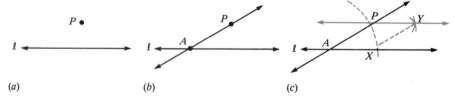

(a)   (b)   (c)

Figure 10-31 shows another way to do the construction. If congruent corresponding angles are formed by a transversal cutting two lines, then the lines are parallel. Thus, the first step is to draw a transversal through P that intersects ℓ. The angle marked α is formed by the transversal. By constructing an angle congruent to α with a vertex at P as shown in Figure 10-31(b), congruent corresponding angles are formed, and therefore, $m \parallel \ell$. Two more ways to construct parallel lines use congruent alternate interior or alternate exterior angles. (These constructions are left as exercises.)

FIGURE 10-31

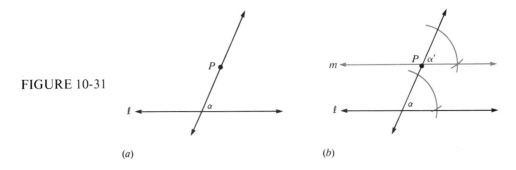

(a)   (b)

Another construction that is based upon a property of a rhombus is that of an angle bisector. In Figure 10-32(a), given $\angle A$, a rhombus having A as a vertex and sides on the rays is constructed. The diagonal of the rhombus through A bisects $\angle A$ as shown in Figure 10-32(b). In other words, $\overrightarrow{AC}$ bisects $\angle A$.

FIGURE 10-32

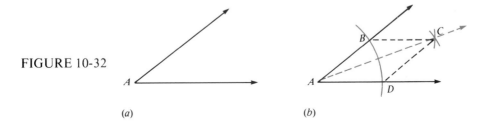

(a)   (b)

In order to construct a line through P perpendicular to line ℓ, where P is not a point on ℓ, as shown in Figure 10-33(a), again use properties of the diagonals of a rhombus. Recall that the diagonals of a rhombus are perpendicular to each other. By constructing a rhombus with a vertex at P and two

FIGURE 10-33

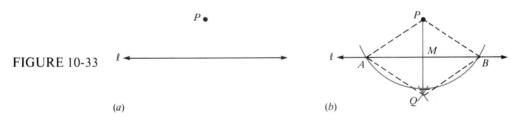

(a)   (b)

vertices A and B on ℓ, as in Figure 10-33(b), the segment connecting the fourth vertex Q to P is perpendicular to ℓ since $\overline{AB}$ and $\overline{PQ}$ are diagonals. To obtain A and B, choose any length longer than the distance between P and ℓ and draw an arc with center P that intersects ℓ. Then, the rhombus with vertices P, A, and B can be completed and the perpendicular determined.

To construct the perpendicular bisector of a line segment $\overline{AB}$ as shown in Figure 10-34(a), use the fact that the diagonals of a rhombus are perpendicular bisectors of each other. The construction yields a rhombus such that $\overline{AB}$ is one of its diagonals. The other diagonal of the rhombus is the perpendicular bisector. Arcs with the same radius and with centers at A and B are drawn. The points P and Q where the arcs intersect are the other vertices of the rhombus since $\overline{AP} \cong \overline{PB} \cong \overline{AQ} \cong \overline{BQ}$. Connecting P and Q gives the perpendicular bisector of $\overline{AB}$ at M.

FIGURE 10-34

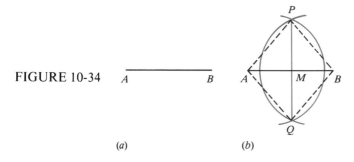

(a)   (b)

Determining a perpendicular to a line ℓ at a point P on ℓ, as shown in Figure 10-35(a) is also based on a property of a rhombus. Determine points A and B on ℓ so that P is the midpoint of $\overline{AB}$. Then, construct any rhombus with two vertices at A and B. In Figure 10-35(b), $ADBC$ is such a rhombus, and $\overleftrightarrow{CD}$ is the required perpendicular. Notice that since point P is given, the required perpendicular could have been determined by connecting C with P.

FIGURE 10-35

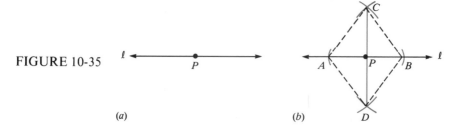

(a)   (b)

This construction is shown in the sample on page 419 from *Mathematics in Our World*, 1979, Grade 8, by Addison-Wesley.

Angles and intersecting lines

Try these constructions. Check the results by measuring the angles with a protractor.

Construct a perpendicular to a line through a point on the line.	**Construct a perpendicular to a line through a point not on the line.**

Step 1   *l* ←——•——→   given point *P* on line *l*

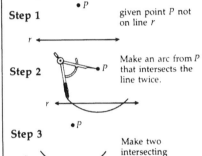

Step 1   given point *P* not on line *r*

Step 2   Make an equal arc on each side of point *P*.

Step 2   Make an arc from *P* that intersects the line twice.

Step 3   Use a larger opening and make intersecting arcs.

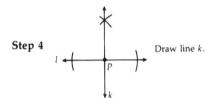

Step 3   Make two intersecting arcs.

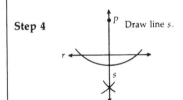

Step 4   Draw line *k*.

Step 4   Draw line *s*.

We say: *k* is perpendicular to *l*.

We write: *k* ⊥ *l*

The angles formed by two perpendicular lines are **right angles.**

Line *s* is perpendicular to line *r*.

We write: *s* ⊥ *r*

The angles formed are right angles.

1. Draw a horizontal line *k* and a point *A* on *k*. Construct line *j* through *A* and perpendicular to *k*.

2. Draw a horizontal line *p* and a point *B* not on *p*. Construct line *q* through *B* so that *q* ⊥ *p*.

3. Do exercises 1 and 2 with lines *k* and *p* drawn vertically.

The perpendicularity constructions can also be completed by paper folding or by using a Mira. A Mira is a plastic device that acts as a reflector so that the image of an object can be seen behind it. The drawing edge of the Mira acts as a folding line on paper. In fact, any construction demonstrated in this text that uses paper folding can be done using a Mira.

To construct a perpendicular to a given line ℓ at a point P on the line using paper folding, fold the line onto itself as in Figure 10-36(a). The fold line is perpendicular to ℓ. To perform the construction with a Mira, place the Mira with the drawing edge on P, as in Figure 10-36(b), so that ℓ is reflected onto itself. The line along the drawing edge is the required perpendicular.

FIGURE 10-36

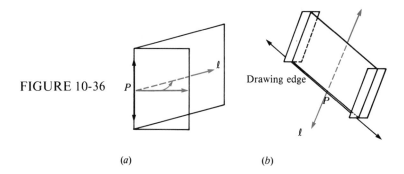

(a)   (b)

Using this same procedure, it is possible to construct any number of lines perpendicular to ℓ. In Figure 10-37, m and n are both perpendicular to ℓ. Since two lines perpendicular to the same line are parallel, $m \parallel n$. Thus, perpendicularity constructions can be used to construct parallel lines.

FIGURE 10-37

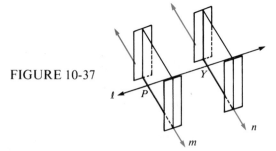

Consider the angle bisector in Figure 10-38. It seems that any point P on the angle bisector is equidistant from the sides of the angle, that is, $\overline{PD} \cong \overline{PE}$. (The distance from a point to a line is the length of the perpendicular from the point to the line.) To prove this, find two congruent triangles that have these segments as corresponding sides. The only triangles pictured are $\triangle ADP$ and $\triangle AEP$. What do we know about these triangles? Since $\overrightarrow{AP}$ is the angle bisector, $\measuredangle DAP \simeq \measuredangle EAP$. Also, $\measuredangle PDA$ and $\measuredangle PEA$ are right angles and are thus congruent. Since $\overline{AP}$ is congruent to itself, $\triangle PDA \simeq \triangle PEA$ by AAS. Thus, $\overline{PD}$ and $\overline{PE}$ are corresponding parts of congruent triangles $\triangle PDA$ and $\triangle PEA$ and hence are congruent. Consequently, *any point P on an angle bisector is equidistant from the sides of the angle.*

FIGURE 10-38

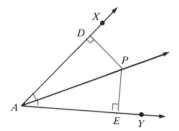

Consider the perpendicular bisector, ℓ, of $\overline{AB}$ and some point P on ℓ as shown in Figure 10-39(a). It appears that P is equidistant from points A and B, that is, $\overline{PA} \simeq \overline{PB}$. To prove this, we must show that the triangles $\triangle PCA$ and $\triangle PCB$, as shown in Figure 10-39(b), are congruent.

FIGURE 10-39

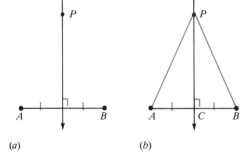

(a)   (b)

Since ℓ is the perpendicular bisector of $\overline{AB}$, $\overline{AC} \simeq \overline{BC}$ and $\measuredangle PCA$ and $\measuredangle PCB$ are congruent right angles. Also, $\overline{PC} \simeq \overline{PC}$ so that $\triangle PCA \simeq \triangle PCB$ by SAS. Hence, $\overline{PA} \simeq \overline{PB}$ since the line segments are corresponding sides of congruent triangles. Since P is an arbitrary point, *any point on the perpendicular bisector of a line segment is equidistant from the endpoints of the segment.*

PROBLEM SET 10-3

1. (a) Given a rhombus $ABCD$, show that diagonal $\overline{AC}$ bisects the angles at A and C.

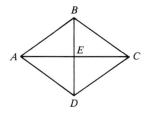

   (b) Use the results of part (a) to show that $\overline{BE} \cong \overline{DE}$.

2. Determine which properties of a rhombus listed in this section are true for any parallelogram.

3. Use a compass and straightedge to construct a line m through P parallel to ℓ using each of the following.
   (a) Alternate interior angles   (b) Alternate exterior angles

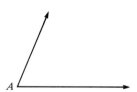

4. Construct each of the following using (i) a compass and straightedge, (ii) paper folding, and (iii) a Mira, if available.
   (a) Bisector of $\angle A$

   (b) Perpendicular bisector of $\overline{AB}$

$\overline{}$
A B

   (c) Perpendicular from P to ℓ

$P \bullet$

$\ell \longleftarrow\!\!\!\longrightarrow$

altitude   5. An **altitude** of a triangle is the perpendicular from a vertex to the opposite side or extended side of the triangle. Construct the three altitudes of each of the following triangles using any method.

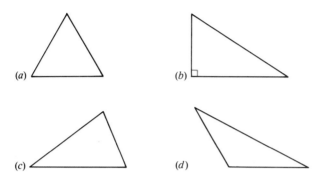

(a)   (b)   (c)   (d)

6. Construct the perpendicular bisectors of each of the sides of the triangles in Problem 5.

median   7. A **median** of a triangle is a segment from a vertex of the triangle to the midpoint of the opposite side. Construct the three medians of each triangle in Problem 5.

8. Prove that the medians of an equilateral triangle are congruent.

9. If two opposite sides of a quadrilateral are parallel and congruent, prove that the quadrilateral is a parallelogram.

10. If both pairs of opposite sides of a quadrilateral are congruent, prove that the quadrilateral is a parallelogram.

11. Prove that the figure formed by joining the midpoints of a rectangle is a rhombus.

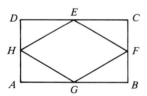

12. Construct a square with $\overline{AB}$ as a side.

A   B

13. Using a compass and straightedge, construct a parallelogram with A, B, and C as vertices.

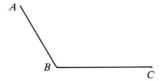

14.   In the accompanying figure, show that $\overrightarrow{PQ}$ is the perpendicular bisector of $\overline{AB}$.

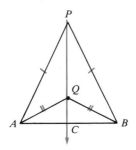

BRAIN TEASER

Given $\overline{AB}$ in the accompanying figure, use a compass and straightedge to construct the perpendicular bisector of $\overline{AB}$. You are not allowed to put any marks outside the border.

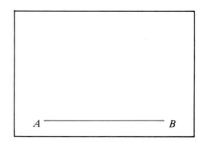

10-4 CONGRUENCE VIA MOTIONS

Euclid seems to have envisioned moving one geometric figure and placing it on top of another to determine if the two figures were congruent. Congruence

FIGURE 10-40

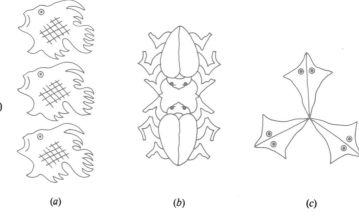

(a)   (b)   (c)

of figures can be studied using the idea of motions. The results of three simple types of motion are illustrated in Figure 10-40.

In Figure 10-41 a child gliding down a slide has moved a certain distance, d, in a certain direction along a line. This type of motion is called a **slide** or **translation.** *A slide (translation) is a motion of a specified distance and direction along a straight line without any accompanying twisting or turning.* Distance and direction of a slide both are indicated by a **slide arrow.**

slide,   translation

slide arrow

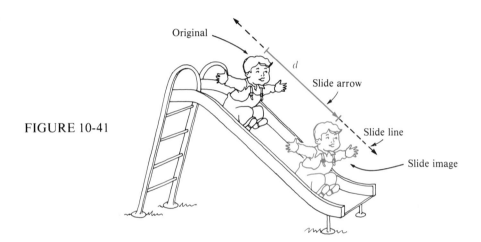

FIGURE 10-41

Figure 10-42 shows a slide of $\triangle ABC$ to $\triangle A'B'C'$. The arrow indicates a slide of d units to the right. The drawing on the piece of paper labeled X is traced

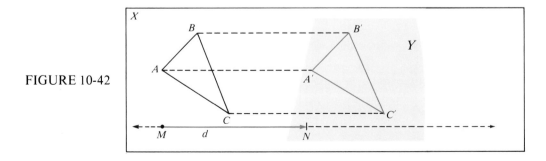

FIGURE 10-42

upon the tracing paper labeled Y. When the tracing paper is slid along $\overleftrightarrow{MN}$, the slide line, until M matches N, the slide images of A, B, and C are A', B', and C'. The physical motion of sliding tracing paper establishes a one-to-one correspondence between the points of plane X and itself such that $AA' = BB' = CC' = d$ and such that $\overline{AA'} \parallel \overline{BB'} \parallel \overline{CC'}$. Notice that any point of plane X has exactly one image point and, moreover, that each point is the image of some point.

Slide images can be constructed using a compass and straightedge. For example, the slide in Figure 10-43(a) takes M to N. By the properties of a slide, the image, A', of A in the slide, must be such that $\overline{AA'} \cong \overline{MN}$ and $\overline{AA'} \parallel \overline{MN}$. Thus, to construct the image A' of point A, construct a line through A that is parallel to $\overline{MN}$ and then construct $\overline{AA'}$ so that $AA' = MN$, as shown in Figure 10-43(b).

FIGURE 10-43

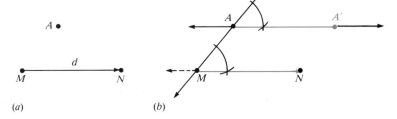

(a)   (b)

flip, reflection   Another transformation is called a **flip** or a **reflection.** One example of a flip often encountered in our daily lives is a mirror image. Figure 10-44 shows a figure with its mirror image. A mirror has perspective; that is, objects close to the mirror have images that appear close to the mirror and objects farther away have images that appear farther away.

FIGURE 10-44

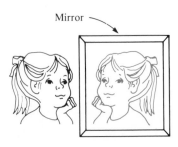

In a plane, we can simulate reflections in various ways. Consider the
half tree shown in Figure 10-45(a). Folding the paper along the **flip line** ℓ and
drawing the image gives the **flip image** of the tree. In Figure 10-45(b), the
paper is unfolded. The figure obtained is symmetric about the fold line in
much the same way that a mirror gives symmetry in space. Another way to
simulate a reflection or flip in a line uses a Mira and is illustrated in Figure
10-45(c).

flip line
flip image

FIGURE 10-45

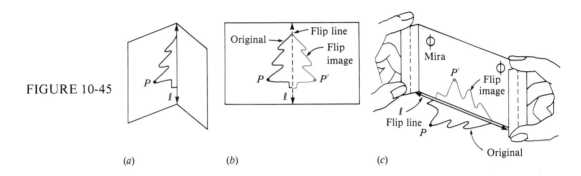

(a)   (b)   (c)

In Figure 10-46(a), the image of P under a flip in line ℓ is P'. In Figure
10-46(b), P is its own image under the flip in line ℓ. In general, *a flip (or
reflection) in a line ℓ is a motion that pairs each point P of the plane with a
point P' in such a way that ℓ is the perpendicular bisector of $\overline{PP'}$ as long as
$P \not\in \ell$. If $P \in \ell$, then $P = P'$.*

FIGURE 10-46

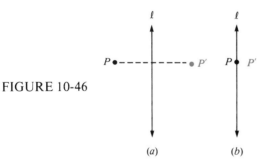

(a)   (b)

To construct the flip image of point P in ℓ using a compass and
straightedge, construct a perpendicular from P to ℓ, namely, m, and mark off
P' so that $\overline{XP'} \cong \overline{PX}$ as shown in Figure 10-47.

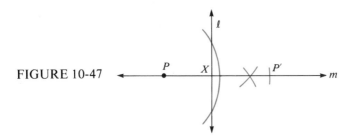

FIGURE 10-47

Given any point A and its flip image A', the flip line ℓ can be found as long as $A \not\in \ell$ because ℓ is the perpendicular bisector of $\overline{AA'}$. This can be done by placing a Mira so that A is reflected onto A' and drawing ℓ along the drawing edge, as shown in Figure 10-48(a). With paper folding, simply fold A onto A' as shown in Figure 10-48(b). The folding line is the required flip line. With a compass and straightedge, construct the perpendicular bisector of $\overline{AA'}$ using the methods of the previous section. This is illustrated in Figure 10-48(c).

FIGURE 10-48

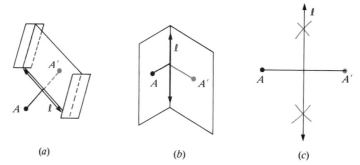

(a)   (b)   (c)

turn, rotation   A **turn** or **rotation** is another kind of motion. In Figure 10-49(a), $\triangle ABC$ and point O are traced on the tracing paper. Holding point O fixed, the **turn image**   tracing paper can be turned to obtain a **turn image**, $\triangle A'B'C'$, as shown in **center of the turn**   Figure 10-49(b). Point O is called the **center of the turn**, and $\angle COC'$ is called **angle of the turn**   the **angle of the turn.**
        In order to determine a turn, three things must be given: (1) the center of the turn, (2) the direction of the turn—either clockwise or counterclockwise, and (3) the amount of the turn. The amount and the direction of the **turn arrow**   turn can be illustrated by a **turn arrow,** as shown with $\angle COC'$ in Figure 10-49(b), or specified as a number of degrees. A counterclockwise turn is indicated by a positive number of degrees; and a negative number of degrees indicates a clockwise turn. In general, *a turn (rotation) is a motion determined by holding one point, the center, fixed and rotating the plane about this point a certain amount in a certain direction.*

FIGURE 10-49

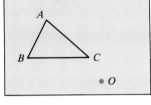

(a)

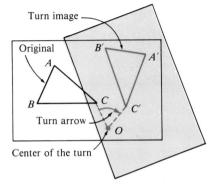

(b)

BRAIN TEASER

Simon and Susan decided to repair a hole in their living room shag carpet. The hole was in the shape of a scalene triangle as shown below. In order to cut a patch, Simon placed his only remnant of the carpet upside down over the hole so that he could cut the triangular shape through the jute backing. When he had cut the patch, he was astonished that it did not fit unless the jute side was up. How can he recut the patch using the minimum number of cuts and piece it together so that it will fit the hole?

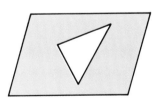

It is possible to construct P', the turn image of a point P under a rotation with center O and angle α as shown in Figure 10-50(a) using a compass and straightedge. Recall that when using tracing paper, the center was fixed and the tracing paper was turned in such a way that if a point was followed through the turn, an arc was formed. In Figure 10-50(b), P', the turn image of P, must be on an arc of a circle with center O and radius $\overline{OP}$. More information is needed to find the exact location of P'. Since $\angle POP'$ must be congruent to the angle of rotation, α, given in Figure 10-50(a), construct $\angle POX$ congruent to α. P' is the point of intersection of $\overrightarrow{O}$ and the circle, as shown in Figure 10-50(b).

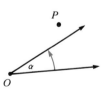

FIGURE 10-50   (a)

(b)

turn symmetry
rotational symmetry

A figure has **turn symmetry** or **rotational symmetry** when the traced figure can be turned less than 360° about its center so that it matches the original figure. In Figure 10-51, the tracing of the fan blade matches after a turn of 120°. Hence, we say that the blade has 120° turn symmetry. Other

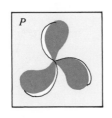

FIGURE 10-51

examples of figures that have turn symmetry are shown in Figure 10-52. Figures 10-52(a), (b), (c), and (d) have 72°, 90°, 180°, and 180° turn symmetry, respectively. (Figures 10-52(a) and (b) also have other turn symmetries.)

FIGURE 10-52

(a)   (b)   (c)   (d)

point symmetry   Any figure that has 180° turn symmetry is said to have **point symmetry** about the center of the turn. Figures with point symmetry are shown in Figure 10-53.

FIGURE 10-53

Suppose P is any point of a figure with point symmetry, such as in Figure 10-54(a). If the figure is turned 180°, there is a corresponding point P' as shown in part (b) of the figure. Points P, O, and P' are collinear, and O is the midpoint of $\overline{PP'}$.

FIGURE 10-54

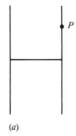

(a)   (b)

line of symmetry

Turns are related to both rotational and point symmetry. Flips are related to line symmetry. A figure has a **line of symmetry** if it is its own image under a flip. The flip line is the line of symmetry. Examples of figures with line symmetry are shown in Figure 10-55. There are three, one, and seven lines of symmetry, respectively, in Figures 10-55(a), (b), and (c).

FIGURE 10-55

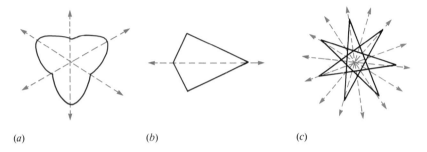

(a)   (b)   (c)

plane of symmetry

A three-dimensional figure has a **plane of symmetry** when every point of the figure on one side of the plane has a mirror image on the other side of the plane. Examples of figures with plane symmetry are shown in Figure 10-56. Solids can also have point symmetry, line symmetry, and turn symmetry. These symmetries are analogous to the two-dimensional symmetries and will be investigated in the exercises.

FIGURE 10-56

  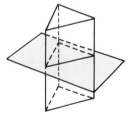

PROBLEM SET 10-4

1. What type of motion is involved in each of the following?
   (a) A circular radio knob is turned from "off" to "on"
   (b) A skier skiing straight down a slope
   (c) A child swinging
   (d) Two children on a teeter-totter
   (e) A leaf floating down a stream
   (f) A page turn in a book

2. Which types of symmetry—point, line, plane, or turn—does each of the following have?
   (a) A ball
   (b) An equilateral triangle
   (c) A regular polygon
   (d) A basketball court
   (e) A football
   (f) A cube

3. For each of the following, name the printed capital letters of the English alphabet having the given property.
   (a) Line symmetry
   (b) Turn symmetry
   (c) Point symmetry

4. (i) Determine the number of lines of symmetry of each flag below.
   (ii) Sketch the lines of symmetry for each flag.

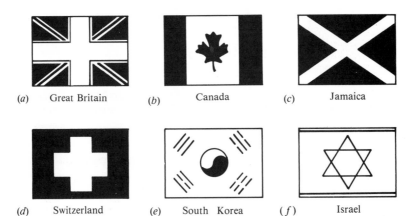

(a)   Great Britain   (b)   Canada   (c)   Jamaica

(d)   Switzerland   (e)   South Korea   (f)   Israel

5. Find the lines of symmetry, if any, for each of the following trademarks.

(a) Shell Oil   (b) The Bell System   (c) The Yellow Pages   (d) Chevrolet

(e) Volkswagen   (f) Chrysler   (g) International   (h) American Automobile
   of America   Corporation   Harvester   Association

6. Answer each of the following. If your answer is no, provide a counterexample.
   (a) If a figure has point symmetry, must it have turn symmetry? Why?
   (b) If a figure has turn symmetry, must it have point symmetry? Why?
   (c) Can a figure have point, line, and turn symmetry? If so, sketch a figure with these properties.
   (d) If a figure has point symmetry, must it have line symmetry? Is the converse true?
   (e) If a figure has both point and line symmetry, must it have turn symmetry? Why?
7. For each of the following, find the image of the given quadrilateral.

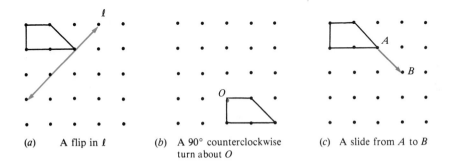

(a)   A flip in ℓ   (b) A 90° counterclockwise   (c) A slide from A to B
                               turn about O

8. How many lines of symmetry do each of the following figures have?
   (a) An equilateral triangle   (b) A square   (c) A rectangle
   (d) A rhombus   (e) A circle
9. In each of the following, complete the sketches so that they have the indicated symmetry.

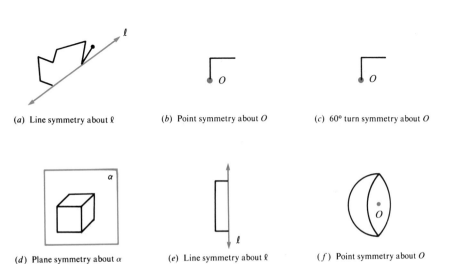

(a) Line symmetry about ℓ   (b) Point symmetry about O   (c) 60° turn symmetry about O

(d) Plane symmetry about α   (e) Line symmetry about ℓ   (f) Point symmetry about O

10. Use (i) tracing paper and (ii) compass and straightedge to construct the images for each of the following:

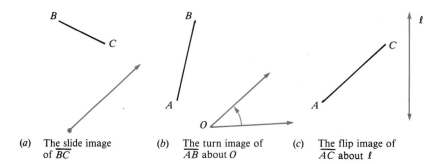

(*a*) The slide image of $\overline{BC}$

(*b*) The turn image of $\overline{AB}$ about O

(*c*) The flip image of $\overline{AC}$ about ℓ

11. For each of the following, use any construction methods to find the image of $\triangle ABC$ if it is flipped about ℓ to obtain $\triangle A'B'C'$ and then $\triangle A'B'C'$ is flipped about m to obtain $\triangle A''B''C''$.

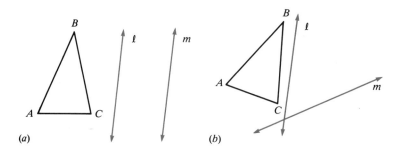

(*a*)   (*b*)

★ 12. What is the relationship between $\triangle ABC$ and $\triangle A''B''C''$ in each part of Problem 11? Can the motions above be described as a single motion?

13. What is the result of performing two successive flips about line ℓ in the figure below?

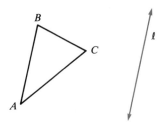

★ 14. Suppose ℓ and m are parallel and $\triangle ABC$ is flipped through ℓ, then m. How does the final image compare to the final image after flipping through m then ℓ? Are the images ever the same?

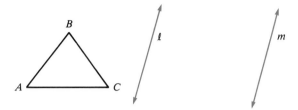

★ 15. (a) Perform in succession the two turns, each with center O, in the figure below.
(b) What is the result of the two turns?
(c) Is the order of the turns important?
(d) Could the result have been accomplished in one turn?

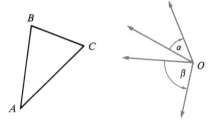

★ 16. A **glide reflection** is defined as the result of a successive slide and flip. Find the image of the footprint in the glide reflection that is the result of a slide from M to N followed by a flip about ℓ.

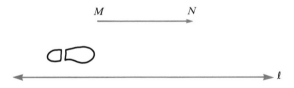

★ 17. If a Mira is available, use it to investigate Problems 11, and 13 through 16.

10-5 SIMILAR TRIANGLES AND SIMILAR FIGURES

If an 8 in. × 10 in. reprint is made of an 8 in. × 10 in. picture, then the two photographs are congruent; that is, they have the same size and shape. However, if an 8 in. × 10 in. picture is blown up to obtain a 16 in. × 20 in.

picture as shown in Figure 10-57, the resulting photographs are not congruent. They have the same shape, but not the same size. When a germ is examined through a microscope, when a slide is projected on a screen, or when a wet wool sweater shrinks when dried in a clothes dryer, the shapes in each case remain the same, but the size is altered. In mathematics we say that two figures that have the same shape but not necessarily the same size are
similar   **similar.**

FIGURE 10-57

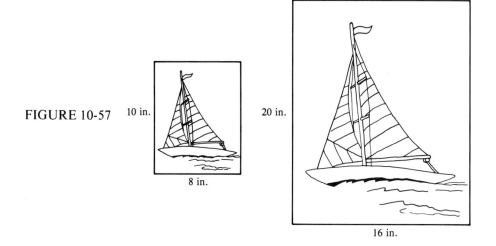

10 in.   20 in.

8 in.

16 in.

For example, if we project an equilateral triangle onto a screen without distortion (so that the same shape is kept), the image on the screen is an equilateral triangle, as shown in Figure 10-58. In this figure, $\triangle ABC$ is
scale factor   enlarged by a **scale factor** of 2 so that the following proportion holds.

$$\frac{A'B'}{AB} = \frac{B'C'}{BC} = \frac{A'C'}{AC} = \frac{2}{1}$$

FIGURE 10-58

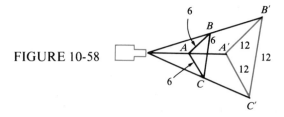

The ratio of the sides is 2 to 1. However, the angle sizes pictured do not change, since both triangles are equilateral and hence equiangular. It is reasonable to assume that *any* triangle projected in this manner will have an image triangle similar to the original. The angle measures remain the same, and the sides are proportional. In general, we have the following definition of similar triangles.

DEFINITION

$\triangle ABC$ is similar to $\triangle DEF$, written $\triangle ABC \sim \triangle DEF$, if and only if $\angle A \cong \angle D$, $\angle B \cong \angle E$, $\angle C \cong \angle F$, and $AB/DE = AC/DF = BC/EF$.

Remark

Note that the one-to-one correspondence obtained from similar triangles is analogous to that obtained with congruent triangles.

Example 10-11

Find a one-to-one correspondence among the vertices of the pairs of similar triangles in Figure 10-59 such that the corresponding angles are congruent. Then, write the proportion for the corresponding sides that follows from the definition.

FIGURE 10-59

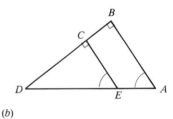

(a)

(b)

Solution

(a) $\triangle ABC \sim \triangle DEF$

$\angle A \cong \angle D$, $\angle B \cong \angle E$,   and $\angle C \cong \angle F$; $\dfrac{AB}{DE} = \dfrac{BC}{EF} = \dfrac{AC}{DF}$.

(b) $\triangle ABD \sim \triangle ECD$

$\angle A \cong \angle E$, $\angle B \cong \angle C$,   and $\angle D = \angle D$; $\dfrac{AB}{EC} = \dfrac{BD}{CD} = \dfrac{AD}{ED}$.

As with congruent triangles, minimal conditions may be used to determine when two triangles are similar. For example, suppose two triangles each have angles with measures of 50°, 30°, and 100°, but the side opposite the 100° angle is 5 units long in one of the triangles and 1 unit long in the other. The triangles appear to have the same shape, as shown in Figure 10-60. The figure suggests that if the angles of two triangles are congruent, then the

FIGURE 10-60

angle, angle, angle (AAA)   sides are proportional and the triangles are similar. There is no easy proof of this statement, but it is true in general. It is called the **angle, angle, angle** property of similarity for triangles and is abbreviated as AAA.

Property | **Angle, Angle, Angle (AAA)**   If three angles of one triangle are congruent to the three angles of a second triangle, respectively, then the triangles are similar.

Remark | Given the measures of any two angles of a triangle, the measure of the third angle can be found. Hence, if two angles in one triangle are congruent to two angles in another triangle, respectively, then the third angles must also be congruent. Consequently, the AAA condition may be

angle, angle (AA) | reduced to **angle, angle (AA)**.

Example 10-12 | For each part of Figure 10-61, determine if the pairs of triangles are similar.

FIGURE 10-61

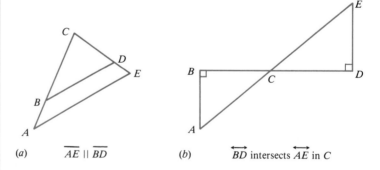

(a) $\overline{AE} \parallel \overline{BD}$ (b) $\overleftrightarrow{BD}$ intersects $\overleftrightarrow{AE}$ in C

Solution | (a)   Since $\overline{AE} \parallel \overline{BD}$, congruent corresponding angles are formed by a transversal cutting the parallel segments. Thus $\angle CBD \cong \angle CAE$, and $\angle CDB \cong \angle CEA$. Also, $\angle C \cong \angle C$, so that $\triangle CBD \sim \triangle CAE$ by AAA.

(b) $\angle B \cong \angle D$ since both are right angles. Also, $\angle ACB \cong \angle ECD$ since they are vertical angles. Thus, $\triangle ACB \sim \triangle ECD$ by AA.

In general, knowing that the corresponding angles are congruent is not sufficient to determine similarity for any two polygons. In fact, two polygons are similar if and only if the corresponding angles are congruent *and* the corresponding sides are proportional.

Example 10-13 In each pair of similar triangles in Figure 10-62, find x.

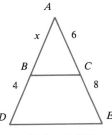

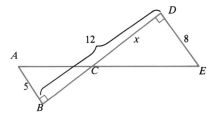

FIGURE 10-62

(a) $\triangle ABC \sim \triangle ADE$ (b) $\triangle ABC \sim \triangle EDC$

Solution (a) Since $\triangle ABC \sim \triangle ADE$,

$$\frac{AB}{AD} = \frac{AC}{AE} = \frac{BC}{DE}$$

Now, $AB = x$, $AD = x + 4$, $AC = 6$, $AE = 6 + 8 = 14$. Thus,

$$\frac{x}{x + 4} = \frac{6}{14}$$

$$14x = 6(x + 4)$$

$$14x = 6x + 24$$

$$8x = 24$$

$$x = 3$$

(b) Since $\triangle ABC \sim \triangle EDC$,

$$\frac{AB}{ED} = \frac{AC}{EC} = \frac{BC}{DC}$$

Now, $AB = 5$, $ED = 8$, and $CD = x$, so that $BC = 12 - x$. Thus,

$$\frac{5}{8} = \frac{12 - x}{x}$$

$$5x = 8(12 - x)$$

$$5x = 96 - 8x$$

$$13x = 96$$

$$x = \frac{96}{13}$$

Similar triangles give rise to various properties. Consider, for example, $\triangle ADE$ in Figure 10-63(a) with $\overline{BC}$ parallel to side $\overline{DE}$. $\triangle ADE \sim \triangle ABC$

FIGURE 10-63

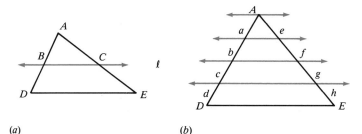

(a)   (b)

(why?) and consequently, $AD/AB = AE/AC$. Subtracting 1 from each side of this equation, we obtain $(AD/AB) - 1 = (AE/AC) - 1$ or $(AD - AB)/AB = (AE - AC)/AC$, which is equivalent to $BD/AB = CE/AC$ or $AB/BD = AC/CE$. The result is summarized in the following property.

Property | If a line parallel to one side of a triangle intersects the other sides, then it divides those sides into proportional segments.

In Figure 10-63(a), if B is the midpoint of $\overline{AD}$ (that is, $AB = BD$) and $\ell \parallel \overleftrightarrow{DE}$, it follows that $AB/BD = 1$, and since $AB/BD = AC/CE$, then $AC/CE = 1$. Consequently, $AC = CE$ and C is the midpoint of AE. Similarly, if parallel lines intersect $\triangle ADE$ as shown in Figure 10-63(b) such that $a = b = c = d$, it can also be shown that $e = f = g = h$. This result is summarized in the following property.

Property | If parallel lines cut off congruent segments on one transversal, then they cut off congruent segments on any transversal.

The preceding property is the basis for separating a line segment into congruent parts. For example, to divide $\overline{AB}$ in Figure 10-64(a) into three congruent parts, draw any transversal $\overrightarrow{AC}$ such that A, B, and C are noncollinear. Mark off three congruent segments on $\overrightarrow{AC}$ as shown in Figure 10-64(b), and connect B with A_3. Then, construct parallels to $\overline{BA_3}$ through A_1 and A_2. The intersections of the parallels with $\overline{AB}$ determine the three congruent parts of $\overline{AB}$.

Not only have similar triangles been used to divide segments proportionately, they have been used to make indirect measurements since the time of Thales of Miletus (ca. 600 B.C.), who is believed to have determined the

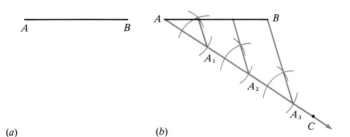

FIGURE 10-64

(a)   (b)

height of the Great Pyramids of Egypt. Most likely he used ratios involving shadows similar to those in Figure 10-65. The sun is so far away it should make approximately congruent angles at B and B'. Since there are right angles at C and C', $\triangle ABC \sim \triangle A'B'C'$. Hence, $AC/A'C' = BC/B'C'$, and since $AC = AE + EC$, the following proportion is obtained.

$$\frac{AE + EC}{A'C'} = \frac{BC}{B'C'}$$

FIGURE 10-65

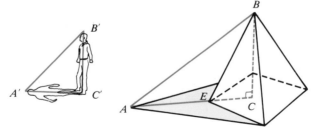

The person's height and shadow can be measured. Also, the length of the shadow of the pyramid AE, can be measured, and EC can be estimated since the base of the pyramid is a square. Each term of the proportion except the height of the pyramid is known. Thus, the height of the pyramid can be found by solving the proportion.

Example 10-14

On a sunny day, a tall tree casts a 40 m shadow. At the same time, a meter stick held vertically casts a 2.5 m shadow. How tall is the tree?

Solution

Look at Figure 10-66. The pictured triangles are similar.

$$\frac{x}{40} = \frac{1}{2.5}$$

$$2.5x = 40$$

$$x = 16$$

FIGURE 10-66

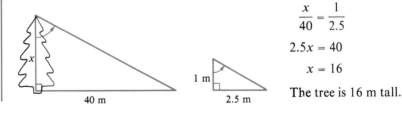

The tree is 16 m tall.

PROBLEM SET 10-5

1. Which of the following triangles is not similar to the other three?

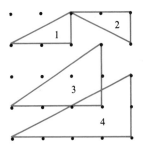

2. Which of the following are always similar?
   - (a) Any two equilateral triangles
   - (b) Any two squares
   - (c) Any two rectangles
   - (d) Any two rhombi
   - (e) Any two circles
   - (f) Any two regular polygons
   - (g) Any two regular polygons with the same number of sides

3. Use a grid like the following one to draw a figure that has sides three times as large as the given figure.

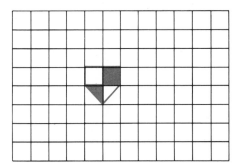

4. (i) Which pairs of the following triangles are similar? If they are similar, explain why.
   (ii) For each pair of similar triangles, find the ratio of the sides of the triangles.

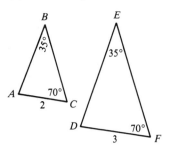

(a)

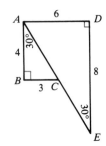

(b)

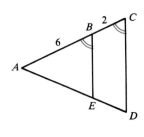

(c)

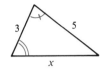

(d)

5. Assume that the triangles in each part are similar and find the measures of the unknown sides.

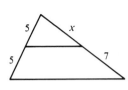

(a)

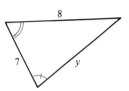

(b)

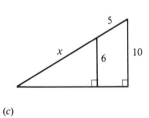

(c)

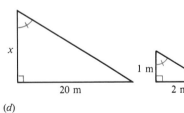

(d)

6. Polly claims that each of the following pairs of triangles are similar. In each part, determine if Polly is right or wrong. Explain why.

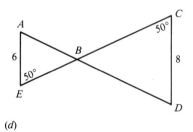

(a)

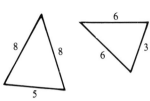

(b)

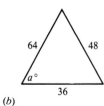

(c)

7. For each of the following, find x.

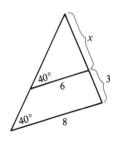

(a)

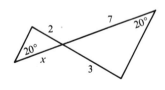

(b)

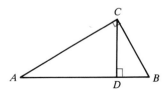

(c)

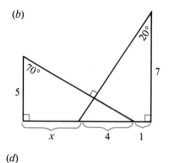

(d)

8. In right triangle ABC, $\overline{CD} \perp \overline{AB}$.

(a) What sets of triangles are similar? Why?
(b) Write the corresponding proportions for each set of similar triangles.
9. Are congruent triangles similar? Why?
10. (a) Construct a triangle with lengths of sides 4 cm, 6 cm, and 8 cm.
    (b) Construct another triangle with lengths of sides 2 cm, 3 cm, and 4 cm.
    (c) Make a conjecture about the similarity of triangles having proportional sides only.
11. (a) Construct a triangle with sides of lengths 4 cm and 6 cm and an included angle of 60°.
    (b) Construct a triangle with sides of lengths 2 cm and 3 cm and an included angle of 60°.
    (c) Make a conjecture about the similarity of triangles having two sides proportional and the included angles congruent.
12. (a) Sketch two nonsimilar polygons for which corresponding angles are congruent.
    (b) Sketch two nonsimilar polygons for which corresponding sides are proportional.

13. Examine several examples of similar polygons to make a conjecture concerning the ratio of their perimeters.

14. Use a compass and straightedge to separate $\overline{AB}$ into five congruent pieces.

A   B

15. Construct a square with a side ⅔ the length of a side of the square below.

16. To estimate the width of a river, a camper puts her tent directly across the river from a tree. She then drives a stake in the ground directly across the river from the tree at point S. Next, she places a stake at point Q directly in line between the tent and a cliff across the river. If the measures are as indicated in the figure, how wide is the river?

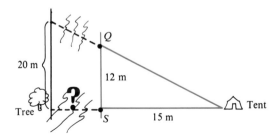

17. Find the distance AB across the pond using the following similar triangles.

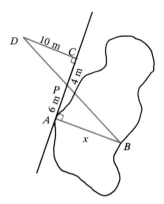

18. In the following isosceles triangle, $\triangle ABC$, $m(\angle A) = 36°$, $\overrightarrow{BD}$ bisects $\angle ABC$, and $\overline{AB} \cong \overline{AC}$. Find two similar triangles in the figure and prove that they are similar.

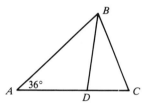

BRAIN TEASER

Two neighbors, Smith and Wesson, planned to erect flagpoles in their yards. Smith wanted a 10-ft pole, while Wesson wanted a 15-ft pole. In order to keep the poles straight while the concrete bases hardened, they agreed to tie guy wires from the tops of the flagpoles to a 6-ft fencepost on the property lines and to the bases of the flagpoles as shown. How far apart should they erect flagpoles for this scheme to work?

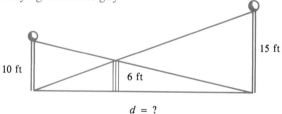

$d = ?$

10-6 PROPERTIES OF CIRCLES AND SPHERES

Recall that a circle is a set of points in a plane that is at a given distance from a given point called the center, as shown in Figure 10-67. The radius is the length of any segment connecting the center with a point of the circle. Any segment with both endpoints on the circle is called a **chord**. A line that contains a chord is called a **secant**. A chord that passes through the center of the circle is called à **diameter**. A diameter is the longest chord of the circle, and its length equals twice the length of the radius.

chord
secant
diameter

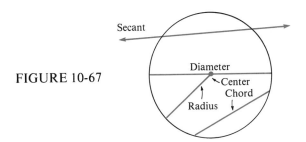

FIGURE 10-67

In Figure 10-68(a), chord $\overline{AB}$ is the diameter of a circle whose center is the midpoint of $\overline{AB}$. For $\overline{AB}$ to be a chord of other circles, both A and B have to be on the circles and, therefore, must be the same distance from the center of the circles. Figure 10-68(b) shows several circles containing both A and B. Every point on the perpendicular bisector of $\overline{AB}$ is equidistant from both A and B. Hence, every point of the perpendicular bisector of $\overline{AB}$ is the center of a circle containing A and B.

FIGURE 10-68

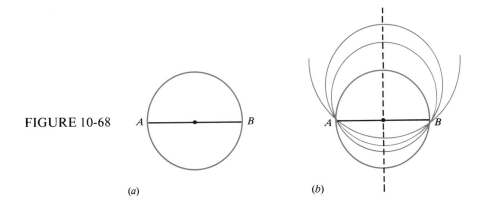

(a)   (b)

THEOREM 10-1

If $\overline{AB}$ is a chord of a circle, then the center of the circle lies on the perpendicular bisector of $\overline{AB}$.

central angles

Congruent chords in a circle seem to intersect the circle so as to form congruent arcs. For example, in Figure 10-69, chords $\overline{AB}$ and $\overline{CD}$ are congruent. The chords or their corresponding arcs determine two angles, $\angle AOB$ and $\angle COD$. These angles are called **central angles** because their vertices are the center of the circle. By performing a turn about O one chord

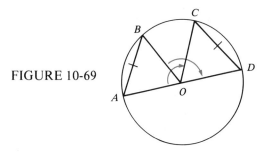

FIGURE 10-69

can be placed on top of the other. The arrows show which way to turn. One outcome of the turn is that $\overarc{AB}$ matches $\overarc{CD}$. Thus, congruent chords have congruent arcs. Also, the turn suggests that $\angle AOB$ is congruent to $\angle COD$. This also follows from the congruence of triangles OAB and OCD. Thus, *congruent chords determine congruent central angles and congruent arcs of the circle.* Conversely, it can be shown that *congruent central angles determine congruent chords and congruent arcs of a circle.*

inscribed polygon   When all the vertices of a polygon are points of a given circle, the polygon is called an **inscribed polygon.** A regular hexagon inscribed in a circle is shown in Figure 10-70(a). Since all sides of a regular hexagon are congruent, the corresponding arcs are congruent and the six corresponding central angles are congruent. Since the sum of the measures of these angles is 360°, the measure of each central angle is 60°. This fact is sufficient to inscribe a hexagon in a given circle using a protractor. A compass and straightedge construction can be accomplished. Look at $\triangle AOB$. Since $\overline{OA} \cong \overline{OB}$, the triangle is isosceles. Hence, the base angles $\angle BAO$ and $\angle ABO$ are congruent. Since the central angle is 60°, then $m(\angle BAO) + m(\angle ABO) = 120°$. Consequently, $m(\angle BAO) = m(\angle ABO) = 60°$, and the triangle is equiangular and equilateral. Thus, $\overline{AB}$ is congruent to a radius of the circle. As a result, to inscribe a regular hexagon in a circle, pick any point P on the circle and mark off chords congruent to the radius. Figure 10-70(b) shows such a construction.

FIGURE 10-70

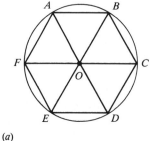

(a)

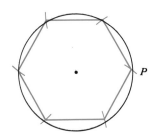

(b)

In a similar manner, to inscribe a regular dodecagon (12 sides) in a circle, construct either twelve congruent chords of the circle appropriately placed or twelve congruent central angles. To find the twelve congruent central angles, bisect the central angles of a regular hexagon as shown in Figure 10-71.

FIGURE 10-71

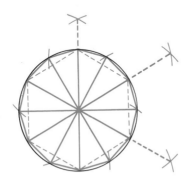

To inscribe a square in a circle, determine four congruent central angles. The central angles must be right angles since the sum of their measures is 360°. Hence, we need only to construct two perpendicular diameters of the circle. Figure 10-72 shows the construction. First, draw any diameter $\overline{PQ}$. Then construct a perpendicular to $\overline{PQ}$ at O and thus determine points R and S. Quadrilateral $PRQS$ is the required square.

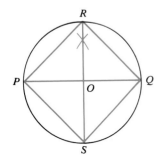

FIGURE 10-72

Determining which polygons can and cannot be inscribed in a circle using only a compass and straightedge has intrigued mathematicians for centuries. In fact, Gauss considered one of his master achievements to be the inscription of a regular 17-gon in a circle, and he wanted a replica of his construction placed on his tombstone. Gauss also proved that a regular n-gon can be inscribed in a circle if all the odd factors of n are distinct and of the form $2^{2^k} + 1$. (It is beyond the scope of this text to prove this result.) Thus, a regular heptagon cannot be inscribed in a circle with a compass and straightedge since 7 is not of the form $2^{2^k} + 1$.

A triangle is inscribed in a circle by connecting any three points of the circle with line segments. Conversely, given three vertices of any triangle, a circle that contains the vertices can be drawn. This process is called **circum-** circumscribing **scribing** a circle about a triangle. For example, in Figure 10-73, circle O is circumscribed about $\triangle ABC$. Such a circle must contain $\overline{AB}$, $\overline{BC}$, and $\overline{AC}$ as chords. Also, it must have $\overline{OA} \cong \overline{OB} \cong \overline{OC}$, since they are all radii. Hence, O must be equidistant from A and B and, consequently O must be on the perpendicular bisector of $\overline{AB}$. Similarly, O is on the perpendicular bisectors of $\overline{BC}$ and $\overline{AC}$. Hence, to find the center of the circle, construct perpendicular bisectors of any two chords. The point of intersection of the chords is the

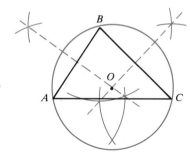

FIGURE 10-73

center of the circle. Segments connecting O with A, B, and C are the radii of the circle. (Note that this construction can be used to find a circle that contains any three noncollinear points.)

tangent

point of contact

A line that intersects a circle in exactly one point is called a **tangent.** In Figure 10-74, it appears that tangent ℓ and the radius pictured form right angles at their point of intersection or **point of contact.** In fact, this is true in general and can be proved. However, we will assume this property of a tangent without proof. Thus, to construct a tangent to a given circle at any

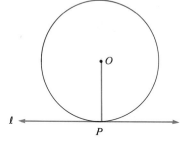

FIGURE 10-74

inscribed

point on the circle, construct a perpendicular to the radius at that point. A circle is **inscribed** in a triangle if it is tangent to the three sides of the triangle. For example, in Figure 10-75(a), circle O is inscribed in $\triangle DEF$ and A, B, and C are the points of contact. Since $\overline{OA}$, $\overline{OB}$, and $\overline{OC}$ are radii, they all have the same length, and they are perpendicular to the three sides of the triangle they each intersect. Thus, O is equidistant from the sides and lies on the bisectors of $\angle 1$, $\angle 2$, and $\angle 3$.

To inscribe a circle in a triangle, first construct the bisectors of two of the angles. Their intersection point O is the center of the inscribed circle. The radius of the circle can be determined by constructing a perpendicular from O to a side of the triangle. Figure 10-75(b) shows the construction. The circle with center O and radius $\overline{OC}$ is the required circle.

FIGURE 10-75

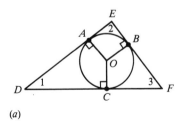

(a)

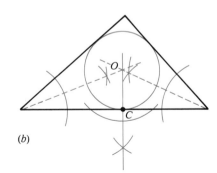

(b)

circumference
pi

The distance around a circle is called its **circumference.** The ancient Greeks discovered that if they divided the circumference of a circle by the length of a diameter, they always obtained approximately the same number, regardless of the size of the circle. The value of the number is approximately 3.14. Today, the ratio of circumference C to diameter d is symbolized as π **(pi).** In the early twentieth century, mathematicians proved that this ratio C/d, or π, is not a terminating decimal but an irrational number.

The relationship $C/d = \pi$ gives a formula for finding the circumference of a circle. Usually, it is written as $C = \pi d$ or $C = 2\pi r$ since the length of a diameter d is twice the radius of the circle. For most practical purposes, π is approximated by $^{22}/_7$, $3\frac{1}{7}$, or 3.14. These values are only approximations and are not accurate values of π. If you are asked for the exact circumference of a circle with diameter 6 cm, the answer is 6π cm.

Example 10-15

Find each of the following.

(a) The circumference of a circle if the radius is 2 m.
(b) The radius of a circle if the circumference is 15π m.

Solution

(a) $C = 2\pi(2) = 4\pi$. Thus, the circumference is 4π m.
(b) $C = 2\pi r$ implies $15\pi = 2\pi r$. Hence, $r = 15/2$. Thus, the radius is $15/2$ m.

sphere

A **sphere** is the three-dimensional analog of a circle. It is defined as the set of all points in space that are the same distance from a given point (called the center). The definitions of chord, secant, and tangent apply to spheres as well as to circles. A plane is tangent to a sphere if it intersects the sphere in exactly one point.

If a plane intersects a sphere in more than one point, then the intersection is a circle as shown in Figure 10-76.

FIGURE 10-76

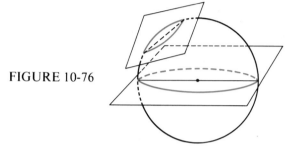

The largest of all such circles, a circle that contains a diameter of a great circle sphere, is called a **great circle.** Any plane containing the center of the sphere intersects the sphere in a great circle. As with circles, spheres have point, line, and turn symmetry. In addition, a sphere has plane symmetry with respect to any plane that passes through its center.

PROBLEM SET 10-6

1. What is the relation between a diameter of a circle and any chord that is not a diameter?
2. If a triangle is drawn in a circle so that one vertex is at the center and the other two vertices are on the circle, what type of triangle must it be? Why?
3. If one side of a triangle is a diameter of a circle and the third vertex is also a point on the circle, what type of triangle must it be? Measure the angles of several such triangles to decide.
4. Use paper folding (or a Mira) to determine the center of the given circle.

5. **Concentric circles** are circles with the same center. Can you construct a common tangent to two distinct concentric circles? Why?
6. Inscribe an equilateral triangle in a given circle.
7. Inscribe a regular octagon in a given circle.

8.　Draw a circle.
　　(a)　Inscribe several quadrilaterials.
　　(b)　Measure the angles of the quadrilaterals from part (a) and find the sums of the measures of pairs of opposite angles.
　　(c)　What seems to be true about the relationship among the angles?
9.　Inscribe a circle in the given square.

10.　Is it possible to inscribe a circle in every quadrilateral? Explain.
11.　Construct a circle with center O which is tangent to ℓ.

• O

ℓ

12.　Construct a circle that is tangent to lines ℓ, m, and n, where $\ell \parallel m$.

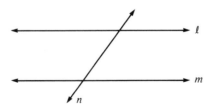

13.　In the accompanying figure, $\overline{AC}$ is a diameter of circle O, and $\overline{CB}$ is a chord of the circle.
　　(a)　What type of triangle is $\triangle OCB$?
　　(b)　Prove that $m(\angle 1) + m(\angle 2) = m(\angle 3)$.
　　(c)　Prove that $m(\angle 1) = \frac{1}{2}[m(\angle 3)]$.

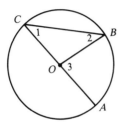

14.　(a)　In how many points can a line intersect a sphere?
　　(b)　In how many points can a plane intersect a sphere?

15. For each of the following circumferences, find the exact length of the radius of the circle.
    (a) 12π cm   (b) 6 cm   (c) $\frac{2}{3}$ cm   (d) 92π m
16. For each of the following, if a circle has the dimensions given, what is its circumference?
    (a) 6 cm diameter   (b) 3 cm radius   (c) $\frac{2}{\pi}$ cm radius   (d) 6π cm diameter
17. What happens to the circumference of a circle if the length of the radius is doubled?
18. The following figure is a circle whose radius is r units. The diameters of the two semicircular regions inside the large circle are both r units, too. Compute the length of the curve that separates the black and white regions.

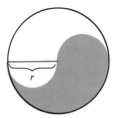

BRAIN TEASER

Suppose a wire is stretched tightly around the earth. (The radius of the earth is approximately 6400 km.) If the wire is cut, its circumference is increased by 20 m, and the wire is placed back around the earth so that the wire is the same distance from the earth at every point, could you walk under the wire?

SOLUTION TO THE PRELIMINARY PROBLEM

Understanding the Problem

A shard of a fragile pottery saucer was found by archaeologists at a dig in Virginia. The border of the shard (shown in Figure 10-77) was part of a circle. In order to reconstruct the saucer, the archaeologists must determine the radius of the circle.

FIGURE 10-77

Devising a Plan

A mathematical model can be used to determine the radius. Trace an outline of the three-dimensional shard on a piece of paper. The result is an arc of a two-dimensional circle as shown in Figure 10-78. To determine the radius, find the center, O. A circle has infinitely many lines of symmetry, and each line passes through the center of the circle where all the lines of symmetry intersect.

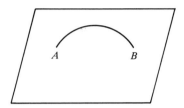

FIGURE 10-78

Carrying Out the Plan

To find a line of symmetry, fold the paper containing $\overset{\frown}{AB}$ so that a portion of the arc is folded onto itself. Then unfold the paper and draw the line of symmetry on the fold mark as shown in Figure 10-79(a). By refolding the paper in Figure 10-79(a) so that a different portion of the arc $\overset{\frown}{AB}$ is folded onto itself, determine a second line of symmetry as shown in Figure 10-79(b). The two dotted lines of symmetry intersect in O, the center of the circle containing $\overset{\frown}{AB}$. To complete the problem, measure the length of either $\overline{OB}$ or $\overline{OA}$. (They should be the same.)

FIGURE 10-79

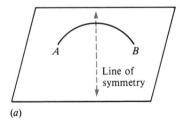
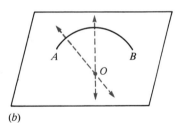

(a) (b)

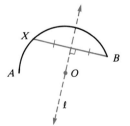

FIGURE 10-80

Looking Back

In the first fold, endpoint B of the arc was folded onto another point of the arc. Label this other point X. The result is shown in Figure 10-80. Since the fold line ℓ is a line of symmetry of the circle containing $\overset{\frown}{AB}$, it must be the perpendicular bisector of $\overline{XB}$ and contain the center of the circle. (See Theorem 10-1, p. 447.) A related problem is: What would happen if the piece of pottery had been a part of a sphere? Would the same ideas still work?

QUESTIONS FROM THE CLASSROOM

1. A student says that since segments can be measured in centimeters, it should be possible to measure angles in centimeters. Is this true?
2. On a test, a student wrote $AB \cong CD$ instead of $\overline{AB} \cong \overline{CD}$. Is this answer correct?
3. A student asks if there are any constructions that cannot be done using a compass and straightedge. How do you answer?
4. A student asks for a mathematical definition of congruence that holds for all figures. How do you respond? Is your response the same for similarity?
5. One student claims that by trisecting $\overline{AB}$ and drawing $\overrightarrow{CD}$ and $\overrightarrow{CE}$ as shown, she has trisected $\angle ACB$. How do you convince her that her construction is wrong?

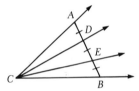

6. In the following drawing, a student claims that polygon $ABCD$ is a parallelogram if $\angle 1 \cong \angle 2$. Is he correct?

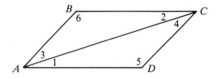

7. A student claims that by connecting the midpoints of the sides of any polygon, a polygon similar to the original results. Is this true?
8. A student asks if the only transformations are flips, slides, turns, or glide reflections. How do you respond?
9. A student asks why $\cong$ rather than $=$ is used to discuss triangles that have the same size and shape. What do you say?
10. A student draws the following figure and claims that since every triangle is congruent to itself, then we can write $\triangle ABC \cong \triangle BCA$. What is your response?

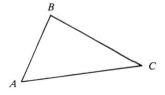

CHAPTER OUTLINE

I. The metric system
   A. A summary of relationships among prefixes and the base unit of linear measure follows.

Prefix	Unit	Relationship to Base Unit	Symbol
kilo	kilometer	1000 meters	km
hecto	hectometer	100 meters	hm
deka	dekameter	10 meters	dam
	meter	1 meter	m
deci	decimeter	0.1 meter	dm
centi	centimeter	0.01 meter	cm
milli	millimeter	0.001 meter	mm

   B. The common units of linear measure are kilometer, meter, centimeter, and millimeter.
   C. The metric system is a base ten or decimal system. To convert from one unit of measure to another in the system, multiply by an appropriate power of 10.

II. Distance
   A. **Distance,** or length, has the following properties, given points A, B, and C.
      1. $AB \geq 0$
      2. $AB = BA$
      3. Triangular inequality:
         $AB + BC \geq AC$
   B. The distance around a two-dimensional figure is called the **perimeter.** The distance around a circle is called the **circumference.**

III. Congruence
   A. Two geometric figures are **congruent** if and only if they have the same size and shape.
   B. Two triangles are congruent if they satisfy any of the following conditions.
      1. Side, side, side (SSS)
      2. Side, angle, side (SAS)
      3. Angle, side, angle (ASA)
      4. Angle, angle, side (AAS)
   C. The simple motions are slides, flips, and turns.
      1. A **slide** (or **translation**) is a motion of a specified distance and direction along a straight line without any accompanying turning and twisting.
      2. A **flip** (or **reflection**) in a line ℓ is a motion that pairs each point P of the plane with a point P' in such a way that ℓ is the perpendicular bisector of $\overline{PP'}$ if $P \notin \ell$, and $P = P'$ if $P \in \ell$.
      3. A **turn** (or **rotation**) is a motion determined by holding one point, the center, fixed and rotating the plane about this point a certain amount in a certain direction.

IV. Types of symmetry
   A. A figure has **line symmetry** if it is its own image under a flip.
   B. A figure has **turn symmetry** when it is its own image under a turn of less than 360° about its center.
   C. A figure that has 180° turn symmetry is said to have **point symmetry.**
   D. A figure has **plane symmetry** when every point of the figure on one side of a plane has a mirror image on the other side of the plane.

V. Similar figures
   A. Two polygons are **similar** if and only if their corresponding angles are congruent and their corresponding sides are proportional.
   B. AAA or AA: If three (two) angles of one triangle are congruent to three (two) angles of a second triangle, respectively, the triangles are similar.

VI. Circles and spheres
  A. A **circle** is a set of points in a plane that are the same distance (radius) from a given point (center).
  B. A **chord** is a segment with endpoints on a circle.
  C. A **secant** is a line that contains a chord of a circle.
  D. A **central angle** of a circle has its vertex at the center of the circle.
  E. A **tangent** is a line that intersects a circle in exactly one point.
  F. A **sphere** is a set of points in space that are the same distance (radius) from a given point (center).
  G. The ratio of the circumference (c) to a diameter (d) of the same circle is the irrational number, π. Thus $C = \pi d$.

VII. Constructions using compass and straightedge
  A. Copy a line segment.
  B. Copy an angle.
  C. Bisect a segment.
  D. Bisect an angle.
  E. Construct a perpendicular from a point to a line.
  F. Construct a perpendicular through a point on a line.
  G. Construct a parallel to a line through a point not on the line.
  H. Divide a segment into congruent parts.
  I. Inscribe regular polygons in a circle.
  J. Circumscribe a circle about a triangle.

CHAPTER TEST

1. In each of the following figures there is at least one pair of congruent triangles. Identify them and tell why they are congruent.

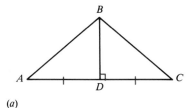

(a)

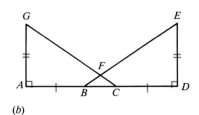

(b)

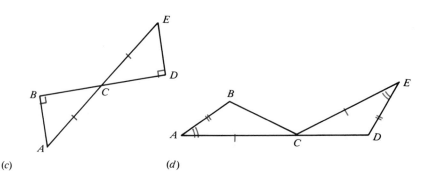

(c)

(d)

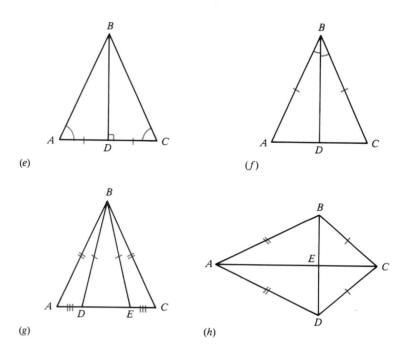

(e)

(f)

(g)

(h)

2. How many lines of symmetry, if any, do each of the following figures have?

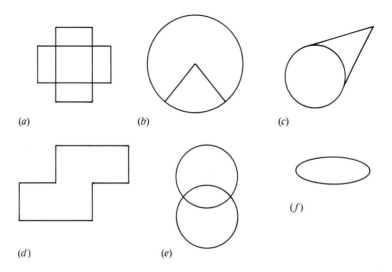

(a)

(b)

(c)

(d)

(e)

(f)

3. For each of the following, identify the types of symmetry (line, turn, or point) the given figure has.

(a)

(b)

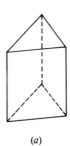

(c)

4. For each of the following, find the number of planes of symmetry.

 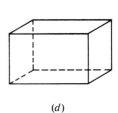

(a)   (b)   (c)   (d)

5. Complete each of the following motions.

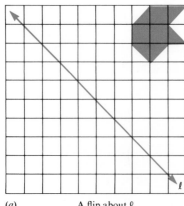 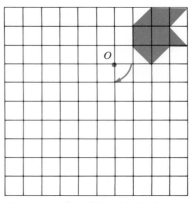

(a)   A flip about ℓ   (b)   A turn about O through the given arc

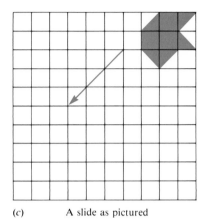

(c)   A slide as pictured

6. For each of the following, construct the image of △*ABC*.

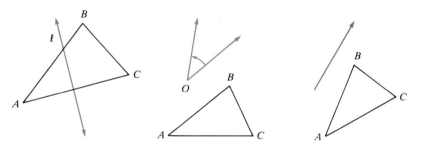

(a) Through a flip about *ℓ*   (b) Through the given turn in *O*   (c) Through the slide pictured

7. Construct each of the following using (i) compass and straightedge, (ii) paper folding.

(a) Bisector of ∡ *A*   (b) Perpendicular to *ℓ* at *B*

• *B*   • *P*

(c) Perpendicular to *ℓ* from *B*   (d) A parallel to *ℓ* through *P*

(e) The perpendicular bisector of $\overline{AB}$

8. For each of the following pairs of similar triangles, find the missing measure.

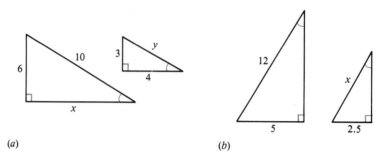

(a)   (b)

9. Divide the segment below into five congruent parts.

A   B

10. Complete the following chart converting metric measures.

	mm	cm	dm	m	dam	hm	km
(a)							0.05
(b)						3.2	
(c)					27		
(d)			2700				
(e)	260 000 000						
(f)				190			

11. For each of the following choose an appropriate metric unit—millimeter, centimeter, meter, or kilometer.
    (a) The thickness of a penny
    (b) The length of a new lead pencil
    (c) The diameter of a dime
    (d) The distance the winner travels in the Indianapolis 500
    (e) The height of a doorknob
    (f) The length of a soccer field
12. Construct a circle containing A and B whose center is on ℓ.

A •
            • B

⟵————————————⟶ ℓ

13. Determine whether each of the following is true or false. If false, explain why.
    (a) A radius of a circle is a chord of the circle.
    (b) A diameter of a circle may be a tangent of the circle.
    (c) If a radius bisects a chord of a circle, then it is perpendicular to the chord.
    (d) Two spheres may intersect in exactly one point.
    (e) Two spheres may intersect in a circle.

14. $\overline{AC}$ and $\overline{BD}$ are diameters of the circle with center P given below.
    (a) Prove that $\overline{AD} \parallel \overline{BC}$.   (b) Prove that polygon $ABCD$ is a rectangle.

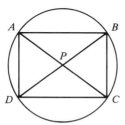

15. A person 2 m tall casts a shadow 1 m long when a building has a 6 m shadow. How high is the building?

16. (a) Which of the following polygons can be inscribed in a circle? Assume all sides of each polygon are congruent and all the angles of polygons (c) and (d) are congruent.
    (b) Based on the answer to part (a), make a conjecture about what kinds of polygons can be inscribed in a circle.

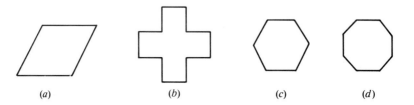

(a)   (b)   (c)   (d)

17. Explain how to inscribe a circle in a regular heptagon using only a compass and straightedge.
18. Explain how to inscribe a circle in a square using only a compass and straightedge.
19. Find the perimeters for each of the following if all arcs shown are semicircles.

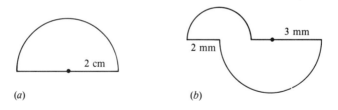

(a)   (b)

20. For each of the following, the length of the diameter of a circle is given. Find the circumference.

   (a) 2π m   (b) $4/\pi$ cm

21. In the circle with center O, $\overrightarrow{AB}$ is tangent to the circle. If $\angle CBA \cong \angle BDA$, prove that $(AB)^2 = (AC)(AD)$.

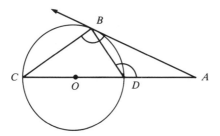

SELECTED BIBLIOGRAPHY

Alexander, F. D. "The Metric System—Let's Emphasize Its Use in Mathematics." *The Arithmetic Teacher,* **20**(May 1973):395–396.

Beamer, J. E. "The Tale of a Kite." *The Arithmetic Teacher,* **22**(May 1975):382–386.

Bohan, H. "Skeeter McGeeter and the Meter." *Arithmetic Teacher,* **26**(December 1978):42–43.

Bruni, J. V. "Geometry for the Intermediate Grades." *Arithmetic Teacher,* **26**(February 1979):17–19.

Bruni, J. V., and H. Silverman. "Developing the Concept of Linear Measurement." *The Arithmetic Teacher,* **21**(November 1974):570–577.

Burton, G. M. "Metrification of Elementary Mathematics Textbooks in the Seventies—the 1870's, That Is." *Arithmetic Teacher,* **27**(December 1979):28–31.

Eccles, F. M. "Transformations in High School Geometry." *The Mathematics Teacher,* **65**(February 1972):103, 165–169.

Edwards, R. "Discoveries in Geometry by Folding and Cutting." *The Arithmetic Teacher,* **24**(March 1977):196–198.

Fisher, R. "Metric Is Here: So Let's Get On With It." *The Arithmetic Teacher,* **20**(May 1973):400–402.

Gast, R. H. "The High School Geometry Controversy: Is Transformational Geometry the Answer?" *The Mathematics Teacher,* **64**(January 1971):37–40.

Hallerberg, A. E. "The Metric System: Past, Present, Future?" *The Arithmetic Teacher,* **20**(April 1973):247–255.

Helgren, F. J. "Schools Are Going Metric." *The Arithmetic Teacher,* **20**(April 1973):265–267.

Henderson, G. L., and C. P. Collier. "Geometric Activities in Later Childhood Education." *The Arithmetic Teacher,* **20**(October 1973):444–453.

Hiatt, A. A. "Problem Solving in Geometry." *The Mathematics Teacher,* **65**(November 1972):595–600.

Hirsch, S. C. *Meter Means Measure.* New York: Viking Press, 1973.

Immerzeel, G. "Geometric Activities for Early Childhood Education." *The Arithmetic Teacher,* **20**(October 1973):438–443.

Johnson, M. "Generating Patterns for Transformations." *The Arithmetic Teacher,* **24**(March 1977):191–195.

Kerr, D. "A Case for Geometry: Geometry Is Important, It Is There, Teach It." *The Arithmetic Teacher,* **26**(February 1979):14.

Kerr, D. R. "The Study of Space Experiences: A Framework for Geometry for Elementary Teachers." *The Arithmetic Teacher,* **23**(March 1976):169–174.

Kidder, R. "Euclidean Transformations: Elementary School Spaceometry." *The Arithmetic Teacher,* **24**(March 1977):201–207.

Krause, M. C. "Wind Rose, the Beautiful Circle." *The Arithmetic Teacher,* **20**(May 1973):375–379.

Leffin, W. W. *Going Metric Grades K–6: Guidelines for the Mathematics Teacher.* Reston, Va; National Council of Teachers of Mathematics, 1975.

Leutzinger, L. P., and G. Nelson. "Let's Do It: Meaningful Measurements, *Arithmetic Teacher,* **27**(March 1980):6–11.

Lindquist, M., and M. Dana. "The Surprising Circle!" *Arithmetic Teacher,* **25**(January 1978): 4–10.

Lindquist, M., and M. Dana. "Wallpaper Capers." *Arithmetic Teacher,* **26**(February 1979):4–9.

Lott, J. W., and I. M. Dayoub. "What Can Be Done with a Mira?" *The Mathematics Teacher,* **70**(May 1977):394–399.

Maletsky, E. M. "Activities: Fun with Flips." *The Mathematics Teacher,* **66**(October 1973):531–534.

Moulton, J. P. "Some Geometry Experiences for Elementary School Children." *The Arithmetic Teacher,* **21**(February 1974):114–116.

Pottinger, B. "Measuring, Discovering, and Estimating the Metric Way." *The Arithmetic Teacher,* **22**(May 1975):372–377.

Reid, J. "Cutting Across a Circle." *Arithmetic Teacher,* **26**(April 1979):27.

Sanok, G. "Living in a World of Transformations." *Arithmetic Teacher,* **25**(April 1978):36–40.

Silverman, H. "Geometry in the Primary Grades: Exploring Geometric Ideas in the Primary Grades." *Arithmetic Teacher,* **26**(February 1979):15–16.

Theissen, D. "Measurement Activities Using the Metric System." *Arithmetic Teacher* **27**(October 1979):36–37.

Thomas, D. "Geometry in the Middle School: Problem Solving with Trapezoids." *Arithmetic Teacher,* **26**(February 1979):20–21.

Threadgill, J. "Let's Metricate Parents, Too!" *Arithmetic Teacher,* **26**(December 1978):18–19.

Trueblood, C. R., and M. Szabo. "Procedures for Designing Your Own Metric Games for Pupil Involvement." *The Arithmetic Teacher,* **21**(May 1974):404–408.

Vance, I. E. "The Content of the Elementary School Geometry Program." *The Arithmetic Teacher,* **20**(October 1973):468–477.

Vervoort, G. "Inching Our Way Towards the Metric System." *The Arithmetic Teacher,* **20**(April 1973):275–279. (Also in *The Mathematics Teacher,* **66**(April 1973):297–302.)

Viets, L. "Experiences for Metric Missionaries." *The Arithmetic Teacher,* **20**(April 1973):269–273.

Woodward, E. "Geometry with a Mira." *The Arithmetic Teacher,* **24**(February 1977):117–118.

Zweng, Marilyn J. "A Geometry Course for Elementary Teachers." *The Arithmetic Teacher,* **20**(October 1973):457–467.

More Concepts of Measurement

PRELIMINARY PROBLEM

A farmer has a field containing three trees, *A*, *B*, and *C*, that form the vertices of a right triangle, which has area 1 hectare. The farmer tethers her animals at the midpoints of the sides of a right

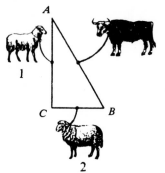

triangle. Her steer is at the midpoint of the hypotenuse and a sheep is at each of the other midpoints. The animals are tied to posts with ropes just long enough to allow them to reach the adjacent vertices. Sheep 1 can reach *A* and *C*; sheep 2 can reach *C* and *B*; and the steer can reach *A* and *B* as in the figure. What is the total area that the two sheep can reach and the steer cannot?

11-1 AREAS OF POLYGONS

area

The term **area** denotes an amount of surface. By the area of a figure we mean the area of the interior region determined by the figure. For example, by the area of a rectangle we mean the area of the rectangular region determined by the rectangle. The most commonly used region for measuring area is the square. For example, a square measuring one inch on each side has area of one square inch, denoted 1 sq. in. A square measuring one centimeter on each side, has an area of one square centimeter, denoted by $1\ cm^2$. A square measuring one meter on each side has area of one square meter, denoted by $1\ m^2$.

To determine how many square centimeters are in a square meter, look at Figure 11-1. Since there are 100 cm in 1 m, each side of the square meter

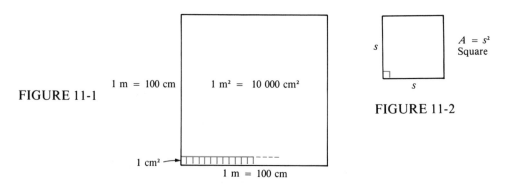

FIGURE 11-1

1 m = 100 cm $1\ m^2$ = 10 000 cm^2

1 cm^2

1 m = 100 cm

s

s

$A = s^2$
Square

FIGURE 11-2

has a measure of 100 cm. Thus, it takes 100 rows of 100 square centimeters each to fill a square meter—that is 100 · 100 or 10 000 cm^2. In general, the area, *A*, of a square that is *s* units on a side is s^2 as given in Figure 11-2.

Other metric conversions of area measure can be developed using the formula for the area of a square. For example, Figure 11-3 shows that $1 \text{ m}^2 = 100 \text{ dm}^2 = 10\,000 \text{ cm}^2 = 1\,000\,000 \text{ mm}^2$. Likewise, Figure 11-4 shows that $1 \text{ m}^2 = 0.01 \text{ dam}^2 = 0.0001 \text{ hm}^2 = 0.000001 \text{ km}^2$. Similarly $1 \text{ cm}^2 = 100 \text{ mm}^2$ and $1 \text{ km}^2 = 1\,000\,000 \text{ m}^2$.

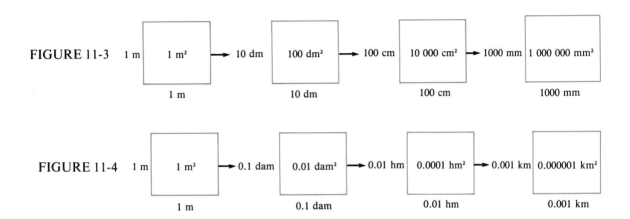

FIGURE 11-3

FIGURE 11-4

Table 11-1 shows the symbols for metric units of area and their relationship to the square meter.

TABLE 11-1

Unit	Symbol	Relationship to Square Meter
Square kilometer	km^2	$1\,000\,000$ m^2
*Square hectometer	hm^2	$10\,000$ m^2
*Square dekameter	dam^2	100 m^2
Square meter	m^2	1 m^2
*Square decimeter	dm^2	0.01 m^2
Square centimeter	cm^2	0.0001 m^2
Square millimeter	mm^2	0.000001 m^2

*means not commonly used

Example 11-1   Convert each of the following as indicated.

(a) 5 cm^2 to mm^2 (b) 1240 m^2 to km^2

Solution

(a)   1 cm^2 = 100 mm^2 implies 5 cm^2 = 5 · 1 cm^2 = 5 · 100 mm^2 = 500 mm^2.

(b)   1 m^2 = 0.000001 km^2 implies 1240 m^2 = 1240 · 1 m^2 = 1240 · 0.000001 km^2 = 0.001240 km^2

One way to measure area is to count the number of units of area contained in any given region. For example, suppose the square in Figure 11-5(a) represents one square unit. Then, the rectangle *ABCD* in Figure 11-5(b) contains twelve nonoverlapping square units, since there are three

FIGURE 11-5

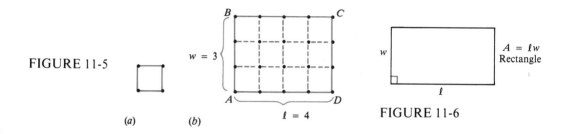

(a)   (b)

FIGURE 11-6

rows of squares with four squares in a row. Hence, the area of rectangle *ABCD* is twelve square units. If the unit is 1 cm^2, then the area of rectangle *ABCD* is 12 cm^2. As with rectangle *ABCD*, the area of any rectangle may be found by multiplying the lengths of two adjacent sides. In general, if *A* represents the area of any rectangle whose adjacent sides have lengths ℓ and w (each in the same unit length), then $A = \ell w$ as given in Figure 11-6.

Example 11-2

Find the area of each rectangle in Figure 11-7

FIGURE 11-7

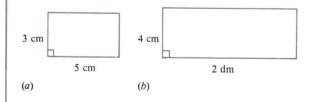

(a)   (b)

Solution

(a) $A = 3$ cm · 5 cm = 15 cm^2

(b)   First, write the lengths of the sides in the same unit of length. Since 2 dm = 20 cm, $A = (4$ cm$)(20$ cm$) = 80$ cm^2. Alternately, 4 cm = 0.4 dm, so $A = (0.4$ dm$)(2$ dm$) = 0.8$ dm^2.

Formulas for areas of various polygons follow from the formula for the area of a rectangle. Consider, for example, the parallelogram *ABCD* in Figure 11-8(a). The parallelogram can be separated into two parts. The shaded triangle can be placed on the right of the parallelogram as in Figure 11-8(b) to obtain a rectangle with length *b* and width *h*. The parallelogram and the rectangle have the same area. (Why?) Since the area of the rectangle is *bh*, the area of the original parallelogram *ABCD* is also *bh*. In general, any

base   side of a parallelogram can be designated as a **base** with measure *b*. We will use *b* to represent either the base or its measure, depending on the context.

height   The **height,** *h*, is always the length of a segment from the opposite side and perpendicular to the base.

FIGURE 11-8

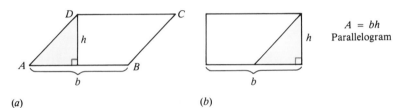

(a)   *(b)*

A formula for the area of a triangle follows from the formula for the area of a parallelogram. In Figure 11-9(a), $\triangle ABC$ has base *b* and altitude *h*. If $\triangle ABD$ is constructed congruent to $\triangle ABC$ and placed as shown in Figure 11-9(b), it can be proved that quadrilateral *BCAD* is a parallelogram. Since the area of parallelogram *BCAD* is *bh*, the area of $\triangle ABC$ is ½*bh*.

FIGURE 11-9

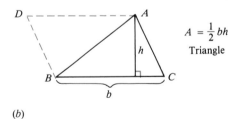

$$A = \frac{1}{2}bh$$
Triangle

(a)   *(b)*

Example 11-3   Find the area of each in Figure 11-10. Assume the quadrilaterals in (a) and (b) are parallelograms.

FIGURE 11-10

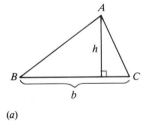
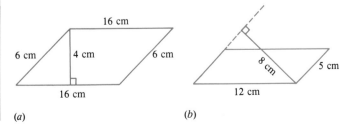

(a)   *(b)*

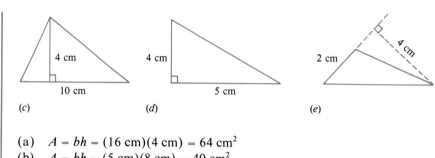

(c)   (d)   (e)

Solution

(a) $A = bh = (16 \text{ cm})(4 \text{ cm}) = 64 \text{ cm}^2$
(b) $A = bh = (5 \text{ cm})(8 \text{ cm}) = 40 \text{ cm}^2$
(c) $A = \frac{1}{2}bh = \frac{1}{2}(10 \text{ cm})(4 \text{ cm}) = 20 \text{ cm}^2$
(d) $A = \frac{1}{2}bh = \frac{1}{2}(5 \text{ cm})(4 \text{ cm}) = 10 \text{ cm}^2$
(e) $A = \frac{1}{2}bh = \frac{1}{2}(2 \text{ cm})(4 \text{ cm}) = 4 \text{ cm}^2$

Areas of other polygons can be found by partitioning the polygons into triangles. Trapezoid $ABCD$ in Figure 11-11(a), has bases b_1 and b_2 and height h. By drawing diagonal $\overline{BD}$ (or $\overline{AC}$), as in Figure 11-11(b), two triangles are formed, one with base $\overline{AB}$ and height $\overline{DE}$ and the other with base $\overline{CD}$ and height $\overline{BF}$. Since $\overline{DE} \cong \overline{BF}$, each has height h. Thus, the areas of triangles ADB and DCB are $\frac{1}{2}(b_1 h)$ and $\frac{1}{2}(b_2 h)$, respectively. Hence, the area of trapezoid $ABCD$ is $\frac{1}{2}(b_1 h) + \frac{1}{2}(b_2 h)$ or $\frac{1}{2}h(b_1 + b_2)$.

FIGURE 11-11

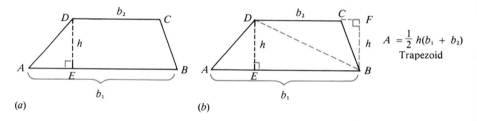

$A = \frac{1}{2} h(b_1 + b_2)$
Trapezoid

(a)   (b)

Example 11-4

Find the areas the trapezoids in Figure 11-12.

FIGURE 11-12

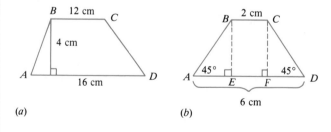

(a)   (b)

Solution

(a) $A = \frac{1}{2}h(b_1 + b_2) = \frac{1}{2}(4 \text{ cm})(12 \text{ cm} + 16 \text{ cm}) = 56 \text{ cm}^2$

(b) $\triangle ABE$ and $\triangle DCF$ are congruent isosceles right triangles. (Why?) Also, polygon $BCFE$ is a rectangle, so $BC = EF = 2$ cm. Thus, $AE + FD = 6$ cm $- 2$ cm $= 4$ cm. Since $\overline{AE} \cong \overline{DF}$, and $\overline{AE} \cong \overline{BE}$, each is 2 cm long. Therefore, the area of the trapezoid is $\frac{1}{2}(2$ cm$) \cdot (6$ cm $+ 2$ cm$) = 8$ cm^2.

Just as the area of a triangle was used to find the area of a trapezoid, it can be used as the basis for finding the area of any regular polygon. For example, consider the regular hexagon pictured in Figure 11-13(a). The hexagon can be separated into six congruent triangles each with a vertex at the center, with side s, and height a. (The height of such a triangle of a **apothem** regular polygon is called the **apothem** and is denoted by a.) The area of each triangle is $\frac{1}{2}as$. Since there are six triangles that make up the hexagon, the area of the hexagon is $6(\frac{1}{2}\ as)$ or $\frac{1}{2}a(6s)$. However, $6s$ is the perimeter p of the hexagon, so the area of the hexagon is $\frac{1}{2}ap$. The same process can be used to develop the formula for the area of any regular polygon. That is, the area of any regular polygon is $\frac{1}{2}ap$, where a is the height of one of the triangles involved and p is the perimeter of the polygon.

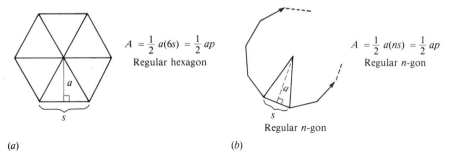

FIGURE 11-13

$$A = \frac{1}{2}\ a(6s) = \frac{1}{2}\ ap$$
Regular hexagon

$$A = \frac{1}{2}\ a(ns) = \frac{1}{2}\ ap$$
Regular n-gon

Regular n-gon

(a)   (b)

The formula for the area of a regular polygon can be used to develop the formula for the area of a circle. Consider, for example, the circle in Figure 11-14(a). The area of a regular polygon inscribed in the circle as in Figure 11-14(b) approximates the area of the circle. The area of any inscribed

FIGURE 11-14

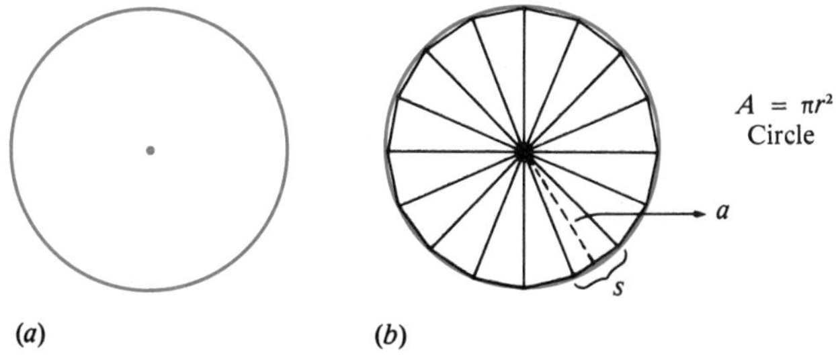

$$A = \pi r^2$$
Circle

(a)   (b)

regular n-gon is $\frac{1}{2}ap$, where a is the height of a triangle of the n-gon and p is the perimeter. If the number of sides, n, is made very large, then the perimeter and the area of the n-gon are close to those of the circle. Also, a is approximately equal to the radius r of the circle and the perimeter approximates the circumference, $2\pi r$. Since the area of the circle is approximately equal to the area of the n-gon, then $\frac{1}{2}ap \doteq \frac{1}{2}r \cdot 2\pi r = \pi r^2$. In fact, the area of the circle is exactly πr^2. (A complete mathematical proof of the formula for the area of a circle requires an understanding of limits and is beyond the scope of this text.)

sector   A **sector** of a circle is a pie-shaped region of the circle. The area of a sector depends upon the radius of the circle and the central angle determining the sector. If the angle has a measure of 90°, as in Figure 11-15(a), the area of the sector is one-fourth the area of the circle or $(90/360)\,(\pi r^2)$. In general, a sector whose central angle has measure θ, has area $(\theta/360)\,(\pi r^2)$, as shown in Figure 11-15(b).

FIGURE 11-15

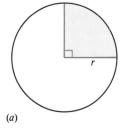

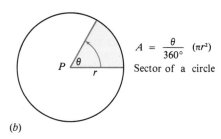

$$A = \frac{\theta}{360°}\,(\pi r^2)$$

Sector of a circle

(a)   (b)

Example 11-5   Find the area of the sector shown in Figure 11-16.

FIGURE 11-16

Solution $A = \dfrac{80}{360} \cdot \pi (5 \text{ cm})^2 = \dfrac{50}{9}\,\pi \text{ cm}^2$

One of the most common applications of area today is in land measure. Old deeds in the United States include land measures in terms of chains, poles, rods, acres, sections, lots, and townships. In the metric system, small land areas are measured in terms of a square unit 10 m on a side (a square dekameter) and called an **are** (pronounced "air"), and denoted by a. Larger land areas, currently measured in acres, are measured in **hectares.** A hectare is 100 a. A hectare, denoted by ha, is the amount of land whose area is

are

hectares

square kilometer

10 000 m², about 2½ acres. One hectare is the area of a square 100 m on a side. For very large land measures, the **square kilometer,** denoted by km², is used. One square kilometer is the area of a square with a side 1000 m long.

Example 11-6

A rectangular field is 200 m by 400 m. Find the area of the field in hectares.

Solution

$A = 200 \text{ m} \cdot 400 \text{ m} = 80\,000 \text{ m}^2 = 8 \text{ ha}$

PROBLEM SET 11-1

1. Choose the most appropriate metric units (cm², m², or km²) for measuring each of the following.
   (a) Area of a sheet of notebook paper
   (b) Area of a quarter
   (c) Area of a desk top
   (d) Area of a classroom floor
   (e) Area of a parallel parking space
   (f) Area of an airport runway
2. Complete the following conversion table.

Item	m²	cm²	mm²
Area of a sheet of paper		588	
Area of a cross section of a crayon			192
Area of a desk top	1.5		
Area of a dollar bill		100	
Area of a postage stamp		5	

3. Estimate, then measure, each of the following using either cm², m², or km².
   (a) Area of door   (b) Area of chair seat
   (c) Area of desk top   (d) Area of chalkboard
4. Explain the difference between a 2 m square and 2 m².
5. Find the areas of each of the following triangles.

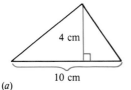

(a)

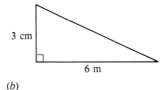

(b)

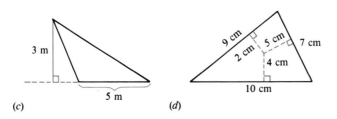

(c)   (d)

6. Find the areas of each of the following quadrilaterals.

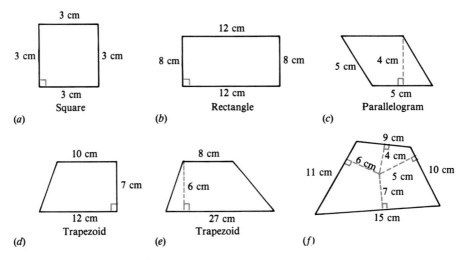

3 cm

3 cm   3 cm

3 cm
Square

(a)

12 cm

8 cm   8 cm

12 cm
Rectangle

(b)

4 cm

5 cm

5 cm
Parallelogram

(c)

10 cm

7 cm

12 cm
Trapezoid

(d)

8 cm

6 cm

27 cm
Trapezoid

(e)

9 cm

4 cm
6 cm
11 cm   5 cm   10 cm
7 cm

15 cm

(f)

7. In the figure below, $\ell \parallel \overleftrightarrow{AB}$. If the area of $\triangle ABP$ is 10 cm², what are the areas of $\triangle ABQ$, $\triangle ABR$, $\triangle ABS$, $\triangle ABT$, and $\triangle ABU$? Explain your answers.

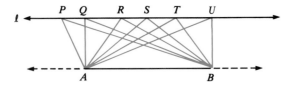

ℓ P Q   R   S   T   U

A   B

8. Find the area of each of the following regular polygons.

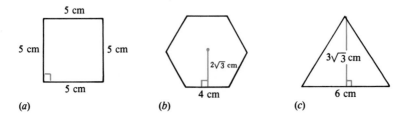

5 cm

5 cm   5 cm

5 cm

(a)

$2\sqrt{3}$ cm

4 cm

(b)

$3\sqrt{3}$ cm

6 cm

(c)

9. Find the area of each of the following. Leave your answers in terms of π.

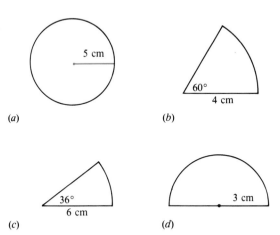

(a) (b)

(c) (d)

10. (a) If a circle has a circumference of 8π cm, what is its area?
    (b) If a circle with radius r and a square with a side of length s have the same area, express r in terms of s.

11. Find the area of each of the following shaded parts. Assume all arcs are circular.

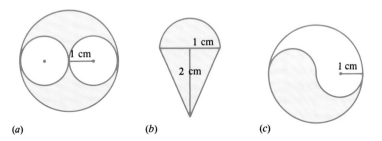

(a) (b) (c)

12. Solve each of the following for x.

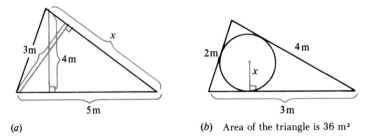

(a) (b) Area of the triangle is 36 m²

13. Find the area of rhombus $ABCD$ if $AC = 6$ m and $BD = 8$ m.
14. Complete each of the following:
     (a) A football field is about 49 m by 100 m or _____ m².
     (b) About _____ ares are in two football fields.
     (c) About _____ hectares are in two football fields.
15. A circular flower bed is 6 m in diameter and has a circular sidewalk around it 1 m wide. Find the area of the sidewalk in square meters.
16. (a) A rectangular piece of land is 1300 m by 1500 m. What is the area in km²? What is the area in hectares?
     (b) A rectangular piece of land is 1300 yards by 1500 yards. What is the area in square miles? What is the area in acres? Compare this problem to part (a).
17. Joe uses stick-on square carpet tiles to cover his 3 m by 4 m bathroom. If each tile is 1 dm on a side, how many tiles does he need?
18. A rectangular plot of land is to be seeded with grass. If the plot is 22 m by 28 m, and if a 1 kg bag of seed is needed for 85 m² of land, how many bags of seed will it take?
19. (a) Find the area of each polygon in the following figure if the area of the figure in the upper right hand corner is one square unit.

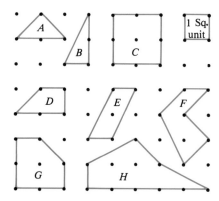

     (b) A polygon, all of whose vertices are points on dot paper, is called a **lattice polygon.** In 1899, G. Pick discovered a surprising theorem involving I, the number of dots *inside* the polygon, and B the number of dots that lie *on* the polygon. The theorem states that the area of any lattice polygon is $I + \frac{1}{2}B - 1$. Check that this is true for the polygons in (a).
20. The area of a trapezoid can be found by constructing a trapezoid (2) congruent to another trapezoid, (1), and placing them to form a parallelogram as follows. Explain how the drawing can be used to determine the formula $A = \frac{1}{2}h(b_1 + b_2)$ for the area of a trapezoid.

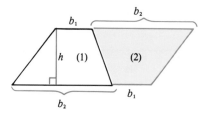

21. Explain how the following drawing can be used to determine a formula for the area of △*ABC*.

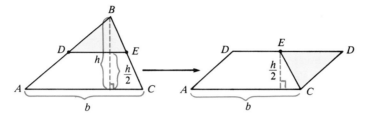

22. A different method for approximating the area of a circle is to separate the circle into congruent sectors and place them as pictured below. Explain how these drawings can be used to approximate the area of the circle.

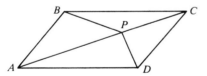

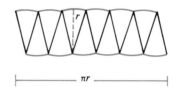

★ 23. In the drawing below, quadrilateral *ABCD* is a parallelogram and *P* is any point on $\overline{AC}$. Prove that the area of △*BCP* is equal to the area of △*DPC*.

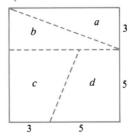

BRAIN TEASER

The accompanying rectangle was apparently formed by cutting the square shown along the dotted lines and reassembling the pieces as pictured.

1. What is the area of the square?
2. What is the area of the rectangle?
3. How do you explain the discrepancy?

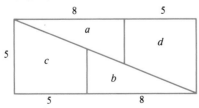

11-2   THE PYTHAGOREAN RELATIONSHIP

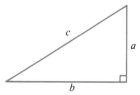

FIGURE 11-17

Pythagoras is one of the two most famous geometers of Greek antiquity (the other being Euclid). Exactly how much geometry Pythagoras himself either discovered or invented is not known, since he was the head of a group known as the Pythagoreans who attributed all of their discoveries to him. One of the most famous discoveries is known as the Pythagorean Theorem.

THEOREM

> **THE PYTHAGOREAN THEOREM**   If a right triangle has legs of lengths a and b and hypotenuse of length c, then $c^2 = a^2 + b^2$.

hypotenuse, legs

In Figure 11-17, the side of the triangle opposite the right angle c is called the **hypotenuse** of the triangle. The other two sides are called **legs**. The hypotenuse is always the longest side of a right triangle.

Interpreted in terms of areas, the Pythagorean Theorem says that the area of a square with the hypotenuse of a right triangle as a side is equal to the sum of the areas of the squares with the legs as sides. This relationship was illustrated on a Greek stamp in 1955, shown in Figure 11-18, to honor the 2500th anniversary of the founding of the Pythagorean School.

There are hundreds of known proofs for the Pythagorean Theorem today. The classic book entitled *The Pythagorean Proposition* contains many of these proofs.

Many proofs of the Pythagorean Theorem involve constructing a square with area c^2 from squares of area a^2 and b^2. For example, Figure 11-19(a)

FIGURE 11-18

FIGURE 11-19

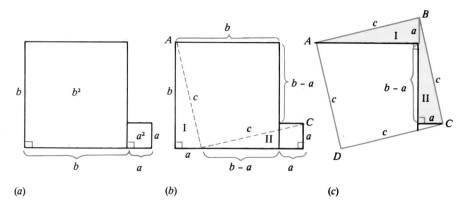

(a)   (b)   (c)

shows two squares with areas a^2 and b^2 side by side. Dissect Figure 11-19(b) along the dotted lines. Then, rotate triangle I counterclockwise 90° about point A, to its new position in Figure 11-19(c). Similarly, rotate triangle II, 90° clockwise about point C, to its new position in Figure 11-19(c). Since quadrilateral $ABCD$, in Figure 11-19(c) is composed of pieces of the squares in Figure 11-19(a), it must have the same area—that is, $a^2 + b^2$. However it can be shown that quadrilateral $ABCD$ is a square with side c, and hence, it has area c^2. Consequently, $a^2 + b^2 = c^2$.

The Pythagorean Theorem can also be proved using similar triangles. This is left as an exercise. (*Hint:* use problem 8 of Problem Set 10-5).

Example 11-7 | For each part of Figure 11-20 find x by using the Pythagorean Theorem.

FIGURE 11-20

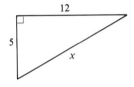

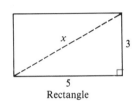

5
Rectangle

(a)   (b)

Solution | (a)   By the Pythagorean Theorem

$$5^2 + 12^2 = x^2$$
$$25 + 144 = x^2$$
$$169 = x^2$$
$$13 = x$$

(b)   In the rectangle, the diagonal labeled x partitions the rectangle into two right triangles with length 5 units and width 3 units

$$5^2 + 3^2 = x^2$$
$$25 + 9 = x^2$$
$$34 = x^2$$
$$\sqrt{34} = x$$

Given a triangle with sides of lengths a, b, and c such that $a^2 + b^2 = c^2$, must the triangle be a right triangle? This is the case and we state the following without proof.

THEOREM	CONVERSE OF THE PYTHAGOREAN THEOREM If $\triangle ABC$ is a triangle with sides of lengths a, b, and c such that $a^2 + b^2 = c^2$, then $\triangle ABC$ is a right triangle with the right angle opposite the side of length c.

Example 11-8 Determine whether or not the following can be the lengths of the sides of a right triangle.

(a) $51, 68, 85$ (b) $2, 3, \sqrt{13}$ (c) $3, 4, 7$

Solution   (a) $51^2 + 68^2 = 7225 = 85^2$, so 51, 68, and 85 can be the lengths of the sides of a right triangle.

(b) $2^2 + 3^2 = 4 + 9 = 13 = (\sqrt{13})^2$, so 2, 3, and $\sqrt{13}$ can be the lengths of the sides of a right triangle.

(c)   Since $3^2 + 4^2 \neq 7^2$, the measures cannot be the lengths of the sides of a right triangle.

PROBLEM SET 11-2

1. Use the Pythagorean Theorem to find x in each of the following.

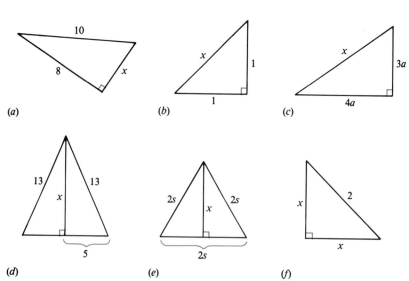

(a)   (b)   (c)

(d)   (e)   (f)

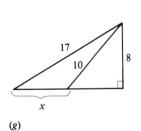

17
10
8
x

(g)

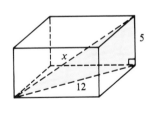

5
x
12

(h)

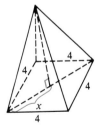

4
4
4
x
4

(i)   Base is a square

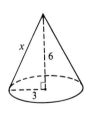

x
6
3

(j)

2. For each of the following, can the given numbers represent lengths of sides of a right triangle?

(a) 10, 24, 16   (b) 2, $\sqrt{3}$, 1   (c) 16, 34, 30

(d) $\sqrt{2}$, $\sqrt{3}$, $\sqrt{5}$ (e) $\sqrt{2}$, $\sqrt{2}$, 2   (f) $\frac{3}{2}$, $\frac{4}{2}$, $\frac{5}{2}$

3. For each of the following, solve for the unknowns.

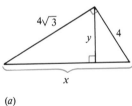

$4\sqrt{3}$
y
4
x

(a)

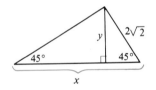

y
$2\sqrt{2}$
45°   45°
x

(b)

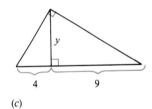

y
4   9

(c)

4. What is the longest line segment that can be drawn in a right rectangular prism that is 12 cm wide, 15 cm long, and 9 cm high?

5. Two cars leave a house at the same time. One car travels 60 km/hr north, while the other car travels 40 km/hr east. After 1 hour, how far apart are the cars?

6. On a square baseball field, 90 feet on each side, a baseball is thrown by the shortstop, who is on the baseline 10 feet from second base, to home plate. How far did he throw the ball?

7. Use the following drawing to prove the Pythagorean Theorem by using corresponding parts of similar triangles, $\triangle ACD$, $\triangle CBD$, and $\triangle ABC$. Lengths of sides are indicated by a, b, c, x, and y.

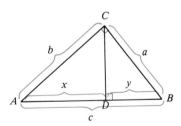

C
b   a
x   y
A   D   B
c

8. Before he was elected President of the United States, James Garfield discovered a proof of the Pythagorean Theorem. He formed a trapezoid like the one that follows and found the area of the trapezoid in two different ways. Can you discover his proof?

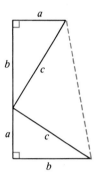

9. Use the following figure to prove the Pythagorean Theorem.

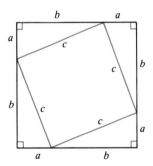

10. Find the area of each of the following.

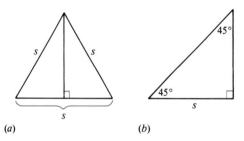

(a) (b)

11. (a)   In the following figure, an equilateral triangle is constructed on each side of a right triangle. Prove that the area of the triangle on the hypotenuse is equal to the sum of the areas of the triangles on the legs.

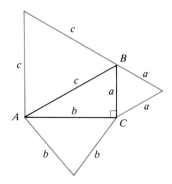

(b)   In the figure accompanying part (a), construct semicircles on △*ABC* with $\overline{AB}$, $\overline{BC}$, and $\overline{AC}$ as diameters. Is the area of the semicircle on the hypotenuse equal to the sum of the areas of the semicircles on the legs.

12.   If the hypotenuse and a leg of one right triangle are congruent to the hypotenuse and a leg of the other right triangle, respectively, must the triangles be congruent?

13.   What is the length of the diagonal of the following cube? (*Hint:* Draw a diagonal of a base.)

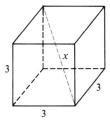

BRAIN TEASER

A spider sitting at *A*, the midpoint of the edge of the ceiling in the room shown, spies a fly on the floor at *C*, the midpoint of the edge of the floor. If the spider must walk along the wall, ceiling, or floor, what is the length of the shortest path the spider can travel to reach the fly?

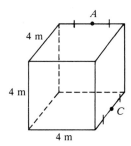

LABORATORY ACTIVITY   The Pythagorean theorem can be demonstrated with paper cutting. Cut along the dotted lines of part (a) of the figure and rearrange the pieces as illustrated in part (b).

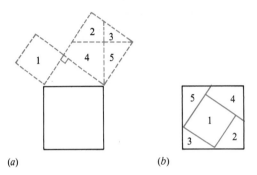

(a)   (b)

11-3 SURFACE AREAS OF POLYHEDRA AND SPHERES

The surface area of a polyhedron is found by adding the areas of each face of the polyhedron. Cubes are the simplest polyhedra. The surface area of the cube in Figure 11-21(a) is the sum of the areas of the faces of the cube. Since each of the six faces is a square of area 16 cm², the surface area is $6 \cdot (16 \text{ cm}^2)$ or 96 cm².

In general, if the edges of a cube are e units, as in Figure 11-21(b), then each face is a square with area e^2 units. Since there are six faces, the surface area of the cube is given by $S.A. = 6e^2$, where e is the length of a side and $S.A.$ is the surface area.

FIGURE 11-21

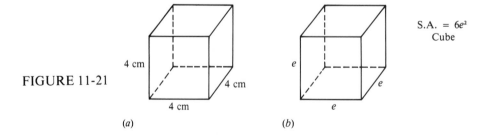

(a)   (b)

To find the surface area of other right prisms, find the sum of the areas of the rectangles that comprise the lateral faces and the areas of the top and

lateral surface area
surface area

bottom. The sum of the areas of the lateral faces is called the **lateral surface area.** Thus, the **surface area** is the sum of the lateral surface area and the area of the bases.

Figure 11-22(a) shows a right pentagonal prism and Figure 11-22(b) shows the figure cut into three pieces. The cuts show the top, the bottom, and the lateral faces. The section formed by the lateral faces is stretched out flat.

FIGURE 11-22

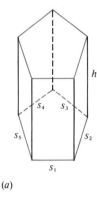

(a)

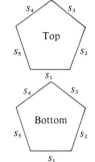

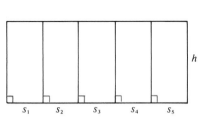

(b)

BRAIN TEASER

How can a stack of fourteen cubes, each having sides of length 1 cm, be arranged so that each touches at least two others and the arrangement has the maximum possible total surface area?

It forms a rectangle whose length is $s_1 + s_2 + s_3 + s_4 + s_5$ and whose width is h. Since $s_1 + s_2 + s_3 + s_4 + s_5$ is the perimeter p of the base of the prism, the lateral surface area is $(s_1 + s_2 + s_3 + s_4 + s_5) \cdot h$ or ph. If B stands for the area of each of the prism's bases, then the surface area ($S.A.$) of the prism is given by the following formula.

$$S.A. = ph + 2B$$

This formula holds for any right prism regardless of the shape of its bases.

Example 11-9 | Find the surface area of each of the right prisms in Figure 11-23.

FIGURE 11-23

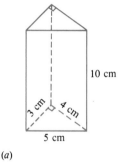

(a)

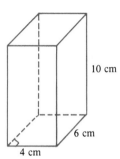

(b)

Solution   (a) Each base is a right triangle. Hence, the area of the bases is $2(\frac{1}{2} \cdot 3 \text{ cm} \cdot 4 \text{ cm})$ or 12 cm². The perimeter of a base is 3 cm + 4 cm + 5 cm or 12 cm. Hence, the lateral surface area is (12 cm) (10 cm) or 120 cm², and the surface area is 132 cm².

   (b) The area of the bases is 2(4 cm) (6 cm) or 48 cm². The lateral surface area is 2(4 cm + 6 cm) $\cdot$ 10 or 200 cm², so the surface area of the right prism is 248 cm².

To find the surface area of the right circular cylinder shown in Figure 11-24(a), cut it into a top and a bottom and the lateral surface shown in Figure 11-24(b). The lateral surface stretched out is a rectangle whose length

FIGURE 11-24

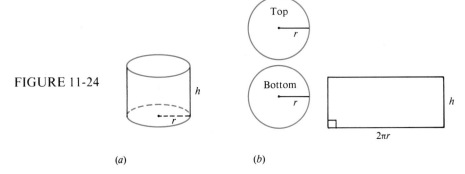

(a)   (b)

is the circumference of the circular base, $2\pi r$, and whose width is the height of the cylinder, h. Hence, the surface area is the sum of the areas of the two circular bases and the lateral suface area.

$$S.A. = 2\pi r^2 + (2\pi r)h$$

slant height   Similarly, the surface area of a right circular cone can be determined by cutting the cone along a **slant height** ℓ, removing the base, and flattening the lateral surface as shown in Figure 11-25. The area of the base is the area of a

FIGURE 11-25

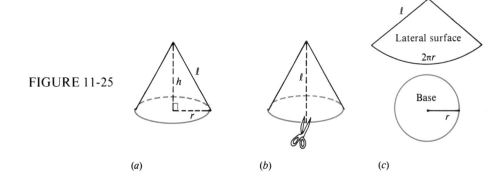

(a)   (b)   (c)

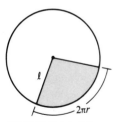

FIGURE 11-26

circle with radius r, namely, πr^2. The lateral surface is the shaded sector of a circle whose radius is ℓ shown in Figure 11-26. To find the area of the sector, assume that the ratio of the area of the circle to the area of the sector is the same as the ratio of the arc lengths of the circle and the sector, respectively. Then, set up the proportion.

$$\frac{A_{\text{sector}}}{A_{\text{circle}}} = \frac{\text{length of arc of sector}}{\text{circumference of circle}}$$

The area of the circle is $\pi \ell^2$, the circumference of the circle is $2\pi\ell$, and the length of the arc of the sector is the circumference of the base of the cone, $2\pi r$. Substitute these values in the proportion and solve for A_{sector}.

$$\frac{A_{\text{sector}}}{\pi \ell^2} = \frac{2\pi r}{2\pi \ell}$$

$$A_{\text{sector}} = \frac{2\pi r(\pi \ell^2)}{2\pi \ell}$$

$$A_{\text{sector}} = \pi r \ell$$

The surface area of the right circular cone is the sum of the areas of the circular base, πr^2, and the lateral surface area, $\pi r \ell$.

$$S.A. = \pi r^2 + \pi r \ell$$

Example 11-10   Find the surface areas of each of the figures in Figure 11-27.

FIGURE 11-27

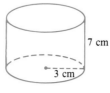
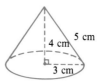

(a) Right circular cylinder   (b) Right circular cone

Solution   (a) $S.A. = 2\pi r^2 + 2\pi r h$
   $= 2\pi(3 \text{ cm})^2 + 2\pi(3 \text{ cm})(7 \text{ cm})$
   $= 18\pi \text{ cm}^2 + 42\pi \text{ cm}^2$
   $= 60\pi \text{ cm}^2$

(b) $S.A. = \pi r^2 + \pi r \ell$
   $= \pi(3 \text{ cm})^2 + \pi(3 \text{ cm})(5 \text{ cm})$
   $= 9\pi \text{ cm}^2 + 15\pi \text{ cm}^2$
   $= 24\pi \text{ cm}^2$

right regular pyramid

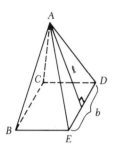

S.A. $= B + \dfrac{1}{2} p\ell$

Right regular pyramid

FIGURE 11-28

The surface area of a pyramid is the sum of the lateral surface area of the pyramid and the area of the base. A **right regular pyramid** is a pyramid such that the segments connecting the apex to each vertex of the base are congruent and the base is a regular polygon. The lateral faces of the right regular pyramid pictured in Figure 11-28 are congruent triangles. Each triangle has an altitude of length ℓ called the slant height. Since the pyramid is right regular, each side of the base has the same length, b. Hence, the lateral surface area of the right regular pyramid pictured is 4 ($\frac{1}{2}b\ell$). Adding the lateral surface area to the area of the base B gives the surface area.

In general, for any right regular pyramid, the surface area is found by adding the area B of the base and the area of the n congruent triangular faces, each with side b and slant height ℓ. The surface area is given by the following formula.

$$S.A. = B + n(\tfrac{1}{2}b\ell)$$

Since nb is the perimeter of the base, the formula reduces to the following.

$$S.A. = B + \tfrac{1}{2}p\ell$$

Example 11-11

Find the surface area of the right regular pyramid in Figure 11-29.

FIGURE 11-29

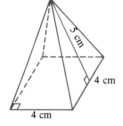

5 cm

4 cm

4 cm

Solution

$S.A. = B + \dfrac{1}{2}p\ell$

$= (4 \text{ cm})(4 \text{ cm}) + \dfrac{1}{2}[4(4 \text{ cm})](5 \text{ cm})$

$= 16 \text{ cm}^2 + 40 \text{ cm}^2$

$= 56 \text{ cm}^2$

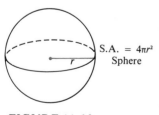

S.A. $= 4\pi r^2$
Sphere

FIGURE 11-30

Finding a formula for the surface area of a sphere is not a simple task using elementary mathematics. The formula for the surface area of a sphere is $S.A. = 4\pi r^2$. That is, the surface area of a sphere is four times the area of the great circle pictured in Figure 11-30.

PROBLEM SET 11-3

1. Find the surface area of each of the following right prisms.

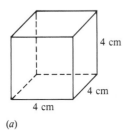

(*a*)   (*b*)

2. Find the surface area of each of the following.

(*a*) Right circular cone   (*b*) Right circular cylinder

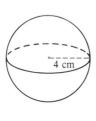

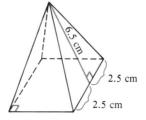

(*c*)   Sphere   (*d*) Right square pyramid

3. Find the surface area of each of the following.

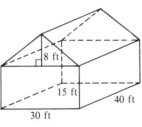

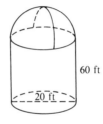

(*a*)   (*b*)   (*c*)

4. How many liters of paint are needed to paint the walls of a room 6 m long, 4 m wide, and 2.5 m tall if one liter of paint covers 20 m^2? (Assume there are no doors or windows.)

5. The napkin ring pictured below is to be resilvered. How many square millimeters of surface area must be covered?

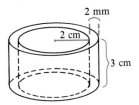

6. Assume that the radius of the earth is 6370 km and the earth is a sphere. What is its surface area?

7. Two cubes have sides of length 4 cm and 6 cm, respectively. What is the ratio of their surface areas?

8. (a) What happens to the surface area of a cube if each side is tripled?
   (b) What is the effect on the lateral surface area of a cylinder if the height is doubled?

★9. Find the total surface area of the following stand, which was cut from a right circular cone.

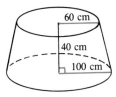

11-4 VOLUME MEASURE AND VOLUMES

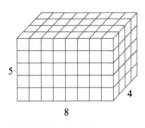

FIGURE 11-31

As area measure is used to describe the interior region of a geometric figure, volume measure is associated with three-dimensional figures. Volume is concerned with how much space a figure occupies. The unit of measure for volume must be a shape that will "fill space." Cubes can be closely stacked with no gaps and fill space. Standard units of volume are based on cubes and are called cubic units. The volume of a rectangular right prism can be measured, for example, by determining how many cubes are needed to build it. One way is to count how many cubes cover the base and then count how many layers of these cubes are used to reach the height of the prism as shown in Figure 11-31. There are 8 · 4 or 32 cubes in the base and five layers.

Hence, the volume of the rectangular prism is 8 · 4 · 5 cubic units. For any rectangular right prism with dimensions ℓ, w, and h measured in the same linear units, the volume of the prism is given by $V = \ell wh$.

In the English system of measurement, a commonly used unit of volume is the cubic foot. The most commonly used metric units are the cubic centimeter and the cubic meter. A cubic centimeter is the volume of a cube whose length, width, and height are each one centimeter. One cubic centimeter is denoted by 1 cm³. Similarly, a cubic meter is the volume of a cube whose length, width, and height are each one meter. One cubic meter is denoted by 1 m³. Other metric units of volume are also symbolized with a raised 3 next to the standard symbol.

Figure 11-32 shows that since 1 dm = 10 cm, 1 dm³ = (10 cm) · (10 cm) · (10 cm) = 1000 cm³.

FIGURE 11-32

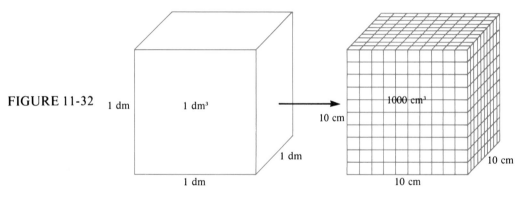

Similarly, Figure 11-33 shows that 1 m³ = 1 000 000 cm³ and 1 dm³ = 0.001 m³.

FIGURE 11-33

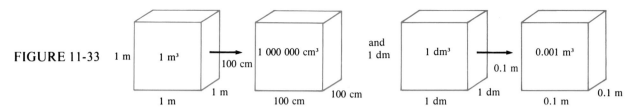

Each metric unit of length is 10 times greater than the next smaller unit. Each metric unit of area is 100 times greater than the next smaller unit. Each metric unit of volume is 1000 times greater than the next smaller unit. Hence, to convert from cubic decimeters to cubic centimeters, multiply by 1000; that is, move the decimal point three places to the right. Also, since 1 cm = 0.01 m, then 1 cm³ = (0.01 × 0.01 × 0.01) m³ or 0.000001 m³. Thus, to convert from cubic centimeters to cubic meters, all that is required is to move the decimal point six places to the left.

Example 11-12 Convert each of the following as indicated.

(a)   5 m³ to cm³   (b)   12 300 mm³ to cm³

Solution

(a)   Since 1 m = 100 cm, then 1 m³ = (100 cm) (100 cm) (100 cm) or 1 000 000 cm³. Thus, 5 m³ = (5)(1 000 000 cm³) = 5 000 000 cm³.

(b)   Since 1 mm = 0.1 cm, then 1 mm³ = (0.1 cm) (0.1 cm) (0.1 cm) or 0.001 cm³. Thus, 12 300 mm³ = 12 300(0.001 cm³) = 12.3 cm³.

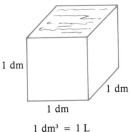

1 cm³ = 1 mL

liter

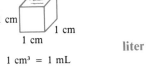

1 dm³ = 1 L

FIGURE 11-34

In the metric system, cubic units may be used for either dry or liquid measure, although units such as liters and milliliters are usually used for capacity measures, that is, for liquids. By definition, one **liter,** symbolized by L, equals one cubic decimeter; that is 1 L = 1 dm³. Note that L is not a universally accepted symbol for liter. However, since the liter is not a standard international unit but derived from other units, there is no proper standard international symbol. In the United States, L is preferred to either ℓ or l.

Since 1 L = 1 dm³ and 1 dm³ = 1000 cm³, then 1 L = 1000 cm³ and 1 cm³ = 0.001 L. Prefixes can be used with all base units in the metric system, so 0.001 L = 1 milliliter = 1 mL. Hence, 1 cm³ = 1 mL. These relationships are summarized in Figure 11-34.

The metric prefixes used with linear measure can also be used with the liter. Both symbols and conversions work the same as they did for length. Table 11-2 shows how metric units involving the liter are related.

TABLE 11-2

Unit	Symbol	Relation to Liter
kiloliter	kL	1000 liters
*hectoliter	hL	100 liters
*dekaliter	daL	10 liters
liter	L	1 liter
*deciliter	dL	0.1 liter
*centiliter	cL	0.01 liter
milliliter	mL	0.001 liter

*not commonly used

Example 11-13 Convert each of the following as indicated.

(a)   27 L to mL   (b)   362 mL to L
(c)   3 mL to cm³   (d)   3 m³ to L

Solution
(a) Since 1 L = 1000 mL, then 27 L = 27 · 1000 mL = 27 000 mL.
(b) Since 1 mL = 0.001 L, then 362 mL = 362(0.001 L) = 0.362 L.
(c) Since 1 mL = 1 cm³, then 3 mL = 3 cm³.
(d) Since 1 m³ = 1000 dm³ and 1 dm³ = 1 L, then 1 m³ = 1000 L and 3 m³ = 3000 L.

Volume of Other Three-Dimensional Figures

The volume of a right rectangular prism is given by $V = \ell wh$, where ℓ and w are the length and width of a base, respectively, and h is the height of the prism. Notice that ℓw is the area of a base of the prism. Hence, using B for the area of the base the formula can written as $V = Bh$. The same formula holds for any three-dimensional figure *if* all cross sections parallel to the base are congruent to the base. The formulas for volumes of right prisms and right circular cylinders are given in Figure 11-35.

FIGURE 11-35

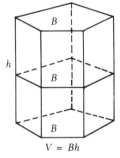

$V = Bh$

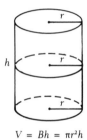

$V = Bh = \pi r^2 h$

Example 11-14

Find the volumes of each of the following in Figure 11-36.

FIGURE 11-36

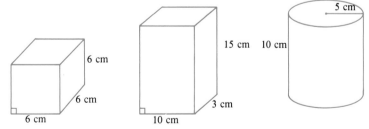

(*a*) Cube   (*b*) Right rectangular prism   (*c*) Right circular cylinder

Solution
(a) $V = Bh = (6 \text{ cm} \cdot 6 \text{ cm}) \cdot 6 \text{ cm} = 216 \text{ cm}^3$.
(b) $V = Bh = (10 \text{ cm} \cdot 3 \text{ cm}) \cdot 15 \text{ cm} = 450 \text{ cm}^3$.
(c) $V = \pi r^2 h = \pi (5 \text{ cm})^2 \cdot 10 \text{ cm} = 250\pi \text{ cm}^3$.

Figure 11-37 shows a right triangular prism with an equilateral triangle as a base. This prism can be separated into three pyramids that have congruent equilateral triangles as bases and heights the same as that of the prism. In this special case, the volume of the right triangular pyramid is one-third the volume of the triangular prism; that is $V = \frac{1}{3}Bh$. In fact, it can be shown that the volume of any pyramid is $\frac{1}{3}Bh$, where B is the area of its base and h is its height.

FIGURE 11-37

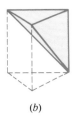 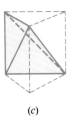

(a)   (b)   (c)

Next, suppose the polygonal base of a pyramid has many sides. The base approximates a circle and the volume of the pyramid is approximately the volume of the cone with the circle as a base and the same height as the pyramid. The area of the base is approximately πr^2, where r is the apothem of the polygon. Hence, the formula for the volume of a cone with a circular base is $V = \frac{1}{3}\pi r^2 h$ or $V = \frac{1}{3}Bh$.

Example 11-15

Find the volumes of each of the following in Figure 11-38.

FIGURE 11-38

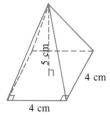 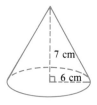

(a) Right square pyramid   (b) Right circular cone

Solution

(a) The figure is a pyramid with a square base whose area is (4 cm · 4 cm) and height 5 cm. Hence, $V = \frac{1}{3}Bh = \frac{1}{3}(4 \text{ cm} \cdot 4 \text{ cm})(5 \text{ cm}) = \frac{80}{3} \text{ cm}^3$.

(b) The base of the cone is a circle of radius 6 cm and height 7 cm. Hence, $V = \frac{1}{3}\pi r^2 h = \frac{1}{3}\pi (6 \text{ cm})^2 (7 \text{ cm}) = 84\pi \text{ cm}^3$.

Volume—pyramid, cone, and sphere

PYRAMID

The volume of a pyramid is $\frac{1}{3}$ the volume of a prism having the same base and height.

Formula $\rangle$ $V = \frac{1}{3} Bh$

CONE

The volume of a cone is $\frac{1}{3}$ the volume of a cylinder having the same base and height.

Formula $\rangle$ $V = \frac{1}{3} Bh$

SPHERE

The volume of a sphere is $\frac{4}{3} \tau$ times the cube of the radius.

Formula $\rangle$ $V = \frac{4}{3} \tau r^3$

$V \approx \frac{4}{3} (3.14)(3.7 \text{ cm})^3$

$V \approx \frac{4}{3}(3.14)(50.653 \text{ cm}^3)$

$V \approx 212.067 \text{ cm}^3$

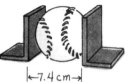

$\mapsto$7.4 cm$\dashv$

$r = 3.7$ cm

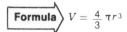

To find the volume of a sphere, imagine that a sphere is composed of a great number of congruent pyramids with apexes at the center of the sphere and the vertices of the base touch the sphere as shown in Figure 11-39. If the

FIGURE 11-39

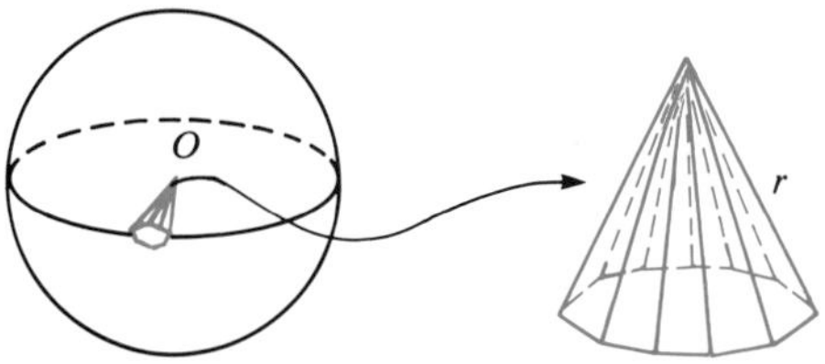

pyramids have very small bases, then the height of each pyramid is nearly the radius, r. Hence, the volume of each pyramid is $\frac{1}{3}Bh$ or $\frac{1}{3}Br$, where B is the area of the base. If there are n pyramids each with base area B, then the total volume of the pyramids is $V = \frac{1}{3}nBr$. Since nB is the total surface area of all the bases of the pyramids and the sum of the areas of all the bases of the pyramids is very close to the surface area of the sphere, $4\pi r^2$, the volume of the sphere is given by $V = \frac{1}{3}(4\pi r^2)r = \frac{4}{3}\pi r^3$.

Example 11-16

Find the volume of a sphere whose radius is 6 cm.

Solution

$$V = \frac{4}{3}\pi(6 \text{ cm})^3 = \frac{4}{3}\pi(216 \text{ cm}^3) = 288\pi \text{ cm}^3.$$

In elementary schools, ideas about volume are taught by filling containers with water or sand. The student page (p. 497 in this text) from *Heath Mathematics*, Grade 8, 1979 uses this method to motivate certain volume formulas.

PROBLEM SET 11-4

1. Complete each of the following.
   (a) 8 m³ = _____ dm³   (b) 500 cm³ = _____ m³
   (c) 675 000 m³ = _____ km³   (d) 3 m³ = _____ cm³
   (e) 7000 mm³ = _____ cm³
2. Why is a unit sphere, a sphere with radius 1 cm, not a "good" unit of volume measure, even for measuring the volume of another sphere?

3. Find the volumes of each of the following.

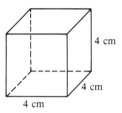

(a)   Right rectangular prism

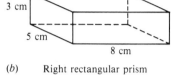

(b)   Right rectangular prism

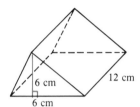

(c)   Right triangular prism

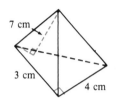

(d) Pyramid with a right triangle as base

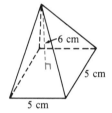

(e)   Square pyramid

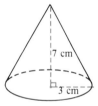

(f)   Right circular cone

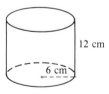

(g)   Right circular cylinder

(h)   Sphere

4. Find the volumes of each of the following.

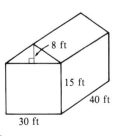

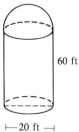

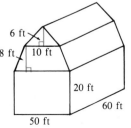

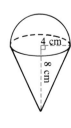

(a)

(b)

(c)   8 ft

(d)

5. What volume of silver is needed to make the napkin ring below out of solid silver? Give your answer in mm³.

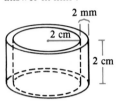

6. Two cubes have sides of lengths 4 cm and 6 cm, respectively. What is the ratio of their volumes?
7. What happens to the volume of a sphere if the radius is doubled?
8. Complete the following.

cm³		500			750	4800
dm³	2					
L		1.5				
mL				5000		

9. Complete the chart for right rectangular prisms with the given dimensions.

	(a)	(b)	(c)	(d)
Length	20 cm	10 cm	2 dm	15 cm
Width	10 cm	2 dm	1 dm	2 dm
Height	10 cm	3 dm		
Volume in cm³				
Volume in dm³				7.5 .
Volume in L			4	

10. Place a decimal point in each of the following to make an accurate sentence.
    (a) A paper cup holds about 2000 mL.
    (b) A regular soft drink bottle holds about 320 L.
    (c) A quart milk container holds about 10 L.
    (d) A teaspoonful of cough syrup would be about 500 mL.
11. A right cylindrical tank holds how many liters if it is 6 m long and 13 m in diameter?

12. If the length of the diameter of the earth is approximately four times the length of the diameter of the moon and both are spheres, what is the ratio of their volumes?

13. A bread pan is 18 cm × 18 cm × 5 cm. How many liters does it hold?

14. An Olympic pool in the shape of a right rectangular prism is 50 m long and 25 m wide. If it is 2 m deep throughout, how many liters of water does it hold?

15. If a faucet is dripping at the rate of 15 drops per minute and there are 20 drops per milliliter, how many liters of water is wasted in a 30-day month?

16. A standard straw is 25 cm long and 4 mm in diameter. How much liquid can be held in the straw at one time?

17. In the drawing below, a marble 12 cm in diameter is resting in a can whose circular base has a radius of 6 cm. If water is poured into the can until the top of the marble is covered and then the marble is removed from the can, how far does the water drop?

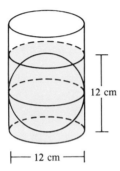

12 cm

├── 12 cm ──┤

18. A theater decides to change the shape of its popcorn container from their regular box to a right regular pyramid and charge only half as much. If the containers are the same height and the tops are the same size is this a bargain for the theater?

19. Which is the better buy (a) a grapefruit 5 cm in radius that costs 22¢ or (b) a grapefruit 6 cm in radius that costs 31¢?

20. A right rectangular prism with base *ABCD* as the bottom is shown below. Suppose *X* is drawn so that $AX = 3 \cdot AP$, where *AP* is the height of the prism, and *X* is connected to *A*, *B*, *C*, and *D*, forming a pyramid. How do the volumes of the pyramid and the prism compare?

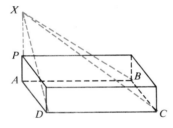

11-5 MASS AND TEMPERATURE

Three centuries ago, Isaac Newton pointed out that in everyday life, the term "weight" is used for what really is mass. He called *mass* a quantity of matter as opposed to *weight,* which is a force exerted by gravitational pull. When an astronaut is in orbit above the Earth, his weight has changed even though his mass remains the same. For common use on Earth, weight and mass are still used interchangeably.

gram

In the metric system, the base unit for mass is the **gram,** denoted by g. A gram is the mass of 1 cm³ of water. An ordinary paper clip or a thumbtack each has a mass of about 1 g.

As with other base metric units, prefixes are added to gram to obtain other units. For example, a kilogram (kg) is 1000 g. Since 1 cm³ of water has a mass of 1 g, the mass of 1 L of water is 1 kg. A person's mass is measured in kilograms. Two standard loaves of bread have a mass of about 1 kg. A newborn baby has a mass of about 4 kg. Another unit of mass in the metric

metric ton

system is the **metric ton** (t), which is equal to 1000 kg. The metric ton is used to record the masses of objects such as cars and trucks. A small foreign car has a mass of about 1 t.

Table 11-3 lists metric units of mass. Metric units of mass are converted in the same way as are units of length.

TABLE 11-3

Unit	Symbol	Relationship to Gram
ton	t	1 000 000 grams
kilogram	kg	1000 grams
*hectogram	hg	100 grams
*dekagram	dag	10 grams
gram	g	1 gram
*decigram	dg	0.1 gram
*centigram	cg	0.01 gram
milligram	mg	0.001 gram

*not commonly used

Example 11-17

Complete each of the following.
(a)   34 g = _____ kg   (b)   6836 kg = _____ t

Solution

(a)   34 g = 34(0.001 kg) = 0.034 kg
(b)   6836 kg = 6836(0.001 t) = 6.836 t

The relationship among the units of volume and mass in the metric system is illustrated in Figure 11-40.

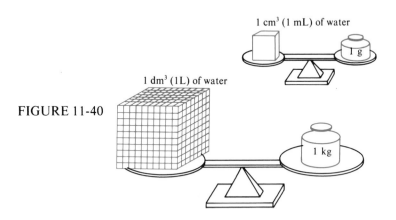

FIGURE 11-40

1 cm³ (1 mL) of water

1 g

1 dm³ (1L) of water

1 kg

Example 11-18

A waterbed is 180 cm wide, 210 cm long, and 20 cm thick.

(a) How many liters of water can it hold?
(b) What is its mass in kilograms when it is full of water?

Solution

(a) The volume of the waterbed is found by multiplying the length times the width times the height.

$$V = \ell wh$$
$$= 180 \text{ cm} \cdot 210 \text{ cm} \cdot 20 \text{ cm}$$
$$= 756\ 000 \text{ cm}^3 \text{ or } 756\ 000 \text{ mL}$$

Since 1 mL = 0.001 L, the volume is 756 L.

(b) Since 1 L of water has a mass of 1 kg, 756 L of water has a mass of 756 kg.

Remark

To see one advantage of the metric system, suppose the bed is 6 ft. by 7 ft. by 9 in. Try to find the volume in gallons and the weight of the water in pounds.

Temperature

degree Kelvin

The base unit of temperature for the metric system is the **degree Kelvin.** However, it is used only for scientific measurements and not for everyday measurements of temperature. For normal temperature measurements in the metric system, the base unit is **degree Celsius,** named for Anders Celsius, the

degree Celsius

Swedish scientist who invented the system. The Celsius scale has 100 equal divisions between zero degrees Celsius (0°C), the freezing point of water, and one hundred degrees Celsius (100°C), the boiling point of water. In the English system, the Fahrenheit scale has 180 equal divisions between 32°F, the freezing point of water, and 212°F, the boiling point of water. Because the Celsius scale has 100 divisions between the freezing point and boiling point of water whereas the Fahrenheit scale has 180 divisions, the relationship between the two scales is 100 to 180 or 5 to 9. Hence, for every 5 degrees on the Celsius scale, there are 9 degrees on the Fahrenheit scale, and for each degree on the Fahrenheit scale, there is $\frac{5}{9}$ degree on the Celsius scale. Figure 11-41 gives some temperature comparisons on the two scales and further illustrates the relationship between them.

FIGURE 11-41

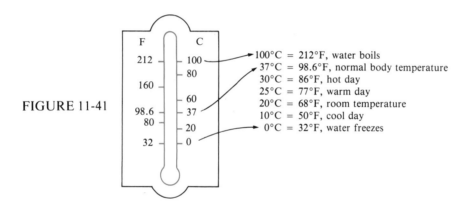

A simple relationship can be developed for converting temperatures between the two scales. Since 50°F is (50 − 32)°F or 18°F above freezing, in degrees Celsius it is [$\frac{5}{9}$ (50 − 32)]°C or 10°C above freezing. In general, C = $\frac{5}{9}$ (F − 32) and F = $\frac{9}{5}$ C + 32.

Example 11-19   Convert 20°C to degrees Fahrenheit.

Solution
$$F = \frac{9}{5}C + 32$$

$$= \frac{9}{5} \cdot 20 + 32$$

$$= 36 + 32$$

$$= 68$$

Thus, 20°C is 68°F.

PROBLEM SET 11-5

1. For each of the following select the appropriate metric unit of measure (gram, kilogram, or metric ton).
   (a) Car   (b) Woman   (c) Can of frozen orange juice
   (d) Elephant   (e) Jar of mustard (f) Bag of peanuts
   (g) Army tank   (h) Cat   (i) Dictionary
   (j) Apple

2. For each of the following, choose the correct unit (milligram, gram, or kilogram) to make each sentence reasonable.
   (a) A staple has a mass of about 340 _____ .
   (b) A professional football player has a mass of about 110 _____ .
   (c) A vitamin has a mass of 1100 _____ .
   (d) A dime has a mass of 2 _____ .
   (e) The recipe said to add 4 _____ of salt.
   (f) One strand of hair has a mass of 2 _____ .

3. Complete each of the following.
   (a) 15 000 g = _____ kg   (b) 8000 kg = _____ t
   (c) 0.036 kg = _____ g   (d) 72 g = _____ kg
   (e) 4230 mg = _____ g   (f) 3 g 7 mg = _____ g
   (g) 5 kg 750 g = _____ g   (h) 5 kg 750 g = _____ kg
   (i) 0.03 t = _____ kg   (j) 0.03 t = _____ g

4. If a paper dollar has a mass of approximately 1 g, is it possible to lift $1 000 000 in the following denominations?
   (a) $1 bills   (b) $10 bills   (c) $100 bills   (d) $1000 bills
   (e) $10 000 bills

5. A fish tank, which is a right rectangular prism, is 40 cm by 20 cm by 20 cm. If it is filled with water, what is the mass of the water?

6. In a grocery store, one kind of meat costs $5.80 per kilogram. How much does 400 g of this meat cost?

7. If a certain spice costs $20 per kilogram, how much does 1 g cost?

8. Abel bought a kilogram of Moxwill coffee for $9 and Babel bought 400 g of the same brand of coffee for $4.60. Who made the better buy?

9. Answer each of the following.
   (a) The thermometer reads 20°C. Can you go snow skiing?
   (b) The thermometer reads 26°C. Will the outdoor ice rink be open?
   (c) Your temperature is 37°C. Do you have a fever?
   (d) If your body temperature is 39°C, are you ill?
   (e) It is 40°C. Will you need a sweater at the outdoor concert?
   (f) The temperature is 35°C. Should you go water skiing?
   (g) The temperature reads ⁻10°C. Is it appropriate to go ice fishing?
   (h) Your bath water is 16°C. Will you have a hot, warm, or chilly bath?
   (i) It's 30°C in the room. Are you uncomfortably hot or cold?

10. Convert each of the following from degrees Fahrenheit to the nearest integer degree Celsius.
   (a) 10°F   (b) 0°F   (c) 30°F
   (d) 100°F   (e) 212°F   (f) ⁻40°F

11. Convert each of the following Celsius temperatures to Fahrenheit temperatures (to the nearest integer).
    (a) 10°C   (b) 0°C   (c) 30°C
    (d) 100°C   (e) 212°C   (f) ⁻40°C

LABORATORY ACTIVITY

1. Record the mass of each U.S. coin. Which coin has the greatest mass? Which of the following sets have the same mass?
    (a) A half-dollar vs. two quarters
    (b) A quarter vs. two dimes and a nickel
    (c) A dime vs. two nickels
    (d) A dime vs. ten pennies
    (e) A nickel vs. five pennies

2. Record the temperature of the room on a Celsius thermometer. Pour 200 mL of water into a liter container. Record the temperature of the water. Add 100 mL of ice to the water. Wait one minute and record the temperature of the ice water.

SOLUTION TO THE PRELIMINARY PROBLEM

Understanding the Problem

A steer is tied to a post at the midpoint of the hypotenuse of a right triangle with area 1 hectare with enough rope to reach the two adjacent vertices A and B. Similarly, sheep are tied to posts at the midpoints of the other sides. The ropes tethering the animals allow each of them freedom to graze. Since each post acts like a center and each rope like a radius, each animal can graze in a circular area. The problem is to find the total area in which the sheep can graze but the steer cannot reach—that is, the shaded crescents in Figure 11-42.

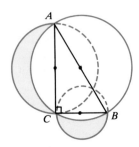

FIGURE 11-42

Devising a Plan

Perhaps the most basic way to attack the problem is to determine whether we can find the area of the shaded portions of Figure 11-42 using the area formulas for triangles and circles. We can find the areas of the three circles and the triangle in Figure 11-42. Observing the drawing, we see that the shaded crescents are outside the larger circle.

If we could find the area of the entire region and subtract the area of the larger circle, then the difference would be the area of the crescents. We can find the area of the entire region by adding the areas of the semicircles determined by diameters $\overline{AC}$, $\overline{BC}$, and $\overline{AB}$ and the area of $\triangle ABC$. To complete the problem, we subtract the area of the circle whose diameter is $\overline{AB}$ to obtain the area of the crescents.

Carrying Out the Plan

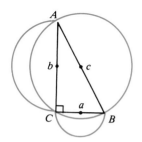

FIGURE 11-43

If we denote the lengths of the sides of $\triangle ABC$ as a, b, and c as shown in Figure 11-43, then the radii of the semicircles with diameters $\overline{BC}$, $\overline{AC}$, and $\overline{AB}$ are $a/2$, $b/2$, and $c/2$, respectively. Hence, the areas of the semicircles are $(1/2)\pi(a/2)^2$, $(1/2)\pi(b/2)^2$, and $(1/2)\pi(c/2)^2$ or $\pi a^2/8$, $\pi b^2/8$, and $\pi c^2/8$. The area of right triangle ABC is $(1/2)(a)(b) = ab/2$. Finally, the area of the circle with diameter $\overline{AB}$ is $\pi(c/2)^2 = \pi c^2/4$. Hence, the area of the crescents is

$$\left(\frac{\pi a^2}{8} + \frac{\pi b^2}{8} + \frac{\pi c^2}{8} + \frac{ab}{2}\right) - \frac{\pi c^2}{4} = \frac{\pi a^2}{8} + \frac{\pi b^2}{8} - \frac{\pi c^2}{8} + \frac{ab}{2}$$

Notice that the area of the crescents can be written as $(\pi/8)(a^2 + b^2 - c^2) + (ab/2)$. Since $\triangle ABC$ is a right triangle with $c^2 = a^2 + b^2$, then $a^2 + b^2 - c^2 = 0$. Hence, the area of the crescents is $(\pi/8) \cdot 0 + (ab/2) = (ab/2)$. Since the area of $\triangle ABC$ is also $ab/2$ and $\triangle ABC$ has area 1 hectare, then the area of the crescents is 1 hectare. Thus, the sheep together have 1 hectare of grazing land that the steer cannot reach.

Looking Back

In solving this problem, we have developed an extension of the Pythagorean Theorem. Recall that to develop the Pythagorean Theorem, we considered the areas of squares constructed on the sides of a right triangle and showed that $a^2 + b^2 = c^2$, where a and b were the lengths of the legs and c was the length of the hypotenuse. From the previous discussion, we found that the areas of the semicircles were $\pi a^2/8$, $\pi b^2/8$, and $\pi c^2/8$. If we multiply each term of the equation $a^2 + b^2 = c^2$ by $\pi/8$, we obtain $\pi a^2/8 + \pi b^2/8 = \pi c^2/8$. Hence, the area of the semicircle constructed on the hypotenuse of the right triangle is equal to the sum of the areas of the semicircles constructed on the legs.

A further extension involves finding what figures can be constructed on the sides of a right triangle in order for the area of the figure constructed on the hypotenuse to equal the sum of the areas of the figures constructed on the legs.

QUESTIONS FROM THE CLASSROOM

1. A student asks if the units of measure must be the same for each term to use the formulas for volumes. How do you respond?
2. In the discussion of the Pythagorean Theorem, squares were constructed on each side of a right triangle. A student asks if different similar figures are constructed on each side of the triangle, does the same type relationship still hold? How do you reply?
3. A student asks, "Can I find the area of an angle?" How do you respond?
4. A student argues that a square has no area since its interior can be thought of as the union of infinitely many line segments, each of which has no area. How do you react?
5. A student asks if the volume of a prism is always a lesser number than its surface area. How do you answer?
6. A student asks, "Why should the United States switch to the metric system?" How do you reply?
7. A student claims that in a triangle with 20° and 40° angles, the side opposite the 40° angle is twice as long as the side opposite the 20° angle. How do you reply?
8. A student interpreted 5 cm^3 using the drawing below. What is wrong with this interpretation?

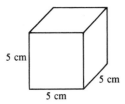

CHAPTER OUTLINE

I. Areas
   A. Formulas for areas
      1. **Square:** $A = s^2$, where s is a side.
      2. **Rectangle:** $A = \ell w$, where ℓ is the length and w is the width.
      3. **Parallelogram:** $A = bh$, where b is the base and h is the height.
      4. **Triangle:** $A = \frac{1}{2}bh$, where b is the base and h is the altitude to that base.
      5. **Trapezoid:** $A = \frac{1}{2}h(b_1 + b_2)$, where b_1 and b_2 are the bases and h is the height.
      6. **Regular polygon:** $A = \frac{1}{2}ap$, where a is the apothem and p is the perimeter.
      7. **Circle:** $A = \pi r^2$, where r is the radius.
      8. **Sector:** $A = \theta\pi r^2/360$, where θ is the measure of the angle formed by the sector and r is the radius of the circle containing the sector.
   B. **The Pythagorean Theorem:** In any right triangle, the square of the length of the hypotenuse is equal to

the sum of the squares of the lengths of the legs.

C. **Converse of the Pythagorean Theorem:** In any triangle, $\triangle ABC$, with sides of lengths a, b, and c such that $a^2 + b^2 = c^2$, $\triangle ABC$ is a right triangle with the right angle opposite the side of length c.

II. Surface areas and volumes

A. Formulas for areas

1. **Right prism:** $S.A. = 2B + ph$, where B is the area of a base, p is the perimeter of the base, and h is the height of the prism.

2. **Right regular pyramid:** $S.A. = B + \frac{1}{2}p\ell$, where B is the area of the base, p is the perimeter of the base, and ℓ is the slant height.

3. **Right circular cylinder:** $S.A. = 2\pi r^2 + 2\pi rh$, where r is the radius of the circular base and h is the height of the cylinder.

4. **Right circular cone:** $S.A. = \pi r^2 + \pi r\ell$, where r is the radius of the circular base and ℓ is the slant height.

5. **Sphere:** $S.A. = 4\pi r^2$, where r is the radius of the sphere.

B. Formulas for volumes

1. **Right prism:** $V = Bh$, where B is the area of the base and h is the height.

    (a) **Right rectangular prism:** $V = \ell wh$, where ℓ is the length, w is the width, and h is the height.

    (b) **Cube:** $V = e^3$, where e is an edge.

2. **Right circular cylinder:** $V = \pi r^2 h$, where r is the radius of the base and h is the height of the cylinder.

3. **Pyramid:** $V = \frac{1}{3}Bh$, where B is the area of the base and h is the height of the pyramid.

4. **Circular cone:** $V = \frac{1}{3}\pi r^2 h$, where r is the radius of the circular base and h is the height.

5. **Sphere:** $V = \frac{4}{3}\pi r^3$, where r is the radius of the sphere.

III. Metric measurement

A. Area measure

1. Units commonly used are the square kilometer, square meter, square centimeter, and square millimeter.

2. Land can be measured using the **are** (100 m^2) and the **hectare** ($10\,000 \text{ m}^2$).

B. Volume measure

1. Units commonly used are the cubic meter (m^3), cubic decimeter (dm^3), cubic centimeter (cm^3), liter (L), and milliliter (mL).

2. $1 \text{ dm}^3 = 1 \text{ L}$ and $1 \text{ cm}^3 = 1 \text{ mL}$.

C. Mass

1. Units of mass commonly used are the milligram (mg), gram (g), kilogram (kg), and metric ton (t).

2. 1 L and 1 mL of water have masses of approximately 1 kg and 1 g, respectively.

D. Temperature

1. The official unit of metric temperature is the **degree Kelvin,** but the unit commonly used is the **degree Celsius.**

2. Basic temperature reference points are the following:
100°C boiling point of water,
37°C normal body temperature,
20°C comfortable room temperature,
0°C freezing point of water.

3. $C = \frac{5}{9}(F - 32)$ and $F = \frac{9}{5}C + 32$

CHAPTER TEST

1. For each of the following, describe how you can find the area of the parallelogram.
    (a) Using *DE*.   (b)   Using *BF*.

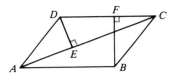

2.   What is the area of the shaded region in the following figure.

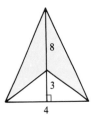

3.   What is the area of the shaded region on the following geoboard if the unit of measure is 1 cm²?

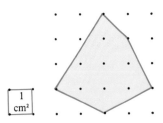

4.   Find the area of the kite.

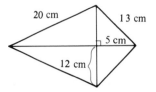

5.   Explain how the formula for the area of a trapezoid can be found using the following pictures.

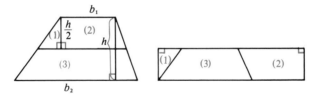

6. Use the figure below to find each of the following.
   (a) The area of the hexagon.
   (b) The area of the circle.

7. Find the areas of each of the following shaded regions.

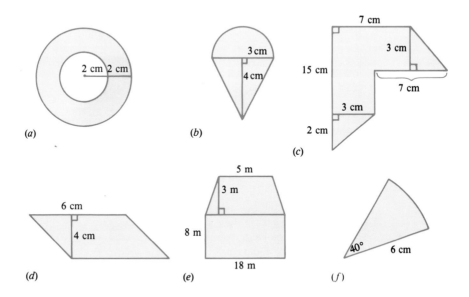

8. For each of the following, can the measures represent sides of a right triangle? **Explain your** answers.
   (a) 5 cm, 12 cm, 13 cm   (b) 40 cm, 60 cm, 104 cm
9. Find the surface areas and volumes of each of the following.

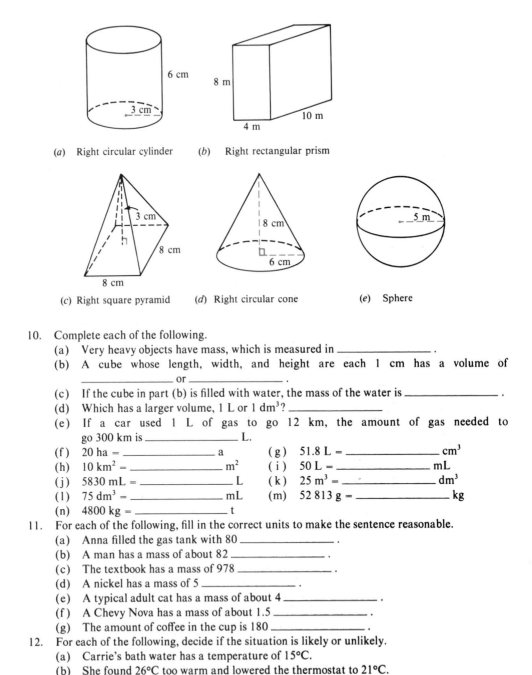

(a)   Right circular cylinder   (b)   Right rectangular prism

(c)   Right square pyramid   (d)   Right circular cone   (e)   Sphere

10.   Complete each of the following.
    (a)   Very heavy objects have mass, which is measured in _____ .
    (b)   A cube whose length, width, and height are each 1 cm has a volume of _____ or _____ .
    (c)   If the cube in part (b) is filled with water, the mass of the water is _____ .
    (d)   Which has a larger volume, 1 L or 1 dm^3? _____
    (e)   If a car used 1 L of gas to go 12 km, the amount of gas needed to go 300 km is _____ L.
    (f)   20 ha = _____ a   (g)   51.8 L = _____ cm^3
    (h)   10 km^2 = _____ m^2 (i)   50 L = _____ mL
    (j)   5830 mL = _____ L   (k)   25 m^3 = _____ dm^3
    (l)   75 dm^3 = _____ mL   (m)   52 813 g = _____ kg
    (n)   4800 kg = _____ t
11.   For each of the following, fill in the correct units to make the sentence reasonable.
    (a)   Anna filled the gas tank with 80 _____ .
    (b)   A man has a mass of about 82 _____ .
    (c)   The textbook has a mass of 978 _____ .
    (d)   A nickel has a mass of 5 _____ .
    (e)   A typical adult cat has a mass of about 4 _____ .
    (f)   A Chevy Nova has a mass of about 1.5 _____ .
    (g)   The amount of coffee in the cup is 180 _____ .
12.   For each of the following, decide if the situation is likely or unlikely.
    (a)   Carrie's bath water has a temperature of 15°C.
    (b)   She found 26°C too warm and lowered the thermostat to 21°C.
    (c)   Jim was drinking water with a temperature of ⁻5°C.
    (d)   The water in the teakettle has a temperature of 120°C.
    (e)   The outside temperature dropped to 5°C, and ice appeared on the lake.

13. Complete each of the following.
    (a) 2 dm^3 of water has a mass of _____ g.
    (b) 1 L of water has a mass of _____ g.
    (c) 3 cm^3 of water has a mass of _____ g.
    (d) 4.2 mL of water has a mass of _____ kg.
    (e) 0.2 L of water has a volume of _____ m^3.

SELECTED BIBLIOGRAPHY

Aman, G. "Discovery on a Geoboard." *The Arithmetic Teacher,* **21**(April 1974):267–272.

Brougher, J. J. "Discovery Activities with Area and Perimeter." *The Arithmetic Teacher,* **20**(May 1973):382–385.

Bruni, J. V. "Geometry for the Intermediate Grades." *Arithmetic Teacher,* **26**(February 1979):17–19.

Burrows, D. "Alan's Geo-Igloo." *The Arithmetic Teacher,* **21**(February 1974):95–97.

Colter, M. T. "Adapting the Area of a Circle to the Area of a Rectangle." *The Arithmetic Teacher,* **19**(May 1972):404–406.

DeTemple, D., and J. M. Robertson. "The Equivalence of Euler's and Pick's Theorems." *The Mathematics Teacher,* **67**(March 1974):222–226.

Ewbank, W. A. "If Pythagoras Had a Geoboard . . ." *The Mathematics Teacher,* **66**(March 1973):215–221.

French, J. E., and R. E. Rea. "Fun with Geometry Through Straw Construction." *The Arithmetic Teacher,* **20**(November 1973):587–590.

Gilbert, E. N. "The Ways to Build a Box." *The Mathematics Teacher,* **64**(December 1971):689–695.

Hawkins, V. J. "Teaching the Metric System as Part of Compulsory Conversion in the United States." *The Arithmetic Teacher,* **20**(May 1973):390–394.

Hirstein, J. J., C. E. Lamb, and A. Osborne. "Student Misconceptions About Area Measure." *The Arithmetic Teacher,* **25**(March 1978):10–16.

Hunt, J. D. "How High Is a Flagpole?" *Arithmetic Teacher,* **25**(February 1978):42–43.

Jamski, W. "So Your Students Know About Area?" *The Arithmetic Teacher,* **26**(December 1978):37.

Jencks, S. M., and D. M. Peck. "Thought Starters for the Circular Geoboard." *The Mathematics Teacher,* **67**(March 1974):228–233.

King, I., and N. Whitman. "Going Metric in Hawaii." *The Arithmetic Teacher,* **20**(April 1973):258–260.

Lichtenberg, D. R. "More About Triangles with the Same Area and the Same Perimeter." *The Mathematics Teacher,* **67**(November 1974):659–660.

Lindquist, M. M., and M. E. Dana. "Let's Do It: Measurement for the Times." *Arithmetic Teacher,* **26**(April 1979):4–9.

Loomis, E. S. The Pythagorean Propositions, Washington, D.C., National Council of Teachers of Mathematics, 1972.

Lott, J. W., and H. Q. Nguyen. "Extremal Problems on a Geoboard." *The Mathematics Teacher,* **72**(January 1979):28–29.

Masalshi, W. J. "An Open-Ended Problem on the Geoboard." *The Mathematics Teacher,* **67** (March 1974):264–268.

Mercaldi, R. W. "An Application of Volume and Surface Area." *The Mathematics Teacher,* **66**(January 1974):71–73.

NCTM Metric Implementation Committee. "Metric, not IF, but HOW." *The Arithmetic Teacher,* **22**(February 1975):103–109.

NCTM Metric Implementation Committee. "Metric Competency Goals." *The Arithmetic Teacher,* **23**(January 1976):70–71.

Prielipp, R. W. "Are Triangles That Have the Same Area and the Same Perimeter Congruent?" *The Mathematics Teacher,* **67**(February 1974):157–159.

Shumway, R. J., and L. Sachs. "Don't Just Think Metric—Live Metric." *The Arithmetic Teacher,* **22**(February 1975):103–109.

Smart, J. R. *Metric Math: The Modernized Metric System (SI).* Monterey, Calif.: Brooks/Cole, 1974.

Thomas, D. "Geometry in the Middle School: Problem Solving with Trapezoids." *Arithmetic Teacher,* **26**(February 1979):20–21.

Wernick, W. "Geometric Construction: The Double Straightedge." *The Mathematics Teacher,* **64**(December 1971):697–704.

Williams, G. A. "The Pythagorean Theorem: A Useful Geometric Tool for Approximating $\sqrt{2}$." *The Arithmetic Teacher,* **24**(April 1977):284–286.

Coordinate
Geometry

PRELIMINARY PROBLEM

One day, Linda left home, *H*, for school, *S*.
Rather than stopping at school, she went on to the
corner, *A*, which is twice as far from home as the
school and on the same street as her home and the
school. Then she headed for the ice cream parlor,

I. Passing the ice cream parlor, she headed straight for the next corner, *B*, which is on the same street as *A* and *I* and twice as far from *A* as *I*. Walking toward the park, *P*, she continued beyond it to the next corner, *C*, so that *C*, *P*, and *B* are on the same street, and *C* is twice as far from *B* as *P*. At this point, she again headed for the school, but continued walking in a straight line twice as far, reaching point *D*. Then, she headed for the ice cream parlor, but continued in a straight line twice as far to point *E*. From *E*, Linda headed for the park but continued in a straight line twice as far to *F* where she stopped. The figure shows the first part of Linda's walk. What is the location of Linda's final stop?

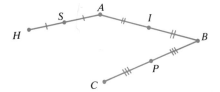

12-1 COORDINATE SYSTEM IN THE PLANE

coordinate geometry
analytic geometry
Cartesian coordinate system

In 1637, René Descartes revolutionized geometry by successfully combining it with algebra. Today, the field that he discovered is known as **coordinate geometry** or **analytic geometry.** Coordinate geometry is based on a coordinate system, often referred to as the rectangular or **Cartesian coordinate system** in honor of Descartes. (In Latin, Descartes is *Cartesius*.)

Every point on a number line corresponds to a real number, and every real number corresponds to a point on the number line. Such a one-to-one correspondence is called a coordinate system for the line. Using a coordinate system, the locations of points on a line can be uniquely described with real numbers. The number corresponding to a given point on the line is called the **coordinate of the point**

coordinate of the point

To uniquely describe the location of a point in a plane, a pair of real numbers is needed. This can be done by using two perpendicular number lines. Take a line *x* in a plane and set up a coordinate system on *x*. This number line is called the ***x* axis.** Next, construct a line *y* perpendicular to the

***x* axis**

origin x axis at the point with coordinate 0, called the **origin.** A coordinate system on line y is then organized in such a way that the zero point on y is also the zero point on x, and the distance between 0 and 1 is the same on both lines. The

y axis   line y is called the **y axis.** The x axis is usually drawn as a horizontal line and the y axis as a vertical line as shown in Figure 12-1.

FIGURE 12-1

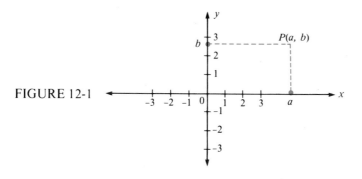

The location of any point P can be described by an ordered pair of numbers as shown in Figure 12-1. If a perpendicular from P to the x axis intersects the x axis at a and a perpendicular from P to the y axis intersects the y axis at b, then we say that point P has coordinates (a, b). The value of a

abscissa x coordinate   is the **abscissa** or the **x coordinate** of P. The value of b is the **ordinate** or **y**
ordinate y coordinate   **coordinate** of P.

In Figure 12-2, the x coordinate of P is $^-3$ and the y coordinate of P is 2. We say P has coordinates $(^-3, 2)$. Similarly, R has an x coordinate of $^-4$ and a y coordinate of $^-3$, which can be written as $R(^-4, ^-3)$. The first number in the parentheses is always the x coordinate, and the second number is always the y coordinate.

FIGURE 12-2

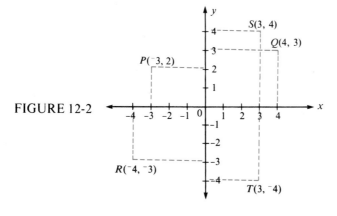

In Figure 12-2, the point with coordinates (4, 3) is Q, whereas the point with coordinates (3, 4) is S. To each point in the plane there corresponds an ordered pair (a, b). Conversely, to every ordered pair of real numbers there corresponds a point in the plane. Hence, there is a one-to-one correspondence between all the points in the plane and all the ordered pairs of real numbers. Such a one-to-one correspondence is called a **coordinate system for the plane.**

Together, the x axis and y axis divide the plane into four parts called **quadrants.** Figure 12-3 shows the four quadrants. The first quadrant can be described as the set of all ordered pairs (x, y), whose x coordinates and y coordinates are positive. The other quadrants can be described in a similar manner.

quadrant I = $\{(x, y) \mid x > 0 \text{ and } y > 0\}$

quadrant II = $\{(x, y) \mid x < 0 \text{ and } y > 0\}$

quadrant III = $\{(x, y) \mid x < 0 \text{ and } y < 0\}$

quadrant IV = $\{(x, y) \mid x > 0 \text{ and } y < 0\}$

Notice that the quadrants do not include points on the axes.

quadrants

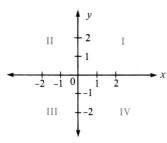

FIGURE 12-3

PROBLEM SET 12-1

1. (a) Give the coordinates of each of the points A, B, C, D, E, F, G, and H of the accompanying figure.

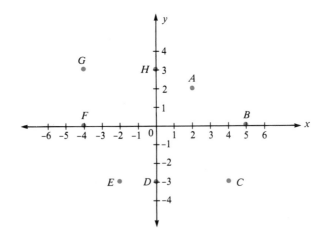

(b) Find the coordinates of another point (not drawn) that is collinear with E, D, and C.

2. For each of the following, name the quadrants in which the ordered pair is located.
   (a) (3, 7) (b) ($^-$5, $^-$8) (c) ($^-$10, 32) (d) (10, $^-$40) (e) (0, 7)
3. For each of the following, find the coordinates of two other points collinear with the given points.
   (a) $P(2, 2), Q(4, 2)$ (b) $P(^-1, 0), Q(^-1, 2)$ (c) $P(^-3, 0), Q(3, 0)$
   (d) $P(0, ^-2), Q(0, 3)$ (e) $P(0, 0), Q(0, 1)$ (f) $P(0, 0), Q(1, 1)$
4. Complete each of the following sentences.
   (a) The y coordinate of every point on the x axis is _____ .
   (b) The x coordinate of every point on the y axis is _____ .
5. For each of the following, give as much information as possible about x and y.
   (a) The ordered pairs ($^-2$, 0), ($^-2$, 1) and (x, y) represent collinear points.
   (b) The ordered pairs ($^-2$, 1), (0, 1) and (x, y) represent collinear points.
   (c) The ordered pair (x, y) is in the fourth quadrant.
6. Consider the lines through $P(2, 4)$ and perpendicular to the x and y axes, respectively. Find both the area and the perimeter of the rectangle formed by these lines and the axes.
7. Plot each of the points $A(^-3, ^-2), B(^-3, 6), C(4, 6)$ and then find the coordinates of a point D such that quadrilateral $ABCD$ is a rectangle.
8. Plot at least six points each having the sum of its coordinates equal to 4.
9. Choose a suitable scale and coordinate system on a graph paper and plot each of the following points: $A(40, 30), B(40, ^-20), C(^-10, ^-20), D(^-10, 30)$.

12-2　THE DISTANCE AND MIDPOINT FORMULAS

One way to approximate the distance between two points in a coordinate plane is to measure it with a ruler that has the same scale as the coordinate axes. Using algebraic techniques, we can calculate the exact distance between two points in the plane. First, suppose the two points are on one of the axes. For example, in Figure 12-4(a), $A(2, 0)$ and $B(5, 0)$ are on the x axis. The distance between these two points is three units.

$$AB = OB - OA = 5 - 2 = 3$$

FIGURE 12-4

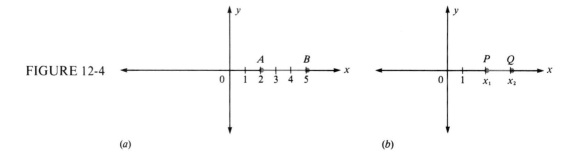

(a)   (b)

In general, if two points P and Q are on the x axis, as in Figure 12-4(b), with x coordinates x_1 and x_2, respectively, and $x_2 > x_1$, then $PQ = x_2 - x_1$. In fact, the distance between two points on the x axis is the absolute value of the difference between the x coordinates of the points. (Why?)

DEFINITION
> Given two points, $A(x_1, 0)$ and $B(x_2, 0)$, the distance between them is given by $AB = |x_2 - x_1| = |x_1 - x_2|$.

A similar definition holds for any two points on the y axis.

DEFINITION
> Given two points, $A(0, y_1)$ and $B(0, y_2)$, the distance between them is given by $AB = |y_2 - y_1| = |y_1 - y_2|$.

Figure 12-5 shows two points in the plane, $C(2, 5)$ and $D(6, 8)$. The distance between C and D can be found by drawing perpendiculars from the points to the x axis and y axis, respectively. In this way the right triangle CDE can be determined. The lengths of the legs are found using horizontal and vertical distances and properties of rectangles.

$$CE = |6 - 2| = 4$$
$$DE = |5 - 8| = 3$$

The distance between C and D can be found by applying the Pythagorean Theorem.

$$CD^2 = DE^2 + CE^2$$
$$= 3^2 + 4^2$$
$$= 25$$
$$CD = \sqrt{25} \text{ or } 5$$

FIGURE 12-5

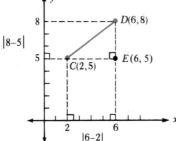

The method described can be used to find a formula for the distance between any two points $A(x_1, y_1)$ and $B(x_2, y_2)$. Construct a right triangle with $\overline{AB}$ as one of its sides by drawing a line through A parallel to the x axis and a line through B parallel to the y axis as shown in Figure 12.6. These lines intersect in point C forming a right triangle ABC. Now apply the Pythagorean Theorem.

FIGURE 12-6

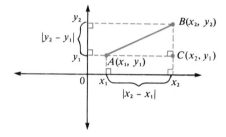

Figure 12-6 suggests that $AC = |x_2 - x_1|$ and $BC = |y_2 - y_1|$. By the Pythagorean Theorem, $(AB)^2 = |x_2 - x_1|^2 + |y_2 - y_1|^2$, and consequently, $AB = \sqrt{|x_2 - x_1|^2 + |y_2 - y_1|^2}$. Since $|x_2 - x_1|^2 = (x_2 - x_1)^2$ and $|y_2 - y_1|^2 = (y_2 - y_1)^2$, then $AB = \sqrt{(x_2 - x_1)^2 + (y_2 - y_1)^2}$. This result is known as the **distance formula.**

distance formula

DISTANCE
FORMULA

The distance between the points $A(x_1, y_1)$ and $B(x_2, y_2)$ is given by the following.

$$AB = \sqrt{(x_2 - x_1)^2 + (y_2 - y_1)^2}$$

Remark

In using the distance formula, it is important to remember that it does not make any difference whether $x_2 - x_1$ or $x_1 - x_2$ is used, since $(x_2 - x_1)^2 = (x_1 - x_2)^2$. The same is true for the y values.

Example 12-1

For each of the following, find the distance between P and Q.

(a) $P(2, 7), Q(3, 5)$ (b) $P(0, ^-3), Q(4, ^-7)$
(c) $P(0, 0), Q(3, ^-4)$

Solution

(a) $PQ = \sqrt{(3 - 2)^2 + (5 - 7)^2} = \sqrt{1 + 4} = \sqrt{5}$
(b) $PQ = \sqrt{(4 - 0)^2 + [^-7 - (^-3)]^2} = \sqrt{16 + 16} = \sqrt{32}$
(c) $PQ = \sqrt{(0 - 3)^2 + [0 - (^-4)]^2} = \sqrt{9 + 16} = \sqrt{25} = 5$

Example 12-2

Show that $A(7, 4)$, $B(^-2, 1)$, and $C(10, ^-5)$ are the vertices of an isosceles triangle.

Solution

Using the distance formula, find the length of the sides.

$$AB = \sqrt{(^-2 - 7)^2 + (1 - 4)^2} = \sqrt{(^-9)^2 + (^-3)^2} = \sqrt{90}$$

$$BC = \sqrt{[10 - (^-2)]^2 + (^-5 - 1)^2} = \sqrt{12^2 + (^-6)^2} = \sqrt{180}$$

$$AC = \sqrt{(10 - 7)^2 + (^-5 - 4)^2} = \sqrt{3^2 + (^-9)^2} = \sqrt{90}$$

Since $AB = AC = \sqrt{90}$, the triangle is isosceles.

Example 12-3

Find all points on the y axis that are ten units away from $C(8, 3)$.

Solution

Suppose P is a point on the y axis satisfying the given requirements. Then P has 0 as its x coordinate. Thus, the coordinates of P are $(0, y)$. Find y so that $PC = 10$.

$$\sqrt{(0 - 8)^2 + (y - 3)^2} = 10$$

Square both sides of the equation and solve for y.

$$(0 - 8)^2 + (y - 3)^2 = 100$$
$$64 + (y - 3)^2 = 100$$
$$(y - 3)^2 = 36$$

Thus, $y - 3 = 6$ or $y - 3 = ^-6$, so $y = 9$ or $y = ^-3$.
Hence, two points, $P_1(0, 9)$ and $P_2(0, ^-3)$, satisfy the condition.

Using the distance formula, it is possible to find the length of a segment if the coordinates of its endpoints are known. In addition, the coordinates of the midpoint of a segment can be found. Given two points $A(x_1, y_1)$ and $B(x_2, y_2)$, the coordinates of the midpoint M of the segment $\overline{AB}$ can be found. First, consider a simpler problem. Let $y_1 = y_2 = 0$. Then, the two points $A(x_1, 0)$ and $B(x_2, 0)$ lie on the x axis as shown in Figure 12-7 with $x_1 < x_2$. To find the x coordinate of the midpoint M, use the given information to write an equation for x in terms of x_1 and x_2 and then solve for x. Since M is the midpoint of $\overline{AB}$, $AM = MB$, which implies that $x - x_1 = x_2 - x$ and therefore

$$2x - x_1 = x_2$$
$$2x = x_1 + x_2$$
$$x = \frac{x_1 + x_2}{2}$$

FIGURE 12-7

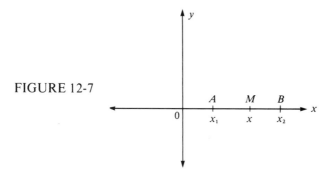

Similarly, for the case where two points lie on the y axis, the two points are $A(0, y_1)$ and $B(0, y_2)$ and the y coordinate of the midpoint is $(y_1 + y_2)/2$.

Now, consider the general case. Let $A(x_1, y_1)$ and $B(x_2, y_2)$ be the endpoints of segment $\overline{AB}$ whose midpoint $M(x, y)$ is shown in Figure 12-8. Since M is the midpoint of $\overline{AB}$, and $\overline{AA_1}$, and $\overline{MM_1}$, and $\overline{BB_1}$ are parallel, M_1 is the midpoint of $\overline{A_1B_1}$. (Why?) Hence, $x = (x_1 + x_2)/2$. By an analogous argument, $y = (y_1 + y_2)/2$.

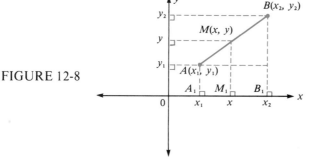

FIGURE 12-8

MIDPOINT FORMULA

Given $A(x_1, y_1)$ and $B(x_2, y_2)$, the midpoint M of $\overline{AB}$ is

$$M\left(\frac{x_1 + x_2}{2}, \frac{y_1 + y_2}{2}\right)$$

Remark

To find the midpoint of a line segment, simply find the average value of the respective coordinates of the two endpoints.

Example 12-4

(a) Find the coordinates of the midpoint of $\overline{AB}$ if A has coordinates $(^-3, 2)$ and B has coordinates $(3, ^-5)$.

(b) Suppose M is the midpoint of $\overline{AB}$, A has coordinates $(2, {}^-3)$, and M has coordinates $({}^-2, 1)$. Find the coordinates of B.

Solution   (a) Let (x, y) be the coordinates of the midpoint of $\overline{AB}$. Then, use the midpoint formula.

$$x = \frac{x_1 + x_2}{2} = \frac{{}^-3 + 3}{2} = 0$$

$$y = \frac{y_1 + y_2}{2} = \frac{2 + ({}^-5)}{2} = \frac{{}^-3}{2}$$

Hence, the midpoint has coordinates $(0, {}^-\!\frac{3}{2})$.

(b) Let the coordinates of B be (x, y) as shown in Figure 12-9. The coordinates of the midpoint M are the average of the respective coordinates of the endpoints of $\overline{AB}$.

FIGURE 12-9

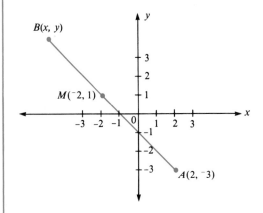

$$^-2 = \frac{x + 2}{2} \qquad\qquad 1 = \frac{y + ({}^-3)}{2}$$

$$^-4 = x + 2 \qquad\qquad 2 = y + ({}^-3)$$

$$x = {}^-6 \qquad\qquad y = 5$$

Consequently, $B({}^-6, 5)$ is the required point.

Example 12-5   Three vertices of a parallelogram are $A({}^-1, 2)$, $B(3, {}^-1)$, and $C(5, 1)$. The fourth vertex D is in the first quadrant. Find the coordinates of D.

Solution   Figure 12-10 shows parallelogram $ABCD$ with the unknown coordinates of D designated by x and y.

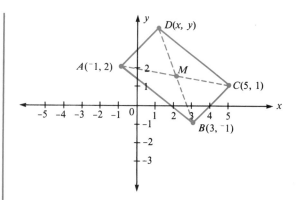

FIGURE 12-10

The strategy is to use the properties of parallelograms to write equations for x and y and then solve the equations. Since the diagonals of a parallelogram bisect each other, the midpoint formula should be useful. In Figure 12-10, M is the intersection point of the diagonals and, hence, the midpoint of each diagonal. If the coordinates of M were known, the midpoint formula could be used to find the coordinates of D.

M is the midpoint of $\overline{AC}$. Thus, M has coordinates $([^-1 + 5]/2, [2 + 1]/2)$ or $(2, 3/2)$. M is also the midpoint of $\overline{DB}$. Thus, $2 = (x + 3)/2$ or $4 = x + 3$, and consequently, $x = 1$. Similarly, $3/2 = [y + (^-1)]/2$ or $3 = y + (^-1)$, and $y = 4$. Hence, D has coordinates $(1, 4)$.

PROBLEM SET 12-2

1. For each of the following find AB.
   (a) $A(0, 3), B(0, 7)$ (b) $A(0, ^-3), B(0, ^-7)$
   (c) $A(0, 3), B(4, 0)$ (d) $A(0, ^-3), B(^-4, 0)$
   (e) $A(^-1, 2), B(3, ^-4)$ (f) $A(4, 0), B(^-3, 0)$
   (g) $A(5, 3), B(5, ^-2)$ (h) $A(0, 0), B(^-4, 3)$
   (i) $A(5, 2), B(^-3, 4)$ (j) $A(4, ^-5), B(2, ^-3)$

2. Find the perimeter of the triangle with vertices at $A(0, 0), B(^-4, ^-3)$, and $C(^-5, 0)$.

3. Show that $(0, 6), (^-3, 0)$ and $(9, ^-6)$ are the vertices of a right triangle.

4. Show that the triangle whose vertices are $A(^-2, ^-5), B(1, ^-1), C(5, 2)$ is isosceles.

5. Find x if the distance between $P(1, 3)$ and $Q(x, 9)$ is 10 units.

6. For each of the following, find the midpoint of the line segment whose endpoints have the given coordinates.
   (a) $(^-3, 1)$ and $(3, 9)$ (b) $(4, ^-3)$ and $(5, ^-1)$
   (c) $(1.8, ^-3.7)$ and $(2.2, 1.3)$ (d) $(1 + a, a - b)$ and $(1 - a, b - a)$

7. One endpoint of a diameter of a circle with center $C(^-2, 5)$ is given by $(3, ^-1)$. Find the coordinates of the other endpoint.

8. Find the lengths of the medians of the triangle whose vertices are given by (0, 0), ($^-$4, 6), and (4, 2). (**A median** is a segment connecting a vertex of a triangle to the midpoint the opposite side.)

★ 9. Three vertices of a parallelogram are given by ($^-$1, 4), (3, 8), and (5, 0). For each of the following, find the coordinates of the fourth vertex if it is in
    (a)   the first quadrant.
    (b)   the second quadrant.
    (c)   the fourth quadrant.

★10. Use the distance formula to show that the points with coordinates ($^-$1, 5), (0, 2), and (1, $^-$1) are collinear.

★11. Use coordinates to prove that the midpoint M of the hypotenuse of a right triangle is equidistant from the vertices. (*Hint:* Use the coordinate system shown in the accompanying figure.)

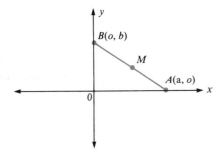

BRAIN TEASER

Among his great-grandfather's papers, José found a parchment describing the location of a hidden treasure. The treasure was buried by a band of pirates on a deserted island that contained an oak tree, a pine tree, and a gallows where the pirates hanged traitors. The map looked like the figure below and gave the following directions.

Count the steps from the gallows to the oak tree. At the oak, turn 90° to the right. Take the same number of steps and then put a spike in the ground.

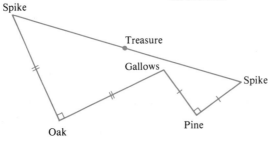

Next, return to the gallows and walk to the pine tree, counting the number of steps. At the pine tree, turn 90° to the left, take the same number of steps, and then put another spike in the ground. The treasure is buried half-way between the spikes.

José found the island and the two trees but could not find the gallows nor the spikes, which had long since rotted. José dug all over the island, but since the island was large, he gave up. Devise a plan to help José find the treasure.

12-3 SETS OF POINTS AND THEIR GRAPHS

Every point on the x axis has a y coordinate of zero. Therefore, the x axis can be described as the set of all points (x, y) such that $y = 0$. The set of points on the x axis is usually denoted by the equation $y = 0$, and we say that the equation of the x axis is $y = 0$. Similarly, the equation $x = 0$ is used to describe a set of points in the plane, (x, y), for which $x = 0$ and y is an arbitrary real number. All such points are on the y axis. Hence, $x = 0$ is the equation of the y axis.

Example 12-6   Sketch the graphs for each of the following.

(a) $x = 2$ (b) $y = 3$ (c) $x < 2$ and $y = 3$ (d) $x < 2$

Solution   (a) The equation $x = 2$ represents the set of all points (x, y) for which $x = 2$ and y is any real number. This set represents a line perpendicular to the x axis at $(2, 0)$ (Figure 12-11).

FIGURE 12-11

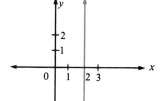

(b) The equation $y = 3$ represents the set of all points (x, y) for which $y = 3$ and x is any real number. This set represents a line perpendicular to the y axis at $(0, 3)$ (Figure 12-12).

FIGURE 12-12

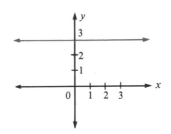

(c) Together, the statements represent the set of all points (x, y) for which $x < 2$, but y is always 3. The set describes a half line as shown in Figure 12-13.

FIGURE 12-13

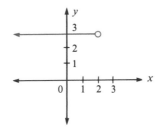

(d) The statement represents $\{(x, y) \mid x < 2 \text{ and } y \in R\}$. Since there are no restrictions on the y coordinates, the coordinates of any point to the left of the line with equation $x = 2$, but not on the line, satisfy the condition. The half-plane in Figure 12-14 is the graph.

FIGURE 12-14

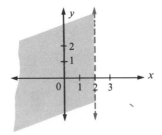

A circle can be described by knowing the location of the center and the length of the radius. Figure 12-15 shows the circle with center $C(5, 4)$ and radius three units long. To find the equation of this circle, consider a point $P(x, y)$ on the circle. The distance from P to the center of the circle is 3 units; that is, $CP = 3$. By the distance formula, $\sqrt{(x - 5)^2 + (y - 4)^2} = 3$ or

$(x - 5)^2 + (y - 4)^2 = 9$. Thus, the coordinates of any point on the circle satisfy the equation $(x - 5)^2 + (y - 4)^2 = 9$.

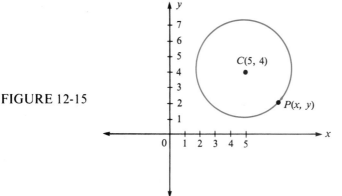

FIGURE 12-15

To find the equation of any circle with center $C(a, b)$ and radius r, proceed in a similar way. Figure 12-16 shows that any point $P(x, y)$ is on the circle if and only if $PC = r$, that is, if and only if $\sqrt{(x - a)^2 + (y - b)^2} = r$. Squaring both sides results in the following *equation of a circle*.

$$(x - a)^2 + (y - b)^2 = r^2$$

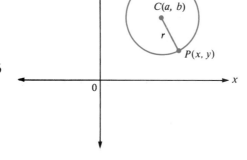

FIGURE 12-16

Example 12-7

    (a)   Find the equation of the circle with center at the origin and radius 4.
    (b)   Find the equation of the circle with center at $C(^-4, 3)$ and radius 5.
    (c)   Sketch the graph of $(x + 2)^2 + (y - 3)^2 = 9$.
    (d)   Write a condition for the set of points in the interior of the circle given in part (c).

Solution   (a) Since the center is at $(0, 0)$ and $r = 4$, the equation $(x - a)^2 + (y - b)^2 = r^2$ becomes $(x - 0)^2 + (y - 0)^2 = 4^2$ or $x^2 + y^2 = 16$.

(b) The equation is $[x - (^-4)]^2 + (y - 3)^2 = 5^2$ or $(x + 4)^2 + (y - 3)^2 = 25$.

(c) The equation $(x + 2)^2 + (y - 3)^2 = 9$ is in the form $(x - a)^2 + (y - b)^2 = r^2$ if and only if $x - a = x + 2$, $y - b = y - 3$, and $r^2 = 9$. Thus, $a = ^-2$, $b = 3$, and $r = 3$. Hence, the center of the circle is at $(^-2, 3)$, $r = 3$, and Figure 12-17 shows the graph of the circle.

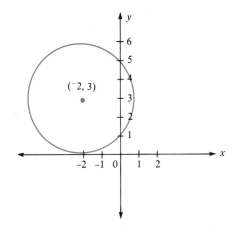

FIGURE 12-17

(d) A point (x, y) is in the interior of the circle if and only if the distance between the point and the center of the circle is less than the radius. In this case $\sqrt{[x - (^-2)]^2 + (y - 3)^2} < 3$ or $(x + 2)^2 + (y - 3)^2 < 9$.

PROBLEM SET 12-3

1. Sketch the graphs for each of the following.
   (a) $x = ^-3$ (b) $y = ^-1$ (c) $x > ^-3$
   (d) $y > ^-1$ (e) $x > ^-3$ and $y = 2$ (f) $y \geq ^-1$ and $x = 0$
2. Find the equations for each of the following.
   (a) The line containing $P(3, 0)$ and perpendicular to the x axis
   (b) The line containing $P(0, ^-2)$ and parallel to the x axis
   (c) The line containing $P(^-4, 5)$ and parallel to the x axis
   (d) The line containing $P(^-4, 5)$ and parallel to the y axis
3. For each of the following, write the equations of the circle given the center C and radius r.
   (a) $C(3, ^-2)$ and $r = 2$ (b) $C(^-3, ^-4)$ and $r = 5$
   (c) $C(^-1, 0)$ and $r = 2$ (d) $C(0, 0)$ and $r = 3$

4. Given the circle whose equation is $x^2 + y^2 = 9$, which of the following points are in its interior, which are in the exterior, and which are on the circle?
    (a) $(3, ^-3)$ (b) $(2, ^-2)$ (c) $(1, 8)$ (d) $(3, 1982)$
    (e) $(5.1234, ^-3.7894)$ (f) $\left(\dfrac{1}{387}, \dfrac{1}{1983}\right)$ (g) $\left(-\dfrac{1}{2}, \dfrac{35}{2}\right)$

5. Find the equation of the circle whose center is at the origin and that contains the point with coordinates $(^-3, 5)$.
6. For each of the following, find the equation of the circle whose center is at $C(4, ^-3)$ and that passes through the point indicated.
    (a) The origin   (b) $(5, ^-2)$
7. Find the equation of the circle with a diameter having endpoints at $(^-8, 2)$ and $(4, ^-6)$.
8. Graph each of the following equations, if possible.
    (a) $x^2 + y^2 > 4$ (b) $x^2 + y^2 \le 4$ (c) $x^2 + y^2 - 4 = 0$ (d) $x^2 + y^2 + 4 = 0$
9. Find the equation of the circle that passes through the origin, the point $(5, 2)$ and has its center on the x axis.
10. Is $2x^2 + 2y^2 = 1$ an equation of a circle? If it is, find its center and radius; if not, explain why not.
11. A treasure was buried on a deserted island with three trees; a pine, an oak, and an olive. A coordinate system was set up so that the x axis was the line through the pine tree and the oak tree. The y axis was drawn through the olive tree perpendicular to the x axis. The coordinates of the treasure satisfy the equation $x^2 + y^2 = 0$. Is it possible to find the exact location of the treasure? If so, find it; if not, explain why not.

12-4 EQUATIONS OF LINES

The graph of the equation $x = a$, where a is some real number, is a line perpendicular to the x axis through the point with coordinates $(a, 0)$ as shown in Figure 12-18. Similarly, the graph of the equation $y = b$ is a line

FIGURE 12-18

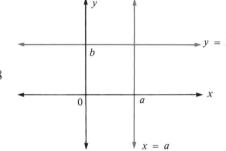

perpendicular to the y axis through the point with coordinates $(0, b)$. To graph the equation $y = x$, plot all points whose x and y coordinates are equal. For example, $(0, 0)$, $(1, 1)$, $(1.3, 1.3)$, $(4, 4)$, $(4.5, 4.5)$, $(10, 10)$ $(^-3, ^-3)$ all belong to the graph. However $(1, ^-1)$ and $(2, 4)$ do not belong to the graph. Plotting some of the points shows that the points lie on a line ℓ as shown in Figure 12-19. In fact, all points represented by the equation $y = x$ lie on line ℓ.

FIGURE 12-19

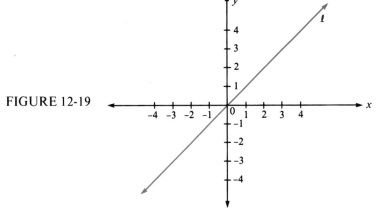

Next, consider the equation $y = 2x$. For any value of x, there is a corresponding value of y. Table 12-1 shows several corresponding values of x and y.

TABLE 12-1

x	$y = 2x$
0	0
1	2
2	4
$^-1$	$^-2$
$^-2$	$^-4$

These five coordinate pairs are plotted in Figure 12-20 along with the graph of $y = x$. The five points appear to be on a straight line. In fact, plotting more points convinces us that all points whose coordinates satisfy the equation $y = 2x$ lie on the same straight line.

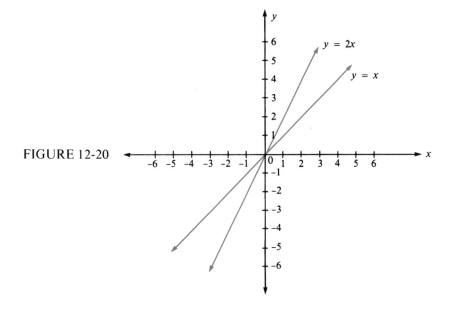

FIGURE 12-20

As Figure 12-20 shows, the graph of $y = 2x$ is *steeper* than the graph of $y = x$. We further explore the notion of steepness by examining the graphs in Figure 12-21.

All six lines in Figure 12-21 have equations of the form $y = mx$, where m takes the values 2, 1, $\frac{1}{2}$, $-\frac{1}{2}$, $^-1$, and $^-2$. The number m is a measure of

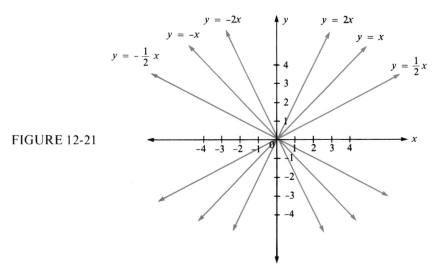

FIGURE 12-21

slope   steepness and is called the **slope** of the line whose equation is $y = mx$. The graph goes up from left to right (increases) if m is positive and goes down from left to right (decreases) if m is negative.

Observe that all six lines in Figure 12-21 pass through the origin. This is true for any line whose equation is $y = mx$. If $x = 0$, then $y = m \cdot 0 = 0$, and hence, $(0, 0)$ is a point on the graph of $y = mx$. Conversely, it is possible to show that any nonvertical line passing through the origin has an equation of the form $y = mx$, for some value of m.

Example 12-8   Find the equation of the line that contains $(0, 0)$ and $(2, 3)$.

Solution   Since the line goes through the origin, its equation has the form $y = mx$. To find the equation of the line, we must find the value of m. The line contains $(2, 3)$, so substitute 2 for x and 3 for y into the equation $y = mx$ to obtain $3 = m \cdot 2$ and thus $m = \frac{3}{2}$. Hence, the required equation is $y = \frac{3}{2}x$.

Next, consider equations of the form $y = mx + b$. To do so, first examine the graphs of $y = x + 2$ and $y = x$. Given the graph of $y = x$, the graph of $y = x + 2$ can be obtained by "raising" each point on the first graph by two units since, for a certain value of x, the corresponding y value is two units greater in $y = x + 2$ than in $y = x$. This is shown in Figure 12-22(a). Similarly, to sketch the graph of $y = x - 2$, first draw the graph of $y = x$ and then lower each point vertically by two units as shown in Figure 12-22(b).

FIGURE 12-22

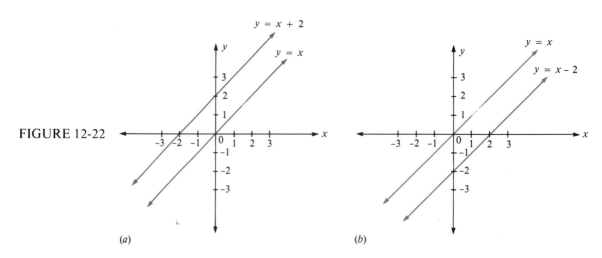

(a)   (b)

The graphs of $y = x + 2$ and $y = x - 2$ are straight lines. Moreover, the lines whose equations are $y = x$, $y = x + 2$, and $y = x - 2$ are parallel. In general, for a given value of m, the graph of $y = mx + b$ is a straight line parallel to the line whose equation is $y = mx$.

The slope m in the equation $y = mx + b$ is a measure of the steepness of the line. There is a geometrical meaning for b, too. The graph of the line $y = mx + b$ can be obtained from the graph of $y = mx$ by sliding the latter b units up as shown in Figure 12-23 for $b > 0$. (If b is positive, the slide is upward; if b is negative, the slide is downward.)

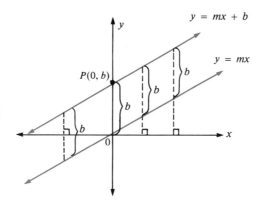

FIGURE 12-23

The graph of $y = mx + b$ in Figure 12-23 crosses the y axis at the point $P(0, b)$. The value of y at the point of intersection of any line with the y axis is *y* intercept called the **y intercept.** Thus, b is the y intercept of $y = mx + b$, and this form slope-intercept form of the equation of a straight line is called the **slope-intercept form.** Similarly, the value of x at the point of intersection of a line with the x axis is called the *x* intercept **x intercept.**

Example 12-9 | Given the equation $y - 3x = {}^-6$, find each of the following.

(a)   The slope of the line.
(b)   The y intercept.
(c)   The x intercept.
(d)   Sketch the graph of the equation.

Solution | (a)   To write the equation in the form $y = mx + b$, add $3x$ to both sides to obtain $y = 3x + ({}^-6)$. Hence, the slope is 3.
(b)   The form $y = 3x + ({}^-6)$ shows that $b = {}^-6$, which is the y intercept. (The y intercept can also be found directly by substituting $x = 0$ in the equation and solving for y.)
(c)   The x intercept is the x coordinate of the point where the graph intersects the x axis. At that point, $y = 0$. Substituting 0 for y in $y = 3x - 6$ gives 2 as the x intercept.

(d)   The y intercept and x intercept give two points located at $(0, ^-6)$ and $(2, 0)$ on the line. Plot these points and draw the line through them to obtain the desired graph as shown in Figure 12-24. Note that any two points of the line can be used to sketch the graph.

FIGURE 12-24

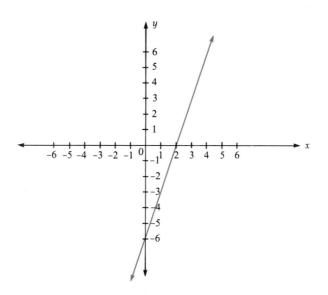

The equation $y = b$ can be written in slope-intercept form as $y = 0 \cdot x + b$. Consequently, its slope is 0 and its y intercept is b. This should not be surprising since the line is parallel to the x axis, and consequently, its steepness should be 0. Any vertical line $x = a$ cannot be written in the slope-intercept form since the slope of a vertical line is undefined (discussed later in this section). Hence, every straight line has an equation of the form $y = mx + b$ or $x = a$. Any equation that can be put in one of these forms is

linear equation   called a **linear equation.**

A line is determined by any two of its points. Hence, given the coordinates of two points on a line, it is possible to find the equation of the line. For example, given $A(4, 2)$ and $B(1, 6)$, find the equation of $\overleftrightarrow{AB}$. Since the line is not perpendicular to the x axis (why?), it must be of the form $y = mx + b$. Substituting the coordinates of A and B in $y = mx + b$ results in the following equations.

$$2 = m \cdot 4 + b, \quad \text{or} \quad 2 = 4m + b$$
$$6 = m \cdot 1 + b \quad \text{or} \quad 6 = m + b$$

To find the equation of the line, find the values of m and b. From the first equation, $b = 2 - 4m$ and from the second, $b = 6 - m$. Consequently, $2 - 4m = 6 - m$ and $m = ^-4/3$. Substituting this value of m in either one of the equations gives $b = 22/3$. Consequently, the equation of the line is $y = (^-4/3)x + 22/3$. The correctness of this equation can be checked by substituting the coordinates of the two given points, $A(4, 2)$ and $B(1, 6)$, in the equation.

Using an analogous approach, it is possible to find a general formula for the slope of a line given two points on a line, $A(x_1, y_1)$ and $B(x_2, y_2)$. If the line is not a vertical line, its equation is given by $y = mx + b$. Substituting the coordinates of A and B into this equation gives the following.

$y_1 = mx_1 + b$ and, therefore, $y_1 - mx_1 = b$

$y_2 = mx_2 + b$ and, therefore, $y_2 - mx_2 = b$

By equating these two values for b and solving for m, the formula for slope results.

$$y_1 - mx_1 = y_2 - mx_2$$

$$mx_2 - mx_1 = y_2 - y_1$$

$$m(x_2 - x_1) = y_2 - y_1$$

$$m = \frac{y_2 - y_1}{x_2 - x_1}$$

SLOPE FORMULA

Given two points $A(x_1, y_1)$ and $B(x_2, y_2)$ with $x_1 \neq x_2$, the slope m of the line $\overleftrightarrow{AB}$ is given by $m = \dfrac{y_2 - y_1}{x_2 - x_1}$.

Remark

In general, $m = \dfrac{y_2 - y_1}{x_2 - x_1} = \dfrac{(y_2 - y_1)(^-1)}{(x_2 - x_1)(^-1)} = \dfrac{y_1 - y_2}{x_1 - x_2}$.

The slope of the line $\overleftrightarrow{AB}$ is the change in y coordinates divided by the corresponding change in x coordinates of any two points on the line. The difference, $x_2 - x_1$, is often called the **run,** while the difference, $y_2 - y_1$, is called the **rise.** Thus, $m = $ rise/run.

Example 12-10

Find the slope of $\overleftrightarrow{AB}$ given $A(3, 1)$ and $B(5, 4)$.

Solution

$$m = \frac{4 - 1}{5 - 3} = \frac{3}{2} \quad \text{or} \quad \frac{1 - 4}{3 - 5} = \frac{^-3}{^-2} = \frac{3}{2}$$

Example 12-11

Find the slope and the equation of the line passing through the points $A(^-3, 4)$ and $B(^-1, 0)$.

Solution

$$m = \frac{4 - 0}{^-3 - (^-1)} = \frac{4}{^-2} = ^-2$$

The equation of the line must be of the form $y = mx + b$. Since $m = ^-2$, $y = ^-2x + b$ and now the value of b must be found. The required line contains each of the given points, and hence, the coordinates of each point must satisfy the equation. Substituting the coordinates of B into $y = ^-2x + b$ gives $0 = ^-2(^-1) + b$ or $0 = 2 + b$. Consequently, $b = ^-2$ and the equation of the line is $y = ^-2x + (^-2)$ or $y = ^-2x - 2$. To check that $y = ^-2x - 2$ is the required equation, we must verify that the coordinates of both A and B satisfy the equation. This is left for the reader.

To examine the slope of a vertical line, pick any two points on the line, (x_1, y_1) and (x_2, y_2). Since the line is vertical, $x_1 = x_2$. Consequently, $m = (y_2 - y_1)/(x_2 - x_1) = (y_2 - y_1)/0$, which is not meaningful. Thus, *the slope of a vertical line is undefined.*

In applications of mathematics, we often need to graph inequalities as well as equations. Consider, for example, the inequality $y - 3x > ^-6$. This inequality is equivalent to $y > 3x + (^-6)$. A point whose coordinates satisfy $y > 3x + (^-6)$ is above the line represented by $y = 3x + (^-6)$. Consequently, the graph of the inequality is the half-plane above the line given by $y = 3x + (^-6)$. The graph is sketched in Figure 12-25. The line itself is not included in the graph and is dotted.

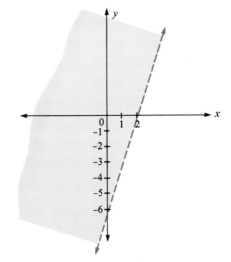

FIGURE 12-25

The graph of any inequality in one of the forms $y > mx + b$ or $y < mx + b$ is a half-plane either above or below the line $y = mx + b$. Thus, in order to graph an inequality like $y - 3x > ^-6$, first graph the corresponding straight line. Then, check some point not on the line to see if it satisfies the inequality. If it does, the half-plane containing the point is the graph, and if not, the half-plane not including the point is the graph. For example, checking $(0, 0)$ in $y - 3x > {}^-6$ gives $0 - 3 \cdot 0 > {}^-6$, which is a true statement. Thus, the half-plane determined by $y - 3x = {}^-6$ and containing the origin is the graph of the inequality as pictured in Figure 12-25.

Example 12-12 | Graph each of the following inequalities.

(a) $x - y > 3$ (b) $x + 3y \le 0$

Solution | (a) Substituting $x = 0$ and $y = 0$ gives $0 > 3$, a false statement. Hence, $(0, 0)$ is not in the required half-plane. Consequently, the graph of $x - y > 3$ is the half-plane determined by $x - y = 3$ and not including the origin, as shown in Figure 12-26.

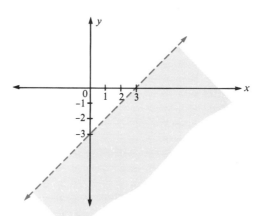

FIGURE 12-26

(b) Substituting $x = 0$ and $y = 0$ gives $0 \le 0$, which is true, and consequently, $(0, 0)$ is on the line represented by $x + 3y = 0$ and not in one of the half-planes. Try another point, for example, the point $(1, 0)$. Substituting these values for x and y in the inequality gives $1 + 3 \cdot 0 \le 0$, a false statement. Hence, the required half-plane does not include $(1, 0)$. We now graph $x + 3y = 0$ and choose the half-plane that does not include $(1, 0)$. The graph is given in Figure 12-27. Notice that the line is not dotted since the inequality $x + 3y \le 0$ is equivalent to $x + 3y < 0$ or $x + 3y = 0$ and, hence, includes the line as well.

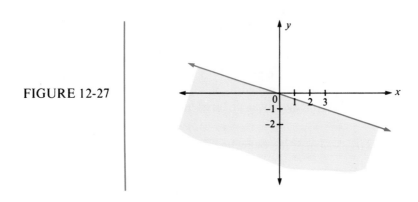

FIGURE 12-27

PROBLEM SET 12-4

1. Sketch the graphs of the equations $y = {}^-x$ and $y = {}^-x + 3$ on the same coordinate system.
2. The graph of $y = mx$ is given in the accompanying figure. Sketch the graphs for each of the following on the same figure.
    (a) $y = mx + 3$ (b) $y = mx - 3$

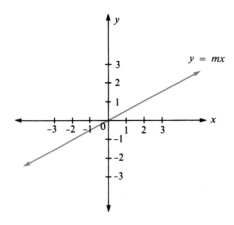

3. Sketch the graphs for each of the following equations.

    (a) $y = \dfrac{{}^-3}{4}x + 3$ (b) $y = 3x - 1$ (c) $y = {}^-3$

    (d) $x = {}^-2$ (e) $y = 15x - 30$ (f) $y = \dfrac{1}{20}x$

4. Find x intercept and y intercept for the equations in Problem 3, if they exist.

5. Write each of the equations below in slope-intercept form.
   (a) $3y - x = 0$ (b) $x + y = 3$ (c) $3x - 4y + 7 = 0$
   (d) $x = 3y$ (e) $x - y = 4(x - y)$

6. For each of the following, find the slope, if it exists, of the line determined by the given pair of points.
   (a) $(4, 3)$ and $(^-5, 0)$ (b) $(^-4, 1)$ and $(5, 2)$
   (c) $(\sqrt{5}, 2)$ and $(1, 2)$ (d) $(^-3, 81)$ and $(^-3, 198)$
   (e) $(1.0001, 12)$ and $(1, 10)$ (f) (a, a) and (b, b)

7. For each of the following, write the equation of the line determined by the given pair of points in slope-intercept form or in the form $x = a$.

   (a) $(^-4, 3)$ and $(1, ^-2)$ (b) $(0, 0)$ and $(2, 1)$ (c) $(0, 1)$ and $(2, 1)$

   (d) $(2, 1)$ and $(2, ^-1)$ (e) $\left(0, \dfrac{^-1}{2}\right)$ and $\left(\dfrac{1}{2}, 0\right)$ (f) $(^-a, 0)$ and $(a, 0)$

8. Use slopes to determine which of the following pairs of lines are parallel.

   (a) $y = 2x - 1$ and $y = 2x + 7$ (b) $4y - 3x + 4 = 0$ and $8y - 6x + 1 = 0$

   (c) $y - 2x = 0$ and $4x - 2y = 3$ (d) $\dfrac{x}{3} + \dfrac{y}{4} = 1$ and $y = \dfrac{4}{3}x$

9. For each of the following, find the equation of a line through $P(^-2, 3)$ and parallel to the line represented by the given equation.
   (a) $y = ^-2x$ (b) $3y + 2x + 1 = 0$ (c) $x = 3$ (d) $y = ^-4$

10. Determine the slopes of each of the following lines.

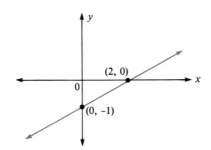

(a)

(b)

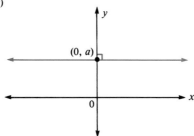

(c)

11. The vertices of quadrilateral $ABCD$ are $A(2, 1)$, $B(3, 5)$, $C(^-5, 1)$, $D(^-6, ^-3)$. Prove that quadrilateral $ABCD$ is a parallelogram.

12. Prove that the points represented by $(0, ^-1)$, $(1, 2)$, and $(^-1, ^-4)$ are collinear.

13. For each of the following, find the equation of the line which passes through the given point and has the given slope.

(a) $(^-3, 0)$ with slope $\dfrac{^-1}{2}$ (b) $(1, ^-3)$ with slope $\dfrac{2}{3}$

14. Show that $(^-1, ^-3)$, $(8, 3)$, $(3, 4)$, and $(0, 2)$ are the vertices of an isosceles trapezoid.

15. Find the x intercept and y intercept of the line whose equation is $x/a + y/b = 1$, where $a \neq 0$ and $b \neq 0$.

16. Find the equation of the flip image of the line $y = 3x + 1$ in each of the following.

(a) The x axis   (b) The y axis

17. Assuming that the relationship between temperature in degrees Celsius and temperature in degrees Fahrenheit is a linear relationship, find a formula that will convert temperature in Fahrenheit into temperature in Celsius if $0°C = 32°F$ and $100°C = 212°F$.

18. Graph each of the following inequalities.

(a) $x - y + 3 > 0$ (b) $2x > 3y$ (c) $x - 2y + 1 \leq 0$

19. The number of chirps made by a cricket is linearly related to the temperature. If a cricket chirped 40 times a minute when it was $10°C$ and 112 times a minute when it was $20°C$, find an equation to describe this relationship.

★20. Use the following drawing and properties of similar triangles to prove that the slopes m_1 and m_2 of two perpendicular lines ℓ_1 and ℓ_2 respectively, satisfy the relationship $m_1 m_2 = -1$.

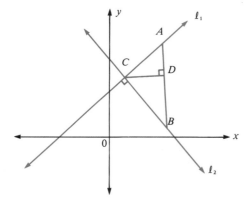

★21. Graph each of the following equations.

(a) $y = |x|$ (b) $|y| = x$ (c) $|y| = |x|$ (d) $|x + y| = 1$

(e) $|x| + |y| = 1$

★22. Find the area enclosed between the curves $x^2 + y^2 = 1$ and $|x| + |y| = 1$.

★23. Find the area of the region defined by $y > |x|$ and $x^2 + y^2 \leq 1$.

12-5 SYSTEMS OF LINEAR EQUATIONS

The mathematical descriptions of many problems involve more than one equation, each involving more than one unknown. To solve such problems, a common solution to the equations must be found. For example, finding the solution to a problem may involve finding all x and y values that satisfy both $y = x + 3$ and $y = 2x - 1$. Together $y = x + 3$ and $y = 2x - 1$ are called a **system of linear equations.** Any solution to the system is an ordered pair (x, y) that satisfies both equations.

system of linear equations

Geometrically, an ordered pair satisfying both equations is a point that belongs to each of the lines. Figure 12-28 shows the graphs of $y = x + 3$ and $y = 2x - 1$. The two lines appear to intersect at $(4, 7)$. Thus, $(4, 7)$ appears to be the solution of the given system of equations. This solution can be checked by substituting 4 for x and 7 for y into each equation. Since $7 = 4 + 3$ and $7 = 2 \cdot 4 - 1$, the ordered pair $(4, 7)$ is a solution. The lines intersect in only one point. Thus, $(4, 7)$ is the only solution to the system.

FIGURE 12-28

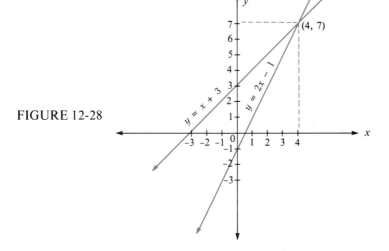

In the upper elementary grades, students learn to graph linear equations. Often, they also learn the relationship between a pair of linear equations and the intersection of two lines as the excerpt on page 544 from the Addison-Wesley text, *Mathematics in Our World,* Grade 8, 1979, shows.

✪ Graphing pairs of equations

Graph on the same coordinate grid
the pair of equations

$$y = x - 2$$

$$y = 4 - x$$

where x and y are rational numbers.

Find the point of intersection
of the graphs.

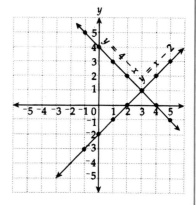

$y = x - 2$

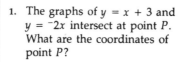

x	5	4	3	2	1	0	-1
y	3	2	1	0	-1	-2	-3

$y = 4 - x$

x	5	4	3	2	1	0	-1
y	-1	0	1	2	3	4	5

Notice that the ordered pair (3, 1)
appears in both tables. The point
(3, 1) is the point of intersection
of the graphs.

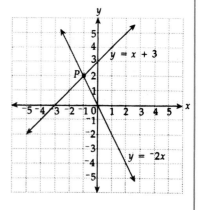

1. The graphs of $y = x + 3$ and
   $y = {}^-2x$ intersect at point P.
   What are the coordinates of
   point P?

2. Substitute the x and y coordinates
   of point P in the equation
   $y = x + 3$. Do you get a true
   statement?

3. Substitute the x and y coordinates
   of point P in the equation
   $y = {}^-2x$. Do you get a true
   statement?

294   Module 11.4

There are certain drawbacks to estimating a solution to a system of equations graphically. The sketch of a graph is often inaccurate, especially if fractions or irrational numbers are involved in the solution. Moreover, the graphic approach is impractical in solving linear equations with three variables and impossible when more than three variables are involved. There are various algebraic methods for solving systems of linear equations. Consider, for example, the system $y = x + 3$ and $y = 2x - 1$. Since the solution (x, y) satisfies each equation, assume that x and y in each equation are the same. Consequently, the expressions $x + 3$ and $2x - 1$ can be equated. The equation $x + 3 = 2x - 1$ has one unknown, x. Solving for x gives $3 + 1 = 2x - x$, and hence, $4 = x$. Substituting 4 for x in either equation gives $y = 7$. Thus $(4, 7)$ is the solution to the given system. As before, this solution can be checked by substitution. This method for solving a system of linear equations

substitution method is called the **substitution method.** It can be applied to any system of linear equations in two unknowns.

Example 12-13

Solve the following system.

$3x - 4y = 5$

$2x + 5y = 1$

Solution

First, rewrite each equation, expressing y in terms of x.

$$y = \frac{3x - 5}{4} \quad \text{and} \quad y = \frac{1 - 2x}{5}$$

Then, equate the expressions for y in terms of x and solve for x.

$$\frac{3x - 5}{4} = \frac{1 - 2x}{5}$$

$$5(3x - 5) = 4(1 - 2x)$$

$$15x - 25 = 4 - 8x$$

$$23x = 29$$

$$x = \frac{29}{23}$$

Substituting $29/23$ for x in $y = (3x - 5)/4$ gives $y = {}^{-}7/23$.
Hence, $x = 29/23$ and $y = {}^{-}7/23$. This can be checked by substituting the values for x and y in the original equations.

Sometimes it is more convenient to solve a system of equations by expressing x in terms of y in one of the equations and substituting the obtained expression for x in the other equation, or by expressing x in terms of y in both equations and solving for y.

Another method for solving systems of equations is based on eliminating one of the variables by adding the original or equivalent equations. This **elimination method** method is called the **elimination method.** For example, consider the system.

$$x - y = {}^-3$$
$$x + y = 7$$

By "adding" the two equations using the addition property of equality, one variable, in this case y, is eliminated. The resulting equation can be solved for x.

$$
\begin{array}{rl}
x - y &= {}^-3 \\
\underline{x + y} &= \underline{7} \\
2x &= 4 \\
x &= 2
\end{array}
$$

Substituting 2 for x in the first equation (either equation can be used) gives $2 - y = {}^-3$ and hence, $y = 5$. Checking this result in the original equations shows that $2 - 5 = {}^-3$ and $2 + 5 = 7$. Consequently, $(2, 5)$ is the solution to the system.

Often another operation is required before equations are added so that an unknown can be eliminated. Consider, for example, the following system.

$$3x + 2y = 5$$
$$5x - 4y = 3$$

Adding the equations does not eliminate either unknown. If the first equation contained $4y$ rather than $2y$, the variable y could be eliminated by adding. To obtain $4y$ in the first equation, multiply both sides of the equation by 2 to obtain the equivalent equation $6x + 4y = 10$. Adding the equations in the equivalent system gives the following.

$$
\begin{array}{rl}
6x + 4y &= 10 \\
\underline{5x - 4y} &= \underline{6} \\
11x &= 16 \\
x &= \dfrac{16}{11}
\end{array}
$$

To find the corresponding value of y, substitute $^{16}\!/_{11}$ for x in either of the original equations and solve for y, or use the elimination method again and solve for y. To eliminate the x values from the original system, multiply the first equation by 5 and the second by $^-3$ (or the first by $^-5$ and the second by 3). Then, add and solve for y.

$$
\begin{array}{rl}
15x + 10y &= 25 \\
\underline{{}^-15x + 12y} &= \underline{{}^-9} \\
22y &= 16
\end{array}
$$

$$y = \frac{16}{22} \quad \text{or} \quad \frac{8}{11}$$

Consequently, $(^{16}/_{11}, {}^8/_{11})$ is the solution of the original system. This solution, as always, should be checked by substitution in the *original* equations.

All examples thus far have had unique solutions. However, other situations may arise. Geometrically, a system of two linear equations has a unique solution if and only if the graphs of the equations intersect in a single point. If the equations represent parallel lines, the system has no solution. If equations have graphs that are the same line, the system has infinitely many solutions.

Consider the following system.

$$2x - 3y = 1$$
$$^-4x + 6y = 5$$

In an attempt to solve for x, multiply the first equation by 2 and then add as follows.

$$4x - 6y = 2$$
$$\underline{^-4x + 6y = 5}$$
$$0 = 7$$

A false statement results. The equation $0 = 7$ actually is $0 \cdot x + 0 \cdot y = 7$. Since there are no x and y values for which $0 \cdot x + 0 \cdot y = 7$, there are no values of x and y that satisfy the original system. In other words, the solution set is $\varnothing$. Geometrically, this situation arises if and only if the corresponding lines are parallel.

Next, consider the following system.

$$2x - 3y = 1$$
$$^-4x + 6y = {}^-2$$

To solve this system, multiply the first equation by 2 and add as follows.

$$4x - 6y = 2$$
$$\underline{^-4x + 6y = {}^-2}$$
$$0 = 0$$

The resulting statement, $0 = 0$, is always true. Rewriting the equation as $0 \cdot x + 0 \cdot y = 0$ shows that all values of x and y satisfy this equation. The values of x and y that satisfy both $0 \cdot x + 0 \cdot y = 0$ and $2x - 3y = 1$ are those that satisfy $2x - 3y = 1$. There are infinitely many such pairs x and y that correspond to points on the line $2x - 3y = 1$ and hence to $^-4x + 6y = {}^-2$.

One way to check that a system has infinitely many solutions is by observing that each of the original equations represents the same straight line. In the preceding system, both equations reduce to $y = \frac{2}{3}x - \frac{1}{3}$. Another way to observe that a system has infinitely many solutions is by observing that one of the equations reduces to the other. Thus, for example, in the system $2x - 3y = 1$ and $^-4x + 6y - 2$, multiplying the first equation by $^-2$ gives $^-4x + 6y = ^-2$, which is the second equation. The solution set of the system is $\{(x, y) \mid 2x - 3y = 1\}$.

Example 12-14 Identify each of the following systems as having a unique solution, no solutions, or infinitely many solutions.

(a) $2x - 3y = 5$ (b) $\dfrac{x}{3} - \dfrac{y}{4} = 1$ (c) $6x - 9y = 5$

   $\dfrac{1}{2}x - y = 1$ $3y - 4x + 12 = 0$ $^-8x + 12y = 7$

Solution One approach is to attempt solving each system. Another approach is to write each equation in the slope-intercept form and interpret the system geometrically.

(a) *First method.* To eliminate x, multiply the second equation by $^-4$ and add the equations.

$$\begin{array}{r} 2x - 3y = 5 \\ ^-2x + 4y = ^-4 \\ \hline y = 1 \end{array}$$

Substituting 1 for y in either equation gives $x = 4$. Thus, $(4, 1)$ is the unique solution of the system.

   Second method. In slope-intercept form, the first equation is $y = \frac{2}{3}x - \frac{5}{3}$. The second equation is $y = \frac{1}{2}x - 1$. The slopes of the corresponding lines are $\frac{2}{3}$ and $\frac{1}{2}$, respectively. Consequently, the lines are distinct and are not parallel and, therefore, intersect in a single point whose coordinates are the unique solution to the original system.

(b) *First method.* Multiplying the first equation by 12 gives $4x - 3y = 12$. The second equation can be written as $^-4x + 3y = ^-12$. Adding the resulting equations gives the following.

$$\begin{array}{r} 4x - 3y = 12 \\ ^-4x + 3y = ^-12 \\ \hline 0 = 0 \end{array}$$

Since every pair (x, y) satisfies $0 \cdot x + 0 \cdot y = 0$, the original system has infinitely many solutions.

   Second method. In slope-intercept form,

$$\frac{x}{3} - \frac{y}{4} = 1 \text{ is } y = \frac{4}{3}x - 4.$$

The second equation $3y - 4x + 12 = 0$ in slope-intercept form is $y = \frac{4}{3}x - 4$. Thus, the two lines are identical and, therefore, the system has infinitely many solutions.

(c) *First method.* To eliminate y, multiply the first equation by 4 and the second by 3 and then add the resulting equations.

$$24x - 36y = 20$$
$$\underline{^-24x + 36y = 21}$$
$$0 = 41$$

Since no pair of numbers satisfies $0 \cdot x + 0 \cdot y = 41$, this equation has no solutions, and consequently, the original system has no solutions.

Second method. In slope-intercept form, the first equation is $y = \frac{2}{3}x - \frac{5}{9}$. The second equation is $y = \frac{2}{3}x + \frac{7}{12}$. The corresponding lines have the same slope $\frac{2}{3}$, but different y intercepts. Consequently, the lines are parallel and the original system has no solutions.

PROBLEM SET 12-5

1. Use the equation $2x - 3y = 5$ to solve each of the following.
   (a) Find four solutions of the equation.
   (b) Graph all the solutions for which $^-2 \le x \le 2$.
   (c) Graph all the solutions for which $0 \le y \le 2$.

2. Solve each of the following systems, if possible. Indicate whether the system has a unique solution, infinitely many solutions, or no solutions.

   (a) $y = 3x - 1$ (b) $2x + 3y = 1$ (c) $3x + 4y = ^-17$
        $y = x + 3$ $3x - y = 1$ $2x + 3y = ^-13$
   (d) $5x - 18y = 0$ (e) $2x - 6y = 7$ (f) $8y - 6x = ^-8$
        $x - 24y = 0$ $3x - 9y = 10$ $9x - 12y = 12$

3. Solve each of the following systems, if possible.

   (a) $y = x + 3$ (b) $\dfrac{x}{3} - \dfrac{y}{4} = 1$ (c) $3x - 4y = ^-x + 3$
        $3x - 4y + 1 = 0$ $x - 2 = 4(y - 3)$

                              $\dfrac{x}{5} - \dfrac{y}{3} = 2$

   (d) $x - y = \dfrac{x}{3}$ (e) $x - y = \dfrac{2}{3}(x + y)$ (f) $\sqrt{2}x - y = 3$
                                                    $x - \sqrt{2}y = 1$

        $y - x = \dfrac{3}{4}y + 1$ $x + y = \dfrac{2}{3}(x - y)$

4. Using the concept of slope, identify whether each of the following systems has a unique solution, infinitely many solutions, or no solutions.

(a) $3x - 4y = 5$ (b) $4y - 3x + 4 = 0$ (c) $3y - 2x = 15$

$$\frac{x}{3} - \frac{y}{5} = 1$$ $8y - 6x + 40 = 0$ $$\frac{2}{3}x - y + 5 = 0$$

5. Show that the lines given by $2x - y + 3 = 0$, $x + 7y + 9 = 0$, and $11x + 2y - 51 = 0$ form the sides of an isosceles triangle. (*Hint:* Find the vertices and then use the distance formula.)

6. The vertices of a triangle are given by $(0, 0)$, $(10, 0)$, and $(6, 8)$. Show that medians, the segments connecting the midpoints of each side to the opposite vertex, intersect in a common point.

7. Two adjacent sides of a parallelogram are on lines with equations $x - 3y + 3 = 0$ and $x + 2y - 2 = 0$. One vertex is at $(0, {}^-4)$. Write the equations of the lines containing the other two sides.

8. The sum of two numbers is ¾. Their difference is ⅞. Find the numbers.

9. The owner of a 5000 gallon oil truck loads his truck with gasoline and kerosene. His profit on each gallon of gasoline is 13¢ and on each gallon of kerosene is 12¢. Find how many gallons of each kind he loaded if his profit was $640.

10. A health food store has two different kinds of granola—cashew nut granola selling for $1.80 a pound and golden granola selling at $1.20 a pound. How much of each kind should be mixed to produce a 200-pound mixture selling at $1.60 a pound?

11. A laboratory carries two different solutions of the same acid, a 60% solution and a 90% solution. How many liters of each solution should be mixed in order to produce 150 liters of 80% solution?

12. A physician invests $80 000 in two stocks. At the end of the year, she sells the stocks, the first at a 15% profit and the second at a 20% profit. How much did the physician invest in each stock if her total profit was $15 000?

★13. (a) Solve each of the following systems of equations. What do you notice about the answers?

(i) $x + 2y = 3$ (ii) $2x + 3y = 4$ (iii) $31x + 32y = 33$
    $4x + 5y = 6$ $5x + 6y = 7$ $34x + 35y = 36$

(b) Write another system similar to those in part (a). What solution did you expect? Check your guess.

(c) Write a general system similar to those in part (a). What solution does this system have? Why?

BRAIN TEASER

A school committee meeting began between 3:00 and 4:00 P.M. and ended between 6:00 and 7:00 P.M. The positions of the minute hand and the hour hand of the clock were reversed at the end of the meeting from what they were at the beginning of the meeting. When did the meeting start and end?

SOLUTION TO THE PRELIMINARY PROBLEM

Understanding the Problem

Linda went for a walk as shown in Figure 12-29. She started at H and walked to A, then to B, from B to C, and from C to D in such a way that S, I, P, and S were the midpoints of $\overline{HA}$, $\overline{AB}$, $\overline{BC}$, and $\overline{CD}$, respectively. From D, Linda continued her walk to E and then to F so that I and P were the midpoints of $\overline{DE}$ and $\overline{EF}$, respectively. We are to find the exact location of Linda's final stop, F.

FIGURE 12-29

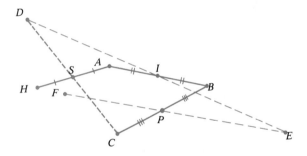

Devising a Plan

Since the entire problem is based on midpoints, one strategy is to use the midpoint formula. For convenience, consider a coordinate system with H at the origin; that is, H has coordinates $(0, 0)$. Let the coordinates of the points S, I, and P be (x_1, y_1), (x_2, y_2) and (x_3, y_3), respectively. Applying the midpoint formula to the midpoint S of $\overline{HA}$, we can find the coordinates of A. Then applying the midpoint formula to the midpoint I of $\overline{AB}$, we can express the coordinates of B using the coordinates of S and I. Continuing in this way, we can express the coordinates of F in terms of the coordinates of S, I, and P.

Carrying Out the Plan

We have to apply the midpoint formula six times and then each time solve the corresponding equation for the coordinates of an endpoint. To reduce the amount of work, we develop a formula to find the coordinates of an endpoint of a segment if we are given its midpoint and the other endpoint. Let M be the midpoint of some segment $\overline{RQ}$ with (x_R, y_R), (x_M, y_M) and (x, y) the coordinates of R, M, and Q as shown in Figure 12-30.

FIGURE 12-30

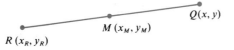

$Q(x, y)$

$M\,(x_M, y_M)$

$R\,(x_R, y_R)$

Using the midpoint formula, we have $x_M = (x_R + x)/2$, which implies $x = 2x_M - x_R$. Similarly, $y = 2y_M - y_R$. We refer to this result as the **endpoint formula.** We now apply the endpoint formula to the six segments $\overline{HA}$, $\overline{AB}$, $\overline{BC}$, $\overline{CD}$, $\overline{DE}$, and $\overline{EF}$, where x_A, x_B, x_C, x_D, x_E, and x_F are the x-coordinates of A, B, C, D, E, and F, respectively.

$x_A = 2x_1 - 0 = 2x_1$

$x_B = 2x_2 - x_A = 2x_2 - 2x_1$

$x_C = 2x_3 - x_B = 2x_3 - (2x_2 - 2x_1) = 2x_1 - 2x_2 + 2x_3$

$x_D = 2x_1 - x_C = 2x_1 - (2x_1 - 2x_2 + 2x_3) = 2x_2 - 2x_3$

$x_E = 2x_2 - x_D = 2x_2 - (2x_2 - 2x_3) = 2x_3$

$x_F = 2x_3 - x_E = 2x_3 - 2x_3 = 0$

Thus $x_F = 0$ and similarly $y_F = 0$, where y_F is the y-coordinate of F. Consequently, F has coordinates $(0, 0)$ and thus Linda stops where she started, at home.

Looking Back

Regardless of the values of (x_1, y_1), (x_2, y_2) (x_3, y_3), the coordinates of F are always $(0, 0)$. Consequently, no matter where S, I, and P are located, Linda's final stop will be at home.

The problem can be extended in different ways. For example, would Linda's final stop be at home if four locations were used rather than three $(S, I,$ and $P)$? If not, how many other locations can be used when Linda's final stop is at home?

QUESTIONS FROM THE CLASSROOM

1. A student asks, "If slope is such an important concept, why is slope of a vertical line undefined?" What is your response?
2. A student argues, "Since 0 is nothing and a horizontal line has slope 0, a horizontal line also has no slope." How do you reply?

3. Trying to find the midpoint, M, of $\overline{AB}$, where A and B have coordinates $(x_1, 0)$ and $(x_2, 0)$ and $x_2 > x_1$, a student argues as follows. "Since $AB = x_2 - x_1$, half that distance is $(x_2 - x_1)/2$ and, since the midpoint M is halfway between A and B, the x-coordinate of M is $(x_2 - x_1)/2$." How do you respond?

4. A student does not understand why, when solving a system of linear equations, it is necessry to check the solution in the original equations rather than in some simpler equivalent equations. How do you respond?

5. A student claims that the graph of every inequality of the form $ax + by + c > 0$ is the half-plane above the line $ax + by + c = 0$, while the graph of $ax + by + c < 0$ is always below the line. How do you respond?

6. A student claims that the distance formula can be further simplified as follows.

$$d = \sqrt{(x_1 - x_2)^2 + (y_1 - y_2)^2} = \sqrt{(x_1 - x_2)^2} + \sqrt{(y_1 - y_2)^2} = |x_1 - x_2| + |y_1 - y_2|$$

How do you respond?

CHAPTER OUTLINE

I. Coordinate system in the plane
   A. Any point in the plane can be described by an ordered pair of real numbers, the first of which is the **x coordinate** and the second the **y coordinate.**
   B. Together the x axis and y axis divide the plane into four **quadrants.**

II. The distance and midpoint formulas
   A. The **distance** between the points (x_1, y_1) and (x_2, y_2) is given by $d = \sqrt{(x_2 - x_1)^2 + (y_2 - y_1)^2}$.
   B. Given $A(x_1, y_1)$ and $B(x_2, y_2)$, the coordinates of the **midpoint M of $\overline{AB}$** are $([x_1 + x_2]/2, [y_1 + y_2]/2)$.

III. Equations of sets of points and notions of slope
   A. The **equation of the circle** with center at (a, b) and radius r is $(x - a)^2 + (y - b)^2 = r^2$.
   B. The **slope** of a line is a measure of its steepness.
      1. Given (x_1, y_1) and (x_2, y_2) with $x_2 \neq x_1$, the slope m of the line through the two points is given by $m = (y_2 - y_1)/(x_2 - x_1)$.
      2. The slope of a vertical line is not defined.
   C. The equation of any nonvertical line can be written in the form $y = mx + b$, where m is the slope and b is the y intercept.
   D. The equation of any vertical line can be written in the form $x = a$.

IV. Systems of linear equations
   A. A system of linear equations can be solved graphically by drawing the graphs of the equations.
      1. If the equations represent two intersecting lines, the system has a unique solution that is the ordered pair corresponding to the point of intersection.
      2. If the equations represent two different parallel lines, the system has no solutions.
      3. If the two equations represent the same line, the system has infinitely many solutions.
   B. A system of linear equations can be solved algebraically either by the substitution method or the elimination method.

CHAPTER TEST

1. Find the perimeter of the triangle with vertices at $A(0, 0)$, $B(^-4, 3)$, and $C(0, 6)$.
2. (a)   Find the midpoint of the line segment whose endpoints are given by $(^-4, 2)$ and $(6, ^-3)$.
    (b)   The midpoint of a segment is given by $(^-5, 4)$ and one of its endpoints is given by $(^-3, 5)$. Find the coordinates of the other endpoint.
3. Show algebraically in at least two different ways that $(4, 2)$, $(0, ^-1)$, and $(^-4, ^-4)$ are collinear points.
4. Graph each of the following.
    (a) $x^2 + y^2 = 16$ (b) $(x + 1)^2 + (y - 2)^2 = 9$ (c) $x^2 + y^2 \le 16$
5. Find the equation of the circle whose center is at $C(^-3, 4)$ and that passes through the origin.
6. Sketch the graphs for each of the following.
    (a) $3x - y = 1$ (b) $3x - y \le 1$ (c) $2x + 3y + 1 = 0$
7. For each of the following, write the equation of the line determined by the given pair of points.
    (a) $(2, ^-3)$ and $(^-1, 1)$ (b) $(^-3, 0)$ and $(^-3, 2)$ (c) $(^-2, 3)$ and $(2, 3)$
8. The vertices of $\triangle ABC$ are $A(^-3, 0)$, $B(0, 4)$, and $C(2, 5)$. Find each of the following.
    (a)   The equation of the line through C and parallel to $\overrightarrow{AB}$
    (b)   The equation of the line through C and parallel to the x axis
    (c)   The point where the line found in part (b) intersects $\overleftrightarrow{AB}$.
9. Solve each of the following systems, if possible. Indicate whether the system has a unique solution, infinitely many solutions, or no solution.

    (a) $x + 2y = 3$ (b) $x/2 + y/3 = 1$ (c) $x - 2y = 1$
          $2x - y = 9$ $4y - 3x = 2$ $4y - 2x = 0$

10. A store sells nuts in two types of containers, regular and deluxe. Each regular container contains 1 lb of cashews and 2 lb of peanuts. Each deluxe container contains 3 lb of cashews and 1.5 lb of peanuts. The store used 170 lb of cashews and 205 lb of peanuts. How many containers of each kind were used?

SELECTED BIBLIOGRAPHY

Arnsdorf, E. "Orienteering, New Ideas for Outdoor Mathematics." *Arithmetic Teacher* **25**(April 1978):14–17.

Bell, W. R. "Cartesian Coordinates and Battleship." *The Arithmetic Teacher,* **21**(May 1974):421–422.

Bergen, S. "A Discovery Approach for the *y*-Intercept." *The Mathematics Teacher,* **70**(November 1977):675–676.

Bruni, J. V., and H. J. Silverman. "Using a Pegboard to Develop Mathematical Concepts." *The Arithmetic Teacher,* **22**(October 1975):452–458.

Burns, M. "Ideas." *The Arithmetic Teacher,* **22**(April 1975):296–304.

Eicholz, R., P. O'Daffer, and C. Fleenor. *Mathematics in Our World.* Reading, Mass.: Addison-Wesley, 1979.

Giles, D. "Graphing Inequalities Directly." *The Arithmetic Teacher,* **18**(March 1971):185–186.

Good, R. G. "Two Mathematical Games with Dice." *The Arithmetic Teacher,* **21**(January 1974):45–47.

Liedtke, W. "Geoboard Mathematics." *The Arithmetic Teacher,* **21**(April 1974):273–277.

Miller, W. A. "Graphs Alive." *The Mathematics Teacher,* **71**(December 1978):756–758.

Nicolai, M. B., "A Discovery in Linear Algebra." *The Mathematics Teacher,* **67**(May 1974):403–404.

Pereira-Mendoza, L. "Graphing and Prediction in Elementary School." *The Arithmetic Teacher,* **24**(February 1977):112–113.

Rainsbury, R. "Where is Droopy?" *The Arithmetic Teacher,* **19**(April 1972):271–272.

Vance, I. E. "The Content of the Elementary School Geometry Program." *The Arithmetic Teacher,* **20**(October 1973):470.

Zweng, M. J. "A Geometry Course for Elementary Teachers." *The Arithmetic Teacher,* **20**(October 1973): 457–467.

Problem Solving Revisited

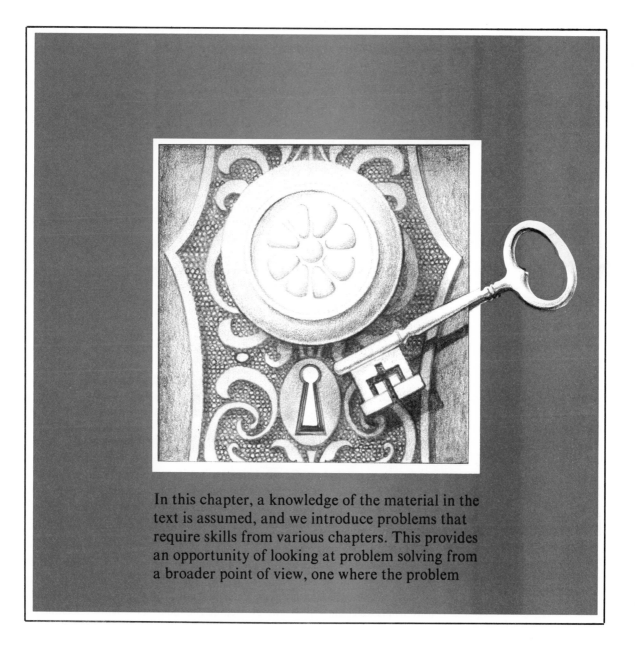

In this chapter, a knowledge of the material in the text is assumed, and we introduce problems that require skills from various chapters. This provides an opportunity of looking at problem solving from a broader point of view, one where the problem solver does not know to which specific topics the problem is related.

Problem-solving skills can be improved by following the discussions in the following examples and by attempting to solve the problems at the end of the section. In the examples, the motives for various steps in a solution are discussed. Although not specifically indicated, problems are solved by following the approach of understanding the problem, devising a plan, carrying out the plan, and looking back.

Example 13-1

In the circle in Figure 13-1, two perpendicular diameters are shown. From a point C on the circle, two segments $\overline{AC}$ and $\overline{CB}$ are drawn so that quadrilateral $ACBO$ is a rectangle. If the diameter of the circle is 10 cm, find the length of $\overline{AB}$.

Solution

$\overline{AB}$ is the hypotenuse of right triangle AOB. One possible way to find $\overline{AB}$ is to use the Pythagorean Theorem. Hence, $(AB)^2 = (AO)^2 + (OB)^2$. Thus, to find $\overline{AB}$, we need to know the lengths of both $\overline{AO}$ and $\overline{OB}$. The lengths of these sides are not given. Moreover, it seems that knowing only the diameter of the circle is not sufficient to determine $\overline{AO}$ and $\overline{OB}$. Thus, using the Pythagorean Theorem does not appear to be a productive strategy.

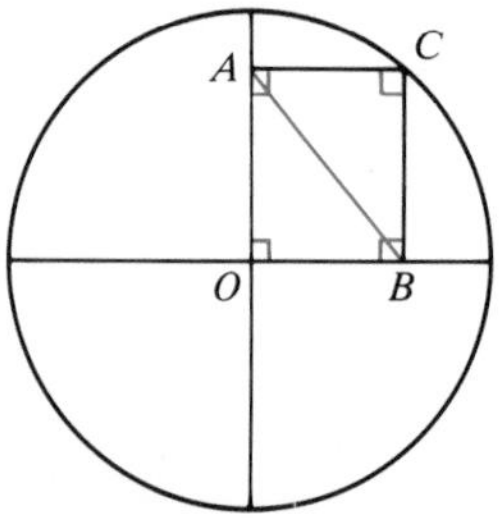

A new strategy is to find parts of a triangle using congruent or similar triangles. Triangle BCA is congruent to $\triangle AOB$. However, there is no more information about $\triangle BCA$ than about $\triangle AOB$. Since Figure 13-1 shows no other triangles, we need to draw an additional segment to define a new triangle. The newly constructed triangle should have sides of known lengths. Since the length of the diameter is 10 cm and the radius is 5 cm, the most natural choice is $\overline{OC}$ as shown in Figure 13-2. The diagonals of a rectangle are congruent. (See Chapter 10. This was shown by proving $\triangle ABO \cong \triangle COB$). Thus, $\overline{OC} \cong \overline{AB}$ and $AB = 5$ cm.

FIGURE 13-1

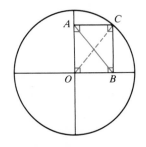

FIGURE 13-2

The solution to Example 13-1 focused on the goal of finding $\overline{AB}$ and relied on previous experiences in solving such problems by trying the Pythagorean Theorem and using congruent triangles. The Pythagorean Theorem approach was abandoned because of insufficient information. Next, a search for appropriate congruent triangles became the focus. This search became the new goal. In the congruent triangle approach, we used all possible information from the problem along with previous definitions and related theorems. The related theorems gave new information that resulted in a solution.

Example 13-2

The king of Ilusia lost a war and was forced to divide his kingdom into a number of smaller countries, no two the same size. The king also had to distribute all 1000 bars of his gold in such a way that each country received one bar more than the next smaller country. No bars could be broken. If the king divided his kingdom into the least number of countries possible and divided his gold as described, how many countries were formed and how many bars of gold did each country receive?

Solution

Each country received one bar more than the next smaller country. Suppose the smallest country received n bars of gold. Then the next larger country received one bar more, and the next larger country two bars more, and so on. That is, the next larger countries, in order of size, received $(n + 1)$ bars, $(n + 2)$ bars, $(n + 3)$ bars, and so on. Since the number of countries is unknown, designate that number by k.

Ordering countries according to size from smallest to largest and making Table 13-1 reveals a pattern. The kth country receives $n + (k - 1)$ bars of gold.

TABLE 13-1

Order of Country	Number of Bars Received
1	n
2	$n + 1$
3	$n + 2$
4	$n + 3$
5	$n + 4$
.	.
.	.
.	.
k	$n + (k - 1)$

The total number of gold bars is 1000. Hence, the total number of bars received by all countries is 1000.

$$n + (n + 1) + (n + 2) + (n + 3) + \ldots + (n + k - 1) = 1000$$

Thus, the problem involves finding a sum of consecutive natural numbers.

Recall that the similar problem of finding the sum of the first 100 natural numbers in Chapter 1 was solved by listing the numbers in the following way and computing the sum (Problem Set 1-2, Problem 13).

$$
\begin{array}{ccccccc}
1 & + & 2 & + & 3 & + & 4 + \ldots + 100 \\
100 & + & 99 & + & 98 & + & 97 + \ldots + \quad 1 \\
\hline
101 & + & 101 & + & 101 & + & 101 + \ldots + 101
\end{array}
$$

Since there are 100 sums of 101 in twice the desired sum, we divide by 2 to obtain $100(101)/2 = 5050$. A similar approach can be used to find the sum $n + (n + 2) + (n + 3) + \ldots + (n + k - 1)$.

$$
\begin{array}{ccccccc}
n & + & (n + 1) & + & (n + 2) & + \ldots + & (n + k - 1) \\
(n + k - 1) & + & (n + k - 2) & + & (n + k - 3) & + \ldots + & n \\
\hline
(2n + k - 1) & + & (2n + k - 1) & + & (2n + k - 1) & + \ldots + & (2n + k - 1)
\end{array}
$$

There are k sums of $2n + k - 1$ shown above and this is twice the desired sum. Hence, divide by 2 to obtain $[k(2n + k - 1)]/2$. This result can be used as follows.

$$ n + (n + 1) + (n + 2) + \ldots + (n + k - 1) = 1000 $$

$$ \frac{k}{2}(2n + k - 1) = 1000 $$

$$ k(2n + k - 1) = 2000 $$

The result is an equation in two unknowns, k and n. To find k and n, we need another equation involving k and n. Unfortunately, no other condition that yields an additional equation is given in the statement of the problem.

An important strategy in solving any problem is to make sure that no important information is neglected. One condition of the problem states that the number of countries k is the least number possible and $k \neq 1$. Also, to be reasonable solutions to the problem, n and k must be natural numbers. Keeping these conditions in mind, focus on $k(2n + k - 1) = 2000$. Since k and $2n + k - 1$ are natural numbers, they are factors of 2000. Since k is the least number possible, start with $k = 2$. If $k = 2$, then $2 \cdot (2n + 2 - 1) = 2000$ and $n = 499\frac{1}{2}$, which is not a natural number. Hence, $k \neq 2$. Similarly, if $k = 4$, the next factor of 2000, then $n = 248\frac{1}{2}$, and hence, $k \neq 4$. However, if $k = 5$, then $n = 198$. Thus, the smallest country receives 198 bars of gold, and, consequently, the five countries receive 198, 199, 200, 201, and 202 bars, respectively.

It is easy to check the solution since $198 + 199 + 200 + 201 + 202 = 1000$. Can the problem be solved if there is a different number of bars? What solutions does the problem have if the number of countries is not minimized?

Example 13-3

In a portion of a large city, the streets divide the city into square blocks of the same size as shown in Figure 13-3. A taxi driver drives daily from point *A* to *P*. One day she drove from *A* to *B* along $\overline{AB}$ and then from *B* to *P* along $\overline{BP}$. If she does not want to cover any distance longer than *AB* + *BP*, how many possible routes are there from *A* to *P*?

FIGURE 13-3

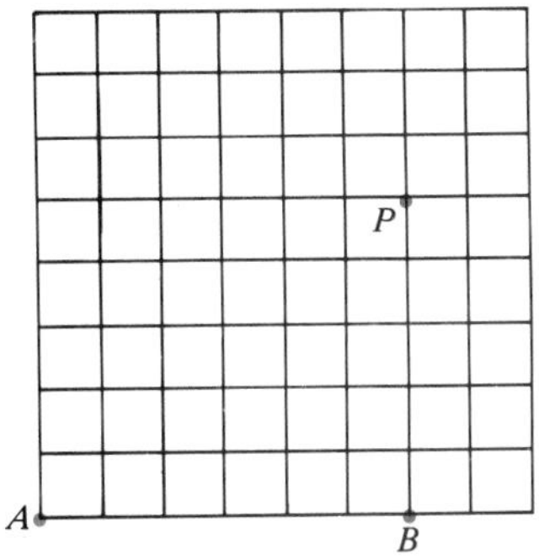

(A grid with P marked near the center, A at bottom-left, B at bottom-middle)

Solution

In order to travel the minimum distance, the taxi driver should only go north (upward) and west (to the right). Two routes are shown in Figure 13-4. For each of the routes, the total length of the horizontal segments is *AB*. Similarly, the total length of the vertical segments is *BP*. Thus, the length of each of the taxi driver's routes from *A* to *P* equals *AB* + *BP*.

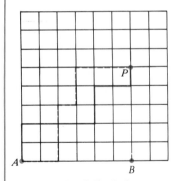

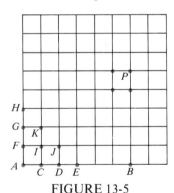

FIGURE 13-4   FIGURE 13-5

One way to solve the problem is by drawing all possible routes from *A* to *P* and counting them. Since that is an enormous task, try looking for simpler versions of the problem. In Figure 13-5, there is only one possible route from *A* to *C* and only one route from *A* to *F*. In fact, each of the points on $\overleftrightarrow{AC}$ and $\overleftrightarrow{AF}$ can be reached via only one route.

Next, examine the routes from *A* to *I*. Two are possible ones, *A–F–I* and *A–C–I*. From *A* to *J* there are three routes, namely, *A–C–D–J*, *A–C–I–J*, and *A–F–I–J*. Similarly, the number of routes to various other points from A can be counted. Figure 13-6 shows the number of possible routes to various points, starting from A.

It appears that the number of routes to any given point from A is the sum of the number of routes to each of its two neighboring points, one immediately to the left and the other immediately below. If this pattern continues, it would be easy to work from point to point until we reach point P. The pattern can be justified since each of the routes from A to point P in Figure 13-6 can be obtained from the two neighboring points L and O. Any route from A to P must pass through either L or O. The number of routes from A to P that pass through L is the same as the number of routes from A to L because, for each route from A to L, there is one single route to P that passes through L. Similarly, the number of routes from A to P that pass through O is the same as the number of routes from A to O. Thus, the number of routes from A to P is the sum of the routes from A to L and from A to O. Since the pattern in Figure 13-6 continues, there are 462 routes from A to P as shown in Figure 13-7.

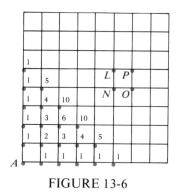

FIGURE 13-6

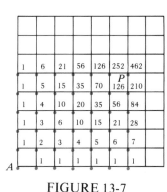

FIGURE 13-7

You may wish to investigate this example further using the concept of combinations discussed in Chapter 7.

Example 13-4

In the central prison of Ilusia, there were 1000 cells numbered from 1 to 1000. All of the cells were occupied, and each had a separate guard. After a revolution, the new king ordered the guards to free certain prisoners based on the following scheme. The guards walk through the prison one at a time, with the first guard opening all 1000 cells. The second guard follows immediately and closes all the cells with even numbers. The third guard follows and changes every third cell, starting with cell 3, closing the open cells and opening the closed cells. Similarly, the fourth guard starts at cell 4 and changes every fourth cell. This process continues until the 1000th guard passes through the prison, at which point the prisoners whose cells are open are freed. How many prisoners are freed?

Solution

The strategy of solving a simpler problem is used. Suppose there are only 20 cells. In the king's scheme, no guard after the 20th touches the first 20 cells.

First, consider the first 20 cells as the first 20 guards pass through. Denote an open cell by *o* and a closed cell by *c*. Table 13-2 shows the state of each cell, as changed by the guards. For example, the fourth guard opens cell 4, opens cell 8, closes cell 12, opens cell 16, and closes cell 20.

TABLE 13-2

Cell Number

Guard Number	1	2	3	4	5	6	7	8	9	10	11	12	13	14	15	16	17	18	19	20
1	o	o	o	o	o	o	o	o	o	o	o	o	o	o	o	o	o	o	o	o
2		c		c		c		c		c		c		c		c		c		c
3			c			o			c			o			c			o		
4				o				o				c				o				c
5					c					o					o					o
6						c						o						c		
7							c							o						
8								c								c				
9									o									o		
10										c										o
11											c									
12												c								
13													c							
14														c						
15															c					
16																o				
17																	c			
18																		c		
19																			c	
20																				c

The table shows that, after 20 guards pass, the only open cells are 1, 4, 9, and 16. Each of these numbers is a perfect square, 1^2, 2^2, 3^2, and 4^2. Will the pattern these numbers suggest continue for 1000 guards and cells? To help answer this question consider cell 25. The cell is opened by guard 1, closed by guard 5, and opened by guard 25, suggesting the answer is yes. (Note that 1, 5, and 25 are the positive divisors of 25.)

What happened to cell 26 (a nonperfect square)? Cell 26 is opened by guard 1, closed by guard 2, opened by guard 13, and closed by guard 26 and, hence, remained closed. In general, observe that a cell is changed only by guards whose numbers divide the cell number.

For the final state of a cell to be open, it must be opened one more time than it is closed; that is, the state is changed an odd number of times. For this to happen, the number of the cell must have an odd number of divisors. We show that the open cells have numbers that are perfect squares by showing that only perfect squares have an odd number of divisors.

Recall that the divisors of a number appear in pairs (see Chapter 5). For example, the pairs of divisors of 80 and 81 are given by the following.

$$80 = 1 \cdot 80 = 2 \cdot 40 = 4 \cdot 20 = 5 \cdot 16 = 10 \cdot 8$$

$$81 = 1 \cdot 81 = 3 \cdot 27 = 9 \cdot 9$$

Thus, 80 has ten distinct divisors or five pairs. On the other hand, the perfect square 81 has five distinct divisors, two pairs of divisors (1, 81 and 3, 27) and a single divisor 9, which is paired with itself. Thus, 81 has an odd number of divisors. By Theorem 5-6 of Chapter 5, if d is a divisor of n, then n/d also is a divisor of n. Consequently, for all divisors d of n, if $d \neq n/d$, then each divisor can be paired with a different divisor and n must have an even number of positive divisors. If, on the other hand, for some divisor d, $d = n/d$, then $n = d^2$, and all the divisors of n are paired with a different divisor, except d. Hence, the number of divisors of n is odd. Since $d = n/d$ occurs only when $n = d^2$, it follows that n has an odd number of divisors if and only if n is a perfect square. As a result, the freed prisoners are in the cells with numbers that are perfect squares less than 1000, namely 1^2, 2^2, 3^2, 4^2, 5^2, 6^2, ..., 31^2. Thus, 31 prisoners are freed.

PROBLEM SET 13-1

Problems 5, 6, 7, 10, 11, 18, and 19 are modifications of the Mathematical Association of America's Annual High School Mathematics Examination problems No. 9 (1972), No. 31 (1970), No. 15 (1971), No. 23 (1971), No. 34 (1970), No. 32 (1970), and No. 34 (1968), respectively. Also, problems 3, 4, and 20 are modifications of problems 190, 153, and 187, respectively, taken from the Comprehensive School Mathematics Program, *Elements of Mathematics, Book B, EM Problem Book,* by CEMREL, Inc. (1975).

1. Without using a calculator, find the number of digits in the number $2^{12} \cdot 5^8$.
2. (a) Discover a pattern for the following sequence of fractions.

$$\frac{3}{5}, \frac{7}{9}, \frac{11}{13}, \frac{15}{17}, \frac{19}{21}, \ldots$$

   (b) Find the 1000th fraction in the sequence.
   (c) Prove that all the fractions (there are infinitely many) in the sequence are in simplest form.
3. Start with a piece of paper. Cut it into five pieces. Take any of the pieces and cut it again into five pieces, and so on.
   (a) What numbers can be obtained in this way?
   (b) What is the number of pieces after the nth experiment?
4. In the figure below, $\overline{BC}$ and $\overline{BE}$ represent two positions of a ladder. How wide is $\overline{AD}$ and how long is the ladder if $AC = 12\ m$, $ED = 9\ m$, $\overline{CB} \simeq \overline{BE}$, and $\overline{CB} \perp \overline{BE}$?

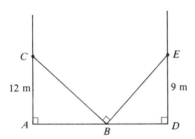

5. Ann and Sue bought identical boxes of stationery. Ann used hers to write one-sheet letters and Sue used hers to write three-sheet letters. Ann used all the envelopes and had 50 sheets of paper left, while Sue used all the sheets of paper and had 50 envelopes left. Find the number of sheets of paper in each box.
6. If a number is selected at random from the set of all five-digit numbers in which the sum of the digits equals 43, what is the probability that the number is divisible by 11?
7. An aquarium is in the shape of a right rectangular prism. It has a rectangular face that is 10 in. wide and 8 in. high. When the aquarium is tilted, the water in it just covers an 8 in. × 10 in. end, but only three-fourths of the rectangular bottom. Find the depth of the water when the aquarium is level on the table.
8. From a wire ten units long, different shapes are constructed: a square, a rectangle with one side two units long, an equilateral triangle, a right isosceles triangle, and a circle.
   (a) Find the area of each shape. Which shape has the greatest area?
   (b) Make a conjecture concerning which figure has the greatest area among all figures with a given perimeter.
9. Susan's executive salary increased each of the past 2 years by 50% over the preceding year. Her present salary is $100 000 per year. To the nearest dollar, how much did she make 2 years ago?
10. Teams A and B play a series of games. The odds of either team winning any game are even. Team A must win two games and Team B must win three games to win the series. Find the odds in favor of Team A winning the series.

11. Find the greatest integer such that when each of the numbers 13 511, 13 903, 14 589 is divided by this integer, the remainders are the same.

12. Take a two- or three-digit number and create a new number by reversing the digits of the original number. Then, subtract the lesser number from the greater. Observe that the difference is divisible by 9. For example, $561 - 165$ is 396, which is divisible by 9. Is this always true? Justify your answer.

13. What is the angle between the clock hands at 2:15?

14. Given a regular hexagon and a point in its plane, and using only a ruler and a compass, construct a straight line through the given point that separates the given hexagon into two parts of equal area.

15. Find the sum of all the digits in the integers 1 through 1 000 000 000.

16. Two adjacent sides of a parallelogram are on the lines given by $3x - 2y = 6$ and $5x + 4y = 21$. One vertex is at $(2, ^-1)$. Without graphing, find the equations of the lines containing the other two sides and the coordinates of the point where the diagonals intersect.

17. Without graphing, find the center and radius of the circle passing through the points with coordinates $(0, 0)$, $(1, ^-3)$, and $(4, 0)$.

18. Starting at the same time from diametrically opposite points, Linda and David travel around a circular track at uniform speeds in opposite directions. They meet after David has traveled 100 meters and a second time 60 meters before Linda completes one lap. Find the circumference of the track.

19. With 400 members voting, the House of Representatives defeated a bill. A revote, with the same members voting, resulted in passage of the bill by twice the margin with which it was originally defeated. The number voting for the bill on the revote was $^{12}\!/_{11}$ of the number voting against it originally. How many more members voted for the bill the second time than voted for it the first time?

20. Find the least possible natural number so that deleting its first digit results in a number that is 57 times smaller than the original number.

21. Lines from the vertices of square $ABCD$ to the midpoints of the sides M, N, O, and P are shown in the following figure.
    (a) Prove that quadrilateral $HGFE$ is a square.
    (b) What is the area of square $HGFE$ if the area of quadrilateral $ABCD$ is 100 cm²? Justify your answer.

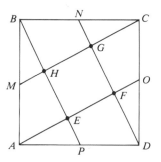

22. The "triangle" on the next page is called the **Pascal triangle,** after the French mathematician Blaise Pascal. Each number in the triangle, except the ones on the "boundary," equals the

sum of two immediate neighboring numbers in the preceding row. (Note how the numbers in the triangle compare with those in Figure 13-6.)

									Row
				1					(1)
			1		1				(2)
		1		2		1			(3)
	1		3		3		1		(4)
1		4		6		4		1	(5)
1	5		10		10		5	1	(6)
1	6	15		20		15	6	1	(7)
1	7	21	35		35	21	7	1	(8)

(a) Continue the triangle by finding two more rows.

(b) Find the sum of the numbers in the first row, the second row, the third row, and the fourth row. Do you notice a pattern? Can you predict the sum of the numbers in the tenth row? Make a general conjecture for the sum of the numbers in the nth row.

(c) Find the "alternate" sum of numbers in each row after row 1; that is, $1 - 1$, $1 - 2 + 1$, $1 - 3 + 3 - 1$, $1 - 4 + 6 - 4 + 1$.

(d) Find other patterns among the numbers in the Pascal triangle.

23. Justify your conjecture in Problem 22(b).

SELECTED BIBLIOGRAPHY

Brown, S., and M. Walter, "Problem Solving and Problem Posing: An Illustration of Their Interdependence." *The Mathematics Teacher,* **70**(January 1977):4–13.

Greenes, C., R. Spungin, and J. Dombrowski. *Problem-Mathics.* Palo Alto, Calif.: Creative Publications, 1977.

Honsberger, R. *Mathematical Morsels.* Washington, D.C.: The Mathematical Association of America, 1978.

Hughes, B. *Thinking Through Problems.* Palo Alto, Calif.: Creative Publications, 1976.

Kordemsky, B. A. *The Moscow Puzzles,* New York: Charles Scribner's Sons, 1972.

Libeskind, S. "A Problem Solving Approach to Teaching Mathematics." *Educational Studies in Mathematics,* **8**(1977):167–179.

Pederson, J. J., and F. O. Armbruster. *A New Twist.* Reading, Mass.: Addison-Wesley, 1979.

Polya, G. *How to Solve It.* Princeton, N.J.: Princeton University Press, 1957.

Polya, G. *Mathematical Discovery.* 2 vols. New York: Wiley, 1962–1965.

Polya, G. *Mathematics and Plausible Reasoning.* 2 vols. Princeton, N.J.: Princeton University Press, 1954.

Salkind, C., and J. Earl. *The Contest Problem Book III.* Washington, D.C.: The Mathematical Association of America, 1973.

Walter, M., and S. Brown. "What If Not." *Mathematics Teaching,* **46**(Spring 1969):38–45.

AI-1 **Statements**

---

statement

Logic deals with reasoning and is a tool used in mathematical thinking. In logic, a **statement** is a sentence that is either true or false, but not both. The following are examples of statements along with their truth values, where T stands for true and F stands for false.

(a)   George Washington is currently the president of the United States. (F)
(b) $2 + 3 = 7$ (F)
(c)   A triangle has four sides. (F)
(d) $2 \cdot (10 + 5) = 30$ (T)

Expressions such as "How tall are you?" "$2 + 3$" or "Close the door" are not statements since they cannot be classified as true or false. The following expressions are also not statements since their truth value cannot be determined without more information.

(a)   She has blue eyes.
(b) $x + 7 = 18$
(c) $2y + 7 > 1$

Each of the preceding expressions becomes a statement if, for (a), "she" is identified, for (b) and (c), values are assigned to x and y, respectively. However, an expression involving *he* or *she* or x or y may already be a statement. For example, "If he is over 210 cm tall, then he is over 2 m tall," and "$2(x + y) = 2x + 2y$" are both statements since they are true no matter who *he* is or what the values of x and y are.

From a given statement, it is possible to create a new statement by forming a negation. Consider the statement "It is snowing." The negation of this statement is "It is not true that it is snowing," or, stated in a simpler form, "It is not snowing." Using the symbol p to represent a statement, the negation   **negation** of p, is the statement, "It is not true that p," denoted by $\sim p$. If a statement is true, then its negation is false. If a statement is false, then its negation is true. Table AI-1 summarizes the truth values for p and $\sim p$.

TABLE AI-1

p	$\sim p$
T	F
F	T

truth table   Table AI-1 is called a truth table. A **truth table** is a table that shows the truth or falsity of a statement for all possible true–false patterns of the statements involved. Truth table AI-1 is used to define negation mathematically.

    The grammatical form, "It is not true that p," sometimes results in an awkward sentence. In many cases, the negation of a statement is more easily stated by simply negating the verb.

Example AI-1 | Negate each of the following statements.

(a) $2 + 3 = 5$
(b)   A hexagon has six sides.
(c)   Today is not Monday.

Solution | (a) $2 + 3 \neq 5$
(b)   A hexagon does not have six sides.
(c)   Today is Monday.

    Are the statements, "The shirt is blue," and "The shirt is green," negations of each other? To check, recall that a statement and its negation must have opposite truth values. If the shirt is actually red, then both of the statements are false and, hence, cannot be negations of each other. However, the statements, "The shirt is blue," and "The shirt is not blue," are negations of each other, since they have opposite truth values no matter what color the shirt really is.

    From two given statements it is possible to create a new statement by using a connective such as *and*. For example, "It is snowing," and "The ski run is open," together with *and* give, "It is snowing and the ski run is open." Other statements can be obtained by using the connective *or*. For example, compound statement   "It is snowing or the ski run is open." In general, a **compound statement** is formed by combining two or more statements with a connective.

Lower case letters are used to represent statements. The symbols $\wedge$ and $\vee$ are used to represent the connectives *and* and *or,* respectively. For example, if p represents, "It is snowing," and if q represents, "The ski run is open," then compound statements involving p and q are:

It is snowing and the ski run is open. $p \wedge q$

It is snowing or the ski run is open. $p \vee q$

It is not snowing and the ski run is open. $\sim p \wedge q$

It is not snowing or the ski run is not open. $\sim p \vee \sim q$

conjunction

The truth value of any compound statement such as $p \wedge q$ is defined using the truth value of each of the simple statements. Since each of the statements p and q may be either true or false, there are four distinct possibilities as shown in Table AI-2. The compound statement p and q, symbolized $p \wedge q$, is called the **conjunction** of p and q and is defined to be true if and only if both p and q are true. Otherwise, it is false.

TABLE AI-2

p	q	$p \wedge q$
T	T	T
T	F	F
F	T	F
F	F	F

Example AI-2

Given the following statements, classify each of the conjunctions as true or false.

p: $2 + 3 = 5$ r: $5 + 3 = 9$
q: $2 \cdot 3 = 6$ s: $2 \cdot 4 = 9$

(a) $p \wedge q$ (b) $p \wedge r$ (c) $s \wedge q$
(d) $r \wedge s$ (e) $\sim p \wedge q$ (f) $\sim(p \wedge q)$

Solution

(a) Since p is true and q is true, $p \wedge q$ is true.
(b) Since p is true and r is false, $p \wedge r$ is false.
(c) Since s is false and q is true, $s \wedge q$ is false.
(d) Since r is false and s is false, $r \wedge s$ is false.
(e) Since $\sim p$ is false and q is true, $\sim p \wedge q$ is false.
(f) Since $p \wedge q$ is true [part (a)], $\sim(p \wedge q)$ is false.

disjunction

The compound statement p or q, symbolized $p \vee q$, is called the **disjunction** of p and q. In everyday language *or* is not always interpreted in the same way. For example, "I will go to a movie or I will read a book" usually means that I will either go to a movie or read, but not do both. On the other hand, if a student says, "I will major in mathematics or in education," the student may major in one or the other or both. In the first statement, the *or* was an *exclusive* or while in the second, it was an *inclusive* or. Either of the meanings for *or* could be adopted, but we use the inclusive meaning. Hence, $p \vee q$ is defined to be false if both p and q are false, and true in all other cases. This is summarized by Table AI-3.

TABLE AI-3

p	q	$p \vee q$
T	T	T
T	F	T
F	T	T
F	F	F

Example AI-3   Given the following statements, classify each of the disjunctions as true or false.

p: $2 + 3 = 5$ r: $5 + 3 = 9$
q: $2 \cdot 3 = 6$ s: $2 \cdot 4 = 9$
(a) $p \vee q$ (b) $p \vee r$ (c) $s \vee q$
(d) $r \vee s$ (e) $\sim p \vee q$ (f) $\sim(p \vee q)$

Solution   (a) Since p is true and q is true, $p \vee q$ is true.
(b) Since p is true and r is false, $p \vee r$ is true.
(c) Since s is false and q is true, $s \vee q$ is true.
(d) Since r is false and s is false, $r \vee s$ is false.
(e) Since $\sim p$ is false and q is true, $\sim p \vee q$ is true.
(f) Since $p \vee q$ is true [part (a)], $\sim(p \vee q)$ is false.

Not only are truth tables used to summarize the truth values of compound statements, they are also used to determine if two statements are **logically equivalent** logically equivalent. Two statements are **logically equivalent** if and only if they have the same truth values. For example, consider $\sim p \vee \sim q$ and $\sim(p \wedge q)$. Table AI-4 shows headings and the four distinct possibilities for p and q. In the column headed $\sim p$, write the negations of the p column. In the $\sim q$ column, write the negation of the q column. Next, use the values in the $\sim p$ and the $\sim q$ columns to construct the $\sim p \vee \sim q$ column. To find the truth values for $\sim(p \wedge q)$, use the p and q columns to find the truth value for $p \wedge q$ and, then, negate $p \wedge q$. Table AI-4 shows the results.

TABLE AI-4

p	q	$\sim p$	$\sim q$	$\sim p \vee \sim q$	$p \wedge q$	$\sim(p \wedge q)$
T	T	F	F	F	T	F
T	F	F	T	T	F	T
F	T	T	F	T	F	T
F	F	T	T	T	F	T

Note that $\sim p \vee \sim q$ has the same truth values as $\sim(p \wedge q)$. Thus, the statements are logically equivalent. The reader will find an analogue to this logical equivalence in Chapter 2. The equivalence between $\sim p \vee \sim q$ and $\sim(p \wedge q)$ along with the equivalence between $\sim(p \vee q)$ and $\sim p \wedge \sim q$ are referred to as DeMorgan's laws.

PROBLEM SET AI-1

1. Determine which of the following are statements and then classify each statement as true or false.
   - (c) $2 + 4 = 8$ (b) Shut the window.
   - (d) Los Angeles is a state.   (d) He is in town.
   - (e) What time is it?   (f) $5x = 15$
   - (g) $3 \cdot 2 = 6$ (h) $2x^2 > x$

2. Complete each of the following truth tables.

   (a)
p	$\sim p$	$\sim(\sim p)$
T		
F		

   (b)
p	$\sim p$	$p \vee \sim p$	$p \wedge \sim p$
T			
F			

   - (c) Based on part (a), is p logically equivalent to $\sim(\sim p)$?
   - (d) Based on part (b), is $p \vee \sim p$ logically equivalent to $p \wedge \sim p$?

3. Write the negation for each of the following statements.
   - (a) The book has 500 pages   (b) Six is less than eight.
   - (c) Johnny is not thin.   (d) Al does not smoke.
   - (e) $3 \cdot 5 = 15$

4. If q stands for, "This course is easy," and r stands for "Lazy students do not study," write each of the following in symbolic form.
   - (a) This course is easy and lazy students do not study.
   - (b) Lazy students do not study or this course is not easy.
   - (c) It is false that both this course is easy and lazy students do not study.
   - (d) This course is not easy.

5. If p is false and q is true, find the truth values for each of the following.
   (a) $p \wedge q$ (b) $p \vee q$
   (c) $\sim p$ (d) $\sim q$
   (e) $\sim(\sim p)$ (f) $\sim p \vee q$
   (g) $p \wedge \sim q$ (h) $\sim(p \vee q)$
   (i) $\sim(\sim p \wedge q)$ (j) $\sim q \wedge \sim p$
6. Find the truth value for each statement in Problem 5 if p is false and q is false.
7. Complete the following truth table.

p	q	$\sim p$	$\sim q$	$\sim p \vee q$
T	T			
T	F			
F	T			
F	F			

8. For each of the following, is the pair of statements logically equivalent?
   (a) $\sim(p \vee q)$ and $\sim p \vee \sim q$
   (b) $\sim(p \vee q)$ and $\sim p \wedge \sim q$
   (c) $\sim(p \wedge q)$ and $\sim p \wedge \sim q$
   (d) $\sim(p \wedge q)$ and $\sim p \vee \sim q$

BRAIN TEASER

An explorer landed on an island inhabited by two tribes, the Abes and the Babes. Abes always tell the truth and Babes always lie. The explorer met three natives on the shore. He asked the first native to name his tribe and the native responded in his native tongue, which the explorer did not understand. The second native stated that the first native said that he was an Abe. The third native then stated that the first native had said he was a Babe. To what tribes do the second and third natives belong?

AI-2 CONDITIONALS AND BICONDITIONALS

Statements like the following are called conditional statements.

If it is raining, then the grass is wet.

If I pass the final, then I will pass the course.

If you mow the lawn, then you can go to the movies.

conditionals
implications

Each of these statements is expressed in the form "if p, then q." **Conditionals** or **implications** are statements that can be written in "if p, then q" form, denoted as $p \rightarrow q$, which can also be read, "p implies q."

Think about an implication as a promise. Suppose Betty makes the promise, "If I get a raise, then I will take you to dinner." If Betty keeps her promise, the implication is true; if Betty breaks her promise, the implication is false. Consider the following four possibilities.

	p	q	
(1)	T	T	Betty gets the raise; she takes you to dinner.
(2)	T	F	Betty gets the raise; she does not take you to dinner.
(3)	F	T	Betty does not get the raise; she takes you to dinner.
(4)	F	F	Betty does not get the raise; she does not take you to dinner.

The only case in which Betty breaks her promise is when she gets her raise and fails to take you to dinner, case (2). If she does not get the raise, she can either take you to dinner or not without breaking her promise. The definition of implication is summarized in the truth table (Table AI-5). Observe that the only case for which implication is false is when p is true and q is false.

TABLE AI-5

p	q	$p \rightarrow q$
T	T	T
T	F	F
F	T	T
F	F	T

Implications may be worded in several ways.

1. If the sun shines, then the swimming pool is open. (if p, then q)
2. If the sun shines, the swimming pool is open. (if p, q)
3. The swimming pool is open if the sun shines. (q, if p)
4. The sun shines implies the swimming pool is open. (p implies q)

Any implication, $p \rightarrow q$, has three related implication statements.

Statement:	If p, then q.	$p \rightarrow q$
Converse:	If q, then p.	$q \rightarrow p$
Inverse:	If not p, then not q.	$\sim p \rightarrow \sim q$
Contrapositive:	If not q, then not p.	$\sim q \rightarrow \sim p$

Example AI-4 | Write the converse, the inverse, and the contrapositive for each of the following statements.

(a)   If $2x = 6$, then $x = 3$.
(b)   If I am in San Francisco, then I am in California.

Solution |
(a)   *Converse:* If $x = 3$, then $2x = 6$.
Inverse: If $2x \neq 6$, then $x \neq 3$.
Contrapositive: If $x \neq 3$, then $2x \neq 6$.
(b)   *Converse:* If I am in California, then I am in San Francisco.
Inverse: If I am not in San Francisco, then I am not in California.
Contrapositive: If I am not in California, then I am not in San Francisco.

As Example AI-4(b) shows, a statement and its converse do not necessarily have the same truth value. On the other hand, an implication and its contrapositive do have the same truth value. Table AI-6 shows that, in general, a conditional statement and its contrapositive are logically equivalent and the converse and inverse of a conditional statement are logically equivalent.

TABLE AI-6

p	q	$\sim p$	$\sim q$	$p \rightarrow q$	$q \rightarrow p$	$\sim p \rightarrow \sim q$	$\sim q \rightarrow \sim p$
T	T	F	F	T	T	T	T
T	F	F	T	F	T	T	F
F	T	T	F	T	F	F	T
F	F	T	T	T	T	T	T

Connecting a statement and its converse with the connective *and* gives $(p \rightarrow q) \wedge (q \rightarrow p)$. This compound statement can be written as $p \leftrightarrow q$ and usually is read "*p* if and only if *q*." The statement "*p* if and only if *q*," is called a **biconditional.** A truth table for $p \leftrightarrow q$ is given in Table AI-7. Observe that $p \leftrightarrow q$ is true if only if p and q have the same truth values; that is, only if both statements are true or both are false.

biconditional

TABLE AI-7

p	q	$p \rightarrow q$	$q \rightarrow p$	$(p \rightarrow q) \wedge (q \rightarrow p)$ or $p \leftrightarrow q$
T	T	T	T	T
T	F	F	T	F
F	T	T	F	F
F	F	T	T	T

Example AI-5 | Given the following statements, classify each of the biconditionals as true or false.

p: $2 = 2$ r: $2 = 1$
q: $2 \neq 1$ s: $2 + 3 = 1 + 3$

(a) $p \leftrightarrow q$ (b) $p \leftrightarrow r$ (c) $s \leftrightarrow q$ (d) $r \leftrightarrow s$

Solution |
(a)   Since $p \rightarrow q$ is true and $q \rightarrow p$ is true, $p \leftrightarrow q$ is true.
(b)   Since $p \rightarrow r$ is false and $r \rightarrow p$ is true, $p \leftrightarrow r$ is false.
(c)   Since $s \rightarrow q$ is true and $q \rightarrow s$ is false, $s \leftrightarrow q$ is false.
(d)   Since $r \rightarrow s$ is true and $s \rightarrow r$ is true, $r \leftrightarrow s$ is true.

PROBLEM SET AI-2

1. Write each of the the following in symbolic form if p is the statement, "It is raining," and q is the statement, "The grass is wet."
    (a)   If it is raining, then the grass is wet.
    (b)   If it is not raining, then the grass is wet.
    (c)   If it is raining, then the grass is not wet.
    (d)   The grass is wet if it is raining.
    (e)   The grass is not wet implies that it is not raining.
    (f)   The grass is wet if and only if it is raining.
2. For each of the following implications, state the converse, inverse, and contrapositive.
    (a)   If you eat Meaties, then you are good in sports.
    (b)   If you do not like this book, then you do not like mathematics.
    (c)   If you do not use Ultra Brush toothpaste, then you have cavities.
    (d)   If you are good at logic, then your grades are high.
3. Construct a truth table for each of the following.
    (a) $p \rightarrow (p \vee q)$ (b) $(p \wedge q) \rightarrow q$ (c) $p \leftrightarrow \sim(\sim p)$
4. If p is true and q is false, find the truth values for each of the following.
    (a) $\sim p \rightarrow \sim q$ (b) $\sim(p \rightarrow q)$ (c) $(p \vee q) \rightarrow (p \wedge q)$
    (d) $p \rightarrow \sim p$ (e) $(p \vee \sim p) \rightarrow p$ (f) $(p \vee q) \leftrightarrow (p \vee q)$
5. If p is false and q is false, find the truth values for each of the statements in Problem 4.
6. Can an implication and its converse both be false? Explain your answer.
7. Tom makes the true statement, "If it rains, then I am going to the movies." Does it follow logically that if it does not rain, then Tom did not go to the movies?
8. Consider the statement, "If every digit of a number is 6, then the number is divisible by 3." Which of the following is logically equivalent to the statement?
    (a)   If every digit of a number is not 6, then the number is not divisible by 3.
    (b)   If a number is not divisible by 3, then every digit of the number is not 6.
    (c)   If a number is divisible by 3, then every digit of the number is 6.
9. Write a statement logically equivalent to the statement, "If a number is a multiple of 8, then it is a multiple of 4."

AI-3   QUANTIFIERS

Abraham Lincoln once said, "You can fool all of the people some of the time, and you can fool some of the people all of the time, but you can't fool all of the people all of the time." The words *all* and *some* in Lincoln's statement are called **quantifiers.** Other examples of quantified statements are as follows.

quantifiers

All men are mortal.

Some students will fail this course.

No triangles are squares.

There exists at least one even prime number.

The quantifiers *all, every,* and *no* refer to each and every element in a set and are called **universal quantifiers.** The quantifiers *some* and *there exists at least one* refer to one or more, or possibly all, of the elements in a set. *Some* and *there exists at least one* are called **existential quantifiers.** Examples with universal and existential quantifiers are as follows.

universal quantifiers

existential quantifiers

All numbers less than 10 are less than 100. (universal)

Every student is important. (universal)

For each counting number x, $x + 0 = x$. (universal)

Some roses are red. (existential)

There exists at least one even counting number less than three. (existential)

There exist women who are taller than 200 cm. (existential)

Quantifiers can be used to give truth values to expressions by making them statements. For example, by itself, the expression $3x = 6$ cannot be classified as true or false. However, quantifiers can be added to $3x = 6$, giving it a truth value.

There exists a counting number, x, such that $3x = 6$. (T)

For all counting numbers, x, $3x = 6$. (F)

Consider the statement, "Some teachers at Paxon School have blue eyes." This means that at least one teacher at Paxon School has blue eyes. It does not rule out the possibilities that all the Paxon teachers have blue eyes or that some of the Paxon teachers do not have blue eyes. Since the negation of a true statement is false, neither "Some teachers at Paxon School do not have blue eyes," nor "All teachers at Paxon have blue eyes," are negations of the original statement. One possible negation of the original statement is, "No teachers at Paxon School have blue eyes."

To discover if one statement is a negation of another, determine if they have opposite truth values in all possible cases. Some general forms of quantified statements with their negations follow.

Statement	Negation
Some *p* are *q*.	No *p* is *q*.
Some *p* are not *q*.	All *p* are *q*.
All *p* are *q*.	Some *p* are not *q*.
No *p* is *q*.	Some *p* are *q*.

Example AI-6

Negate each of the following statements.

(a)   All students like hamburgers.
(b)   Some people like mathematics.
(c)   No professor has red hair.
(d)   Some graduates will not find jobs.

Solution

(a)   Some students do not like hamburgers.
(b)   No people like mathematics.
(c)   Some professors have red hair.
(d)   All graduates will find jobs.

To show that an existentially quantified statement is false, it is necessary to show that the statement is false for all possibilities. To show that a universally quantified statement is false, it is necessary to show that there is at least one case for which the statement is false.

Negations of quantified statements involving mathematical expressions are made using the rules given earlier. Consider the following statements.

There exists a counting number x such that $3x = 6$.
For all counting numbers x, $3x = 3x$.

Two possible negations of these statements follow.

There does not exist a counting number x such that $3x = 6$.
There exists a counting number x such that $3x \neq 3x$.

Statements involving universal quantifiers can be expressed in the form, "if p, then q." For example, all men are mortal," can be expressed as, "If you are a man, then you are mortal." A statement such as, "No elementary teacher is rich," can be rewritten as, "If you are an elementary teacher, then you are not rich."

Reasoning situations develop when certain given statements are used to deduce another statement called a **conclusion.** The reasoning is said to be **valid** if the conclusion follows unavoidably from the given statements, the **hypotheses.** Consider the following example.

conclusion, valid
hypotheses

Given:	All roses are red.
	This flower is a rose
Conclusion:	Therefore, this flower is red.

A circle can be used to represent all roses and another circle to represent all red objects. The statement "All roses are red," can then be pictured with a diagram as in Figure AI-1.

The information, "This flower is a rose," implies that this flower must belong to the circle containing the roses, as pictured in Figure AI-2. This flower also belongs to the circle containing the red objects. Thus, the reasoning is valid because it is impossible to draw a picture satisfying the hypotheses and contradicting the conclusion.

Consider the following argument.

Given:	All elementary teachers are rich.
	Some rich people are not thin.
Conclusion:	Therefore, no elementary teacher is thin.

Let E be the set of elementary teachers, R be the set of rich people, and T be the set of thin people. Then the statement, "All elementary teachers are rich," can be pictured as in Figure AI-3. The statement, "Some rich people are not thin," can be pictured in several ways. Three of these are illustrated in Figure AI-4.

According to Figure AI-4(c), it is possible that some elementary teachers are thin, and yet the given statements are satisfied. Therefore, the

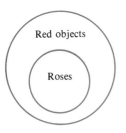

FIGURE AI-1

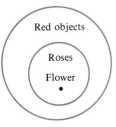

FIGURE AI-2

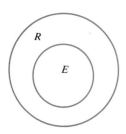

FIGURE AI-3

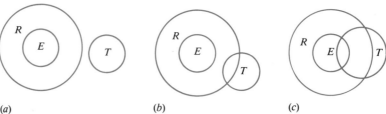

FIGURE AI-4   (*a*)   (*b*)   (*c*)

conclusion that "No elementary teacher is thin," does not follow from the given hypotheses. Hence, the reasoning is not valid.

If a picture can be drawn to satisfy the hypotheses of an argument and contradict the conclusion, the argument is not valid. However, all possible pictures must be considered to show that there are no contradictions if an argument is valid.

PROBLEM SET AI-3

1. Use quantifiers to make each of the following true where x is an integer.
   (a) $x + 8 = 11$ (b) $x + 0 = x$ (c) $x^2 = 4$ (d) $x + 1 = x + 2$
2. Use quantifiers to make each equation in Problem 1 false.
3. Write the negations for each of the following.
   (a) Some people have blond hair.
   (b) All dogs have four legs.
   (c) Some cats do not have nine lives.
   (d) No dogs can fly.
   (e) All squares are rectangles.
   (f) Not all rectangles are squares.
   (g) All Mary's crayons are broken.
4. Write the negations for each of the following.
   (a) For all integers x, $x + 3 = 3 + x$.
   (b) There exists an integer x such that $3 \cdot (x + 2) = 12$.
   (c) Every counting number is divisible by itself and one.
   (d) Not all integers are divisible by 2.
   (e) For all integers x, $5x + 4x = 9x$.
5. Investigate the validity of each of the following arguments.
   (a) All men are mortal.
       Socrates was a man.
       Therefore, Socrates was mortal.
   (b) All squares are quadrilaterals.
       All quadrilaterals are polygons.
       Therefore, all squares are polygons.
   (c) All teachers are intelligent.
       Some teachers are rich.
       Therefore, some intelligent people are rich.
   (d) All x's are y's.
       Some z's are x's.
       Therefore, all z's are y's.
   (e) If a student is a freshman, then she takes mathematics.
       Jane is a sophomore.
       Therefore, Jane does not take mathematics.

(f) If *A*, then not *B*.
   If not *B*, then *C*.
   Therefore, if *A* then *C*.

(g) All fat people are jolly.
   Some thin people are intelligent.
   Therefore, no fat people are intelligent.

(h) All *x*'s are *y*'s.
   Some *z*'s are *x*'s.
   Some *z*'s are not *y*'s.
   Therefore, some *z*'s are *y*'s.

6. For each of the following, form a conclusion which logically follows from the given statements.

(a) All college students are poor.
   Helen is a college student.

(b) Some freshman like mathematics.
   All people who like mathematics are intelligent.

(c) If I study for the final, then I will pass the final.
   If I pass the final, then I will pass the course.
   If I pass the course, then I look for a teaching job.

SELECTED BIBLIOGRAPHY

Andree, R., and J. Andree. *Logical Thinking* Norman, Okla.: University of Oklahoma Press, 1977.

Boyer, L. "On Validity and the Use of Truth Tables." *School Science and Mathematics,* **69**(March 1969):553–560.

Exner, R. and P. Hilton. "Should Mathematical Logic Be Taught Formally in Mathematics Classes?" *The Mathematics Teacher,* **64**(May 1971):388–401.

Harnadek, A. *Mathematical Reasoning,* Unit 4, Troy, Mich.: Midwest Publications, 1972.

Kattsoff, L. "Symbolic Logic and the Structure of Elementary Mathematics." *The Mathematics Teacher,* **55**(April 1962):269–275.

Masse, M. "More Problems Please." *Arithmetic Teacher,* **26**(December 1978):11–14.

National Council of Teachers of Mathematics. *Topics in Mathematics for Elementary School Teachers,* Booklet Number 12, *Logic,* 1968. Washington, D.C.: NCTM.

Poincare, H. "Intuition and Logic in Mathematics." *The Mathematics Teacher,* **62**(March 1969): 205–212.

Roberge, J. "Negation in the Major Premise as a Factor in Children's Deducting Reasoning." *School Science and Mathematics,* **69**(March 1969):715–722.

Suppes, P. and S. Hill. *First Course in Mathematical Logic.* Boston: Ginn, 1966.

Appendix II

Calculator Usage

INTRODUCTION

In 1976, the National Council of Teachers of Mathematics (NCTM) adopted the following position on the use of hand-held calculators (see *The Mathematics Teacher,* January 1976, 92–94).

> With the decrease in cost of the minicalculator, its accessibility to students at all levels is increasing rapidly. Mathematics teachers should recognize the potential contribution of this calculator as a valuable instructional aid. In the classroom, the minicalculator should be used in imaginative ways to reinforce learning and to motivate the learner as he becomes proficient in mathematics.

To assist teachers in their implementation of calculators in the classroom by complementing the existing curriculum, the Instructional Affairs Committee of NCTM developed the following list of possible uses for calculators (see *The Mathematics Teacher,* January 1976, 92–94).

1. To encourage students to be inquisitive and creative as they experiment with mathematical ideas.
2. To assist the individual to become a wiser consumer.
3. To reinforce the learning of the basic number facts and properties in addition, subtraction, multiplication, and division.
4. To develop the understanding of computational algorithms by repeated operations.
5. To serve as a flexible "answer key" used to verify the results of computation.
6. To be a resource tool that promotes student independence in problem solving.

7. To solve problems that previously have been too time consuming or impractical.
8. To formulate generalizations from patterns of numbers that are displayed.
9. To decrease the time needed to solve difficult computations.

The authors feel that calculators should be used in classrooms and that prospective teachers must be exposed to them. This appendix contains a section on features to look for in a calculator, a section of example problems for calculator usage arranged by subject matter, and a section on the use of flowcharts.

AII-1   FEATURES OF CALCULATORS

Once a teacher or school system has decided to use calculators with students, the most important problems become, which calculator best fits the expected usage and which can be integrated in the curriculum with the fewest problems. The choice of calculator certainly depends upon the grade level in which it will be used. There are a number of features a calculator should have.

Type of Logic

The type of logic built into a calculator determines how a problem is entered into the calculator. For example, the most natural way to enter $2 + 4 \cdot 5 - 4 \div 2$ on a calculator is exactly as it is written. With different types of logic, this may or may not do the problem.

Arithmetic Logic. With arithmetic logic, there is no $\boxed{=}$ key. The keys with the "equals" symbol are $\boxed{\pm}$ and $\boxed{=}$. A problem like $3 + 4$ is entered as $\boxed{3}$ $\boxed{\pm}$ $\boxed{4}$ $\boxed{\pm}$. This logic is confusing for most elementary students and probably should not be used. Arithmetic logic is becoming obsolete and probably will not be found on the majority of calculators.

Algebraic Logic. With algebraic logic, the problem may be entered exactly as written. The calculator processes the operations in the order in which they are entered. For example,

$$2 + 4 \cdot 5 - 4 \div 2$$

would be evaluated as

$$6 \cdot 5 - 4 \div 2$$

then as

$$30 - 4 \div 2$$

and finally as

$$26 \div 2 = 13$$

Remembering, however, that multiplication and division are done before addition and subtraction, the correct solution to the problem $2 + 4 \cdot 5 - 4 \div 2$ is $2 + 20 - 2 = 22 - 2 = 20$. Algebraic logic is used in many models and is adequate if both teacher and students are aware of the order in which operations must be performed.

Algebraic Operating System. Many calculators with algebraic logic also include a feature called an **algebraic operating system.** It evaluates parentheses first, then multiplications and divisions, and then additions and subtractions. For example, in the problem $2 + 4 \cdot 5 - 4 \div 2$, if ② ⊞ ④ is entered, the calculator will not perform the addition. If ② ⊞ ④ ⊠ is entered, no calculations will be completed. After ② ⊞ ④ ⊠ ⑤ ⊟ is entered, the display will show 22. In other words, the calculator performs 4 × 5 before adding 2. A calculator with the algebraic operating system feature will complete the original problem $2 + 4 \cdot 5 - 4 \div 2$ and give the desired answer of 20 if the problem is entered in the order it is written.

Reverse Polish Notation. In a calculator that uses Reverse Polish Notation (RPN), all operations are entered after the numbers have been entered. For example, to find $2 + 4$ on a machine that uses RPN, both 2 and 4 must be entered before the operation of addition. There is an ENTER button on a calculator with RPN. To compute $2 + 4$, the buttons are pushed as follows:

② ENTER ④ ⊞

The display shows 6. No ⊟ key is necessary since the computation is completed when the operation button is pushed.

Number of Functions

The *minimal* number of functions a calculator should perform is four. These functions are ⊞ , ⊟ , ⊠ , and ⊡ . There are other function keys that are desirable, including ⬚%⬚ and ⬚√⬚ , but they are not absolutely necessary. They will be further discussed under special keys.

Display

A calculator display should have at least an eight-digit readout. Two types of displays commonly available are the light emitting diode (LED) and the liquid crystal display (LCD). There are various advantages and disadvantages to each of these. Typically, the LED machine uses 9-volt batteries with a short life, while the LCD machine uses the longer lived, but more expensive, silver oxide battery. Also, the LCD machine is more expensive than the LED machine. In addition, the LCD calculator requires some reflected room light to be seen. The LED calculator can be seen in the dark but is very hard to see in bright light. For classroom purposes a machine must be easily readable from a wide viewing angle, regardless of the type of display.

Keys and Keyboard

Each key should have only one purpose and should give some indication that it has been pressed—click, beep, etc. There should be an easily accessible off–on switch. The position of the keys on the keyboard may vary, but they should be adequately spaced and of a large enough size that fingers hit no more than one key at a time. Also, the calculator should have separate clear and clear-entry keys. On some calculators, pressing the clear key once clears the display while pressing it a second time clears the whole calculator.

Decimal Notation

The calculator should have a floating decimal point. For example, when ⬚1⬚ ⬚÷⬚ ⬚3⬚ ⬚=⬚ is entered, the display should show 0.3333333, rather than 0.33 as some displays do on fixed point machines. Be aware of how a calculator rounds decimals, if it does. For example, in ⬚2⬚ ⬚÷⬚ ⬚3⬚ ⬚=⬚ , the display with a floating decimal may show 0.6666666 or 0.6666667. If the display shows 0.6666667, the round-off is apparent. If it shows 0.6666666, then multiply by 3 and observe the result, which may be either 1.9999998, 1.9999999 or 2. If 1.9999998 appears, there is no round-off by the calculator. If 1.9999999 or 2 appears, there is an internal round-off.

  Also, when considering decimal notation, determine if the calculator uses scientific notation and, if so, how it works. Recall that in scientific notation a number like 238 000 is written as a number between 1 and 10 multiplied by a power of 10. Thus 238 000 = 2.38 × 10⁵. For upper-grade students, scientific notation is desirable. Students should consult their owner's manual to see how scientific notation is displayed.

Error Indicator

There should be some signal on the calculator to indicate when an "illegal" operation is entered. For example, ① ÷ ⓪ ⊟ should cause the display to show an error. This indicator should also show when the computing limit of the calculator is exceeded.

Special Keys

There are several special keys that are convenient for elementary school usage. The first of these is the constant key Ⓚ, which allows an operation to be repeated without pushing all the buttons each time. For example, the calculator might be designed so that if ① ⊞ Ⓚ is entered, then 1 is added to whatever appears on the display each time ⊟ is pushed. This allows kindergarten or first-grade students to count by ones. Some machines have automatic constants built into them, rather than a separate constant key. In such cases, the owner's manual should be consulted.

The second of the convenient special keys is a "change the sign" key, ⌊+/−⌋. This allows for the entry of negative numbers. Normally, each number entered into a calculator is positive. Pushing ③ ⌊+/−⌋ changes 3 to ⁻3. This key is especially important if integers are to be studied using the calculator. (It is desirable that the negative sign immediately precede a number to denote a negative number rather than leaving a space between the sign and the number.)

The third and fourth special keys are the parentheses keys, ⌈(and ⌉) . With parentheses keys, operations may be ordered as desired. A calculator with parentheses keys will perform operations inside the parentheses before any others. For example, there is no confusion to the problem 2 + 4 · 5 − 4 ÷ 2 if parentheses are added as shown: 2 + (4 · 5) − (4 ÷ 2).

The fifth special key is the percent key, ▨% . This key may operate in a variety of ways, depending on the calculator. It may change a percent to a decimal. For example, pushing ⑥ ▨% may give 0.06 on the display. On other machines the ▨% key may be a function key. For example, pushing ② ⌧× ③ ▨% may yield 0.06 without using the ⊟ key. If the ⊟ key is used, the display might show 2.06, which is 2 + 2(3%). The user should carefully check how the ▨% key operates. In many cases, a more thorough understanding of percents takes place by not using a percent key.

Other keys that may be convenient are $\boxed{\sqrt{}}$, the square root key, and $\boxed{x^2}$, the squaring key. There are numerous other keys available that an individual school system or teacher may find useful. Regardless of the type of machine and keys selected, the teacher should be thoroughly familiar with the owner's manual.

Memory

The memory feature is particularly important in using the calculator in upper elementary grades. Many calculators use a two-key memory system—$\boxed{\text{STO}}$ used for storing a displayed number in the memory and $\boxed{\text{RCL}}$ for recalling a number from the memory. This arrangement is adequate for most uses.

Other machines have four-key memories. These are usually memory-plus $\boxed{\text{M+}}$, which allows addition to be performed on the content of a memory register, "memory-minus $\boxed{\text{M−}}$, which does subtraction from the content of a memory register, memory recall $\boxed{\text{MR}}$, and memory clear $\boxed{\text{MC}}$.

Other Considerations

There are many other considerations involved in choosing calculators for students. Among these are the size, shape, and weight of the machine, the power source, cost, durability and warranty, and reliability of the vendor and/or the manufacturer. These are individual items upon which the teacher or the school system must decide.

Topics for Calculator Usage

Many of the topics in the following problem set have been developed in schools for years without the use of calculators, but calculators can be used to reinforce some concepts and to introduce other topics more effectively. It is divided into basic concepts and computations with text explanations only where absolutely necessary. The divisions of the material correspond to chapters in the text with suggested grade levels in the margins. The instructor may wish to allow students to explore problems on their own and only give explanations if needed.

We will assume that the calculator being used has algebraic logic, an eight-digit display, the four basic function keys $\boxed{+}$, $\boxed{−}$, $\boxed{\times}$, $\boxed{÷}$, a change of sign key, separate clear and clear entry keys, and a constant feature. For some specific problems, we assume that the calculator has other features. These will be noted when they appear.

PROBLEM SET AII-1

Grade Level   **Place Value**

1. Display the following on a calculator. Press the CLEAR button after completing each part of the problem.
   (a) A three-digit number with 7 as the units digit
   (b) A two-digit number with 3 as the tens digit
   (c) A four-digit number with 0 as the hundreds digit
   (d) A five-digit number with 6 as the thousands digit and 3 as the tens digit
   (e) The number thirty-six
   (f) The number five hundred three
   (g) The number two thousand twenty-seven
   (h) A six-digit number that has five zeros as digits

1–2

2. Make your display read 123456. Now, push an operation button (+ , − , × , or ÷), enter some number (possibly multidigit), and then push = to make the display read 120456.

2–4

3. Make a calculator display numbers that have the following values.
   (a) Seven tens
   (b) Nine thousands
   (c) Eleven hundreds
   (d) Fifty-six tens
   (e) Three hundred forty-seven tens

1–2

4. Use only the buttons 1 , 2 , 3 , 4 , 5 , 6 , 7 , 8 , 9 , for each of the following.
   (a) Fill the display to show the greatest number possible; each button can be used only once.
   (b) Fill the display to show the least number possible; each button can be used only once.
   (c) Fill the display to show the greatest number possible if a button may be used more than once.
   (d) Fill the display to show the least possible number if a button may be used more than once.

1–3

3

5. Display the greatest number that has exactly seven digits with no two digits repeated.

Grade Level   **Counting**

K

6. In the display 12456789, which digit is missing?
7. Make a calculator count to 100. (Use a constant operation if available.)
   (a) By 1's
   (b) By 2's
   (c) By 5's

1–2

8. Make a calculator count backwards to 0 from 27. (Use a constant operation if possible.)
   (a) By 1's
   (b) By 3's
   (c) By 9's

1–2

K–8

1–2

K–8

2–3

9. Find the greatest possible number that can be displayed on a calculator. (The solution to this problem depends upon the student and the sophistication of the machine.)

10. If a calculator is made to count by 2's starting at 2, what is the thirteenth number in the sequence?

11. Find out what happens on a calculator when the nine-digit number 123456789 is entered.

12. Display a number for each of the following
   (a) The number comes before 4362
   (b) The number comes after 9089
   (c) The number comes after 6099

Grade Level

Addition of Whole Numbers

2–3

2–3

2–3

2–3

13. On a calculator practice adding each of the following.
   (a) 375 + 24 =   Answer 399
   (b) 506 + 702 =   Answer 1208
   (c) 99 + 9 =   Answer 108
   (d) 27 + 98 =   Answer 125

14. The Mississippi delta is famous for its rich _____. To answer this, add the following. Once the sum is found, turn the calculator upside down and read the answer.
   103 + 2589 + 406 + 1642 + 2365 =

15. Find the sum of the following numbers: three thousand two hundred fifty-six, four hundred twenty-seven, and four thousand six.

16. Fill in the blanks to make a magic square. The sum of each row column, and diagonal must be the same.

10	3	8
5		
	11	

17. The following is a supermagic square taken from an engraving called *Melancholia* by Dürer (1514).

1–2

16	3	2	13
5	10	11	8
9	6	7	12
4	15	14	1

   (a) Find the sum of each row, the sum of each column, and the sum of each diagonal.
   (b) Find the sum of the four numbers in the center.
   (c) Find the sum of the four numbers in each corner.

18. Add 11 to the numbers in each square of the following magic square. **Is the result a magic square?**

4	9	5	16
15	6	10	3
14	7	11	2
1	12	8	13

19. Add the following on a calculator.

$$92\ 345\ 679 + 9\ 999\ 555$$

What is the result?

20. Determine if the order of addition is important. For example, are sums like **493 + 566 and** 566 + 493 equal?

21. Find the missing numbers in each of the following.

(a)
```
    _ _ 1
  + 4 2 _
  _____
    4 0 2
```

(b)
```
    _ 0 2 5
    1 1 _ 6
  + 3 1 4 8
  _____
    6 _ 6 _
```

(c)
```
    1 _ 6 9
    2 _ 9 4
    9 5 4 6
    9 _ _ 3
  + 7 _ 6 4
  _____
    2 8 7 7 6
```

(d)
```
      2 _ 1
      4 5 _
  +   _ 8 4
  _____
    1 3 2 6
```

22. Arrange eight 8's so that the sum is 1000.

23. The following is one version of a game referred to as NIM. Two players are needed with one calculator. Player 1 pushes ① or ② and ⊞. Player 2 pushes ① or ② and ⊞. The players take turns until the target number of 21 is reached. The first player to make the display read 21 is the winner. Determine a strategy for deciding who always wins.

24. Try the game of NIM, referred to in Problem 23, using the digits 1, 2, and 3, with a target number of 24. Is the winning strategy basically the same?

25. Try a game of NIM using the digits 3, 5, 7, with a target number of 73. The first player to exceed 73 loses. Is the winning strategy basically the same?

26. In the song, "The Twelve Days of Christmas," the person received a partridge in a pear tree the first day, two turtle doves and a partridge in a pear tree the second day, three French hens, two turtle doves, and a partridge in a pear tree the third day, and so on. How many gifts did the person receive the twelfth day? What is the total number of gifts the person received in "The Twelve Days of Christmas"?

27. Consider the following additions.

    1 + 11 =
    1 + 11 + 111 =
    1 + 11 + 111 + 1111 =

(a) What is the pattern?
(b) How many addends are there the first time the pattern no longer works?

28. (a) Use a calculator to place the whole numbers given below in the empty circles so that the sum of the values of the numbers in the circles connected by each line is the same. The whole numbers are 24, 25, 26, 27, 28, 29, 30, 31, 32, and each may be used exactly once.

5–8

(b) How many solutions are there?

29. Place the digits 7, 6, 8, 3, 5, 2 in the boxes to obtain (a) the greatest sum, and (b) the least sum.

3–8

1

30. Display any number on a calculator. Add 0. What is the result? Does this work in general?

Grade Level

Subtraction of Whole Numbers

2–3

31. Find the following.
Three thousand four hundred eighty-two minus nine hundred sixty-eight = _?_

32. Given the following magic square, if 11 is subtracted from the numbers in each square, is the result a magic square?

2

27	14	13	24
16	21	22	19
20	17	18	23
15	26	25	12

33. There is a famous set of children's stories known as Mother _?_ Rhymes. To find the answer, complete the following problem, turn the calculator upside down and read the display to find the missing word.

3–4

$$67\ 845 - 32\ 839 = \underline{\ ?\ }$$

34. Is 13 632 greater than or less than 19 169? Work the following problem, turn the calculator upside down, and read the display to find the answer.

$$19\ 169 - 13\ 632 = \underline{\ ?\ }$$

35. Find the missing numbers for each of the following.

(a)   87693   (b)   8135   (c)   3 _ _   (d)   1 _ _ 6
    − _ _ _ _ _   − 4682   − 1 5 9   − 8 3 0 9
    ─────────   ────────   ─────   ─────────
      41279   _ _ _ _   _ 2 4   4 9 8 7

36. In the game of NIM discussed earlier, two players are needed with one calculator. Player 1 pushes ① or ② and ⊞ . Player 2 pushes ① or ② and ⊞ , and both try to reach the target number of 21. Now, play Reverse NIM. Instead of ⊞ , use ⊟ . Put 21 on the display. Let the new target number be 0. Determine a strategy for winning Reverse NIM.

37. Try Reverse NIM using the digits 1, 2, and 3, and starting with 24 on the display. The target number is 0. What is the winning strategy?

38. Try Reverse NIM using the digits 3, 5, and 7, and starting with 73 on the display. The first player to display a negative number loses. What is the winning strategy?

39. Display any number on a calculator. Subtract 0. What is the result? Is this true for all numbers?

40. Given the following addition problem, replace nine digits with 0 so that the sum of the numbers is 1111.

$$
\begin{array}{r}
999 \\
777 \\
555 \\
333 \\
\underline{111}
\end{array}
$$

41. Place the digits 7, 6, 8, 3, 5, 2 in the boxes to obtain (a) the greatest difference, and (b) the least difference.

$$
\begin{array}{r}
\square\ \square\ \square \\
-\ \square\ \square\ \square
\end{array}
$$

Multiplication of Whole Numbers

42. Investigate the relation between addition and multiplication by comparing $14 + 14 + 14 + 14 + 14$ and $5 \cdot 14$.

43. If you multiply any odd whole number by 5, the units digit of the product is __?__

44. If you multiply any even whole number by 5, the units digit of the product is __?__

45. Use the constant feature on a calculator to determine the value of $9 \times 9 \times 9 \times 9 \times 9 \times 9 \times 9$ or 9^7.

Grade Level

3-4

3-4

2-8

2-8

2-8

1

4-6

3-8

Grade Level

3

3

3

3-4

46. Complete the following chart and try to discover how to square any two-or-more-digit number having 5 as the units digit (at least up to 105).

    $15 \times 15 =$

    $25 \times 25 =$

    $35 \times 35 =$

    $45 \times 45 =$

    $55 \times 55 =$

    $65 \times 65 =$

    $75 \times 75 =$

    $85 \times 85 =$

    $95 \times 95 =$

    $105 \times 105 =$

47. Find all pairs of whole numbers whose product is 36.

48. Complete the following problems.

    (a) $43 \times 10 =$ (b) $43 \times 100 =$ (c) $43 \times 1000 =$ (d) $43 \times 10\,000 =$

    (e) Form a conjecture based on parts (a) through (d) for multiplication by a power of 10.

49. Use a calculator to find the missing numbers.

    (a)
    ```
        3 7
      × 4 3
      ------
      - - -
      - - - -
      ------
      _ 5 9 1
    ```
    (b)
    ```
        _ _
      × 3 6
      ------
        5 5 8
      2 7 9 0
      ------
      _ _ _ _
    ```
    (c)
    ```
        _ _ _
      ×   _ _
      ------
      1 5 7 2
      3 1 4 4 0
      ------
      3 3 0 1 2
    ```
    (d)
    ```
          3
      × 5 _
      ------
      2 5 8
      2 1 5 0
      ------
      2 4 0 8
    ```

50. Place the digits 7, 6, 8, 3 in the boxes to obtain (a) the greatest product, and (b) the least product.

    □ □ □
    × ___ □

51. Place the digits 7, 6, 8, 3, 2 in the boxes to obtain (a) the greatest product, and (b) the least product.

    □ □ □
    × □ □

52. Guess the greatest product in each of the following and then check the answer.

    (a) 24×11 (b) 20×30

         25×11 30×40

         26×11 40×50

53. In the Winter Olympics, one of the most dangerous events is the   ?   race. Complete the following problem, turn the calculator upside down, and read the display to determine the answer.

    $$144 \times 349\,832 =$$

54. Describe the pattern in the answers of the following products.

$$1 \times 1$$
$$11 \times 11$$
$$111 \times 111$$
$$1111 \times 1111$$

Through how many steps does this pattern continue?

55. How many minutes are in a decade?
56. How many times does your heart beat in 1 day?
57. Which is a better deal, a ton of dimes or a ton of quarters?
58. The work on a test paper follows. Use a calculator to determine why it is wrong.

$$
\begin{array}{r}
4\,3\,5 \\
\times\, 8\,3 \\
\hline
1\,3\,0\,5 \\
3\,4\,8\,0 \\
\hline
4\,7\,8\,5 \\
\end{array}
$$

59. Enter any number on a calculator. Multiply by 0. What is the result? Is this true in general?
60. Investigate the following numbers.

$$2^{(3^7)} \text{ and } (2^3)^7$$

Are they equal? Is exponentiation associative?

61. Suppose a person can spend $1 per second. How much can that person spend in a minute? An hour? A day? A week? A month? A year? Twenty years?
62. Compare $2 \cdot 13$ and 2^{13}. Which is greater?
63. Find $1 \cdot 2 \cdot 3 \cdot 4 \cdot 5 \cdot 6 \cdot \ldots \cdot 10$. This product is called 10 **factorial** and is written as 10!
64. For each of the following, try to find a number which multiplied times itself equals the given number.

    (a) 36   (b) 361   (c) 1764   (d) 3721

65. Suppose a friend chooses a number between 250 000 and 1 000 000. What is the fewest number of questions that must be asked in order to guess the number if the friend only answers yes or no to the questions?

Grade Level

Division of Whole Numbers

66. How many 7's are in 98?
    (a) Use the constant feature to count backward from 98 to 0 by 7's, and count the number of 7's subtracted.
    (b) Count forward from 0 to 98 by 7's.
    (c) Use a calculator to find: $98 \div 7$.
67. (a) Find all whole numbers that divide 36.
    (b) Find all whole numbers that divide 144.

68. Given the following problems, find all the possible whole number divisors.

(a) $\overline{)123}$
    -9
    $\overline{33}$
    -27
    $\overline{6\,R}$

(b) $\overline{)147}$
    -100
    $\overline{47}$
    -45
    $\overline{2\,R}$

(c) $\overline{)146}$
    $\overline{}$
    $3\,R$

(d) $\overline{)335}$
    $\overline{}$
    $2\,R$

69. Use the digits 7, 6, 8, and 3 and place them in the boxes to determine (a) the greatest quotient, and (b) the least quotient.

$$\square \,\overline{)\,\square\ \square\ \square}$$

70. Jack watched 492 minutes of television last week. How many hours and minutes did Jack watch television?

71. If a cow produces 700 pounds of hamburger, and there are 4 quarterpounders to a pound, how many cows does it take to produce the 21 billion hamburgers that MacDonald's has sold, assuming they are all quarterpounders?

72. Suppose two people play a target number game on the calculator. They take turns entering numbers and pressing the multiplication button. The scoring of the game is achieved by finding the positive difference in the product and the target number. For example, the target number is 75, and the first person pushes $\boxed{8}$ $\boxed{\times}$. If the second person pushes $\boxed{9}$ $\boxed{=}$, the display shows 72. The difference, $75 - 72 = 3$, is the first person's score for the first round. Now, the second player enters $\boxed{25}$ $\boxed{\times}$ and the first player enters $\boxed{3}$ $\boxed{=}$, the display shows 75. The second player's score for the first round is $75 - 75$ or 0, and the first player wins. Start again. Suppose the target number is 75, what natural number must the first player enter to assure the highest possible score?

73. When the tramp wanted money, he would stand on the street corner and   ? .
Complete the problem $2552 \div 4 =$. Turn the calculator upside down and read the display to determine the answer.

74. Enter any three-digit number on the calculator, for example, 243. Repeat it, 243 243. Divide by 7. Divide by 11. Divide by 13. What is the answer? Try it again with any other three-digit number. Will this always work? Why?

75. Estimate which of the following division problems have quotients between 20 and 50? Use a calculator to verify the answers.
(a) $436 \div 13$ (b) $4368 \div 131$ (c) $4368 \div 13$ (d) $436 \div 131$

76. The division algorithm states that for any two whole numbers, a and b, with $a > b$, $a = b \cdot q + r$, where $0 \le r < b$. Use a calculator to find the whole number remainder for each of the following.
Example: $7 > 5$. On the calculator $\boxed{7}$ $\boxed{\div}$ $\boxed{5}$ $\boxed{=}$ yields 1.4. To find the whole number remainder, ignore the decimal portion of 1.4, multiply $5 \cdot 1$, and subtract this product from 7. The result is the remainder.

(a) 28 and 5   (b) 32 and 10   (c) 29 and 3
(d) 41 and 7   (e) 49 382 and 14

Grade Level   ## Mixed Operations on Whole Numbers

In Problems 77–80, use only the designated number keys. Use any function keys on the calculator.

4–6   77.   Use the buttons $\boxed{1}$, $\boxed{9}$, $\boxed{7}$ exactly once in any order and use any operations available to write as many of the whole numbers as possible from 1 to 20. For example, $9 - 7 - 1 = 1$, and $1 \cdot 9 - 7 = 2$.

4–6   78.   Use the $\boxed{4}$ button as many times as desired with any operations to make the display read 13.

2–3   79.   Use the $\boxed{2}$ button three times with any operations to make the display read 24.

4–6   80.   Use the $\boxed{1}$ button 5 times with any operations to display 100.

81.   Use the digits 7, 6, and 8, and place them in the boxes to determine the greatest whole number answer.

(a) $\square \boxed{\times} \square \boxed{-} \square \boxed{=}$

3–4   (b) $\boxed{(}\ \square \boxed{+} \square \boxed{)} \boxed{\times} \square \boxed{=}$

(c) $\square \boxed{\times} \boxed{(}\ \square \boxed{-} \square \boxed{)} \boxed{=}$

(d) $\boxed{(}\ \square \boxed{\times} \square \boxed{)} \boxed{-} \square \boxed{=}$

(e) $\square \boxed{\times} \boxed{(}\ \square \boxed{+} \square \boxed{)} \boxed{=}$

82.   Find all pairs of positive integers that, when substituted for $\square$ and $\triangle$, make the equations true.

4–5
(a) $(7 \cdot \square) + (5 \cdot \triangle) = 110$

(b) $(9 \cdot \square) + (6 \cdot \triangle) = 108$

Grade Level   ## Integers

83.   To find the additive inverse of a number, enter the number on the display and then push the $\boxed{+/-}$ key. For example, entering 7 and pushing $\boxed{+/-}$ yields -7 on the display. Find the additive inverses for each of the following.

6
(a)   14   (b)   24

(c) $^-2$ (d) $^-5$

84.   Complete each of the following integer arithmetic problems on the calculator making use of the $\boxed{+/-}$ key. For example, $^-5 + ^-4 =$ is entered as $\boxed{5}\ \boxed{+/-}\ \boxed{+}\ \boxed{4}\ \boxed{+/-}\ \boxed{=}$

(a) $^-12 + ^-6 =$ (b) $^-7 + ^-99 =$

(c) $^-12 + 6 =$ (d) $27 + ^-5 =$

6
(e) $3 \times ^-14 =$ (f) $^-7 - ^-9 =$

(g) $^-12 - 6 =$ (h) $16 - ^-7 =$

(i) $^-27 \times 3 =$ (j) $^-46 \times ^-4 =$

(k) $^-26 \div 13 =$ (l) $^-26 \div ^-13 =$

For elementary school students, exercises like the preceding ones can be used to demonstrate the patterns used to develop the properties of integers.

85. The formula for converting Fahrenheit (F) to Celsius (C) is

$$C = \frac{(F - 32) \cdot 5}{9},$$

Find the Celsius temperatures corresponding to each of the following Fahrenheit temperatures. (The order of operations is important.)
(a) 212°   (b) 32°
(c) 68°   (d) ⁻4°
(e) ⁻40°

6–8

86. Finite differences were used in Chapter 1 to find patterns. Find the seventeenth term of the following using the calculator.

6

⁻20, ⁻17, ⁻14, ⁻11, ⁻8, . . .

★87. Begin at X, end at Y. Find a path such that by adding the numbers in circles and subtracting the numbers in squares, the result upon leaving Y must be 24.

3–8

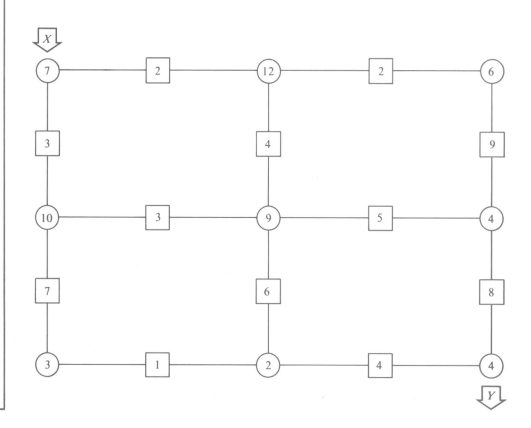

Grade Level   **Number Theory**

6–7

6–7

6–7

6–7

6–7

5

6–8

4

7–8

88. Use the calculator to list all factors for each of the following.
   (a)   24   (b)   36
   (c)   64   (d)   144

89. Find the prime factorizations for each of the following.
   (a)   24   (b)   36
   (c)   64   (d)   144
   (e)   45   (f)   1286

90. Find the greatest common divisor, GCD, for each of the following.
   (a)   24 and 36   (b)   36 and 45
   (c)   45 and 144   (d)   18 and 81

91. Find the least common multiple, LCM, for each of the following.
   (a)   24 and 36   (b)   36 and 45
   (c)   45 and 144   (d)   18 and 81

92. Compare the products of each of the pairs of numbers in Problem 91 with the product of the GCD and LCM of each of the pairs. What is true?

93. The calculator may be used to test for divisibility of one number by another. Test the divisibility of the first number by the second in each of the following.
   (a)   490 by 2   (b)   575 by 5
   (c)   353 by 3   (d)   4907 by 7
   (e)   4074 by 4   (f)   123 123 by 11

94. For each of the following, find all possible missing digits to make the numbers divisible by 6.
   (a)   5_32   (b)   49_8
   (c)   617_   (d)   _391

95. Palindromes are words or numbers that read the same backwards as forwards. Examples are "Mom," "Dad," "1881," "Madam I'm Adam," and "Able was I ere I saw Elba." An interesting problem is to turn numbers into palindromes.
   (a)   Write any two-digit number.
   (b)   Reverse the digits and add the result to the original number.
   (c)   If the sum is not a palindrome, repeat the process.
   (d)   Sometimes the process must be repeated several times before a palindrome is obtained.
   For example,
   (a)   76
   (b)   67 + 76 = 143
   (c)   341 + 143 = 484
   Try this procedure on several numbers. It is an unsolved problem whether or not for an n-digit number, a palindrome can always be obtained.

96. Mathematicians have tried for centuries to find a general formula for primes. One of the formulas that yields several primes is $n^2 + n + 17$.
   (a)   Substitute $n = 1, 2, 3, \ldots, 17$ in the formula and find which of the resulting numbers are primes and which are composite.
   (b)   Find a value of n, $n > 100$, for which $n^2 + n + 17$ yields a prime number.

Grade Level

Rational Numbers

A rational number is defined as a number that can be written in the form a/b, where a and b are integers and $b \neq 0$. It can also be defined as a repeating or terminating decimal. Because most calculators treat rational numbers as decimals, the problem emphasis in this section is on decimals. However, we try to relate decimals to the a/b form of rationals. The first group of problems investigates the fact that a rational number in the form a/b must be either a repeating or terminating decimal and vice versa.

97. This exercise helps determine which fractions can be expressed as terminating decimals and which as repeating decimals. Column I in Table A will be used later. Leave it blank for now. Use a calculator to divide the numerator of each fraction by the denominator. Enter the resulting decimal equivalent in Column III, then place a check in Column IV or V, whichever is true for that fraction.

Table A

I	II Common Fraction	III Decimal Equivalent	IV Terminating	V Repeating
	½			
	⅓			
	¼			
	⅖			
	⅙			
	2/7			
	⅝			
	⅑			
	3/10			
	1/11			
	1/12			
	4/15			
	9/16			
	1/18			

6–8

Table A (Continued)

I	II Common Fraction	III Decimal Equivalent	IV Terminating	V Repeating
	$^{13}/_{20}$			
	$^{17}/_{22}$			
	$^{23}/_{24}$			
	$^{23}/_{25}$			

To discover a pattern that helps tell which fractions represent terminating decimals and which represent repeating decimals, do each of the following in Table A.

(a) Find the prime factorization of each denominator and write it in the space in Column 1.

(b) Look at the fractions that have terminating decimal equivalents. What two numbers always appear in the prime factorization of their denominators?

(c) If the denominator has any prime factors other than 2 and 5, is the result a terminating decimal or is it a repeating decimal?

By using the prime factorization of the denominator, it is possible to tell *how many* decimal places are needed to achieve the terminating decimal. Find the decimal equivalents of the fractions in Table B, find the prime factorization of their denominators, and fill in the other columns.

Table B

I Prime Factorization of Denominator	II Common Fraction	III Decimal Equivalent	IV Denominator Is What Power of 2?	V Number of Decimal Places in III
	$^{1}/_{2}$			
	$^{3}/_{4}$			
	$^{1}/_{8}$			
	$^{5}/_{16}$			
	$^{3}/_{32}$			
	$^{9}/_{64}$			

Table B (Continued)

I Prime Factorization of Denominator	II Common Fraction	III Decimal Equivalent	IV Denominator Is What Power of 5?	V Number of Decimal Places
	$\frac{1}{5}$			
	$\frac{3}{25}$			
	$\frac{7}{125}$			
	$\frac{393}{625}$			

Does the same number always result in Columns IV and V? _____
Try the same process with the fractions, in Table C.

Table C

I Prime Factorization of Denominator	II Fraction	III Decimal	IV Power of 2	V Power of 5	VI Greater of the Numbers in IV or V	VII Number of Decimal Places in III
	$\frac{3}{10}$					
	$\frac{7}{20}$					
	$\frac{9}{40}$					
	$\frac{17}{50}$					
	$\frac{29}{80}$					
	$\frac{1}{250}$					
	$\frac{1}{500}$					

Are the numbers always the same in the last two columns? _____

98. This group of exercises concentrates on finding repeating decimals.
    (a) Use a calculator to find decimals for each of the following.
        (1) $^1/_7 =$ Do this by entering $\boxed{1}$ $\boxed{\div}$ $\boxed{7}$ $\boxed{=}$.
        (2) $^2/_7 =$
        (3) $^3/_7 =$
        (4) $^4/_7 =$
        (5) $^5/_7 =$
        (6) $^6/_7 =$
    How many places were used before each decimal repeated?
    (b) To find the repeating decimal for $^5/_{17}$, divide 5 by 17 to obtain .29411765. Find the result of multiplying .29411765 by 17. If 5 does not appear on the display, then (1) the machine has rounded the decimal quotient, (2) kept part of the decimal internally, (3) truncated the decimal, or (4) a combination of all of these. Recall that, since the divisor is 17, there could be a 16 digit repetend (repeating part of the decimal). One way to recover the rest of the decimal follows.
        (1) Truncate .29411765 to .2941176, since the last digit may have been rounded.
        (2) Multiply .2941176 · 17 to get 4.9999992.
        (3) Subtract 5 − 4.9999992 to get 0.0000008.
        (4) Divide 8 ÷ 17 to get .47058824.
        (5) Truncate the decimal .4705882.
        (6) Multiply 17 · .4705882 to get 7.9999994.
        (7) Subtract 8 − 7.9999994 to get 0.0000006.
        (8) Divide 6 ÷ 17 to get .35294118.
        (9) The process continues until the decimal repeats.
    Using the standard division steps, this problem looks as follows

    ```
             Step 1      Step 2  Step 3
            ⏜⏜⏜⏜⏜⏜⏜   ⏜⏜⏜⏜⏜⏜   ⏜⏜
      0.2 9 4 1 1 7 6 4 7 0 5 8 8 2 3 5
    1 7)5.0 0 0 0 0 0 0 0 0 0 0 0 0 0 0 0 0
      4 9 9 9 9 9 9 2
                  8 0 0 0 0 0 0 0
                  7 9 9 9 9 9 9 4
                              6 0 0
                              5 9 5
                                  5
    ```

    (c) Use this procedure to find repeating decimals for each of the following.
        (1) $^3/_{13}$ (2) $^3/_{23}$
        (3) $^{12}/_{19}$ (4) $^4/_{17}$
    Another method of finding repeating decimals for rational numbers in the form of a/b, where a and b are integers and $b \neq 0$ is given in "Fun with Repeating Decimals" by Sue Wagner in *The Mathematics Teacher*, March 1979, pp. 209–212.

    6–8

    *The procedure given here must be adapted for various problems. The number of digits to be truncated varies depending on partial products in the divisions.

99. One problem involving fractions is to decide when one fraction is greater than another, less than another, or whether one is really a different name for the other fraction. For example, is $\frac{1}{2} = \frac{1098}{2196}$? There are two ways to decide using the calculator. The first is simply to convert both to decimals and compare the decimals. Since the displays for both $\boxed{1}\ \boxed{\div}\ \boxed{2}\ \boxed{=}$ and $\boxed{1}\ \boxed{0}\ \boxed{9}\ \boxed{8}\ \boxed{\div}\ \boxed{2}\ \boxed{1}\ \boxed{9}\ \boxed{6}\ \boxed{=}$ are 0.5, then $\frac{1}{2} = \frac{1098}{2196}$.

6

The second is to use a notion developed in Chapter 6. That is, $a/b = c/d$ if and only if $ad = bc$ with $b \neq 0$ and $d \neq 0$. Using this notion we have the following.

Since both $\boxed{1}\ \boxed{\times}\ \boxed{2}\ \boxed{1}\ \boxed{9}\ \boxed{6}\ \boxed{=}$ and $\boxed{2}\ \boxed{\times}\ \boxed{1}\ \boxed{0}\ \boxed{9}\ \boxed{8}\ \boxed{=}$ yield a display of 2196, then $\frac{1}{2} = \frac{1098}{2196}$.

Compare each of the following rational fractions using both methods.

(a) $\frac{24}{31}$ and $\frac{23}{30}$ (b) $\frac{86}{75}$ and $\frac{85}{74}$ (c) $\frac{3}{11}$ and $\frac{2}{9}$

100. Try the following problem on a calculator.

$$\boxed{2}\ \boxed{\div}\ \boxed{0}\ \boxed{=}$$

What did the calculator do?

Some calculators show an error sign, some give a blank display, and some flash wildly. To understand why the calculator cannot do this problem, investigate what happens when a given number n is divided by an *increasingly smaller* set of divisors, x. Complete the following table:

n	$\div$	x	$=$	y
2	$\div$	2	$=$	1
2	$\div$	1	$=$	2
2	$\div$	0.5	$=$	
2	$\div$	0.2	$=$	
2	$\div$	0.001	$=$	
2	$\div$	0.00001	$=$	

6–8

(a) What happens to the answer y as 2 is divided by smaller and smaller numbers?
(b) Is the divisor x getting closer and closer to zero?
(c) What happens to the quotient y as the divisor x gets closer and closer to zero?
(d) How large do you think the answer y will be when the divisor x reaches zero?
(e) What can be determined about division by zero?
(f) Explain why the calculator reacts the way it does.

101. When trying to add fractions on a calculator, there are two major problems. The first problem is the order in which the calculator handles the operations entered. For example, to add $\frac{1}{4} + \frac{3}{4}$, the following sequence of buttons might be pushed

$$\boxed{1}\ \boxed{\div}\ \boxed{4}\ \boxed{+}\ \boxed{3}\ \boxed{\div}\ \boxed{4}\ \boxed{=}$$

The answer obtained depends totally on the order in which the machine performs the

6–8

operations. If the correct order of operations is built into the machine, then 1 appears on the display. If not, the display is 0.8125 because the calculator performs the following computations.

$$1 \div 4 = 0.25$$
$$0.25 + 3 = 3.25$$
$$3.25 \div 4 = 0.8125$$

The answer 0.8125 is the one that will appear on most machines used. Since it is obviously the wrong answer, something must be done to alleviate the problem. If the calculator has a memory, then use the following sequence.

$$\boxed{1}\ \boxed{\div}\ \boxed{4}\ \boxed{=}\ \boxed{\text{STO}}\ \boxed{3}\ \boxed{\div}\ \boxed{4}\ \boxed{=}\ \boxed{+}\ \boxed{\text{RCL}}\ \boxed{=}$$

The display should be 1. Note that when using a calculator without memory, anything to be stored may be written on paper and can be used when the sequence shows a recall $\boxed{\text{RCL}}$.

The second problem dealing with addition of fractions has to do with the manner in which a calculator changes the fractions to decimals. Since a calculator has a limited display, every repeating decimal is terminated with the number of places shown on the display. Thus, $\frac{1}{3} = 0.3333333$ and $\frac{2}{3} = 0.6666666$ (or 0.6666667 depending upon the machine). Hence, $\frac{1}{3} + \frac{2}{3}$ might appear as 0.9999999, which is obviously wrong. As a result, any sum of two fractions can be wrong if at least one of the fractions represents a repeating decimal.

Add the following fractions using a calculator. Are the correct answers obtained?
  (a) $\frac{1}{2} + \frac{1}{3}$
  (b) $\frac{1}{3} + \frac{1}{7}$
  (c) $\frac{1}{7} + \frac{1}{11}$

102. Try to discover a way to add two fractions on a calculator without using the memory or writing down intermediate answers.

103. Subtract each of the following pairs of rational numbers.
  (a) $\frac{1}{2} - \frac{1}{3}$
  (b) $\frac{1}{3} - \frac{1}{7}$
  (c) $\frac{1}{7} - \frac{1}{11}$

104. Recall the procedure for multiplying fractions.

$$\frac{a}{b} \cdot \frac{c}{d} = \frac{a \cdot c}{b \cdot d}$$

To multiply fractions on a calculator the following sequence may be used.

$$\boxed{a}\ \boxed{\div}\ \boxed{b}\ \boxed{\times}\ \boxed{c}\ \boxed{\div}\ \boxed{d}\ \boxed{=}$$

Try this technique with each of the following problems.
  (a) $(\frac{2}{3}) \cdot (\frac{1}{5})$
  (b) $(\frac{1}{19}) \cdot (\frac{4}{17})$
  (c) $(\frac{3}{1}) \cdot (\frac{2}{3})$
(Note that the answer on the display may not be accurate depending on round-off.)

105. (a) Find the product of 0.22 and 0.35 on the calculator. How does the placement of the decimal point in the answer on the calculator compare with the placement of the decimal point using the rule in Chapter 6? Explain.
  (b) Similarly, investigate placement of the decimal point in the quotient obtained by performing the following division, 0.2436 ÷ 0.0006.

6–8

6–8

6–8

6–7

106. On the average, in America, each adult uses the following.
    46.5 gallons of water per day
    10 glass bottles each month
    12.5 gallons of gas each week
    120 aluminum cans each year
    520 lbs. of wood products each year
    Assume that you are average and find the amount of these products that you use in a day, week, month, and year.

6–8

107. My paycheck has a hole in it!
    Suppose the boss said, "Yesterday's salary was $1.00 per hour; today's salary is $.50 per hour; tomorrow's salary will be 2½ times today's salary minus yesterday's salary." Each day the next day's salary will be recomputed. Compute a salary for twelve days starting with yesterday's salary. In Column A, suppose the boss rounds everything up to the nearest dime. In Column B, suppose the boss rounds everything down to the nearest dime.

6–8

	Nearest Dime	
Day	A	B
1	1.00	1.00
2	0.50	0.50
3	0.30	0.20
4		
5		
6		
7		
8		
9		
10		
11		
12		

108. Comparison of Metric vs. Customary Calculations

7–8

Customary System

(a) A new water bed is 6 feet wide, 7 feet long, and 9 inches thick. How many gallons of water will it hold? How many pounds will it weigh when it is full of water? (*Hint:* One cubic foot of water weighs 62.5 pounds. There are 1728 cubic inches in a cubic foot and 231 cubic inches in a gallon.)

(b) Some property is 1500 yards long and 1200 yards wide. How many square miles of property are there?

Metric System

(c) A new water bed is 183 centimeters wide, 23 centimeters thick, 213 centimeters long. How many liters of water will it hold? What is its mass in kilograms when it is full of water? There are 1000 cm^3 in 1L and 1L of water has a mass of 1 kg.

(d) Some property is 1400 meters long and 1100 meters wide. How many square kilometers of property are there?

6–7

109. Look through several grocery store ads for products and prices of containers of various sizes. For example, suppose one store charges 79¢ for the 16-ounce size of a product and another store advertises the 12-ounce size of the same item for 59¢. Find a way to use the calculator to decide which is the best buy.

6–8

110. A snail can crawl 0.523 foot in 240 seconds. In the same amount of time, a man can run 5280 feet, a race car can go 52 800 feet, and an airplane can fly 528 000 feet. How far can each travel in 1 second?

6–8

111. The greatest distance ever walked nonstop is 230.8 miles in 68.5 hours near Napier, New Zealand, on September 11–14, 1971, by John Sinclair, 54, of Great Britain. What is Mr. Sinclair's average walking speed in miles per hour?

6–8

112. Which is a better buy, two 10-inch circular pizzas at $2.00 each or one 14-inch circular pizza for $4.00?

Grade Level

Percents

Different calculators compute percents in various ways. To investigate this, try the following.

6

113. $5(6\%) = ?$ If the following sequence of buttons is pushed, does it work? Is your answer 0.3?

$$\boxed{5}\ \boxed{\times}\ \boxed{6}\ \boxed{\%}\ \boxed{=}$$

6

114. Push $\boxed{6}\ \boxed{\%}\ \boxed{\times}\ \boxed{5}\ \boxed{=}$. Is the answer 0.3?

6

115. Calculate what percent of your television-watching time is taken up by commercials.

6

116. Make a list of your classmates' first names. What percent of the class names begin with a vowel? What percent of the names begin with a consonant?

6

117. Look through the ads in a newspaper and list five items that have been marked down. Compute the discount from the marked price and the original price. Express this savings as a percent.

6

118. Look for newspaper advertisements that make claims like "25% off." Use the calculator to see if the prices are as advertised.

6

119. Sally bought a dress marked "20% off." The regular price was $28.00. What was the sale price?

6

120. What is the sale price of a softball if the regular price is $6.80 and there is a 25% discount?

7

121. Joe weighed 9 pounds when he was born. At 6 months, he weighed 18 pounds. What was the percent of increase in Joe's weight?

7

122. In 1965, there were 728 eagles counted in Glacier Park. Five years later, there were 594 counted. What is the percent of decrease in the number of eagles counted?

8

123. Ms. Jackson borrowed $42 000 at 13% simple interest to buy her house. If she won the Irish Sweepstakes exactly 1 year later and was able to repay the loan without penalty, how much interest did she owe?

8

124. Carolyn went on a shopping spree with her Bankamount card and made purchases totaling $125. If the interest rate is 1.5% per month and she did not pay this debt for one year, how much interest did she owe at the end of the year?

Grade Level   ## Other Application Problems

6–8

125.   At a local bank, two different systems are available for charging for checking accounts. System A is a "dime-a time" plan, as there is no monthly service charge and the charge is 10¢ per check written. System B is a plan with a service charge of 75¢ per month plus 7¢ per check written during that month.
   (a)   Which plan is the most economical if an average of 12 checks per month is written?
   (b)   Which system is the most economical if an average of 52 checks per month is written?
   (c)   What is the "break-even point" as to the number of checks written (that is, the number of checks for which the cost of the two plans are as close as possible)?

6–8

126.   A bank statement from a local bank shows that a checking account has a balance of $83.62. The balance recorded in the checkbook shows only $21.69. After checking the canceled checks against the record of these checks, the customer finds that the bank has not yet recorded six checks in the amounts of $3.21, $14.56, $12.44, $6.98, $9.51, $7.49. Is the bank record correct? (Assume the person's checkbook records *are* correct.)

127.   Sooner or later, most people are faced with the task of buying a number of items at the store, knowing that they have just barely enough money to cover the needed items. In order to avoid the embarrassment of coming up short and having to put some of the items back, they must use their estimating or rounding skills. For each of the following sets of items, estimate the cost. If you are short of funds, tell what must be returned to come just under the allotted amount to be spent.

6–8

(a)   Amount on hand—$2.98
   2 packs of gum at 24¢ ea.
   3 Kojak suckers at 10¢ ea.
   1 licorice at 4 for 20¢
   1 soft drink at 35¢
   1 pack dental floss at 99¢

(b)   Amount on hand—$20.00
   7 gal. gas at $1.089 per gal.
   2 qts. oil at $1.05 per quart
   a car wash at $1.99
   a new headlight at $3.39
   air in a tire at 0¢ lb.
   air freshener at 99¢
   starter fluid at 99¢
   parking ticket at $1.00
   windshield wiper at $1.59
   Coke for your date at 35¢

(c)   Amount on hand—$5.50
   2 hamburgers at $1.45 each
   a double shake at 80¢
   large order fries at 70¢
   popcorn at 75¢
   apple turnover at 40¢
   onion rings at 55¢

(d)   Amount on hand—$10.00
   2 lb. hamburger at $1.89/lb.
   1 loaf French bread at 3 for $2
   1 head lettuce at 3 for $1
   1 package of salad dressing at 2 for $1.89
   6-pack of soft drinks at $1.89
   1 lb. fresh mushrooms at $1.69/lb.

(e)   Amount on hand—$55.00
      3 shirts at $10.89 ea.
      2 pairs socks at 3/$2
      2 ties at 2/$11
      1 pair slacks at $17.99

(f)   Amount on hand—$89¢
      candy bar at 18¢
      kite string at 29¢
      pencil at 7¢
      tablet at 19¢
      eraser at 4¢
      1 Twinkie at 2/25¢

128.   The winner of the big sweepstakes has 15 minutes to decide whether to receive $1 000 000 cash immediately or to receive 1¢ on the first day of the month, 2¢ on the second day, 4¢ on the third, and so on each day receiving double the previous day's amount, until the end of a 30-day month. However, only the amount received on that last day may be kept and all the rest of the month's "allowance" must be returned. Use a calculator to figure which of these two options is more profitable, and figure out *how much* more profitable one way is than the other.

129.   The DEC-20 computer can perform 10 operations in 5 microseconds (1 microsecond is 0.000001 second). How long does it take the computer to do 1 000 000 operations?

130.   Suppose that the price of gold is $605 per ounce and the price of silver is $48 per ounce. Use a calculator to solve each of the following problems.

    (a)   A box is 1 ft × 1 ft × 2 ft. What weight of gold will it hold? What weight of silver will it hold? (*Hint:* Gold weighs 1204 pounds per cubic foot and silver weighs 655 pounds per cubic foot.)

    (b)   How much is a cubic foot of gold worth? How much is a cubic foot of silver worth?

    (c)   A box 1 ft × 2 ft × 2 ft is full of gold. How much is the gold worth? If it was full of silver, how much would the silver be worth?

Grade Level   **Other Problems**

131.   In a Math 131 class at DiPaloma University, the grades on the first exam were as follows:

$$
\begin{array}{ccccccc}
96 & 71 & 43 & 77 & 75 & 76 & 61 \\
83 & 71 & 58 & 97 & 76 & 74 & 91 \\
74 & 71 & 77 & 83 & 87 & 93 & 79
\end{array}
$$

    (a)   Find the mean average

$$\left(\overline{x} = \frac{x_1 + x_2 + \ldots + x_n}{n} \right)$$

    (b)   Find the median score.

    (c)   Find the mode.

    (d)   Find the variance of the scores if

$$v = \frac{(x_1 - \overline{x})^2 + (x_2 - \overline{x})^2 + \ldots + (x_n - \overline{x})^2}{n}$$

    (e)   Find the standard deviation of the scores if $s = \sqrt{v}$.

6–8

6–8

6–8

8

132. Recall that π is an irrational number that can be approximated by a decimal. One way to find an approximation for π is to use the sequence given by

$$\frac{\pi^2}{6} = 1 + \frac{1}{2^2} + \frac{1}{3^2} + \frac{1}{4^2} + \frac{1}{5^2} + \cdots ,$$

7–8

and then compute π as

$$\sqrt{6\left(1 + \frac{1}{2^2} + \frac{1}{3^2} + \frac{1}{4^2} + \frac{1}{5^2} + \cdots\right)}$$

  (a)   Find an approximation of π using the first 20 terms.
  (b)   Compare the answer in (a) to 22/7, which is often used as a value for π.

7–8

133. Given that the measures of the sides of a triangle are 24 cm, 26 cm, and 28 cm, can the triangle be a right triangle? (Recall the Pythagorean theorem, $a^2 + b^2 = c^2$.)

AII-2 USE OF FLOWCHARTS

To work a complicated problem in mathematics successfully requires an organized plan of attack. There are many ways to organize the processes necessary to do a problem. One of the most fundamental methods for use with **flowchart**   calculators or computers is the construction of a **flowchart**. A flowchart is a schematic step-by-step procedure for solving a problem using the geometric diagrams like the ones in Figure AII-1.

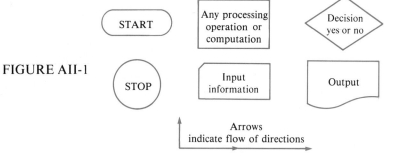

FIGURE AII-1

The flowchart in Figure AII-2 organizes the steps for sharpening a pencil.

1. Given a pencil and a sharpener.
2. Put pencil in sharpener.
3. Turn handle clockwise.
4. Take pencil out.
5. Is pencil sharp? If yes, go to Step 6, if no, go to Step 2.
6. Stop.

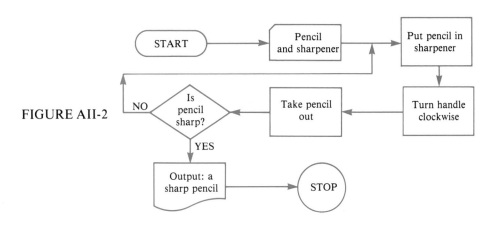

FIGURE AII-2

The flowchart in Figure AII-2 contains two important parts, subroutine and loop, that should be noted. Consider the first processing diagram.

Put pencil in sharpener

subroutine

loop

This diagram assumes that the user of the flowchart can determine which end of the pencil goes in the sharpener and that the user can decide where to insert the pencil into the sharpener. This capability of the user, which has been assumed, is called a **subroutine.** If the flowchart user cannot complete the subroutines in the diagram, then the flowchart may have to be rewritten.

The flowchart in Figure AII-2 also illustrates a **loop.** The loop is used each time the decision, the pencil is *not* sharp, is made. This loop might be used several times before the pencil is sufficiently sharp and a different branch of the flowchart is reached. A flowchart may or may not contain a loop.

Example AII-1

Arrange the following steps for preparing gelatin into a flowchart.

1. Ingredients: One package of gelatin, boiling water, bowl, spoon.
2. Put gelatin in bowl.
3. Put 1 cup of boiling water in bowl.
4. Stir contents of bowl for 3 minutes.
5. Is gelatin dissolved? If yes, go to Step 6. If no, go to Step 4.
6. Add 1 cup of cold water.
7. Refrigerate for 30 minutes.

8.   Remove bowl from refrigerator.
9.   Is gelatin set? If yes, go to Step 10. If no, go to Step 7.
10. Gelatin is set.

Solution | Figure AII-3 shows the solution.

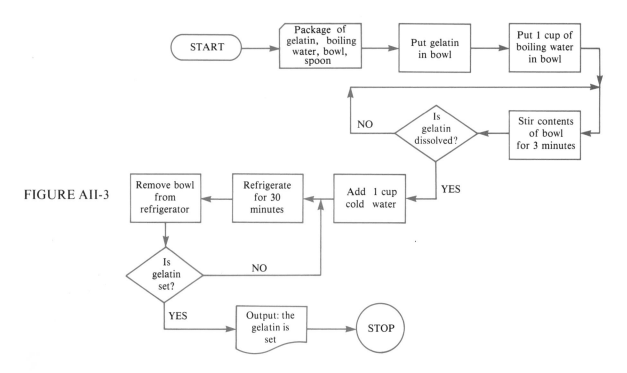

FIGURE AII-3

Example AII-2 | Arrange the diagrams in Figure AII-4 into a flowchart for deciding which of two distinct numbers is larger.

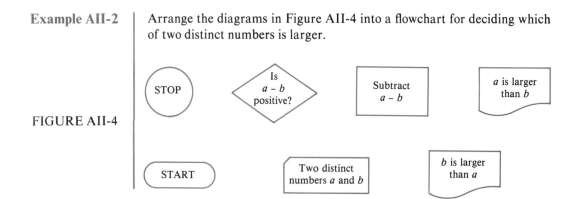

FIGURE AII-4

Solution   Figure AII-5 shows the solution.

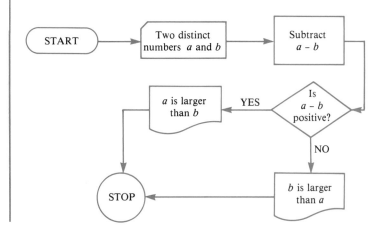

FIGURE AII-5

The flowchart in Figure AII-6 is important in mathematics. The flowchart pictured is for assigning the absolute value to any integer. (This topic is treated in Chapter 4.)

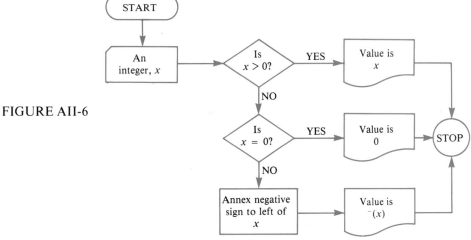

FIGURE AII-6

Example AII-3   Use the flowchart in Figure AII-6 to solve each of the following.

(a) Find the absolute value of 5.
(b) Find the absolute value of 0.
(c) Find the absolute value of $^-5$.

Solution   (a) 5   (b) 0   (c) $^-(^-5)$

PROBLEM SET AII-2

1. Follow the accompanying flowchart. Input various values to see if the result is always the same.

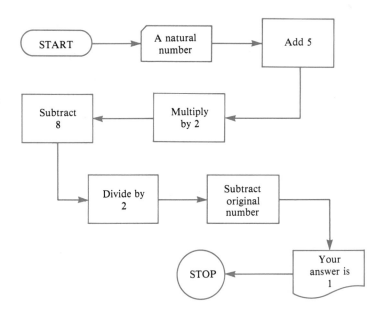

2. Organize the following steps into a flowchart for placing a phone call to a friend.

    Look up number.
    Lift receiver.
    Wait for dial tone.
    Dial number.
    Is there a busy signal?
    If so, hang up.
    If not, does anyone answer?
    If not, hang up.
    If so, is it your friend?
    If yes, have conversation; then hang up.
    If no, can the friend be called to the phone?
    If yes, have friend called to phone; have conversation; then hang up.
    If no, hang up.

3. Page 615 shows a chapter review page from *The Random House Mathematics Program,* Grade 8. Complete all the exercises.

CHAPTER REVIEW

1. Make a flow chart that lists in proper order the steps for putting on shoes and socks.

PUT FEET INTO SHOES
PUT ON SOCKS
STOP
TIE SHOESTRINGS
START

2. Make a flow chart for solving the equation $3n - 5 = 13$.

3. Copy and complete the flow chart, placing in proper order these steps for eating a candy bar.

REMOVE WRAPPER
STOP
CHEW AND SWALLOW
TAKE A BITE
DOES SOME OF BAR
  REMAIN?

4. By placing these steps in order, make a flow chart for arranging six objects into three rows of two objects.

ARE THERE THREE ROWS
  OF TWO OBJECTS?
PUT OBJECT IN A FIRST
  POSITION
STOP
PUT OBJECT IN A SECOND
  POSITION
START

5. What is wrong with this flow chart for rounding to the nearest whole number?

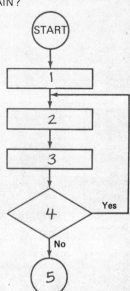

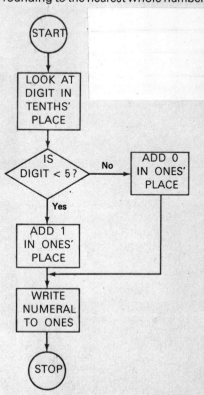

4. Determine what the accompanying flowchart does. What should be in the blank in the output statement?

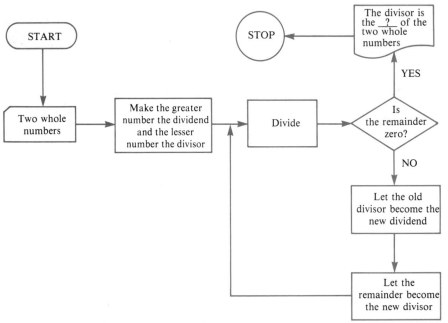

5. The accompanying flowchart is for the addition of two two-digit numbers. Use it to add 94 and 89 and tell what happens at each step.

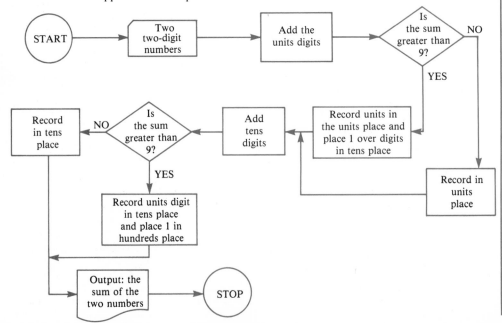

6. Extend the flowchart in Problem 5 to add two three-digit numbers.

SELECTED BIBLIOGRAPHY

Ahl, D. H. (ed.). *The Best of Creative Computing.* Vol. 1. Vol. 2. Morristown, N.J.: Creative Computing Press, 1976 and 1977.

Aidala, G. "Calculators: Their Use in the Classroom." *School Science and Mathematics,* **78**(April 1978):307–311.

Aidala, G., and P. Rosenfeld. "Calculators in the Classroom." *The Mathematics Teacher.* **71**(May 1978):434–435.

Aviv, C. A. "Pattern Gazing." *The Mathematics Teacher.* **72**(January 1979):39–43.

Bell, M. S. "Calculators in Elementary Schools? Some Tentative Guidelines and Questions Based on Classroom Experience." *The Arithmetic Teacher,* **23**(November 1976):502–509.

Billstein, R., and J. W. Lott. "When Does a Fraction Yield a Terminating Decimal?" *Calculators/Computers,* **2**(January 1978):15–19.

Bitter, G. G., and T. H. Metos. *Exploring with Pocket Calculators.* New York: Julian Messner, (Distributed by Simon and Schuster), 1977.

Boyle, P. J. "Calculator Charades." *The Mathematics Teacher,* **69**(April 1976):281–282.

Bright, G. "Ideas." *Arithmetic Teacher,* **25**(February 1978):28–32.

Bruni, J. V. and H. J. Silverman. "Let's Do It!—Taking Advantage of the Hand Calculator." *The Arithmetic Teacher,* **23**(November 1976):494–501.

Buckwalter, L. *100 Ways to Use Your Pocket Calculator.* Greenwich, Conn.: Fawcett Publications, 1975.

Caravella, J. R. *Minicalculators in the Classroom.* Washington, D.C.: National Education Association, 1977.

Davidson, J. *Let's Start to Calculate.* New Rochelle, N.Y.: Cuisenaire Company of America, 1976.

DeMent, G. *Calculator Capers: An Introduction to the Calculator for Primary Grades.* Englewood Cliffs, N.J.: Prentice Hall Learning Systems, Inc., 1977.

Denman, T. "Calculators in Grades K–3: Why? What? How?" *Calculator Information Center,* **6**(January 1979).

Dolan, D. T. *Let's Calculate.* San Leandro, Calif.: Lakeshore Curriculum Materials Co., 1976.

Drake, P. M. "Calculators in the Elementary Classroom." *Arithmetic Teacher,* **25**(March 1978):47–48.

Fisher, B. "Calculator Games: Combining Skills and Problem Solving." *Arithmetic Teacher,* **27**(December 1979):40–41.

Gardner, M. "Mathematical Games: Fun and Serious Business with the Small Electronic Calculator." *Scientific American,* **335**(July 1976):126–129.

Gawronski, J. D. "Leading a Calculator Workshop." *Calculator Information Center,* **5**(December 1979).

Gawronski, J. D., and D. Coblentz. "Calculators and the Mathematics Curriculum." *The Arithmetic Teacher,* **23**(November 1976):510–512.

Gibb, E. G. "Calculators in the Classroom." *Today's Education,* **64**(November–December 1975):42–44.

Goodhue, J. F. "Calculator Crossword Puzzle." *The Mathematics Teacher,* **71**(April 1978):279–282.

Gregory, J. "Santa Takes a Calculated Risk." *The Mathematics Student,* **22**(December 1974):1–2.

Hallerberg, A. E. "Squaring the Circle—For Fun and Profit." *The Mathematics Teacher,* **71**(April 1978):247–255.

Hobbs, B. F., and C. H. Burvis. "Minicalculators and Repeating Decimals." *Arithmetic Teacher,* **25**(April 1978):18–20.

Immerzeel, G. "It's in Your Hands." *The Arithmetic Teacher,* **23**(November 1976):493.

Immerzeel, G. *Ideas and Activities for Using Calculators in the Classroom.* Dansville, N. Y.: The Instructor Publications, Inc., 1976.

Jones, M. H., and R. C. Bosley. "Calculators and Instruction: An Information Bulletin for Administrators." *Calculator Information Center,* **4**(December 1978).

Judd, W. *Games Calculators Play.* New York: Warner Books, 1975.

Judd, W. *Games, Tricks, and Puzzles for a Hand Calculator.* Menlo Park, Calif.: Dymax, 1974.

Judd, W. "Instructional Games with Calculators." *The Arithmetic Teacher,* **23**(November 1976):516–518.

Judd, W. "Rx for Classroom Math Blahs: A New

Case for the Calculator." *Learning,* **3**(March 1975):41–48.

Kerr, S. D. "Who Is Quickest with Mind and Fingers?" *The Mathematics Teacher,* **72**(February 1979):123–126.

Keller, C. "Using Tables to Teach Mathematics." *The Mathematics Teacher,* **71**(November 1978):655–656.

Lappan, G., and M. J. Winter. "A Calculator Activity That Teaches Mathematics." *Arithmetic Teacher,* **25**(April 1978):21–23.

Lazarus, M. "Reckoning with Calculators." *National Elementary Principal,* **7**(January 1978):71–77.

Meyer, P. I. "When You Use a Calculator You Have to Think!" *Arithmetic Teacher,* **27**(January 1980):18–21.

Michelow, J. S., and B. R. Vogeli. "The New World of Calculator Functions." *School Science and Mathematics,* **78**(March 1978):248–254.

Morris, J. "More About Repeating Decimals." *Calculators/Computers,* **2**(April 1978):64–68.

Morris, J. "Problem Solving with Calculators." *Arithmetic Teacher,* **25**(April 1978):24–26.

Moursund, D. *Calculators, Computers, and Elementary Education for Teacher Education.* Salem, Ore.: The Math Learning Center, 1977.

Munson, H. R. "Your District Needs a Policy on Pocket Calculators!" *The Arithmetic Teacher,* **25**(October 1977):46.

"Minicalculators in Schools." *The Arithmetic Teacher,* **23**(January 1976), 72–74. *The Mathematics Teacher* **69**(January 1976):92–94.

National Council of Teachers of Mathematics *NCTM.* "Position Statements: Use of Minicalculators." *The Mathematics Teacher,* **71**(May 1978):468.

Nicolai, M. B. "Sum of the Integers." *The Mathematics Teacher,* **71**(April 1978):271–273.

Number Sense and Arithmetic Skills. Palo Alto, Calif.: Creative Publications, 1977.

Ockenga, E. "Calculator Ideas for the Junior High Classroom." *The Arithmetic Teacher,* **23**(November 1976):519–522.

Ockenga, E., and J. Duea. "Ideas." *Arithmetic Teacher,* **25**(May 1978):28–32.

Ockenga, E., and J. Duea. "Ideas." *Arithmetic Teacher,* **26**(January 1979):28–32.

Palmer, H. B. A. "Minicalculators in the Classroom—What Do Teachers Think?" *Arithmetic Teacher,* **25**(April 1978):27–28.

Pollak, H. O. "Hand-Held Calculators and Potential Redesign of the School Mathematics Curriculum." *The Mathematics Teacher,* **70**(April 1977):293–296.

Prigge, G., and J. D. Gawronski. *Calculator Activities.* Big Spring, Texas: Math-Master, 1978.

Report of the Conference on Needed Research and Development on Hand-Held Calculators in School Mathematics. National Institute of Education and National Science Foundation, 1977.

Reys, R. E., et al. *Keystrokes: Calculator Activities for Young Students: Addition and Subtraction.* Palo Alto, Calif.: Creative Publications, 1979.

Riden, C. "Less Than Ten on a Calculator." *School Science and Mathematics,* **75**(October 1975):529–531.

Rising, G. R., B. J. Krist, C. Roesch, and W. Jewell. *Using Calculators in Mathematics.* National Institute of Education Contract No. 400-78-0013. State University of New York at Buffalo, 1978.

Schmalz, R. "Calculator Capers." *The Mathematics Teacher,* **71**(May 1978):439–442.

Schmalz, R. "Calculators: What Difference Will They Make?" *Arithmetic Teacher,* **26**(December 1978):46–47.

Schultz, J. E. "How Calculators Give Rise to a New Need for Skills in Algebra." *School Science and Mathematics,* **78**(February 1978):131–134.

Schultz, J. E. "Using a Calculator to Do Arithmetic in Bases Other Than Ten." *Arithmetic Teacher,* **26**(September 1978):25–27.

Sharp, J. N. C. *The Calculator Workbox.* Reading, Mass.: Addison-Wesley, 1977.

Suydam, M. N. *Electronic Hand Calculators: The Implications for Pre-College Education.* Final Report, Grant No. EPP 75-16157, National Science Foundation, February 1976.

Teitelbaum, E. "Calculators for Classroom Use?" *Arithmetic Teacher,* **26**(November 1978):18–20.

Usiskin, Z. "Are Calculators a Crutch?" *The Mathematics Teacher,* **71**(May 1978):412–413.

Wagner, S. "Fun with Repeating Decimals." *The Mathematics Teacher,* **72**(March 1979):209–212.

Waits, B. K. "Using a Calculator to Find Rational Roots." *The Mathematics Teacher,* **71**(May 1978):418–419.

Woodburn, D. "Can You Predict the Repetend?" *The Mathematics Teacher,* **69**(December 1976):675–678.

Zakariya, N., M. McClung, and A. A. Warner. "The Calculator in the Classroom." *Arithmetic Teacher* **28**(March 1980):12–16.

Answers to the Odd-numbered Problems

CHAPTER 1

Problem Set 1-1

1. **(a)** 22, 26, 30   **(b)** 25, 30, 35   **(c)** $5 \times 6, 6 \times 7$, 7×8 **(d)** 000000, □□□□□□□, 00000000   **(e)** 45, 41, 37   **(f)** 15, 20, 26   **(g)** 26, 37, 50   **(h)** 1/16, 1/32, 1/64   **(i)** X, Y, X (answers vary)   **(j)** 1, 18, 1   **(k)** 8, 13, 21   **3.** **(a)** 299, 447, 664   **(b)** 56, 72, 90   **(c)** 108, 190, 304   **5.** **(a)** $1 + (n - 1)2$ or $2n - 1$ **(b)** $2n$ **(c)** $9 + (n - 1)4$ or $4n + 5$ **(d)** n^3 **(e)** $2 \cdot 3^{n-1}$ **7.** **(a)** 3, 6, 11, 18, 27   **(b)** 4, 9, 14, 19, 24

Problem Set 1-2

1. None. There is no dirt in a hole.   **3.** 1 hour: clock can't tell A.M. and P.M.   **5.** 3

7.

9. 1 hour, 20 minutes = 80 minutes.   **11.** There is no extra dollar since there is no reason for the second column to add to $50.   **13.** Yes: same answer. It has the advantage of working with an even or odd number of numbers.   **15.** $1.19: one 50¢, one 25¢, four 10¢, and four 1¢.   **17.** 325   **19.** 12   **21.** 5 inches   **23.** 10 boys, 12 dogs   **25.** 16 days   **27.** 1, Applejack; 2, Null Set; 3, Fast Jack; 4, Lookout; 5, Bent Leg.   **29.** **(a)** 11   **(b)** 63   **31.** No. To do so each domino must cover a black and a white square. Since there are only 30 white squares while there are 32 black squares, this is impossible.

CHAPTER 2

Problem Set 2-1

1. (c) and (d) are well defined; (a) and (b) are not.   **3.** **(a)** $B = \{x, y, z, w\}$ **(b)** $3 \notin B$ **(c)** $\{1, 2\} \subset \{1, 2, 3, 4\}$ **(d)** $D \not\subseteq E$ **5.** **(a)** $\not\subseteq$,   **(b)** $\not\subseteq$,   **(c)** $\not\subseteq$,   **(d)** $\not\subseteq$,   **(e)** $\subseteq$,   **(f)** $\not\subseteq$,   **(g)** $\subseteq$,   **(h)** $\subseteq$,   **(i)** $\not\subseteq$,   **(j)** $\not\subseteq$.   **7.** **(a)** $S = \{x \mid x$ is a state in the United States$\}$ **(b)** $E = \{x \mid x$ is an elementary teacher$\}$ **9.** $2^n - 1$ **11.** One if $B = \emptyset$.   **13.** No. $\emptyset \not\subseteq \emptyset$.   **15.** **(a)** T.   **(b)** F. $\{\emptyset\}$ has one element and hence it is not empty.   **(c)** T.   **(d)** F. A could equal B.   **(e)** T.   **(f)** F. Suppose $A = \{1\}$ and $B = \{1, 2\}$, then $A \subseteq B$ but $A \neq B$.

Problem Set 2-2

1. **(a)** $\{f, i, n, a, l, s, r, e\}$ **(b)** $\{a\}$ **(c)** $\{o, v, e, r\}$ or C **(d)** $\emptyset$ **(e)** $\{f, i, n, a, l, s, o, v, e, r\}$ **(f)** $\{a\}$ **(g)** $\{f, i, n, a, l, s, o, v, e, r\}$ or U **(h)** $\emptyset$ **(i)** $\{o, v\}$ **(j)** $\{f, i, n, l, s, o, v, e, r\}$ **3.** **(a)** B **(b)** A **5.** **(a)** $B - A$ or $B \cap \overline{A}$ **(b)** $\overline{A \cup B}$ or $\overline{A} \cap \overline{B}$ **(c)** $A \cap B \cap C$ **(d)** $A \cap B$ **(e)** $(A \cap C) - B$ or $(A \cap C) \cap \overline{B}$ **(f)** $(A - B) \cup (C - B) \cup (A \cap C)$ **7.** **(a)** U **(b)** U **(c)** S **(d)** $\emptyset$ **(e)** S **(f)** U **(g)** $\emptyset$ **(h)** S **(i)** $\overline{S}$ **(j)** S **9.** **(a)** A **(b)** $\emptyset$ **(c)** $\emptyset$ **(d)** $\emptyset$

11. **(a)**
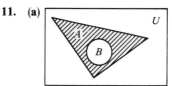

(b)

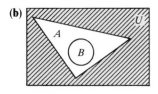

(c)

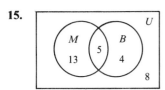

13.   (a) is the set of all students at Paxson School taking band but not choir. (b) is the set of all students at Paxson taking both band and choir. (c) is the set of all students at Paxson taking choir but not band. (d) is the set of all students at Paxson taking neither choir or band.

15.

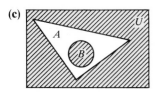

4 have a class in biology but not mathematics.

17.

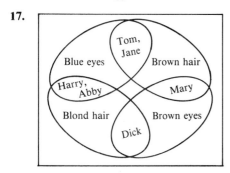

The two families are Tom, Jane, Mary and Abby, Harry, Dick.

Problem Set 2-3

1.   **(a)** Not equal, examples vary. The following Venn diagrams show that in general the expressions are not equal.

(b)

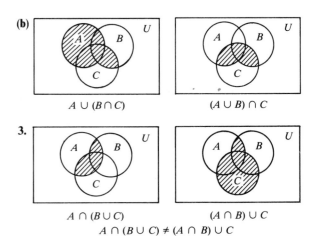

$A \cup (B \cap C)$ $(A \cup B) \cap C$

3.

$A \cap (B \cup C)$ $(A \cap B) \cup C$
$A \cap (B \cup C) \neq (A \cap B) \cup C$

5.   **(a)** T   **(b)** F   **(c)** F   **7.**   **(a)** Equal
(b) Equal   **(c)** Equal   **(d)** Not equal   **(e)** Not equal   **(f)** Equal   **9.** $A = B$

Problem Set 2-4

1.   Only the pairs (a) and (c).   **3.** $4 \cdot 3 \cdot 2 \cdot 1 = 24$, $5 \cdot 4 \cdot 3 \cdot 2 \cdot 1 = 120$, $n(n - 1)(n - 2) \cdot \ldots \cdot 3 \cdot 2 \cdot 1$
5.   **(a)** $\{1, 3, 5, 9, \ldots, 2n - 1, \ldots\}$
$\qquad \updownarrow \updownarrow \updownarrow \updownarrow \qquad\quad \updownarrow$
$\qquad \{3, 5, 7, 11, \ldots, 2n + 1, \ldots\}$

(b) $\{100, 101, 102, 103, \ldots, n + 99, \ldots\}$
$\qquad \updownarrow \ \ \updownarrow \ \ \updownarrow \ \ \updownarrow \qquad\quad \updownarrow$
$\qquad \{101, 102, 103, 104, \ldots, n + 100, \ldots\}$

7.   **(a)** Cardinal   **(b)** Ordinal   **(c)** Ordinal
(d) Cardinal   **(e)** Cardinal and then ordinal.

Problem Set 2-5

1.   **(a)** $\{(x, a), (x, b), (x, c), (y, a), (y, b), (y, c)\}$
(b) $\{(0, a), (0, b) (0, c)\}$ **(c)** $\{(a, x), (a, y), (b, x),$
$(b, y), (c, x), (c, y)\}$ **(d)** $\varnothing$ **(e)** $\{(0, 0)\}$ **(f)** $\varnothing$
(g) $\{(x, 0), (y, 0), (a, 0), (b, 0), (c, 0)\}$ **(h)** $\{(x, 0),$
$(y, 0), (a, 0), (b, 0), (c, 0)\}$ **(i)** $\varnothing$ **(j)** $\varnothing$
3.   **(a)** 3   **(b)** 6   **(c)** 9   **(d)** 20   **(e)** $m \cdot n$
(f) $m \cdot n \cdot p$ **5.** 5   **7.** 12   **9.** 60
11.   **(a)** $\{(x, y) \mid y = x^2\}$, ordered pairs vary.
(b) $\{(x, y) \mid x$ is the wife of $y\}$ **(c)** $\{(x, y) \mid x$ is the small printed letter in the English alphabet and y is the corresponding printed capital letter$\}$ **(d)** $\{(x, y) \mid y$ is the cost of x candies$\}$ **13.**   **(a)** $3n - 1$ **(b)** $n^2 + 1$

(c) $n \cdot (n + 1)$ or $n^2 + n$ **15. (c)** Domain = $\{1, 2, 3\}$ Range = $\{a, b\}$ **17. (a)** 5 **(b)** 11 **(c)** 35 **(d)** $3a + 5$ **19.** Answers vary. For example,

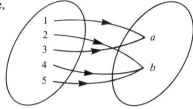

Problem Set 2-6

1. (a) None of the properties hold. **(b)** Reflexive, symmetric, and transitive, and thus an equivalence relation. **(c)** Reflexive, symmetric, and transitive, and thus an equivalence relation. **(d)** Symmetric and transitive. **(e)** Reflexive, symmetric, and transitive, and thus an equivalence relation. **(f)** Symmetric **3. (a)** Reflexive and transitive **(b)** Symmetric **(c)** Reflexive, symmetric, and transitive **5. (a)** {Abe, Aza}, {Ben, Betty}, {Carolyn}, {Doug, Dax}, {George}, {Laura}, {Mike, Mary}, {Sue}, {Zachary} **(b)** {Abe, George, Sue, Mike}, {Laura, Aza}, {Ben, Carolyn}, {Betty, Zachary, Mary}, {Dax}, {Doug} **(c)** {Abe, Ben, Sue, Dax, Aza}, {Doug, Mike, Mary}, {Laura, Betty}, {George}, {Zachary, Carolyn}

Chapter Test

1. (a) $\{a, b, c, d, e\}$ **(b)** $\{x \mid x$ is one of the first five letters of the English alphabet} **3. (a)** $\overline{A}$ is a person living in Montana who is less than 30 years old. **(b)** $A \cap C$ is a person living in Montana. **(c)** $A \cup B$ is a person living in Montana. **(d)** $\overline{C}$ is a person living in Montana who doesn't own a gun. **(e)** $\overline{A \cap C}$ is a person living in Montana younger than 30 or who doesn't own a gun.

5. (a)   **(b)**

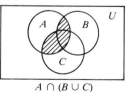   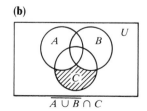

$A \cap (B \cup C)$ $\overline{A \cup B} \cap C$

7. $2^6 - 1 = 63$
9. $A \cap (B \cup C) \neq (A \cap B) \cup C$

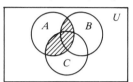   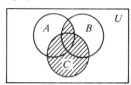

11. (a) This is a function from $\{a, c, e, f\}$ to $\{b, d, a, g\}$. **(b)** This is not a function since the elements a and b are paired with more than one element. **(c)** This is a function from $\{a, b\}$ to $\{a, b\}$. **13. (a)** $\{3, 4, 5, 6\}$ **(b)** $\{14, 29, 44, 59\}$ **(c)** $\{0, 1, 4, 9, 16\}$ **(d)** $\{5, 9, 15\}$ **15. (a)** F. Suppose $A = \{1\}$ and $B = \{a\}$. Then $A \not\subset B$ and $B \not\subset A$. **(b)** F. It is not a proper subset of itself. **(c)** F. Suppose $A = \{1, 2\}$ and $B = \{a, b\}$. Then $A \sim B$ but $A \neq B$. **(d)** F. It is an infinite set. **(e)** F. Infinite sets are equivalent to proper subsets of themselves **(f)** F. Consider $A = \{1, 2, 3, 4, \ldots\}$ and $B = \{1, 2\}$. $B \subset A$ and B is finite. **(g)** T **(h)** F. Consider $A = \{1, 2\}$ and $B = \{a\}$. $A \cap B = \emptyset$. **(i)** F. $\emptyset$ has no elements. **(j)** T

CHAPTER 3

Problem Set 3-1

1. (a) ▼ ▼ < ▼ ▼; 𓀀 𓀀 𓀀 ??? ∩∩∩ ∩∩∩ ‖; MMMDCLXXII

(b) 602; ??? ‖ ; DCII

(c) 1223; << <<▼▼▼; MCCXXIII

(d) 1667; << ▼▼▼▼ ▼▼▼ << ▼▼▼▼ << ▼▼▼ ; 𓀀 ??? ∩∩∩ ∩∩∩ ‖‖‖‖ ‖‖‖

3. (a) MCML; MCMXLVIII **(b)** $\overline{\text{MII}}$; $\overline{\text{M}}$ **(c)** M; CMXCVIII **(d)** << <▼▼; << <

(e) 𓀀 ?? |; 𓀀 ꝯ ∩∩∩∩∩ ‖‖‖‖‖ ∩∩∩∩ ‖‖‖‖

5. (a) Hundreds **(b)** Tens **(c)** Thousands **(d)** Hundred thousands **(e)** Ten thousands **(f)** Hundred thousands **7.** Discussion should include place value, the number of symbols used, and the use of a symbol for 0.

Problem Set 3-2

1.   5 is farther to left on number line than 7. 6 is farther to right on number line than 3.   **3.**   No. If $k = 0$, we would have $k = 0 + k$ implying $k > k$.

5.

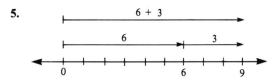

7. **(a)** No. $1 + 1 \notin A$.   **(b)** Yes   **(c)** Yes
(d) Yes   **(e)** No. $1 + 3 \notin R$.   **(f)** Yes
9. **(a)** "Siamese cat show" versus "Siamese show cat."   **(b)** "Going to school I saw the kids" versus "I saw the kids going to school."
11.

	0	1	2	3	4	5	6
0	0	1	2	3	4	5	6
1	1	2	3	4	5	6	10
2	2	3	4	5	6	10	11
3	3	4	5	6	10	11	12
4	4	5	6	10	11	12	13
5	5	6	10	11	12	13	14
6	6	10	11	12	13	14	15

Problem Set 3-3

1.

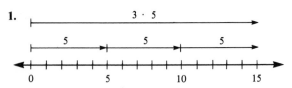

3. $16.00   **5.** $8 \cdot 3 = (6 + 2) \cdot 3$
$$= 6 \cdot 3 + 2 \cdot 3$$
$$= 18 + 6 = 24$$

7. **(a)** 303   **(b)** 24   **(c)** $ac + ad + bc + bd$
(d) $3x + 3y + 15$ **(e)** $\Box \triangle + \Box \bigstar$ **(f)** $x^2 + xy + xz + yx + y^2 + yz$ or $x^2 + 2xy + xz + y^2 + yz$
(g) $x^2 + 2xy + 2xz + y^2 + 2yz + z^2$ **9.** **(a)** $5x$
(b) $14x$ **(c)** $5(x + 1)$ or $5x + 5$ **(d)** $a(b + 1)$
(e) $m(b + c + 1)$ **(f)** $(2 + x)(x + 3)$ **11.**   No. When $a = 0$ and b and c are any values.
13. **(a)** **(i)** $a^2 + ab + ba + b^2 = a^2 + 2ab + b^2$
(ii) 1508

(b) $(m + n)(x + y) = (m + n)x + (m + n)y$
$$= (mx + nx) + (my + ny)$$
$$= mx + (nx + my) + ny$$
$$= mx + my + nx + ny$$

Problem Set 3-4

1.

$$\begin{array}{c} 3\ 7\ 8\ 9 \\ 9_3 2_1 9_8 6_5 \\ 6\ 8\ 4_2 3 \\ \hline 1\ 9\ 9\ 2\ 8 \end{array}$$

3.   The columns separate place value and show that $7 + 8 = 15$ and $20 + 60 = 80$. Finally, $15 + 80 = 95$.
5.   Diagonals separate place value as placement does in the traditional algorithm.

7. **(a)**
$$\begin{array}{r} 4\ 2\ 6 \\ \times\ 7\ 8\ 3 \\ \hline 1\ 2\ 7\ 8 \\ 3\ 4\ 0\ 8 \\ 2\ 9\ 8\ 2 \\ \hline 3\ 3\ 3\ 5\ 5\ 8 \end{array}$$
(b)
$$\begin{array}{r} 3\ 2\ 7 \\ +\ 9\ 8\ 1 \\ \hline 1\ 3\ 0\ 8 \end{array}$$

9.   Answers will vary.

11. **(a)**

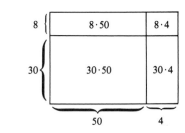

(c)

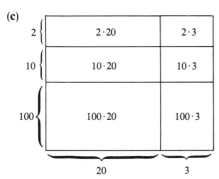

20   3

13. **(a)** $293 \cdot 476 = 139\,468$ **(b)** Placement still indicates place value.

(c)
```
   3 6 3
 ×  8 4
 ─────────
 2 9 0 4
 1 4 5 2
 ─────────
 3 0 4 9 2
```

15. $2^2 + 2^3 = 4 + 8 = 12$ but $2^{2+3} = 2^5 = 32$.

Problem Set 3-5
1. **(a)** 3   **(b)** 3   **(c)** 13   **(d)** a **(e)** 0   **(f)** $\{3, 4, 5, 6, 7, 8, 9\}$ **(g)** $\{10, 11, 12, \ldots\}$ **3.** **(a)** $x = 119 + 213$ **(b)** $213 = x + 119$ **(c)** $213 = 119 + x$
5. It is a different approach to subtraction, but the number of balloons left after the one-to-one correspondence is made is the difference.
7. **(a)** $a = b$ **(b)** $c = 0$ **(c)** $a = 0$ **(d)** All whole numbers values of a, b, and c for which $b - c$ is meaningful.   **9.** **(a)** $40 = 8 \cdot 5$ **(b)** $362 = 2 \cdot x$
(c) $48 = x \cdot 16$ **(d)** $x = 5 \cdot 17$ **(e)** $a = b \cdot c$
(f) $(48 - 36) = 6x$
11. **(a)** $a = b \neq 0$ **(b)** $b \neq 0$ **(c)** $b \neq 0$
(d) $b \neq 0$ **13.** \$32   **15.** 2; 3 left.
17. **(a)**

□	△
0	34
1	26
2	18
3	10
4	2

(b) △ = 66

(c)

□	△
25	1
5	1
1	5
1	25

19. See answers in Appendix II.

Problem Set 3-6
1. **(a)** $1 + 20 + 336 = 357$
Check: $357 + 79 = 436$
(b) $1 + 900 + 1 = 902$
Check: $902 + 99 = 1001$
3. **(a)** 7 tens   **(b)** 20 tens   **5.** Yes. No. Not all at dinner.   **7.** 12 km   **9.** Yes, because a subtraction such as $a - b$ becomes $(a + 10^n) - (b + 10^n)$.

Problem Set 3-7
1. **(a)** 1, 10, 11, 100, 101, 110, 111, 1000, 1001, 1010, 1011, 1100, 1101, 1110, 1111   **(b)** 1, 2, 10, 11, 12, 20, 21, 22, 100, 101, 102, 110, 111, 112, 120   **(c)** 1, 2, 3, 10, 11, 12, 13, 20, 21, 22, 23, 30, 31, 32, 33   **(d)** 1, 2, 3, 4, 5, 6, 7, 10, 11, 12, 13, 14, 15, 16, 17   **3.** 20
5. **(a)** 3212   **(b)** 1177   **(c)** 12 110   **(d)** 100 101
(e) 1 431 304   **(f)** 1E3T4   **(g)** 9000E0
7. **(a)** 6   **(b)** 1   **(c)** 9   **9.** 1 hour 34 minutes 15 seconds   **11.** 4; 1, 2, 4, 8; 5; 1, 2, 4, 8, 16.

Problem Set 3-8
1. **(a)** 2144   **(b)** 121_{five} **(c)** 14_{five} **(d)** 14_{five}
(e) 11_{two} **(f)** $1E16_{\text{twelve}}$ **3.** **(a)** 9 hours 33 minutes 25 seconds   **(b)** 1 hour 39 minutes 40 seconds
5. **(a)** nine   **(b)** four   **(c)** six   **(d)** Any base greater than or equal to 2.

Chapter Test
1. **(a)** 400 044   **(b)** 117   **(c)** 1704   **(d)** 11
(e) 1448   **3.** **(a)** 3^{17} **(b)** 2^{21} **(c)** 3^5 **5.** **(a)** $3 < 13$ since $3 + 10 = 13$.   **(b)** $12 > 9$ since $12 = 9 + 3$.   **7.** **(a)** 1119   **(b)** $173E_{\text{twelve}}$ **9.** **(a)** 5 R 243
(b) 91 R 10   **11.** **(a)** 3 tens   **(b)** 3 thousands
(c) 3 hundreds

13. **(a)**

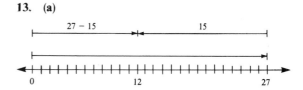

(b)

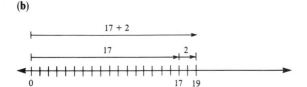

15. (a) Addition, 25   (b) Division, 8
(c) Multiplication, 72   (d) Subtraction, $26.

CHAPTER 4

Problem Set 4-1

1. (a) $^-2$ (b) 5   (c) ^-m (d) 0   (e) m
(f) $^-(a + b)$ **3.** (a) 7   (b) $^-2$ (c) 0   (d) 0
(e) $^-10$ (f) 2   (g) 2   **5.** (a) $^-17 + 10 = ^-7$
(b) $^-10 + 8 = ^-2$ (c) $5000 + ^-100 = 4900$
(d) $^-200 + 100 + ^-50 = ^-150$ (e) $^-2 + 7 + 0 +$
$^-8 = ^-3$ **7.** (a) 5   (b) 10   (c) 3   (d) 7
(e) $^-5$ **9.** (a) $^-9$ (b) $^-10$ (c) 13   (d) $^-4$
11. (a) $^-9$ (b) 3   (c) 1   (d) $^-19$
13. (a) Yes   (b) Yes   **15.** (a) 5   (b) 5
(c) 0   (d) $^-7$

Problem Set 4-2

1. (a) 12   (b) $^-15$ (c) $^-15$ (d) 0   (e) 30
(f) $^-30$ (g) 0   (h) 16   (i) 30   **3.** (a) $^-10$
(b) $^-40$ (c) a if $b \neq 0$ (d) $^-10$ (e) a if $b \neq 0$
(f) $^-32$ (g) $^-5$ (h) 0   (i) Impossible   (j) $^-4$
(k) Impossible   (l) 13   (m) $^-1$ (n) $^-9$ (o) $^-2$
5. (a) $^-2$ (b) 2   (c) 0   (d) $^-6$ (e) $^-36$
(f) 6   (g) $x \in I$, but $x \neq 0$.   (h) $x \in I$, but $x \neq 0$.
(i) Impossible   (j) 3, $^-3$ (k) Impossible   (l) $x \in$
I, but $x \neq 0$.   **7.** (a) $3(^-4) + 3 \cdot 4 = 3(^-4 + 4) =$
$3 \cdot 0 = 0$ (b) $(^-4)(^-3) + (^-4)3 = ^-4(^-3 + 3) =$
$^-4 \cdot 0 = 0$
(c) $n(^-m) + nm = n(^-m + m) = n \cdot 0 = 0$
(d) $(^-n)(^-m) + (^-n)m = (^-n)(^-m + m) = (^-n) \cdot 0 = 0$
9. (a) Yes   (b) Yes   (c) Yes   (d) Yes
11. $^-15°C$

Problem Set 4-3

1. (a) 12   (b) 0   (c) $^-5$ (d) 19   (e) 9
(f) $^-9$ (g) $^-13$ (h) $^-8$ (i) $^-8$ (j) $^-16$
(k) 16   **3.** (b) and (c); (d) and (e); (g) and (h).
5. (a) $^-2x + 2$ (b) $^-2x + 2y$ (c) $x^2 - xy$
(d) $^-x^2 + xy$ (e) $^-2x - 2y + 2z$ (f) $^-x^2 + xy +$
$3x$ (g) $^-25 - 10x - x^2$ (h) $x^2 - y^2 - 2y - 1$
(i) $^-x^4 + 3x^2 - 2$ **7.** No. It is not of the form
$(a - b)(a + b)$.   **9.** (a) $(x + y)^2 = x^2 + 2xy + y^2$
(b) $(x - y)^2 = x^2 - 2xy + y^2$ **11.** If $a - b = c$, then
$a = b + c$ by the definition of subtraction.   Since $a = b$
$+ c$, then

$$a + (^-b) = (b + c) + (^-b) \text{ Addition Property of Equality}$$
$$= b + (c + ^-b) \text{ APA}$$
$$= b + (^-b + c) \text{ CPC}$$
$$= (b + ^-b) + c \text{ APA}$$
$$= 0 + c \text{ Additive Inverse}$$
$$= c \qquad\qquad \text{ IPA}$$

Thus, $a + (^-b) = c$ and $a - b = c$, so that $a + (^-b) =$
$a - b$.
13. (a) Prove: $^-(^-a) = a$. Proof: The additive inverse of
^-a is a. Also, the additive inverse of ^-a is $^-(^-a)$. Since
additive inverses are unique, then $^-(^-a) = a$.
(b) Prove: $^-a + ^-b = ^-(a + b)$. Proof: The additive
inverse of $^-(a + b)$ is $a + b$. Also,

$$(^-a + ^-b) + (a + b) = (^-a + a) + (^-b + b)$$
$$= 0 + 0$$
$$= 0$$

Thus, the additive inverse of $(^-a + ^-b)$ is $(a + b)$.
Hence, $^-a + ^-b = ^-(a + b)$ since the additive inverse is
unique.

Problem Set 4-4

1. (a) $^-20, ^-13, ^-5, ^-3, 0, 4$ (b) $^-6, ^-5, 0, 5, 6$
(c) $^-100, ^-20, ^-15, ^-13, 0$ (d) $^-3, ^-2, 5, 13$
3. (a) $^-18$ (b) $\{^-17, ^-16, ^-15, \ldots\}$ (c) 18
(d) $\{17, 16, 15, \ldots\}$ (e) $^-18$ (f) $\{^-18, ^-19, ^-20, \ldots\}$
(g) $^-7$ (h) $\{^-8, ^-9, ^-10, ^-11, \ldots\}$ (i) $^-2$ (j) $\{^-2,$
$^-1, 0, 1, 2, \ldots\}$ (k) $^-1$ (l) $\{^-2, ^-3, ^-4, ^-5, \ldots\}$
(m) $^-2$ (n) $\{^-4, ^-5, ^-6, \ldots\}$ **5.** (a), (c), (d), and
(e) are always true.   **7.** (a) 1, 0, $^-2$ (b) 9

(c) $^-6$, $^-7$　(d) $^-3$, $^-2$, $^-1$, 0, 1, 2, 3　9.　(a) Prove: If $a > b$ and $b > c$, then $a > c$. Proof: $a > b$ implies $a = b + k$ where $k > 0$. $b > c$ implies $b = c + m$ where $m > 0$. Thus, $a = (c + m) + k = c + (m + k)$, but $m + k > 0$ so that $a > c$.　(b) Prove: If $a > b$, then $a + c > b + c$. Proof: $a + c > b + c$ if and only if $(a + c) - (b + c) > 0$. Now $(a + c) - (b + c) = a - b$. But $a - b > 0$ since $a > b$, so the proof is complete.　(c) Prove (i): If $a > b$ and $c > 0$, then $ac > bc$. Proof: $ac - bc = (a - b)c$. Since $a > b$, we have $a - b > 0$. Since $c > 0$, then $(a - b)c > 0$ and, therefore, $ac - bc > 0$, which implies $ac > bc$. Prove (ii): If $a > b$ and $c < 0$, then $ac < bc$. Proof: $ac - bc = (a - b)c$. Since $a - b > 0$ and $c < 0$, then $(a - b)c < 0$ and, consequently, $ac < bc$.　11.　(a) Yes. $x^2 + y^2 \geq 2xy$ if and only if $x^2 - 2xy + y^2 \geq 0$ and $x^2 - 2xy + y^2 = (x - y)^2 \geq 0$　(b) $x = y$　13.　No. $^-5 < 2$ but $(^-5)^2 \not< 2^2$.　15.　(a) $\{^-3, ^-2, ^-1, 0, 1\}$　(b) $\{^-2, ^-3, ^-4, ^-5, \ldots\}$

Problem Set 4-5

1.　$^-19$　3.　Rick has \$100; David has \$300.
5.　A, 2800 cars; B, 1400 cars; C, 3100 cars
7.　524　9.　78; 80; 82　11.　Eldest \$30 000;
middle \$24 000; youngest \$10 000

Chapter Test

1.　(a) $^-3$　(b) a　(c) 0　(d) $^-(x + y)$　(e) $x - y$
3.　(a) 3　(b) $^-5$　(c) $x \in I$; $x \neq 0$
(d) Impossible　(e) $^-41$　(f) $x \in I$

5.　(a)
$$\begin{aligned}
(x - y)(x + y) &= (x - y)x + (x + y)y \\
&= (x^2 - yx) + (xy + y^2) \\
&= (x^2 + {}^-yx) + (xy + y^2) \\
&= x^2 + ({}^-yx + xy) + y^2 \\
&= x^2 + ({}^-xy + xy) + y^2 \\
&= x^2 + 0 + y^2 \\
&= x^2 + y^2
\end{aligned}$$

(b) $(^-2 - x)(^-2 + x) = (^-2)^2 - x^2$
$\qquad\qquad\qquad\qquad = 4 - x^2$

7.　(a) $x(1 - 3) = ^-2x$　(b) $x(x + 1)$　(c) $5(1 + x)$
(d) $(x - y)(x + 1 - 1) = (x - y)x$　9.　1010 seniors, 895 juniors, 2020 sophomores, 1790 freshmen.
11.　$^-7°C$　13.　14 pounds

CHAPTER 5
Problem Set 5-1

1.　(a) T　(b) T　(c) T　(d) T　(e) T　(f) F
3.　(a) Theorem 5-3　(b) Theorem 5-1(b)
(c) None　(d) Theorem 5-1(b)　(e) Theorem 5-3
5.　(a) $d \mid 13a$ by Theorem 5-3, $d \mid 21b$ by Theorem 5-3, and $d \mid (13a + 21b)$ by Theorem 5-1(a)　(b) Proof is similar to 5(a).　7.　(a) T　(b) F　(c) F
(d) T　(e) T　(f) F　(g) T　9.　(a) $7 \mid 805$
(b) $7 \mid 6405$　(c) $7 \mid 2002$　(d) $7 \nmid 20\,002$
11.　(a) No. Suppose that the number is divisible by 10; then it must be divisible by 5, a contradiction.
(b) Yes. Example $5 \mid 5$ but $10 \nmid 5$.　13.　If the digit d appears three times, then $3d$ appears in the sum of all the digits. This is true for each digit of the number, so the number must be divisible by 3.　15.　$a \cdot 10^4 + b \cdot 10^3 + c \cdot 10^2 + d \cdot 10 + e = (10\,000a - a + a) + (1000b + b - b) + (100c - c + c) + (10d + d - d) + e = (10\,000a - a) + (1000b + b) + (100c - c) + (10d + d) + (a - b + c - d + e)$.　17.　Let $N = a_4 \cdot 10^4 + a_3 \cdot 10^3 + a_2 \cdot 10^2 + a_1 \cdot 10^1 + a_0$.

$9 \mid 9$ implies $9 \mid 9a_1$
$9 \mid 99$ implies $9 \mid 99a_2$
$9 \mid 999$ implies $9 \mid 999a_3$
$9 \mid 9999$ implies $9 \mid 9999a_4$

Thus, $9 \mid (9999a_4 + 999a_3 + 99a_2 + 9a_1)$. Since $N = 9999a_4 + a_4 + 999a_3 + a_3 + 99a_2 + a_2 + 9a_1 + a_1 + a_0$, then $9 \mid ((9999a_4 + 999a_3 + 99a_2 + 9a_1) + (a_4 + a_3 + a_2 + a_1 + a_0))$ if and only if $9 \mid (a_4 + a_3 + a_2 + a_1 + a_0)$.　19.　See answers for Appendix II.

Problem Set 5-2

1.　(a) $2^3 \cdot 3^2 \cdot 7$　(b) $3^2 \cdot 5^2 \cdot 11$　(c) $2 \cdot 3^2 \cdot 5^4$
3.　73　5.　See page 184 for primes less than 100. Others are 101, 103, 107, 109, 113, 127, 131, 137, 139, 149, 151, 157, 163, 167, 173, 179, 181, 191, 193, 197, 199　7.　27 720　9.　3 and 5; 11 and 13; 17 and 19; 29 and 31; 41 and 43; 59 and 61; 71 and 73; 101 and 103; 107 and 109; 137 and 139; 149 and 151; 179 and 181; 191 and 193; 197 and 199.　11.　(a) Yes
(b) No. $4 \mid 2 \cdot 2$ but $4 \nmid 2$.

13.   **(a)** $5! + 2 = 122$ and $2 \mid 122$

$5! + 3 = 123$ and $3 \mid 123$

$5! + 4 = 124$ and $4 \mid 124$

$5! + 5 = 125$ and $5 \mid 125$

(b) The numbers are composite since 11! is divisible by each of the integers 2 through 11, and hence $11! + 2$ is divisible by 2, $11! + 3$ by 3, $11! + 4$ by 4, ..., and $11! + 11$ by 11.   **15.**   **(a)** 1, 2, 4, 8, 16, 32, 64, 128, 256 **(b)** 1, 3, 9, 27, 81, 243   **(c)** 54 **(d)** $(k + 1)(m + 1)$ **17.**   If any prime q in the set $\{2, 3, 5, \ldots, p\}$ divides N, then $q \mid 2 \cdot 3 \cdot 5 \cdot \ldots \cdot p$. Since $q \nmid 1$ by Theorem 5-1 part b, $q \nmid (2 \cdot 3 \cdot 5 \cdot \ldots \cdot p + 1)$, that is, $q \nmid N$.

Problem Set 5-3

1.   **(a)** 2; 90   **(b)** 12; 72   **(c)** 4; 312   **3.**   **(a)** 4 **(b)** 1   **(c)** 16   **5.**   **(a)** 160 820   **(b)** 158 433 320 **(c)** 941 866 496   **7.**   **(a)** 1   **(b)** GCD of any two consecutive integers is 1.   **(c)** Let $d = \text{GCD} (n, n + 1)$. $\text{GCD} (n + 1, n) = \text{GCD} (n, 1) = 1$, by Theorem 5-9. **9.**   **(a)** T. If a and b are both even, then GCD (a, b) is at least 2.   **(b)** T. If GCD $(a, b) = 2$, then $2 \mid a$ and $2 \mid b$.   **(c)** F. For example, $a = 12$, $b = 20$.   **(d)** F. If $a = 8$, $b = 4$, then LCM $(a, b) = 8$ and GCD $(a, b) = 4$ and $8 \nmid 4$.   **(e)** T. LCM $(a, b) \cdot$ GCD $(a, b) = ab$. **11.**   No. GCD $(2, 4, 6) = 2$. LCM $(2 \cdot 4 \cdot 6) = 12$; $2 \cdot 12 = 24 \neq 2 \cdot 4 \cdot 6$.   **13.**   36   **15.**   **(a)** 1, 2, 3, 4, 5, 6, 7, 8, 9, 10, 11, 12   **(b)** All integers x such that $0 < x < p$ are relatively prime to p.   **(c)** $p^2 - (p - 1)$ since there are $p - 1$ multiples of p less than or equal to p^2. **17.**   Let GCD $(a^2, b^2) = d$. Since $d \mid a^2$, $d \mid a$. Similarly, $d \mid b^2$ implies $d \mid b$, but since GCD $(a, b) = 1$, $d = 1$. Thus GCD $(a^2, b^2) = 1$.   **19.**   See the answers in Appendix II.

Problem Set 5-4

1.   **(a)** 3   **(b)** 2   **(c)** 6   **(d)** 8   **(e)** 3   **(f)** 4 **(g)** Impossible   **(h)** 10

3.   **(a)**

$\oplus$	1	2	3	4	5	6	7
1	2	3	4	5	6	7	1
2	3	4	5	6	7	1	2
3	4	5	6	7	1	2	3
4	5	6	7	1	2	3	4
5	6	7	1	2	3	4	5
6	7	1	2	3	4	5	6
7	1	2	3	4	5	6	7

(b) 6; 4   **(c)** Each addition problem, $a - b = x$, can be rewritten as $a = b + x$. Since every number x shows up exactly once in every row and column, no matter what a and b are, then x can be found.

5.   **(a)**

$\otimes$	1	2	3
1	1	2	3
2	2	1	3
3	3	3	3

$\otimes$	1	2	3	4
1	1	2	3	4
2	2	4	2	4
3	3	2	1	4
4	4	4	4	4

$\otimes$	1	2	3	4	5	6
1	1	2	3	4	5	6
2	2	4	6	2	4	6
3	3	6	3	6	3	6
4	4	2	6	4	2	6
5	5	4	3	2	1	6
6	6	6	6	6	6	6

$\otimes$	1	2	3	4	5	6	7	8	9	10	11
1	1	2	3	4	5	6	7	8	9	10	11
2	2	4	6	8	10	1	3	5	7	9	11
3	3	6	9	1	4	7	10	2	5	8	11
4	4	8	1	5	9	3	6	10	3	7	11
5	5	10	4	9	3	8	2	7	1	6	11
6	6	1	7	2	8	3	9	4	10	5	11
7	7	3	10	6	2	9	5	1	8	4	11
8	8	5	2	10	7	4	1	9	6	3	11
9	9	7	5	3	1	10	8	6	4	2	11
10	10	9	8	7	6	5	4	3	2	1	11
11	11	11	11	11	11	11	11	11	11	11	11

(b) 3 and 11   **(c)** If n is prime, divisions can be performed.   **7.** Wednesday   **9. (a)** 4   **(b)** 0   **(c)** 0   **(d)** 7   **11. (a)** $24 \equiv 0 \pmod 8$ **(b)** $^-90 \equiv 0 \pmod 3$ **(c)** $n \equiv 0 \pmod n$ **13. (a)** 1   **(b)** 5   **(c)** 10   **15.** Let $N = a_k \cdot 10^k + a_{k-1} \cdot 10^{k-1} + \cdots + a_2 \cdot 10^2 + a_1 \cdot 10^1 + a_0$. $4 \mid N$ if and only if $4 \mid (a_1 \cdot 10 + a_0)$. Proof: $100 \equiv 0 \pmod 4$. Hence, $N = 100(a_k 10^{k-2} + a_{k-3}10^{k-3} + \cdots + a_2) + a_1 10 + a_0 \equiv a_1 10 + a_0 \pmod 4$. Consequently, $4 \mid N$ if and only if $4 \mid (a_1 10 + a_0)$.
17. (a) For example, $2 \cdot 3 \equiv 2 \cdot 1 \pmod 4$, but $3 \not\equiv 1 \pmod 4$.   **(b)** For example, $2^2 \equiv 4^2 \pmod 6$, but $2 \not\equiv 4 \pmod 6$.

Chapter Test

1. (a) F   **(b)** F   **(c)** T   **(d)** F   **(e)** F
3. (a) 83 160 is divisible by 2, 3, 4, 5, 6, 7, 8, 9, and 11.   **(b)** 83 193 is divisible by 3 and 11.   **5.** $N = a \cdot 10^2 + b \cdot 10 + c = (99a + 9b) + (a + b + c)$. Since $9 \mid 9(11a + b)$, then $9 \mid N$ if and only if $9 \mid (a + b + c)$ using Theorem 5-1.   **7.** The number must be divisible by both 8 and 3. Since $3 \mid 4152$ and $8 \mid 4152$, then $24 \mid 4152$.   **9. (a)** $2^4 \cdot 5^3 \cdot 7^4 \cdot 13 \cdot 29$ **(b)** $278 \cdot 279$

CHAPTER 6

Problem Set 6-1

1. (a) The solution to $8x = 7$ is $7/8$.   **(b)** Jane ate seven-eighths of Jill's candy.   **(c)** The ratio of boys to girls is seven to eight.   **(d)** $7/8$ is a rational number.
3. (a) $4/18, 6/27, 8/36$ **(b)** $^-4/10, 2/^-5, ^-10/25$ **(c)** $0/1, 0/2, 0/4$ **(d)** $2a/4, 3a/6, 4a/8$ **5.** Only the fractions in (d) and (e) are not equal.   **7.** Only the fractions in $d, e,$ and f are not equal.   **9.** Let $i \in I. \ i = i/1$ and $i/1 \in Q$.   **11.** See Appendix II for answers.

Problem Set 6-2

1.

$$\frac{1}{5} + \frac{2}{3} = \frac{13}{15}$$

$$\frac{1}{5} = \frac{3}{15}, \qquad \frac{2}{3} = \frac{10}{15}$$

$$0 \qquad \frac{3}{15} \qquad\qquad \frac{13}{15} \quad 1$$

3. (a) $^-31/20$ **(b)** $58/35$ **(c)** $^-19/40$ **(d)** $(5y - 3x)/xy$ **5. (a)** $18\tfrac{2}{3}$ **(b)** $2\tfrac{4}{5}$ **(c)** $^-(2\tfrac{93}{100})$ **(d)** $^-(5\tfrac{7}{8})$ **7. (a)** $7/12$ **(b)** $49/12$ **(c)** $41/24$ **(d)** $71/24$ **(e)** $^-23/3$ **(f)** $^-23/12$
9. $17\tfrac{7}{12}$ yd   **11. (a)** Yes   **(b)** No   **(c)** No   **(d)** No   **(e)** No   **(f)** Yes   **13. (a)** Let (a/b) and $(c/d) \in Q$

$$\frac{a}{b} + \frac{c}{d} = \frac{ad + bc}{bd} \in Q$$

since $ad + bc$ and $bd \in I$ and $bd \neq 0$.
(b) Let a/b and $c/d \in Q$

$$\frac{a}{b} + \frac{c}{d} = \frac{ad + bc}{bd} \qquad \text{definition of addition of rationals}$$

$$= \frac{bc + ad}{bd} \qquad \text{CPA}$$

$$= \frac{cb + da}{db} \qquad \text{CPM}$$

$$= \frac{c}{d} + \frac{a}{b} \qquad \text{definition of addition of rationals}$$

(c) We are trying to show that if $a/b = c/d$, then $a/b + e/f = c/d + e/f$ where $a/b, c/d,$ and $e/f \in Q$. Now $a/b + e/f = (af + be)/bf$. Also, $c/d + e/f = (cf + de)/de$. Thus, $a/b + e/f = c/d + e/f$ if and only if $(af + be)/bf = (cf + de)/df$, which is true if and only if $(af + be)df = bf(cf + de)$ or $adf^2 + bdef = bcf^2 + bdef$, or $adf^2 = bcf^2$, or $ad = bc$, which is true since $a/b = c/d$.   **(d)** Let $a/b, c/d, e/f \in Q$.

$$\left(\frac{a}{b} + \frac{c}{d}\right) + \frac{e}{f} = \frac{ad + bc}{bd} + \frac{e}{f}$$

$$= \frac{(ad + bc)f + (bd)e}{(bdf)}$$

$$= \frac{adf + bcf + bde}{bdf}$$

$$= \frac{a}{b} + \frac{cf + de}{df}$$

$$= \frac{a}{b} + \left(\frac{c}{d} + \frac{e}{f}\right)$$

Problem Set 6-3

1. (a) $1/4 \cdot 1/3 = 1/12$ (b) $2/5 \cdot 3/5 = 6/25$
3. (a) $3/4$ (b) $3/8$ (c) $1/5$ (d) b/a
(e) $^-5a/3b$ (f) za/x^2y **5.** (a) $10\frac{1}{2}$ (b) $8\frac{1}{3}$
7. (a) 27 (b) $8/7$ (c) $^-6/7$ (d) y/x
9. (a) $21/8$ (b) $1/5$ (c) $3/35$ (d) $15/32$
(e) $^-56/5$ (f) $^-45/28$ **11.** 12 and 63 **13.** 45
days   **15.** $1/6; 1/1008$ **17.** $1\frac{1}{3}$ days
19. (a) Let a/b and $c/d \in Q$. $a/b \cdot c/d = ac/bd$ and
$ac, bd \in I$. $bd \neq 0$. Thus $ac/bd \in Q$.   (b) Let a/b
and $c/d \in Q$.

$$\frac{a}{b} \cdot \frac{c}{d} = \frac{ac}{bd}$$
$$= \frac{ca}{db}$$
$$= \frac{c}{d} \cdot \frac{a}{b}$$

(c) Let $a/b, c/d, e/f \in Q$.

$$\left(\frac{a}{b} \cdot \frac{c}{d}\right) \cdot \frac{e}{f} = \left(\frac{ac}{bd}\right)\frac{e}{f}$$
$$= \frac{(ac)e}{(bd)f}$$
$$= \frac{a(ce)}{b(df)}$$
$$= \frac{a}{b} \cdot \frac{ce}{df}$$
$$= \frac{a}{b} \cdot \left(\frac{c}{d} \cdot \frac{e}{f}\right)$$

(d) Let $a/b \in Q$.

$$\frac{a}{b} \cdot 0 = \frac{a}{b} \cdot \frac{0}{1} = \frac{a \cdot 0}{b \cdot 1} = \frac{0}{b \cdot 1} = \frac{0}{1}$$

since $0/1 = 0$. Then, $a/b \cdot 0 = 0$. By commutativity of
multiplication, $0 \cdot a/b = 0$.   (e) Let $a/b, c/d$ and e/f
$\in Q$.

$$\frac{a}{b}\left(\frac{c}{d} + \frac{e}{f}\right) = \frac{a}{b}\left(\frac{cf + de}{df}\right)$$
$$= \frac{a(cf + de)}{b(df)}$$
$$= \frac{acf + ade}{bdf}$$
$$= \frac{acf}{bdf} + \frac{ade}{bdf}$$
$$= \frac{ac}{bd} + \frac{ae}{bf}$$
$$= \left(\frac{a}{b}\right)\left(\frac{c}{d}\right) + \left(\frac{a}{b}\right)\left(\frac{e}{f}\right)$$

Problem Set 6-4

1. (a) $>$; (b) $>$; (c) $<$; (d) $<$; (e) $=$; (f) $=$ **3.**
(a) $x \le 27/16$ (b) $x \ge 115/3$ (c) $x < 17/5$
(d) $x \ge 141/22$ **5.** (a) No. Multiplication by bd,
which is negative, reverses order.   (b) Yes. Multiplication by bd, which is positive, retains same order.
7. 40 **9.** $3/2$ **11.** $16/9$ **13.** 2469
15. 270 miles   **17.** (a) $1/2$ (b) Let $a/b = c/d =$
$e/f = r$. Then

$a = br$
$c = dr$
$e = fr$

So that $a + c + e = br + dr + fr$

$$a + c + e = r(b + d + f)$$
$$\frac{a + c + e}{b + d + f} = r$$

Thus,

$$\frac{a}{b} = \frac{c}{d} = \frac{e}{f} = \frac{a + c + e}{b + d + f}.$$

19. (a) Prove: If $a/b > c/d$ and $c/d > e/f$, then $a/b >$
e/f. Proof: $a/b > c/d$ and $c/d > e/f$. Hence

$$\frac{a}{b} = \frac{c}{d} + \frac{g}{h} \text{ where } \frac{g}{h} > 0$$

$$\frac{c}{d} = \frac{e}{f} + \frac{i}{k} \text{ where } \frac{i}{k} > 0$$

$$\frac{a}{b} = \left(\frac{e}{f} + \frac{i}{k}\right) + \frac{g}{h}$$

$$\frac{a}{b} = \frac{e}{f} + \left(\frac{i}{k} + \frac{g}{h}\right) \text{ but}$$

$$\frac{i}{k} + \frac{g}{h} > 0 \quad \text{so} \quad \frac{a}{b} > \frac{e}{f}.$$

(b) Prove: If $a/b > c/d$ then $a/b + e/f > c/d + e/f$. Proof: $a/b > c/d$ if and only if $a/b = c/d + g/h$ where $g/h > 0$.

$$\frac{a}{b} + \frac{e}{f} = \left(\frac{c}{d} + \frac{g}{h}\right) + \frac{e}{f}$$

$$\frac{a}{b} + \frac{e}{f} = \left(\frac{c}{d} + \frac{e}{f}\right) + \frac{g}{h}$$

$$\therefore \frac{a}{b} + \frac{e}{f} > \frac{c}{d} + \frac{e}{f}$$

(c) Prove: If $a/b > c/d$ and $e/f > 0$, then $a/b \cdot e/f > c/d \cdot e/f$. Proof: $a/b > c/d$ implies $a/b = c/d + g/h$ where $g/h > 0$.

$$\frac{a}{b} \cdot \frac{e}{f} = \left(\frac{c}{d} + \frac{g}{h}\right) \cdot \frac{e}{f} = \frac{c}{d} \cdot \frac{e}{f} + \frac{g}{h} \cdot \frac{e}{f},$$

but $g/h \cdot e/f > 0$ since $e/f > 0$ and $g/h > 0$. Therefore, $a/b \cdot e/f > c/d \cdot e/f$.
Prove: If $a/b > c/d$ and $e/f < 0$, then $(a/b) \cdot (e/f) < c/d \cdot e/f$. $g/h \cdot e/f < 0$ since $g/h > 0$ and $e/f < 0$. Thus, $a/b \cdot e/f = c/d \cdot e/f + g/h \cdot e/f$ implies $a/b \cdot e/f < c/d \cdot e/f$.

Problem Set 6-5

1. **(a)** $1/3^{13}$ **(b)** 3^{13} **(c)** 5^{11} **(d)** 5^{19}
(e) $1/(^-5)^2$ or $1/5^2$ **(f)** a^5 **(g)** a^2 **3.** **(a)** False. $2^3 \cdot 2^4 \neq (2 \cdot 2)^{3+4}$ **(b)** False. $2^3 \cdot 2^4 \neq (2 \cdot 2)^{3 \cdot 4}$ **(c)** False. $2^3 \cdot 2^3 \neq (2 \cdot 2)^{2 \cdot 3}$ **(d)** False. $a^0 = 1$ if $a \neq 0$ **(e)** False. $(2 + 3)^2 \neq 2^2 + 3^2$ **(f)** False. $(2 + 3)^{-2} \neq 1/2^2 + 1/3^2$ **(g)** False. $a^{mn} = (a^m)^n \neq a^m \cdot a^n$ **(h)** True. $(a/b)^{-n} = 1/(a/b)^n = 1/(a^n/b^n) = b^n/a^n = (b/a)^n$ **5.** $2 \cdot 10^{11}$; $2 \cdot 10^5$

7. **(a)** $(1 - x)^2/x$ **(b)** $(x^2y^2 - 1)/y^2$ **(c)** $(1 + y)^6/y^3$ **(d)** $6x^2 + 4x$ **(e)** $(3a - b)^2$ **(f)** $8x^2 + 67a^3$ **(g)** $x^2y/(y + 3x^2)$

Problem Set 6-6

1. **(a)** $0 \cdot 10^{-1} + 2 \cdot 10^{-2} + 3 \cdot 10^{-3}$ **(b)** $2 \cdot 10^2 + 0 \cdot 10^1 + 6 \cdot 10^0 + 0 \cdot 10^{-1} + 6 \cdot 10^{-2}$ **(c)** $3 \cdot 10^2 + 1 \cdot 10^1 + 2 \cdot 10^0 + 0 \cdot 10^{-1} + 1 \cdot 10^{-2} + 0 \cdot 10^{-3} + 3 \cdot 10^{-4}$ **(d)** $0 \cdot 10^{-1} + 0 \cdot 10^{-2} + 0 \cdot 10^{-3} + 1 \cdot 10^{-4} + 3 \cdot 10^{-5} + 2 \cdot 10^{-6}$ **3.** **(a)** 536.0076
(b) 3.008 **(c)** 0.000436 **(d)** 5 000 000.2
5. **(a)** Yes **(b)** Yes **(c)** Yes **(d)** Yes
(e) Yes **(f)** Yes **(g)** No **(h)** No **(i)** No
7. **(a)** 39.202 **(b)** 230.697 **(c)** 168.003
(d) $^-$390.6313 **(e)** 1.49093 **(f)** 0.0575763
(g) $^-$10.4 **(h)** 4.681 **(i)** $^-$0.00399 **9.** **(a)** 46.3; 4630; 463 000 000 **(b)** 0.4; 40; 4 000 000 **(c)** 463; 46 300; 4 630 000 000 **(d)** 4630; 463 000; 46 300 000 000 **(e)** 0.0463; 4.63; 463 000
(f) 0.000000463; 0.0000463; 4.63 **(g)** 7.9; 790; 79 000 000 **(h)** 62; 6200; 620 000 000
11. Because lining up decimals acts as using place value. **13.** 1.679 **15.** 0.8 in. **17.** The number of digits in the terminating decimal is the greater of m or n.

Problem Set 6-7

1. **(a)** $0.\overline{4}$ **(b)** $0.\overline{285714}$ **(c)** $0.\overline{27}$ **(d)** $0.0\overline{6}$
(e) $0.02\overline{6}$ **(f)** $0.\overline{01}$ **(g)** $0.8\overline{3}$ **(h)** $0.\overline{076923}$
2. **(a)** $3.2\overline{3}, 3.\overline{23}, 3.23, 3.\overline{22}, 3.2$ **(b)** $^-1.45, ^-1.454, ^-1.45\overline{4}, ^-1.\overline{454}, ^-1.4\overline{54}$ **5.** **(a)** $1/1$ **(b)** No positive number k can be found such that $0.\overline{9} + k = 1$ or $1 + k = 0.\overline{9}$. **(c)** $1/3 = 0.\overline{3}$ implies $3 \cdot (1/3) = 3 \cdot 0.\overline{3}$ or $1 = 0.\overline{9}$. **7.** **(a)** 3.25 **(b)** 462.245 **(c)** 0.01515 **(d)** $462.2\overline{43}$

Problem Set 6-8

1. **(a)** 789% **(b)** 3.2% **(c)** 19 310% **(d)** 20%
(e) $83.\overline{3}\%$ or $83\frac{1}{3}\%$ **(f)** 15% **(g)** $1.\overline{3}\%$ or $1\frac{1}{3}\%$
(h) 571.43% approximately or $571\frac{3}{7}\%$
3. **(a)** 2.04 **(b)** 50% **(c)** 60 **5.** $16 960
7. **(a)** Bill, 221 **(b)** Joe, 90% **(c)** Ran, 265
9. January 1, 1992 **11.** (1) $20 (2) $11.25 (3) $100 (4) $210 **13.** Approximately 89.7%

15.   **(a)** 3.325×10^3 **(b)** 4.632×10^1 **(c)** 1.3×10^{-4} **(d)** 9.30146×10^5 **17.** See Appendix II answers.

Problem Set 6-9

1.   Answers vary, one possibility is $0.232233222333\ldots$ **3.**   **(a)** Yes   **(b)** No   **(c)** No   **(d)** Yes   **(e)** Yes   **(f)** Yes   **5.**   **(a)** 4.12   **(b)** 2.65   **(c)** 4.58   **(d)** 0.11   **(e)** 4.51   **(f)** 1.28   **7.**   No $\sqrt{9 + 16} \neq \sqrt{9} + \sqrt{16}$.   **9.**   Suppose $\sqrt{3}$ is rational.

$$\sqrt{3} = \frac{a}{b}$$

$$3 = \frac{a^2}{b^2}$$

$$3b^2 = a^2$$

a^2 has an even number of 3's in its prime factorization but $3b^2$ has an odd number of 3's in its prime factorization, and this is impossible. Thus $\sqrt{3}$ is irrational.   **11.**   **(a)** m is a perfect square.   **(b)** Use the result of Problem 10.   **13.**   See answers in Appendix II.

Problem Set 6-10

1.   **(a)** $6\sqrt{5}$ **(b)** 23   **(c)** $11\sqrt{3}$ **(d)** $6\sqrt{7}$ **(e)** 13/14   **(f)** 7/14 or 1/2   **3.**   **(a)** $2\sqrt{3} + 3\sqrt{2} + 6\sqrt{5}$ **(b)** $2\sqrt[3]{5}$ **(c)** $30 + 12\sqrt{6}$ **(d)** $1/\sqrt{2}$ or $\sqrt{2}/2$ **(e)** $17\sqrt{2}$ **(f)** $\sqrt{6}$ **5.**   **(a)** 4   **(b)** 1/4   **(c)** 9   **(d)** 1/9   **(e)** 32   **(f)** 4   **(g)** 9   **(h)** 32   **(i)** 1/256   **(j)** 10   **(k)** 9   **7.**   **(a)** 2^{10} **(b)** 2^{11} **(c)** 2^{12}

Chapter Test

1.   **(a)**

(b)

3.   **(a)** 6/7   **(b)** ax/b **(c)** 0/1   **(d)** 5/9   **(e)** b **(f)** 2/27   **5.**   **(a)** 11/10   **(b)** 13/175   **(c)** 10/13   **(d)** 25/24   **(e)** 50/9   **(f)** 45.454   **(g)** 0.8294   **(h)** 12.3   **(i)** 38.811   **(j)** 15.362   **7.**   **(a)** 6/1   **(b)** 5/4   **9.**   *Hint:* Use place value.   **11.**   **(a)** 25%   **(b)** 192   **(c)** $56\frac{2}{3}$ **13.**   **(a)** 0.60   **(b)** $0.00\overline{6}$ **(c)** 1   **15.**   **(a)** No. $^-\sqrt{2} + \sqrt{2} = 0$ **(b)** No. $\sqrt{2} - \sqrt{2} = 0$ **(c)** No. $\sqrt{2} \cdot \sqrt{2} = 2$ **(d)** No. $\sqrt{2} \div \sqrt{2} = 1$ **(c)** $0.\overline{076923}$ **19.**   **(a)** 4.26×10^5 **(b)** 2.37×10^{-6} **21.**   **(a)** $11\sqrt{2}$ **(b)** $12\sqrt{2}$ **(c)** $6\sqrt{10}$ **(d)** $3\sqrt[3]{6}$

CHAPTER 7

Problem Set 7-1

1.   **(a)** $S = \{m, a, t, h\}$ **(b)** $S = \{1, 2, 3, 4\}$ **(c)** $S = \{$Red, Blue$\}$ **(d)** $S = \{(1, \text{Red}), (1, \text{Blue}), (2, \text{Red}), (2, \text{Blue}), (3, \text{Red}), (3, \text{Blue}), (4, \text{Red}), (4, \text{Blue})\}$ **(e)** $S = \{$HHH, HHT, HTH, HTT, THH, THT, TTH, TTT$\}$ **(f)** $S = \{$(Red, 1), (Red, 2), (Red, 3), (Red, 4), (Red, 5), (Red, 6), (Blue, 1), (Blue, 2), (Blue, 3), (Blue, 4), (Blue, 5), (Blue, 6)$\}$ **(g)** $S = \{(1, 1), (1, 2), (1, 3), (1, 4), (2, 1), (2, 2), (2, 3), (2, 4), (3, 1), (3, 2), (3, 3), (3, 4), (4, 1), (4, 2), (4, 3), (4, 4)\}$ **3.**   **(b)** $P(A) = 5/10$ or $1/2$ **(c)** $P(C) = 5/10$ or $1/2$ **(d)** $P(D) = 9/10$ **5.**   **(a)** $P(\text{Brown}) = 4/12$ or $1/3$ **(b)** $P(\text{Either black or green}) = 8/12$ or $2/3$ **(c)** $P(\text{Red}) = 0/12 = 0$ **(d)** $P(\text{Not black}) = 6/12$ or $1/2$ **7.** $P(\text{Vowel}) = 5/26$, $P(\text{Consonant}) = 1 - 5/26 = 21/26$ **9.**   210   **11.**   10

Problem Set 7-2

1.   **(a)** 1/216   **(b)** 1/120   **3.**   1152/39 916 800 or 1/34 650   **5.** $P(\text{SOS}) = 1/3$ with Box 1 and $P(\text{SOS}) = 1/5$ with Box 2, so choose Box 1.   **7.**   64/75   **9.**   She should play Billie-Bobby-Billie, then the probability of winning two in a row is 3/5.   **11.** $P(\text{at least 3 H}) = 5/16$ **13.**   **(a)** $P(\text{3 plums}) = 25/8000$ or $1/320$ **(b)** $P(\text{3 oranges}) = 126/8000$ or $63/4000$ **(c)** $P(\text{3 lemons}) = 0$ **(d)** $P(\text{no plums}) = 4275/8000$ or

171/320   **15.** Since there are only two colors of socks, no three socks can be of different color. Among any three socks, at least two have to be the same color. Consequently, the probability of getting a matching pair is one.

Problem Set 7-3

1. The odds in favor of drawing a face card are 12/40 or 3/10. The odds against drawing a face card are 40/12 or 10/3.   **3.** 15/1   **5.** $P(\text{win}) = 5/8$ **7.** No. It is not a fair game. The payoff would have to be $6.00.   **9.** $3.50   **11.** 3 hours

Problem Set 7-4

1. 224   **3.** 32   **5.** 1352 with 3 letters and 35 152 with 4 letters   **7.** (a) T   (b) F   (c) F   (d) F   (e) T   (f) T   (g) T   **9.** 15   **11.** (a) 24 360   (b) 4060   **13.** 9! = 362 880   **15.** 45   **17.** 3840   **19.** 720

Chapter Test

1. (a) $S = \{$Sunday, Monday, Tuesday, Wednesday, Thursday, Friday, Saturday$\}$ (b) $E = \{$Tuesday, Thursday$\}$ (c) $P(T) = 2/7$ **3.** (a) $P(\text{Black}) = 5/12$ (b) $P(\text{Black or white}) = 9/12$ or 3/4   (c) $P(\text{Neither red nor white}) = 5/12$ (d) $P(\text{Not red}) = 9/12$ or 3/4   (e) $P(\text{Black and white}) = 0$ (f) $P(\text{Black or white or red}) = 1$ **5.** (a) $P(3W) = 64/729$ (b) $P(3W) = 24/504$ or 1/21   **7.** $P(L) = 6/25$ **9.** 7/45   **11.** 3/3 or 1/1   **13.** 30¢   **15.** 900   **17.** 24   **19.** 5040

CHAPTER 8

Problem Set 8-1

1. (a) November, 30 cm   (b) October, 15 cm; December, 25 cm; January, 10 cm.

3. (a)

Number of children	Tally	Frequency
0	ⅠⅣⅠ	6
1	Ⅰ	1
2	ⅠⅣ ⅠⅠⅠ	8
3	ⅠⅣ ⅠⅠ	7
4	ⅠⅣ	5
5	ⅠⅠⅠ	3
6	ⅠⅠⅠⅠ	4
7	Ⅰ	1
8	Ⅰ	1
9		0
10	Ⅰ	1
11		0
12		0
13		0
14	Ⅰ	1
		38

(b) 2

5. (a)

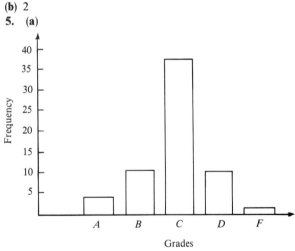

(b)

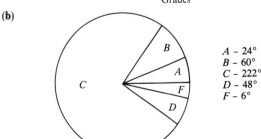

A – 24°
B – 60°
C – 222°
D – 48°
F – 6°

7. When the radius of a circle is doubled, the area is quadrupled, which is misleading since the population has only doubled   **9.** Answers vary   **11.** The line graph is more helpful since we can approximate the point midway between 8:00 A.M. and 12:00 noon and then draw a vertical line upward until it hits the line graph. An approximation for the 10:00 A.M. temperature can then be obtained from the vertical axis.

Problem Set 8-2

1. (a) mean = 6.625, median = 7.5, mode = 8
(b) mean = $13.\overline{4}$, median = 12, mode = 12
(c) mean ≈ 19.8, median = 18, mode = 18 and 22
(d) mean = 81.4, median = 80, mode = 80   (e) mean = $5.8\overline{3}$, median = 5, mode= 5   **3.** 1500
5. $78.\overline{3}$ **7.** mean = $22\ 700$, median $20\ 000$, mode = $20\ 000$ **9.** No, since there may be extreme values.   **11.** 2.59   **13.** $320   **15.** $41\ 275
17. See Appendix II answers.

Problem Set 8-3

1. (a) Range, 8; Variance, 8; Standard deviation, 2.8.   (b) Range, 80; Variance, 730.4; Standard deviation, 27.02.   **3.** 68/100   **5.** (a) 1020
(b) 1425   (c) 15   (d) 7.5 so approximately 8.
7. (a) $S = 0$ (b) Yes

9. $$v = \frac{(x_1 - \overline{x})^2 + (x_2 - \overline{x})^2 + \cdots + (x_n - \overline{x})^2}{n}$$

$$= \frac{(x_1^2 - 2\overline{x}x_1 + \overline{x}^2) + (x_2^2 - 2\overline{x}x_2 + \overline{x}^2) + \cdots + (x_n^2 - 2\overline{x}x_1 + \overline{x}^2)}{n}$$

$$= \frac{(x_1^2 + x_2^2 + \cdots x_n^2) - 2\overline{x}(x_1 + x_2 + \cdots + x_n) + n\overline{x}^2}{n}$$

$$= \frac{x_1^2 + x_2^2 + \cdots + x_n^2}{n} - \frac{2\overline{x}(x_1 + x_2 + \cdots + x_n)}{n} + \frac{n\overline{x}^2}{n}$$

$$= \frac{x_1^2 + x_2^2 + \cdots + x_n^2}{n} - 2\overline{x}^2 + \overline{x}^2$$

$$= \frac{x_1^2 + x_2^2 + \cdots + x_n^2}{n} - \overline{x}^2$$

Chapter Test

1. If it said the average is 2.41 children, then the *mean* average is being used. If it said 2.5, then the *mean* or the *median* might have been used.   **3.** (a) mean = 30, median = 30, mode = 10   (b) mean = 5, median = 5, modes = 3, 5, 6.

5. (a)

Weight	Tally	Frequency
39	||	2
40	||	2
41	||	2
42	||||	4
43	||	2
44	|	1
45	|	1
46	|	1
47	|	1
48	|	1
49	|||	3
		$\overline{20}$

(b)

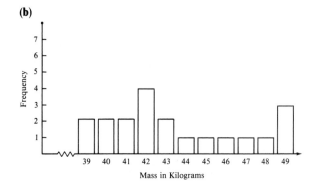

7.

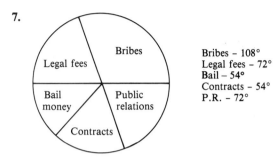

Bribes – 108°
Legal fees – 72°
Bail – 54°
Contracts – 54°
P.R. – 72°

9. $2840   **11.** (a) $P_{16} = 525$ (b) $D_{50} = P_{50} =$ 600   (c) $P_{84} = 675$

CHAPTER 9

Problem Set 9-1

1. (a) $\{C\}$ (b) $\varnothing$ (c) $\{C\}$ (d) $\varnothing$ (e) $\overline{CE}$
(f) $\overrightarrow{AB}$ (g) $\overrightarrow{BA}$ (h) $\overleftrightarrow{AD}$ **3.** (a) $\overleftrightarrow{EF}$ and $\overleftrightarrow{DC}$
(b) $\overleftrightarrow{EF}$ and α are parallel.   (c) (i) $\overleftrightarrow{AB}$ (ii) $\overleftrightarrow{BC}$
(iii) $\overleftrightarrow{BD}$ (d) No. E, F, and B determine β. D is not in β.   **5.** (a) An infinite number   (b) One
7. (a) Yes. If ℓ and m were not parallel, they would intersect in a point common to planes α and β, which contradicts the fact that α and β are parallel.   (b) No. See the following figure.

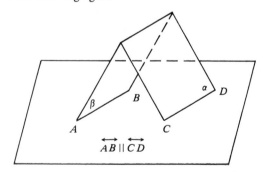

$\overleftrightarrow{AB} \parallel \overleftrightarrow{CD}$

(c) Yes. If the planes were not parallel, they would intersect in a line ℓ, and at least one of the given lines would intersect ℓ and hence the plane α, which contradicts the fact that the given lines are parallel to α.   **9.** (a) 4   (b) 6   (c) 8   (d) $2(n-1)$
11. (a) 3   (b) 6   (c) 10   (d) $1 + 2 + 3 + \cdots + (n-1) = n(n-1)/2$.   **13.** If the lines of

intersection are not parallel, they would meet at some point P, which would be in both planes. This is a contradiction since the planes are parallel. (The lines of intersection cannot be skew lines since they are contained in the third plane.)

Problem Set 9-2

1. (a) $\angle ABD$, $\angle DBC$, $\angle EBC$, $\angle EBA$ (b) $\overrightarrow{BE}$
(c) $\{B\}$ (d) $\angle EBC$ (e) No   **3.** (a) $\angle 1$ and $\angle 2$ are adjacent, $\angle 3$ and $\angle 4$ are vertical.   (b) $\angle 1$ and $\angle 2$ are vertical, $\angle 3$ and $\angle 4$ are adjacent.   (c) No vertical or adjacent angles marked.   (d) $\angle 1$ and $\angle 2$ are adjacent.   **5.** (a) 1, 2, 3, 5, 6, 7, 8, 9, 11, 12
(b) 1, 2, 5, 7, 8, 9, 11   (c) 1, 2, 5, 7, 8, 9, 11   (d) 1, 2, 7, 8, 9, 11   (e) 7, 8   (f) 2, 9, 11   **7.** No. Two segments will not determine a closed curve.
9. (a) 2   (b) 5   (c) 9   (d) $n(n-3)/2$
11. (a) 8   (b) 16   **13.** (a) F. The triangle in 12(b) is isosceles but not equilateral.   (b) T   (c) T
(d) T   (e) T   (f) F. In a rhombus, the angles do not have to be congruent.   **15.** (a) and (c) are convex. (b) and (d) are concave.

Problem Set 9-3

1. (a) 42°   (b) 117°   **3.** (a) 41°31′30″
(b) 79°48′47″   **5.** $m(\angle 1) = 120°$, $m(\angle 2) = 60°$, $m(\angle 3) = 120°$, $m(\angle 5) = 120°$, $m(\angle 6) = 60°$, $m(\angle 7) = 120°$, $m(\angle 8) = 60°$.   **7.** (a) Yes. A pair of corresponding angles are 50° each.   (b) Yes. A pair of corresponding angles are 70° each.   (c) Yes. A pair of alternate interior angles are 40° each.   (d) Yes. A pair of corresponding angles are 90° each.   **9.** (a) No, since two or more obtuse angles will produce a sum of more than 180°.   (b) Yes. For example, each angle may be 60°.   (c) No. Then the sum of the measures of the three angles would be more than 180°.   (d) No, since it may have an obtuse or a right angle as well.
11. (a) 540°   (b) 720°   (c) 18   **13.** (a) 5 · 180° − 360° = 540°   (b) The sum of the measures of the angles in all n triangles is $n \cdot 180°$. Subtracting the measures of all nonoverlapping angles whose vertex is P, we obtain $n \cdot 180° − 360° = (n-2) 180°$.

15.

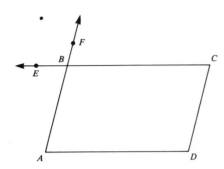

(a) $m(\angle A) = m(\angle FBC)$ (corresponding angles). $m(\angle B) + m(FBC) = 180°$ (supplementary angles). Thus, $m(\angle B) + m(\angle A) = 180°$ (substitution).
(b) $m(\angle A) = m(\angle ABE)$ (alternate interior angles). $m(\angle ABE) = m(\angle C)$ (corresponding angles). Hence, $m(\angle A) = m(\angle C)$. Likewise, $m(\angle B) = m(\angle D)$.
17. Let $ABCD$ be a quadrilateral with $m(\angle 1) = m(\angle 3)$ and $m(\angle 2) = m(\angle 4)$.

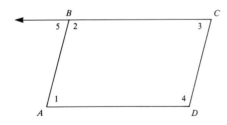

We are given that $m(\angle 1) = m(\angle 3)$ and $m(\angle 2) = m(\angle 4)$. Also, we know $m(\angle 1) + m(\angle 2) + m(\angle 3) + m(\angle 4) = 360°$. Substituting, we have $m(\angle 1) + m(\angle 2) + m(\angle 1) + m(\angle 2) = 360°$. Thus, $2m(\angle 1) + 2m(\angle 2) = 360°$ or $2[m(\angle 1) + m(\angle 2)] = 360°$ and so $m(\angle 1) + m(\angle 2) = 180°$. Since $m(\angle 5) + m(\angle 2) = 180°$, then $m(\angle 1) + m(\angle 2) = m(\angle 5) + m(\angle 2)$. Subtracting the $m(\angle 2)$ from both sides, we have $m(\angle 1) = m(\angle 5)$. Now, since alternate interior angles are congruent, we have $\overleftrightarrow{AD} \parallel \overleftrightarrow{BC}$. Similarly, it can be shown that $\overleftrightarrow{AB} \parallel \overleftrightarrow{DC}$.

19.

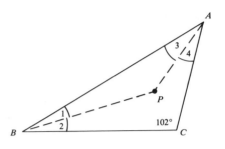

Let $m(\angle 1) = m(\angle 2) = x$ and $m(\angle 3) = m(\angle 4) = y$. Then $m(\angle BPA) = 180° - (x + y)$. In $\triangle ABC$, $2x + 2y + 102° = 180°$, so $2x + 2y = 78°$. Thus, $2(x + y) = 78°$ and $x + y = 39°$. Hence, $m(\angle BPA) = 180° - (x + y) = 180° - 39° = 141°$.

Problem Set 9-4

1. (a) Yes. Since m is perpendicular to α, m is perpendicular to every line in α through C. Consequently, $m \perp \overleftrightarrow{BC}$ and $m \perp \overleftrightarrow{AC}$, and angles DCB and DCA are right angles. Thus triangles BDC and ADC are right triangles. (b) No. Since $\triangle DPC$ will be a right triangle with a right angle at C, no other angle can be 90° or more. (c) Yes, since it contains the line m which is perpendicular to α. **3.** (a) Quadrilateral pyramid (b) Quadrilateral prism (c) Pentagonal pyramid **5.** (a) T (b) F (c) T (d) F (e) F (f) F (g) F (h) T

9.

	Pyramid	Prism
(a)	$n + 1$	$n + 2$
(b)	$n + 1$	$2n$
(c)	$2n$	$3n$

(d) Pyramid: $(n + 1) + (n + 1) - 2n = 2$

11. (a) $ABFE$ is a parallelogram. $\overleftrightarrow{AB} \parallel \overleftrightarrow{CD}$ and $\overleftrightarrow{CD} \parallel \overleftrightarrow{EF}$, hence $\overleftrightarrow{AB} \parallel \overleftrightarrow{EF}$. Also, $\overleftrightarrow{BF}$ and $\overleftrightarrow{AE}$ are parallel since (1) these lines are in parallel planes, and (2) they cannot be skew lines since they are in the plane determined by $\overleftrightarrow{AB}$ and $\overleftrightarrow{EF}$. Thus, $ABFE$ is a parallelogram.
$ABFE$ is a rectangle. $\overleftrightarrow{AB} \perp \overleftrightarrow{AD}$ since $ABCD$ is a square. Likewise $\overleftrightarrow{AB} \perp \overleftrightarrow{AH}$. Since $\overleftrightarrow{AB}$ is perpendicular to two lines in plane ADE, it is perpendicular to the plane ADE. Thus $\overleftrightarrow{AB}$ is perpendicular to every line passing through the point of intersection, which is A. Hence, $\overleftrightarrow{AB} \perp \overleftrightarrow{AE}$. Similarly, $\overleftrightarrow{AB} \perp \overleftrightarrow{BF}$. It can also be shown in the

same manner that $\overleftrightarrow{EF}$ is perpendicular to $\overleftrightarrow{AE}$ and $\overleftrightarrow{BF}$, and so $ABFE$ is a rectangle.   **(b)** The planes determined by ABC, DCF, HGF, ABG, ABF, and HDC.   **(c)** Yes. If $\overleftrightarrow{CD}$ intersects the plane ABF, it must intersect it along $\overleftrightarrow{AB}$ since $\overleftrightarrow{CD}$ is in the plane determined by ABC, and any point common to both planes is on $\overleftrightarrow{AB}$. This is a contradiction since $\overleftrightarrow{AB}$ and $\overleftrightarrow{CD}$ are parallel.

Problem Set 9-5

1.   (a), (b), (c), (e), (g), (h), (j), and (k) are transversable.

(a)

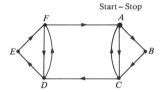

Path: $ABCACDEFDFA$. Any point can be a starting point.

(b)

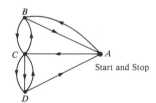

Path: $ABACBCDCDA$. Any point can be a starting point.

(c)

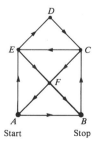

Path: $ABCFAEDCEFB$. Only points A and B can be starting points.

(e)

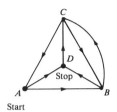

Path: $ABCBDCAD$. Only points A and D can be starting points.

(g)

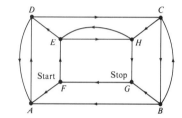

Path: $FADABCBGFEDCHEHG$. Only points F and G can be starting points.

(h)

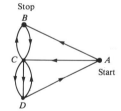

Path: $ACBCDCDAB$. Only points A and B can be starting points.

(j)

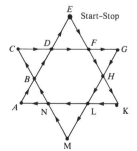

Path: $EFHKLNABDFGHLMNBCDE$. Any point can be a starting point.

(k)

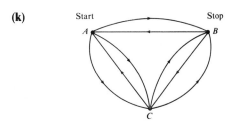

Path: *ABACACBCB*. Only points *A* and *B* can be starting points.

(b) Network (i) is not traversable since it has 4 odd vertices. Network (ii) has 2 odd vertices so it is traversable as shown below.

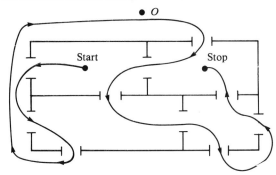

3. (a)

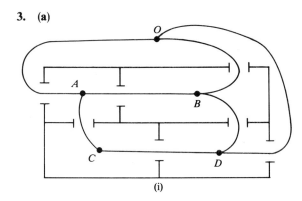

5. (a)

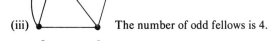

(i)   The number of odd fellows is 0.

(ii)   The number of odd fellows is 2.

(iii)   The number of odd fellows is 4.

(iv)   The number of odd fellows is 4.

(b) The number of even fellows may be either even or odd.

Chapter Test

1. (a) $\overleftrightarrow{AB}, \overleftrightarrow{BC}, \overleftrightarrow{AC}$ **(b)** $\overrightarrow{BA}, \overrightarrow{BC}$ **(c)** $\overline{AB}$ **(d)** $\overline{AB}$ **(e)** $\overrightarrow{AB}$ **3. (a)** Three noncollinear points   **(b)** Two distinct intersecting lines   **(c)** Two distinct parallel lines   **(d)** A line and a point not on the

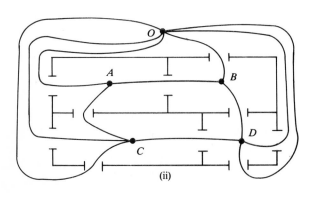

line   **5.** Answers vary   **7.** **(a)** No. The sum of two obtuse angles is larger than 180°, which is the sum of the measures of the angles in the triangle.   **(b)** No. The sum of the measures of the four angles in a parallelogram must be 360°. If all the angles are acute, the sum would be less than 360°.   **9.** **(a)** Given any convex *n*-gon, pick any vertex and draw all possible diagonals from this vertex. This will determine $(n - 2)$ triangles. Since the sum of measures of the angles in each triangle is 180°, the sum of the measures of the angles in the *n*-gon is $(n - 2)180°$.   **(b)** 90 sides **11.** 6 **13.** **(a)** 60° **(b)** 120° **(c)** 120° **15.** 48°

CHAPTER 10

Problem Set 10-1

1. **(a)** 20; 2   **(b)** 36; 3.6   **(c)** 45; 4.5   **(d)** 5; 0.5 **(e)** 6.2; 0.62   **(f)** 7.9; 0.79   **(g)** 0.93; 9.3   **(h)** 11.9; 119   **(i)** 144; 14.4   **(j)** 1.69; 16.9   **3.** **(a)** 100 **(b)** 10   **(c)** 0.1   **5.** **(a)** 3.5; 35; 3500   **(b)** 16.3; 163; 1630   **(c)** 0.035; 0.35; 3.5   **(d)** 0.1; 10; 100 **(e)** 2; 20; 200; 2000   **7.** 6 m, 5218 mm, 52 dm, 38 dm, 245 cm, 700 mm, 91 mm, 8 cm   **9.** **(a)** 8 cm **(b)** 12 cm   **(c)** 9 cm   **(d)** 20 cm   **11.** **(a)** 13 cm   **(b)** $(a + b + c)$ cm   **(c)** $3s$ **(d)** $4s$ **(e)** $2\ell + 2w$ **(f)** ns

Problem Set 10-2

1. **(a)** Yes. ASA   **(b)** Yes. AAS   **(c)** No **(d)** Yes. SAS   **(e)** Yes. SSS   **(f)** No **3.** **(c)** Right triangle   **(d)** Impossible **7.** **(a)** $\measuredangle ABD \simeq \measuredangle CBD$, Definition of angle bisector; $\overline{AB} \simeq \overline{CB}$, Definition of isosceles triangle; $\overline{BD} \simeq \overline{BD}$, Reflexive property. $\triangle ABD \simeq \triangle CBD$, SAS; $\overline{AD} \simeq \overline{CD}$, CPCTC.*   **(b)** $\measuredangle ADB \simeq \measuredangle CDB$, CPCTC using (a) above; $\measuredangle ADB$ and $\measuredangle CDB$ are adjacent, Definition of adjacent angles; $m(\measuredangle ADB) + m(\measuredangle CDB) = 180°$ since

*CPCTC: Corresponding parts of congruent triangles are congruent.

$\measuredangle ADC$ is a straight angle. $m(\measuredangle ADB) = m(\measuredangle CDB)$, Definition of $\simeq$ angles. $m(\measuredangle ADB) = m(\measuredangle CDB) = 90°$.   **9.** **(a)** Congruent sides   **(b)** Lengths are congruent, and widths are congruent.   **11.** **(a)** Use 10(c)   **(b)** $\measuredangle CDA$ is a right angle since $\measuredangle BAD$ is right, and interior angles on the same side of a transversal are supplementary. $\overline{AB} \simeq \overline{DC}$ by 10(b); $\overline{AD} \simeq \overline{AD}$, Reflexive property; $\triangle ABD \simeq \triangle DCA$, SAS; $\overline{BD} \simeq \overline{CA}$, CPCTC.

13. **(a)**

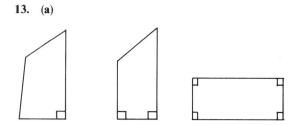

(b) Sum of the angles of a convex quadrilateral is 360°.   **(c)** No. Any parallelogram with a pair of right angles must have its other pair of angles as right angles and hence be a rectangle.

Problem Set 10-3

1. **(a)** $\overline{AB} \simeq \overline{BC} \simeq \overline{AD} \simeq \overline{DC}$, Definition of rhombus; $\overline{AC} \simeq \overline{AC}$, Reflexive property; $\triangle ABC \simeq \triangle ADC$, SSS; $\measuredangle BAC \simeq \measuredangle DAC$ and $\measuredangle BCA \simeq \measuredangle DCA$ by CPCTC. **(b)** $\measuredangle BAC \simeq \measuredangle DAC$ by 1(a); $\overline{AE} \simeq \overline{AE}$, Reflexive property; $\overline{AB} \simeq \overline{AD}$ Definition of rhombus; $\triangle ABE \simeq \triangle DAE$, SAS; $\overline{BE} \simeq \overline{DE}$, CPCTC.   **5.** **(a)** and **(c)** Altitudes should meet at a point in the interior of an acute triangle.   **(b)** Altitudes meet at a vertex of the right angle of a right triangle.   **(d)** Altitudes meet in the exterior of an obtuse triangle.   **7.** Medians meet at a point (centroid).   **9.** Let $ABCD$ be a quadrilateral with $\overline{AB} \simeq \overline{CD}$ and $\overline{AB} \parallel \overline{CD}$. $\measuredangle ABD \simeq \measuredangle CDB$, alternate interior angles of parallel lines; $\overline{BD} \simeq \overline{BD}$, Reflexive property; $\triangle ABD \simeq \triangle CDB$, SAS; $\measuredangle ADB \simeq \measuredangle CBD$, CPCTC; $\overline{BC} \parallel \overline{AD}$, congruent alternate interior angles determine parallel lines.

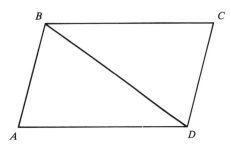

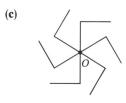

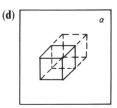

11. $\overline{AD} \simeq \overline{BC}$ and $\overline{DC} \simeq \overline{AB}$, Opposite sides of a parallelogram are congruent; $\overline{HD} \simeq \overline{AH} \simeq \overline{CF} \simeq \overline{BF}$; $\overline{DE} \simeq \overline{CE} \simeq \overline{BG} \simeq \overline{AG}$; also $\angle A$, $\angle B$, $\angle C$, and $\angle D$ are right angles. Hence, $\triangle DEH \simeq \triangle CEF \simeq \triangle BGF \simeq \triangle AGH$, SAS; $\overline{HE} \simeq \overline{FE} \simeq \overline{GF} \simeq \overline{GH}$, CPCTC.

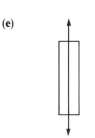

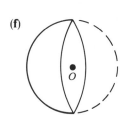

Problem Set 10-4

1. **(a)** Turn   **(b)** Slide   **(c)** Turn   **(d)** Turn
(e) Slide   **(f)** Flip   **3.** Answers vary depending on how letters are made.   **5.** **(a)** 1 vertical   **(b)** 1 vertical   **(c)** 1 vertical   **(d)** None   **(e)** 1 vertical   **(f)** 5 lines   **(g)** 1 vertical   **(h)** 1 vertical

7. **(a)**   **(b)**

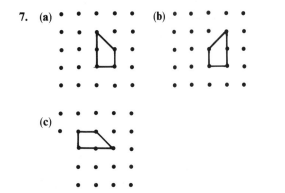

(c)

13. Last image is original image.   **15.** **(b)** A turn   **(c)** No   **(d)** Yes, a turn with center 0 through $\beta - \alpha$.

Problem Set 10-5

1. Triangle 3
3.

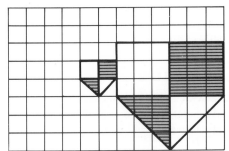

9. **(a)**   **(b)**

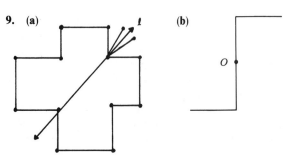

This illustration is one possibility.   **5.** **(a)** $x = 7$ **(b)** $x = 24/7$ **(c)** $x = 15/2$ **(d)** $x = 10$ m   **7.** **(a)** 9   **(b)** 14/3   **(c)** $7\frac{1}{2}$ **(d)** 3   **9.** Yes. Corresponding angles are congruent.   **11.** **(c)** If in $\triangle ABC$ and $\triangle DEF$ we have $AB/DE = AC/DF$ and $\angle A \simeq \angle A$, then $\triangle ABC \sim \triangle DEF$.   **13.** Ratio of the perimeters is the same as the ratio of the sides.   **17.** 15 m

Problem Set 10-6

1. Diameter is the longest chord of a circle.
3. Right triangle **5.** No. The tangent line will intersect one circle in two points. **7.** *Hint:* first inscribe a square in the given circle. **9.** *Hint:* The center of the circle is at the intersection point of the diagonals. **11.** *Hint:* Draw perpendicular from O to ℓ to obtain radius of the circle. **13.** **(a)** Isosceles
(b) $m(\angle 3) + m(\angle COB) = 180°$. $m(\angle 1) + m(\angle 2) + m(\angle COB) = 180°$. Hence, $m(\angle 1) + m(\angle 2) = m(\angle 3)$. **(c)** $m(\angle 1) = m(\angle 2)$ ($\triangle OBC$ is isosceles). Since $m(\angle 1) + m(\angle 2) = m(\angle 3)$, it follows that $m(\angle 1) + m(\angle 1) = m(\angle 3)$, $m(\angle 1) = (1/2) m(\angle 3)$.
15. **(a)** 6 cm **(b)** $3/\pi$ cm **(c)** $1/3\pi$ cm
(d) 46 cm **17.** Doubled

(b)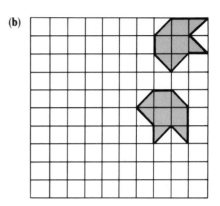

Chapter Test

1. **(a)** $\triangle ABD \simeq \triangle CBD$ by SAS **(b)** $\triangle AGC \simeq \triangle DEB$ by SAS **(c)** $\triangle CBA \simeq \triangle CDE$ by AAS
(d) $\triangle ABC \simeq \triangle EDC$ by SAS **(e)** $\triangle ABD \simeq \triangle CBD$ by ASA or by SAS **(f)** $\triangle ABD \simeq \triangle CBD$ by SAS
(g) $\triangle ABD \simeq \triangle CBE$ by SSS, $\triangle ABE \simeq \triangle CBD$ by SSS **(h)** $\triangle ABC \simeq \triangle ADC$ by SSS. Possibly others if the pair listed is used to establish that corresponding parts of congruent triangles are congruent.

3. **(a)** Line and turn **(b)** Line, turn, and point
(c) Line

(c)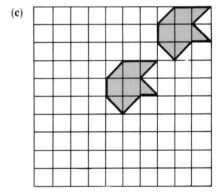

5. **(a)**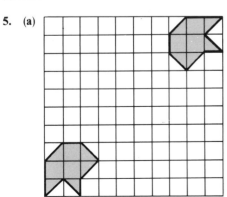

11. **(a)** mm **(b)** cm **(c)** mm **(d)** km
(e) cm **(f)** m **13.** **(a)** False. A chord has its endpoints on the circle. **(b)** False. A diameter intersects a circle in two points and a tangent intersects it in only one point. **(c)** True **(d)** True **(e)** True
15. 12 m **17.** Find the point of intersection of the perpendicular bisectors of the sides. This is the center of the circle. A radius has length which equals the distance from the center to any vertex of the heptagon.
19. **(a)** $(4 + 2\pi)$ cm **(b)** $(6 + 5\pi)$ mm
21. $\angle CBA \simeq \angle BDA$ given $\angle A \simeq \angle A$, Reflexive property; $\triangle ABD \simeq \triangle ACB$, AA; $AB/AC = AD/AB$, Corresponding sides of similar triangles are proportional. $(AB)^2 = (AC)(AD)$, Multiplication property of equality.

CHAPTER 11

Problem Set 11-1

1. (a) cm² (b) cm² (c) cm² (d) m² (e) m²
(f) km² 3. Answers vary 5. (a) 20 cm²
(b) 900 cm² or 0.09 m² (c) 7.5 m² (d) 46.5 cm²
7. The area of each triangle is 10 cm² since they all
have the same base, $\overline{AB}$, and the same height.
9. (a) 25π cm² (b) (8/3)π cm² (c) 3.6π cm²
(d) 4.5π cm² 11. (a) 2π cm² (b) [2 + (π/2)] cm²
(c) 2π cm² 13. 24 m² 15. 7π m²
17. 1200 19. (a) $A = 1, B = 1, C = 4, D = 1\frac{1}{2},$
$E = 2, F = 3, G = 3\frac{1}{2}, H = 5\frac{1}{2}$. (b) Pick's theorem
holds for all polygons in (a), for example, in G, I +
(1/2) B − 1 = 1 + (1/2)(7) − 1 = 3½ 21. Rotate
the shaded region 180° clockwise about point E. The
area of the triangle is the same as the area of the
parallelogram. Thus $A = (h/2) \cdot b$.
23.

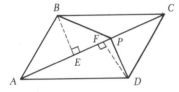

Draw altitudes $\overline{BE}$ and $\overline{DF}$ of triangles BCP and DCP,
respectively. $\triangle ABE \cong \triangle CDF$ by AAS. Thus, $\overline{BE} \cong \overline{DF}$.
Since $\overline{CP}$ is a base of $\triangle BCP$ and $\triangle DCP$, and since the
heights are the same, the areas must be the same.

Problem Set 11-2

1. (a) 6 (b) √2 (c) 5a (d) 12 (e) √3s
(f) √2 (g) 9 (h) 13 (i) √32/2 or 2 √2
(j) √45 or 3 √5 3. (a) $x = 8, y = 2\sqrt{3}$ (b) $x = 4$,
$y = 2$ (c) $y = 6$ 5. √5200 km or 20 √13 km ≐
72.1 km 7. $\triangle ACD \sim \triangle ABC$. Thus $b/x = c/b$
implies $b^2 = cx$. $\triangle BCD \sim \triangle BAC$. Thus $a/y = c/a$
implies $a^2 = cy$. Consequently, $a^2 + b^2 = cx + cy =$
$c(x + y) = c^2$. 9. The area of the large square is
equal to the sum of the areas of the smaller square and
the four triangles. Thus, $(a + b)^2 = c^2 + 4(ab/2); a^2 +$
$2ab + b^2 = c^2 + 2ab; a^2 + b^2 = c^2$. The reader should
also verify that the smaller quadrilateral is a square.
11. (a) The area of the triangle of side length c is

$\sqrt{3}c^2/4$ (see 10(a)). From the Pythagorean Theorem,
$c^2 = a^2 + b^2$. Thus $\sqrt{3}c^2/4 = (\sqrt{3}/4)(a^2 + b^2) = (\sqrt{3}/4)a^2 + (\sqrt{3}/4)b^2$. Since $(\sqrt{3}/4) a^2$ and $(\sqrt{3}/4) b^2$ are the
areas of the two smaller triangles, the proof is
complete. (b) Yes 13. √27 or 3 √3

Problem Set 11-3

1. (a) 96 cm² (b) 236 cm² 3. (a) 4900 sq ft
(b) 1500π sq ft (c) 32π + 16 √5π or (32 + 16 √5)π
5. 2688π mm² 7. 16/36 or 4/9 9. (6400 √2π
+ 13 600 π) cm²

Problem Set 11-4

1. (a) 8000 (b) 0.0005 (c) 0.000675
(c) 3 000 000 (e) 7 3. (a) 64 cm³ (b) 120
cm³ (c) 216 cm³ (d) 14 cm³ (e) 50 cm³
(f) 21π cm³ (g) 432π cm³ (h) (500/3)π cm³
5. 1680π mm³ 7. It is multiplied by 8.

9.

Height	10	3	20	25
cm³	2000	6000	4000	7500
dm³	2	6	4	7.5
L	2	6	4	7.5

11. 253 500π L 13. 1.62 L 15. 32.4 L
17. 8 cm 19. (b) is a better buy.

Problem Set 11-5

1. (a) t or kg (b) kg (c) g (d) t (e) g
(f) g (g) t (h) kg or g (i) kg or g (j) g
3. (a) 15 (b) 8 (c) 36 (d) 0.072
(e) 4.230 (f) 3.007 (g) 5750 (h) 5.750
(i) 30 (j) 30 000 5. 16 000 g or 16 kg
7. $0.02 9. (a) No (b) No (c) No
(d) Yes (e) No (f) Yes (g) Yes (h) Chilly
(i) Hot 11. (a) 50°F (b) 32°F (c) 86°F
(d) 212°F (e) 414°F (f) ⁻40°F

Chapter Test

1. (a) Find the area of $\triangle ADC$ and double it, that is, A
$= 2(\frac{1}{2} \cdot DE \cdot AC)$ (b) $A = b \cdot h = DC \cdot FB$.
3. 8½ 5. The area of the trapezoid is equal to the

area of the rectangle from its component parts. The area of the rectangle is $(h/2)(b_1 + b_2)$, which is the formula for the area of a trapezoid.   **7.** (a) 12π cm^2 (b) $(12 + 4.5\pi)$ cm^2 (c) 64.5 cm^2 (d) 24 cm^2 (e) 178.5 m^2 (f) 4π cm^2 **9.** (a) $S.A. = 54\pi$ cm^2, $V = 54\pi$ cm^3 (b) $S.A. = 304$ m^2, $V = 320$ m^3 (c) $S.A. = 144$ cm^2, $V = 64$ cm^3 (d) $S.A. = 96\pi$ cm^2, $V = 96\pi$ cm^3 (e) $S.A. = 100\pi$ m^2, $V = (500/3)\pi$ m^3 **11.** (a) L   (b) kg   (c) g   (d) g   (e) kg (f) t   (g) mL   **13.** (a) 2000   (b) 1000   (c) 3 (d) 0.0042   (e) 0.0002

CHAPTER 12

Problem Set 12-1

1. (a) $A(2, 2)$; $B(5, 0)$; $C(4, ^-3)$; $D(0, ^-3)$; $E(^-2, ^-3)$; $F(^-4, 0)$; $G(^-4, 3)$; $H(0, 3)$ (b) Answers vary, e.g., $(2, ^-3)$ **3.** Answers vary (a) $(0, 2)$ and $(1, 2)$ (b) $(^-1, 1)$ and $(^-1, 3)$ (c) $(5, 0)$ and $(6, 0)$ (d) $(0, 1)$ and $(0, ^-1)$ (e) $(0, 2)$ and $(0, 3)$ (f) $(2, 2)$ and $(3, 3)$ **5.** (a) $x = ^-2$; y is any real number.   (b) x is any real number; $y = 1$.   (c) $x > 0$ and $y < 0$; x and y are real numbers.   **7.** D has coordinates $(4, ^-2)$.   **9.** The choice of scale is up to the individual.

Problem Set 12-2

1. (a) 4   (b) 4   (c) 5   (d) 5   (e) $\sqrt{52}$ or $2\sqrt{13}$ (f) 7   (g) 5   (h) 5   (i) $\sqrt{68}$ or $2\sqrt{17}$ (j) $\sqrt{8}$ or $2\sqrt{2}$ **3.** Let A, B, and C have coordinates $(0, 6)$, $(^-3, 0)$, $(9, ^-6)$, respectively. $AB = \sqrt{45}$; $BC = \sqrt{180}$; $AC = \sqrt{225}$. Since $(\sqrt{45})^2 + (\sqrt{180})^2 = (\sqrt{225})^2$, then $(AB)^2 + (BC)^2 = (AC)^2$ and A, B, and C are the vertices of a right triangle.   **5.** $x = 9$ or $^-7$ **7.** $(^-7, 11)$ **9.** (a) $(9, 4)$ (b) $(^-3, 12)$ (c) $(1, ^-4)$ **11.** m has coordinates $(a/2, b/2)$

$$BM = \sqrt{\left(\frac{a}{2}\right)^2 + \left(\frac{b}{2} - b\right)^2} = \sqrt{\frac{a^2}{4} + \frac{b^2}{4}}$$

$$AM = \sqrt{\left(\frac{a}{2} - a\right)^2 + \left(\frac{b}{2} - 0\right)^2} = \sqrt{\frac{a^2}{4} + \frac{b^2}{4}}$$

$$MO = \sqrt{\left(\frac{a}{2} - 0\right)^2 + \left(\frac{b}{2} - 0\right)^2} = \sqrt{\frac{a^2}{4} + \frac{b^2}{4}}$$

Therefore, M is equidistant from A, B, and O.

Problem Set 12-3

1. (a)

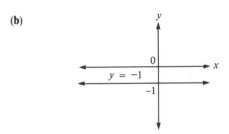

(b)

(c)

(d)

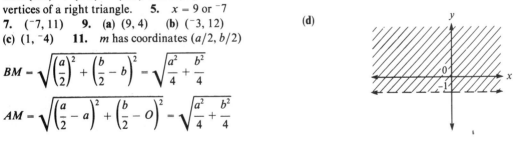

(e)

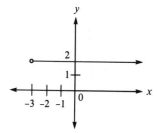

3. (a)

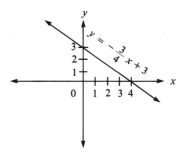

(f)

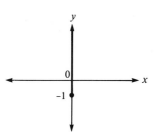

(b)

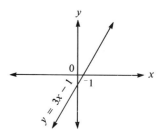

3. (a) $(x - 3)^2 + (y + 2)^2 = 4$ **(b)** $(x + 3)^2 + (y + 4)^2 = 25$ **(c)** $(x + 1)^2 + y^2 = 4$ **(d)** $x^2 + y^2 = 9$ **5.** $x^2 + y^2 = 34$ **7.** $(x + 2)^2 + (y + 2)^2 = 52$ **9.** $[x - (29/10)]^2 + y^2 = (29/10)^2$ **11.** The treasure is at $(0, 0)$, that is, the point of intersection of the line connecting the pine and the oak tree and the line through the olive tree perpendicular to the first line.

(c)

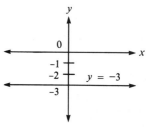

Problem Set 12-4

1.

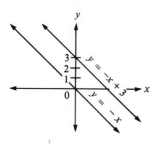

(d)

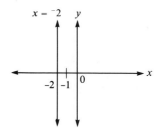

(e)

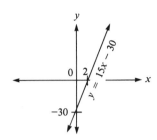

(b)

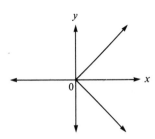

(f)

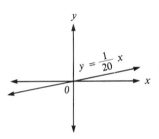

(c)

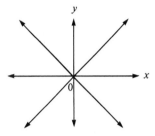

5. **(a)** $y = (1/3)x$ **(b)** $y = {}^-x + 3$ **(c)** $y = (3/4)x + (7/4)$ **(d)** $y = (1/3)x$ **(e)** $y = x$ **7.** **(a)** $y = {}^-x - 1$ **(b)** $y = (1/2)x$ **(c)** $y = 0 \cdot x + 1$
(d) $x = 2$ **(e)** $y = x - (1/2)$ **(f)** $y = 0 \cdot x + 0$
9. **(a)** $y = {}^-2x - 1$ **(b)** $y = {}^-(2/3)x + (5/3)$
(c) $x = {}^-2$ **(d)** $y = 3$ **11.** Slope of $\overline{BC}$ and $\overline{DA}$ is $1/2$, which implies $\overline{BC} \parallel \overline{DA}$. Slope of $\overline{CD}$ and $\overline{BA}$ is 4, which implies $\overline{CD} \parallel \overline{BA}$. Thus, $ABCD$ is a parallelogram.   **13.** **(a)** $y = {}^-(1/2)x - (3/2)$
(b) $y = (2/3)x - (11/3)$ **15.** x intercept is a; y intercept is b **17.** $C = (5/9)(F - 32)$ **19.** Let T and C be the respective temperature and number of chirps. $T = (5/36)C + (40/9)$

21. **(a)**

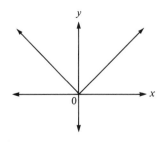

(d)

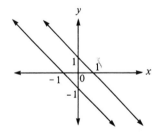

(e)

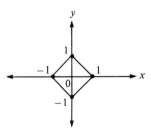

23. $\pi/4$ square units

Problem Set 12–5

1. (a) $(0, ^-\!{}^5\!/_3)$; $(^5\!/_2, 0)$; $(1, ^-1)$; $(2, ^-\!{}^1\!/_3)$
(b)

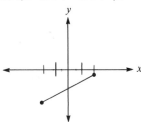

(c)

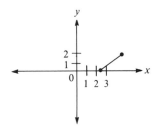

3. (a) $(^-11, ^-8)$ (b) $(^-30\!/_{11}, ^-84\!/_{11})$ (c) $(^{13}\!/_3, ^{43}\!/_{12})$
(d) $(^-\!{}^6\!/_5, ^-\!{}^4\!/_5)$ (e) $(0, 0)$ (f) $(^-1 + 3\sqrt{2},$
$3 - \sqrt{2})$ **5.** The lines intersect at $A(^-2, ^-1)$,
$B(3, 9)$, and $C(5, ^-2)$. $AB = BC = \sqrt{125}$, so the triangle
is isosceles.   **7.** $y = {}^1\!/_3 x - 4$ and $y = ^-\!{}^1\!/_2 x - 4$.
9. 4000 gallons of gasoline and 1000 gallons of
kerosene.   **11.** 100 liters of 90% solution and 50 liters
of the 60% solution.   **13.** (a) The answers are all
$(^-1, 2)$.

(b) $\begin{cases} 13\,x + 14\,y = 15 \\ 16\,x + 17\,y = 18 \end{cases}$

The solution is $(^-1, 2)$.

(c) $\begin{cases} ax + (a + 1)y = a + 2 \\ (a + 3)x + (a + 4)y = a + 5 \end{cases}$

has solution $(^-1, 2)$ as does the system:

$\begin{cases} ax + (a + d)y = a + 2d \\ (a + 3d)x + (a + 4d)y = a + 5d \end{cases}$
Substitute to check.

Chapter Test

1. 16   **3.** (i) The slopes of the three segments
determined are each $3/4$.   (ii) Labeling $(4, 2)$, $(0, ^-1)$
and $(^-4, ^-4)$ as A, B, and C, respectively, we find that
$AB = 5$, $AC = 10$, and $BC = 5$ so that $AB + BC = AC$.
Hence, A, B, and C are collinear.   **5.** $(x + 3)^2 +$
$(y - 4)^2 = 25$ **7.** (a) $y = ^-(4/3)x - (1/3)$
(b) $x = ^-3$ (c) $y = 3$ **9.** (a) $(^{21}\!/_5, ^-\!{}^3\!/_5)$ is the unique
solution.   (b) $(^{10}\!/_6, ^4\!/_3)$ is the unique solution.   (c) No
solution

CHAPTER 13

1. The number of digits is 10.   **3.** (a) 1, 5, 9, 13, 17,
21, ...   (b) $4(n - 2) + 5$ or $4n - 3$ **5.** 150
sheets of paper in each box.   **7.** Water depth is 3
inches.   **9.** Approximately $44 444
11. $d = 98$ **13.** $30° - 7° \, 30' = 22° \, 30'$.
15. 40 500 000 001   **17.** Center at $(2, ^-1)$, $r = \sqrt{5}$
19. 60   **21.** (a) *Hint:* Show that $\overleftrightarrow{BP} \parallel \overleftrightarrow{ND}$,
$\overleftrightarrow{MC} \parallel \overleftrightarrow{AO}$, and that $\triangle BHM \approx \triangle CGN \approx \triangle DFO \approx$
$\triangle AEP$.   (b) 20 cm^2; show that $AO = {}^5\!/_2 EF$ and apply
the Pythagorean Theorem to $\triangle ADO$. The area of $HGFE$
is ${}^1\!/_5$ of the area of $ABCD$.   **23.** Answers vary.
That the sum of the numbers in any row is given by 2^{n-1}
can be justified by noticing that the sum of the numbers
in each row is really twice as much as the sum in the
preceding row. For example, consider the fourth and
fifth row as shown below.

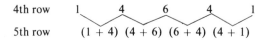

4th row

5th row

Each of the numbers in the 4th row appears twice as
many times in the sum of the numbers in the 5th row.
Consequently, the sum of the number in any row is twice
as large as the one in the preceding row. Since the sum in
row one is $1 = 2^0$, then the next sums are given as shown
at the top of the next column.

row	sum
1	$1 = 2^0$
2	$2 = 2^1$
3	$4 = 2^2$
4	$8 = 2^3$
5	$16 = 2^4$
.	.
.	.
.	.
n	2^{n-1}

APPENDIX I

Problem Set AI-1

1. (a) False statement   (b) Not a statement
(c) False statement   (d) Not a statement   (e) Not a
statement   (f) Not a statement   (g) True
statement   (h) Not a statement   **3.** (a) The book
does not have 500 pages   (b) Six is not less than eight
or six is greater than or equal to eight.   (c) Johnny is
thin.   (d) Al does smoke.   (e) $3 \cdot 5 \neq 15$
5. (a) F   (b) T   (c) T   (d) F   (e) F   (f) T
(g) F   (h) F   (i) F   (j) F

7.

p	q	$\sim p$	$\sim p \vee q$
T	T	F	T
T	F	F	F
F	T	T	T
F	F	T	T

Problem Set AI-2

1. (a) $p \rightarrow q$ (b) $\sim p \rightarrow q$ (c) $p \rightarrow \sim q$
(d) $p \rightarrow q$ (e) $\sim q \rightarrow \sim p$ (f) $q \leftrightarrow p$

3. (a)

p	q	$p \vee q$	$p \rightarrow (p \vee q)$
T	T	T	T
T	F	T	T
F	T	T	T
F	F	F	T

(b)

p	q	$p \wedge q$	$(p \wedge q) \rightarrow q$
T	T	T	T
T	F	F	T
F	T	F	T
F	F	F	T

(c)

p	$\sim p$	$\sim(\sim p)$	$p \rightarrow \sim(\sim p)$	$\sim(\sim p) \rightarrow p$	$p \leftrightarrow \sim(\sim p)$
T	F	T	T	T	T
F	T	F	T	T	T

5. (a) T   (b) F   (c) T   (d) T   (e) F   (f) T
7. No. Tom can go to the movies or not and the
implication is still true.   **9.** Answers may vary. For
example, "If a number is not a multiple of 4, then it is
not a multiple of 8."

Problem Set AI-3

1. (a) There exists an integer x such that $x + 8 =$
11.   (b) For all integers x, $x + 0 = x$, or there exists
an integer x such that $x + 0 = x$.   (c) There exists an
integer x such that $x^2 = 4$.   (d) For no integers x, $x + 1$
$= x + 2$.   **3.** (a) No person has blond hair.
(b) Some dogs do not have four legs.   (c) All cats have
nine lives.   (d) Some dogs can fly.   (e) Some squares
are not rectangles.   (f) All rectangles are squares.
(g) Some of Mary's crayons are not broken.
5. (a) Valid   (b) Valid   (c) Valid   (d) Invalid
(e) Invalid   (f) Valid   (g) Invalid   (h) Valid

APPENDIX II

Problem Set AII-1

3. (a) 70   (b) 9000   (c) 1100   (d) 560
(e) 3470   **5.** 9 876 543   **7.** Depends on the keys
available.   **9.** Depends on the calculator, but use
scientific notation if available.   **11.** Depends on the
calculator.   **15.** 7689   **17.** (a) 34; 34; 34

(b) 34   **(c)** 34   **19.** Depends on the calculator if the answer appears.

21.   **(a)** 981
+421
——
1402

(b) 2025
1196
+3148
——
6369

(c) 1069
2094
9546
9003
+7064
——
28776

(d) 291
451
+584
——
1326

23. Play second and make sure that the sum when you hand the calculator to your opponent is a multiple of 3.   **25.** Play first; push 3. After that, on your turn make the sum 3 plus a multiple of 10.   **27.**   **(a)** 12; 123, 1234; 12345, . . .   **(b)** 10

29.   **(a)** Possibly 863
+752

  (b) Possibly 368
+257

31. 2514   **33.** 35 006; GOOSE
35.   **(a)** 46 414   **(b)** 3453

(c) 383
−159
——
224

(d) 13296
−8309
——
4987

37. Play second; use a strategy similar to number 36 but use a multiple of 4.   **39.** The original number displayed; yes.

41.   **(a)** 876   if positive numbers
−235   only are used.

  (b) 623
−587

43. 5   **45.** 4 782 969   **47.** 1 · 36; 2 · 18; 3 · 12; 4 · 9; 6 · 6

49.   **(a)** 37
×43
——
111
1480
——
1591

(b) 93
×36
——
558
2790
——
3348

(c) 786
×42
——

(d) 43
×56

51.   **(a)** 732   **(b)** 378
×86   ×26

53. 50 375 808; BOBSLEDS   **55.** It depends on when the decade starts and how many leap years are involved, but approximately 5 259 600.   **57.** The ton of dimes. Check weights.   **59.** 0; yes.   **61.** $60; $3600; $86 400; $604 800; approximately $18 144 000; approximately $31 557 600; approximately $631 152 000   **63.** 3 628 800   **65.** 19
67.   **(a)** 1, 2, 3, 4, 6, 9, 12, 18, 36   **(b)** 1, 2, 3, 4, 6, 8, 9, 12, 16, 18, 24, 36, 48, 72, 144   **69.**   **(a)** $3\overline{)876}$
(b) $8\overline{)367}$ **71.** 7 500 000 cows   **73.** 638; BEG
75.   **(a)** Yes   **(b)** Yes   **(c)** No   **(d)** No
77. These answers depend entirely on your calculator and the buttons it contains.

$3 = 1 + 9 - 7$ $11 = 7 + 1 + \sqrt{9}$
$4 = 1^7 + \sqrt{9}$ $12 = 19 - 7$
$5 = 7 - \sqrt{9} + 1$ $13 = 91 \div 7$
$6 = 7 - 1^9$ $14 = 7(\sqrt{9} - 1)$
$7 = 7 \cdot 1^9$ $15 = 7 + 9 - 1$
$8 = 7 + 1^9$ $16 = (7 + 9) \cdot 1$
$9 = 1^7 \cdot 9$ $17 = 7 + 9 + 1$
$10 = 1^7 + 9$ $18 = \sqrt{9}\,(7 - 1)$
                 $19 = ?$
                 $20 = 7\sqrt{9} - 1$

79. $22 + 2 =$ **81.**   **(a)** $7 \cdot 8 - 6 =$ **(b)** $(7 + 6)8 =$ **(c)** $8(7 - 6) =$ **(d)** $(7 \cdot 8) - 6 =$
(e) $8(7 + 6) =$ **83.**   **(a)** $^-14$ **(b)** $^-24$ **(c)** 2
(d) 5   **85.**   **(a)** 100   **(b)** 0   **(c)** 20   **(d)** $^-20$
(e) $^-40$ **87.** One possible solution is given in the accompanying path. There are infinitely many others.

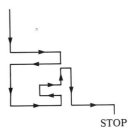

STOP

$7 - 3 + 10 - 3 + 9 - 3 + 10 - 7 + 3 - 1 + 2 - 1 + 2 - 6 + 9 - 6 + 2 - 4 + 4 = 24$ **89.**   **(a)** $2^3 \cdot 3$

(b) $2^2 \cdot 3^2$ (c) 2^6 (d) $2^4 \cdot 3^2$ (e) $3^2 \cdot 5$ (f) $2 \cdot 643$ **91.** (a) 72 (b) 180 (c) 720 (d) 162
93. (a) Yes (b) Yes (c) No (d) Yes (e) No (f) Yes **95.** There are many possibilities.

97. (a)

I	II	III	IV	V
2^1	½	0.5	✓	
3^1	⅓	$0.\overline{3}$		✓
2^2	¼	0.25	✓	
5^1	⅖	0.4	✓	
$2^1 \cdot 3^1$	⅙	$0.1\overline{6}$		✓
7^1	2/7	$0.\overline{285714}$		✓
2^3	⅝	0.625	✓	
3^2	1/9	$0.\overline{1}$		✓
$2^1 \cdot 5^1$	3/10	0.3	✓	
11^1	1/11	$0.\overline{09}$		✓
$2^2 \cdot 3^1$	1/12	$0.08\overline{3}$		✓
$3^1 \cdot 5^1$	4/15	$0.2\overline{6}$		✓
2^4	9/16	0.5625	✓	
$2^1 \cdot 3^2$	1/18	$0.0\overline{5}$		✓
$2^2 \cdot 5^1$	13/20	0.65	✓	
$2^1 \cdot 11^1$	17/22	$0.7\overline{72}$		✓
$2^3 \cdot 3^1$	23/24	$0.958\overline{3}$		✓
5^2	23/25	0.92	✓	

(b) 2's and 5's (c) Repeating

Table B

I	II	III	IV	V
2^1	½	0.5	1	1
2^2	¾	0.75	2	2
2^3	⅛	0.125	3	3
2^4	5/16	0.3125	4	4
2^5	3/32	0.09375	5	5
2^6	9/64	0.140625	6	6
5^1	⅕	0.2	1	1
5^2	3/25	0.12	2	2
5^3	7/125	0.056	3	3
5^4	393/625	0.6288	4	4

yes

Table C

I	II	III	IV	V	VI	VII
$2^1 \cdot 5^1$	3/10	0.3	1	1	1	1
$2^2 \cdot 5^1$	7/20	0.35	2	1	2	2
$2^3 \cdot 5^1$	9/40	0.225	3	1	3	3
$2^1 \cdot 5^2$	17/50	0.34	1	2	2	2
$2^4 \cdot 5^1$	29/80	0.3625	4	1	4	4
$2^1 \cdot 5^3$	1/250	0.004	1	3	3	3
$2^2 \cdot 5^3$	1/500	0.002	2	3	3	3

yes

99. (a) $\dfrac{24}{31} > \dfrac{23}{30}$ (b) $\dfrac{86}{75} < \dfrac{85}{74}$

(c) $\dfrac{3}{11} > \dfrac{2}{9}$

101. (a) No (b) No (c) No **103.** (a) 1/6 (b) 4/21 (c) 4/77 **105.** (a) 0.077; it seems misleading since 0 is truncated from 0.0770. (b) 406; it is accurate.

107.

Day	A	B
4	0.30	0
5	0.50	⁻0.20
6	1.00	⁻0.50
7	2.00	⁻1.00
8	4.00	⁻2.00
9	8.00	⁻4.00
10	16.00	⁻8.00
11	32.00	⁻16.00
12	64.00	⁻32.00

109. Is 79/16 greater or less than 59/12? Greater.
111. Approximately 3.37 mph **119.** $22.40
121. 100% **123.** $5460 **125.** (a) dime-a-time (b) System B (c) 25 **127.** (a) Okay
(b) No. Don't buy your date a coke. (c) No. Go on a diet and cut the fries. (d) Okay (e) No. Only buy 1

shirt.   **(f)** No. Forget the eraser.   **129.**   0.5 sec
131.   **(a)** Approximately 76.81   **(b)** 76   **(c)** 71
(d) 156.82   **(e)** 12.52   **133.**   No

Problem Set AII-2

1. It is always the same.

3. (1)

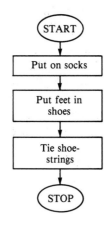

(3)

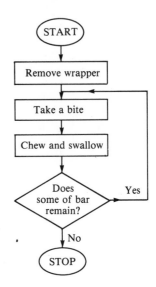

(2)

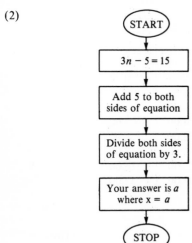

(4)

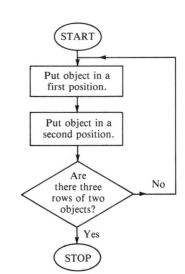

(5) If digit in tenths place is less than 5, you do not add
1 to the ones place.

5.

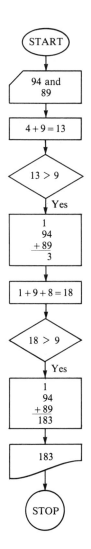

Index